The First Tank Crews

The Lives of the Tankmen who fought at the
Battle of Flers–Courcelette 15 September 1916

Stephen Pope

Helion & Company Limited

Helion & Company Limited
26 Willow Road
Solihull
West Midlands
B91 1UE
England
Tel. 0121 705 3393
Fax 0121 711 4075
Email: info@helion.co.uk
Website: www.helion.co.uk
Twitter: @helionbooks
Visit our blog http://blog.helion.co.uk/

Published by Helion & Company 2016
Designed and typeset by Mach 3 Solutions Ltd, Bussage, Gloucestershire
Cover designed by Paul Hewitt, Battlefield Design (www.battlefield-design.co.uk)
Printed by Gutenberg Press Limited, Tarxien, Malta

ISBN 978-1-910777-77-0

British Library Cataloguing-in-Publication Data.
A catalogue record for this book is available from the British Library.

For details of other military history titles published by Helion & Company Limited contact the above
address, or visit our website: http://www.helion.co.uk.

We always welcome receiving book proposals from prospective authors.

For Kate and Lu

Contents

List of Photographs

In Colour Plate Section

1   From Leuze Wood looking SE showing Purdy's route towards Combles (centre).
2   From Dickens' Cross looking SE showing Arnold's route towards Bouleaux Wood (right).
3   From Dickens' Cross looking north to the Quadrilateral (low trees central on horizon).
4   From south of Ginchy looking ENE showing Henriques, Macpherson and Murphy's route towards Quadrilateral (low trees central on horizon).
5   From the Quadrilateral looking south towards Leuze Wood showing how the position dominates ground.
6   From the Quadrilateral looking south west towards Guillemont and the tanks' approach route.
7   From Ginchy looking NE across the ground crossed by the Guards Division accompanied by Clarke and Smith who reached the wood line (second left breaching the skyline).
8   From the Guards Memorial looking west towards Delville Wood (left) and High Wood (centre).
9   Looking NW toward Delville Wood showing Mortimore's route to eastern edge.
10   From the German artillery position, on the Bulls Road, looking south towards Delville Wood.
11   Sunken lane, used by Blowers to avoid artillery fire, looking north towards Gueudecourt.
12   Flers, looking north from the New Zealand memorial, showing the attack routes.
13   Looking north towards Martinpuich, towards Colle's objective on the east of the village.
14   Drader's route from the SW west towards Martinpuich; he halted on the left by the crops.
15   Looking north from the Sugar Trench to Courcelette (behind trees) and factory (right).
16   Looking south from the Courcelette Sugar Factory, showing Inglis' route from Pozières.

List of Maps in colour section

Acknowledgements

My greatest supporters in publishing this history have been my wife Kate, who suggested that I turn my research into a book and my daughter Lu for putting up with an absent father as I have immersed myself in the story of the First Tank Crews for the past thirteen years.

I would also wish to acknowledge the help and guidance of Duncan Rogers at Helion & Co, his commissioning editor Dr Michael LoCicero as well as George Anderson who converted my rather simplistic diagrams into the superbly clear battlefield maps. Army colleagues have played a key part in encouraging my research. These include Major Fraser Martin who introduced me to the Somme battlefield and Colonel Ben Edwards with whom I followed the tracks of his grandfather Gerald who commanded the tank *Dalliance* at Cambrai. Lieutenant Colonel Alistair Mack, my *boss* for the past three years, not only encouraged me but also reviewed each chapter and made suitable suggestions as to how the work could be improved. Lieutenant Colonel Geoffrey Vesey-Holt, the RTR historian, who introduced me to Duncan Rogers and who photographed the locations of the tank actions which are included as coloured pictures, has been a unparalleled source of information and guidance about the Tank Corps and their later actions.

I would acknowledge the assistance and encouragement of my neighbour Robert Wilkinson-Latham, who has published a series of original books on British bladed weapons and militaria, and who edited each chapter of this book. In addition to David Fletcher, I would like to thank the curator David Willey and the staff of the Tank Museum Archives (TMA), in particular Stewart Wheeler, Jonathan Holt and Katie Thompson for their sustained help in obtaining original photographs of tanks and crewmen as well as access to copies of the RTR journal *Tank* and unit histories. I would also wish to acknowledge the support of Sarah Lambert, not just in her role as Exhibitions Officer at Bovington but also for her personal help in providing pictures of Cyril Coles from the Skinner Street United Reformed Church. Accessing the letters of Walter Atkins, which are held by the Herbert Gallery at Coventry and which form the backbone of Chapter 2, could not have been possible without the initiative of Huw Jones who, as a Keeper of Collections, made contact through my website. It was very much a "quid pro quo" as it enabled me to support the superb exhibition which commemorated the lives of the soldiers from Coventry who died in the Great War. Last but not least, I acknowledge the families of the First Tank Crews who have aided me in bringing the lives of their relatives to light and for their assistance in providing the original photographs for publication for the first time.

1

The Forgotten Pioneers

The premier Baronet of England; a champion rose grower; a grandson of the social reformer Joseph Rowntree; a street-car electrician from Toronto; the chemist who introduced science into the whisky distilling process and a Liverpool mathematics teacher who awarded John Lennon detention – six men with nothing apparently in common. Yet, within three months of seeing a tank for the first time in July 1916, these men and the other members of the First Tank Crews had deployed to France and taken part in the first tank battle in history. The action was not a wholesale success as many of the tanks and their drivers were unable to cope with the shell damaged ground. Although only thirteen Tankers were killed on the 15 September, others were so badly injured, in this and later battles, that they could no longer serve in fighting units. Others, both wounded and unharmed, were employed as instructors and became part of the equipment supply chain whilst those who were badly injured were discharged to allow them to take up civilian employment. The remainder formed the backbones of the tank battalions that fought at the Battles of Arras, Ypres, Cambrai and Amiens and who eventually forced the German Army back to its 1914 start-point on the Belgian border.

The story of the First Tank Crews has never been fully told. In April 1916, this ad-hoc group of people were bought together for gunnery training at the Bisley ranges in Surrey. They included motorcyclists who had never seen action, civilians who volunteered under the Derby Scheme to avoid conscription into the infantry and newly commissioned officers with limited battle experience. In May these men were formed into six companies and, in June 1916, moved to a secret training ground at Elveden on the border of Norfolk and Suffolk. The tanks themselves started to arrive shortly afterwards from factories in Birmingham and Lincoln. These prototype tanks were uncomfortable, unproven and unreliable. Their drivers, mainly from the Army Service Corps (ASC) tractor depot at Avonmouth, were stunned by their first task – to offload from a train, at night, vehicles about which they had no previous experience. It was not a good start but they soon got the hang of the job.

Less than three months later, the First Tank Crews went to France. As individuals the crews knew their jobs but they were far from ready for war. The drivers had no opportunity to learn to operate across shell damaged ground and had never driven their tanks at full battle weight. The Tankers had little opportunity to train together as formed crews and had only limited training for operations at night. Before they left for France, the tanks were already starting to show mechanical frailty; there were few spare parts and not enough time to prepare them for battle. When the Crews arrived in France, there was little opportunity to practice tactics with the infantry divisions whom they would support. Furthermore, what limited time was available was regularly disrupted by "demonstrations" to senior officers and politicians.

Despite this unpromising start, the First Tank Crews went into action on Friday 15 September 1916. Of the forty-nine tanks, which deployed on the opening day of the Battle of Flers-Courcelette, almost half did not make it to their start points. More were damaged by artillery fire or became stuck in shell holes as they made their way across no man's land. The few tanks that did break through the German defences had a superb impact on the morale of the units they supported but the reaction of the German troops was quite the opposite. One Canadian soldier who saw the tanks go into action at Courcelette later described that *"several Huns, minus rifles and equipment, got out of their trench and were beating it back over the open, terrified at the approach of the tank"*.

The tanks were used on several occasions in the next two months and their crews gained substantial battle experience. Despite dreadful weather conditions, sodden ground, massive shell holes and the need to cannibalise wrecks to keep their tanks operational, the crewmen aided the slow push by the British and Empire units through the German Army's rearmost defences. As a result, the German Army were forced to withdraw from positions which they had held for two years and planned a new defensive position near Cambrai.

The story of the First Tank Crews is, like much of the success of the Allied offensive of autumn 1916, virtually unknown. The aim of this book is to tell the story of the 500 brave men who crewed the first tanks, both prior to and after their first action on the Somme battlefield. It is about engineers and clerks; merchants and apprentices, drapers and farm workers. Sixty-nine of the 500 crewmen, who served at the Battle of Flers-Courcelette, on 15 September to 1 October 1916, lost their lives in battle as a result of wounds or from sickness before the war ended. The remainder of these pioneers returned to civilian life and carried on as if their part in the first tank action had not occurred. As we approach the centenary of the first tank action, this book remembers those who fought in them on 15 and 16 September 1916 and who have almost been forgotten – the First Tank Crews.

2

Alpacas go to war

The first tank units were formed in May 1916 at the Motor Machine Gun Service (MMGS) Depot at Bisley Camp. There were originally six tank companies in the Heavy Section of the Machine Gun Corps (HS MGC) and the tank crewmen were mainly volunteers from the MMGS. Other crewmen came from those training at the MGC Depot near Grantham whilst the "skippers", selected by Colonel Ernest Swinton, started to arrive either from reserve infantry battalions or directly from officer training units in Oxford and Cambridge.

Ernest Swinton was the focus for the development of tanks. It was he who identified the requirement during the autumn battles of 1914 when the British Regular Army was reduced to cadre strength as it fought the German Army to a standstill near Ypres. Through his friendship with Maurice Hankey, the secretary of the Committee for Imperial Defence, Swinton was able to press for the development of a vehicle able to cross trench-lines, breach German strongpoints and destroy machine guns. He also determined the original specifications for the new vehicles, which were designed by William Tritton, an agricultural engineer from Lincoln, and Walter Wilson, an automotive engineer who was serving in the Royal Naval Air Service. Swinton also selected officers for employment in tank units, developed tactics for their use and was a regular visitor to tank training locations.

Lionel McAdam (left) during Vickers machine training at Bisley Camp spring 1916.
(McAdam Family Toronto)

The majority of the initial training was delivered using experienced instructors from the MMGS Depot. Most crewmen were already trained on the water-cooled Vickers machine guns which were to be fitted to the female tanks – see Annex B. These MGC crewmen were also trained on the Hotchkiss light machine guns. These guns fired bullets linked together in small strips and were mainly used by machine gun sections supporting cavalry regiments. Each tank commander was provided with a Hotchkiss machine gun which was also fitted to "male" tanks in addition to their main armament, the Hotchkiss 57mm gun which fired a six pound shell. This quick-firing (QF) gun had been designed to defeat attacks by motor torpedo boats on warships and its modification for use on male tanks was quite simple. Dry training on the Hotchkiss 57mm gun, that is training undertaken without live ammunition, was originally undertaken at Bisley under the supervision of Royal Navy instructors. For a short time, the gunners also fired live ammunition on the Stickledown Range, which at 1,200 yards was the longest at Bisley, but the practice stopped when ricocheting shells left the range area and landed close near a group of cottages on the Chobham Ridges. Thereafter live fire training on the QF gun was undertaken on Royal Navy warships in the English Channel and at the artillery ranges at Larkhill to the north of the ancient monument of Stonehenge.

There is little by way of official records about the events which took place during the formation of the tank companies but one crewman's description of the training system has survived. Walter Atkins, who was to serve with the "Black Cat Crew" at Martinpuich, wrote letters to his mother Ann from his arrival at Bisley in late March 1916 until just before he departed for France in early September 1916. Walter was one of the many motorcyclists and mechanics that had joined the MMGS through *The Motor Cycle* whose offices were in his home town of Coventry. He exchanged letters, on an almost daily basis, to reassure his mother of his good health as he was her only and much loved son. Having arrived at Bisley on 28 March, Walter's first letter reveals that he had travelled by train via Euston Station in London where he had joined other soldiers at a free refreshment stand, before catching the train from Waterloo to Brookwood and therefore arriving after the evening meal had been served. Walter spent his first few nights in a large wooden shed with seventy other recruits. It was snowing when he arrived at Bisley and, despite the fact that he had seven blankets and there were three stoves in the hut, Walter felt the cold. Breakfast was not provided until 7:50 a.m. but Walter was pleased by the menu of porridge, fish, and two slices of bread and butter with as much tea as he could drink. Walter was well fed at home and he was pleased that this continued at Bisley. In one of his early letters he reveals that Walter recognised one officer from Coventry, Lieutenant Alfred Wheeler, who would later command the tank *Champagne* at Courcelette on 15 September 1916. Alfred was a drapers' son who lived in the nearby village at Foleshill.

There were many other motorcyclists from the Coventry area at the MMGS Depot and Walter soon met up with Roland Elliott, a butcher's assistant from Foleshill. Walter and Rol, as he was known, already knew each other by sight and they soon became best friends. They lived in the same hut for initial training which primarily consisted of weapon handling and fitness training, much being achieved through route marching as well as the expected foot drill. The MMGS uniform was similar to that worn by the majority of British soldier but the Crews wore riding breeches, short greatcoats and leather gaiters as protection when riding motorcycles.

Walter Atkins wearing the distinctive leather gaiters worn by MMGS soldiers. (Herbert Art Gallery and Museum, Coventry)

Whilst this made the MMGS men feel different to other soldiers, there was to be little opportunity to ride motorcycles as they were soon posted to the Armoured Car Section of the MGC. Like most recruits, Walter was short of cash before he was first paid and, although fed well at Bisley, he missed the cakes, biscuits and other fancies available at the various canteens nearby so he borrowed money for these from his mother. He also purchased a plain leather waist belt, and a walking out stick, which were *de-rigueur* amongst the MMGS soldiers as can be seen from the photo of a machine-gun crew in training on page 15. Rol Elliott and Walter not only continued to live and train together in the Armoured Car Section; they also attended chapel together, visited Woking which was the nearest large town and, whenever possible, travelled home to Coventry for weekend leave. Rol, as he was known to Walter, is mentioned in many letters, Walter normally confiding to his mother than they were both "in the pink". Despite this, Ann Atkins remained worried that her son did not enough to eat and sent regularly food parcels as well as the other items Walter needed including a replacement for the Army issue shaving brush which was not to his liking.

In May 1916, the Armoured Car Section was re-named the Heavy Section MGC and both Rol and Walter were posted to F Company. This unit was billeted at a specially established tented camp near the Siberia range. Despite its name, and the fact that the tented camp was established in early April, the warmth of eleven bodies in each tent made living conditions tolerable. The name Siberia caused some confusion to some of the newly arriving officers. When Lieutenant Basil Henriques was told the camp's name when he first arrived at Brookwood Railway Station, early that month, he was concerned that he had missed his new unit's deployment and was unsure how he would get to Russia. The camp was however only a few mile's walk, as the crow flies, across the Surrey heathlands. In May 1916, Walter and Rol were posted to D Company whose headquarters was established at Bullhousen Farm which was located just north of the Siberia range. On 22 May, Walter started to learn to fire the QF gun at Bisley and, at the end of the month, was sent to HMS *Excellent* at Whale Island for live fire training with the Royal Navy. His journey to Portsmouth was faithfully reported to his mother, as was the large amount of food which was "piled up just as I get it at home". Walter also mentioned that the live fire training was undertaken from a warship in the English Channel. His does not name the vessel on which the firing took place, presumably to avoid the risk of being in trouble for revealing secrets. He did tell his mother that he saw Nelson's flagship HMS *Victory* which was afloat in Portsmouth harbour and that he was sleeping in a sprung bed which was a major change from sleeping on the floor boards of a bell tent.

Although Bisley was located on the edge of a major training area, the large number of trees made it unsuitable for tank training. Ernest Swinton tasked a fellow regular Royal Engineer officer, Major Maurice O'C Tandy, to find a suitable location, which was not only sufficiently large but was also away from public view. Tandy identified a suitable area within Lord Iveagh's estate at Elveden, near Thetford, and the First Tank Crews were sent there in early June 1916. Another Royal Engineer officer, Gifford Martel, designed and supervised the construction of an extensive nine row trench system replicating the German defences at Loos, which was used for battle practices. Entrances to the so-called "Elveden Explosives Area" were guarded by members of the Defence Corps and cavalry patrolled the perimeter to ensure no-one could observe the tanks whilst training. Everyone visiting was escorted and the tank crewmen were issued with identity passes and were warned that the new unit's activities must be totally secret. It was originally planned that the crewmen would be confined to the training area but this proved impracticable. As a result, the nearby market town of Bury St Edmunds soon became their weekend destination and it was here too that Walter and Rol went when they could not get home at the weekend.

The first "tank" to be seen by the crewmen, which later was known as *Mother*, was the prototype built at the Foster's factory in Lincoln which had been demonstrated to the War Cabinet at Hatfield House in early February 1916. She arrived at Elveden on 4 June and was used for demonstrations to C Company three days later. On 7 June 1916, driving classes started but there was little opportunity

HMLS *Centipede*, later known
as *Mother*, at Hatfield House
January 1916.

for the crewmen to get much experience until the arrival of the first production tanks on 18 June. These tanks, which were mainly built at the Metropolitan Carriage Company in Birmingham, were offloaded at a specially built siding at night. Although all the crewmen had expected to drive the new vehicles, it was agreed that trained ASC personnel would be the "first driver" in each tank crew. These drivers mainly came from the ASC depot at Avonmouth where Holt caterpillar tractors were received from America and then sent to ASC and artillery units in France to tow stores and artillery pieces. The ASC drivers joined a new unit, known as 711 (Mechanical Transport) Company, which had been formed on 3 June 1916, together with engineering officers and NCO mechanics who would supervise the maintenance and repair of the tanks. The ASC men were not all volunteers and not all were suited to the task. The task of offloading the tanks from a train, at night in darkness, is very difficult. Each tank had to be offloaded using an end ramp, each driver having to drive the tanks along the length of the line or "rake" of rail flats and then ease the 26 ton machine down the ramp to the ground. It took a long time and was certainly "character forming". Rail offloading later became a standard feature of tank driver training and is taught to drivers of armoured fighting vehicles to this day.

Demonstrations and other distractions

Tactical training took place at Elveden on the specially constructed "battle zone" and these were also the location of a number of demonstration arranged for senior officers. On 21 July a mock battle involving twenty tanks took place which was observed by the Minister of Munitions David Lloyd George. Five days later, King George V visited Elveden and was again provided with a tactical demonstration. Driver training was limited to movement by day after an early attempt to drive at night using compasses proved unsuccessful. It was also rare for the tanks to be driven whilst fitted with the gun sponsons fitted to either side of the tank and, whilst the drivers practiced crossing trenches, the sandy ground and lack of deep muddy shells meant that they were wholly unprepared for the dreadful conditions the drivers would encounter during the Battle of Flers-Courcelette. .

The name "tank" had been developed to shield the nature of the new vehicles from German intelligence staffs. However, the crews called their vehicles "cars" or "buses" and it is clear that, from his letters, that Walter Atkins' mother could not understand why specialist drivers were necessary. It was probably not helped when Walter described the "cars" as being parked across three fields. As it was, the arrangements for training were such that tank crews rarely had the same ASC driver during practice periods and the split command and control arrangement made the development of esprit de corps almost impossible. One exception to this was the crew of the

Mark I male tank, without sponsons, negotiating an obstacle at Elveden. (Tank Museum Bovington)

tank *Casa*, commanded by Lieutenant Victor Smith who took his soldiers to Bury St Edmunds where they were photographed together (see page 82). Some tank skippers certainly looked after their men but their discipline was much lighter than in most Army units. Gunner Archie Richards recalled that his skipper Alfred Enoch used his Christian name, which was almost unknown in the rest of the Army, whilst Walter Atkins told his mother that his tank's commander Harry Drader provided cakes when Harry felt his crewmen had done well. Walter's best friend Rol Elliott had become Harry's servant which meant that Walter was sometimes "in the know" about the plans for the company's deployment. One regular area of discussion in Walter's letters were his trips back to his home at Bell Green and, from July onwards, whether he would be granted a final period of leave before D Company deployed to France. The need to get the tanks to France to aid the soldiers fighting on the Somme meant that block leave, a common feature of modern military operations, was not granted. In part, this lack of leave was also due to the number of visits by senior officers that started to increase and arrival of more tanks. The visits included demonstrations of the tank's mobility across country but it was rare for the senior officers to travel inside the tank. An exception was made for King George V who was driven by Pte Harry Tate – the journey was short as the King soon decided that he had experienced enough of the new vehicle!

In comparison with modern tanks, the Mark I tanks driven by the First Tank Crews were primitive. They had no suspension and the engine, located in the centre of the tank, was not in a separate compartment. As a result the tank's interior became hot as well as full of gasses as there were neither exhaust pipes nor a silencer. The crew were almost deafened and had to use hand signals to communicate as driving the tank was also a team effort – see Appendix 2. Walter Atkins described the sensations of being a tank crewman to his mother: "It is exciting like rolling around in a ship. Oh the sensation when we go down a steep pit and climb the other side. The sides of the pit are about twice as steep as a roof." The tanks were also unreliable; the ride Walter described was undertaken in the tank of another crew as his own was unserviceable. Basil Henriques later recalled that his own crew never trained together in their allocated tank until they reached France. There were also only limited live firing opportunities for QF gun at Elveden so training continued to take place at Larkhill. In another letter to his mother, Walter Atkins described a trip when he left Thetford early one morning, travelled by train to Salisbury, was then driven by lorry past Stonehenge to the firing range and was back at Elveden, having crossed London, that evening. Walter was amazed at having to travel so far and walk so little.

On Sunday 13 August, Colonel Ernest Swinton addressed C Company just before the crews started to load their tanks onto rail waggons. Two days later the first train departed and the unit's advance party deployed to France, led by Lieutenant Sir John Dashwood and accompanied by a few members of D Company under Lieutenant Heady Head. The tanks were sent by rail, in two groups, to Avonmouth and then to Le Havre but the crewmen took a more direct route to the continent. They travelled by train from Thetford Bridge to Liverpool Street Station and then marched across London to Waterloo Railway Station. Arriving in Southampton that evening, the crews crossed to Le Havre where they stayed in a tented camp. Four days later, the first set of tanks arrived at Le Havre on 21 August and, after offloading, was sent by train to Contreville which was the nearest railway station to their new training area. The train stopped en route whilst at Rouen and Gunner Fenwick Styan managed to buy a postcard and send it to his fiancée Doris Shipley at Driffield.

The second party were photographed as they marched between Liverpool Street and Waterloo Railway Stations. Archie Holford-Walker is on the far left, near the centre of the road, then George Macpherson and Basil Henriques but I have been unable to identify the officer closest to the camera. The smiling civilian on the pavement was one of the members of Basil Henriques' Boys Club in the East End of London. The second party sailed overnight from Southampton to Le Havre and their tanks arriving on 25 August. The C Company advance party had set up their base at St Riquier close to where the training area had been established at Yvrench. This area contained a number of old French and German trench lines which enabled a range of training exercises

C Company officers and men marching to Waterloo Railway Station London. (Tank Museum)

and field demonstrations to take place. On 26 August, just five days after their arrival in France, five tanks from C Company supported 7th Battalion Middlesex Regiment in a demonstration of an attack. This was observed by the British Commander in Chief, General Douglas Haig, who was accompanied by his Army Commanders Lieutenant Generals Henry Rawlinson and Hubert Gough. Haig was encouraged by the tanks' cross country capability but was concerned that the tactics for the tanks had yet to be finalised. Other units of 56th Division, which C Company would support on 15 September, took part in later exercises but this was the only collective training undertaken before the tanks were used in action. It was also during this time that Lieutenant Basil Henriques was able to select the driver and train his crew as a team. He was offered the choice of two drivers from 711 (MT) Company; one had an attitude which Henriques did not like and he therefore chose the "quiet man" despite the fact that the driver had no experience of driving tanks. It was also during these final exercises that the shortage of spare parts and lack of tools became fully clear. One tank could not be sent to the Somme because it had a broken track plate which could not be replaced; the tank hulk was left at Yvrench after it had been cannibalised by C Company to provide spare parts. Major Allen Holford-Walker also sent one of his men back to England to collect fifteen sets of spanners which his wife had purchased in London at his request.

Whilst C Company were practising in France, D Company were completing their final preparations for deployment. They had painted their tanks to a design by the Royal Academician Sir Solomon J Solomon who had been accepted by the British General Staff as an expert on such matters. On Saturday 19 August, Walter Atkins' crew was "issued with a new car fitted with guns; all gun layers had to fire a certain number of rounds of a new type". That morning, Walter had been issued with a gas mask, goggles, jack knife and haversack and, according to a letter sent to his mother at 1:00 p.m., was preparing for a kit inspection at 3:00 pm. He had been given two weeks' pay that morning whereas the crewmen in Numbers 1 and 2 Sections being paid only one week as they, with the company pay staff, were to deploy to France the following week. That afternoon, D

Mark I female tank, painted in a camouflage pattern designed by Sir Solomon J Solomon.
(Tank Museum)

Company held a sports day at which Rol Elliott was a favourite to win one event. The following evening, Walter wrote to his mother confirming Rol won a prize and that his crew had also taken their new car to the firing range for more practice. The crew did not get a meal until 6:30 p.m. after which they returned to the car to clean it and the guns. The D Company crewmen were wholly unaware of the preparations being undertaken in France and were still hoping for the chance of some final leave. Walter was also worried that he would get his motorcycle home to Bell Green and when he could get to a railway station. A few crewmen did get away and several were married by special licence just before they deployed. Tragically two of those brides were widowed within a month. On Tuesday 22 August, Walter told his mother that the crew had been issued with new leather helmets. These specially designed hats were most distinctive and the cause of much comment by onlookers as the tank crewmen marched across London. The following day, Walter wrote that some crewmen had been selected to send signals to tanks from observation balloons behind the British front lines and that this would delay his departure owing for need to train signallers. On Friday 25 August, D Company's officers were given orders to deploy which was mentioned in Walter's second letter of the day. He wrote "Have heard some good news. A chap who drives a car has been told by the major that we may go over any time now but that we shall not use the cars till the spring as we have a lot of practice and manoeuvring to do".

The following day, Lieutenant Jefferson Wakley, who was D Company's Tank Park Officer, departed for Avonmouth with thirteen tanks for No 1 and 2 Sections which were loaded to the recently built SS *Ilston*. On Sunday, Arthur wrote to his mother confirming he would get no more leave and that he "has been issued revolver, pays books and ID discs. The section is away at the ASC camp fitting sponsons, left at 1230 and expected to back by six." Atkins had time to write home as he had been tasked by his tank skipper, Harry Drader, to mend his motorcycle's puncture. In a second letter, written late evening, Walter suggested that, if his mother wished to see him before he left for France, she should travel to Ingham Station which was only three miles away from Elveden. She does not however appear to have made the trip. On Monday 28 August, the first 155 men from the D Company HQ with No 1 and 2 Sections departed Elveden at 6:00 a.m. and, like C Company, travelled by rail from Thetford to London, marched to Waterloo Station then travelled by train to Southampton docks. They sailed that evening for Le Havre on the troop ship SS *Caesarea*. Their deployment was described in Walter's next letter in which he records he had been ordered to take over running the Company canteen which provided drinks and food for the soldiers each evening. He was also part of a working party tasked to tidy up the camp whilst the rest of his section was preparing the tanks for departure. In a letter the next day, Walter reported to his mother that "he will be leaving on Friday (1 Sep); that the cars will be taken to the station that evening at 9.00 pm." From his statement that he would not drink alcohol whilst running the canteen, it is clear that his mother was worried about her son's moral health. This letter was his last before he was wounded on 15 September.

Alpacas travel by rail

On Friday 1 September, a loading party led by Lieutenant Billy Sampson which included the tank drivers, departed for Avonmouth with the remaining twelve tanks belonging to D Company. The next morning, the 106 men from No 3 and 4 Sections departed Thetford Bridge for London and then onto Southampton. That same night, when the Germans launched the largest aerial bombing attack of the war using twelve Zeppelin airships, one of the massive aircraft bombed the nearby village of Culford. The Germans were aware of the development of the new heavy armoured cars but, despite much comment after the event about German spies at Elveden, there is no evidence that the raid on Culford was based on intelligence about the new vehicles being in the area. To keep the tank's secret, whilst being moved to France, the vehicles were known by the code-name *Alpaca*.

Having arrived and been unloaded at Le Havre, D Company's *Alpacas* were loaded to trains but their departure for Contreville was delayed by a number of men going absent in France. Their military conduct sheets show they were punished by being confined to camp rather than imprisoned as trained crewmen were few in number and every man would be needed very shortly.

The first party of D Company personnel arrived at their new billets ay Yvrench on 1 September, having marched from their railway station at St Riquier. Their tanks arrived at Contreville on 3 September and their crews spent the next two days refitting the sponsons and checking the tanks were mechanically in good order. By this time, C Company had been giving demonstrations on an almost daily basis to senior officers including Edward, Prince of Wales who was serving in France. The future King Edward VIII was not impressed by the tanks but he was by their crews: "They are good toys but I don't have much faith in the success. But their crews of one officer and seven Other Ranks are damned brave men". No 3 and 4 Sections of D Company, including Walter Atkins arrived at Contreville on 6 September. C Company were preparing to leave Contreville for the Somme battlefield using two trains, the first leaving on the evening of 7 September and the other the following morning. D Company's tanks continued to give demonstrations including one on 8 September to the British Prime Minister Anthony Asquith whose son Raymond was serving with the Grenadier Guards and who would be in action supported by tanks from C Company on 15 September.

Like C Company, the D Company crews moved to the Somme in two groups; the first on 9 September and the remainder of 10 September. After a train journey lasting twenty-four hours, the tanks arrived at the Loop railhead to the north of Bray-sur-Somme. The Company's motor transport moved to the Loop under the command of Lieutenant Billy Brannon in a journey taking only ten hours. After being offloaded, the D Company tanks were driven to join their comrades in C Company at Happy Valley to the south of Fricourt. Their arrival was an open secret and, whilst the crews carried out their pre-battle preparations, they had many visitors. D Company was visited

C Company tanks being prepared for action. (Tank Museum)

by the Prince of Wales on 10 September who escorted by Captain Bill Huffam who was the cousin of a tank commander Victor Huffam. As he entered Victor's tank Dolly, the Prince banged his head and the air, if not the blood, was certainly blue! Other visitors to the tanks included Will Dawson's two brothers who were serving with the Coldstream Guards and George Macpherson's friend Lieutenant Geoffrey Wyatt with whom he attended Winchester College, and probably Hugh Bell's brother, Harold who was serving as a chaplain in 47th London Division.

The crews were making final preparations, including loading ammunition into the machine guns, the huge amount of stores needed to keep the tank in action and, in the case of C Company, fitting anti-grenade roof cover to their tanks' roofs which had started to arrive in France. Basil Henriques and George Macpherson borrowed bicycles to undertake a reconnaissance of the local area whilst the section commanders were attending briefings and being told of the attack plans. Final orders were delivered on 13 September but these were amended as the tanks started to move to their starting points the following day. There was little opportunity for the tank skippers to see the ground over which they were to deploy and only one map and set of orders per six tank commanders. As the tanks moved forward, several broke down and had to be replaced from the ten spare tanks which had arrived at the Loop, direct from England, on 10 September. Rather than to allow the tanks to travel across country, they were sent along the same roads as the guns, infantry and supporting units all tried to get to their forming up points. The crews were very tired before they started to go into action; they had no sleep on the night of either the 13 or 14 September and their final approach was often subjected to enemy artillery fire. It was not a good way for a new unit to go to war.

3

First into Action

It was no coincidence that the first tank to go into action on 15 September 1916 was *Daredevil*. It was not just because she was manned by tank Crew D1, the first crew of the first section of D Company, nor because her skipper, Captain Harold Mortimore, was also the section's commander. *Daredevil* was tasked to undertake a preliminary attack, before the main assault, to clear a system of German trenches to the east of Delville Wood which was expected to create heavy casualties amongst the attacking British troops (see map 7). Major Frank Summers had to make sure that the attack was a success so he selected a man he could trust. Frank Summers did know his tank commanders to any great degree. He first met them in May 1916 as he was appointed to command D Company. Many had less than a month's experience as officers so Frank, like his fellow company commander Allen Holford-Walker, looked for experienced officers from other units to lead each tank section. Summers found one such officer in Harold Mortimore with whom he had earlier served in the Royal Naval Division (RND).

Not long after first light, at 5:20 a.m. on Friday 15 September, *Daredevil* left her start point which was about 200 yards south of the Ginchy to Longueval Road. (see picture 9) The tank passed through the waiting infantry in their "jumping-off" trenches and, in the pre-dawn light, crossed no man's land. As the tank reached the eastern edge of Delville Wood, where it joined a trench known as Hop Alley, *Daredevil* fired its 6 pdr QF guns as a signal to the waiting infantry and then turned east, away from the Wood driving parallel to the Hop Alley trench and firing at the defending German infantry. Two British companies from 6th Battalion King's Own Yorkshire Light Infantry (KOYLI) then emerged from Delville Wood and, following the tank, cleared the German front line trenches. One of them, Len Lovell later recalled "We were equipped with bombs, we didn't have rifles but, if we knocked a few Germans out who were wounded we had to finish them off with what was basically a lump of lead piping. So all we had to do was keep following the tank, keep peering around the side. The Germans were as terrified of the tank as we appeared to be. They stayed there until they realised they had to get out of the way or else be squashed. The Germans got out of the way but those who couldn't or wouldn't – well, the tank just went over them and they were squashed". *Daredevil* turned north at the junction of Hop Alley with Beer Trench and then followed Ale Alley, which was a German communications trench, firing at the remaining German defenders so that they fled back towards Flers. Harold Mortimore later told John Foley "I managed to get astride one of the German trenches in front of the wood and opened with the Hotchkiss machine gun. There were some Germans in the dugouts and I shall never forget the looks on their faces as they emerged and saw my tank across the trench". *Daredevil* then drove north to join the main attack on Gueudecourt but, as it made its way through the British barrage, a shell hit the left hand rear track sprocket and *Daredevil* was out of action. Fortunately none of her crew was hurt but the tank had to be abandoned. *Daredevil* was never recovered and was blown apart, in early 1919, during the battlefield clearances.

Harold Mortimore, or Morty as he was known to his family, was born on 12 September 1891 at Chiswick. His father was an engineer on a Thames steamship. Morty, who had two older sisters

Harold Mortimore in summer 1916.
(Dr Tilly Mortimore)

and a younger brother called Bob, was educated at the Latymer School at Hammersmith and then worked as a ledger clerk at the Brentford Gas Company. Morty was a determined and physically active young man who had represented Middlesex in both athletics and football. In 1910, Morty joined the City of London Yeomanry, a Territorial Force which provided him with comradeship, sports and social life as well as the chance of a paid summer holiday at their Annual Camp. On the outbreak of war, Morty joined the RND; this was probably because Yeomanry units were tasked to undertake home defence duties and Morty wanted to see action. He enlisted on 1 September 1914 and, because of his experience as a clerk, was appointed as an Ordinary Seaman 3rd class writer. Assigned to the RND Transport Company, he deployed to Antwerp less a month later where the RND defended the port against the advancing Germans. It was here that he met Frank Summers who had been appointed Adjutant of the RND Transport Company.

After the fall of Antwerp, Morty was sent to Ieper where the RND Transport Company supported the British infantry who held the trench lines against German attacks. Morty was soon identified as having officer potential and was sent back to England on 26 August. Commissioned as a sub lieutenant in the Royal Naval Air Service (RNAS), he was later selected for pilot training and posted to the Naval Flying School at Eastbourne in February 1916. Morty was flying by the end of the month but he had great difficulty in his new role. He was continuously airsick and, on one occasion, demolished a hut whilst landing one aircraft. When he was approached by Frank Summers to volunteer for "a secret and dangerous mission", Morty did so reasoning that nothing could be worse than flying. Morty's naval commission was terminated on 19 May 1916 and two days later he was commissioned into the Heavy Section MGC. The photo above was taken at Eastbourne about this time.

Morty joined D Company at Elveden less than a month before they deployed to France. Promoted acting Captain on 11 August 1916, Morty was sent with the Advance party to Le Havre where he organised the offloading of the tanks. After leading his section in training at Contreville, he moved to the Somme, celebrating his twenty-fifth birthday as he prepared his section for their first attack. It was on 13 September that he was told he had been selected to clear the trenches near Delville Wood and, as a result, Harold Mortimore was the first tank commander to go into action. Although some other crewmen were in action on 26 September and 1 October, I can find no evidence that any of Morty's crew was used. On 4 October he accompanied Frank Summers to Hébuterne, to the north of the River Ancre, to establish a new company HQ and stores location. Morty then undertook recces of attack routes near Beaumont-Hamel and led a section of six tanks to Auchonvillers on 12 November during which he was gassed. On 14 November, he commanded a composite section of six tanks as they went into action near Beaumont-Hamel. Two days later, this time whilst he was supporting the RND, Morty was gassed again. Refusing medical treatment; he remained at duty and moved with the Company HQ to Blangy-sur-Ternoise within the newly established Tank Administrative area. It was there, on 1 December 1916, that Morty signed off the final entry in the D Company War Diary. Unlike several of the tank skippers, Morty did not receive a medal for his part in the first action but he was mentioned in Sir Douglas Haig's Despatches for gallant and distinguished services in the field. When D Battalion was formed, Morty was initially appointed to command No 11 Company. This command was short lived as Morty was sent back to England for Christmas leave and, in early January 1917, took over as adjutant of F Battalion which had formed at Bovington with Frank Summers as the first CO.

Morty returned to France with F Battalion on 20 May but, on 30 June 1917 as F Battalion was deploying to the Ypres Salient, he was relieved of his post because of poor health. Certainly his lungs were in a very bad state, due to the November gassing, but he may also have been suffering from stress. Morty later told his daughter Tilly that, whilst in Belgium, he saw new troops arriving by train and, to his horror, recognised one as his fourteen year old brother Bob. Bob had lied about his age when he joined the Army but there was nothing Morty could do to keep him from danger. Bob was sent to the trenches and, when Bob later became lost in no man's land, Morty went forward to find him. Bob did survive the war but his health was permanently affected as was Morty's. On 12 July 1917, Morty was admitted to 1st Eastern General Hospital at Cambridge where he was diagnosed with tuberculosis. After a month he was sent to a convalescent hospital at Blackpool. On 18 October 1917, a Medical Board stated that his condition resulted from severe gas shelling near Auchonvillers and recommended he undertake a home service posting. He was sent to the Tank Corps Depot Battalion at Wareham but, by December 1917, Morty's health was so bad that he was admitted to another Convalescent Hospital, this time at Summertown near Eastbourne. There, on 18 February 1918 at Eastbourne Parish Church, he married Dorothy Moorhouse, a local girl whom he had probably met whilst learning to fly in 1916. He had recovered some of his health by the summer although one medical report in July 1918 stated his right lung was still sodden. Morty was then appointed as the adjutant at the Convalescent Hospital in which role he served for a further two years during which time, Dorothy gave birth to the couple's only son, Anthony, at Eastbourne on 4 January 1919. In March 1919, Morty's de-mobilisation was published in the *London Gazette* but the RAMC colonel commanding the hospital at Eastbourne sought his retention as he wished for an officer to manage the administration of the unit. Morty therefore was not released for a further twelve months, his final posting being to Queens Mary's convalescent centre at Woodcote Park near Epsom.

When he did leave the Army on 22 March 1920, Morty was one of the many ex-officers who could not find employment. He therefore sought work overseas and, on 28 June 1922, Morty, Dorothy and their three year old son Anthony, travelled to Johannesburg. Morty later told his daughter Tilly that South Africa "was the most beautiful country in the world but I could not live in a place which labeled benches for whites only". Dorothy and Anthony returned to the UK on 18 December 1922, Morty returning seven months later. Morty then gained a position as a private secretary before joining a firm of maltsters at Sawbridgeworth in Hertfordshire where he later became the company secretary. Sadly his first marriage failed after Dorothy had an affair; Morty suing her for divorce in May 1938. Morty soon found love again and on 20 January 1939, he married Mary Boning who was twenty years his junior. With the outbreak of the Second World War, Morty formed the Home Guard at Sawbridgeworth, and later became Chairman of the Eastern Region of the Confederation of British Industry. On 15 September 1950, Morty again became a father. Just after his fifty-ninth birthday, his daughter Tilly was born on the forty-fourth anniversary of the day he took *Daredevil* into action. The photograph was taken about this time.

Harold Mortimore in his later years.
(Dr Tilly Mortimore)

In 1959, at the age of sixty-eight, Morty retired with Mary to her home town of Torquay where his health deteriorated. When the Devon branch of the Tank Corps Old Comrades Association (OCA) was formed in 1962, Morty was elected Vice President in absentia. Although there were several other men, who had fought at the Battle of Flers-Courcelette, they never met as Morty's poor health prevented him from attending meetings. He died aged seventy-six on 17 July 1967.

Morty described his second in command Sergeant H Davies as "the oldest of the crew"; he fired the starboard QF gun as well as commanding the other gunners. Davies, who was born in October 1883, had enlisted into the MMGS on 18 May 1915. He suffered from shell-shock on 15 September, when the tank went into action at Delville Wood, and had to be removed from the tank for treatment by the RAMC. He was later discharged due to wounds on 23 November 1917 but sadly I can find no further information about him thereafter.

Davies' loader was Gunner Fred Hobson who was probably from Preston. Ten years younger than his sergeant, Fred joined the MMGS in November 1915 and later served with the Heavy Branch MGC and then the Tank Corps. He must have been badly wounded, during actions in the Ypres Salient, as he was discharged from the Army on 28 February 1918. He probably died aged thirty-nine in Stockport in 1932.

The portside gun crewmen were also both from Preston. Albert Smith, the QF gunner, was born on 27 July 1884. He was the youngest of seven children, five of his of siblings being girls and two having died before he was born. Albert married Ann Arkinstall on 18 April 1908 at St Mark's Preston Church in Preston and their only daughter Elsie was born on New Year's Eve 1909. In 1911, the family were living in Priory Street in Ashton on Ribble and Albert was working as a loom overlooker or supervisor. Before he enlisted in August 1915, Albert had changed trade to loom mechanic. After the first tank actions, on the night of 23 September, Albert went back to *Dinnaken*, with his skipper and the rest of the crew, to remove her machine guns. Whilst this task was underway, Stuart Hastie was asked to send two crewmen to remove the guns from *Dolly* which was sitting in no man's land, and thus prevent them being used by the Germans against the British troops who were to attack Gueudecourt. Albert and Roy Reiffer volunteered and accompanied an infantry patrol from 15th Battalion Kings Liverpool Regiment to Grass Lane, between Flers and Gueudecourt. Whilst the infantry provided local protection, and Roy stood in the door of the tank keeping watch, Albert entered *Dolly* and made sure the Vickers machine guns were unusable. Albert also removed the commander's Hotchkiss gun which he took back to Green Dump and which was later sent to the tank's commander, Victor Huffam, who was in hospital suffering from shell-shock. Albert was awarded the Military Medal for this action on 13 November. The next day he transferred to D Battalion and served with them for the rest of the war, eventually serving as a motorcycle despatch rider at the Battalion Headquarters. Never promoted, he left the service but must have kept in contact with his comrades. In 1957, he was located by Victor Huffam who was trying to meet up with those who fought at the first tank action. The two were pictured in *Lancashire Evening Post* on 26 July 1957, whilst Albert was living at Mill Street in Farrington near Leyland, but that is the last date time I can find anything about him.

Albert's loader, Arthur Day, also survived the war. Born in October 1892, Arthur lived about half a mile from Arthur's home at Ashton on Ribble. Arthur, who was a wood turner, was attested on 24 October 1915 at Preston and enlisted in the MMGS, reporting to their Depot at Bisley the following day. Captain Woods recorded in his note book that Arthur was slightly wounded in the hand on 15 September but he remained at duty. After the first tank battles, Arthur continued to serve with D Battalion, joining No 10 Company where he re-trained as a driver. He probably fought during the Battle of Arras, during the attack on the German defensive position on Telegraph Hill near Beaurains. Arthur was wounded on 4 October, during the Third Battle of Ypres, and was evacuated to the UK. He was treated at 2nd Western General Hospital in Manchester until 16 February 1918, when he was sent on leave for a fortnight. He never served overseas again, having been medically down-graded. Although he did not originally claim a pension, Arthur was far from good health and, in December 1919, he was awarded a 20% disability pension for deafness, worth eight shillings a week. Arthur's home of Preston was one of the 482 towns which were presented with a tank after the war to mark the financial contribution made by the townspeople through the purchase of War Bonds. Sadly, by 1929, the tank was in poor condition because of lack of maintenance and there was a local campaign for the tank to be removed from its place of honour in a local park. Arthur's letter for it to be retained, published on 9 October in the *Lancashire Daily Post*, was not heeded and the tank was later scrapped. Arthur was last mentioned in print at the time of the Fortieth Anniversary of the Battle of Cambrai when *The Tank* confirmed that he was still alive and living in Preston. Sadly, after that, he disappears from view.

Standing next to Alfred, when *Daredevil* went into action, was Gunner Ewart Doodson. Ewart was one of two gearsmen, who not only assisted the driver to manoeuvre the tank but also supplied the gunners with ammunition. Ewart was born in Eland in West Yorkshire in November 1898. After the early death of his parents, he was adopted by a couple named Tyas and Morwenna Woods from Ravensthorpe. Ewart, who worked as a junior clerk at the Yorkshire Electric Power Company, joined the MGC in October 1915. After the first action at Delville Wood, Ewart's letter to his adoptive parents was published in the local paper. He recalled "we went over almost before it was first light on Friday morning, and our tank was out of action with a shell through our driving wheels within almost half an hour. It was supposed to be an exceptionally difficult position and hot too.....Fritz simply bunked and well he might to see this thing (the tank) coming on him in the half light. We got through this redoubt and were well towards the German main trench when we got hit. There was plenty of flames and smoke but no one was hurt".

Ewart then mentions that a friend from Eland, Fred Gomersall who was a crewman in *Dinnaken*, helped remove the machine guns from *Dolly*. Two weeks later, on 1 October 1916, Ewart was wounded in the leg and face, possibly during the attack at Eaucourt L'Abbaye, and was sent for treatment at the Australian General Hospital at Rouen. He soon recovered and, when D Battalion was formed at Blangy at the end of 1916, Ewart was posted to join No 12 Company. On the opening day of the Battle of Arras, Ewart was a crewman in one of eight tanks which supported the Canadian and British assault at Vimy Ridge. Because of the poor conditions, four of the tanks then become stuck in a sunken track and the remainder in the German trenches. As the crew tried to get their tanks back in action, Ewart was fatally wounded. James Anderson, who was in the same tank crew, wrote to Ewart's family and told them that three of the crew of the tank had "got outside to make a necessary adjustment and were working together when a shell dropped a yard behind us. Ewart and the sergeant were immediately unconscious. The sergeant [MacNamee] died in a few minutes and Ewart lived for about half an hour but never regained consciousness and had no pain whatever. The wound was in his skull. I was with him till the end with his head on my knee. Every possible aid was given." The two crewmen were buried close by the tank but their graves were subsequently lost.

Daredevil's other gearsman was killed two days later during the first Battle of Bullecourt. Gunner Harry Leat, who was born at Westcott near Dorking in early 1895, was the ninth of ten children of a bricklayer's assistant. His two older brothers both died before they were five years old leaving Harry as the only son. The family had moved to Aldershot in 1897, where Harry's younger sister Bella was born and he was educated at the East End school. On leaving school, Harry gained as an apprenticeship at the local printers Gale and Polden. His wages must have been extremely useful to his

Harry Leat as a young man. (Sue Chifney)

family after his father died of tuberculosis in May 1910, all of his sisters being in domestic service. Having completed a seven year apprenticeship, Harry worked in the letterpress department at the printers who undertook a large amount of both official and private work for the units in the garrison town. Harry assumed the role of head of the house, completing the 1911 census return and placing his own details immediately below his mother's and above that of his four sisters who were also living at 1 Halimote Road.

The family attended the recently built Aldershot Presbyterian Church in Victoria Road and Harry, like many of the First Tank Crews, rode a motorcycle. His apprenticeship provided Harry with a great deal of mechanical expertise and he must have easily passed the MMGS trade tests at Coventry when he enlisted in December 1915. His training at Bisley was only ten miles from his home so he must have been home most weekends.

Like most of the First Tank Crews, Harry had a photograph taken in his new uniform wearing the distinctive leather gaiters worn by his unit. Having completed his tank training with D Company at Canada Farm at Elveden, Harry deployed to France in early September 1916 and, after the first actions, joined D Battalion. Assigned to No 11 Company, Harry and the small number of former D Company soldiers were crucial to the formation of the new unit. His company commander, Major Willie Watson, later wrote in his book *A Company of Tanks* that those in the company "were of three classes. First came the "Old Tankers," those who had been trained with the original companies. They had been drawn for the most part from the ASC. Some had been once or twice in action; some had not. They were excellent tank mechanics. Then came the motor machine gunners – smart fellows, without much experience of active operations. The vast majority of officers and men were volunteers from the infantry – disciplined fighting men."

Harry Leat before he deployed to France. (Sue Chifney)

During the Battle of Arras, in No 11 Company's first action, Harry was killed. The first attack at Bullecourt, planned for 10 April 1917, was abandoned at the last minute as the tanks were unable to get to the start line on time; severe snow creating problems during their approach march. The next day, against a background of snow and with the Germans being fully ready for the attack, No 11 Company went into action in support of two Australian infantry brigades. The unarmoured tanks were riddled with German machine gun bullets which ripped through the front and sides of the vehicles. As a result, eight out of eleven tanks were destroyed and almost half of the crewmen were killed, missing or injured. The Australians, who suffered more than 3,300 casualties with a further 1,170 becoming prisoners of war, blamed their losses equally on their British commanders who decided not to undertake a preliminary artillery bombardment, relying on tanks to crush the German wire defences, and on the tanks, which were unable to cope with the sodden ground conditions. When Harry's mother Sarah was informed Harry was missing, she appealed for information in the local newspaper about her youngest boy but nothing more could be found. Harry's grave was never identified and he was later commemorated on the Arras Memorial to the Missing. He was also commemorated at the Aldershot Presbyterian Church together with nine other local men who "obeyed the call of their Country". When the Church was demolished in the 1960s, as Aldershot town centre was "modernised", this memorial was transferred to St Andrew's Garrison Church on Queen's Avenue in the heart of South Camp.

The final member of *Daredevil's* crew was the driver Albert Wateridge. He was born on 27 February 1884 at Cranham in Essex but was bought up in southeast London at Lambeth and South Norwood. As a youth Albert worked as porter in a draper's shop but he later became a milkman. In summer 1915 he married Elizabeth Mundy and, on 11 December 1915, Albert joined the ASC. He learned to drive a lorry at the Mechanical Transport Depot at Grove Park. Albert and Elizabeth's elder daughter Winifred was born in the summer of 1916, just before Albert deployed to France. After the first tank battles, Albert was one of the ASC drivers who transferred to the MGC. Promoted Lance Corporal, Albert fought at Vimy Ridge in the same company as Ewart Doodson. He then fought at Second Battle of Bullecourt on 3 May 1917 driving an unarmoured tank. The supporting infantry failed to get forward and the skipper, Second Lieutenant Charles Knight was forced to retire as most of the crewmen were injured by German armour-piercing bullets. Despite the loss of his comrades, Albert refused to give up his post and, having gained replacement gunners, drove the tank back to the German trenches, supporting the British infantry attack. Albert was later awarded the Military Medal for conspicuous gallantry. He was later promoted sergeant and, despite being "no longer physically fit for war service", was not discharged until 2 May 1919. He returned to South Norwood, where his younger daughter Margaret was born in the autumn of 1921. Albert was unable to work and the family had to survive on his Army pension. In 1923, he became seriously ill and his health deteriorated even further in 1926. He died, aged only 46, at St James' Hospital, in Portsmouth on 15 July 1929.

Crew C24 and Clan Cameron

A second tank was tasked to support the preliminary attack at Delville Wood but did not get reach its objective. This tank, known as *Clan Cameron*, was from C Company and its commander was Harold Cole. After the action on 15 September, Major Allen Holford-Walker attempted to clarify exactly what Harold Cole had done but was unable to do so as Cole "was in a very jumpy condition" and had him sent back to England. He did not return to operational service for the rest of the war.

Harold Cole, who was born on 7 August 1884 in Fulham, was the eldest son of a railway guard named Ralph Cole and his wife Harriet. Educated at Latymer School at Hammersmith, albeit some years before Harold Mortimore, Harold Cole originally worked a railway booking clerk but later became a commercial traveler living with the family at Chiswick. On 19 April 1908, Harold married Edith Forrest, the daughter of a railway policeman at St Simon's Church in Paddington. The couple's elder daughter Winifred was born the following year. In 1910, the family was living in Action but, by the time of the 1911 census, the family had moved to Plymouth where, Harold worked as the Devon and Cornwall manager for the German Typewriter Manufacturer Blickensderfer. The couple's younger daughter Phyllis was born in December 1912 but she died the following year.

On the outbreak of the Great War, Harold volunteered to join the Army and served with the Plymouth Garrison Headquarters Royal Engineer Signals Section where he was promoted to the rank of sergeant and placed in charge of the motorcycle dispatch riders. In April 1916, Harold was commissioned into the Heavy Section MGC. Like several of the original tank officers he was a tall man, at six feet one inch, which made it difficult for him to enter *Clan Cameron* as the entry door was less than two feet tall. Following the action on 15 September Harold lost his memory and suffered from shell shock. He was initially admitted to the Duchess of Westminster's hospital at Étaples and then evacuated to King's College Hospital in London. On 16 October, Harold wrote to Colonel Ernest Swinton asking to be returned to his unit but Swinton advised him to rest. On

HMLS *Clan Cameron* after the action. (TPC)

20 December, again seeking to return to duty, Harold wrote to the War Office stating that his tank was destroyed whilst near Delville Wood – a clear sign of his loss of memory. On 28 February 1917, his medical records show that he was experiencing bad dreams but, three months later, he had recovered sufficiently to be fit for duty. Promoted lieutenant on 15 October 1917, he did not serve overseas again. In March 1918, Harold was initiated as an Apprentice Mason in the Lodge of Sincerity at Plymouth, his father William joining the Lodge five months later.

At the end of the war, Harold was serving at the Tank Corps Training Centre at Bovington but was not immediately demobilised. On 27 July 1919, Harold volunteered to join the British tank training team sent to the Baltic to support anti-Bolshevik forces in western Russia. Harold served as finance and messing officer and, during the time in the Baltic, was admitted to the hospital in Narva. Before his collapse, Harold must made major contribution to the team's success as he was later awarded the MBE. Harold was demobilised on February 1920 and was presented with his award by King George V at Buckingham Palace. Harold retired to Westcliffe on Sea and in 1921, as a result of suffering from Reynaud's Disease, sought an increase in his war pension. He claimed that his injuries were the result of his tank being been hit by shellfire in 1916; the claim was turned down but a subsequent Medical Board did reveal that Harold was malnourished and suffering from poor circulation. By 1925, Harold and his family had settled at Prittlewell and lived in Essex until his death, aged fifty-seven years old, at Southend municipal hospital on 2 January 1942. As for his crew, due to the lack of records kept by C Company, I have been unable to identify no details whatsoever.

Crew D5 and *Dolphin*

A third tank was allocated to the preliminary action at Delville Wood, approaching from the north as Daredevil attacked from the south. This tank, named *Dolphin* was commanded by Second Lieutenant Arthur Blowers. The crew had to get to its starting point at the north of Delville Wood in total darkness and the route selected was straight through the wood. By the middle of 15 September 1916, after two months of continuous fighting, the wood was in ruins, the trenches were smashed and the trees had been reduced to stumps. The ground was also littered with unexploded shells and unburied corpses but the route was marked with white tape, which the commanders could follow. Arthur Blowers managed to lead *Dolphin* through the wood, including over a store of unexpected French mortar shells, but the tank ditched in a large shell hole as it tried to get out of its northern edge. Towed out by a tank commanded by Lieutenant Heady Head, Arthur realised he was too late to support *Daredevil* and therefore set off in a north easterly direction, past the eastern side of Flers and towards the final objective of Gueudecourt (see maps 8 and 9).

Dolphin was well behind the first waves of infantry as it crossed the German front line trenches. Despite being slowed by the badly damaged ground, and by its steering wheels which were being dragged uselessly behind, *Dolphin* reached the second objective – a German defensive position known as Gap Trench, which protected the southern entrance to the village of Flers. *Dolphin* crossed the barbed wire and defensive trench and, passing Flers to the east, moved north towards the final objective of Gueudecourt following the track from Ginchy. The tank destroyed two abandoned German artillery pieces as she moved north, using a sunken track to keep out of sight of other German guns positioned to the east of Flers on the Bulls Road (see picture 11). *Dolphin* pushed on northwards and reached the next German trench line (see map 9). As the British infantry were now well behind him, and as tank commanders had been ordered to ensure that their tanks did fall into enemy hands, Arthur turned *Dolphin* south towards its rally point near Delville Wood. On the way back, the tank was stopped by an infantry runner, who asked the crew to destroy a German strong point which was stopping progress to the east of Flers. Arthur Blowers accordingly turned *Dolphin* west towards the village and crossed the sights of the German 77mm guns that were still in position along the Bulls Road. *Dolphin* was moving slowly and she was side-on to the German gunners who had clear view all the way to Delville Wood (see picture 10). The tank was an easy target and one of the shells created an explosion and the tank caught fire. One crewman Leslie Gutsell died immediately whilst Edgar Barnsby was badly injured and died of his wounds after he was dragged from the burning hulk. Arthur Blowers and two more crewmen were also injured but, helped by the three others, managed to make their way back to their own lines despite having to avoid the ongoing British artillery bombardment.

Arthur Blowers was one of the few battle-hardened soldiers amongst the First Tank Crews. Born on 5 November 1891, at Pattles Farm in Knodishall, he was the thirteen of fourteen of a tenant farmer. Arthur, however, shone at school and was awarded a scholarship to the Northgate Grammar School in Ipswich and then gained a place of St Luke's teacher training college in Exeter. A keen sportsman Arthur had played hockey and football for the local teams at Leiston and he played hockey for the college. He was capped by Devon and played soccer for Exeter City football club as an amateur. Arthur was also a keen motorcyclist and served in 4th (Territorial) Battalion the Devonshire Regiment. Returning to Suffolk, he was employed by the local education board and he taught in Grundisburgh, Snape and Hollesley

At the start of the Great War, Arthur immediately re-enlisted and joined 1st/4th Battalion Suffolk Regiment. He was appointed lance corporal on 10 October and deployed to France on 9 November 1914. He was again promoted and, by 16 March 1915, was a sergeant. Arthur was a good shot and was tasked to kill German snipers operating in the opposing trenches. Equipped with a steel faceguard to reduce his own chances of being killed, on 24 April, he identified a sniper and tried to engage him; the German however shot first and hit Arthur's faceguard. Arthur was later admitted to hospital suffering from shock and deafness.

Arthur Blowers in France 1915. (Tank Museum)

Arthur Blowers on commissioning 1916. (Roger Blowers)

He returned to his unit within a month and was soon serving on the front line again. On 25 July 1915 Arthur accidently shot off the top of his second left finger after he fell off the fire step. Although he had been firing at the German trenches his injury was investigated on account of the prevalence of self-inflicted wounds amongst soldiers in the trenches. His CO recorded that no board of enquiry was necessary. Arthur was returned to Britain and treated in Cardiff for six weeks. Having recovered to full fitness, and posted to a battalion training at Tring, Arthur applied for a commission on 31 December and, on 25 February 1916, was posted to the Pembroke College Cadet Unit in Cambridge where he trained alongside many of his future comrades. Arthur was commissioned into the MMGS on 15 April and, after training at Bisley and Elveden, returned to France on 29 August.

Recalling his first tank action, Arthur told his son Roger that he sat in *Dolphin* firing his Webley revolver at German infantry. "I fired over a hundred rounds. None of the targets was more than about 10 yards away, so I didn't miss many". Arthur was awarded the MC "for conspicuous gallantry in action, He fought his Tank with great gallantry, reaching his final objective. On several occasions he assisted the infantry and enabled them to advance". Arthur also told Roger that he was awarded the MC because he rescued his driver, George Thomas, from the wreck of the burning *Dolphin*. However local newspaper reports following award of the medal states Arthur set fire to *Dolphin* after he had sustained a gunshot wound to the head, after he left the tank, and had to be evacuated back to England. He recovered quickly and was photographed in Trafalgar Square in February 1917 being presented by a ribbon from a "Maid of Alsace-Lorraine" who was raising money for charity. Other pictures at the Tank Museum show him instructing at Bovington and then at a party in Bere Regis in July 1917.

On 18 July, Arthur was declared fit for active service. Although he still suffered from severe headaches, he was appointed section commander in the newly formed H Battalion. The unit deployed to France one month later and, having been equipped with its tanks, trucks and all its equipment, moved to Wailly for driver training. On the day of their arrival, 5 September 1917, Arthur was badly injured when a petrol container exploded inside a tank he was inspecting. After initial treatment in France, Arthur was evacuated back to the UK where his injuries were declared as severe but not life threatening. Late in 1917, he was moved to a convalescent hospital at Ashton Court on the outskirts of Bristol, where he took part in the Christmas pantomime. Apparently Arthur found it difficult to sleep in the quiet of a country house so his doctors arranged for him to travel from Bristol to London by train and back again. Whilst travelling, Arthur was able to sleep quite soundly but he was far from well and probably suffering from post-traumatic stress disorder. In May 1918, just after the poet Wilfred Owen was released from Craiglockhart hospital in Scotland, Arthur was admitted to the special hospital near Edinburgh. A Medical Board at Craiglockhart declared Arthur was unfit for further service and, on 25 July, he relinquished his commission.

Returning to Norfolk, Arthur married his fiancée Rosa Fisher the following spring. Their son Harry was born on 9 February 1920 and his sister Brenda was born on 5 June 1921. Arthur was given six months to live in 1920 and was offered a lump sum in place of his pension rights which he refused. During the ongoing treatment for his head injuries he became hooked on heroin. Determined to beat this addiction, Arthur lived in a tent in the orchard on his father's farm and weaned himself off the drug replacing it with large amounts of beer! He made a complete recovery without becoming an alcoholic.

Sadly Rosa died in 1924 of tuberculosis but Arthur married again two years later, he and his second wife Dorothy having five more children. On demobilisation he worked for British Petroleum and in the motor trade in Ipswich and Norwich before returning to the teaching profession in 1926. After a short period at Halesworth, he became headmaster at Ilketshall St Lawrence in 1927. Promotions saw him appointed successively headmaster at Hollesley, a

Lowestoft school for unemployed youths, Ilketshall St James and Snape. He was appointed headmaster of Leiston Modern School in 1939 – a post he held until his retirement in 1954. One pupil remembers he had a rhinoceros tail which appeared in his hand if school children were late in getting ready for school.

Arthur also served as an officer in the Air Training Corps, the local unit being based at his school. Arthur also rode for the Triumph works motorcycle trials team and in 1926, rode a lap of the Isle of Man Tourist Trophy course. Arthur remained a keen sportsman and spent many years as chairman of Leiston Football Club and as an official for Suffolk Amateur Athletic Association. Retiring from teaching in 1954, he worked as a researcher for the Conservative Association, as well tidying up others' gardens for pocket and petrol money. He played his last game of hockey on his sixtieth birthday and regularly attended reunions at St Luke's College at Exeter. At one gathering he presented his cap to the college; his black and light blue college blazer having fallen to pieces as a result of frequent wear. In 1979 he was diagnosed with cancer and, after a very short illness, Arthur died at Spixworth on 10 January 1980 aged eighty nine.

Arthur's second in command, Corporal Ted Foden was born on 12 February 1897 at Wolstanton near Newcastle under Lyme and was therefore the youngest member of *Dolphin*'s crew. When he left school, Ted lived with his grandparents and worked as an apprentice at their butcher's shop in Etruria, the housing estate built by the Wedgewood Company. On 14 October 1915, Ted volunteered to join the MMGS. He was tall for his age and also for a Tanker, just short of six feet tall. Within two days of enlisting, Ted was at the MMGS Training Centre at Bisley. He volunteered to join the Armoured Car Section and was transferred to the Heavy Section MGC on 4 May. The next day he was appointed lance corporal and promoted full Corporal on 5 August. During *Dolphin*'s assault on 15 September Ted was wounded in the ankle and right hand by shell splinters, this was probably as he tried to make his way back to safety. He was evacuated to a hospital in Rouen the next day, and then back to England the UK arriving in Birmingham three days later. Ted was released from hospital on 11 November, shortly after which it was announced that he had been awarded the Military Medal for his actions.

Ted Foden wearing the Military Medal.
(John Foden)

Ted made a full recovery from his wounds but, despite further treatment at to the Lancashire Military Convalescent Hospital at Clift's Park Blackpool, his ankle remained stiff and he gained a permanent limp. Despite this he did not claim a disability pension. As it was determined that Ted would not return to D Battalion. A character reference was requested of Lieutenant Colonel Frank Summers who was by now at serving at Bovington. On 9 March 1917, Summers assessed Ted as "sober, reliable, intelligent and very level headed". Released from hospital on 31 March, and granted ten days leave, Ted was declared fit for service at home but not overseas. He was posted to MGC Depot at Bovington on 16 April 1917, as a corporal, and then to the Tank School of Instruction on 28 July, he served as a Lewis gun instructor. He was later promoted acting sergeant on 1 September 1918. Discharged on 21 February 1919, he returned to live with his grandparents at Burslem. Ted married Elsie Roberts in the summer of 1926 and their son Edward, who was known as John, was born eighteen months later. Elsie and Ted lived at 27

St John Street in Hanley throughout their marriage. Ted eventually became a master butcher and worked at the shop in Etruria until he retired in 1966. He never moved from Stoke on Trent and he died there, aged eighty-two, on 18 March 1978.

Regrettably I have been not able to discover much about the two crewmen who died on 15 September 1916 after *Dolphin* was hit by German artillery to the east of Flers. Gunner Edgar Barnsby was born 28 March 1891 in Chelmsford. His father William, who was a master watchmaker, had married Emma Perks at St Saviour's Church in Birmingham in June 1884. The couple eldest son William was born in Birmingham as were Edgar's elder sisters but the family later moved to Chelmsford which was Emma's home town. They must have kept their links to Birmingham as it was here that Edgar enlisted in April 1916. Having been trained on machine guns at Bisley and then at Elveden, Edgar managed to get to Birmingham during his final leave. He married a local nurse named Edith Phazey, who like Edgar was twenty-five years old, on 5 August at St James' Parish Church in Edgbaston. Less than six weeks later, Edith was widowed when Edgar was fatally wounded on 15 September, his legs being shattered by the shells which penetrated *Dolphin*. He had been dragged from the hulk by William Hodgson but he died soon afterwards. He was commemorated in the National Roll of Great Britain within the Birmingham section as well as in the Birmingham Book of Remembrance.

The other fatality, Gunner Leslie Gutsell, was born in Dorchester High Street on 27 January 1896. Leslie's father Robert was a draper's manager who moved to Basingstoke where he later became the managing director of a furnishing company. The family later moved to Shaftesbury where Robert set up his own drapery business. Leslie became the assistant scoutmaster of the 1st Shaftesbury Boy Scout troop and was also, according to a *Western Gazette* article published after his death, a good musician who would be relied upon to assist others. Leslie joined the MMGS on 3 November 1915 so he must also have been a competent motor cyclist. His service record have not survived so there are no details about his Army life until he was killed aged just nineteen on 15 September. His body was recovered on 30 September by a party from D Company and was buried with Edgar Barnsby near the tank hulk. Sadly both graves were subsequently lost and both men are commemorated on the Thiepval memorial. Leslie's death was also commemorated on a bookcase, which was presented to the Shaftesbury Scout troop. By a strange quirk of fate, the plate from the bookcase came into the possession of a Great War enthusiast Martin Pegler and it is now kept with Leslie's medals and death plaque at Combles, only two miles from where Leslie lost his life.

Gunner William Hodgson, who helped get Edgar Barnsby out of *Dolphin* and put him in a shell hole for safety, managed to get back to the British front line without injury. William had enlisted on 19 February 1916 into the MGC; he later served with the Tank Corps as a lance-corporal but was discharged, as a result of sickness on 5 June 1918. Captain Graham Woods' recorded that Gunner Frank Plant received slight wounds on 15 September and was treated in the camp at the Loop, the site of the railway siding where the tanks were first offloaded. Frank, who was born in Castle Church in Staffordshire in the spring of 1896, was the youngest child of a leather curer Thomas Plant and his wife Harriet. As a young man, Frank worked as a clerk at the County Asylum in Stafford. Whilst he was in France, Frank probably met up with his elder brother Clem who was serving as a bombardier signaller in 287 Siege Battery of the Royal Garrison Artillery. Clem was fatally wounded on 29 June whilst serving in the Ypres Salient and died the following day. Clem was later buried at the Lijssenthoek military cemetery. In the summer of 1917, Frank moved from D Battalion into 2nd Salvage Company, which repaired and recovered broken down and damaged tanks, often under enemy fire. Shortly arriving in the Ypres Salient, Frank was injured whilst riding a motorcycle, near Vlamertinghe on 21 August 1917 and, according to the unit War Diary, was sent to hospital. He survived the war and initially settled at Clyde Street in Leicester with his eldest brother James. After he married Elsie in the early 1920s, they initially lived at 17 Second Avenue in Selly Oak. Later they settled at 18 Heathlands Road in Sutton Coldfield where he died, aged sixty-nine on 23 December 1965. His medals are now held by Simon Payne.

Dolphin's driver, Private George Thomas, was injured on 15 September but was not evacuated to England. The eldest son of a shoemaker, George was born at Royston in Hertfordshire in late 1891. He was only twenty, and working as a hotel porter, when he married Minnie Poulter, on 18 November 1911. Their two children Lily and Thomas were born at Royston in 1912 and 1913. In 1915, George, who was employed as a motor driver, enlisted into the ASC at Hitchen but, as far as I can tell, did not deploy to France until he was serving with the tanks in September 1916. He was awarded the Military Medal for his action on 15 September. After he recovered from his injuries, George rebadged to the MGC and served with No 12 Company of D Battalion with Albert Wateridge and James Anderson. He probably fought at Thelus on Vimy Ridge, on 9 April, during the opening day of the Battle of Arras. Like Albert Wateridge, he drove an unarmoured tank into action at the second Battle of Bullecourt, on 3 May 1917. He was killed as the tanks pressed home their attack on the Hindenburg line defences. Sadly the site of George's grave is unknown and he is commemorated on Arras war memorial as well as the Royston war memorial.

The final member of *Dolphin*'s crew was the splendidly named Faraday Mendelssohn Sladdin. Born on 1 November 1878 in Brighouse in West Yorkshire, he was the son of a silk spinner who later established his own clothing company. Faraday, who became a shoulder pad manufacturer in his own right, was the oldest member of the crew at thirty-eight years of age. He had enlisted at Halifax on 9 December 1915 but was not mobilized until 28 April 1916. As Faraday deployed overseas on 28 August, only four months later, his training was limited. I cannot confirm if he fought on the Somme, after 15 September, but he was transferred to D Battalion in November 1916. Faraday joined No 11 Company under the command of Major Willie Watson and probably fought at the first Battle of Bullecourt, a "bloodbath" resulted in the large number of Australian and British troops becoming casualties as they were easily targeted by German artillery and machine guns against a background of snow. The tanks were equally badly affected with only two of the eleven tanks rallying; the remaining nine were knocked out. The Company also fought during the Third Battle of Ypres near St Julian and also at Poelcapelle on 9 October 1917 when the tanks had to use what remained of the local roads. The countryside on either side was a quagmire after three months of artillery bombardment, heavy rain and a fine soil which had turned into a swamp. Faraday, who had retrained as driver, drove a tank into action the Battle of Cambrai on 20 November when No 11 Company broke through the Hindenburg Line to the west of Flesquières. He also fought at the battle to capture Bourlon village and Bourlon Wood on 23 November; although all the tanks rallied, most suffered significant levels of damage with all Lewis guns being disabled by enemy fire.

On 1 December, Faraday's close friend Alfred Walters was killed in action. Faraday was granted home leave soon afterwards and, whilst there, wrote to Alfred's parents about his death enclosing a money order for £30 which he had removed from his body. When D Battalion was re-designated 4th Battalion, in January 1918, Faraday was classified as a first class tank mechanic. Faraday served with the unit until the end of the war and moved with them to Germany where he worked in the Battalion HQ. He returned to England on 19 February 1919 for demobilisation and returned to Brighouse. Three years later, he married Edith Gaudin, a local woman who had moved to Brighouse as a girl. The couple lived in Brighouse until 1935 when they moved to Devoran near Truro naming their house Mount View after Faraday's home in Brighouse. Sadly Edith died in 1946 but, two years later, Faraday married Eleanor Denham. They lived on at Mount View until Faraday's death on 16 August 1953 at the age of seventy-four.

4

Fighting for their lives

D Company provided the tanks for the centre of the attack on 15 September 1916 and C Company provided the tanks on each flank. No 1 Section supported the Canadians near Courcelette whilst No 3 and No 4 Sections supported the British attacks on the eastern flank between Ginchy and Combles, where they worked alongside the French Army. Three tank crews were allocated to support the attacks near Combles: crew C13 commanded by Sir John Dashwood, C14 commanded by Frank Arnold and C16 commanded by Eric Purdy (see map 4). The tank manned by the C13 crew broke down near Angle Wood as it made it way by night to its start point. The other tanks not only got to their start points at Leuze Wood but also crossed no man's land ahead of the British infantry in accordance with their orders. Once they had reached their objectives, both sets of crewmen had to fight for their lives for several hours after their vehicles had become stuck in German front-line trenches.

Crew C13

When Major "Boney" Fuller became Chief of Staff at the Tank Headquarters, he described officers serving with newly formed tank battalions as "the biggest Band of Brigands I have ever met". Whilst this may have an apt description for the 18th century "Hellfire Club", led by the infamous Sir Francis Dashwood, it was wholly inappropriate for his descendant Sir John Dashwood. This twenty year old aristocrat commanded No 3 Section of C Company as well as tank crew C13 on 15 September. He was the Premier Baronet of England, having been born on 25 April 1896 at West Wycombe Park in Buckinghamshire and succeeding to the title when he was only twelve years old. He was educated at Wellington College and Magdalen College Oxford where he was studying as war was declared. A member of the University of Oxford OTC, Sir John applied for a commission in his local regiment, the Oxfordshire and Buckinghamshire Light Infantry. Commissioned on 14 September 1914, aged only eighteen, he was posted to 10th Battalion Argyll and Sutherland Highlanders (A&SH) where he served with Allen Holford-Walker, his future commander in C Company. They deployed to France in May 1915 and fought at the Battle of Loos on 25 September 1915. This was the first time that the British Army undertook a set piece attack against a major German defensive position. Ten British infantry and one Indian Army divisions were committed to the attack including four divisions formed from Field Marshal Herbert Kitchener's volunteer battalions. Two of these Divisions were Scottish and they took large numbers of casualties. The 9th Scottish Division, in which Sir John served, was tasked to capture the colliery complex known as Fosse 8 which was fortified by the Germans. The Battalion history reports, after the assaulting companies had captured their objective at Peking Trench, the nineteen year baronet bought up two Vickers machine guns, their crews and the associated equipment and ammunition, to assist in subduing German counter-attacks. It says much for Sir John's leadership and the determination of his men as they could only reach their comrades by crossing the bullet-swept no man's land. They were successful but later that afternoon, the German formations re-captured the British held trenches using a combination of artillery fire, well-practiced counter attack plans and their extreme lethal stick grenades proved too much for the inexperienced formations.

In comparison to other units in the Division, Sir John's battalion lost relatively few other ranks but many of its officers were wounded. Sir John was consequently appointed acting Captain on 8 October but must have either have been wounded or fell ill as he later returned to England. On 15 May 1916, Sir John transferred to the MMGS probably at Allen Holford-Walker's instigation as, like Frank Summers of D Company, he had major concerns about over the lack of battle experience amongst the junior officers sent to him. Originally appointed to command C Company's Reserve section, Sir John led the advance party to Le Havre. He arrived on 8 August 1916 and, with Captain Richard Trevithick, organized the offloading of the tanks. Moving by rail to the training area at Yvrench, Sir John took over No 3 Section when Richard Trevithick injured his knee. On 14 September, whilst commanding tank crew C13, he led the two other crews (C14 and C16) to their start point near Leuze Wood to the northwest of Combles. C13's track broke near Angle Wood, half way to the start point.

As his tank could not be immediately recovered, Sir John Dashwood was then given command of tank crew C20 whose original skipper, George Macpherson, had died on 15 September. Gunner Will Dawson, who served in the C20 crew, later wrote that on 23 September, Sir John was again tasked to support 56th Division in company with tank crew C23 under Second Lieutenant Andrew Henderson. On 24 September, the two tanks moved to the point of assembly at Wedge Wood. They were unable to move on 25 September as Sir John was seeking a replacement for Andrew Henderson who had sprained his ankle. Second Lieutenant Len Bates was sent up with a consignment of petrol which was delivered using animal transport – the poor state of the ground making it impossible to use the Company's motor vehicles for replenishment. The two tanks then advanced in

Officer instructors in Spring 1917. (TPC)

support of 168th Brigade but Dashwood's tank became stuck in a sunken road and took no further part in the battle. On 30 September, after the crew returned to the vehicle, the tank was dug out and returned to the Loop. Thereafter Sir John acted as a Liaison Officer for the rest of the actions on the Somme. Sir John joined C Battalion in November 1916, as the unit was withdrawn from the Somme battlefield and, unusually, was granted home leave. In early 1917, whilst at St Pol Sur Ternoise, Sir John was appointed to instruct at the newly formed Central School.

Sir John is pictured standing in the rear rank, second from the left, just behind Stuart Hastie who commanded *Dinnaken* on 15 September 1916 at Flers. Also in the rear rank second from the right is Alec Arnaud whose tank became ditched whilst trying to get to his start point that morning. The school was vital for ensuring that new commanders and crewman, who joined the four new tank battalions being formed in France, were trained for the operations which were due to take place later that spring. On 27 March 1917, he was sent to the local hospital with an inflamed knee but was released in time to command a section during the Battle of Arras which started on Easter Monday. There is no detailed record of his role in that battle but his service record reveals Sir John was again granted home-leave in early May. He returned to C Battalion where he continued to serve as a section commander. He attended the F Battalion dinner night on 27 June where he met with many of the tank skippers who fought at Flers-Courcelette. He obviously attracted Frank Summers' attention that evening as Sir John was attached to F Battalion on 29 July, the first day of the Third Battle of Ypres, and assumed the post of Adjutant on 1 August 1917 after Harold Mortimore was sent back to England owing to sickness.

Appointed substantive Captain on 17 November 1917, Sir John served with F Battalion throughout the Battle of Cambrai. He stayed with the Battalion after the unit was re-roled onto Whippet tanks and harried the German forces as they pushed the British and French forces back across the ground they captured in 1916 and 1917. Sir John was again in action during the Battle of Amiens but was then detached, when the unit was still in action, from 24 August until 9 September 1918 to the Inter-Allied Tankodrome. He only rejoined 3rd Battalion, as it had become known, after the 100 day advance which caused the German to sue for peace. Having been appointed a company commander, Sir John entered hospital for a knee operation in January 1919. He left 3rd Battalion on 2 February 1919 and returned to England three days later when he was demobilised.

Sir John was busy with estate business for the next two years until 13 December 1920, when he was appointed Third Secretary in the Diplomatic Service. In the New Year, he attended 3rd Battalion's second annual dinner at the Cannon Street Hotel on 29 January 1921 at which Eric Purdy was also present. On 20 December 1922, he married Helen Eaton, whose Canadian father had died of wounds on 11 April 1917, whilst commanding 8th Bde Canadian Field Artillery whilst in direct support of the 3rd Canadian Division during the assault on Vimy Ridge. On 1 January 1923, Sir John was appointed as Second Secretary at the British Embassy in Brussels.

His daughter Maud was born on 23 February 1924 and his son Francis, the 11th Baronet, was born on 7 August 1925. Sir John served with the Foreign Office until 1927 and, after a brief period as a stockbroker, retired to his West Wycombe estate. In March 1929, Sir John and Lady Moira travelled to South Africa but had returned to England for the birth of their younger son John on 16 June 1929. On 1 August 1933, he was appointed Assistant Marshal of the Diplomatic Corps, acting as a link between the Royal Household and the diplomatic community in London, in which role he served until his death. Having been appointed Sherriff of Buckinghamshire in 1934, a role which held for the usual twelve months, Sir John was granted a Reserve commission in the RAF on 9 November 1938. He served with 907 (County Of Middlesex) Balloon Squadron in which role held continued to serve after the outbreak of war. In 1942, he returned to the Foreign Office, became the Chief Security Officer for the Diplomatic Service in 1943 and, amongst other tasks, investigated the CICERO spy scandal in Ankara in January 1944, after a German spy named Elyesa Bazna gained employment as the valet to the British Ambassador Sir Hughe Knatchbull-Hugessen. His

Sir John and Lady Helen Dashwood and their daughter Maud. (National Portrait Gallery)

service to the Royal Household was recognised then through his appointment as a Commander of Royal Victorian Order. In 1952, Sir John opened the West Wycombe caves where his ancestor Sir Francis had entertained the Hellfire club two hundred years earlier. Six years later, he was also appointed an Extra Gentleman Usher to the Queen from 2 August 1958 in which role he served until his death aged seventy on 9 July 1976. Lady Helen lived at West Wycombe until her death, aged eighty-nine, on 26 June 1989.

Crew C16

The tank, supporting the Londons on their attack towards Combles on 15 September 1916, was a female variant which was possibly called *Corunna*. Commanded by Lieutenant Eric Purdy, the tank attacked the German positions on the northwest of the village of Combles. Starting from the south-east corner of Leuze Wood (see coloured image 1), the tank had moved on time, downhill across no man's land, to the junction of the German Loop and Combles trenches, on the outskirts of the village of Combles. Arriving well before the British infantry, the tank crewmen neutralized enemy machine gun and rifle fire as the Londons made their way across no man's land. The tank was hit by German artillery defensive fire but the crew fought on for five hours despite being attacked by Germans at very close range. Eventually, after they had run out of ammunition, the crew set fire to the tank before being abandoned in accordance with orders.

The crew's skipper, Eric Purdy, was born on 5 September 1894 at Newtown to the southwest of Sydney in New South Wales. He was educated at Sydney Grammar School and then, after the family moved to London, at the South West Polytechnic in Chelsea. From 1911, he studied at Ardingly College in Sussex where he served in the OTC. When he left school, Eric followed his father into the hotel business. Soon after the declaration of war, on 8 September, Eric enlisted as a private soldier in 23rd Battalion London Regiment. He deployed to France on 14 March 1915 and, twelve days later, was commissioned, in the field, into the Northamptonshire (Northants) Regiment. Eric returned to England on 3 May 1915 and joined 6th Battalion. He returned to France on 5 September 1915 and, six weeks later, was badly wounded whilst serving with 1st Battalion Northants on 13 October, during the final stages of the Battle of Loos. The War Diary records that his unit suffered heavy losses after their trenches were struck by three direct hits whilst waiting the order to advance. The company commander was wounded and handed command over to Eric. Eric was later badly wounded in the shoulder and practically half the company was either killed or wounded in the space of a few minutes. He was evacuated to Southampton on 16 October and, after being treated at St Thomas' Hospital in London, was granted leave for three months.

Joining 8th Battalion Northants at Colchester on 22 January 1916, Eric transferred to the Armoured Car Section MGC two months later, no doubt having volunteered for the "secret and dangerous mission". He returned to France on 16 August 1916 and was awarded the Military Cross for his conspicuous gallantry in action near Combles on 15 September. Promoted Temporary Lieutenant on 1 October 16. Eric was a popular officer who appeared in performances by the the the *Willies*, the concert party of C Battalion, often playing a curate.

Eric fought in the early stages of the Battle of Arras but, on 28 April 1917, he was sent home on duty to the UK. His stay was extended on 13 May to enable him to attend his medal investiture and again extended the next day for "VIP affairs". On 19 May, Eric returned to C Battalion and was placed in command of tank no 2728 driven by Private William Piper. After his tank crew completed driver training at Wailly between 10 and 19 June, Eric took over command of No 10

Section of No 9 Company. On 31 July 1917, he commanded No 12 Section at the Third Battle of Ypres when his four tanks took part in the assault on the Frezenberg redoubt. Eric initially commanded his section from the tank *Chili* which became ditched twice. He then transferred to the tank *Crusader* and caught up with the Gordon Highlanders he was supporting, successfully dealing with many machine gun, snipers and strong points he encountered.

On 20 November, on the opening day of the Battle of Cambrai, Eric's section supported the attack on the Pam-Pam Farm which dominated the Bonavis Ridge and the road from Peronne to Cambrai. Ten tanks from C Battalion were needed to subdue the German garrison who were in four mutually supporting bunkers, the bunkers being cleared by members of two infantry battalions who then set the farm on fire. Eric then

Eric Purdy 1917. (TPC)

led his tanks north up the Cambrai Road to Le Quennet Farm to the north west of Lateau Wood. After the position was taken, the section was pushing north towards Masnieres when one of Eric's section *Comet II* was destroyed. Amongst its crew was Harry Tiffin who had been present at Flers-Courcelette, his death being witnessed by his close friend Bob Tate, who had served with Archie Holford-Walker in *Clan Leslie* on 15 September. On 23 November Eric commanded one of two composite sections from C Battalion who supported the attack on Fontaine Notre Dame, the other being commanded by Andrew Henderson who was the skipper of *Clan Ruthven* at High Wood on 15 September 1916. One of Eric's tanks, named *Cayenne*, was hit by direct fire at the start of the attack but managed to get back to its rallying point. The two others made their way from Bourlon Wood to the north of the village, suppressing German fire from Fontaine en route to their objective to the north-east of the village. They then returned to Bourlon Wood and patrolled its north-east edge looking for targets. Finding no German infantry, they then made their way back to the rally point and assisted a group of British infantry who were pinned down in a sunken lane to the west of the village, and then protected them whilst the village was mopped up.

Granted home leave, immediately after the tanks were withdrawn, Eric returned to London from 2 to 16 December 1917. He returned to the newly designated 3rd Light Battalion and trained his crews to operate the newly issued Whippet tanks. On 25 March 1918, Eric again commanded No 12 Section which defended Colincamps during the great German offensive known as the "Kaiserschlacht". Although his three Whippet tanks were only in action for two hours, they each fired over 200 rounds of machine gun ammunition. Two of the tanks dispersed about two hundred Germans advancing towards Auchonvillers whilst the third ran over a machine gun and dispersed another fifty troops who subsequently abandoned a further five machine guns. Unusually granted leave in England between 18 July and 1 August 1918, Eric was again in command of No 12 Section during the Battle of Amiens, personally commanding one of the four Whippet tank named *Cayenne*. Commanding one of the Whippets named *Chili* was Sergeant George Kennedy, who had fought in C Company on the Somme in 1916 and who had won the Military Medal during the Battle of Arras. Tasked to support 7th Dragoon Guards, Eric's section followed the cavalry until the horses were stopped by heavy machine gun fire. The tanks then went forward and cleared the machine guns and their supporting troops which were well dug into woods either side of Beaucourt, and then pushed them further back. The tanks then patrolled the newly captured ground until the 4th Canadian Division could take over. The tanks then rallied. On 21 August, Eric and his four tanks were again in action near Achiet-le-Grand, this time attacking under the cover of thick mist. The tanks were successful until the mist lifted and seven of the tanks were knocked out, many after their machine guns had jammed due to overheated barrels.

On 25 August, when fifteen Whippets were committed to support an attack on Bapaume to Arras road, the Germans stopped the tanks in their tracks. Although most managed to rally, three tanks were knocked out. Eric Purdy was wounded in the left thigh and arm and was evacuated back to England on 1 September 1918. After treatment in London, he was released on 18 September but declared as unfit for three months. He was released from the Army on 2 January 1919 and settled on Wandsworth Common. The following summer, he married Margaret Wainwright at Maidenhead where the couple made their home. On 29 January 1920, Eric attended the second annual dinner held by officers of the 3rd Battalion, one of the other officers present being his section commander on the Somme, Sir John Dashwood.

Having served in the Army Reserve for 30 months, Eric eventually relinquished his commission on 1 September 1921. He had returned to the hotel business and initially managed the Naval and Military Hotel in South Kensington. From 1925, he was a member of C Battalion OCA committee. His daughter Tonia was born the following autumn at Maidenhead, her brother Graham born in March 1929 and their younger sister Josephine the following year. In addition to running the Norfolk Hotel in Kensington, Eric served in the RAF Volunteer Reserve (VR) as General Duties

Flying Officer from 16 September 1926 for ten years but did not lose touch with his tank comrades, attending the annual Cambrai Dinner in November 1938. On the outbreak of hostilities in 1939, Eric was again commissioned in the RAF VR. Concerned for their children's safety, Margaret and Eric sent their children to Toronto in July 1940 and therefore missed the London Blitz. Graham returned to England in late 1943, Tonia just after D Day and Josephine in 1945. In 1948, Eric visited Australia with his elder daughter and returned to England the following year. He returned to Australia in 1953 and the following year, undertook a long sailing trip. A Brisbane newspaper, reported that "the 55-year-old Sydney sloop, Heartsease, which is being sailed on a three month Barrier Reef cruise by her skipper-owner, Mr Eric Purdy. Mr Purdy recently retired from running a chain of London Hotels. Mr Purdy, Sydney born, celebrated his 61st birth day yesterday shortly after arriving in port". He returned to England but, after his wife Margaret died on 5 April 1958, returned to Australia. He initially lived in the Sydney suburb of Bondi until 1980 and died aged eighty-nine on 1 May 1984 at Townsville.

Although none of the other crew members of the C16 are listed in any official documents, I am convinced that Gunner William Piper was on board as a result of reading a scrapbook he kept which is now held by the Tank Museum. William Piper, who was born in Oxford in 1880, was the fourth child and second son of an Oxford college messenger who lived next door to Worcester College. By the age of 21, William was working as a club messenger but 10 years later, he had become a college messenger and living with his brother in law and sister at 46 Abingdon Road. He was living at 67 Woodstock Road in Oxford when he volunteered to serve with the MMGS. Enlisting at Coventry on 21 March 1915, in the same week as Gerald Pattinson, William's scrap book records his tank was tasked to assault Leuze Wood so he probably fought with Lieutenant Purdy. He must have re-trained as a driver as his scrapbook also records he served with Eric Purdy, as a driver until May 1917, and then he was tasked to crew the tank, *Crab*, with Captain Hiscocks and Corporal Alsopp. Later transferred to the Tank Corps, William was injured during the Third Battle of Ypres and evacuated to the UK, eventually being treated at Norwich. He was discharged from hospital around 24 September 1917 and released from the Army on 15 April 1918. I can find no other records of this early tanker but you can see his scrapbook, which was purchased at an auction in the late 1990s, in the Tank Museum archives.

Crew C14

The other crew that got into action on 15 September did their best to ensure the infantry broke through the enemy front lines. Like their comrades near Combles, they were involved in close quarter fighting for several hours, before they abandoned the tank as 56 London Division could not make progress.

Tom Bernard, who described the action in his diary written later on 7 October, said

> We went into action on September 15 with D and C Company and altogether fifty cars. My car No 509, which was a female car, went over (the British frontline) to the left of Leuze Wood. The ground was awful, all shell holes, and that very loose. We went over our first line at 6.08 a.m. and roved about "no man's land" and over the enemy trenches, backed up the infantry. Unfortunately at about 9.15, our diff [differential gear} got stripped and we could only proceed with the diff locked which caused our steering to lock. The officer Second Lieutenant Arnold consulted us on the matter and we decided to stick the action – we were signaled by a sergeant of our infantry that they were being attacked by a party of bombers from Leuze Wood so we came stern first to attack these bombers and, just as we got within twenty yards of them, the car got stuck in a large shell hole which, had we had our steering gear been in order, we would easily have got out of.

The hulk of C14 with Bouleaux Wood to its east. (Tank Museum)

The officer then asked for volunteers to go out and try to dig the car out. Corporal Pattinson, Gunner Winter, Gunner Williams and myself went out of the back door and made a start. The shell hole in which we were stuck was connected to the trench in which were the German bombers. After about ten minutes digging, a bomb fell at Corporal Pattinson's feet. He picked it up and tried to throw it away but it exploded in his hands, killing him and wounding Gunner Winter.

Williams and I rushed down the trench towards the bombers and, at the corner of the traverse trench, came into one [German soldier] with a bomb in his hand and was in a position to throw it. I had my revolver our ready and let him have two [bullets], unfortunately Williams had left his revolver in the car so we rushed back to the car. Winter also got wounded through the shoulder by a sniper. The Officer [Frank Arnold] then went out and managed to get to a captain of the infantry to try to get some men to try to assist to dig the car out. During the time he was away, Gunner Ritchie took one machine gun and Williams took another and occasionally have them have burst [of fire] but unfortunately, we were in such a position that we could not train them [the guns] on the Germans. Still it reminded them that we were awake and I was potting away with revolvers through the loop holes of the conning tower and all this time the German artillery was giving us a very warm time.

At about 4:00 p.m. we decided to abandon the car and we made for a short trench about 40 yards away which had been made by connecting a few shell holes, We were being sniped all the way, I got nearly to where Mr Arnold was and reported to him. He then got me that the [machine gun] locks would have to be removed to make the guns useless in case the enemy should get inside [the tank] in which case they could sweep the field [with bullets]. I went back and took Gunner Williams with me and left Gunner Ritchie, Giles and Winter in the trench with Mr Arnold and Private Sleath [Owen Sleath the ASC driver]. We got back to the car and effectively jammed with guns fetching the locks back with us, not without some difficulty.

We arrived where Mr Arnold was but he had left. We were in a shell hole with a lieutenant and corporal of the infantry and stayed there until dark which was about 7:30 p.m. During this time a chap was hit whilst crawling over my knees and it was rather cold. At dark, the enemy artillery made a tremendous bombardment on our second line trenches and we decided to wait a while. At 7:50 p.m. Williams, myself and about six infantryman, who had been wounded, made a dash across the two hundred yards to the second line trench. As the star [illuminating] shells came, we dropped to the ground so as not to be seen and then up and ran again. I fell over a French parapet but Williams had not arrived. I got along the communications trench which was an awful sight with dead and wounded and eventually got to the 8th Battalion Bedfordshire headquarters and was directed to a valley where two of our tanks were waiting. I was glad to see them, at about 11 p.m. and managed to get a few hours' sleep.

In the morning I proceed to our headquarters and reported to the Adjutant. During the afternoon the OC sent for me and congratulated me on coming through. At night Mr Arnold came and took me back to camp. He and Private Sleath of the ASC had got through although both we shaken up.

I have since ascertained that Gunner Ritchie is at Abbeville hospital and hoping to get to England shortly. Gunner Winter is at Boulogne hospital and is almost blind in the left eye, which I hope it only temporary, and the other wound through the shoulder in progressing satisfactorily. Gunner Giles was killed whilst trying to get back to our second line. Gunner Williams is also in hospital and is recovering from shellshock. I have been to the dressing station and recovered the gun locks left there by him.

The tank had crossed the start- line, at the north east corner of Leuze Wood on time and reached the German front line known as Beef Trench well ahead of infantry (see map 4). There, her crew used their four belt-fed Vickers machine guns to suppress the Germans' fire as the Londons crossed no man's land and reached the German trench. Their skipper Second Lieutenant Frank Arnold then directed his driver to move deeper into German territory (see coloured image 2). Moving slowly because of the poor ground condition, the tank had reached at the end of Bouleaux Wood by 8.00 a.m. Tank crew C14 had driven more than 1,200 yards through the German defences reaching their third objective at northeast corner of Bouleaux Wood. Finding he was well ahead of the infantry, Frank took his tank back to Beef Trench twice to lead the infantry forward; the final time approaching stern first perhaps to give covering fire as it moved off again. It was then that the tank became ditched in a shell hole and could not be driven out. They then fought off the Germans for over eight hours before Frank Arnold decided to evacuate the tank

Following the action, Tom Bernard and Billy Williams were both awarded the Military Medal for putting the tank's machine guns out of use whilst Frank Arnold was awarded the Military Cross. Major Allen Holford-Walker recommended Corporal Gerald Pattinson for the Victoria Cross but this was not approved because there were no independent witnesses to the action which, as he later pointed out, said a great deal about how far the tank crew was ahead of the infantry unit they were supporting.

As the VC was, at the time, the only gallantry medal which could be awarded posthumously, Gerald Pattinson's bravery was never formally recognised. He was born in Sunderland on 26 March 1885; his German mother Helene was from Hamburg and his English father Charles was a rope-walker's traveller. Gerald was working overseas as a marine engineer at the start of the war but returned to England on 7 May 1915. He enlisted into the MMGS at Coventry in July 1915 and deployed to France on 24 August 16. In October 1916, after the British managed to push the Germans back and capture the tank hulk, his body was recovered and buried close to the tank. Later his remains were removed, during the battlefield clearances, and buried at Combles Communal Cemetery Extension. His sister, despite her grief, sent Christmas gifts to Gunner Denton Winter who was in hospital

Denton Winter, who was born in 1890, was bought up in Potter Newton in Leeds. At six feet, he was much taller than the average crewmen. Before he enlisted into the MMGS on 11 December 1915, Denton worked as a dental mechanic at Church Street in York. He was wounded in his side, left eye and shoulder on 15 September by German grenade splinters and it later took him 2½ hours to crawl back to his own lines. Denton was evacuated to No 13 Stationary Hospital at Boulogne where, at Christmas, he received the gifts from Emily Pattinson. Despite losing the sight of his left eye, Denton was not discharged from the Army but, probably at his own request, was posted to the Training and Reinforcement Depot on 27 May. He stayed at Dannes-Camiers, which was close to Étaples, for two months where he retrained as a driver. Whilst Denton might have expected to be sent back to C Battalion, to join his old comrades, he was sent to D Battalion and allocated to No 10 Company which also contained many of the First Tank Crews. He arrived with his new unit, just as it was going into action in the Ypres Salient. D Battalion suffered many casualties during the Third Battle of Ypres and also had a good number of tanks destroyed on 20 November near Flesquières on the first day of the Battle of Cambrai.

On 21 November, Denton again sustained multiple wounds from German artillery fire and was sent back to England on 25 November. Admitted to the Reading War Hospital, by 17 December, he recovered sufficiently to be granted leave over Christmas. Denton also decided to spend New Year with his parents and therefore did not return to duty until 3 January 1918. As a result he was found guilty of being Absent without Leave and forfeited seven days' pay. Posted onto the strength of the Command Depot at Catterick, Denton was again admitted to hospital on 4 February 1918 suffering with influenza. On 13 April he was discharged but his health had been compromised and his medical standard was accordingly reduced to B2 – that is fit for employment on the Lines of Communication overseas. He was posted to the Tank Corps Depot at Wareham but Denton never became sufficiently well to be fully fit for operations. He therefore remained at the Depot until he was demobilised on 5 February 1919.

Despite his low medical category, Denton was retained in the Z Reserve for a further year. On 31 July 1919, he was awarded a pension of 16/6d for seventy weeks as a result of the loss of his left eye. Denton became engaged to Sarah Howes whose home at Hamilton Avenue was only half a mile from Reginald Terrace where Denton was now working as a dentist. They married on 29 April 1922 at St Martin's Church in Potterworth and their son Herbert was born on 22 March 1925. Sarah's father owned a number of wine shops in Leeds and Denton took over the management of one of them. The family lived at the Moorland Wines Store on the Harrogate Road for many years but, according to one relative, the combination of his war-time experiences and the ready access to alcohol had a distinct impact on his life. Denton died aged seventy in Leeds on 21 July 1960.

Gunner Bertie Arthur Garnett Giles, who was the youngest crewman in C14, was killed as he tried to return to the British trenches on 15 September. Known by his crewmates as Bag, he was born on 9 July 1898 at Barking. His father had been a Regular soldier but, when his second son Bertie was born, he was working a Gas Works gate and timekeeper. By 1911, the family had moved to Colchester and, although he was still at school, Bertie was also working as a grocer's errand boy. He enlisted into the MMGS in 1915, aged just seventeen and was killed when he was only eighteen years old. Although his body was later recovered, his grave was subsequently lost and BAG is commemorated on the Thiepval memorial.

The tank's driver, Private Owen Sleath suffered from shell-shock as a result of the fighting at Bouleaux Wood but recovered and transferred to the Tank Corps with whom he served for the remainder of the war. Owen, who was born in Warwick in early 1892, was the second son of a machine agent named Alfred Sleath and Louisa Parkinson. He was baptised on 8 August at St

Mary's Church which was the obvious place for the family as they were living at 50 Brook Street in Warwick. As a young man Owen learned to drive and, by 1911, was working as a chauffeur in Leamington Spa. I have been unable to find out exactly when he joined the ASC but he later was attached to 711 MT Company which formed on 3 June 1916. Just before he deployed to France with the tanks from Elveden, Owen returned to Warwick where he married his sweetheart Eveline Gumbley, a cashier who was two years his junior.

Owen's service record has not survived but, from his service number, it is clear he transferred from the ASC to the Heavy Branch MGC in early 1917. The *Midlands Daily Telegraph* later reported that Owen was again wounded in October 1917 – this would have been in the Ypres Salient. Owen eventually reached the rank of Machinist Staff Sergeant, the senior driver and mechanic in each tank company. Returning to Warwick after the war, Eveline and Owen had two children; their daughter Kathleen was born in early 1920 and their son Norman who was born in December 1922 whilst Owen was living in St Paul's Close in the centre of Leamington. The family then moved to Brook Street in the town before moving to Stratford upon Avon where Owen worked as a theatre attendant in the local hospital. His son Norman died, aged only forty-eight, on 9 April 1962 in Leamington Spa, his wife Eveline died the following year on 22 August 1963 at Stratford upon Avon Hospital and Owen himself died just eleven months later, aged seventy-two, in the same hospital on 11 August 1964.

I have been unable to find out nothing about Gunner Billy Williams despite the fact that he was awarded the Military Medal for his bravery during the first tank actions. He was initially reported as "missing" but was later found, suffering from shock, and taken to a hospital. Gunner Arthur Ritchie, who was fatally injured in the action, died almost two months later. Born on 28 October 1895, Arthur was the only child of a Scottish doctor David Ritchie and Alice Osbourn, a butcher's daughter from Hunslet. The couple met when David moved to England and set up his practice in Alice's parents' house. They married on 17 August 1891 at St Jude's Church in Hunslet where Arthur was baptised on 12 February 1896. David Ritchie died, just before Arthur's second birthday, but his mother Alice remar-

ried and had a daughter Elsie and two more sons. Arthur initially worked as a pawnbroker's assistant but, by the time he enlisted at Halifax, he was running his own business in Todmorden. Arthur Ritchie suffered severe shrapnel wounds in his back during the action on 15 September and was evacuated to a base hospital at Abbeville where he celebrated his twenty-first birthday. However his injuries did not respond to treatment and, when he became dangerously ill, the War Office arranged for his mother and his stepsister Elsie to visit him in France. They were present when he died on 14 November 1916.

Frank Arnold, the tank's skipper, was the son of a school teacher named William and his wife Sarah. Frank was baptised at St Mark's Church in Bow on 26 January 1896 and educated at Christ's Hospital School at Horsham. He then worked for the Metropolitan Asylums Board as a clerk on the Training Ship *Exmouth* which was

Frank Arnold. (*Sphere Magazine*)

moored off the town of Grays on the north bank of the River Thames. This specially built ship was one of several sailing vessels which providing schooling for pauper children, as well as vocational training which enabled them to join the Royal and Merchant Navies. Frank volunteered to enlist and initially served as a private in one of the Public Schools Battalions, the 19th Battalion Royal Fusiliers. He served in France as a Lance Corporal in France from 12 November 1915 alongside Alec Arnaud and then returned to England on 19 March, after his Battalion was disbanded to provide junior officers. Frank and Alec were commissioned into the MGC on 15 April 1916 and both allocated to C Company.

According to Allen Holford-Walker, Frank Arnold "had never seen a shot fired in wrath in his life" before the first tank action and the C Company commander was not initially convinced that he should recommend Frank for a gallantry award following the action at Bouleaux Wood. Allen only did so after he followed the tracks of the tank, across the battlefield and noted how far the tank had advanced into the enemy defences without infantry support as well as his bravery into deciding to return twice to Beef Trench bring the Londoners forward. As a consequence, Frank was awarded the Military Cross. Frank joined C Battalion, on its formation in November 1916 and served with No 9 Company. At the Battle of Arras, Frank commanded tank crew C45 in *Cayenne*. This was one of six tanks which became ditched in the morass on the move-up to the start point near Achicourt on 9 April 1917. The tank was recovered but did not go into action that day. Frank again commanded *Cayenne*, this time a Mark IV tank, on 31 July 1917 on the opening day of the Third Battle of Ypres. The tank initially failed to start and, after the crew had got it moving, it subsequently became stuck on a tree and did not get into action. Frank was appointed temporary lieutenant on 15 October 1917 but does not appear to have been in action during the Battle of Cambrai. However, he stayed with C Battalion as it was re-designated 3rd Light Battalion and was re-equipped with Whippet Tanks. Frank fought with the unit during the opening of the Battle of Amiens in August 1918 and was appointed to command a section in C Company from 1 September until 19 October 1918.

Frank, who was the only officer to serve with C Battalion and then 3rd Light Tank Battalion for the duration of the war, only relinquished his commission on completion of service on 1 September 1921. He did not lose contact with his former friends in C Battalion as he is listed in the 1925 Old Comrades Association membership even though he was living in Mexico where his contact address was the Tuxpam Bar in Veracruz. Frank must have returned shortly to England afterwards as, in the summer of 1927, he married Evelyn Waghorn near her home of Lewisham. Frank became a traveller for a company of manufacturing chemists and Evelyn gave birth to their only son Raymond on 25 April 1934 by which time they had settled at Bromley in Kent. Frank remained in the TA Reserve of Officers and, following the outbreak of the Second World War, was commissioned, in the rank of Captain into the Royal Armoured Corps on 2 September 1939. He served with the Eighth Army in North Africa but I can find nothing of his later war service. Returning to work as a commercial traveller, Frank remained in the Reserve until he relinquished his commission having exceeded the age-limit on 16 April 1949, when he was granted the rank of honorary rank of captain. Evelyn and Frank later moved to Somerset where he died, aged only 61 on 19 April 1957 at Bleadon Hill near Weston Super Mare.

The final member of the crew was Gunner Tom Bernard who described the action in his diary on 7 October. Tom, who was born at Harwich on 27 April 1895, was the third son of Charles Bernard who had established a naval uniform manufacturing company in the Suffolk seaport. When Charles died in 1908, Tom's mother Mary took over the business and two years later, when Tom was just fifteen years old, sent him to the Scottish naval base at Invergordon to get orders for the family firm. It was here that he met Elizabeth Mackenzie, from nearby Fortrose whom he later married. When war was declared, Tom volunteered to serve as a naval canteen assistant and was appointed to HMS *Hogue*. Joining the ship on 4 September 1914, this armoured cruiser was one of

Tom Bernard 1917. (Tank Museum)

three Royal Navy warships which supported the Royal Marines at Ostend. All three ships were sunk by a German submarine *E-9* on 22 September but, although 374 of the crew died, Tom was rescued by the crew if HMS Lowestoft having only in the water for thirty-five minutes; he did however lose his diary.

Tom was returned, fortuitously, to Harwich where, after a single day at home, he went back to Invergordon to work again for the family firm. Tom lived in rented accommodation for some six months and had a "glorious time" spending the weekends at Fortrose with Elizabeth. Whilst he was in Invergordon, Tom's elder brother Charlie joined the MMGS. Tom however returned to sea this time on HMS *Fearless* for four months before being sent to Jarrow to super-intend the export of goods to ships overseas.

After three months Tom decided to join the Army and followed his brother into the MGC but sadly, his service papers have not survived. Having got safely back unharmed to the British lines, on the evening of 15 September 1916, for the second occasion, Tom returned to the tank wreck in early October 1916 and found it had been rifled by the Germans. His diary, which he had left in the hulk, was later used to provide intelligence about the formation of the tank and their organisation.

The Tank Museum has an image of Tom with his crew taken in France, probably after the first action given the state of the ground. Sadly none of the crew is named and so we cannot determine which is which of the crew, certainly I do not believe the officer to be Frank Arnold but I could be wrong. Tom served on in the MGC and later in the Tank Corps. Tom's elder brother Charles was tragically Killed in Action on 28 March 1918 as the British tried to hold back the German forces as they advanced from Cambrai to Albert. Charles was still serving with the MMGS, as a gunner, and his body was subsequently buried at the Peronne Communal Cemetery Extension. I believe it likely that Tom would have visited his brother's grave. Although there is no written proof, I also believe that he later served with 8th Battalion as Tom struck up a long lasting correspondence with the padre, the Reverend Lawrence Chamberlen who was awarded the Military Cross for his service with the Battalion. More tangible evidence of Tom's service with 8th battalion is the description of the work of a section commander's orderly at the battle in 1918 (see Annex C).This document, which was found by Tom's son in his papers, neatly describes the action of 8th battalion at the Battle of Hamel on 4 July 1918 in which the unit played a key role.

On 1 October 1918, whilst on home leave, Tom was presented with the Military Medal by the Mayor, Alderman Saunders, at a special ceremony at the Harwich Guildhall. According to a report in the *Chelmsford Chronicle*, the Mayor stated that "the whole town is proud of you". When Tom returned to Harwich, at the end of the war, he took over the family firm. He married his childhood sweetheart, Elizabeth, on 7 November 1921 at Fortrose and they had two children, Dorothy in the summer of 1922 and Tom five years later. They settled in Dovercourt from where Tom senior not only ran the naval outfitting company, he was also appointed a Tax Commissioner in 1927 and

Tom Bernard and his crew 1916. (Tank Museum)

Tom Bernard 1941. (Tom Bernard)

later Chairman of the General Commissioners of Income Tax. A member of the Star in the East Lodge no 650, Tom was elected master in 1933. He was also elected to the local council and was subsequently appointed alderman, becoming the youngest Mayor of the Borough of Harwich. He also represented HM Treasury on the Harwich Harbour Conservancy Board.

In the build-up to the Second World War, during which his company was to become the biggest naval outfitter in the country, Tom organised the local Civil Defences and was involved in the care of survivors following the sinking of the Dutch ship Simon Bolivar which struck a naval mine on18 November 1939. The level of his commitment to his town's defences, during the war, was recognised on 29 December 1944, when he was awarded the MBE. After the war, he was appointed Justice of the Peace and served as Chairman of the local bench of magistrates for many years. His wife Margaret died aged only 62 in 1964. Tom died aged seventy-five, after a life time of service, in his home at Dovercourt on 29 January 1971. Subsequently his son Tom found a hidden side to his father's activities during the Second World War when he located a secret wireless in the cellar of the family home. Subsequent investigations revealed Tom was a member of the ultra-secret British Resistance Organisation which was tasked to disrupt the activities of the occupying force in the event of a successful German invasion in the 1940s.

5

David and Jonathan

Whilst No 3 Section supported the 56th (London) Division for their attacks near Leuze and Bouleaux Woods, on the right flank of the attack on 15 September 1916, four tanks from No 4 Section were tasked to support 6th Division capture the Quadrilateral, a strong point approximately 750 yards to the north of Leuze Wood (see maps 4 and 5) which dominated the road from Ginchy to Morval.

Clan Leslie

No 4 Section's commander was Captain Archie Holford-Walker, the younger brother of the C Company commander. Archie was also the skipper of Crew C19 who manned the male tank Clan *Leslie*. As this male tank moved forward from the section base at Chimpanzee Valley towards its start point, on the evening of 14 September, a series of photographs were taken which are often used to illustrate the first use of tanks. Sadly I have not been able to identify the Tanker, standing to the right of the picture who was leading the tank but he must have been one of the Archie's crew. *Clan Leslie* was accompanied by two other tanks, tank crew C22 commanded by Basil Henriques

HMLS *Clan Leslie* leaving Chimpanzee Valley 14 September 1916. (Tank Museum)

and tank crew C23 under George Macpherson. En route to the start point, *Clan Leslie's* steering tail was damaged by German artillery and a repair team from 711 MT Company ASC was sent forward to carry out repairs. They used parts from Tom Murphy's tank but, despite this, *Clan Leslie* did not get into action and she was abandoned. As Archie lead the remaining two tanks forward, George Macpherson's tank also broke down and repairs commenced. Informed that Basil's tank was running short of fuel, Archie arranged for his brother, Allen, to bring petrol cans forward in his staff car. As a result, Basil Henriques and tank crew C22 were able to achieve their mission whilst Archie made sure that George Macpherson's tank was repaired and able to be brought into action later on 15 September 1916.

Archie Holford-Walker was born in 20 June 1893 at Hartley Witney in Hampshire. He was the third son of a Royal Artillery officer, Edgar Holford-Walker and his second wife Maria who was of the Scottish Leslie clan – hence Archie called his tank *Clan Leslie*. Known by the family as Bo, Archie was commissioned into 3rd (Reserve) Battalion King's Own Shropshire Light Infantry (KSLI) on 15 August 1914 only eleven days after Great Britain declared war on Germany. He deployed to France in February 1915 where he served with 2nd Battalion KSLI in the Ypres Salient. This had been a Regular Army unit which had been recalled from India on the outbreak of the war. 2nd KSLI arrived in Flanders in December 1914 and was used to reinforce the defences around Ypres where the British had fought the German Army to a standstill over the previous month. On 22 April 1915 the Germans launched a major assault during which they used chlorine gas, a first for the Western front and which enabled them to initially take much more ground than they expected. On the day of the initial attack, 2nd KSLI were in reserve but, when the Germans broke through the French forces, they were sent forward to prevent further ground being taken. Archie was wounded during a counter-attack in the early hours of 28 April near the village of St Julian and was sent back to England on 30 April 1915. Archie was attached to the Heavy Section MGC in April 1916 and joined C Company before his brother Allen took command so it may have been it was Archie who prompted the move.

Having lost all his tanks on 15 September, Archie was allocated three other tanks commanded by John Clarke, Jethro Tull and Victor Smith. On 25 September, these supported 5th Division in their assault on Les Boeufs and Morval. On 18 October, after C Company had moved north of the River Ancre to the area around Beaussart, Archie was allocated two tank crews from A Company commanded by Capt the Lord Rodney and Capt James Bennewith. Although the weather was good in the early part of the month, the persistent rain caused all attacks to be postponed. Five days later, these tanks including one commanded by Herbert Elliot were tasked to assist in an attack near Serre but, again due to a combination of heavy rain and sodden ground, the tanks could not get into action. On 11 November, Archie was tasked to take part in an assault, with a tank crew commanded by Len Bates, but this again did not take place due to the ground conditions.

On 18 November 1916, as the British attacks on the Somme were abandoned for the winter, C Company started to move into its winter quarters, at Erin and Tilly Capelle to the west of St Pol Sur Ternoise, and became the basis of C Battalion. Archie stayed with the Battalion on its formation and, with several other original Tankers including Eric Purdy, became a member of the *Willies* concert party, Archie performing conjuring tricks. There is no record of his being in action at the Battle of Arras but official records rarely show the names of the section commanders. His signature is however shown on a menu card for the F Battalion dinner night on 27 June, just before the tanks deployed to Belgium to participate in the Third Battle of Ypres. On 1 August, following the opening actions of the Third Battle of Ypres, Archie was sent back to England. Having recovered from sickness, Archie was tasked to report to Bovington Camp where he joined L Battalion. On 5 December, Archie's family was plunged into mourning when his only sister Audrey, known as Stubby died on 5 December aged only twenty-one. Spirits must however have risen when Archie became engaged to Nea Grimshaw on 17 December 1917. In L Battalion, Archie was serving as a section commander alongside Billy Sampson who fought at High Wood on 15 September 1916. Archie and Billy returned to France, with No 36 Company on 5 January 1918, accompanied by Jack Clarke who had served in Archie's section in 1916.

On 17 July 1918, as plans were being developed for the massive combined arms attack near Amiens, Archie was granted home leave during which he and Nea were married at Holy Trinity Church in Guildford. Billy Sampson witnessed the event so he was probably the best man. Returning to France, Archie took his section in action on 21 August 1918 during the Battle of Amiens. Unlike other units, who were equipped with the new Mark V tanks, L Battalion fought through the German Hindenburg Line and on towards the Belgian border in older, less powerful Mark IVs taking on German tanks operating British tanks which had been captured at Cambrai. Archie took command of a company in 12th Battalion on 2 November 1918 and on 1 March 1919 he changed his name by deed poll to Bruce (To avoid confusion, I have chosen to use his birth name in this book). Archie was, by then, serving at Bovington alongside Billy Sampson and was pictured with his godson Tony Sampson by the coast.

Transferring to the Regular Army, on 3 March 1920, Archie was appointed adjutant of the newly formed 19th (Lothian and Borders Horse) Armoured Car Company in which role he served until 11 September 1923. Nea gave birth to their elder son Paul on 19 August 1920 and their second son Bruce on 19 July 1923. Whilst serving as adjutant, Archie organised the first C Battalion all ranks dinner night and then on 11 September 1923, he joined 3rd Light Tank Battalion at Lydd. He was posted to B Company and, on 16 November that year, Archie deployed to Buxteiler, which is five miles to the northeast of Trier, where his unit took up occupation duties as part of the original British Army of the Rhine. On 7 February 1924, Archie was sent to Bovington join No 2 Armoured Car Company on its formation but later that year, was posted to join 10th Armoured Car Company in India. Here he again took up the role of section commander, again serving alongside Billy Sampson and also Len Bond who commanded tank crew D18 at Flers on 15 September 1916.

Archie Holford-Walker in India 1924.
(Stuart Sampson)

Archie took part in several operations in armoured cars on the North West Frontier before being appointed personal assistant to Colonel RTC at the Indian Army HQ on 21 November 1927. The following year, he was joined in India by Nea and their younger son Bruce. On 1 April 1931, Archie and his family returned to England, where he assumed a staff captain's post on 2 November 1931 in the Aldershot area. In 1934 Archie was then appointed to command a tank company, probably at Bovington. Sadly his marriage ended in divorce in 1935, his wife Nea having lived with a brother Tank Corps officer, Adrian Gatehouse, for the previous two years.

On 27 November, Archie was promoted to the rank of substantive major on 27 November 1936 whilst living at Farnborough. He retired just before the start of the Second War but was soon was recalled to duty. He joined 4th Battalion Royal Tank Regiment, which was commanded by Adrian Gatehouse, and was appointed to command C Company. On 19 September 1939, the unit deployed through Cherbourg to the area around Vimy Ridge. Equipped with the heavily armoured but slow Matilda Mark I tank, they were the first armored regiment to serve with the British Expeditionary Force. They carried out recces near Cambrai as well as further north in Belgium, near Ypres, and then moved to the Somme. Archie returned to England during the Phoney War and, having been promoted to lieutenant colonel on 4 July 1940, served with the Army recruiting organisation for the remainder of the war. In May 1941, Archie married Ada Barrow who had been born in Santiago Chile in May 1918, and they had two children. On 23 July 1946, Archie again retired from the Army and was granted the rank of colonel. The family settled on Hayling Island, close to his elder brother Leslie but sadly neither Leslie nor Archie lived to see his new family become adults. Leslie died in Lugarno in Switzerland, aged sixty on 8 July 1951 whilst Archie died at Bishopstoke in Hampshire, aged only fifty nine years, on 5 October 1951.

Unusually for a C Company tank, we know the identity of one of Archie's crew. Gunner Bob Tate was one of the Great War veterans interviewed by Peter Liddle as part of his North East England oral history project and the tapes of his interviews are held in the University of Leeds. Bob, who was the son of a blacksmith, was born in August 1894 in Sunderland, and was the eldest of seven children. At the start of the Great War, Bob was working as a chauffeur for the Sunderland Gas Company. He volunteered for military service and, as he was training as a mechanic, tried to join the ASC. When the Recruiting Staff told him they needed older men for the ASC, Bob travelled to Leeds to join the Royal Flying Corps (RFC). This time he was rejected as "RFC ground crew were considered as non-combatants" and "only married men were acceptable". On his way home, Bob bought a copy of *The Motor Cycle* and saw an advertisement about the MMGS. He applied to join and travelled to Coventry where he undertook a series of tests with about seventy other applicants. Only twenty-seven passed and these were immediately sent by train to Bisley. Bob undertook training on the Vickers, Lewis and Hotchkiss machine-guns for two months before being posted to the tank training area at Elveden. He later recalled that the crews had initially trained on *Little Willie*, then *Mother* then the tanks they were to take into action. Training included cross-country driving and night drives using compasses but this part of the programme failed due to the inability of the inboard compasses to cope with the deflection of metals from other tanks. Bob says he was present at a number of demonstrations for dignitaries including Lloyd-George and he also recorded that he drove King George V during one visit to Elveden.

Bob's service records that he was late back from his pre-deployment leave by twenty-four hours and was awarded seven days field punishment. He deployed to France on 16 August 1916 but "broke out of camp" at Le Havre five days later and was awarded 14 days confined to camp. Sadly Bob recalled little about the first tank action on 15 September other than the tank's wheels were blown off as he went into action but this supports other accounts of *Clan Leslie's* deployment. When the tanks were withdrawn from the Somme, in November 1916, Bob joined C Battalion and probably fought at the Battle of Arras. Between 11 to 23 June, he attended a driver training camp and was one of the select few appointed as a driver. He recalls any of the actions in 1917, other than the

Battle of Cambrai when he saw his friend Harry Tiffin's tank destroyed. This means Bob must have been serving in Eric Purdy's section on the Cambrai to Peronne Road and was probably a crewman in *Cayenne,* one of the two tanks of his unit which got furthest north on 20 November.

As a result of casualties during the battle, Bob was appointed First Class Tank Machinist back-dated to 20 November 1917. He stayed with C Battalion, as it re-rolled to a Light Tank unit, and later drove Whippets. As casualties grew during the Final Advance, Bob was promoted paid lance corporal on 26 October 1918. He was also injured by mustard gas in the last three weeks of the war and, as a result, was in a UK hospital at the time of the Armistice. Bob was granted leave after being discharged from hospital but he was lost his stripe on 17 December 1918 after, again returning late from leave. Bob served on after the war at Bovington and was again promoted Lance Corporal just before he married Violetta Cockburn on 22 May 1919 at St Mark's Parish Church at Millfield. He was demobilised from Ripon on 9 September 1919 and returned home to Deptford near Sunderland. Their daughter Dorothy was not born until 1933 and the family was still living in Sunderland, when he was interviewed by Peter Liddle in 1974. Bob, who also remained in touch with the family of tank crewman Harry Tiffin who lived close by, died aged ninety-seven in 1981.

Tank Crew C 22

Having refuelled their tank, in the early hours of 15 September 1916, Tank Crew C22 was the only one of Archie Holford-Walker's sub-section to get into action on time that morning. Basil Henriques, who was the tank's skipper and was injured in the action, was born on 17 October 1890. He was the youngest son of a successful Jewish businessman named David Henriques and his wife Agnes. David was almost blind and Agnes lame but they had five children who were bought up in a wealthy home. As a child Basil was sent to preparatory schools at Elstree and then at Locker's Park school near Hemel Hempstead, as was his great friend George Macpherson albeit eight years later. Basil then went to Harrow School but he suffered from ill-health from about the age of fifteen and had to be tutored at home. Before he entered the University of Oxford, Basil spent a year in Versailles, at the home of the sister of his Harrow French master where he later wrote that "he learned to think out problems for himself". As a student at University College, he read "Across the bridges" by Alec Paterson, in which he leant about the destitution amongst East End families and the work of Oxford graduates to relieve their suffering. Around the same time, Basil became convinced of the need to expound the doctrines of Liberal Judaism. Whilst his father's sudden death in July 1912 gave Basil the opportunity to follow his ambition, it also triggered a breakdown. Basil was sent to recover in Bermuda where his older brother Ronald was serving with the Queen's Regiment. This was, in Basil's words, "my last glorious fling of social life" although his diary for the next few years shows that he still enjoyed an extremely privileged life.

On his return to Oxford, he received a letter asking if he and other undergraduates could assist in establishing a Jewish boys' club in Stepney, an invitation which ultimately led to his life's work amongst Jewish people living in the East End of London. On leaving Oxford, Basil first worked with Christian social workers at Toynbee Hall, gaining an understanding of the difficulties in which the poor lived. In early 1914, he established a boys' club in the Whitechapel slums designed keep Jewish teenagers from crime and to integrate the children of foreign born Jews into British society. It became a centre for social care and development. One of the first club helpers was a talented pianist and artist named Rose Loewe who also taught first aid to the boys. The following year, at Basil's suggestion, Rose founded the first club for Jewish girls which was similarly successful.

As the conscription act approached, Basil volunteered to join the infantry and was commissioned into the East Kent Regiment on 10 October 1915. Basil had premonitions that he would be blinded during his service and had practiced walking blindfold around the club. Rose, who took over the running of the two youth clubs for the rest of the war, trained as a nurse perhaps as a result

Rose and Basil Henriques at their wedding 1916. (Jewish Museum, London)

of Basil's fears. After two months training at the officer cadet battalion in Oxford, Basil was sent to Dover to join 3rd Battalion the Buffs. It was there that he met George Macpherson with whom he developed a close relationship based on a common spirituality, Colin Hardy later describing the pair as *David and Jonathan* in allusion to the relationship between the future King of Israel and his "brother in arms" who was the son of Saul. They were recommended by their CO for the "secret and dangerous mission" and, on 13 April 1916, were interviewed by Colonel Ernest Swinton at Wellington Barracks in London. Despite their lack of knowledge of either motor vehicles or machine guns, both Basil and George were approved and sent to Bisley arriving the next day at Brookwood Railway station. It was here that Basil found that his unit had been sent to Siberia but was relieved when he ascertained that this was a rifle range not part of the Russian Empire.

Whilst at Bisley, Basil decided that he could not manage singlehandedly with running the club after the war but that he and Rose could so together. The couple became engaged on 27 June and, on 19 July, married at St John's Wood Synagogue. After a twenty-four hour honeymoon near Sevenoaks, Basil returned to Elveden for final training. Basil and George deployed to France on 24 August and were photographed as they marched across London to Waterloo Station on their way to Southampton docks (see page 20). Having undertaking some limited training at Yvrench, the section moved by train to the Somme. Soon after their arrival, they were told that they were soon to go into action so George and Basil used bicycles to recce the route from their forward base in the Chimpanzee Valley to their RV at Wedge Wood to the south of Guillemont (see map 5). They were not however able to see the ground over which they were to fight nor meet the units they would be supporting.

Their task for 15 September was to neutralise the Quadrilateral, which was the name given to a major German defensive position which dominated no man's land south towards Bouleaux and Leuze Wood, to the south west towards Guillemont and to the north west of Ginchy (see coloured images 4-6). During the move to the start point, first Archie's tank and then George's vehicle broke down and Basil's tank used more than half its fuel. Archie realised that Basil needed more full if he were to get into action. He obtained sixteen gallons of petrol which were bought forward by his brother Allen in the company staff car arriving at 2:30 a.m. Whilst refueling was underway at his RV at Wedge Wood, Basil walked north to recce the route to his start point, after which he returned to his tank where his crew were trying to rest. He received new orders, which ordered him to wait at the RV, for an hour longer than expected. He then followed a tape, which identified the route in the darkness. Despite having to encourage his driver to squash German bodies, which were on their route forward, Basil's tank reached a point 500 yards behind the British front line by 5:00 a.m. where he stopped. By 5:45 a.m. Basil moved up to the British jumping-off trenches but then reversed twenty yards to avoiding the infantry in the area being hit by German artillery fire aimed at the tank.

As Basil moved up to the start point, his tank crew fired on soldiers of the 9th Norfolks, believing they were enemy, and created several casualties. Basil then sought the aid of a company commander of 9th Norfolks to make sure he headed in the right direction to get to his objective. Basil then followed the old French railway line across no man's land arriving at the Quadrilateral on time at zero hours. There the tank dominated the German position; the crew using their four belt-fed Vickers machine guns to suppress the German defenders whilst the British infantry advanced. Whilst this reduced casualties amongst the attackers, it did not prevent the Germans using their artillery to decimate the attacking British units, the losses being increased because of the lanes in the British barrage to facilitate the advance of three tanks. Before the soldiers from 6th Division reached the Quadrilateral, Basil took his tank north to clear a German communication trench but it was badly damaged by German armour piercing bullets which penetrated the sides of the tank. All of the C22 crewmen became wounded or took cover on the floor of the tank. Basil Henriques and his driver were also partially blinded – Basil by a piece of glass from the tank's periscope – but he got his gunners back into action. Despite this Basil was eventually forced to withdraw and the tank was hit by German artillery fire as she returned to her rallying point.

Although several were wounded, none of Basil's crew was killed. On the way back to the C Company base, Basil met George at 168 Brigade Headquarters near Guillemont. George's tank had been repaired by the mechanics from 711 (MT) Company ASC and, having received new orders, was now was on his way to the start point for a follow-on attack planned for noon. Basil recorded that his visible wounds caused George severe distress but that he smiled as they parted.

Basil was initially evacuated to a hospital at Rouen and then back to Southampton arriving on 19 September in London. Rose, who had been warned by Basil in a telegram that he was to be treated for eye injuries, made her way to Waterloo where she saw Basil get off the train with his eyes bandaged. She was worried that Basil's fear of being blinded had come true so, standing in the middle of the road, she stopped the car. Getting into the vehicle, Rose was relieved to find her husbands' injuries were not as bad as she feared. However Basil Henriques was desperately affected by the loss of George Macpherson, who had died on 15 September, and suffered from post-traumatic stress disorder. Having recovered from his physical injuries, which included wounds to his legs, Basil appealed to Colonel Swinton to be allowed to return to France. However, he was sent home for several weeks to recover and await new orders which did not assist him overcoming feelings of guilt for the loss of his friends and the many infantrymen from 6th Division which Basil believed was due to his disobeying the orders he had received. In early 1917, Basil was sent to the new training area at Bovington where he joined the recently formed G Battalion. His company commanders was Allen Holford-Walker who managed to convince Basil that he had not caused large numbers of casualties amongst the attacking infantry, rather he had followed his orders correctly. At Bovington Basil instructed officers in map reading and, more importantly on 6 February 1917, gave a lecture on his experience as a tank commander which provided unparalleled insight to those training to be tank skippers. In early April, Basil returned to France as part of his training as a company recce officer but was back to Bovington by 23 April.

Basil deployed back to France with No 19 Company in late May. On 7 July, he met many of those who fought at Flers-Courcelette at D Battalion's sports day including members of George's crew. All spoke highly of George including one who had been given his pistol as he left his tank – this certainly gives lie to the suggestion that George took his own life. Basil served with G Battalion throughout the Third Battle of Ypres. He was then promoted captain and appointed as G Battalion's recce officer, a role he undertook during the Battle of Cambrai, and for which he was awarded the Italian Silver Medal in January 1918. Now serving with the re-designated 7th Battalion, in April 1918, Basil was sent with a detachment of Lewis gunners to stem the German advance near the Lys canal. There he was directed by Brigadier General Hugh Elles, who was close to the front line, to form a new unit from retreating troops and re-establish the line. Basil achieved this and for his success was Mentioned in Despatches. Later that year Basil, who continued to lead a highly spiritual life, wrote a series of "Prayers for Trench and Base" for use by Jews serving with the Armed Forces. This collection, in addition to a brief section entitled "daily prayers", contained specially adapted prayers for those in danger, for "the dead on the field of battle" as well as for sincerity, for strength and for purity. The prayers were approved, and subsequently published, by the office of Chief Rabbi.

At the end of August 1918, he was sent back to Wareham to train new recce officers, a task he undertook until the end of the war. Retained by the Army until July 1919, Basil returned to social work in Whitechapel and, with Rose, established St George's Settlement and Synagogue at Berners Street from where they ran a pioneering joint youth club. The Settlement, which was on the site of one of the Ripper Murders only thirty years earlier, was opened by the local MP and future Prime Minister Major Clement Attlee with whom Basil had served for a short time in G Battalion at Bovington. In addition to his social work, including visiting prisoners, Basil served as a magistrate and was Chairman of the East London Juvenile Court from 1936 to 1955. From 1925, Rose and Basil lived at Southcote Cottage near Linslade which they rented from the Rothschild family. As well as providing the East End children with education, vocational training, recreation and holidays in the country, the childless but philanthropic couple opened their large house to sick and deprived Jewish children at Southcote for twenty-five years. During the Second World War, Basil continued his youth work, initially sleeping each night at the club as a fire watcher during the London Blitz. Rose not only supported his work but, at the end of the war, led one of the first Jewish relief units into the concentration camp at Bergen-Belson. For the next five years, she served as the head of the Germany section of the Jewish Committee for Relief Abroad. Basil retired from his work as Warden of the club in 1947 but continued his work with young people, being appointed vice-chairman of the National Association of Boys' Clubs. He was also a prolific author on youth work and allied subjects which included the causes and cure of crime.

Basil was awarded the CBE in 1948 and knighted in January 1955 for his lifetime of service. In November 1961 he had a heart attack and died on 2 December 1961. He left funding in his will for many charities including a scholarship for a graduate of University College Oxford to support his studies on theological and social work. Basil's own service to the community of the East End was permanently marked by the local council who renamed Berners Street in his memory.

Basil described the first action in some detail in his first book, *Indiscretions of a Warden* including that his driver was wounded. Sadly he does not give his name – he does however, record that he was selected whilst the crew was training at Yvrench. Basil describes him as a "quiet gentleman" who had never seen action but who was wholly honest. He also describes being having to coax the driver

Basil Henriques in his later years. (Jewish Museum, London)

to run over the bodies of dead men as they went into action and he was hit by machine gun fire which penetrated the tank. Sadly Basil does not name any of his crew but Rose Henriques mentions three of the crew including his second in command, Corporal Roger Paterson. Roger was born in 1895 in Edinburgh and was an engineer. He enlisted into the MMGS on 10 August 1915, having been attested at the South Edinburgh Unionist Association at 71 Princes Street. He was posted to C Company as an acting Lance Corporal on 27 May and promoted acting Corporal one month later. Judging from Basil's subsequent description of the action at the Quadrilateral, Roger Paterson was probably the left hand gearsman. He remained with C Battalion, in the rank of Corporal, when it was formed on 18 November 1916 but later he trained as a driver. Sadly his service record is sparse but it does show he was posted to the Central Workshops on 18 January 1918 which probably indicates that he had served in C Battalion's Workshop Company in 1917. As Roger was appointed a First Class Tank Machinist on 29 January 1918, this would also make sense. We know little more of his service other than he returned to England on 4 May 1919 and was transferred to the Z Reserve on 5 June 1919. The formation of this Reserve, from amongst experienced soldiers, was an short term measure designed to ensure that the British Government could quickly assemble should the German government renege on the conditions agreed as part of the Armistice. Sadly I can find no other information about this soldier.

The other named crewmen were Gunner Frank Raynor and Reg Fisher whose service numbers are consecutive which indicates that they transferred to the Tank Corps on the same day and served in the same unit. Frank, who was from Heighington near Grimsby, was the eldest son of a joiner and was bought up in Worksop in Nottinghamshire. He was one of the youngest crewmen, being born on 23 October 1898. Frank joined the MMGS on 23 March 1916 and was only seventeen years of age when he went into action at the Quadrilateral. He served with C Battalion, after the tanks were pulled back to Tilly, and was one of the crewmen who met Basil Henriques on 7 July. He later served with 16th Battalion, who were in almost constant action in September and October 1918, and reached the rank of sergeant. After the war, Frank returned to Grimsby and, in summer 1922, married Ethel Hill from nearby Spilsby. The local business guide for 1923 shows Frank was working in the retail fish industry at Grimsby and birth records reveal that, in 1925 Ethel gave birth to their child Dorothy. He later settled near Boston and lived until his seventy-four year, dying in the summer of 1972.

Reg Fisher was born at Hackford by Reepham in Norfolk in late March 1897. He was the youngest child of the local grocer and draper whose shop was located in the Market Square. His elder brother Harry was a motor engineer and Reg was almost certainly knowledgeable about machines. Reg was attested at Norwich and volunteered for service with the MMGS at Coventry where his medical was undertaken on 14 March 1916. Reg passed the trade test and moved to Bisley two days later. After the first actions, Reg also transferred to C Battalion. The twenty year old gunner was wounded on 9 April 1917, the first day of the Battle of Arras, but remained at duty. The following month Reg attended a course on the 6 pdr QF cannon, fitted to male tanks, at the 2nd Tank Brigade School from 19 to 26 May and then at the Tank Driving School at Wailly from 11 to 16 June. I believe that Reg fought during the Third Battle of Ypres and he certainly fought at Cambrai as he was appointed lance corporal on 21 November 1917 after Lance Corporal Bentley was wounded so badly he had to leave C Battalion. He was then granted home leave from 15 to 30 December. He remained with 3rd Battalion for the remainder of the war, serving in the light (Whippet) role, eventually reaching the rank of sergeant. He moved with 3rd Battalion into Germany, after the Armistice and was granted Christmas leave in the UK. In January 1919 Reg returned to Germany where he was transferred to 12th Battalion and served with the newly established British Army of the Rhine. As he had only volunteered for the duration of the war, Reg actively sought his discharge. When he failed he sought the help of a local supporter over delays to his demobilization. Enquiries were set up by Tank Corps Record Office but Reg was not released from service until November 1919. Five years later, in the autumn of 1924 he married Eva Leonard. They initially lived at Reepham but, in the 1930s, moved to Barnham Broom where Reg's father died in 1933. Reg was, by now, in business in his own right and the family lived there until his death aged fifty-seven on 22 March 1954; Eva survived until she was eighty-one and died in the autumn of 1977.

Tank Crew C20

Basil Henriques' close friend, George Macpherson, managed eventually to get his tank into action on 15 September. It had reached the RV at Wedge Wood at 7:00 am but broke down again after travelling 100 yards. Having been again repaired George was tasked to move forward, this time in company with Tom Murphy whose tank was tasked to deploy without a steering tail, something which had been previously considered impossible before the tanks went into action. As Basil's tank came out of action, George met Basil at 16th Brigade Headquarters at Wedge Wood to the south of Guillemont where he was to receive his final briefing. George was concerned for his friend's sight as he was more than aware that Basil feared that he would be blinded in the war. Having been briefed that his objective remained the Quadrilateral, George and Tom followed the road north to Guillemont cross roads and then north to the railway line (see map 5).

The Germans at the Quadrilateral would have been able to see the two tanks as they reached the cross roads just before noon and as they moved to their start point. The two tanks went forward on time and managed to reach their objective as ordered; however the infantry did not follow as their attack had been cancelled. As the tanks reached the Quadrilateral, they were fired upon by German machine guns on other positions which were now equipped with armour piercing bullets,

George Macpherson shortly after being commissioned. (Tank Museum)

which easily penetrated the tank's armour. Having stayed for a period on the objective, both tanks withdrew and eventually returned the way they had come to 16th Brigade headquarters at Wedge Wood.

George Macpherson was the only son of a coal and iron master. Born at Penn near Wolverhampton on 7 May 1896, George was, like Basil, was educated at Locker's Park School at Hemel Hempstead albeit some years later. He then was educated at Winchester College, where he was head boy and a member of the College's rugby and football team. George intended to become ordained after he had completed his studies at the University of Cambridge but, like many young men, put these plans aside on the outbreak of war. Shortly after leaving Winchester, George was commissioned into The Buffs on 15 October 1915, the same day as Basil.

They were to become the closest of friends and Basil recognised George's spirituality, describing his faith as "the purest and plainest". Also serving with 3rd Battalion was another Wykhamist named Geoffrey Wyatt who was to be killed on the same day at George. In early 1916, when Ernest Swinton was looking for officers for the tanks, George and Basil were sent to Wellington Barracks at Westminster for an interview. Despite their lack of mechanical knowledge and lack of expertise with machine guns, both were accepted and were attached to MGC from 14 April 1916. Joining the same company, they deployed to France on 24 August 1916 and, having undertaken training at Yvrench, George and Basil moved with their tanks to the Somme. The tanks were offloaded at the Loop and undertook final preparations including fitting anti-grenade roof protection to their tanks. On Sunday 10 September, George was visited by Geoffrey Wyatt and they spent four hours together. Geoffrey was now serving with 1st Battalion East Kent which was also to go into action on 15 September. They were part of 6th Division and their objective was the Quadrilateral, the German defensive position which George and Basil were tasked to neutralize.

After George bought his tank back from its action on the afternoon of 15 September, he was seriously injured. One of his crewmen, Gunner Will Dawson, later wrote that George was told to report to the headquarters and, whilst there, was fatally injured by German artillery fire. Other second hand accounts state that George took his own life, something Basil believed to be impossible. George was unconscious when he evacuated to 34 Casualty Clearing Station where he died four hours later. His body is now buried at Grove Town Cemetery near Meulte and commemorated at St Bartholomew's Church at Penn. George's parents received the news of their only son's death whilst staying at their estate in Aberdeenshire and a memorial service was held shortly afterwards at Glass Parish Church. The former organist of Westminster Abbey, Sir Frederick Bridge, who was staying locally, played a special composed arrangement of the Scottish lament, the Flowers of the Forest at the ceremony. Five years later, the family presented a bronze memorial tablet to the church at Glass at a service which was attended by large numbers of their tenants and the lament was again played by Sir Frederick Bridge. George's mother Hilda contributed to the cost of the Tank Memorial at Pozières; nor did Basil forget his brother-in-arms for, in the South West Essex synagogue is a lectern on which is inscribed the name of George Macpherson HSMGC. The Synagogue is a successor to the Berners Street Jewish Settlement which was established by Basil in the 1920s and the inscription on the memorial lectern was a clear symbol of the spiritual bond between the two men.

Gunner Will Dawson, who described the battle and his subsequent service in a manuscript held by the Tank Museum, is the only crewman who is known to have served in the C22 crew. He was born on 22 March 1888 in Boston in Lincolnshire and was the eldest of four children, his younger sister being named Audrey and two younger brothers George and Thomas. When Will was eleven, his Master Mariner father was drowned at the age of forty-nine in Boston Deeps together with two other pilots. On leaving school, Will worked as a younger shipping company clerk and with his brothers sustained the family. George and Thomas joined the Coldstream Guards in 1915 but Will, who was a keen motorcyclist, volunteered to join the MMGS. Having attended an oral examina-

tion at Coventry, William enlisted on 2 February 1916 and was sent to Bisley for initial training where he was later allocated to B Company HS MGC. He sent a postcard of his fellow recruits in No 7 Tent at Siberia Camp, where he not only trained on the Vickers and Hotchkiss machine guns but also the 6 pdr QF Hotchkiss gun with the Royal Navy. Posted to C Company, Will later recorded that his journey to Norfolk in June 1916 ended with a nine miles march in pouring rain to the new training area at Elveden. Having carried out initial tank training, Will was granted a short, pre-deployment leave to say farewell to his family and records travelling by motorcycle with his friend Cecil Kaye as far as Sleaford where they managed to obtain petrol en route by convincing suppliers that they were despatch riders on official duty.

Will met his brothers at Happy Valley in the last couple of days before he went into action. A Guards SNCO had seen the tanks whilst collecting stores from the area where demonstrations were being given to senior officers. He described what he had seen to his comrades and George and Thomas realised that the strange sight

Will Dawson in 1917, probably taken in France. (Rosemary Mitchell)

could only be the armoured vehicles described by their brother. Will's description of the first tank action give no real detail of events other than the tank was damaged by machine gun fire and that George Macpherson left the tank to report to the local commander after the battle. After George's death, Will's crew was commanded by Sir John Dashwood. They went back into action on 26 September, in support of 56th Division. In his manuscript, Will described how the tank became stuck on a tree as it approached the village of Morval and how the crew subsequently recovered the vehicle four days later. According to his family Will fought at Beaumont-Hamel on 13 November so he must have been attached to D Company at this time. After the initial actions, Will joined C Battalion and served with No 8 Company. He fought at the Battle of Arras taking part in the assault on the Harp on 9 April 1917 – Will being the only battle-experienced crewman in his tank. The tank became ditched on the first objective and was struck by enemy artillery; one round passing between the driver and the skipper Lieutenant Charles Ambrose who had also fought with C Company in September 1916. The shell must have been solid short as it did not explode and the crew was able to get the tank out. The tank was repaired and resumed the advance after 4 hours only to become ditched for a further ninety minutes near the Cambrai road. The tank eventually caught up with the attacking infantry who were held up by the Germans but it was too dark for the tank to provide assistance. Two days later morning, Will's tank was one of three which attacked the German positions at Monchy-le-Preux from the south west. The tank, again commanded by Lieutenant Ambrose, reached the crossroads on the Arras to Cambrai road at La Bergère where it was set upon by enemy bombers and penetrated by armour piercing bullets. All the gunners were wounded but they nevertheless managed to force the enemy to take cover in a sunken road. The tank then fought its way towards Monchy but was immobilised by bombs exploding under its tracks; it then received a direct hit from a shell which blew in a sponson. The enemy once more surrounded the tank but were again driven off by Lewis gun fire and the tank was then abandoned. Of the seven crewmen, three were killed and Will and his skipper Charles Ambrose badly wounded.

Will Dawson was sent to a dressing station and then by ambulance train to hospital in Rouen. After recovering, Will was sent to a rest camp at Étaples when he was photographed. He then returned to C Battalion where he was allocated to No 9 Company. He was met on arrival by his section commander, Captain Andrew Henderson who had commanded C23 at High Wood, and with whom he had served on 26 September the previous year. Will was allocated as the driver to Lt Johnny Walker and on the opening day of the Third Battle of Ypres, on 31 July 1917, drove the tank *Challenger* which reached the Frezenberg redoubt on the Ieper to Zonnebeke Road. Sir Phillip Gibbs, in his daily newspaper report, drew particular attention to their success which occurred before the rains made the reclaimed marsh virtually impossible for the tanks to be used effectively. Will's skillful driving was mentioned in the C Battalion War History and he was subsequently awarded a Tank Corps Certificate of Merit, being told, at its presentation by Brigadier General Hugh Elles, that he deserved a medal but the Corps had not been issued sufficient. Will was appointed lance corporal in early August then promoted corporal on 13 September 1917. He fought at Cambrai, again with No 9 Company, where his section fought its way past Bleak House on the eastern flank of the British attack towards the fourth German defensive line near Masnieres. On 23 November Will's tank *Challenger* lead the section which assaulted Fontaine Notre Dame; Andrew Henderson was also on board and *Challenger* was the only tank which was not destroyed. On 30 November 1917, as the Battle of drew to its close, Will and some other crewmen in C Battalion were told they would be sent on home leave, their first leave since their deployment in August 1916. After the Germans counter-attacked, the crewmen were told that only officers could be spared and that the crewmen's leave was cancelled. This unfairness created significant disquiet amongst the crewmen and Captain Victor Smith, who had commanded *Casa* in 15 September 1916, intervened on their behalf with the result that William and the others were released to go home.

Will Dawson during a visit to 1 RTR 1967. (Rosemary Mitchell)

Will was back with No 9 Company for Christmas, by which time it had been announced that it would operate Whippet tanks in 1918. He had been recommended for a commission and was due to leave the renamed 3rd Battalion in February 1918 but he was taken ill and hospitalised at Meulte for three weeks. Returning to the UK on 5 March 1918, Will initially trained at the Tank Corps officer cadet unit at Wareham before undertaking a second period of training at Hazeley Down. Will was commissioned on 3 March 1919 and served in the Army Reserve until 1921, his two brothers also surviving the war. After he was demobilised, in 1919, Will joined the Liverpool based shipping brokers Bahr Behrend and Company. Settling at Liscard on the Wirral, Will married May Elliott on 1 September 1924. The couple had two daughters, Audrey who was born in 1925 and Sybil nine years later, who both became teachers, Audrey a deputy headmistress and Sybil a headmistress. Will became a Fellow of the Institute of Chartered Shipbrokers and served on the Liverpool committee for a number of years as chairman and also was elected national vice president for a year. He also became an associate of the Royal Photographic Society and relaxed by fly-fishing and watercolour painting.

Will remained a keen motorcyclist and, in the 1950s, was involved in an accident whilst crossing some wet railway lines. He was subsequently admitted to the Countess of Chester hospital where X-rays revealed he still had shrapnel from the Great War in the back of his head. Will kept in touch with a number of tank comrades and regularly attended the Battle of Cambrai commemorative parades held at the Cenotaph in Whitehall. In 1965, at the age of seventy-seven, Will was invited to visit 1st RTR, who were based in Hohne in Germany, for five days. He drove a Centurion tank and later recalled 'the welcome and hospitality by all ranks was overwhelming". In September 1966, he was one of the First Tank Crewmen who attended the Fiftieth Anniversary Veterans' dinner at Caxton Hall in London and in July 1967, returned to Germany for the mounted revue of the RTR by Queen Elizabeth II. He also visited 1 RTR at Catterick Barracks for their Cambrai Day celebrations in November 1967 and again drove a Centurion tank. In 1971 May died aged seventy-nine whilst Will died two years later at the age of eighty-five years.

Tank Crew C21

Although rarely mentioned, there was another tank allocated to the attack on the Quadrilateral. Originally one of the tanks kept as part of the Corps Reserve, first at the Company headquarters and then at Trônes Wood, the tank moved forward on the night of 14 September to support a new infantry assault planned for 1.30 p.m. Tank Crew C21, commanded by Lt Harold Vincent, reached their RV at the Guillemont crossroads but could not move forward. Harold Vincent then sent a message back to his Company Headquarters "My tank No 749 is completely ditched near crossroads, cannot move at all. Have abandoned same and am in a refuge in a shell hole". It was sadly not the only tank so abandoned.

Harold Vincent was one of the oldest tank skippers having been born in 1881. He had a remarkable life before he was commissioned into the MMGS on 14 April 16. In his teens he had enlisted in the British South African Police and, when the Boer War broke out, volunteered for active service taking part in the relief of Ladysmith in 1900. After the war ended, Harold stayed in South Africa and took a degree. He later became a teacher at a native school but later returned to police duty when it is reported that he arrested Mahatma Gandhi at Durban. Harold then worked as an engineer at the Rhodesian gold mines in Zimbabwe and subsequently returned to England. Harold was promoted lieutenant on 1 July 1916 and deployed to France on 17 August 1916, where he was designated commander of three tanks held in Corps Reserve. He did not remain with the tanks after the new battalions formed but served with the Royal Irish Regiment from 31 January 1917. There must have been a major incident at a later stage, which caused him to be cashiered on 14 August 1918 but he was still able, in 1922, to successfully apply for his medals.

At this time, Harold was living in North Kensington. A keen sunbather, at a time when the pastime was considered most unusual, Harold had founded the Sun Ray Club in London. In order to publicise sunbathing, he proposed a march through Hyde Park by 200 naked men and women which created a major scandal. In 1927 he was charged with contravening the Royal Parks Regulations by sunbathing whilst wearing only shorts. Described as a schoolmaster when he appeared before the Marlborough Street court, the stipendiary magistrate Mr Mead stated that "to expose the upper torso of the body was likely to shock people of normal sensibilities". In 1930 he again appeared before Mr Mead and was sentenced to eleven days imprisonment for begging; the charge being linked to his distributing leaflets supporting sunbathing for which he sought donations. Harold was also sentenced for three other offences committed in 1929 to another twenty-one days. In the summer of 1930, the members of the Sun Ray Health Club and New Life Society indulged in semi-clad and nude sunbathing, again led by Harold Vincent. Angry protesters turned up at the Welsh Harp, near Hendon, to challenge them even though they were on private property and well away from any public area or footpath. The police were called on a number of occasions because, although the naturists were not breaking any law, they were in danger from the crowd by continuing to sunbath.

In August 1932, Harold was convicted of obstructing Policewoman Annie Matthews, assaulting her and damaging her uniform. Harold is reported to have presented a striking appearance in the dock at Marlborough Street Magistrates' Court described in the newspapers as "over six feet in height with his skin bronzed to a deep copper hue through continual exposure to the sun". Harold wore only a tennis shirt open at the neck, grey flannel trousers, and canvas shoes with no socks – certainly not clothing expected to be worn by a defendant in a magistrate's court. Harold had objected to Annie Matthews removing children who were swimming in the Serpentine and had damaged her uniform when Harold pushed her into the water. This time the Magistrate, Mr Mead, sentenced Harold to three months imprisonment. After his release, Harold disappeared from public life but he continued to live in northwest London near the Edgeware Road. In his eighties, his health declined and from 1964 -1965, he lived at the Redhill House Hospital. He died aged eighty-five years, from kidney failure, on 25 June 1966, just before nudity was about to create more newspaper headlines following the opening of the theatrical musical "*Hair*".

6

Disaster at Ginchy

The Guards Division was formed in August 1915 from Guards battalions serving with other forma- tions. It was soon in action at the Battle of Loos where it attacked enemy positions at Hill 70 on the third day of the battle. The Division took heavy casualties, in particular the 1st Battalion Scots Guards who lost 474 men killed or wounded. The Division then held the line in the Ypres Salient before being committed to the fighting on the Somme in September 1916. Tasked to break through the German defences between Ginchy and Morval, the Guards were expecting a hard fight. As a result, unlike 6th and 56th Divisions which only had three tanks each, ten tanks were allocated to the Guards. Their initial objective was the village of Les Beoufs, a village a mile to the north east of Ginchy (see map 6).

The nine tanks were organized into three groups of three, under the overall command of Captain Herbert Hiscocks, with a tenth commanded by Lieutenant Harold Cole whose exploits are recorded in Chapter 3. The tanks' initial assembly area on 14 September was at Trônes Wood and they had to make their way, without lights, to their rendezvous at Ginchy to arrive at 2:20am, four hours before zero at 6:20am. Owing to mechanical breakdown, almost half of the tanks did not support the attack. Every one of the central tanks, known as "D", "E" and "F", failed to get into action. Hiscocks' own tank "D" ditched before it could cross the start line, Tom Murphy's steering gear was damaged on the move up to the rendezvous and Alec Arnaud's tank "E" became ditched on route to the start point. Frustrated and embarrassed by failure of his section, Herbert Hiscocks went to forward on foot to ensure that the tanks attacking on the Guards' left flank set off in the right direction; "A", commanded by Jethro Tull, damaged its steering wheels as it crossed no man's land and had to return to the Start Point. Jack Clarke in "B" and Victor Smith in "C" deployed in the correct direction, across no man's land towards the Guards' objective but then went north in same direction as the Guards, who had diverted from their correct axis of attack, eventually reaching their second objective. Of the third group of tanks, "K" under the command of Charles Ambrose had steering and engine problems which prevented him from reaching the start point but "G" commanded by Len Bates and "H" commanded by Herbert Elliot, not only crossed no man's land and through the German front line trenches, but also moved onto their second objective near Pound Trench.

D Tank

Herbert Hiscocks, the section commander, was one of the "Empire-men" who returned to England to join the Army on the outbreak of war. He was born on 11 November 1892 in Bombay but educated at Littlehampton. Herbert had entered the Sandhurst entrance examinations in 1911 but was unsuccessful and moved to Sri Lanka where he worked on a tea-plantation. After the outbreak of war in1914, Herbert joined the local volunteer infantry unit known as the Ceylon Planters' Rifle Corps (CPRC). Together with seventy other CPRC volunteers, he travelled to London arriving on 13 December 1914 and enlisted that same day at the Rifle Brigade Depot at Winchester. Herbert was commissioned five weeks later into the North Lancashire Regiment. His medal index card records he was part of 35th Division which was made up of Bantam units; this would have been an interesting sight as Herbert stood over six feet tall and the Bantams were all at least nine inches shorter.

On 5 July 1915 Herbert was promoted to the rank of acting captain, the same day that he attended his sister Ethel's marriage at St Dunstan's Church in East Acton. He deployed to France on 22 September 1915 but I cannot identify why he returned to England and joined the Heavy Section MGC. It is likely that Herbert was one of the "stiffeners" bought in to provide Section Commanders as the companies trained at Elveden. Having undertaken tank crew training in Norfolk, Herbert travelled with the first section of tanks leaving Avonmouth on 16 August 1916 and arriving at Le Havre five days later. After travelling to Yvrench by train, and undertaking final training, he deployed to the Somme area, where he was tasked to command ten tanks at the first tank action. This was the largest number of tanks under the command of one man on the opening day of the Battle of Flers-Courcelette.

Herbert's driver was insufficiently trained to cope with the dreadful ground conditions in the area around Ginchy and, as a result, the tank became stuck before it could cross the start-line. With the other two tanks in his sub-section also out of action. Herbert went forward into no man's land to ensure that Jack Clarke and Victor Smith were travelling in the right direction towards their objectives. The combined efforts of the Guards and their tanks were not enough so, on 25 September, the Guards Division were again tasked to capture Les Boeufs, supported by Hiscocks' section. The section set off for its objective of Morval at 12:35 p.m. on 25 September. The next morning two of the tanks were east of Delville Wood and one at Trônes Wood; at 1:40 p.m. the tanks were deployed towards Mutton Trench to assist with an assault towards Morval which was a success. In October Herbert commanded another section, this time of five tanks, in support of 2nd Division to the north of the River Ancre near Serre. The planned attacks were constantly postponed due to the bad weather which had made the ground impossible for tanks. William Dawson, who was with him, described the ground as "shell holes within shell holes, all full of water".

In the middle of November, after C Company moved back to Erin, Herbert joined C Battalion and unusually he was permitted to return home for Christmas. Shortly after he returned to France, he temporarily took command of No 8 Company. Although he is not named in any of the contemporary records, Herbert probably fought during the attack at the Harp near Beaurains in 9 April 1917. His section undertook a driving course from 11 to 19 June 1917 at the recently established driving school at Wailly and shortly after, just before the tank units deployed into the Ypres Salient, he attended the F Battalion dinner on 27 June where many of the original tank skippers were present.

During the opening days of the Third Battle of Ypres, which started on 31 July, Herbert commanded No 7 Section which formed the Corps Reserve located at Oosthoek Tankodrome. On 16 August, he was sent back to the UK to provide the battle experience so badly needed by newly established battalions. Herbert joined K Battalion, which formed at Bovington, and deployed back to France on Christmas Eve 1917. In February 1918, he was appointed second in command of B Company in the re-designated 11th Battalion. In early March 1918 Herbert was admitted to hospital for three weeks and so was not involved in the opening stages of the great German offensive or "Kaiserschlacht". By the time he returned, 11th Battalion had lost all its tanks. As a result on 11 April 1918, Herbert was tasked to command a party of 4 officers and 56 gunners, working as teams of Lewis Gunners, to stem the German offensive near Le Bassee, a role he undertook for three days. Remarkably, Herbert was granted UK leave from 7 to 21 August 1918 and therefore did not take part in the opening part of the Battle of Amiens. However, he was soon in action again with one of two composite companies; each with only a few tanks, which were committed to action on 27 August and again on 2 September in support of the Canadians fighting towards Cambrai to the north of the Arras road. Herbert remained with the unit until 25 October when it reorganized itself for the final push. By this time the Battalion was down to less than 20 tanks, so Herbert was granted local leave, returning to the unit just in time for the Armistice. He stayed in France until 3 March 1919 and was released from military duty three days later.

Herbert was subsequently awarded the Military Cross, in the King's Birthday Honours list on 3 June 1919 for service with 11th Battalion. Returning to Sri Lanka, Herbert worked as a tea planter on the Ekkeralle Estate. On 3 April 1924, he married Mary Bradford at the Holy Trinity Church in Nuwara Eliya, the holiday resort built by the British in the heart of the tea country. It is fairly likely that Herbert met up with Jethro Tull whom he had served in C Company, as he also had returned to Sri Lanka. Mary and Herbert's only daughter Rosemary was born on 26 July 1925 at East Preston in Sussex. The family followed the common routine of ex-patriots by returning to England every three to four years. Herbert and Mary eventually settled in England in the late thirties but sadly Herbert died, aged forty-six years at St Lawrence's Hospital in Bodmin on 3 July 1940.

E Tank

The second of the three tanks was commanded by a former member of a Public School's Battalion. Alec Arnaud was born on 9 August 1892 in Bromley in Kent, where his family were builders. Before the war, he worked for the family firm as a book-keeper. Alec initially joined 19th Battalion Royal Fusiliers, deploying as a private solider to France on 14 November 1915 and probably fighting at Le Bassee. When the Battalion was disbanded in early 1916, Alec was selected for officer training. He was commissioned into the Heavy Section MGC on 15 April 1916. Having failed to get into action on 15 September, Alec again commanded the "male" tank no 772 on 25 September in support of the Guards Division follow-on attack. His advance was delayed when water was found in the fuel tank but his crew was quickly able to effect repairs and the tank crew arrived at their start point on time. However, the tanks were not called upon to assist in the attack. On 23 October, Alec was the skipper of another "male" tank No 706 which was one of five under Herbert Hiscocks' command to the north of the River Ancre.

After the company was withdrawn from the Somme, Alec was selected to be one of the instructors who taught the newly formed tank battalions the rudiments of tank operations near St Pol Sur Ternoise. Alec served as an instructor for the remainder of the war but he also commanded a section of tanks at the Battle of Cambrai; the crews being formed from NCO instructors from the driving school at Wailly. On 20 November, Alec's section was in support of 1st Tank Brigade who pushed north from Havrincourt Wood towards the bridges at Marcoing, ripping away German barbed wire in order that the British and Canadian troops could advance.

After the Battle of Cambrai, he returned to instructor duties for which his sustained service was recognised by the award of the Military Cross in the King's Birthday Honours list in May 1918. Soon afterwards, whilst on home leave, Alec married Winifred Pearce who was a builder's daughter from Beckenham. He was appointed Acting Captain on 1 September 1918 whilst still undertaking instructional duties; a role he continued until completion of his service on 20 February 1920. Settling at 93 High Street on Wimbledon Common, Winifred and Alex's elder son Roy was born in 1922 – Roy was to serve as a Royal Artillery officer during the Second World War. In 1925, Alec and Winifred's younger son Anthony was born. Alec was employed by a motor car company, French and Foxwell Ltd who were located at Walton on the Hill between Epsom and Reigate. Alec later worked as a factory manager before he retired to Reigate and he died, aged seventy-seven, on 12 May 1970 in Redhill; Winfred dying two years later.

Alec Arnaud (standing left).
(Tank Museum)

F Tank

The final tank of the central group was commanded by Lieutenant Tom Murphy. Born at Deal on 5 April 1891, Tom was the son of a Customs and Excise officer from Banteer in County Cork. Whilst a schoolboy, the family moved to Bromley where he may have met Alec Arnaud. Tom was educated at the Coopers' Company's School in the Mile End area of London and then studied at the East London College, now Queen Mary's London, where he obtained a science degree. Tom also served in the London University OTC. Having moved with the family to Snaresbrook, Tom followed his father into the Customs and Excise department. On the outbreak of war, Tom was yet another future tank commander who enlisted into 18th Battalion Royal Fusiliers. He deployed to France on 14 November 1915 as a machine gunner, and when the unit was disbanded, returned to England. After training at No 2 MGC Officer Cadet Battalion at Cambridge, Tom was commissioned into HS MGC on 15 April 1916. He was at Bermersfield camp, at Elveden, with C Company by 21 June and deployed to France on 24 August.

On the move-up to the RV on the night of 14 September, Tom's female tank became damaged – probably by enemy artillery fire – near Trônes Wood. The steering gear was removed and fitted to *Clan Leslie* which later became damaged on the route forward. After many of the other tanks failed to get into action, Tom's crew proved that they could steer their tank despite the lack of the tail and were tasked to support a follow-on attack by 6th Division in the afternoon of 15 September.

Working in concert with George Macpherson and crew C22, Tom and his crew attacked the German defensive position at the Quadrilateral, to the east of Ginchy, and then on towards Morval. Both tanks were hit by armour piercing rounds as they went forward but both managed to return to the British Lines having completed their tasks. During the action, Tom received gunshot wounds to his back and he was admitted to a dressing station on 18 September but was released the same day. Tom commanded the same tank on 25 September, during attacks on Les Boeufs in support of the Guards who this time successfully captured their objectives. In October, Tom went north, with a group of tanks, to the area around Serre and commanded another female tank No 524, again under Herbert Hiscocks' command, on 23 October 1916. Owing to the awful ground condition the attacks were called off and the tanks were not used.

In the middle of November, as the tank companies were withdrawn, Tom was transferred to B Battalion with John Allan and Alfred Wheeler who had fought with No 1 Section at Courcelette on 15 September. Given the few men or tanks available to B Battalion, there was little action for the officers to do and Tom was granted home leave from 21 to 31 December. He was also sent to UK from 7 to 16 February on a course of instruction. As part of the Battalion's preparation for summer operations, Tom's company was sent on a driving course from 12 to 15 May at Wailly. He served with No 6 Company commanding Tank B44 at the Battle of Messines. On 7 June, he was due to form part of the second wave but Tom's tank ditched, at 4.00 a.m. in the German front line on the way to its jumping off point and did not get into action. After the battle, Tom was reassigned to No 5 Company. On 26 July 1917, during the preparations for the 3rd Battle of Ypres, as his company made their way towards their RV near Zillebeke, they were bombarded for two hours by German artillery using a mix of explosives and mustard gas. Most of the officers were affected as they were outside their tanks, guiding them forward. Tom was temporarily blinded by the gas and sent to a hospital at Le Touquet. He was then evacuated to 2nd Western Hospital in Manchester arriving on 2 August. A Medical Board on 19 August pronounced he was unfit for general service and was granted 3 weeks leave. When he was examined on 15 September by the Senior Medical Officer at Wareham, the burns had healed and Tom was declared fit for active service.

Promoted Temporary Lieutenant one month later, Tom was one of the four tank commanders who were sent to Dublin in November to assist with peacekeeping duties. Just after he arrived, Len Bates who commanded "G" tank on 15 September 1916 was killed in an accident. Tom gave evidence at the subsequent Board of Inquiry and was almost certainly at the funeral at Grangegorman, which was held on 14 November with full military honours. It was soon recognised that the deployment of tanks to Ireland was a failure and Tom and the crews were sent back to Bovington. He was posted to 14th Battalion as a tank commander and, returning to France in April, fought at the Battle at Amiens. On 8 August, he served with B Company in a Mark V male tank called *North Berwick*, reached the second objective and returned his tank to the rally point. The next day, whilst in a composite company in support of 5th Canadian Brigade, his tank was hit by direct fire between the second and third of objectives. Tom was captured and held as a prisoner of war by the Germans. In his subsequent statement, taken once he had been released, Tom recalled that he was captured near Mehacourt at 5.00 p.m.; his tank having been stopped by direct fire after being hit by the third shell from an artillery battery in front of the village. Tom had been unable to identify the enemy battery's location despite it previously hitting another tank. Two men were wounded inside the tank; one was killed and another wounded whilst trying to escape. As he was well ahead of the attacking infantry, Tom took shelter in a German trench with his crew. As they tried to get back to British lines, they were quickly surrounded by a "strong party of Germans". As he was the only of his crew who was armed, and only with a revolver, Tom saw no choice but to surrender. By 26 August, he had been transferred to the POW camp at Karlsruhe where appears to have spent the rest of the war. Tom was repatriated by the Germans on 13 December 1918 and, following the routine investigation into his capture, was completely exonerated. Sadly, after he left the Army, I can find no other details of his life.

Western Group

The western group of tanks (G, H & K) were to start west of Ginchy and move up Lager Trench to their first objective, the Green Line, They were then to move east along Serpentine trench then north-east following Calf Alley to their final objective at Les Boeufs. They were due to be joined by the tenth reserve, *Clan Cameron*, commanded by Lieutenant Harold Cole but, as described in Chapter 3, he did not return from his preliminary task to clear the trenches near Delville Wood. Charles Ambrose in "K" did not get far before his "car" broke down with steering and engine problems. As Len Bates in "G" and Herbert Elliot in "H" went forward, they were unable to see and engage the German machine guns dug into the banks along the Ginchy to Flers Road. As a result, when the 2nd and 3rd Coldstream advanced, these machine guns created tremendous casualties. The Guards pressed home their attack and the CO of 3rd Coldstream, Lieutenant Colonel Campbell won the VC leading an attack against these guns. Like the 1st Coldstream further to the right, Bates and Elliott swung north in their attack, pushing up on 6th Division's boundary (see map 6). This incorrect advance line caused them to believe that the trenches they had now taken were their objective on the Blue Line. After some time the tank commanders realised the error and resumed their advance in the correct direction, taking the second objective and later returning to their rally point.

G Tank

Len Bates was born on 11 August 1885 at Oxton on the Wirral. The youngest son of a marine insurance secretary, Len was educated with his elder brother William at Birkenhead School. Len studied at the University of Liverpool and at the Camborne School of Mines. He then worked for three years as a coal mining engineer at Aspartia in Cumberland, after which, in 1904 he claimed fellowship of the Royal Geographical Society. Len then worked overseas as an engineer in Lobitos in Northern Peru. Following the outbreak of war, Len returned from Peru, the final stage of his journey being on the ill-fated liner *Lusitania*. Arriving in England on 18 December 1914, he enlisted into 18th Battalion Royal Fusiliers on two occasions; firstly at Epsom on 30 December after which he was discharged as medically unfit on 5 February 1915 and then again on 26 April 1915 at Epsom. He was appointed lance corporal on 1 September 15 and deployed to France as a machine gunner. Len returned to England when the Battalion was disbanded and, together with Tom Murphy and Alec Arnaud who has served in the same battalion, completed initial officer training in March 1916 at Cambridge. It was whilst he was at Cambridge, on 23 March, that his eldest brother William died of wounds whilst serving with 25th (Nova Scotia) Battalion Canadian Infantry and was buried in Loker Churchyard Cemetery.

Len was commissioned on 15 April 1916 and joined the newly formed Heavy Section of the MGC at Bisley. Deploying to France, Len wrote his will on 12 September whilst near the railhead at the Loop. Following his abortive first action, Len commanded tank no 710 under the command of Herbert Hiscocks on 27 September. He was sent sick on 8 October but was soon sufficiently well to return to duty, moving with the bulk of the Company north of the River Ancre. Len was also part of Archie Holford-Walker's section at Beaussart in November 1916. He continued to serve with C Battalion, on its formation, and was granted home leave from 23 December to 2 January 1917. Initially allocated to No 9 Company, with many of those who had fought on the Somme, Len later commanded No 12 Section during the Battle of Arras. Like most officers he attended the driving camp at Wailly in early June and was then appointed to command No 1 Section of 7 Company for the Third Battle of Ypres. On 31 July, Len led his section in an attack on the area at Bremen Redoubt and Boston Farm; the ground conditions being so bad that he could not command from a tank. He therefore walked between the tanks, indicating targets and assisting those crews hurt in the action to safety. For this action, he was awarded the Military Cross for conspicuous gallantry and devotion to duty. The citation states that "On several occasions he guided them over difficult country, frequently under heavy machine-gun and shell fire. It was greatly due to his exertions that the tanks of his section reached their objectives and rendered valuable assistance to the infantry, notably in the vicinity of Beck House. His conduct throughout was most gallant."

On 20 August Len handed over command of his section and returned on leave to England for 10 days leave after which he reported to the tank training centre at Bovington. Appointed acting Captain from 15 October, Len was invested with the Military Cross by King George V at Buckingham Palace on 31 October, the same day as Harry Drader and Eric Robinson of D Company. Len then deployed to Ireland with a Special Service Company to support peace-keeping operations and arrived in Dublin on 8 November. Two days later,

Len Bates 1916. (Birkenhead School)

Len was fatally injured in an accident at the railway siding at Remount Depot at Ballsbridge. He died six hours after being admitted to the Royal City of Dublin Hospital. At the subsequent inquest, the coroner recorded that "Whilst directing operations in the unloading of a tank at Ballsbridge Railway siding, (Bates] was [fatally injured] by reason of the tank slipping and crushing him between it and the platform. Cause of death was shock and hemorrhage". Amongst the witnesses at military inquiry were Billy Sampson, who commanded *Delilah* at High Wood on 15 September 1916, together with Charles Ambrose and Tom Murphy who served with him in No 2 Section; all of whom had also deployed with tanks to Ireland. Len's body was buried with full military honours on 14 November at the Grangegorman Military Cemetery in Dublin. His loss was commemorated in the Roll of Honour of the Birkenhead School where his memorial is opposite that of his brother William, even though Len's death was not as a direct result of conflict.

H Tank

Lieutenant Herbert Elliot, who commanded "H" tank, was born at Elmer's End in Beckenham, Kent on 28 January 1890. The fourth son on an electrical engineer, Hebert could claim descent from William the Conqueror through his mother Sara. Despite these connections, as a twenty-one year old, he was working as a traveller for a firm of publishers and printers. On 27 September 1913, he married Isabel Palmer who was the daughter of a butler, at her Parish Church at Spratton to the north of Northampton. By this time Herbert had become an advertisement manager and was also a keen motorcyclist. On 4 October 1915, he was commissioned as temporary second lieutenant in the MMGS and was pictured driving a motorcycle combination at Bisley in the 22 June 1916 edition of *The Motor Cycle*.

Having successfully taken "H" Tank into action on 15 September, he commanded Tank no 505 supporting the Guards Division twelve days later and then again on 23 October north of the River Ancre. After transferring to C Battalion, in November 1916, Herbert was appointed a section commander in No 8 Company and led them during the assault on the Harp Feature near Beaurains on 9 April 1917. Promoted acting Captain on 12 April 1917, Herbert again commanded No 8 Section at the 3rd Battle of Ypres before returning to England in September 1917. He joined 11th Tank Battalion and, returning to France, on 27 December, served alongside Henry Hiscocks as a section commander. On 4 July 1918, Isabel gave birth to the couple's only son John at 122 Castle Hill in Reading. Herbert probably fought at the Battle of Amiens in August 1918 and was then appointed an Assistant Instructor on 1 September 1918. He stayed in this role until 5 February 1919 and then served until he relinquished his commission on 21 September 1921. Herbert returned to advertising, the family initially living at Leigh on Sea in Essex and then, in 1927, moving a newly built house in Wembley Park. Two years later, and now a company director, Herbert and his family have moved to Great Berkhamstead and in December 1930, he visited Capetown on business. In the 1930s, the family moved to Hampstead and Herbert supported the National Advertising Benevolent Society. He returned to active service on 20 May 1941 when he was commissioned into the RAF Training Branch where he served for the rest of the war. His son John, who was later to become a well-respected BBC drama producer, served in the Royal Army Medical Corps, initially as a SNCO and then as an officer. When John married a WAAF officer named Margaret Haynes in 1945, Herbert and Isobel were living in Petts Wood. They then moved to Hildenborough near Tunbridge Wells, in the 1950s, before settling in Crowborough Sussex where Herbert died, aged seventy-five on 4 August 1965.

K tank

On 15 September 1916, "K" tank commanded by Second Lieutenant Charles Ambrose, failed to reach start point due to steering tail and engine problems. Charles, who was known for his exceptionally blond hair, was born on 7 November 1896 in Dulwich. He was the second child and eldest son of a fruit and flower merchant. Initially educated at Sutton Valence School near Maidstone, he then attended Dulwich College where he played rugby in the Second XV. Charles served in the Officer Training Corps from 25 September 1913 to 8 April 1915. He volunteered to join the Army on leaving school and, whilst serving with 10th Battalion Border Regiment, applied for commission on 1 June 1915. Charles was sent to the Cambridge UOTC on 21 June 1915 and subsequently commissioned into the MMGS.

After the false start of 15 September 1916, Charles again commanded Tank No 760 on 25 September during attacks in the Morval, Quadrilateral and the Bouleaux wood area. He also commanded the female tank No 522 on 27 September.

When C Company was expanded to a battalion in November, he stayed with the unit. On 2 January 1917, he was admitted to 12 Stationary Hospital at St Pol sur Ternoise but he was back with his unit in ten days – this early contact with what came known as Spanish influenza later killed many across France and the UK. Like most of the original C Company officers and men, Charles served with No 8 Company at the Battle of Arras. On 9 April 1917 he took part in the Battle of the Harp, near Beaurains, when he commanded tank crew C36 which included Will Dawson who fought with George Macpherson at the Quadrilateral in 1916. His tank crossed the German front line and engaged the enemy, but ditched before reaching the Blue line. The tank was recovered but not before it had been hit by British artillery fire. Although Charles was suffering from shock, he took the tank back into action four days later at Monchy-le-Preux. His tank reached the crossroads at La Bergère, well ahead of the British infantry, where it was attached by German infantry using grenades and armour piercing bullets. All the gunners were wounded but they managed to force the enemy to take cover in a sunken road. The tank pushed on towards Monchy but was immobilised by grenades exploding under its tracks; it also received a direct hit from a shell which blew in a sponson. The enemy once more surrounded the tank but were again driven off by Lewis gun fire. When the tank was eventually abandoned, three men were killed and two wounded. Charles was subsequently awarded the Distinguished Service Order for conspicuous gallantry and devotion to duty.

Charles attended the 2nd Tank Brigade gunnery school from 15 to 19 May and the following month deployed to the tank driving school at Wailly. He was admitted to hospital on 28 June 1917 suffering from tonsillitis. Discharged on 19 July, he was sent to England for leave on 9 August 1917. Suffering from recurrent tonsillitis, Charles admitted himself to 4th London General Hospital at Denmark Hill on 19 August 1917. He was not fit for duty for a further month and, on 20 September tasked to report to the Tank Depot at Wareham. There he was ordered to join M Battalion on 17 October 1917 and, on his arrival, he was selected to serve with Len Bates and Tom Murphy with the Special Service Company. Four tank crews were sent to Dublin to assist with internal security duties which arrived on 8 November. After Len's death, Charles was made a member of the Committee of Adjustment and given the unenviable task of sorting out Len Bates' effects.

Charles again became ill whilst in Dublin and was not fit for duty until 22 January 1918. Charles returned to England and joined 13th Battalion Tank Corps whose officers included Herbert Hiscocks Nine days later, he embarked from Southampton on 31 January with the unit and was soon back in action. Like Herbert Hiscocks, Charles commanded several sections of Lewis Guns, from C Company, during the German offensive near Vierstraat in the Ypres Salient on 26 April. Although he is not mentioned in the Battalion history Charles also probably took part in the successful attack, by the Australians, at Hamel on 4 July 1918. He was not present at the start of the Battle of Amiens as he was granted UK leave from 1 to 15 August 1918. However he fought during the Final Advance when 13th Battalion was fully engaged in operations. Following the Armistice, Charles was posted to the Tank Driving and Maintenance School at Bovington where he served as an assistant instructor from 28 November 1918 until 14 January 1919. He served on until September 1920. On 2 October 1920, having found employment as a secretary, he married Gwendoline Jarratt at Christchurch in Streatham. They had a daughter and two sons but sadly their marriage broke up due to the trauma created by his wartime experiences. After the Second World War, Charles moved to Huntingdon where he worked for a while as a Post Office telephonist. He later settled at Hartford and died, in straitened circumstances on 21 February 1964 at Huntingdon, his wife Geraldine having died two months earlier at Hailsham.

Eastern Group

The final group of tanks, who supported the Guards on the right, was commanded by Jethro Tull, Jack Clarke and Victor Smith. They were due to set off fifty minutes before the Guards attack. As the tanks deployed, across no man's land, the ground was covered in low fog but they were put on their right course by Herbert Hiscocks who, having no longer in command of his own tank, went forward on foot to ensure that the Eastern group deployed in the right direction. (see coloured image 7) Jethro Tull's steering mechanism was damaged before reaching the German front line but he was able to get the tank back across no man's land to the rally point – the commanders being under strict orders not to allow the tanks to be captured. Jack Clarke and Victor Smith's tanks reached the German front line well ahead of the attacking infantry. The two skippers would have seen the artillery barrage come down on the first objective or Green Line, which ran along the Serpentine trench at zero hour (6:20 a.m.) as the infantry left their trenches. The artillery plan called for a barrage to be laid down 100 yards in front of the infantry, and for this to creep forward at fifty yards a minute. The plan also included a 100 yards wide gap in the barrage for the expected advance line of the tanks, which were luckily within their lane or they would have been hit by their own artillery.

Despite the presence of the tanks, the Guards met a hail of bullets from Straight Trench as well as enfilade fire from the Quadrilateral to their east. Captain Sir Iain Colquhoun, who was commanding a company of Grenadiers, recorded what happened thus: "

> Sept 15th. Started digging 2.30am, finished 3.15am. Went round all my Company to see they were all in their right places, etc. Anyone can see that there must be hopeless confusion when

we start. Lay down in a shell hole at 4 am. About 4.30am the Tanks began to arrive behind us. The Germans heard them and sent up many rockets and shelled slightly. At 5.40am the Tanks started and went through our front line. At 6.30am the entire British Line advanced, the 1st Guards Brigade on our left the 6th Division on our right. As we anticipated the entire wave formation had disappeared before we had crossed our own front line, and we advanced in a great mass, Grenadiers, Coldstream, Irish and Scots Guards all inextricably mixed up. Within 30 yards I found myself in front of the Grenadiers with a few of my men. Our barrage was about 50 yards in front of us, and the whole landscape was obscured by smoke, and it was impossible to see anything or keep direction. About 100 yards on we found a few Germans lying in shell holes. I shot one and clubbed one. We then came under heavy machine-gun fire, and the Lines disappeared into shell holes.

Both Jack Clarke and Victor Smith's tanks are believed to have got to the area of Low Road, which was also the German's second line trench. The tanks used machine guns to keep the German defenders down so that the British infantry could advance. Victor Smith got on a little further but neither tank made it to Les Boeufs. The Guards suffered badly during their 2,000 yards advance and lost more than 25% casualties amongst the division. 2,000 men were killed, including Lieutenant Raymond Asquith, the eldest son of the Prime Minister and a further 3,000 were wounded including the future Prime Minister Harold MacMillan.

A Tank

Lieutenant Jethro Tull's tank's steering tail was wrecked whilst traversing no man's land and did not have any real effect on the Germans. This male tank was again used, on 25 September, during attacks in the Morval, Quadrilateral and the Bouleaux wood area. The tank stopped due to problems with the engine electrics, the platinum coming off the contact breaker, but by 7:00 a.m., this had been repaired by the crew. The tank then moved forward to the Quadrilateral Ridge where it became ditched after a trench caved in. Jethro eventually managed to withdrew his tank despite it being bracketed by German artillery fire.

Jethro, who was the second son of a London brewer, was born on 17 December 1886 in Pimlico. He was educated at Westminster School before he, like Henry Hiscocks, emigrated to Sri Lanka to work as a planter. He was employed at Haloya Estate near Peradiny and joined the Ceylon Planters' Rifles Corps in 1912. He left Sri Lanka immediately war was declared and, on 15 September 1914, enlisted as a private soldier into 18th Battalion Royal Fusiliers – the battalion having been formed only four days earlier at Epsom. Due to his previous military training in Sri Lanka, Jethro was immediately promoted to the rank of corporal. He applied for a commission whilst the Battalion was at Tidworth and was commissioned into the MMGS on 26 August 1915. I can find no record of Jethro being involved in any further action on the Somme but he stayed with C Battalion when the original company was expanded on 18 November 1916.

Allocated to No 7 Company, Jethro was appointed acting Captain on 12 April 1917 after being placed in command of a section. There is no record of which section he commanded during the Battle of Arras. In June 1917, he took his section to the driver training school at Wailly where the old trench lines were used to train new drivers. Jethro commanded the section of supply tanks in No 7 Company during the opening actions of the 3rd Battle of Ypres. He relinquished command of that section on 20 August 1917 when he returned to the UK to join the newly forming J Battalion. There is no record of him serving with the unit in France; however by September 1918, he had transferred and was serving with 16th Battalion in France. He commanded a section in B Company operating the much longer Mark V and V* tanks during the Battle of St Quentin Canal in support of 3rd Australian Division. His company was attached to 13th Tank Battalion to assist in exploiting

Australian success. On 29 September, One of his tank commanders was killed and a second declared missing; he had been captured by the Germans. A third commander was injured as was Jethro who suffered splinters in his right eye. Evacuated to England on 5 October, Jethro was treated at 3rd London General Hospital at Wandsworth where his damaged eye was removed. Although he was promoted Temporary Captain on 19 October 1918, he did not return to active service.

Before he was discharged from the Army, Jethro purchased two false eyes on 14 April 1919 and then sailed to Sri Lanka. Jethro returned to the Haloya Estate and worked for the Gildon Hall Tea and Rubber Co Ltd. He applied for a pension on 29 December 1919 and was granted £100 per year. He later married an American woman, Katherine who was ten years his junior. They returned to England and in 1938 travelled to the United States for a three week holiday, going out on the RMS *Queen Mary* and returning on SS *Normandie* arriving at Southampton on 17 October 1938. The couple lived in Sri Lanka during the Second World War, Jethro continuing his work as a planter but the couple returned to the UK from Colombo on 14 August 1945. Five years later, Katherine died whilst on holiday in Cornwall, and Jethro moved to Bentley in Hampshire where he died at Vine Cottage on 4 May 1953. His body is buried at Brookwood Cemetery.

C 17 *Campania* or B tank

On 15 September 1916, Lieutenant Jack Clarke commanded crew C17 who manned the male tank number 746 which has recently be identified as HMLS *Campania*. The tank successfully crossed no man's land, with the female tank C18 known as *Casa* under the command of Victor Smith, and after crossing the German Front line trench turned north to reach the first objective at Low Road, which was the German support trench. The tank crew then returned to refuel as the shell damaged ground conditions made the fuel consumption very high. Jack, whose full name was John Peard Clarke, was born at Staplegrove near Taunton on 28 March 1897. He was the son of a local solicitor whose firm is still in business. He was educated at Malvern College between 1910 and 1913; his final year spent in Germany resulting in Jack speaking German fluently. On 4 September 1914, Jack enlisted into the Somerset Light Infantry (SLI) with his older brother Geoffrey. Jack was appointed lance corporal on 9 February 1915 and later served with 6th Battalion SLI at Witley Camp near Godalming where he applied for a commission. Jack was commissioned into the SLI on 6 April 1915, nine days after his eighteenth birthday, and was attached to the MMGS on 10 October 1915. He later joined C Company and deployed to France on 16 August.

After the action on 15 September, Jack again commanded tank 746, on 25 September, during attacks in the Morval, Quadrilateral and the Bouleaux wood area. He must have been injured and evacuated home because Reg Legge's service file contains a report written by Jack at 2nd Southern General Hospital in Bristol. Granted leave at the end of the year, Jack returned to France and joined C Battalion. However, he had to be sent back to England on 4 February 17 due to an ingrowing toe nail. He was treated at the officers' convalescent hospital at the Ilfracombe Hydro but was not declared fit for light duties on 31 May which indicates that he may have required other treatment, perhaps related to his wounds in 1916. After three weeks leave, Jack was sent to Bovington and became one of the first members of 12th Battalion. He returned to France on 5 January 18 with the renamed L Battalion whose section commanders included Archie Holford-Walker. At the end of February, Jack was attached to the Mechanical School for a week.

As one of the Battalion's more experienced officers, Jack was promoted acting Captain on 11 June 1918 and appointed to command a section. During the third Battle of the Somme, on 23 August 1918, as the British troops forced the Germans back over the ground they had captured during the "Kaiserschlacht", Jack commanded a tank in addition to his section. Whilst this was common in 1916, it was most unusual by 1918. Although it was high summer, there was a lot of ground mist and Jack followed Herbert Hiscocks' example from the first tank action. To quote from his medal citation: "During the early hours of the attack there was a good deal of mist, and Captain Clarke realised that there was a great danger of his tanks losing direction. He therefore led them on foot, walking in the open under machine-gun and shell fire. In doing this he was twice wounded, once in the arm and once in the leg, but he refused to leave his section and guided them safely to the starting-point. He then entered his tank and led his section into action, advancing through the village of Hamelincourt and clearing it of enemy machine guns, thus enabling the infantry to advance with few casualties. Throughout the action he showed a complete disregard of personal safety and was a splendid example to all ranks in his section." His conspicuous gallantry and devotion to duty was subsequently recognised through the award of a Military Cross.

As a result of his wounds, Jack sent to hospital and sent back to England on 29 August, being admitted to the Horton War Hospital at Epsom. He was suffering from gunshot wounds to his left forearm plus two light flesh wounds to his left leg. He was not released from hospital until 30 November 1918 when he was sent on three weeks leave, after which he was employed with 593 Agricultural Company ASC based at Taunton. A report from the Medical Board, held at Taunton on 23 December 1918 shows him as "Quite well" and fit for general duties. Jack was not released from Army service until 7 May 1919 when he returned to Staplegrove. After the war, Jack trained as an engineer in Leeds. In 1921 he became a member of the Yorkshire Ramblers Club and climbed the three peaks, Pen-y-ghent, Whernside and Ingleborough in the North Yorkshire Dales. On completion of his studies, he returned to his home near Taunton, where he was living in 1925, but soon set off for India. On 27 January 1927, the office of the Commander in Chief India at Simla sought records of his service following Jack's request to join the Indian Army Reserve of Officers and he was later listed amongst the officers serving with the Tank Corps in India. In 1928, he returned from Bombay but he did not stay in England for long. In 1934 Jack moved to Kenya, much later than many of the unemployed ex-officers who moved there immediately after the Great War. By 1936 he had established himself as a farmer at Endebess in the Kenyan Rift Valley and he lived there until he died, sadly young at forty-eight, on 30 April 1944.

Exceptionally we know the name of Jack's driver on 15 September due to the survival of a letter, sent to his family, which describes his part in the battle. The letter, which is now held by the Imperial War Museum, was written by Leonard Viner and initialed by Jack Clarke prior to being posted to England as being free of any sensitive material. Len Viner was much older than most of the First Tank Crews, being born on 5 November 1879. He was the elder son of a bank clerk from Battersea who, by the age of twenty-one, was living in Dunstable working as a photographer's assistant. Three years later, he had become a chauffeur for the Jamieson family of The Wells at Epsom. In 1907, he married Maude Davies in Warwick and they had three children: Alan, Violet and Noel. Leonard was a keen rifle shot and, in 1915, regularly fired on the National Rifle Association's ranges at Bisley which remained open to rifle clubs for the majority of the war. Later in 1915, Len joined the ASC in 1915 as a motor transport driver and, in June 1916, was posted to 711 MT Company which supported the first tank companies. In his letter to Maude, written on 18 September 1916, Len explains that the tank was hit by shrapnel and bullets and that the prisms, which provided vision for the driver and commander, were broken during the action. He also tells her that the crew was very tired but otherwise unhurt. Remarkably Len also told Maude that he had fired a 6 pdr QF which seems a most unusual task for an ASC driver. He also reports that two infantrymen were bought back in the tank –one of whom was shot in the jaw.

Len was later injured during the actions on the Ancre, in October, and perhaps it was as a result of this injury that he stayed with the ASC, rather than transfer to the MGC. After the war, Leonard moved to Coventry and, according to his son Noel's wedding certificate, worked as a test driver. On 11 June 1940, the family moved to Calcutta and Leonard died at Cossipore in north Calcutta on 7 February 1942.

C 18 *Casa*

The final tank in the group of eastern tanks was commanded by Lieutenant Victor Smith who called his tank *Casa* after his boyhood home. The female tank left its start to the east of Ginchy point on time, crossed the open ground of No Man's Land and then breached the German Front Line and then, having lost contact with the Guards, supported an attack by the Leicesters on a strip wood about 1,000 yards into the German held ground (see the long wood on the horizon in the centre of coloured image 7). However Victor was forced to withdraw from action when his tank's engine bearings started to seize due to a lack of lubrication. He managed to get *Casa* back to the rally point at Guillemont Railway Station, where he sent a message by carrier pigeon for assistance from Theodore Wenger, the ASC engineer officer who led the maintenance and repair team for C Company.

Victor Smith was born on 15 December 1890 in Erleigh Road in Reading. He was the elder son of an architect Reginald Smith, who was a Justice of the Peace, and a grandson of a former mayor of Reading in 1875. The family home *Casa* was built in 1903 on the Elmhurst Road on the boundary of the Whiteknights estate which now forms the campus of Reading University. It would have been a short walk downhill to Reading School where Victor was first educated; later he was attended the Leighton Park School which is also only a ten minute walk from *Casa*. On leaving school, Victor joined his father's firm as an architect's pupil. Victor did not volunteer to join the Army until 1916 which may have stemmed from Victor's Quaker-based education at Leighton Park. He was attested at Reading on 13 March 1916 and shortly afterwards sent to No 5 Cadet Battalion at Cambridge for officer training. In a letter sent to his younger sister Vera, written on Wednesday 22 March shortly after he arrived at Trinity College, Victor reveals that he did not have a uniform and was sleeping on the floor in a straw-staffed mattress. He was also being paid as a private soldier. Shortly

Casa crewmen at Bury St Edmunds 1916 Standing rear John Witty, Pte Stewart, William Scott, George Caffrey. seated; Douglas Gardiner, Victor Smith, John Webby, Sitting front Harry Greenberg. (Tank Museum)

afterwards, Victor was interviewed by Colonel Ernest Swinton and commissioned into the Heavy Section MGC on 15 April 1916. Given that he had completed officer training in less than 3 weeks, it is reasonable to assume that Victor had previously undertaken some military training in the OTC at Reading School.

Victor joined C Company whilst it was still under the command of Captain Napier as Allen Holford-Walker did not take command until May 1916. Victor deployed to France on 24 August 1916, his tank which had arrived at Le Havre earlier being the first to be off-loaded in France. After the initial action on 15 September *Casa* was repaired and Victor was in sent back in action ten days later this time supporting 5th Division. *Casa* became ditched in a dug out as it deployed forward the start point but the crew extracted it. By the time the tank crew got forward to the valley facing Morval, the objective had been taken and Victor was tasked to return to the start point by his section commander, Archie Holford-Walker. Victor transferred to C Battalion, as it formed in November 1916, and joined No 7 Company which was initially under command of Allen Holford-Walker. Four months later, on the opening day of the Battle of Arras, 9 April 1917, Victor was serving with No 7 Company commanding tank crew C7, his tank almost certainly being called *Casa*. His section was tasked to support 9th (Scottish) Division's assault from St Nicholas towards the village of St Laurant Blangy, a port on the River Scarpe. Victor was tasked to break through the German front line defences in concert with tank C8 whose commander is not known. The C8 tank became ditched as she tried to cross the German trenches but Victor used *Casa* to drag her out. Both then moved on until C8 received a direct hit but *Casa* achieved its objective and returned to its rally point. On 23 April, again whilst commanding tank crew C7, Victor supported the 51st Highland Division's attack on Mount Pleasant Wood near the village of Roeux. His approach was delayed up at a railway arch which was full of wounded and blocked by a sandbag barricade. However *Casa* eventually caught up with the infantry at the southern end of Mount Pleasant Wood. The infantry were held up by machine-gun fire so *Casa*'s crew engaged the enemy in the northern part of the wood and cleared it. Victor then proceeded towards Roeux and, entering the village, destroyed a number of machine-guns that were stopping the infantry advance; he also used *Casa*'s 6 pdr QF guns to clear the German held buildings. It was not, however, all one-way fire and *Casa* was damaged and four of the crew wounded by armour-piercing bullets which penetrated the tank. Having achieved his mission, Victor withdrew *Casa* and returned to the rally point. For this action, Victor was awarded the Military Cross.

Victor returned to England on duty from 28 April until 15 May 1917 before attending a driving camp at Wailly from 10 to 19 June. There is no record of his commanding a tank during the Third Battle of Ypres so he was possibly serving as the company recce officer. He was promoted lieutenant on 15 October and commanded No 2 Section at the Battle of Cambrai where his tanks broke through the Hindenburg line to the east of La Vacquerie near Pam-Pam Farm. One of the Reserve tanks, in his company, was called *Casa*. Victor is not mentioned during the No 7 Company's follow-on attacks on 23 and 27 November but he was present near Gouzeaucourt as the remaining C Battalion tanks were being withdrawn from the battlefield on 30 November. According to Will Dawson, there was an argument after some crewmen, who had been promised UK leave, were told they have to remain to crew tanks which were to be used to push back the German counter-attack. Their officers were permitted to leave but Victor intervened to ensure that the crewmen could be released. He himself went on leave on 2 December, returning to the Battalion at its base at Auchy on 19 December.

By this time, C Battalion was starting to convert to drive Whippet tanks and redesignated 3rd Light Battalion. The first two months of 1918 were spent training to operate the new vehicles, during which Victor accompanied Brigadier General Hugh Elles on a trip to the Foster's factory in Lincoln to see Whippets under construction. One of the new C Company tanks was designated *Casa* but Victor ceased the role of section commander on 3 July 1918 so would not have commanded

Victor Smith (centre on steps with Graham Woods to the left) Mers-les-Bains Spring 1919.
(Mrs Paddi Lilley)

it in action. He was sent to command the Officers' Company at the Reinforcement and Training Depot at Mers-les-Bains. After the Armistice, he was promoted major and served as Commandant of the Depot. One of his final actions, before he returned to England for demobilisation, was to present a tank to the town in recognition of the local people's support. The officer who represented HQ Tank Corps at the event was Lieutenant Colonel Graham Woods who was the Adjutant of D Company in September 1916.

In March 1920, Victor won a silver cup for Bath to Land's End motorcycle race. Later that year, Victor met his future wife Barbara Abram at a History Pageant in Reading which had been organised by her father who was the mayor. On 28 April 1921, the couple was married at St Luke's Church Reading. Victor and Barbara were children of two very prominent Reading families; Barbara's father, Stewart, was the senior physician at the Royal Berkshire Hospital, as well as a JP, who was knighted in 1922 for his service as the founder and controller of the War Hospital in Reading. The wedding reception was held at Reading town hall and more than 300 guests travelled from the church to the feast in specially decorated tram cars. Using public transport for this purpose was a first and the local paper commented most positively about the sight of gentlemen in silk top hats and their ladies in the latest fashions travelling through the centre of the town. Victor and Barbara later had four children; three daughters and a son.

Victor became a successful businessman as well as becoming involved in politics and local affairs. He was a member of the senior management team of Huntley and Palmers, the Reading-based biscuit makers, and was managing director of the biscuit tin manufacturing company, Huntley, Boorne and Stevens for 24 years. In 1927 the firm, which is famous for their specially designed and highly-coloured biscuit tins, produced a special tank shaped tins containing iced-gem biscuits. The company history site states the tin was based on the Mark 1 medium tank, which was introduced in the mid 1920s and it is probably fair to say that Victor ensured the model was as accurate as possible. In 1928, shortly after the death of his father-in-law, Victor was elected to Reading Council representing the Abbey ward. He served on the Council until 1946 when he was appointed alderman. He also actively supported education both at Reading School and Reading University which was, and still is, heavily linked to the business community. Victor also became a director of Olympia, the long-established dance hall in London Street, Reading and was also a vice chairman of the Confederation of British Industry. Awarded the OBE for political and public services in Berkshire in the 1953 Queen's Coronation awards, Victor and Barbara attended the investiture at Buckingham Palace on 28 October.

Forty years after he went into action near Ginchy, Victor appeared with Victor Huffam on a BBC TV panel game show called *what's the Link?* This was the catalyst for Victor Huffam to find surviving members of the crews and provide some of the original information upon which this book is based. Victor remained heavily involved in local politics but after Barbara's death, he retired to his son's farm near Henley on Thames where he died, aged eighty seven, on 21 December 1977.

Unusually we know all the names of the *Casa* crew as the result of a photograph taken at Bury St Edmunds before they deployed to France in 1916. Bury St Edmonds was the nearest large town to the tank training ground at Elveden and was regularly visited by the members of C and D Companies when given time away from training. The photograph, which was later presented to the Tank Museum in the late 1960s by one of the crewmen, William Scott, is exceptional because

John and William Scott (seated) 1917.
(Geoffrey Churcher)

the back is annotated with their names. I have not been able to identify the ASC driver, Private Stewart but Gunner William Scott, who was born on 11 February 1897, was the son of John and Fanny Scott from Horsham. Usually he was not christened until he was fifteen months old. When he left school, William worked for a nurseryman which his older brother John was a cycle engineer. John was one of the earliest members of the MMGS having enlisted in January 1915. William was attested at Bisley on 23 May 16, just three months before he deployed to France. He wrote his will as the tanks moved to their assembly areas on 13 September, leaving everything to his mother. He remained with C Battalion on its formation; his elder brother John joining the unit in November 1916 after which they served together in No 8 Company.

John was awarded the Military Medal in November 1917; the citation read"on 22 August 1917 when serving near Hill 35. "When his tank was isolated in front of the infantry, this NCO volunteered to go through heavy machine and sniper fire for further orders and information to the section commander. He successfully accomplished his mission. Through the action he displayed courage and initiative in a marked degree."John and William fought No 8 company during the Battle of Cambrai and then with B Company of 3rd Battalion operating Whippets. In the summer of 1918, William returned to the UK to join the newly forming 22nd Light Battalion at Bovington. In March 1919, whilst John was discharged having married the previous month, William was posted to Dublin to join the 17th Armoured Car Battalion which had been sent on internal security duties. William was discharged in Dublin in September 1919 and returned to Horsham after which he disappears until 1969 when he presented the photograph of the crew to the Tank Museum as well as his ID tags, a flag and his protective facemask.

Gunner Harry Greenberg joined the MMGS in 1915 and served with that unit again after the first action. There is no record that he later transferred or to link of his service in the Tank Corps; indeed when he was discharged from the Army on 20 February 1919, he was still a gunner in the MMGS. The tank's second in command was also a MMGS man. Corporal Douglas Gardiner was born in Cardiff on 14 November 1894, the only son amongst seven children born to Andrew and Elizabeth Gardiner. Douglas was working as an insurance clerk, and living at Fairfield in Llanishen, when he volunteered to join the MMGS on 23 March 1916 at Coventry. The medical records from that day show he was five feet nine inches in height; weighed just under twelve stones pounds and a chest measurement of forty inches when expanded which made him a much broader man than most of his comrades. Douglas was posted to C Company on 25 May 16, appointed acting lance corporal on 27 June then substantive corporal on 7 August. Douglas embarked from Southampton on 24 August 1916 and disembarked the next day at Le Havre.

Following the first tank actions, Douglas was transferred to C Battalion on its formation on 18 November 1916 but he did not stay with the unit for long. Douglas was posted to the MGC Base Depot at Dannes-Camiers, near Étaples, on 24 January 17 and reverted to rank of gunner. On 22 June 1917, Douglas was posted to the Infantry Branch of the MGC and remained at the Depot undertaking instructional duties. He was detached to the training grounds at Étaples in April and May 1918 followed by twenty days attached to the American Forces. Eventually reaching the rank of acting Sergeant on 9 November 1918, he was demobilised on 28 January 1919. Douglas married Helen Tobin in Cardiff on 30 September 1924. Their eldest son Peter was born the following year but died when he was just two years old. The couple did however have a further three children, Although I can find little about his life after that, he kept in contact with his Tank Corps comrades and was present at the 50th Anniversary Dinner, held at Caxton Hall in London on 15 September 1966. Douglas was one of the longest surviving tank crewmen; he and Helen moved to the Isle of Wight where she died on 13 February 1989. Douglas died exactly nine months later on the day before his ninety-fifth birthday at Cowes on the Isle of Wight.

Gunner George Caffrey sadly did not survive the war. Like Douglas Gardiner, George was a Welshman but he came from the mid Welsh town of Machynlleth. Born in early 1895, George was the eldest of six children of a railwayman after whom he was named, and his wife Minnie. He joined the MMGS at Coventry in August 1915 and went to train at Bisley that same month. Although his service record did not survive the London Blitz, details of George's service was recorded in the local newspaper the *Cambrian Times*. His part in the first tank action was mentioned on 29 September, presumably after he had written home to his parents. The paper also reported that he was serving with the Heavy Section in October 1916. Shortly afterwards he was wounded and evacuated to England. His wounds were not serious and he was granted leave in early November. He did not return to France until after April 1917 probably with G Battalion which had formed earlier that year at Bovington. He was later burned when his tank caught fire; this was probably during the Battle of Cambrai when a number of tanks were "brewed up" after being hit by German artillery. He again recovered from his injuries and returned to France where he was given home leave just before the Battle of Amiens in July 1918. George was killed on 2 September 1918 whilst C Company of 7th Battalion was supporting the 5th British Division attack to the north of Beugny between Bapaume to Cambrai. Of the six Mark IV tanks deployed in this action, only one was hit. Both George and his "skipper" Lieutenant George Adney, another Welshman who been awarded the Military Cross after the battle at Bourlon Wood on 23 November 1917, were killed. They were initially buried near where they were killed to the northwest of Beugny, Later, during grave concentration, their remains were relocated and they are now buried side by side at the Vaux Hill cemetery. On 20 September 1918, the *Cambrian Times* reported:

> The sad news reached Mr and Mrs George Caffrey last week, of the death in action of their eldest son, Arthur, aged 23 years, a gunner in the Tank Corps. He had been on active service for many months. Some time ago his tank caught fire and he was badly burnt. After treatment in this country he was again sent out, but was home on leave about six weeks ago. His quiet and unassuming manner won him a host of friends. His loss will also be keenly felt at the Presbyterian Chapel, where he was a member. Much sympathy is felt with Mr and Mrs Caffrey, the brothers (one of whom is on active service), and the sisters, and Miss Katie Jones, his fiancée.

John Webby, who was the oldest member of the crew, survived. Born at Honiton in late September 1887, John was the eldest son of a schoolmaster, Tom Pearce Webby and his wife Hannah. Like Arthur Blowers, John trained as a teacher and also served for a while in the local Territorial Army unit, 4th Devons, whilst he trained at St Luke's College. John was working as a teacher in Yeovil when he enlisted on 3 December 1915 expressing a preference to serve with 7th (Cyclist) Battalion of the Devonshire Regiment. He was not however called up until 16 March 1916 when he was allocated to the MGC and sent to Bisley for training. He was posted to C Company in 27 May 1916 and deployed to France with his crewmates on 24 August 1916. After the first actions, John joined C Battalion when it formed in November 1916 and undertook driver training at a course at Wailly between 10 and 18 June 1917. I do not know that whether he fought at the Battles of Arras and Ypres in 1917 but; given he was granted home-leave from 4 to 18 December 1917 John must have been in action during the Battle of Cambrai.

Three days after returning to England, he married Grace Pembroke at Croydon Registry Office. He returned to France and served with 3rd Battalion for the rest of the war, eventually being promoted acting Sergeant on 6 January 1919. He returned to UK on 21 January and having been demobilized at Fovant, returned to Yeovil. John returned to teaching after the war and he and Grace had two daughters; Vivien who was born in Yeovil in 1923 and Audrey who was born near Axminster in 1926. The family later moved to Seaton, where John named their house *Elveden* after the tank training ground in Norfolk which says much about the happy memories he had of his time with the tanks. John died, aged sixty-seven years old, on 2 December 1955 at the Royal Devon and Exeter Hospital; Grace surviving him until 27 May 1979 when she also died in Exeter.

John Witty, who joined the MMGS at Coventry on the same day as John Webby, was born in late March 1888 at Middleton on the Wolds in North Yorkshire. John was the son of a railway labourer who moved his family to Leeds by 1891. Initially John worked as a tailor's shop assistant but, by the time of his marriage, had become a commercial traveler. He married Effie Stanley on 1 March 1913 at Wesleyan School Chapel at Holbrook and their elder daughter Florence was born on 8 February 1914 at Hunslet. John enlisted at Leeds on 11 December 1915 and was mobilized on 16 March 1916 which was the same day as John Webby. He remained with C Battalion on its formation and served in No 9 Company and 3rd Battalion until February 1919. He attended the same driving course as John Webby in June 1917. On joining the Tank Corps in July 1917 John was granted ASC rates of pay when he qualified as a first class tank mechanic and driver in August 1917. He was granted the same period of home leave as John Webby which again indicates he fought at Cambrai. Serving on with C Battalion, after it renumbered to 3rd Battalion and converted to a light tank unit, John was appointed paid lance corporal on 25 July 1918.

John was wounded on 8 August 1918, the opening day of the Battle of Amiens, but this was not sufficiently serious to prevent his taking part in later actions. John was awarded the Military Medal for his subsequent bravery. According to the medal citation: "During the action near Achiet-le-Petit, on Aug 21, 18, this man as driver of his tank displayed the greatest skill and daring under extremely heavy artillery and machine-gun fire. Owing to his skill in manoeuvring his tank he enabled his gunners to inflict heavy casualties on the enemy. This man has driven a tank in every action of his Company or Battalion since the formation of the Tank Corps with the greatest gallantry and skill, and was especially brought to notice for gallantry in action on Aug 8, 18." John was promoted corporal on 28 October 1918 and then sergeant on the same day which demonstrates the numbers of casualties being suffered by the 3rd Tank Battalion as the British Army pushed the Germans back towards the Belgian border. John served on France until 10 February and dispersed on 12 February 1919 from Clipstone back to his home in Leeds. Effie died in 1944, whilst living at the Plough Hotel in Yetholm in the Scottish Borders. John lived on, as a widower for a further twenty-two years until he died aged seventy-nine, in Whitley Bay.

7

Death of a Fire-eater

---

15 September 1916 was to be a frustrating day for the tank crew D4. They had become stuck in Delville Wood on the way to their start point for their attack and, despite hours of hard work, could not get the tank into action. They would however prove their fighting ability on 26 September at Gueudecourt. The remainder of Captain Harold Mortimore's section managed to cross no man's land, and get into action. Tank D3, which dragged *Dolphin* out of Delville Wood was badly damaged by German artillery fire after it had got amongst the German trenches and had to return to British lines. *Dolphin*, whose actions are described in Chapter 3, was later destroyed as was the final tank, manned by crew D6, which reached the outskirts of Gueudecourt where it was destroyed by German artillery (see maps 8 and 9).

Tank Crew D4

The skipper of the D4 crew, Charles Storey, was much older than most tank skippers. The son of a stockbroker, Charles was born on 16 February 1877 at Brompton in West London, and brought up in Hackney. He was educated at Cranleigh School in Surrey. His father died when Charles was young and his mother who settled in Southend died in 1897. By this time Charles was working in London but he travelled to South Africa as a young man and served with the locally raised 2nd Imperial Light Horse Regiment during the Second Anglo-Boer War. Returning to England in 1902, he continued to work in London and served with the London Rifle Brigade for three years. Prior to outbreak of war in 1914, Charles was working in Argentina as a clerk in the stores of a British run railway company. He immediately decided to return to England, and travelling via Montevideo on the SS *Ionic* arrived home on 24 August. He enlisted on 3 September 1914 into the 18th Battalion Royal Fusiliers, where he served alongside Tom Murphy in the Machine Gun Platoon. Their battalion entered France on 14 November 1915 and served at the infamous Cuinchy brick stacks, on the front line of the Loos battlefield.

When the battalion was disbanded, Charles was selected for officer training and joined No 4 Officer Cadet Battalion at Oxford on 24 March. After less than three weeks training, he was commissioned into the HS MGC. Now aged thirty-eight, despite being a bachelor, Charles became known to his younger comrades as "Father". Although his tank did not get into action on 15 September, Charles and his crew were not safe from danger; indeed Charles was slightly injured as he tried to get his tank out of Delville Wood and into action. On 24 September Charles was tasked to take a new tank into action in support of 21st Division attack on guns protecting Gueudecourt. Three other tanks, commanded by Heady Head, Graeme Nixon and Stephen Sellick, were also allocated to the attack, which was to take place on 25 September but none of the tanks was called forward. The next day, however, his tank played a key role in breaching the defences at Gueudecourt and capturing 500 prisoners. The Company War Diary records that Charles and four other crewmen were wounded in this action although amongst the infantry losses were also very light at only two killed and two injured which is remarkable when compared with the dreadful numbers of dead and injured elsewhere. Charles, who was awarded the Distinguished Service Order for his action, lost his right eye and was evacuated to Queen Alexandra's Military Hospital on London's Millbank on 29 September 1916.

When he was declared fit, on 13 February 1917, he was "claimed" by Frank Summers who was now commanding the newly formed F Battalion. Promoted Captain on 12 April, Charles returned to France in late May 1917 with No 17 Company. He commanded No 6 Section on 31 July 1917 during the fighting at St Julian; all of his tanks getting to their objective. During this action he was again wounded, this time in his left eye, but not so badly that he was sent back to England. He was discharged from hospital on 8 August and returned to duty. It is not recorded whether he went into action again during the 3rd Battle of Ypres but he relinquished the rank of acting Captain when he lost command of his section on 8 October. Charles had been granted UK leave, probably as a result of the injury to his left eye, and was tasked to attend a Medical Board on 15 October. Four days later, he was presented with the insignia of the DSO, by King George V, at Buckingham Palace.

On 12 January 1918, Charles took command a company at the Tank Training Centre at Bovington and later that year, on 27 April, married a widow named Constance Knapp in London. Charles served as a major throughout 1918 and relinquished his commission on account of ill-health resulting from his wounds in March 1919. When Constance and Charles' daughter Josephine was born in the summer of 1924, the family were living in Godstone in Kent. During the 1930s, the family lived at Oxted in Surrey. It was at this time that Charles was fined five shillings for failing to comply with a traffic sign but there is no evidence as to whether he could actually have seen it. The family then moved to Hindhead in the 1940s where Charles died on 27 July 1943. The family were clearly in financial difficulty at this time as Constance appealed for a Regular Officer's pension; it may be that he had returned to active service during the Second World War but I can find no record of this.

Charles' second in command, on 15 September, was a lance corporal may have been named Hawker. I have found it impossible to identify him and it is possible he was called actually James Hawkins as the Adjutant's writing in his note book is unclear. James certainly served with the Tanks in 1916. Gunner Tom Beardmore, who came from Stafford, was the only son of a locomotive fitter. Tom, who was named after his grandfather, and his younger sister Mary lived at 84 Grey Friars in the centre of Stafford where he worked as a hairdresser's assistant. After the first actions, Tom, retrained as a driver and was posted to 7th Battalion Tank Corps who were brigaded with 4th battalion for much of the war. Tom was awarded the Military Medal for his actions during the break-in battles on the Hindenburg Line. According to the citation, on 27 September 1918, he had to cross the Canal du Nord near Inchy. He drove his tank with splendid judgement and coolness across the Canal du Nord and, despite the fact that his skipper was wounded, succeeded in reaching his objective. In a similar citation, it was noted that the canal was considered nearly impassable to cross with a Mark IV tank by many competent judges. Two days later, after his tank received a direct hit near Tilloy, Tom and his commander succeeded in getting the injured away, under heavy shell fire. Throughout all operations, he showed a complete disregard of personal danger and a willing and cheerful spirit. He was subsequently promoted to the rank of sergeant. The Stafford Roll of Honour records that he was gassed twice and wounded on another occasion but, although it confirms he returned to Stafford, I cannot find anything about his life other than he probably died in 1944.

Gunner Clement Heath initially joined D Battalion, after his company was withdrawn from the operations on the Somme but he was later posted to 5th Battalion Tank Corps where he was appointed as a lance corporal. There are no records of his service but, as there is also no mention of him in the Tank Corps Book of Honour or list of Soldiers who died in the Great War, I am confident that he survived the war but cannot positively identify him. Private William Shortland, the tank's driver, rebadged from the ASC to the Heavy Branch MGC in the spring of 1917 and later served in the Tank Corps. He served with B Battalion then 2nd Battalion but was never promoted but he also survived the war. Gunner Roberts was probably Private F J Roberts, who was awarded the Military Medal for his actions during the autumn of 1916 but, as there is no citation for this medal, I cannot confirm what he did to merit the honour other than take part in the attack at Gueudecourt.

There was also a gunner named Morrison or Merrison in the crew. I believe that this was Edward Merrison who joined the MMGS in the last week of March 1916. Edward, who was born in Brundall in Norfolk in 1896, was the younger son of a farmer named George and Anna Merrison who lived at Baybridge Farm. When he left school, Edward worked with his father and his elder brother Benjamin as a farmhand. Having served with the Heavy Section, Edward was transferred to the Labour Corps, probably due to illness. In the summer of 1918, Edward married Grace Breach at her home village of Mutford near Lowestoft. Their son Alan was born in Blofield the following year and their daughter Jean in 1922. Edward later took over the farm at Baybridge. He died aged seventy-one, in the summer of 1968, and is buried in the grounds of St Andrew and St Peter's Church at Blofield.

I have only been able to identify Gunner Oswald Clayton because he was killed in action in 1917. Oswald was older than most tank crewmen, having been born in the spring of 1882 in Great Harwood in Lancashire. Oswald and his family were all cotton weavers, he married a local girl called Elizabeth in early March 1906 and in 1911 they were living at 56 Mercer Street. Oswald enlisted into the MGC at Great Harwood and, after the first actions, continued to serve with D Battalion. He probably fought at the Battle of Vimy Ridge in support of the assault on Thelus on 9 April 1917. He was in action at the second Battle of Bullecourt on 3 May where like George Thomas, was killed in action. His body was never found and his commemorated on the Arras memorial and at the War Memorial in Great Harwood.

D3

The tank which towed *Dolphin* out of the hole in Delville Wood was commanded by Lieutenant Heady Head. His route through the remains of Delville Wood, by night, was marked by white tape but it took the tank over a number of unexploded French 60lb mortar bombs. The crews started to move these out of the way but they were forced to give up when a German artillery barrage including gas shells, made the work unbearable. Heady then discussed the situation with Arthur Blowers who was following the same route with *Dolphin* after which they stood on the mortar bombs to see it they would bear their weight. Finding they did, Heady ordered his driver, George Simpson, to drive the tank over the shells which sank into the smashed and soaked ground. *Dolphin* followed up without the bombs exploding and the two tanks slowly moved to the edge of the wood; a journey which took more than nine hours to complete. Having pulled *Dolphin* out of the shell hole and, crossing the start line, Heady's tank made its way across no man's land and through the German Front Line defences. The tank then followed a German communications trench towards the eastern outskirts of Flers, firing at the defenders. However the tank was crippled by German artillery fire and Heady ordered the tank to be driven to a bank known as the Rideau de Filoires. The crew were forced to stay there for ten hours as the Germans constantly used their artillery to prevent the attackers bringing up reinforcements up the Flers road. Three days later, the tank was brought back to the D Company advanced base at Green Dump. Heady was later awarded the Military Cross for "conspicuous gallantry in action. He handled his Tank with great courage and skill, remaining out for over an hour under heavy fire, and accounting for many of the enemy".

Heady was born on 12 February 1895 at Great Dean in Holdenhurst, a village five miles north east of Bournemouth. He was the youngest son of a Yorkshire-born bricklayer who later established

Heady (left) with Stuart Hastie sitting in tent – summer 1916. (Tank Museum)

a building and decorating business in the recently established resort of Bournemouth. Heady was initially educated at St Paul's elementary school but then attended the newly opened Bournemouth School where he was a member of the OTC. On leaving school, he worked as a clerk to an architect and then for his father's firm. On the outbreak of war, Heady and several of his friends from Bournemouth School enlisted into the Hampshire Cyclist Battalion. Heady was soon commissioned into the Hampshire Regiment and served with 12th (Service) Battalion. These were all volunteers who joined the Army in response to Lord Kitchener's demand the "Britain needs you!" On 12 September 1915, Heady married Vera Osmonde at the Warminster Register office; Heady being stationed at Sutton Veny Camp. Their son David was born at 10 Grange Road in Buxton on 15 May 1916, just after his father joined D Company. As a result, Heady became known as "Young Father" as, being only twenty years with a son, was exceptional for a junior officer.

Whilst training at Bisley, Heady must have been relieved to hear that his eldest brother, Edgar who was a professional Royal Navy officer, had survived the Battle of Jutland. According to an interview at the Tank Museum in 1986, Heady then deployed to France on 15 August 1916; this date was well ahead of the main body of D Company and matches the arrival of the C Company advance party. Heady described that he then moved to Yvrench where he awaited the arrival of the tanks; this may indicate that he was one of the party that prepared the vehicles for their repainting and final exercises. Heady described the action on 15 September 1916 in a letter to his family which was later published in the *Bournemouth Visitor's Directory Newspaper*.

We went over (the front line) the first time on 15th September. We started at 8.30 the night before but the ground was so bad that by the time we had traversed half a mile, it was 5.30 a.m. and at 6 o'clock we started. Three cars were detailed for the job; one broke down before it had gone far, one got hit and only mine got through to the German second line. Then we were hit and we were put out of action for 10 hours, and during the whole time we were under incessant shell fire.

After the tank had been recovered by the ASC on 18 September, Heady was tasked to take it into action again on 25 September 1916. This time, Heady could not get into action because a track broke whilst moving its start point. On 18 October, whilst most of D Company was fighting to the north of the River Ancre, Heady was in action to the north of Flers. His section commander was Arthur Inglis who commanded *Crème de Menthe* on 15 September at Courcelette and the other tanks were commanded by Stuart Hastie of *Dinnaken* who captured Flers on 15 September and George Pearsall who commanded *Die Hard* which was destroyed the following morning. Only two tanks were allocated to support the attack on 18 October; a male commanded by Heady and a female commanded by Stuart Hastie. Hastie's tank initially failed to get into action but later joined in the battle; Heady's crew was on time and dominated the German trenches permitting the attacking infantry to take their objectives. Both the division and brigade's record state that the tank reached the initial objective of Gird Trench, ahead of the infantry, and remained there for twenty-three minutes during which the 6 pdr guns destroyed a German machine gun position. Heady's own machine guns caused significant casualties amongst the German defenders. Realising that there was no German effective defence, Heady got out of the tank and signalled the infantry to come forward. He then advanced to the German second line trenches, again clearing the defenders with his machine guns, and remaining in position for ten minutes for the infantry follow-up. He then returned to the 21st Brigade HQ, who reported that his "work was most effective". Heady's own description in the local paper includes that his driver was driving for fifteen hours; this included the journey from the base at Green Dump and back again, and that that two of his crewmen were killed. Sadly I have been unable to identify either of these men as there is no record of any tank crewmen killed on that day.

When D Battalion was formed in the middle of November, Heady joined No 12 Company with several of his original crew. He was granted leave at Christmas and returned to Bournemouth where he visited his old school. According to the school journal, he spoke "very modestly of his performance". The Journal also describes another event which probably occurred north of the River Ancre but for which there is no other record.

> On one occasion when he was in action, and his tank in "No Man's Land" it was struck by a German shell, which destroyed the clutch. Unable to move the machine, he and his men were obliged to abandon it and retire to their own trenches. When night came they returned to the tank with the tools and spare parts necessary to undertake the repairs, but they were "spotted by a German searchlight and, the neighbourhood having become 'unhealthy,' they were obliged to discontinue their work and again retire. They by no means gave up hope of retrieving their derelict, however, and the next day, under the cover of a friendly fog, they went out again, completed the repairs, and brought back the Tank in triumph."

Heady was awarded the Military Cross for his action on 18 October and, after the award was announced, his school granted the pupils a half day holiday in celebration.

On the opening day of the battle of Arras, Heady was in command of No 10 Section, supporting the British attack near Thelus Ridge on 9 April 1917, but all his tanks became ditched due to the poor ground conditions. Appointed acting Captain three days later, Heady again commanded No 10 Section at the second Battle of Bullecourt on 3 May 1917. All of his four tanks managed to get across no man's land and fire into the German trenches but none managed to penetrate the defence line. Many of his men were killed and injured as they were crewing unarmoured tanks. Amongst them were several who fought at Flers-Courcelette including George Thomas and Oswald Clayton who were killed, Jack Choules who received severe wounds to his scalp, James Anderson who was temporarily blinded but later awarded the Distinguished Conduct Medal, and Albert Wateridge who was awarded the Military Medal for taking his tank back into action after having been wounded.

On 20 September, during the Third Battle of Ypres, Heady commanded No 12 Section during their attack on Rose House and, on the opening day of the Battle of Cambrai, he was again in command of a section. Two other section commanders serving in No 12 Company had served with Heady in D Company on 15 September 1916; Graeme Nixon who led No 3 Section and Alfred Enoch was the skipper of crew D7 on 15 September. Heady commanded No 10 Section for the assault on Flesquières, two of his tanks being knocked out by German artillery as they approached the western side of the village near the Cemetery – the episode being described in JC Macintosh's book *Men in Tanks*. Although the tank in which he was travelling burst into flames, Heady escaped unhurt; sadly this was not the case for many crewmen – the action at Flesquières causing great loss amongst the tanks of D and E Battalions.

In March 1918, during the great German advance known as the Kaiserschlacht, Heady was still in command of No 10 Section. Alfred Enoch was in command of No 9 Section and their two sections fought together as they tried to stem the German advance which was to recapture all the ground won by the British in 1916 and 1917. On 22 March 1918, Heady's three tanks attacked from the area of Spur Quarry at 7.45 a.m. Unsupported by infantry the tanks drove into the enemy inflicting severe casualties. Four days later, having lost all his tanks, Heady was placed in command of twenty Lewis Guns teams, formed from tank machine gunners, under the command of 106th Brigade. Placed on the Bray to Albert Road, his unit was in position for six hours, fighting back even though he was outflanked by the Germans, until he was ordered to withdraw. On 30 June 1918 Heady was in command of C Company of 4th Battalion but, after the initial stages of the Battle of Amiens, left the Battalion on 23 August 1918 for the UK to train with the RFC. Heady qualified as an aircraft observer but did not transfer to the RFC, probably because of the reduc-tion in demand for aircrew at the end of the war. He retired at the end of May 1919 and retained the rank of Captain.

Heady returned to Bournemouth with the aim of working his father's firm. It was a successful for a while but he craved independence. As a result, Heady and Vera moved to Cornwall and managed the Prince of Wales Hotel at Penzance for many years. Their son David, who initially attended his father's old school in Bournemouth, attended Penzance Grammar School and finally, as a boarder, Bromyard Grammar School. David then joined the Royal Tank Corps, as a private soldier, and soon became a PT instructor. Returning to Bournemouth, in the 1930s, Heady established a confectionary and tobacco shop at 656 Christchurch Road in 1935. The following year David, who was now twenty-two years old and had been promoted to corporal, married Edith Smith, who was a cashier and book-keeper at a local Bournemouth swimming pool.

On the outbreak of the Second World War, Heady joined the RAF VR as an air traffic controller and served as a squadron leader on 138 and 161 Squadrons whose aircraft supported Special Operation Executive

Heady in 1945 (Tony Head)

covert operations in Europe. David, who was initially commissioned in the Royal Hussars, served in India and Burma. He transferred into 16th Light Cavalry Regiment of the Indian Army, which was the first horse unit to transfer to tanks, and served in Burma as Deputy Provost Martial and then at the General HQ during the assault on Rangoon.

After the war, Heady and Vera moved to Devon and settled in a hamlet called Compton Marldon on the outskirts of Paignton. In 1946, they established a small confectionary and tobacconist shop called the *Cranny*. Vera died the following year but, after three years, on 21 November 1949, Heady married a nursing sister named Phyllis Bowden from nearby Kingkerswell. By this time Heady also had become the co-proprietor of a pleasure cruiser named the *Trevarno* which operated from the Princess Pier at Torquay and also from Dartmouth. In the 1960s, Phyllis and Heady moved to Torquay but, although he had retired, he had retained his passion for fast cars and his zest for life. He was the only D Company officer present at the 50th Anniversary dinner night at Caxton Hall in London on 15 September 1966 although there were a number of crewmen including Robert Frost from nearby Teignmouth, who had fought in D10 and who, like George, later served in the RAF. Heady maintained a clear memory of the events at Flers, twenty years later, which he recounted when he visited the Tank Museum on 15 September 1986, the 70th anniversary of the battle. Phyllis, who was 14 years younger than her husband, died in the summer of 1988; Heady died the following year on 28 November 1989, almost the last crewman to survive.

Heady's second in command was Corporal William McNicoll who, in 1918, not only served as a tank commander but was also awarded the Distinguished Conduct Medal for his actions in that role. William was born on 13 March 1894 at Kinettles, to the south of Forfar where his father Adam was an estate manager. On leaving school he was apprenticed as a clerk to a solicitor's firm named Thomas Thornton in Dundee. He joined the MGC in 1916 and was soon appointed corporal. In 1917, William saw action at Arras, Ypres and Cambrai with D Battalion. He served on with the renamed 4th Battalion and, in the summer of 1918, William was one of the first sergeants selected to serve as a tank commander. During the Battle of Amiens, on 8 August 1918, he commanded a tank and "took it five miles into hostile territory. When nearing Cayeux, it was put out of action by two direct hits which seriously wounded William and all his crew except one gunner. William immediately ordered the crew to evacuate the tank but he himself remained and covered the withdrawal of his wounded crew with machine gun fire during which time the enemy opened heavy machine gun fire upon his derelict tank. Eventually, when the infantry arrived, he himself was able to withdraw and was taken to a dressing station". For this conspicuous action, William was awarded the Distinguished Conduct Medal and, when he returned to Kinettles on leave in October 1918, was presented with a gold watch purchased by the local parishioners. Returning to Kinettles after the war, he qualified as a solicitor and moved to Glasgow. There, on 10 April 1925, he married Margaret Smith and became a senior partner in the Glasgow law firm of Keyden, Strange and Company. Margaret and William later settled in Bearsden, where he died, aged sixty-seven, just after midnight on 20 October 1961.

Gunner William Barrie was also a Scot from the Borders. Born on 14 April 1897, he was the only son of Maggie and Matthew Barrie, a grocer's assistant living in the High Street at Melrose. William grew up at Largs in Fife where his younger sister Dolina was born. When William was attested into the MMGS on 22 November 1915 in Edinburgh, he working as a grocer's assistant. William was soon training at Bisley and, after tank training at Elveden, deployed overseas on 28 August. He was wounded on 15 September but not seriously. William was again wounded on 18 October, probably during the action at Bayonet Trench between Flers and Gueudecourt, and admitted to Edgehill Casualty Clearing Station the following day. Presumably the wounds were not serious as he was able to return to duty after three days. He then served with D Battalion, serving as a lance corporal from 7 August 1917 and was promoted to corporal after the Battle of Cambrai. William later served with the renamed 4th Battalion, latterly serving with C Company – this was originally No 12 Company so he probably fought in the 1917 actions at Thelus, Bullecourt and Flesquières. He was appointed paid acting sergeant on 5 October 1918, as the Battalion was being withdrawn from action during the Final Advance. He voluntarily reverted to the rank of corporal on 2 December and returned to Melrose, after de-mobilisation, and was transferred to the Z Reserve on 20 March 1919. William took over his father's grocer's shop in October 1924 and, on 1 October 1928, married Margaret Lawson at the Royal Hotel in Galashiels where Margaret was living. William's sister Dolina died on 18 September 1952 at the Peel Hospital at Galashiels; William, who was her executor, remarried in 1953 to Christine Steedman, at Morningside in Edinburgh but he died shortly after from a brain haemorrhage on 2 September 1953 aged fifty seven.

There is little recorded in the D Company records about Gunner Bentley other than he was wounded in the hands by a splinter from a high explosive shell on 15 September; this probably occurred as the crew tried to get back to safety after their tank was abandoned at Rideau de Filoires. I believe that he was Gunner William Bentley who was from Forest Gate in East London. According to the *Chelmsford Chronicle*, William was captured by the Germans on 22 August 1917 whilst serving with D Battalion. This links to a prisoner of war record for Private William Bentley who served with No 12 Company and who captured during their attack from St Julian towards the Frezenberg during one of the British attacks in the Third Battle of Ypres. William, who was a draper in 1911, was held by the Germans until the end of the war. Thereafter I can find nothing about him nor have I been able to identify any details about the driver, Private George Simpson, other than on 25 September 1916 when he was the driver of the ad hoc B Crew attached to the Reserve Army for attacks near Thiepval. He rebadged from the ASC to the MGC in early 1917 and served on with the Tank Corps, as a private soldier, until the end of the war.

The service records of the last three members of the crew have survived. Gunner Cecil Chalfont, who was born in Willesden, north London on 19 May 1896, was the son of a printer and worked in the family firm of Chalfont and Sons who were based in High Holborn. Cecil joined the MMGS on 3 November 1915 and arrived at the Motor Machine Gun Training Centre at Bisley on 23 November. After machine gun training at Siberia camp and tank training at Elveden in Norfolk, Cecil deployed to France on 28 August. He joined D Battalion on 18 November 1916 and served with them until 11 September 1917 when he was posted to G Battalion. At this time, the two units were brigaded and his transfer was possibly undertaken to reinforce G Battalion which had taken large number of losses during the 3rd Battle of Ypres. Cecil was soon afterwards detached to the Driving School at Wailly, probably to retrain as a driver. Unusually Cecil was granted home leave during the Battle of Cambrai, returning to his unit on 29 November. On 4 April 1918 Cecil was posted to 11th Battalion, serving with C Company for six months, before being posted to HQ 1st Tank Brigade as a batman on 16 September 1918. Granted home leave in October 1918, he was later sent to the Tank Corps HQ at Bermison, again to serve as a batman. Cecil later served with the 3rd Tank Group Inspectorate in Germany, before returning home to London and being transferred to Z Reserve on 18 February 1919. Cecil married Maud Briant at Hendon in northwest London, in the summer of 1926 and they had three sons, Roy, Roger and Kenneth. By 1934, Cecil had become a master printer and head of the family business but he died young, aged only forty-seven, at Red Hill Hospital on 6 April 1943.

Gunner Willie Shelton survived until his eightieth year. Born at Droitwich on 20 November 1885, his father and mother's marriage failed when Willie was very young and his mother died when he was seven. By the age of fifteen, he was living with his maternal grandmother in York Place in Worcester, where he had found work as a draper's clerk. By 1911, Willie had moved to Balsall Heath where he worked as a cashier. The following year, aged twenty-seven, he married Alice Butcher at Kings Heath Registry Office on 23 January 1912. Their eldest daughter Vera was born 13 September 1912 and their son Manfred, who was soon to become known as Bill, on 4 March 1914.

Willie Shelton with his hand built machine. (Shelton family)

A keen motorcyclist, who built his own machines, Willie was still working as a cashier when he enlisted into the MMGS at Coventry on 10 December 1915. He then returned to his family who were living in 144 Tenby Road in Moseley. Willie was not mobilised until 23 March and was originally posted to E Company of the Armoured Car Section MGC. He was granted leave after a month's service but failed to get back to Bisley by the stipulated time and was charged with absence. Allocated to D Company on 27 May, Willie embarked for France on 28 August and, after the first actions, was posted to D Battalion on 18 November. Like his former skipper Heady Head, Willie served with No 12 Company and probably fought at Thelus during Battle of Vimy Ridge on 9 April 1917. Willie was wounded in the back on 3 May 1917 during 2nd Battle of Bullecourt, when the tanks tried vainly to penetrate the German defences. Although Willie originally refused to be evacuated, the wounds were so serious that he was admitted to a Field Ambulance and later evacuated to No 47 Hospital at Le Tréport on 8 May. After ten days treatment, Willie was released to the Reinforcement Depot, and after a period of convalescence and refresher training, returned to D Battalion on 8 June. Soon afterwards, he was detached for special duty on 18 June possibly in support of Operation HUSH – the proposed invasion of the Belgian coast when tanks were to be used to scale the sea walls. I can find no evidence that he fought during the Third Battle of Ypres although he is pictured in a photograph of the crew of *Dragonfly III* which was commanded by Lt Herbert Chick which was taken about this time.

On 6 November, Willie returned to the Tank Depot at Wareham. He was attached to newly forming N Battalion on 8 November together with Frank Steer from tank crew D6. In December 1917 and early 1918, Willie served as a crewman with the training tank *Nelson* which toured

Willie Shelton standing rear right and the crew of *Dragonfly III*. (Tank Museum)

Yorkshire and North East England supporting sales of War Bonds. His family have a picture of him with *Nelson* at Bradford. Like Frank Steer, he was then posted to 16th Battalion on 3 January 1918 where he also served with James Anderson from D Battalion and William Lock who had fought with C Company on 15 September 1916. Willie, who had retrained as a driver in England, was appointed lance corporal on 28 March 1918 and then promoted corporal on 19 September, ten days after the Battalion had arrived in France and at the same time the Battalion was being issued with its tanks. Only another ten days later, Willie fought with B Company of 16th Battalion as part of the Final Advance. His bravery during the Battle of the Selle was recognised through the award of the Distinguished Conduct Medal. The citation states that on "on 17th October 18. When his tank was ditched, he worked under heavy fire for three hours and subsequently drove his tank for 6 hours, showing excellent skills in manoeuvring, so that many machine gun nests holding up the infantry were destroyed." After the Armistice, Willie was promoted acting sergeant on 20 November. He returned to England on 31 January 1919; was demobilised through Chisenden and then transferred to Z Class Reserve on 3 March. The award of the DCM was announced in the *London Gazette* on 13 June 1919; the medal being sent by post in July 1919 to his home.

   Although, according to his family, he was entitled to a war pension, Willie refused to take it. His daughter Lucy was born in February 1920 and, by November 1921, he was working as a cashier at Walsall branch of Armour. Willie and Alice had a further two children, Peter born in 1923 and Beryl in 1926. In his spare time Willie continued to build motorcycles and the couple took the children on holidays in a motorcycle-sidecar combination, travelling as far as Llandudno, Rhyl, Bristol and Malvern. A supporter of the Labour party, Willie used to read the *Daily Mirror* on a daily basis. Sadly his wife Alice died during the extremely harsh winter on 1946/47; this hit the sixty-one year old Willie very hard as he had paid into a private pension to allow him to retire comfortably with Alice. He settled with his youngest daughter Beryl in Addenbrooke Street in Walsall, where he died aged seventy-nine, on 12 April 1964.

The anti-German sentiments, which became widespread after the invasion of Belgium in 1914, resulted in the final member of the D3 crew changing his middle name. William Fritz Steer was born on 11 October 1895 at Milton near Sittingbourne. The younger son of a paper dryer, Willie had become a fruiterer by the time he enlisted into the MMGS on 17 November 1915 at Coventry. His attestation form shows he had moved to Teynham and that he changed his middle name from Fritz to Frank – a change mirrored by Willie Shelton's son who became known as Bill rather than Manfred. Although William's service record has survived, it reveals little about his service in D Company. He deployed to France with No 2 Section on 28 August and, after the first actions was posted to D Battalion on 18 November 1916. Like Willie Shelton, just prior to the Battle of Cambrai, he was sent back to the Tank Corps Training Centre at Bovington on 6 November 1917 "on special duty". William was posted to the recently formed N Battalion on 8 November but was not sent to Ireland. Rather he was however granted eight days leave from which he got back late. Charged for the offence, he was subsequently punished by being confined to barracks for seven days.

On 3 January 1918, together with Willie Shelton and James Anderson who had also fought with No 12 Company at Thelus and Bullecourt, he was posted to B Company of the newly formed 16th Light Battalion. Appointed lance corporal on 23 March 1918, William returned to France on 9 September 1918, having retrained as a driver. Only twenty days later, his unit went into action at the Battle of the St Quentin Canal. William's previous experience clearly was useful to his unit as they took part in the Final Advance, fighting in four more bloody actions. He was appointed paid lance corporal on 30 October and finally acting corporal on 30 November which reveals the levels of casualties sustained during the three weeks 16th Battalion was in action. Having been sent to the Tank Corps Training and Reinforcement Depot at Mers-Les-Bains, William returned to the UK on 7 February. When he transferred to Z Reserve on 10 March, he was living at the wonderfully named *Eldorado* in London Road, Sittingbourne. In early 1927, he married Adelaide Coward, who had been born in Milton in 1902, and they lived at Eltham between the wars. By the late 1950s, the couple returned to Sittingbourne where William ran a grocery shop on Rock Road. He and Adelaide later moved to Richmond upon Thames where Adelaide died in 1977. William lived for another eleven years, dying aged ninety-two in April 1988. His family registered his death using his original middle name of Fritz; the difficulties once associated with a German name having been long forgotten.

Crew D6

Reginald Legge commanded tank crew D6, who fought in support of the 41st Division attack to the east of Flers. On 15 September, the female tank left the Company Base at Green Dump and made its way around the western edge of Delville Wood to its start point and then followed the main road north toward Flers (see maps 8 and 9) . As it approached the German front lines, the tank passed Sergeant Norman Carmichael, of 21st Battalion Kings Royal Rifle Corps (KRRC) who described it "lumbering past on my left, belching forth yellow flames from her Vickers gun and making for the gap where the Flers Road cut through the enemy trench!" This was the German Switch Trench, which was half way between Delville Wood and Flers village. The tank then turned to the east and then skirted Flers as it made its way towards its next objective on the Bull's Road. On the way, the D6 crew used its guns to aid the attacking British infantry. According to Lieutenant Colonel William North, CO of 26th (Bankers) Battalion Royal Fusiliers: "This tank was of the greatest material use and the party in charge of it distinguished themselves considerably."

Despite the obvious dangers from the Germany 77mm artillery pieces, which were positioned in depth around the village, Legge pressed on north, away from the protection of the infantry who were unable to advance beyond the Bulls Road. Following Goode Street, the tank approached Gird Trench which was only 500 yards from the centre of Gueudecourt which was their final objective. Here the tank was engaged by a German 77mm field gun battery which the crew engaged and destroyed one gun. The tank was then hit by a high explosive artillery shell; only one crewman died in the tank but two were killed after they left the burning hulk and two more died of wounds. Surprisingly, despite the fact that the tank was over a mile behind the German front lines, and they had to avoid the British and German artillery bombardment on the way, the three remaining crewmen managed to reach safety uninjured. The hulk could not be recovered and was blown up during the battlefield clearances. Part of the superstructure and the right hand track adjuster was subsequently located by the tank historian Philippe Gorczynski whilst he was visiting the battle-fields with Trevor Pidgeon, the author of the *Tanks at Flers*. Both items are now on display in the Tank Museum.

The tank's skipper, Reginald Legge was born on 18 February 1882 in Brighton. He was the second son of a military tailor and was educated at Brighton Grammar School. By 1901, Reginald had moved to London where he was worked as a draper's assistant. He then moved overseas, to the British Gold Coast colony – now part of Ghana – where he worked as an agent for Mullens Ltd. Following the outbreak of war, Reginald left the main settlement of Sekundi and returned to England arriving on 6 January 1915. Although he openly admitted he was not a good horseman, he enlisted in the Royal Buckinghamshire Hussars. Reginald Legge was appointed lance corporal on 24 March 1915 and served with 2/1st Regiment, who were training unit. Later selected for commissioning, from 4 March 1916, he attended six weeks officer training at No 5 Officer Cadet Battalion at Trinity College Cambridge with Arthur Blowers and several other tank skippers. Reginald asked to join his country regiment, the Royal Sussex, but he was posted to Heavy Section MGC. He was much older than most of the tank skippers, who later described him as being a "quartermaster type". This was a particularly arrogant comment by his peers as only one officer in either C or D Company had been commissioned through the Royal Military College. On 15 April, Reginald was commissioned into the MGC. He joined D Company and trained with them, firstly at Bisley and then at Elveden where he wrote his will whilst living at John O'Groats Camp on 25 August. This was the base of D Company and it was witnessed by his section commander Harold Mortimore and Hugh Bell who commanded tank crew D2.

After his tank was hit on 15 September, he ensured that the survivors got out and were well clear of the hulk. He was last reported as seen alive by Gunner Herbert Clears in a shell hole where the crew had taken shelter. Later declared missing by the British Army, his family sought details of their son. It was not until his ID disc was sent by the German Red Cross to Geneva, and the disc and a quantity of money were subsequently received by the War Office in February 1918, that his family was formally notified of his death. It was later confirmed that he had died of his wounds on 16 September 1916 and buried by the Germans the same day although the details of the location of his grave were not made known. Reginald Legge was considered, by his comrades, to be a "fire eater", in the belligerent sense, and they were not surprised that he got his tank so far forward. "Good old Legge" recalled Arthur Blowers "he came so close to being great".

Legge's details were recorded in the War Diary of 1st Battalion of the 10th Bavarian Infantry Regiment who captured him at Gueudecourt and later probably buried his body. The Germans also buried the other three dead crewmen but the location of their graves is also unknown as is much about their lives. Gunner George Cook was named after his barman father. George and his wife Sarah Goodwin were married, by special licence, on 17 June 1886 at Camberwell Parish Church. Sarah's father was a boot manufacturer who died shortly after her marriage. George was born in Westminster in the autumn of 1887 but sadly his parents' marriage failed. By 1891, he was living with his 30 year old mother and his widowed grandmother who had taken over her husband's boot shop at 32 Buckingham Palace Road. George was living at Camberwell when he enlisted into the MGC but otherwise his service record is not known. He is commemorated on his mother's grave near Laycock Abbey, where she had settled by 1919, as well as on the Memorial to the Missing at Thiepval. George is also commemorated on the war memorial at Bowden Hill Church.

Gunner John Garner was born at Long Eaton in Nottinghamshire. He was the youngest son of a lace maker, also named John, and his wife Sarah Bexton, and was christened on 15 April 1891. Ten years later, the family was living at 18 Park Street in Long Eaton and later at 51 Breeden Street, where John, his father and two of his three brothers all worked as lace makers. I can find no records of his service other than he enlisted into the Machine Gun Corps. His life is commemorated at the Long Eaton war memorial and on the Memorial to the Missing at Thiepval. The third crewman, killed that day, was Gunner Fred Bardsley. Born in Oldham in early 1882, and christened on 10 April at St Andrew's Church, Fred was the only child of grocery shop manager John Bardsley and his wife Margaret. By 1911 Fred was working as a commercial clerk with the Cooperative society: his father being an assistant grocery manager with the same company. He enlisted, in the MGC, at Chadderton into the west of Oldham. On 14 October 1916, the Oldham Evening Chronicle reported his parents received a letter from Gunner John Wells, probably of crew D24, stating that Fred's had come to grief and he feared for the safety of the crew who had been reported missing. He is commemorated on the memorial to those who worked at the headquarters of the Cooperative Wholesale Society as well as in his home town of Oldham and the Memorial to the Missing at Thiepval.

Herbert Clears, who was captured by the Germans on 15 September, was the oldest member of the D6 tank crew. Born in September 1877, in London, he was the third son of a pawnbroker. Baptized on 9 October 1877 at the Trinity Church in Marylebone; Herbert followed his father David into pawn broking. In 1901 he was living in South Hammersmith and assisting his father but ten years later, he had become a jewellers' salesman living with his parents on the Earls Court Road in Kensington. Unusually, when he joined the MGC, he trained both as machine gunner and a mechanic and so was employed as a gearsman. Although Herbert suffered head injuries on 15 September, these were not serious and he was interrogated by the German who sought details of the training he had received as well as the capabilities of the tank. He was later held at the Friedrichsfeld POW camp near the town of Wesel on the Rhine where he was visited by Red Cross officials in August 1917. After his release at the end of the war, Herbert originally returned to Kensington but, by 1920, he had moved to Woking where he successfully established himself as a jeweller. He probably met up with members of the crew of *Champagne* who also lived in the town. By 1930, Herbert had made sufficient money to take his youngest sister Minnie on a Mediterranean cruising holiday from Southampton. He never married but later lived with Minnie, in a large five bedroom detached house in Woking from 1932 until 1964. He died two years later aged ninety-one, at Paddington.

The three crewmen who got back to the British lines were Legge's second in command, his driver and one of the machine gunners. Of these three, only the latter Robert Beesley survived the war. Born on 22 August 1890 in Coventry, Robert was the second son of a watch movement maker. When he enlisted into the MMGS on 28 March 1916, Robert was working as a plumber and painter. He was a short man only five feet one inch tall and less than nine stone in weight. Robert was sent to Bisley for initial training the same day and he followed the normal pattern of joining the Armoured Car Section, then the Heavy Section and then D Company. Robert was wounded in face, during the fighting on 15 September, but this was not sufficiently serious to require hospital treatment. Robert remained with D Company and then transferred to D Battalion where, like Harry Leat, he joined No 11 Company commanded by Major Willie Watson. Watson's book *A Company of Tanks* describes the difficulties of pulling together a group of disparate soldiers, with very little equipment into a fighting unit in less than 3 months. They fought their first action, on 11 April 1917, at the first Battle of Bullecourt where the unit was badly mauled. Half the crews were killed or injured; Harry Leat was killed and Robert suffered gunshot wounds to his right arm, left hand and under his armpit. This may indicate that he was manning a Lewis gun during the battle. Robert was first treated in France and then from 23 April at Tooting Hospital. During his treatment which lasted forty days, foreign bodies were removed by surgery; these were probably metal fragments from the tank's armour which detached when the outside of the tank was hit by machine gun bullets.

Granted ten days home leave after he was released from hospital, Robert reported to the Tank Depot at Worgret Camp near Wareham on 14 June 1917. He was at the Depot for almost nine months and joined 17th Armoured Car Battalion as a despatch-rider just three days before they deployed to France on 27 April 1918. During the Battle of Villers-Brettoneux, Robert was again wounded, this time whilst taking orders to the forward units on a motorcycle. He was soon back in action, both during the Battle of Amiens when he was once again wounded, and as the Armoured Cars took part in the Final Advance to the German border. He was awarded the Military Medal

for great gallantry and devotion to duty during the continuous fighting from 10th June up to the cessation of hostilities. This soldier acted as despatch rider to the armoured cars. Without the protection which the armoured cars possess, he has taken despatches to them in the most exposed positions, having on one occasion on 9th August being wounded and still carrying on. His determination of getting to his objective is most marked, He was never failed to deliver his dispatch under any circumstances.

17th Armoured Car Battalion was the first British unit to enter Germany and they crossed the River Rhine at Cologne on 6 December. They remained in the area over Christmas and Robert served in Cologne until 23 January 1919 when his Battalion was sent to Ireland to assist in subduing the uprising. Robert served with A Company at Limerick which one of the most active areas in the Irish War of Independence. Robert did not wish to serve on in the Army and sought his discharge on the basis that he had been wounded three times. After a lengthy investigation about his wounding near Flers, he was eventually discharged on 20 September 1919. Robert returned to Coventry and, the following spring, married the eighteen-year old Winifred Lole from nearby Nuneaton. The couple had three children, Robert who was born in the summer of 1920, Veronica in 1925 and Peter two years later. Robert became a successful builder and the family lived at Mary Herbert Street. Robert died, aged sixty-four, in the Alcock Hospital at Keresley on 15 August 1955 – Winifred living until her death in Coventry in 1978.

Lance Corporal Wilfred da Cunha Brooks, who was the tank's NCO, had been offered a commission in 1914 but surprisingly declined the opportunity. He was born in Sale in Cheshire in 1891 where his father Arthur was the manager in shipping merchant's office. Wilfred attended grammar schools at Bolton, Sale and Manchester before studying for City and Guilds qualifications at the Manchester School of Technology. He also served in the Manchester University OTC from 1 February 1909 to 30 September 1911. Having graduated, Wilfred worked as an assistant manager of a cotton warehouse. Because of his previous military experience, he was offered a commission at the outbreak of war but was unable to accept. He then joined the Westinghouse Company as an Inspector of Munitions in their artillery shell fuse department. Eventually Wilfred enlisted into the MMGS on 30 April 1916 and, after initial training, was appointed as an instructor. On 15 September, after his tank was destroyed, he only managed to get back to safety after passing through both enemy and British barrages. He then volunteered to join another tank crew and went back into action on 1 October 1916 at Eaucourt L'Abbaye. His tank was put out of action when the gearing became entangled with barbed wire which provided the objective. Leaving the tank, he attempted to cut the wire to allow the tank to be extracted but was shot by the German defenders. Having been ordered to abandon the tank by his skipper, probably Captain George Bown, Wilfred set fire to it but whilst escaping, he was wounded in the right forearm by a grenade.

For his action at Eaucourt L'Abbaye, he was awarded the Military Medal. Wilfred was evacuated to the Bangour War Hospital, near Edinburgh, where he stayed for more than a year. Although he recovered from his wounds, he was not fit to return to active duty until November 1917, so was put in charge of the workshops of the hospital's X-ray Department. Having been promoted Corporal, he was sent to the Tank Corps Depot at Worgret Camp. There he contracted cerebra-spinal menin-gitis and died shortly afterwards at the Weymouth Isolation Hospital on 2 February 1918. He was buried in Weymouth but his life is commemorated at St Ann's Church on Sale Moor and at the Manchester Grammar School.

The ASC driver, and the final member of the crew, was also an NCO. Herbert Thacker, who was born on 5 March 1883 at Tonbridge, was the eldest son of a bank manager. He was educated at the Whitgift Grammar School in Croydon and later became a partner in the East Kent Motor company. When the war started, Herbert joined as an Army Special Enlistment on 4 August 14 and, nine days later, was serving in France with 2nd Division's Ammunition Park. Herbert took part in the retreat from Mons and remained in France until early 1916. During this time he was promoted twice and served with 62 Company ASC. Herbert returned to the UK in March 1916 for hospital treatment and lost his rank. He then joined 711 (MT) Company, which formed on 13 June, and was appointed corporal on 21 June and acting sergeant on 30 July. Herbert deployed on SS *Ilston* from Avonmouth on 29 August with the first group of D Company tanks – he presum-ably was a key member of the party which worked under Morty Mortimore to offload the tanks at Le Havre. Following the action on 15 September 1916, Herbert suffered from shellshock. On 18 September was admitted to 11th Stationary Hospital before being invalided back to the UK on the Hospital Ship *Aberdonian*. It was routine for those who were evacuated back to the UK, who were not expected to return to their unit, to receive a character reference. Herbert's reference, signed by Captain P K Edkins stated he was "exceedingly temperate; particularly reliable and an excellent NCO at all times having his men under command; intelligent energetic and efficient. Style of man who could adapt himself to almost anything being bright and keen to learn. He displayed great coolness and skills whilst in action".

This report, together with the award of the Military Medal, resulted in Herbert being selected for officer training. Herbert spent a short while at Bulford Camp after he recovered and was then sent to the Grove Park Officer Training Centre from 28 January 1917. His commissioning form tells us a little about his physical appearance: he was just over six feet tall with blue eyes and just over eleven stones in weight. Commissioned into ASC, six weeks later, on 4 March 1917, he was posted to No 3 Section of 904 MT Company which supported a heavy artillery unit. Herbert was then selected to deploy to Egypt, probably as part of the force which was to eject Turkish forces from Palestine. On his way out, Herbert drowned when his ship SS *Arcadian* was sunk by a torpedo on 15 April 1917. Herbert body was never recovered and his life is commemorated on the Mikra memorial near Thessaloniki which records the loss of over 500 nurses, officers and men drowned in the eastern Mediterranean. After his death there was copious correspondence between his father and the War Office as to the whereabouts' of his son's Military Medal and his will. The medal, which had been sent to Bulford, had not been presented as he served in four units in as many months. It was eventually located and presented to his father by the Duke of Connaught – his father's request that it be presented by King George V being refused.

8

The tank "which made headlines"

The fortified village of Flers was expected to create a major obstacle to the British attack on 15 September. It was also protected by a series of trenches and wire entanglements, which is why ten tanks were allocated to assist three infantry divisions tasked to capture the stronghold. The task of taking the village was given to 41st (London) Division with 14th Division taking the ground to the east and the recently formed New Zealand Division to the west. Three tanks were tasked to enter the village, *Dolly* with the D9 crew commanded by Victor Huffam, the D14 crew whose skipper was Gordon Court and *Dinnaken* with the D17 crew commanded by Stuart Hastie. Only *Dinnaken* crossed No Man's Land and reached the village as the other tanks became stuck in the British front line trench. They were dug out that afternoon by pioneers from 4th Battalion South Lancashire Regiment. Victor Huffam recalls being *"given a rocket"* by his OC Major Frank Summers and then was told that he and Gordon Court, were to support a follow-on attack the next day. During this action, both tanks were destroyed and many of the crewmen were killed and injured.

Crew D17 and *Dinnaken*

Dinnaken was behind D9 and D14 as the three tanks started their advance from Delville Wood on 15 September. After her skipper, Stuart Hastie, saw the leading tanks become stuck in the British front line, he pressed on alone (see map 8). As the tank followed the Flers Road north from Delville Wood, across No Man's Land, *Dinnaken*'s rear steering gear was smashed by German artillery fire. Stuart Hastie ordered the trailing wheels to be raised off the ground and changed the direction by using the brakes on the tank's tracks. One report says that Hastie followed Reginald Legge in *Dolphin* up the main road towards the Switch Trench, the first of the defensive trenches. This was crossed without difficulty and *Dinnaken* then followed the road towards the village; Legge turning east and then going northeast towards Gueudecourt.

In a BBC interview, recorded in 1963, Hastie does not mention that the attacking infantry were unable to get through the German protective wire in front of the village. However, other reports state it was only after *Dinnaken* crushed the wire and then stopped astride the German defensive trench, known as the Flers Trench, that the British infantry were able to take this objective. *Dinnaken* then drove through Flers village, using her 6 pdr QF guns to destroy German strong points whilst the machine gunners engaged German troops positioned in the eaves of the houses. *Dinnaken* was spotted by an observer of the RFC aircraft as she drove through the village and a report was passed back. Although the phrase "A tank is walking down the High St of Flers with the British Army cheering behind" was subsequently reported in several newspapers, it was however, far from accurate. *Dinnaken* was well ahead of the infantry as she made her way through the village. Having reached the tiny square, towards the north of the village, Hastie paused until the infantry caught up and then turned his vehicle through 180 degrees, a feat which according to an early history of the Tank Corps took almost an hour, and then withdrew, as ordered, towards his start point. He stopped *Dinnaken* as he left the village, at Flers Trench, and got out of the tank to speak to the infantry there. He was asked by an officer to leave his machine-guns so that they could be used against the expected German counter-attack. However, as the guns were only capable being used in the tank's mountings, Hastie was unable to assist and he was concerned about the engine, which was also knocking badly.

Dinnaken followed the road southwards back toward Delville Wood and eventually reached the Rideau de Filoires, the chalk bank where Heady Head's tank had been abandoned. Here *Dinnaken*'s engine failed and the crew had to remain in the tank, for the rest of the day, as German artillery fire continued to target the road and prevent the British sending reinforcement to the village. Eventually, in the evening, they made their way back to the D Company base at Green Dump. Until she was recovered later in the year, *Dinnaken* was used as a headquarters but she was eventually recovered and used during the Third Battle of Ypres, as a wireless tank, providing reports on progress during the British attacks.

Stuart Hastie in 1917. (TPC)

Stuart Hastie was born on 7 September 1889 in Edinburgh. Sons of an ironmonger, both Stuart and his younger brother Harold were educated at George Heriot's School. Stuart then studied Chemistry at Edinburgh University for four years, during which he served in the Officer Training Corps being appointed a cadet corporal in his final year. After graduating in 1914, Stuart initially worked as a chemist but then applied for a commission on 22 March 1915. Standing over six feet tall, twenty-five years old and effectively trained as a platoon commander, Stuart was quickly accepted by the Highland Light Infantry and commissioned into 4th (Special Reserve) Battalion. On 16 April 1915, he had married Agnes Bonnez at the Church of the Holy Trinity in St Andrews. Agnes was the daughter of a Danish master mariner and their only son Douglas was born the next year at Cramond.

In October 1915, Stuart was seconded to the MMGS and later trained alongside Heady Head when the two men served with D Company (see page 92).

For his actions on 15 September, at Flers, Stuart was awarded the Military Cross "for conspicuous gallantry in action. He fought his Tank with great gallantry, reaching the third objective. Later, he rendered valuable service in salving a Tank lying out under very heavy fire". This latter phrase refers to Stuart's work to recover Charles Storey's tank which was destroyed on 26 September. In October, Stuart served under Captain Arthur Inglis at Green Dump, Inglis having been detached from C Company when the majority of tanks were sent to assist in clearing the German positions north of the River Ancre. On 18 October, Stuart Hastie and Heady Head were tasked to support an attack on the Bayonet trench to the north of Flers. Heady was commanding the male tank he fought on 15 September whilst Stuart was commanding a female; either the one previously commanded by George Macpherson or that commanded by Basil Henriques on 15 September. Whilst Heady was able to get into action, as described in the previous chapter, Stuart failed because of the dreadful ground conditions over the route he was required to take.

Stuart stayed with D Battalion as it was formed in November 1916 but, on 21 January 1917, he was appointed to command the Tank Driving School near St Pol. His fellow instructors included Alec Arnaud and Sir John Dashwood (see page 40). Stuart remained in this role when the school was moved to Wailly where the tank battalions were trained at a German trench complex captured in April 1917. On 30 September, Stuart was sent back to England on special duty for 10 days, probably to visit the tank factories where the new Mark V tanks were being developed. During the Battle of Cambrai, on 20 November 1917, the instructors from the Driving School crewed tanks which were used to rip up the German wire entanglements and allow the cavalry to deploy. Stuart Hastie was in overall command of all three sections and he had several of the First Tank Crews under command including Alec Arnaud who was one of his section commanders.

In January 1918, Stuart was appointed Chief Instructor of Driving and Maintenance School in France in January 1918, a post he held for a year and for which he was awarded the OBE in the Honours List in June 1919. As he approached demobilisation, in February 1919, Stuart was offered a Regular Army commission by Brigadier General Hugh Elles but as the long term future of the Tank Corps was uncertain, he declined. After demobilisation Stuart joined the brewing firm of William Younger in Edinburgh. In the early 1920s, he took charge of Sir Peter Mackie's new laboratory at the Campbeltown distillery. Stuart's work of applying chemistry to the whisky production process created major savings and he soon became a senior member of staff. During his time working for Distillers, he would have regularly met Geordie Campbell, who commanded *Cognac* on 15 September and who became Sir Peter's son in law and was later Chairman of White

Stuart Hastie in later years. (TPC)

Horse Distillers. In 1923, Agnes and Stuart's daughter Katherine was born. In 1926, his research into distilling whiskey was published following a lecture to the London Engineers' Club and, in 1928 Stuart published an article in the Journal of the Institute of Brewing which is quoted in several studies of the industry. In 1936, Stuart was tasked to head up an inquiry into the state of Scottish barley growing and he was also called as an expert witness at a court case in 1938, when he gave details of analytical work undertaken at Campbeltown which had been copied by Japanese manufacturers.

Stuart's expertise as a chemist was clearly matched by his business acumen as in 1930 he was appointed a director of the Distillers Company. In his spare time he was a keen freshwater fisherman and taught his son Douglas to fish. In 1935, Stuart became Managing Director of Scottish Malt Distillers Limited: a post he held for twenty years. The following year, his son Douglas became a student member of the Institute of brewing whilst working for William McEwan's in

Edinburgh. There are no records of Stuart serving during the Second World War but Douglas served in the RNVR. He was commissioned as a temporary Sub Lieutenant on 5 February 1942. Promoted Lieutenant one year later, he ultimately commanded the American built minesweeper HMS Byms 2036 from 21 February 1945 for a year. From 1947, just after his daughter Katherine moved to Canada, Stuart gave a series lectures to members of the wine trade in London and Birmingham which were to form the basis of a book "From Burn to Bottle", which was published in 1951 by the Scottish Whiskey Association. He also corresponded with Liddell Hart in 1957, during his research into the formation of the Tank Corps, and was interviewed by the BBC in 1963; one of several veterans recalling their service – the recording is available in the Imperial War Museum. Stuart and Agnes then retired to Elgin, probably to be near his son Douglas who was living in the ancient city. Agnes died aged eighty-five, in 1976 at Elgin and Stuart remarried the following year at Laurencekirk; his second wife was Margaret Cameron. Douglas died in 1979 and Stuart died the following year, on 27 October 1980 at Spynie Hospital. As for how the tank was named, Stuart's step-daughter Fiona claims that, after the first tank action, Stuart was asked by a newspaper reporter for the name of his tank to Hastie replied *Dinnaken* – Scottish for "I don't know".

In comparison with *Dinnaken*'s skipper, there is little information available about his second in command Corporal Edward Sheldon who controlled the gunners, other than he served on with the Tank Corps eventually reaching the rank of sergeant. Gunner Eric Blake was probably a gearsman, who eventually reached the rank of WO1 and Gunner William Sugden operated a machine gun on the port side was commissioned. He was blinded by flakes from interior of tank and hospitalized. William Sugden was later promoted sergeant in the Tank Corps and was commissioned on 8 October 1918 He later settled on the Manchester Road in Wilmslow at a cottage called "Finney Dene".

Gunner Eric Blake, who was born at Putney on 21 March 1889, was the eldest son of a solicitor's clerk named Herbert Blake and his wife Edith, Herbert later becoming a tax officer at the Royal Courts of Justice. Eric was baptized at St Mary's Parish Church on 28 April 1889 and educated at Highgate School in London before starting work as a clerk with the Canadian Bank of Commerce (CBC) on 11 November 1907. Eric was living in Addiscombe where he married Dorothy Thompson on 22 November 1913 and the couple had a daughter named Betty Bouchard who was born on 8 August in the following year. Eric enlisted in the MMGS in London on 16 January 1916, whilst working at the CBC City of London branch in Lombard Street. Like most soldiers, Eric kept in touch with his work friends when he deployed to France. On 28 September, he wrote a letter about his time after the attack on Flers which was published by the CBC in their periodical *Letters from the Front*. Eric gives no information about *Dinnaken*'s action on 15 September although he does try to counter some of the more hyperbolic reports of the event.

You will probably have seen in the papers how things have been going on lately and also about the Tanks. A great deal of it is true about them but I am afraid a certain amount is somewhat exaggerated. However their moral effect on Fritz the first time we went into action is undoubted, as was also their fighting ability, but I can assure you that the feeling of being boxed up like that whilst under intensively heavy shell fire takes some getting used to.

Our infantry is absolutely splendid. It is quite a sight seeing them going over the parapet as if it was nothing in the world like enemy machine guns or a barrage of fire. We went over with some Imperial battalions and the New Zealanders. I have not seen the Canadians in action: they were some distance away on our left. I hear they did splendid work. Well they could not beat our New Zealanders. They are magnificent.

I was out on a working party two or three days ago when quite suddenly a "coal box" [a German 5.9 inch heavy shell] burst right amongst us doing rather bad damage to some of our boys and killing one outright" [Gunner Fred Horrocks]. I had my tunic unbuttoned and flying loose and one side is now quite riddled with splinter holes. A night later I was walking along a road with a message when a shell burst five or six yards away from me. The concussion knocked me over and very luckily too as otherwise I would have probably stopped a piece of flying shell.

The papers will tell you more than I am allowed by an eagle eyed censor but I notice that the papers say very little about the poor devils who made the success of the tanks possible, namely the crews. I can assure you that it was a splendid test of a man's pluck and you might be pleased to hear that, whatever the tanks have been through at any time, there has never been once any sign of panic amongst any crew. Not a bad thing to be able to say for absolutely raw soldiers and some of us have been through it a bit too.

The CBC also published a record of service which states Eric fought at Courcelette in1916. He then fought at Bullecourt in May 1917, where he suffered burns and shock, which would indicate he was serving with No 12 Company. Eric was appointed lance corporal in July 1917 before he fought, and was wounded, in the Ypres Salient. He was subsequently promoted sergeant in November 1917, probably as a result of casualties taken at Cambrai. Eric took part in the delaying actions during the Kaiserschlacht and then was again slightly wounded at Villers-Bretonneux which indicates he was serving either with 8th or 13th Battalion. He was promoted to company sergeant major before the end of the war.

Exceptionally, after having been demobilized, Eric re-enlisted as a Regular soldier on 26 September 1919 into the Tank Corps. He served through the ranks, working his way to the rank of Warrant Officer Class 1 finally completing more than 30 years of Colour service. He retired through ill health in 1946 and settled at Duncan Crescent in Bovington. Eric then became a civil servant and worked at the Driving and Maintenance School in the Administrative Squadron in which role he also looked after civilians in the school. He was a staunch member of the Bovington Branch of the RTR OCA and was an honorary member of several Sergeants' Messes in the Garrison. He died suddenly, aged sixty-six, at his home in Cologne Road on 15 July 1954. Following his funeral on 20 July 1954, which was attended by many members of the Regiment, Eric was buried in Wool Churchyard.

Dinnaken's driver, an ASC private called Charles Wescomb, transferred to the Tanks in early 1917. The eldest son of a coastguard, also known as Charles, he was born on 30 April 1887 at Sandown on the Isle of Wight. By the time he was four, the family had moved to a new home at

Erdagh in Country Kerry, where Charles' father served as a coastguard. Bought up in Ireland, Charles and his family later returned to the Isle of Wight and, by 1911, he was working as a domestic gardener at Bembridge. His younger brother Harold had joined the Royal Engineers Territorial Force from 1910 and he was the first of three brothers to volunteer for war service, Charles followed in 1915 and Alfred later again. Harold deployed to France with the British Expeditionary Force in 1914 but was evacuated to England in early 1916 owing to persistent illness; he was discharged in February of that year. By this time Charles was already serving with the ASC. After he joined the tanks, his younger brother Alfred also volunteered to join having previously served with the Hampshire Regiment. All the brothers survived the war and most of the family continued to live on the Isle of Wight. Charles married Lily Tourle from East Preston in Sussex in 1922 and they settled

Eric Blake in 1946 at Bovington.
(*Tank Magazine*)

in Reigate where their son Peter was born in 1926. Sadly Charles did not see his son become a teenager; he died aged only fifty, on 30 October 1937 at the East Surrey Hospital in Redhill.

I found out about Gunner Fred Gomersall through his friendship with Ewart Doodson of *Daredevil*. Fred, who was the younger son of a butcher Abraham Gomersall and his wife Annie, was born on 13 May 1894 at Pudsey. He was christened at the parish church on 8 July. The family soon moved to Ravensthorpe when his father set up in business in his own right. When he left school, in May 1908, Fred did not join the family business like his older brother but worked in Dewsbury as a clerk for an accountant named Arthur Greenwood. By the time he enlisted into the MMGS at Coventry, on 22 October 1915, he was almost six feet tall and was qualified as an accountant. He went through the standard training package at Bisley and Elveden before he deployed to France on 28 August. When *Dinnaken* went into action, he was the gunner on the port side 6 pdr QF gun, using it to "good effect as the tank drove through the village of Flers". The next day, he was in a party which salvaged the guns from his friend Ewart Doodson's tank *Daredevil*. Fred later served with D Battalion and probably fought at the Battle of Bullecourt on 11 April. Unusually he was granted home leave in early July 1917 but returned to D Battalion serving in No 11 Company under Maj Willie Watson. Fred also changed trade from a machine gunner to driver as he qualified as a First Class mechanic in August 1917, No 11 Company having trained more drivers in May at Wailly. Fred was also given home leave after the Battle of Cambrai but not until late January 1918; this is possibly because he had been home in the previous summer.

From his company conduct sheet, which was replaced in March 1918 after HQ 4th Battalion was destroyed by enemy shelling, it is clear he remained serving with B Company which had formerly been known as No 11 Company. Fred was detached for two months to the Training and Reinforcement Depot from 7 July to 15 September 1918, and therefore missed the Battle of Amiens. However, he served with 4th Battalion as they fought their way past the German defenders during the Final Advance, but was send home, as the battalion was withdrawn from battle and joined the Tank Corps Depot. He was then attached to London District (Labour Centre) as acting RQMS – the NCO responsible for clothing and equipment accounting on 28 December 1918 and then four days later, posted to Shrewsbury as acting RQMS at 308 Protection Company of the Royal Defence Corps for two months. Finally he was appointed RQMS of 19th Battalion Tank Corps, at Bovington, which had several other Flers veterans amongst its members. When he was demobilised, he appears to have returned to work in Dewsbury. Sadly there are no records of him until his marriage at Barkston Ash to Rebe Harrison in the spring of 1972; he died at Barkston the following year aged seventy nine.

The 6 pdr gunner on the other side of *Dinnaken* was a seventeen year old named Percy Boult who became known for his keen eyesight and good shooting. Roy Reiffer, who fought alongside him in the starboard sponson, states he shot down a German observation balloon as well as causing large numbers of casualties amongst the German troops in the eaves of the houses in Flers. Percy, who was born in Hanley which is now part of Stoke on Trent on 17 August 1897, was the youngest surviving son of a merchant tailor. He joined the MMGS on 24 November 1915 at Coventry where he met Roy for the first time. On 15 September, as *Dinnaken* fought through Flers, he was temporarily blinded by metal flakes from interior of tank hull from German gunfire and hospitalised. He stayed with the tanks and was commissioned on 25 March 1918. During the Final Advance, whilst serving with 9th Battalion, he was awarded two gallantry awards in just over a month, the citations clearly explaining why he earned them.

> During the operations near Joncourt on October 1, '18, when his tank was stopped and under heavy shell fire, 2nd Lieut Boult put out a smoke bomb to cover the tank. The bomb, however, stuck, and burst partly inside the tank. Thinking that the tank was on fire, 2nd Lieut Boult ordered his crew to evacuate it. This he was able to do, but not seeing his crew, who were in

a shell-hole close by, he drove on into the fight. He was stopped by the infantry, who asked for his support. He explained he was alone and asked for a volunteer crew. An officer and two privates of the 2nd Manchester Regt volunteered to go with him; he then drove the tank on into action. As the infantry did not understand the Hotchkiss gun, he continually had to leave the driver's seat and help to load and explain it. During the fight he noticed a signal from another tank (I. 29) which had been hit and was under heavy fire, so drove his tank alongside and took off three gunners. As the infantry had retired, he drove back to their line, when the three infantry volunteers rejoined their unit. I cannot speak too highly of this officer's resourcefulness and courage. For the action he was awarded the MC.

Percy Boult was awarded a bar to the MC for his remarkable actions at a time when the British Army was running out of serviceable tanks and in what was to be the last major tank action of the war.

> During the action near Mormal Forest on 4th November '18, his tank broke a track near the front line before zero, but he got it into action up to time. He directed his Tank on foot during the greater part of the action, showing marked gallantry and disregard of danger, and in a thick fog thus kept direction to an important objective. He fought his Tank with four guns out of action later in the day, with two of his crew wounded, and undoubtedly by his devotion to duty saved the infantry many casualties.

After the war, Percy served for a further three years before settling in Ashton under Lyne. He had married Ethel Birch in his home town of Stoke on Trent in early 1919; their only daughter Beryl was born in Ashton on 25 February 1926. Percy later became a partner in a clothing manufacturing firm named Boult Brothers. In September 1935, whilst living in Roundhay, Percy wrote to the *Yorkshire Evening post*, and confirmed Roy Reiffer's claim that he had shot down the balloon near Flers having fired six 6 pdr shell at the target. Following the outbreak of the Second World War he was commissioned into the RAOC on 8 April 1940 but had to leave the Army on account of ill-health eleven months later. After the war, Edith and Percy moved to Mill Hill on the outskirts of London. Their daughter Beryl, who served for four years with the British delegation to the United Nations in New York, married an American physicist, Loran Bittman, at Shrewsbury in 1955 and the young couple settled in Pennsylvania. Percy and Edith returned to Stoke where Percy died in late 1971.

The final member of *Dinnaken*'s crew was Percy's loader Roy Reiffer. He was born on 21 October 1896 in Lewisham and worked as a clerk to the Port of London Authority. He was living at Sydenham when he was attested on 15 November 1915. Ten days later, when he went to Coventry to report for duty for the MMGS, he met Percy Boult and four days later, they were training at MMGS Depot at Bisley. Roy provided details about the battle in a manuscript he later wrote for the Tank Museum just before his death in 1970. This includes that the tank crew stripped to the waist for the first action.

On 23 September, Roy was one of a party tasked to remove the guns from *Dinnaken*. As they were working at the tank, Stuart Hastie was asked to send some men to remove the guns from the hulk of *Dolly*. Roy stepped forward and, with Arthur Smith and Fred Gomersall, accompanied an infantry patrol from 15th Battalion Kings Liverpool Regiment. Moving at midnight into no man's land, the patrol reached the hulk and the infantry watched as the two Tank Crews removed the machine guns from the hulk which was now a complete wreck. During the time they were by the tank, they were subject to German rifle and machine gun fire. Roy was awarded the MM for "clearing the wreckage of D9, on 23 Sept 16; the local Brigade Commander fearing the hulk had been converted to a defensive position". Continuing to serve with D Battalion, in No 10 Company, he retrained as a driver.

Roy fought at the Battle of Arras with Second Lieutenant Frederick Rankin and crew D11 on 9 April, reaching the German front line near Neuville Vitasse before it became ditched. Having been recovered two days later, the tank was again in action on 23 April as one of a pair – again under the command of Second Lieutenant Rankin. Rankin's crew cleared four to five hundred of two lines of trenches, firing 3,000 rounds of ammunition before the tank broke down with radiator trouble. The tanks was hit by German artillery fire and Frederick Rankin, got through to the German support trenches before it took a direct hit and was burnt out. Lieutenant Rankin and Gunner James Miller were killed and their remains buried in a single grave at Wancourt Military Cemetery. One other crewman was badly burned and three others injured in the action.

After the battle, Roy attended a gunnery course at Merlimont from where on 17 May he was admitted to hospital at Étaples. He rejoined D Battalion on 1 June 1917 and probably fought in the opening actions of the 3rd Battle of Ypres. Roy was promoted corporal on 27 August 1917 and, three weeks later, was posted to the Driving School at Wailly as an instructor. He later claimed that this was due to the influence of his former skipper, Stuart Hastie. Roy also fought at Cambrai in one of the crew of the wire pulling tanks which cleared a route for the cavalry. The crews of these tanks were withdrawn after the British assault petered out and Roy was granted leave in the UK from 28 November, the day before the Germans launched their counter attack which took back so much of the ground captured the week before. Roy rejoined the Mechanical School staff and in March 1918, during the Kaiserschlacht, brought back a sponson-less tank to safety; many other tanks having been lost or abandoned as the tank battalions fought to delay the advancing Germans. Returning to instructor duties he was transferred to Tank Corps Training and Reinforcement Depot at Merlimont on 19 July 1918. Roy was on leave in the UK at the time of the Armistice; he had been due to Return to Unit on 11 November but Roy overstayed returning on 14 November. Naturally he was charged for the offence but was simply admonished and his pay accordingly lost. With courses being cancelled at Merlimont, but with the need to train up the new Tank Battalions forming in England, Roy was transferred to the Central Schools at Bovington on 11 December. He served there for four months and was transferred to the Z Reserve on 6 May 1919.

Although he initially went home to Sydenham, he soon returned to Bovington and, by 1920, was running a taxi firm with a fellow driving instructor Owen Rowe, who fought at Martinpuich in *Daphne,* and another Tank Corps NCO named Frederick Hillier. Owen died in 1922 but Roy expanded the Red Garage at Bovington to look after the cars and motorcycles of soldiers living in the local areas as well as running a charabanc service to Wool Railway Station and to large town in the area. One of the Tank Corps soldiers stationed at Bovington in the 1920s was Thomas Lawrence, better known as Lawrence of Arabia, who became a regular customer at the Red Garage after he joined the Royal Tank Corps in 1923 under the pseudonym of TE Shaw. Between 1923 and 1925, when Lawrence returned to the RAF, the two men became good friends. Roy also provided storage for Lawrence's Brough motorcycles which were maintained at the Red Garage by the Runyard brothers, two young mechanics from Wool who were employed by Roy. Lawrence loaned Roy one of the Broughs, known as *George II* fitted as a motorcycle combination, so Roy could to court his fiancée Nora Chick. Roy and Nora, who was a farmer's daughter from nearby Winfrith, were married at St Christopher's Church at Winfrith-Newburgh on 11 April 1925. They had three sons, Michael, Donald and David, and later moved to Broadmayne which is about ten miles away from Bovington. Lawrence, who had made his home at Cloud's Hill cottage to the north of Bovington whilst he served in the RAF, continued to be a customer at the Red Garage where Roy stored the series of Brough motorcycles he was loaned by well-wishers.

Roy was one of the last people to see Lawrence alive. Around noon on 13 May 1935, Lawrence called at the Red Garage for fuel for his Brough before making his way to Wareham. Lawrence was fatally injured that afternoon during his return journey to his cottage at Cloud's Hill. Roy and the Runyards were present at the inquest, on 21 May, which took place the morning before Lawrence's

Roy Reiffer on one of TE Lawrence's Brough motorcycles. (Huntington University CA)

funeral at Moreton Church. Roy continued to run the Red Garage at Bovington until 1942 when he and Nora moved to Llyswen; a village between Hay on Wye and Brecon, where he again ran a motor garage at Green Pit. On the day after the BBC television programme, "Find the Link", on 3 September 1956, Roy wrote to Victor Huffam who visited him in Wales. In 1962, Roy retired from the motor repair business moving back to Dorset where he and Nora ran owned a boarding house at 25 East Street in Weymouth where he was again visited by Huffam. About this time, Roy wrote to his former skipper Stuart Hastie and in 1963 both men were interviewed by the BBC. In early 1970, Roy lodged a manuscript called "Recollections of life in the Tank Corps and TE Lawrence" shortly after which he died, in Weymouth aged eighty-four.

Dolly and Crew D9

15 September was a day which should have been memorable to Victor Huffam and the crew of *Dolly* for all the right reasons. As it was, he not only failed to get into action but did so in the most embarrassing way. He was following Gordon Court, in Tank D14, from the start point to the north of Delville Wood towards Flers when he saw the leading tank stopped as it crossed the British front line trench. D14 had the misfortune to drive over a shelter in the trench which collapsed. Victor decided that he would pull the stricken tank clear so they could both get into action. Manoeuvring close to the ditched tank, so that cables could be connected between them, Dolly also became stuck. The crews tried everything they could to extract the two 28 ton machines but to not avail. It

D9 *Dolly* and D14 stuck in the British trench – 15 September 1916. (Tank Museum)

was not until later afternoon that, following the intervention of the Divisional pioneers battalion, that they were removed. Court and Huffam were then tasked to take their tanks into action the following day.

In the very early hours of 16 September, as ordered by Frank Summers, *Dolly* left her start point near Delville Wood and made her way northwards along the Flers road and linked up with attacking infantry by 5:30 hrs. Victor Huffam and his crew were to be in the centre of assault on Germans to north of Flers with George Pearsall and *Die Hard* on the left and Gordon Court in D14 to the right. As the three tanks advanced, *Dolly* cleared the German trench complex known as Cox and Box before heading for the Gird Trench, which protected the front of the village of Gueudecourt. D14 was to follow the track known as Good Street and attack the northwest of the village. As *Dolly* moved eastwards towards the Grass Lane, Victor saw his friend's tank destroyed by German artillery fire as she crossed the Gird Trench. *Dolly* then turned north and assisted a New Zealand attack on a German position near what is now the Australia Imperial Force Cemetery. As *Dolly* moved north up Grass Lane, she was too hit by Germany artillery fire, on the left hand gun sponson, killing two machine gunners and wounding Victor and four other crewmen who managed to make their way to safety. To prevent her guns being used by the Germans against subsequent British attacks, they were removed by members of *Dinnaken*'s crew on 23 September but the hulk itself could not be moved and *Dolly* was blown apart after the end of the war.

Victor Huffam was born on 18 May 1890 at Heaton Chapel near Stockport. The eldest of eight children, he was educated at Hessle in East Yorkshire and then at Buxton College. His father was an engineer who also acted as a company secretary. Victor also decided to become an engineer and, from 1905 to 1908, was apprenticed at Crossley's whilst studying in the evenings at Manchester Technical College. Crossley's were pioneers in the production of internal combustion engines and also manufactured motor cars. In 1909, aged nineteen, Victor travelled to Western Australia, with his brother Gordon, to find work. Victor worked as a technician and agent with an engineering firm Saunders and Stuart in the gold fields; the firm was an agent of Crossley's so Victor's apprenticeship made him perfect for the job. Victor also joined 18th Battalion Australian Light Horse as a trooper. Having been overseas for five years, Victor returned to England on leave in July 1914 and spent time at his parents' home in Norwich. Following the British declaration of war, on 4 August, Victor travelled to London to seek advice from the Australian High Commission as to whether he should join his unit in Western Australia. At this time, his state had not been tasked to provide mounted units for the Australian Expeditionary Force and, given the option of going back or joining the British Army, Victor enlisted in 18th Battalion Royal Fusiliers on 30 August 1914.

Victor was subsequently commissioned on 11 May 1915, into 3rd (Reserve) Battalion Norfolk Regiment and was employed at Felixstowe with 9th Battalion of the Norfolks who were known as *Ninth Holy Boys*. Victor, who according to his service records, was only four feet seven inches tall, recalled that most of the two hundred soldiers in his company were ex-Regular soldiers who had already seen action in France and some were twice his age. Frustrated by the lack of action, he volunteered for a "secret duty" in January 1916, along with 300 other volunteers. Victor was interviewed by Colonel Ernest Swinton at Wellington Barracks in Westminster and was one of twenty eight selected, presumably because of his engineering background. He returned to Felixstowe and, having been told to keep ready for training, did not accompany the members of D Company of the Ninth Holy Boys when they returned to France. Victor was attached to the Heavy Section MGC on 17 April. He then trained at Bisley and Elveden with D Company. Victor was related to an Aide to Camp to the Prince of Wales, Capt Bill Huffam, and it was probably through this link that the future Edward VIII visited C Company both at Yvrench and later D Company as they undertook their final preparations at the Loop Railway siding in early September 1916.

After *Dolly* was destroyed, Victor was so badly shaken that Frank Summers sent him to a Casualty Clearing Station; Billy Sampson also recalled that Victor's hair turned white overnight. Victor was visited by Frank Summers and his cousin Bill Huffam and, after a short period at a rest camp, rejoined D Company at Green Dump. On 21 October, he was sent to establish another stores dump, near Auchonvillers, to support attacks to the north of the River Ancre. After the attack on Beaumont-Hamel, on 14 November, in which both supporting tanks were ditched, Victor was sent forward with a party to look after the hulks. It was here, according to Victor that he was badly gassed. Harold Mortimore, who was gassed on the same date, later stated that Victor had lost his nerve. Whatever the cause, Victor was sent to a hospital at Doullens where he was again visited by Frank Summers. Victor was considered no longer fit for active service and was sent back to England.

Victor was initially treated in a hospital at Oxford where he was visited by Gordon Court's mother. She only knew her son was missing and Victor had to break the news that he had seen his friend's tank destroyed. Later Victor visited one of his crewmen, Harry Saunders, in a hospital in Kent where he was pleased to see his driver recovering albeit in a wheelchair. Victor was then sent to Bovington to join one of the new battalions being formed and met up with Harry Drader whilst there. Expecting to return quickly to France, Victor decided to marry his sweetheart Dorothy Vincent in early 1917. Dorothy, after whom the tank *Dolly* was probably named, was a nineteen year old bank clerk and the pair was married at the local Register Office on 24 February 1917. However Victor was deemed not well enough to return to active service and was employed therefore at the new Ministry of Munitions. Victor's subsequent application to join the Institute of Chartered Engineers reveals he was employed with the inspection of aircraft engines and was in charge of seventy five inspectors.

Dorothy and Victor's only son John was born in Norwich on 28 July 1919. Having been released from the Army in early 1920, Victor and his father took over an engineering company at Norwich. Later, Victor moved to London and established another engineering firm, called the Temple Fortune Works, at Golders Green. It became a successful company and Victor travelled extensively overseas. Sadly his marriage to Dorothy failed in 1922 and they divorced after she had an affair. During the Second World War John Huffam served as a Royal Navy Engine Room Artificer. He survived and, on 25 October 1945, he married Daphne Green, the daughter of a captain in the Coldstream

D Company officers at Canada Farm Summer 1916.
Standing left to right: Reginald Legge (D6), Arthur Blowers (D5), Eric Robinson (D21), Len Bond (D18), George Bown (D8), Harry Drader (D20), Jack Bagshaw (D15), Arthur Arnold (D16), Stuart Hastie (D17), Harold Darby (D10), Hugh Bell (D2), Charles Storey (D4) and George Pearsall (D11)
Seating left to right: Eric Colle (D25), Alfred Enoch (D7), Graeme Nixon (D12), George Mann (D23), Stephen Sellick (D19), Frank Summers (OC), Graham Woods (Adjutant), Harold Mortimore (D1), unknown, Jeff Wakley and Walter Stones (D24). On ground left to right: Victor Huffam (D9), Alex Sharp (D22); Gordon Court (D6) and Heady Head (D3). Absent: Bill Sampson (D13). (Tank Museum)

Guards at St George's Church Hannover Square. That same year, Victor married Mabel Verral and they settled in Stanmore. Mabel accompanied Victor on his overseas trips throughout the 1950s and almost forty years after the first tank action, Victor Huffam appeared with Victor Smith on a BBC game show called *Find the Link*. This programme led to his correspondence with the author of the RTR history, Sir Basil Liddell Hart, who was keen to make contact with surviving members of the First Tank Crews. As a result of his enquiries, it was Victor who provided the photograph of the D Company officers taken at Canada Farm at Elveden in August 1916

In 1960, Victor was one of the Great War Tank veterans were presented to the Queen at Buckingham Palace. It was also about that time that Victor and Mabel decided to retire to South Africa. They had visited the country on several occasions and settled at Scottburgh to the south of Durban. Victor was soon in touch with Arthur Arnold, who had commanded tank Crew D16 on 15 September 1916 and who was living near Bloemfontein. Victor prompted Arthur to write an article about the first tank action which was published in the *Tank* in 1963. Victor, who had a passion for polo, later visited Arthur to buy some ponies. The South African coastal climate was to benefit Victor's health and the couple lived there for a further twenty years, Victor dying ten days after Mabel, on 31 July 1982 at the age of ninety-two.

Harry Saunders, who was Victor's second in command, had enlisted on 31 October 1914 and, as such was one of the first to join the MMGS. He originally undertook training at Bisley which including driving a 750cc Clyno motorcycle with a Vickers machine gun in the sidecar. During the action at Flers, he was one of the two gearsmen in the tank. In a written letter to Basil Liddell Hart, on 1 September 1957, Harry states that the move-up on the night of 13 September took place in torrential rain and at speed of two miles an hour. The following day, the tank halted in a valley beyond Longueval but I have been unable to identify its location. Harry Saunders' recall of other events, forty years previously, was not wholly accurate in other respects and I believe that the tank stopped at Green Dump to the southwest of the village. Harry recalled that there was very little in the way of food for the tank crews apart from some meat, probably tinned beef, onions and army biscuit. In his report he recalled "As corporal and second in command, after viewing the rations, I put it to the vote if we should eat, drink and be merry and consume the rations we had, or make those rations spread out over a period. It was agreed that we should consume the rations forthwith. We lit a wood fire and proceeded to make the best we could. We cooked the meat and onions on the lid of a biscuit tin. I can recall taking a portion to Mr Huffam. He took one look and said to me 'I am afraid I could not eat that!"

Harry states that the tank had got no further than 800 yards, on 15 September, before it ditched in a communications trench and "after vainly trying to dig out tank out, for some hours, a party of the navvy battalion came to our assistance and we managed to get moving". These were soldiers from 4th Battalion the South Lancashire Regiment who were Divisional pioneers. By the time the tank was extracted, it was too later for the crew to be re-tasked so they stayed where they were stranded for the rest of the day. The next day, Harry Saunders was trapped in the tank after it had been hit by the German artillery. He managed to escape through the rear escape hatch and throw himself on the ground and crawl to a shell-hole where Victor Huffam and the rest of the crew were taking shelter. Victor recalls seeing his shins sticking and using morphine as well as shell dressing from other crewmen to treat Harry's injuries. Harry wrote that he owed his life to Victor's heroic action whilst Victor recalled he had to drag Sanders to safety across no man's land, using his Sam Browne belt from shell-hole to shell-hole, to avoid the large amount of small arms fire being directed at the tank. This is more than possible as Grass Lane was in clear view of the German infantry in the Gird Trench which dominates the ground over which *Dolly's* crew had to escape. Harry was evacuated from France and treated in a hospital in Kent where he was visited by Victor in early 1917. Harry's wounds were however so bad that he was demobilised on 31 May. The two men kept in contact after the war and in September 1957 when he was in correspondence with Basil Liddell Hart in connection with his history of the Tank Corps, Harry was living at 130 Stoney Lane in Yardley in Birmingham. Thereafter I can find no record of him.

The two crewmen, who were killed when a German shell hit *Dolly's* port sponson on 16 September, were Gunners Alfred Andrew and Ronald Chapple. Alfred was born on 6 July 1887 on the Green at Barnes in Surrey. Like his company commander, and several more of the First Tank Crews, Alfred was the eldest child of a draper after whom he was named. His mother Maria Syms was a dressmaker; she had four children but sadly only Alfred and his sister Winifred survived infancy. By 1901, the family had moved to West Ashford in Kent and, ten years later, were living in Station Road in Preston, a suburb of Brighton, where Alfred was employed as a cycle maker in a local works. His sister was a dressmaker but, unlike her mother who worked independently from home, Winifred worked for a costumier. Ronald Chapple was born on 17 July 1897 at 68 Ivy Road in St Denys which is a village near Southampton. He was the eldest son of a telegraphist, Charles Chapple who had married Gertrude Caplen earlier that year. By 1911 Ronald was living at 9 Egham Street in Cardiff where his father was a post office sorting clerk and telegraphist. Ronald joined the MMGS whilst working in Coventry but his service record has not survived. Neither has the record of the location of his grave and both Alfred and Ronald are commemorated on the Thiepval Memorial but there are no family details for Alfred. However, I have recently found, in the Army Record of Soldier's Effects, his widow was named Lily and this has led me to the record of a marriage between Alfred and Lily Streeter who were married at Tonbridge Register Office on 20 December 1915. Alfred's occupation was shown as a motor mechanic and Lily was a domestic cook.

Lance Corporal George Sanders, who drove the tank on 15 September, was not the original driver. This was, according to Graham Woods' notebook, a corporal named George Mullis. George Mullis did not go into action on either 15 or 16 September but he did stay with the tanks when some other drivers returned to the ASC. George Mullis rebadged to the MGC, with several other members of 711 (MT) Company, and later served with the Tank Corps as a private soldier until the end of the war. George Sanders, who drove the tank on 15 and 16 September, also survived and served with the ASC for the rest of the war but I can find no details of him.

Lance Corporal Arthur Archer was born in October 1894 at Stapenhill, near Burton upon Trent. The second child and eldest son of a postman, he was working as a brewers' clerk at Allsops Brewery in Stoke on Trent when he enlisted into the MMGS on 11 November 1915. A fortnight later, he was at the MMGS Depot at Bisley where he undertook initial training. Fairly tall for a tanker at 5 feet 10¾ inches, he was posted to D Company on 27 May. He was appointed lance corporal on 5 August, whilst training at Elveden, and deployed on 28 August 1916. When the tank went into action on 16 September, with no ASC driver available, Arthur drove *Dolly* until he was temporarily blinded by splinters. Arthur was then moved back to the gun stations and, after the tank was hit, was wounded in the right arm by small arms fire as he made his way to safety. Initially treated by the New Zealanders, and hospitalised the next day, he was evacuated on Hospital Ship *Jan Breydal* on 19 September and treated at No 2 General Hospital at Bristol. He reverted to the rank of Gunner on 23 January 1917, presumably when it was realized he would not return to active service. He was admitted to a hospital at Wool, near Bovington, on 7 February suffering with severe paralysis to the right arm as well as atrophy to the lower arm muscles. Despite treatment, this could not be overcome and he was released from hospital on 15 March and discharged from the Army on 28 April 1917. Arthur married Sarah Wild in the autumn of 1919 at Burton upon Trent but they do not appear to have been parents. Arthur died, aged only forty two, in early 1938 also at Burton upon Trent.

Gunner Ernie Powell was the only crewman to escape injury on 16 September. He originally served with the Royal Fusiliers before he transferred to the MMGS. He was born on 13 August 1895 at Merthyr Tydfil. He was the youngest of three children of a saddler named Thomas Powell and his wife Mary Morgan and the family originally lived at their shop at 21 High Street. By 1911, the family was living at 6 Park Terrace. Ernie was educated at the County Grammar School in Merthyr and then worked as a junior clerk at the Llandeillo branch of London and Provincial Bank. In September 1915, he enlisted at Ammanford and but, surprisingly, joined 26th (Bankers) Battalion of the Royal Fusiliers. He undertook recruit training at Loughton in the Epping Forest and then served at Aldershot where he became a member of the machine gun crew. Ernie told his family that he was selected to transfer to the HS MGC because of his height; he was five feet six inches, and because he learnt some French at school. Although he did not get into action on 15 September, he saw his old pals in the Bankers battalion fight their way into Flers as part of 14th Division.

Ernie stayed with the tanks for the rest of the war and fought at Ypres in the summer of 1917 and at Amiens the following year. He was detached to Fontainebleau, to the Allied Tank School where he served as an orderly room clerk. Never promoted, he was demobilised on 3 March 19 and returned to his old job in a bank. He initially worked in Ebbw Vale then Aberdare and Taunton. He later moved to the London suburbs and become a branch manager for Barclays in Croydon and West Wickham. Ernie married Mary Williams at St Mary Magdalene Church in Addiscombe on 22 August 1931; they were both aged thirty-six years and Mary was the daughter of a tailor. The couple had two children: a daughter Jennifer and a son Graham. During the Second World War, Ernie served in both the Home Guard and the Royal Observer Corps. Later Ernie and Mary settled in Bickley and, although he did not appear to maintain links with his Tank Corps comrades, he regularly attended reunion dinners with the Royal Fusiliers. He died on 16 March 64 at Bromley Hospital.

The final member of the crew was Reg Laverty. Born on 19 August 1893 in Winchester, Reg was the tenth child and youngest son of a self-employed cabinetmaker James Laverty. James employed most of his children in the family firm although his third son William, who was ten years older than Reg, joined the Army and served with the King's Royal Rifle Corps for eighteen years. William fought in the second Anglo-Boer War and was present at the Relief of Mafeking in May 1900. Reg, who worked for his father alongside his brothers as a cabinet maker, joined the Territorial Force and served for four years in the Army Service Corps, probably in the Wessex Division Supply and Transport Column. Reg would also have been involved in the making of souvenirs, which his father sold to raise funds for the restoration of Winchester Cathedral, using fragments of masonry extracted from under the building by the diver William Walker whose five years of work in pitch-black water filled pits saved the south side of the huge Norman Cathedral from collapse.

Following the outbreak of the Great War, Reg's elder brother John volunteered to join the Army on 8 October 1914 at Winchester and joined 10th Battalion Rifle Brigade, one of the many service battalions which resulted from Lord Kitchener's poster-appeal for 100, 000 volunteers. John was however discharged after only nineteen days service. His brother Edwin volunteered to join the Royal Navy on 9 November 1915 as a carpenter, and after three months training in HMS *Fishguard* in Portsmouth Harbour, served for three years in HMS *Monarch* which fought at the Battle of Jutland in May 1916. Reg enlisted at the MMGS Depot at Bisley on 19 January 1916. He was extremely tall at 6 feet 2½ inches and was also unusual in that he had previous military service. Following initial training as a machine gunner at Bisley, he voluntarily transferred to the Armoured Car Section. He was granted leave in mid May and, although there is a direct rail line from Winchester to Bisley, was charged with being late from leave on 27 May; the same day he was posted to D Company at Bullhousen Farm. He was also late from leave on 2 July by which time D Company was based at Canada Farm within the secret tank training area at Elveden in Norfolk.

Reg deployed to France on 28 August. On 16 September, after *Dolly* had been hit and he was making his way back to the British lines, he was caught in the blast of an exploding German artillery shell and knocked out. Reg was admitted to the 2/2nd London Casualty Clearing Station and then transferred to Convalescent Depot at Étaples on 21 September. He had recovered by 26 October when he was graded A1 Medical health and returned to his unit. Transferring to D Battalion one month later, he went with the unit back to their new base at Blangy-sur-Ternoise from where, on 6 January 1917, he was sent on a course to 3rd Army School of Cookery. D Battalion was growing and they needed men who could support them whilst not on operations. The following month, as the British started the 1917 offensive on the Somme, Reg's brother William was Killed in Action. He was now serving as a sergeant in 1st Battalion KRRC and was killed near Miraumont on 17 February as the British again attempted to drive the Germans back towards Bapaume. 1st KRRC was part of 6th Division, which with 18th (Eastern) and 63rd (Royal Naval) Divisions, forced the German to withdraw but took heavy casualties. William's body was originally buried close to where he was killed but after the war, it was reinterred at the Regina Trench cemetery to the northwest of Courcelette. His loss is also commemorated in the tiny church of St Swithin's Church upon Kingsgate where a small but beautiful wooden memorial plaque was placed having been made by his family.

He served with D Battalion through the Battle of Arras and 3rd Ypres but unusually, Reg was granted UK leave from 2 – 16 November rejoining the Battalion on 20 November just after the unit went into action. This demonstrates just how effective were the systems in place to ensure a soldier returned to his unit despite the fact that it had moved three times whilst he was on leave. According to his family, Reg was wounded on three occasions whilst serving with the tanks; the lower parts of his face were also badly scarred by the impact of small fragments of steel, or scabs, which peeled from the inside of the tank when machine gun bullets hit the exterior of the tank hull. Reg fought with the renamed 4th Battalion until he was taken ill on 27 August 1918. Evacuated to a hospital in France, he made a full recovery and was posted to the Reinforcement Depot at Mers-les-Bains on 15 September, exactly France two years to the day he was first in action. Reg served with the Reinforcement Depot until his discharge on 16 January 1919, when he was sent back to England.

Those offered firm employment were often released and his father actively sought Reg's return to the family business in Winchester. Returning home on 18 January, Reg lived with his family at 1 College Street and, in addition to working for the family firm, taught wood carving to the boys of Winchester College as well as the local College of Art. He married a young singer named Beatrice Ragless and they made their home at Old Down Cottages near Morstead, a village three miles south east of Winchester. The couple had three children; two daughters and a son Peter, who studied at Winchester Art School, became a celebrated artist and was appointed director of the New South Wales Art Gallery. Beatrice died in 1938 when she was only thirty years old. Reg, who was still suffering from the effects of the Great War, was unable to bring up the children on his own so Peter and his sisters, Janet and Margaret, lived with other members of the family. Reg later settled at Longwood, near Oswelbury, and had three more children, Victor, John and Irene with his housekeeper, Queenie Norgate. After Victor Huffam appeared on the BBC *Find the Link* programme, Reg made contact and they met at Winchester, probably at his house at 20 St Swithin's street. Reg died, aged seventy-one, on 26 March 1965 at the Royal Hampshire County Hospital and was buried in the same plot as his wife Bea in Morstead churchyard.

Crew D14

The tank, manned by the D14 crew, was also recovered on 15 September and tasked to support 21st Division on 16 September as they advanced towards Gueudecourt. The tank advanced some 1,100 yards before it was forced to stop at Gird Trench, a location which was to be the scene of continuous fighting for the next week. The Gird Trench would have been registered by the German defenders for "final protective fire", designed to disrupt any enemy attack which managed to break through their defences. After the sergeant, Robert Pebody, and the driver, Laurence Upton, got out to determine how to cross the obstacle, the tank was hit by artillery fire which caused an explosion killing all within the tank and mortally wounding both Pebody and Upton.

Gordon Court, the tank's commander, was born on 9 May 1889 at Milton near Sittingbourne in Kent. The son of a farmer, Gordon was educated at the Queen Elizabeth Grammar School at Faversham and the Herne Bay College, before he moved to Southern Africa. Gordon served in the British South African Police as a trooper from 2 October 1909; the unit providing security against possible rebellion by the local Africa tribes. When the British decided to capture the German colony in what is now Namibia, Gordon joined the locally raised 1st Rhodesia Regiment on 20 October 1914 and fought with them during the South West Africa Campaign until 31 July 1915. When the unit was disbanded, Gordon returned to England arriving in London on 16 February 1916. Volunteering to join the MMGS, he was immediately selected for an officer's appointment and was sent to Trinity College Cambridge on 9 March 1916 where he trained alongside Reginald Legge and Arthur Blowers. Commissioned on 15 April 1916 into the Heavy Section of the MGC, he was killed just over six months later – his tank being only three hundred yards from Legge's tank which was destroyed the previous day. Like all those who were killed inside the tank, Gordon's body was never recovered.

Gordon's second in command was Sergeant Robert Baden Pebody. Born in Warwick in early 1896, shortly after Robert Baden-Powell achieved fame in Matabeleland, there is unusually no record of his birth or of his parents. He was raised in Rugby by his uncle, John Pebody, who was a post office clerk. The Pebody family had been working as post office employees for several generations and John later lived with his grandfather at the post office in Braunston near Daventry. Robert enlisted at Coventry in 1915, joined D Company and was quickly promoted to the rank of Acting Sergeant – quite remarkable progress for a twenty old. It was also unusual that Robert served in Court's crew as a sergeant normally served with the Section Commander. There is no record of Robert's actions when the tank ditched on 15 September. After the tank was forced to stop on 16 September, at the Gird Trench, Robert got outside with the driver, Lawrence Upton, to work out how to get across the obstacle. When the tank exploded, the two men were killed. His body was recovered and is now buried in the AIF Burial Ground, within sight of where the tank was destroyed. Robert is not only commemorated on the Rugby war memorial gates but also at Daventry close to his childhood home of Braunston.

The Post Office post office, as well as their deaths on 16 September, also links Robert with Lawrence Upton. Born at Kirk's Terrace in Chesterfield on 21 October 1892, Lawrence was the only child of a coal-hewer William Upton and his wife Mary. By 1901, the family had moved to Worksop but ten years later, they had moved to Ashover, near Matlock, where father and son both worked as postmen. Lawrence later moved to Bradford. He enlisted into the ASC in 1915 at Doncaster close by to where his widowed mother Mary was living at Barnby Dun. Lawrence became engaged to the local schoolmistress, Bertha Smith, who was a 33 year old daughter of a labourer who worked on the nearby Aire and Calder navigation. Lawrence was posted to 711 (MT) Coy and sent to Elveden for training. Lawrence soon realised he would be sent to France so Bertha arranged for the Banns to be announced and on Sunday 27 August, the weekend before he deployed overseas, on the couple married at the Barnby Dun parish church. Three weeks later, Bertha was tragically widowed. Lawrence's body was initially buried at some distance from the tank, and apart from Robert Pebody, on the southeastern outskirts of Gueudecourt. During the battlefield clearances; his body and that of Sergeant Robert Pebody was exhumed and later moved to the AIF Burial ground where they are now buried albeit some rows apart.

Sadly there are very no service records for the others who were killed in 16 September. Gunner William Barber was born on 15 March 1881 at Broomfield in Smethwick. William was the only son of an edge tool manufacturer; he was named after his father and his middle name was also his mother's maiden name Henty. William had two younger sisters Mary and Winifred being five and ten years his junior. By the turn of the century, his father business had expanded into the production of ornamental ironwork whilst William, now aged twenty one, was employed as a music teacher. As his father grew older, William joined his father's firm. After the action near Flers, his body was not recovered, possibly because the tank was burnt out. He is commemorated on the Thiepval Memorial to the Missing and also listed at the Birmingham Hall of Memory. The CWGC records no family details of Lance Corporal Thomas Cromack but the register of Army Register of Soldier's effects, his widowed mother's name was Charlotte. This has enabled me to confirm that Thomas was born in South Hackney in January 1879. He was the sixth of seven children of a carpenter Edwin Cromack and his wife Charlotte. Sadly Charlotte was widowed four years later when her youngest child Richard was only two. The 1901 census reveals that Thomas was still living in Hackney and working as a bus conductor but ten years later he was employed as an insurance collector and living in Homerton. Thomas enlisted into the MGC at South Hackney and was thirty-seven, and unmarried, when he was killed in action on 16 September. His mother was later awarded a war gratuity of £3.00 in early 1919 which was only eleven pence more than his balance of pay, which was also sent to her twelve months earlier when the Government accepted that Thomas was dead, not missing in action. Gunner Andrew Lawson was also a Londoner. Born in 1895, in Kingsland, he was the eldest son of fancy box manufacturer also named Andrew Thomas and his wife Eliza. He was bought up in Finchley where he worked as a commercial clerk for a paper merchant. He enlisted at Wood Green in Essex and joined the MGC, being transferred to the Heavy Section to serve with D Company. Sadly, other than the reports of his death and details of his effects, there are no other records of his Army service.

George Mann killed in action 15 September 1916. (Tank Museum)

Gunner Joseph Crowe, who was the son of George Crowe and Ann Elliott Crowe, was born in the summer of 1892, at Low West House Farm in County Durham. He was bought up by his grandmother at 25 Bridge Street in the nearby village of Tow Law where he later worked as a rope-guide for a stationery steam engine at the local collier. At the time of the 1911 census he was living with his aunt, at 62 High Street. He enlisted at Tow Law into the MGC but, as his service has not survived, there is nothing known of his service until he was declared missing. After he was presumed dead in January 1917, the outstanding balance of his pay was sent to his mother Jane. He is commemorated at the Thiepval Memorial and also on the village war memorial at Tow Law. George Mann was also from a farming family; he was born on 13 March 1892 at Burn Farm at Avoch in Rossshire. He was the only son of a farmer's daughter named Christine Mann and was bought up on his grandparents' farm on the Black Isle. In 1912 George gained a Technical Bursary from the Glasgow Highland Society worth £25 a year and commenced his studies at the Royal Technical College, Glasgow, aiming to become a chartered engineer. He did not however complete his studies as, after three years, he volunteered to join the MMGS. He was twenty four years old when he was killed and, like the others who were in the tank when it exploded, his body was never recovered. His photograph (above) is held by the University of Glasgow as part of their memorial to those students who lost their lives in the Great War.

9

Ditched, damaged and destroyed

The attack on Flers was undertaken by three divisions supported by ten tanks. Like the Guards Division, these were to be in three groups of three with a singleton on one flank. The singleton was Reginald Legge's tank whose exploits are described in Chapter 7. The remaining nine tanks were soon reduced to four which actually engaged the German defenders; the others becoming ditched, damaged or destroyed. The ten tanks were commanded by Capt Stephen Sellick. He also commanded the group of tanks known as E Group; these three crews were D2 commanded by Lt Hugh Bell, D15 commanded by Lt Jack Bagshaw and D19 commanded by Sellick himself. Sadly none of them were got to their objective. Hugh Bell's tank came stuck or "ditched" in one of the many shell holes within Delville Wood as it made its way in the darkness to the start point; Stephen Sellick's tank made it through the wood but then ditched on its way to the start line, whilst Jack Bagshaw's tank was destroyed by artillery fire as it crossed the German front line.

Crew D2

Lieutenant Hugh Bell was the fourth of five children borne to the Reverend Samuel Bell and his wife Elizabeth. Hugh was born on 7 May 1879 in Pimlico where his father was curate at St Saviour's Church. The salary offered to a curate was not sufficient to support five children so the Reverend Bell supplemented his income by acting as an Army tutor preparing aspiring candidates for the entrance examinations to the Royal Military College at Sandhurst. Hugh attended St Paul's Cathedral Choir School in Kensington from 1887 to 1893 and then St Paul's School at Hammersmith until 1898. Although he was intelligent enough to acquire an Oxford & Cambridge Certificate, and so be exempted from Responsions at Oxford, his academic performance at school was erratic. One master wrote of him

> Though without much capacity, he has generally done as much as he could: he can write intelligently, knowing more Greek and Latin than the rest of the form, but is not a very consistent worker. There is a long way between his best and his worst work.

Hugh's forte was singing and he was awarded the first prize for this in July 1898. An obituarist wrote of him:

> He was a good musician and came to St Paul's as an experienced chorister. In due time he developed an alto voice of unusual quality, most valuable in the men's quartettes which often marked our concerts. He was also a keen member of the Musical Society and on leaving school gained a place in the renowned Magdalen choir.

Before joining the choir at Magdalen College at Oxford, Hugh was a non-collegiate student – that is he did not live in the College as this would have attracted fees which his family could not support. His elder brother Harold had recently become a clergyman and the family had to support him whilst he had completed his studies at King's College London. Hugh matriculated at New College, Oxford, on 15 October 1898. He then joined the high renowned Magdalen College choir as an Academical Clerk, singing alto on 16 December 1898. Hugh passed the First Public Examination in the Hilary and Trinity Terms of 1899 and three Groups of the Final Pass School in Michaelmas Term 1900. On 2 December 1900 the Tutorial Board agreed to make a special grant of £10 to Hugh to aid his studies which confirms that his family was not well off. On leaving Oxford Hugh became an assistant master at Yardley Preparatory School at Somerfield, near Tonbridge, where he established a very popular and successful "Singing Class" with concerts each summer. He then taught at a school in Sutton Coldfield before teaching at Trent College public school at Long Eaton in Derbyshire from June 1910.

From 25 February 1913 to April 1915, Hugh served as a lieutenant in the Trent College OTC. He had been commissioned into the Junior Division of the OTC on 1 June 1910 and was promoted lieutenant on 25 February 1913. He did not immediately volunteer to join the Army on the outbreak of war but he was commissioned into the MMGS in 2 September 1915. Arriving on the Somme, twelve months later, Hugh almost certainly met his eldest brother Harold who was serving as a chaplain in 47th (2nd London) Division. This Division was also in action on 15 September attacking the German trenches in High Wood, just over one mile north from Delville Wood. As Hugh attempted to get his tank out of the Wood, that same morning, he was wounded by artillery shrapnel but not sufficiently seriously that he was sent to a medical unit. As his tank failed to get into action that day, Hugh was tasked by Frank Summers to support the follow-up attack on Gueudecourt on 16 September but Hugh's tank was not fit for use and only George Pearsall, Gordon Court and Victor Huffam went forward; all three tanks being destroyed in the subsequent action.

Hugh and his crew did however get into action on 7 October, when they supported the attack on the village of Le Sars. The village sat astride the Pozières to Bapaume road behind the Germans most rearmost defensive line. The attack, which was undertaken by 12th Battalion Durham Light Infantry, included the destruction of a German defensive position called the Tangle. Hugh Bell carried out his task to the letter and, having assisted in cleared the Tangle, moved into Le Sars. Sadly, his tank was hit by German artillery fire and disabled. Three of the crewmen were injured by high explosive shell fragments and, after they abandoned it, the tank was destroyed by artillery fire. The capture of the village was considered to be a striking success in the official history; Hugh Bell's crew being also praised for the excellent service in helping to achieve it. On 14 November, during the last tank action of the year, Hugh commanded a reserve tank supporting an attack by 63rd (Royal Naval) Division on a German strongpoint north of Hamel. After Eric Robinson's tank became ditched, Hugh Bell took his tank forward and supported Harry Drader in *Daphne*. The infantry could not make their way forward and suffered dreadful losses but both tanks

Hugh Bell killed in action 3 September 1918. (The Sphere)

pushed on until they became stuck in the appalling ground conditions. Hugh's tank stuck in the middle of no man's land and Harry Drader on the German front line. The tank crews continued to fire on the German machine gun posts using their 6 pdr guns which caused the Germans to surrender in large numbers. As however the Germans did not move out of the redoubt, and the British infantry were along way behind, Hugh and Harry lead their crews forward armed with their revolvers. They cleared the German trenches, as well as a redoubt and succeeded in capturing more than 400 Germans, some of whom had to be winkled out of the deep underground chambers. It was a superb action, which showed just how effective tank crews could be. As a result of his actions at Le Sars and Hamel, Hugh was Mentioned in Despatches.

Hugh joined D Battalion on its formation and served with No 10 Company as a section commander. On 9 April 1917, on the opening day of the Battle of Arras, Hugh led three tanks from 3 Section during an attack on the heavily defended position of Telegraph Hill near Beaurains. The units they supported were from 14th Division, which had also taken part in the attack on Flers on 15 September. Hugh's section gained its objective on this element of the Hindenburg Line without any great difficulty. The following day, Hugh again commanded his section, this time in support of 30th Division – the tanks going forward ahead of the infantry and getting amongst the enemy trenches, patrolling them and keeping the German troops from resisting the British attacks for over five hours. Again, they attacked on 12 April at Henin-sur-Congeul as the British slowly fought their way through the Hindenburg Line to the south east of Arras. It was that day he was promoted acting Captain.

Like many of the experienced section commanders, Hugh was then sent back to the UK to provide the command structure for one of the newly forming battalions. He joined 11th Battalion and, with Herbert Hiscocks and Herbert Elliott who had served with C Company the previous summer, Hugh returned to France on 27 December 1917. He was promoted acting Major on 20 April 1918, the same day Hugh took command of a company. He commanded a company during the Battle of Amiens; the battalion's losses being so great that the unit was reformed with only two sub-units. From the evening of 28 August, Hugh commanded one of these two composite companies, consisting of only nine tanks, in action at Neuville Vitasse for three days. On the afternoon of 2 September 1918, as the battalion fought its way towards Cambrai, he took forward a group of four tanks towards Dury which it was reported that the infantry had failed to hold. Whilst passing through Haucourt the following day at about 1:00 p.m. Hugh was killed by a stray shell. His body was later recovered and he was buried at Cabaret Rouge British Cemetery at Souchez. His loss was reported in *The Sphere*; the picture on the previous page, showing him in MGC uniform which was probably taken before he deployed to France for the first time. His medals were claimed by his brother Harold.

Hugh's tank NCO was probably Corporal William Walden, who was the son of a dairyman John Walden and his wife Anna, who came from Holcombe near Bridport. William was born at Chilcombe in early 1887 and baptised at the local parish church on 20 March 1887. William later moved to Belvedere in Kent where, in 1911, he worked as an assistant teacher employed by the local urban council. His service record has not survived but the Army medal rolls confirm he served with the Tank Corps until the end of the war achieving the rank of acting sergeant. In the autumn of 1920, William married Florence Hall, who was six years his junior, in her home town of Lichfield. The couple settled in Erith in Kent but do not appear to have children. After William died in the local hospital on 18 November 1945, aged only 58, Florence stayed in the area until her death, near Dartford, in summer 1960

Fortunately there is much more information available about the rest of his crew. Gunner James Adamson was the son of a journeyman watchmaker from Cupar in Fifeshire. Although he was only born in 1898, he claimed he had just celebrated his nineteenth birthday when he enlisted into the MMGS in 1915. Being an apprentice motor mechanic he had no difficulty passing the mandatory selection tests at Coventry. Called up on 15 March 1916, James trained at Bisley as a machine gunner and became a member of the Armoured Car Section before he joined D Company. After the first action, he joined D Battalion on 18 November 1916. James undertook training at the Gas school from 25 to 30 January 1917 and then also trained as a driver. I can find no details his section or whether he was in action during the Battle of Arras in April 1917. From 16 to 21 May, James was hospitalised with an ulcer but soon returned to D Battalion. Shortly after the start of the Third Battle of Ypres, he was appointed a Second Class mechanic on 6 August 1917. James must have fought at the Battle of Cambrai as he was sent on leave to UK from 11 to 25 December 1917. In January 1918 James was appointed a First Class tank mechanic. As the German Army pushed the British Army back across the ground captured during the battles of the Somme and Cambrai, D Battalion tried to delay their advance. Gilbert was captured near Epehy on 22 March. From an account given after his release, he was in one of two tanks which deployed forward in heavy mist for two hours without meeting any opposition. As the mist lifted however, the tanks observed the advancing Germans and used their deadly effect. The other tank was hit and all the crewmen killed, James' tank was also hit but not put out of action. As the tank tried to get back, they became surrounded and having made their guns unusable, attempted to reach the British lines on foot. All the crew were however captured.

Initially tasked to move wounded Germans to the rear, as part of the German casualty treatment plans, James was later sent to the German garrison town of Dulmen, between Dusseldorf and Osnabruck, when a POW camp had been established. Initially James was put to work at a colliery but he injured his shoulder which took three months to heal after which, then to use his own words, he was sent to an easy job in a factory. He was paid ten pence a day and "apart from the food life was not too bad". Cigarettes could be bought for only three pence a packet but these "gassed you" and everything else was exceptionally dear. Released from captivity, he returned to Scotland by 8 December. Although he had only volunteered for the duration of the war, James was compulsorily retained in the Army on 1 February 1919. He caught syphilis whilst he was serving at the Tank Corps Depot, and was hospitalised for three weeks, and then treated for a further five weeks. On 4 June, he was demobilised and returned to his family in Cupar. James stayed there for three years before he set off for California. He arrived at Montréal on 1 July 1923 en route for Ventura. There he worked in a jewellery store as a watchmaker; his elder brother Harry joined him in 1925 and they both worked as jewellers. James soon married an English girl from Canterbury, Adelina Pattison, and their only son Douglas was born in 1931. They settled on Mill Drive off Highway 399. Adelina died in December 1957 and was buried at Ivy Lawn Memorial Park. James lived in Ventura for a further ten years until his death on 30 June 1968 when he was buried alongside his wife Adelina.

The other Scotsman in the crew was from Edinburgh. According to Scottish family records, James Brunton was born at 8.00 p.m. on 9 September 1889 at 15 Murdoch Street in the west of the city. He was the eldest son of a cooper, also called James, and his wife Maggie. James Junior was working as a pattern maker when he enlisted into the MMGS on 30 October 1915; two days later, he had started his training at Bisley. Like several of the First Tank Crews, James managed to get home and marry his fiancée before he deployed to France. On 5 August, he married Isabella Russell Marshall from Clerk Street in Loanhead, a small town to the south of Edinburgh. When he returned from leave, James was awarded 3 days Confined to Barracks for failing to attend for a parade; he had been on tank guard beforehand so he possibly had overslept. Posted overseas on 27 August 1916, James was unhurt on 15 September but was wounded during the attack on Le Sars on 7 October. Admitted to 13th Casualty Clearing Section, James was sent to 9th General Hospital at Rouen on 10 October. Fortunately his wounds were not serious and two weeks later was transferred to No 2 Convalescent Camp. Exactly two months after the first action, James was sent back to re-join D Company. He arrived as D Battalion was being formed and, over the winter, James re-trained as a driver and mechanic. His service record does not provide details of the battles in which he fought; however we know he was a member of No 11 Company which means he almost certainly fought at the First Battle of Bullecourt, where nine tanks were knocked out as they supported the Australians attempting to break through the Hindenburg line on 11 April 1917.

James was admitted to hospital during the summer but it is unclear as to the reasons; certainly his wife did not know as she later sought information about it so that she could claim on his insurance. He must have been back with this unit by 10 July as this is when he was appointed paid Lance Corporal on 10 July 17; he was still driving at this stage as he was paid as First Class Tank Mechanic less than a month later. James fought at the Battle of Cambrai and was appointed paid acting Corporal on 24 November 1917; replacing Corporal Frederick who had been injured during the opening actions of the Battle of Cambrai. He was also appointed Tank Mechanic Class 1, with the associated rise in pay and then promoted substantive Corporal on 29 November. This was followed by a period of home leave from 18 to 30 December. James was back with his unit on 1 January 1918, which shows just how good rail communications were at this stage. James stayed with the re-numbered 4th Battalion and served with them during their fight to delay the German advance. He was promoted Sergeant on 29 April 1918, on the death of Sergeant Sydney Chave in action the previous day near Morbeque. James must also have fought through the battles of Amiens and the battles to break the Hindenburg line. On 29 September, he was fighting in support of the 30th US Division when he was injured; his hand being caught between water tins and guide brackets on the roof of the tank. From this description, it would appear that James was commanding the tank from its roof, as it moved across broken ground. The wounds were quite severe; he was immediately taken to the American casualty clearing section and later admitted to the 72nd General Hospital in Trouville. James was not fit for release until 13 December when he was sent to the Tank Corps Reinforcement Depot at Mers-Les-Bains and then back to D Battalion one week later. By now, Christmas leave was underway and James was granted home leave from 27 December until 10 January 1919. He did not return on time owing to his being sick and, as a result his unit started absence procedures. It was soon identified that James had recovered and he was discharged from the Army, without being required to return to France, on 8 February. He returned to his old trade of pattern maker and later became a foreman. He continued to live in Edinburgh until the 1950s when he moved to his wife's hometown of Loanhead. He died there, as a result of throat cancer at 4:30 pm in 14 January 1953 aged sixty-three years.

Most of the crews had men from Birmingham or Coventry and this tank crew was no exception. Walter Bell was born in August 1895 in Kings Norton Birmingham; he was one of sixth children of Arthur Bell, a warehouseman at a boot factory, and his Annie Dawson. Walter was baptized on 21 August at St John's Church in Ladywood. His brothers Ernest later served on *HMS Warspite* and Frank served with Royal Warwickshire Regiment during the Great War. Walter was initially employed as a liner in the cycle manufacturing business but, by the time he enlisted in the MMGS on 20 October 1915 in Birmingham; he was working as a motor fitter. Walter initially trained at Bisley as a machine gunner with E Company but he was posted to D Company on 27 May 16 and deployed overseas on 28 August. He was wounded during the attack on Le Sars, sufficiently seriously to be sent to 10 General Hospital at Étaples. Walter was discharged on 16 October but he did not get back to D Company until 4 November. He then served with No 10 Company of D Battalion and must have fought near Beaurains on the first day of the Battle of Arras. By this time, he was trained as a 6 pdr gunner as well as able to operate Lewis guns. On 23 April 1917, Walter was again in action, under the command of Captain Heady Head. He was again wounded suffering gunshot wounds to his right hand and right thigh when eight tanks attacked north from Henin-sur-Coeur. Walter was so badly injured that he was returned to the UK on 1 May and hospitalised at Dundee until 29 June. Granted leave until 9 July, and categorized as BII medical standard, Walter was posted to the Command Depot, at Catterick, until he was declared fully fit for duty. Rebadged to the Tank Corps, he was posted to the Tank Depot at Wareham on 19 September. Walter served initially with N Battalion on 8 October and then joined 15th Battalion after which he returned to France. He was appointed acting Lance Corporal on 24 August with that unit, this was probably as a result of the casualties experienced during the Battle of Amiens. He was sent back to the UK on 16 October, where he joined 19th Battalion – this was another newly formed unit expected to be deployed to France to take place in the 1919 campaign. Walter was re-graded A1; that is fully fit for duty, and promoted to the rank of Sergeant by the time of the Armistice. He was discharged in March 1919 and returned to his home in Leslie Road Edgbaston, where he lived until 1935, when he moved to Gravelly Hill. He died the following summer, aged only forty-one.

Gunner Arthur Branfield was born on 27 April 91 at Bascote Heath near Coventry but, by the time he was ten, his family had moved to Hornsey in North London. He became a clerk and was married at twenty-one, on Boxing Day 1912, to a schoolteacher's daughter named Dorothy Watt at St John the Evangelist Church in Wembley. The couple moved to St Albans and Arthur worked as a commercial traveller employed by William Hoare and Co of Basinghill Street in the city of London. Although he enlisted on 15 December 1915, Arthur was not mobilised until 28 March the following year. He joined the MGC Armoured Car Section at Bisley on 4 April 1916 and transferred to the Heavy Section MGC exactly one month later. Arthur was posted to D Company on 27 May and trained at Elveden as part of No 1 Section. Whilst there, like James Brunton, he was charged with failing to report for a parade, following tank guard duty, on 11 August and was sentenced, by Lieutenant Harold Mortimore, to be Confined to Barracks for three days. He deployed to France on 27 August.

Although Arthur escaped injury at Delville Wood on 15 September, he was like James Brunton, wounded in the left hand by small arms fire on 7 October – this almost certainly means he was serving with Hugh Bell and the rest of the original D2 crew at Le Sars. He returned to the UK on the Hospital Ship *Brighton* and was treated at Western General Hospital in Newport in Monmouthshire until 16 January 1917. When Arthur was posted to No 20 Company in the recently formed G Battalion on 2 February 1917, he was found to be suffering from ringworm and was hospitalised. He was then posted to the Tank Depot at Worgret Camp, near Wareham, where he served until 21 November when he was posted to HQ J Battalion which was in the final stages of preparing to deploy to France. Arthur returned to France on 19 December 1917, with several former D Company officers including Captains Harry Drader and Eric Robinson, and served with now renamed 10th Tank Battalion in France until the end of the war. He was granted leave from 14 December and was discharged two weeks later, having received an offer of re-employment with his old company. Sadly his marriage to Dorothy was dissolved in 1925 after she had an affair; eight years later Arthur married Mary Ann Brufton in St Albans and they later settled in Dorking where Arthur died on 7 March 1960.

The final two crewmen also survived the war. Gunner John Letts was a shop assistant from Plymouth. Born in May 1897, he volunteered to join the Devonshire Royal Garrison Artillery on 27 September 1915 perhaps hoping to avoid overseas service. John was immediately embodied into the Regular Army and then transferred to the MGC. Like Walter Bell, he was initially posted to E Company HS MGC then to D Company on 27 May 1916. According to the notebook of D Company's adjutant, John was a replacement for Gunner Eric Forward who did not go into action on 15 September. John was transferred to D Battalion on its formation and served with the unit for the duration of his service. John probably fought at Arras, then in the Ypres Salient and at Cambrai, after which he was granted UK leave from 16 to 30 December, returning to duty with his unit on 1 January 1918. John was serving as a private with B Company of 4th Battalion during the German offensive known as the Kaiserschlacht when he again went into action. To quote the citation:

at Chapel Hill, south of Gouzeaucourt on March 21, when all his crew, with the exception of the NCO, had become casualties, he went into action with his tank on two occasions. He combined the duties of second and third drivers in addition to instructing the infantrymen who were acting as Lewis gunners how to fire from a tank. Had it not been for this man's assistance and keenness it would not have been possible for the NCO to have taken the tank into action and to have driven off the enemy infantry with casualties.

John gained more driving expertise and was appointed as a first driver. He went into action again on the opening day of the Battle of Amiens, 8 August 1918, and was awarded a bar to the Military Medal. Again, to quote a medal citation:

this man behaved in a most cool and collected manner when in action on the morning of August 8, 18. After several casualties had occurred and the officer was firing the gun himself, this man (under the directions of his officer) continued to act as first driver and crew NCO, maintaining most accurate direction. After the tank was knocked out near Lemaire Wood he rendered great assistance to his officer, though himself wounded by being blown in the air by the explosion of a second shell.

The injuries to this chest and back resulted in his being evacuated to the American hospital at Le Tréport. He recovered and was posted back to 4th Battalion on 29 September. John was promoted corporal in place of William Hogarth who had served in tank D10 on 15 September 1916. John served with 4th Battalion during the Final Advance, as a 1st class Tank Mechanic, and after the Armistice. John returned to the UK on 12 January 1919; the award of the bar to his MM being published on 21 January. There was clearly an administrative error in France after William had returned to the UK as the unit sought the assistance of the Plymouth police in locating him – they reported that he has been demobilised. John declined to have his Military Medal and Bar presented and the medal was received by post on 10 March 1919; his other medals received on 29 June 1921. Two years later, John married Dorothy Hooper in Plymouth; their son John being born in Devonport in the autumn 1924. The family settled at 45 Fisher Street in Stoke, Plymouth and John Junior married Barbara Davies in 1951. John Senior died the following year, aged fifty-five, at the South Devon and East Plymouth Hospital on 9 February 1952.

The final crewman was the tank's driver acting Corporal Ernest Keats of the Army Service Corps. Born in Tincleton, Dorset on 31 March 1887, Ernest was the fourth child, and third son, of a carter named James Keats and his wife Rosina. In 1891 and 1901 the family was living at the village of Moreton which is about 3 miles to the west of what is now Bovington camp. As a young man, James worked as an agricultural labourer but he soon moved to Weymouth. In 1911 he was living at 10 Royal Terrace, working as a coachman for the Lithegow family. In 1915, he joined the ASC as a Mechanical Transport driver. Trained at Grove Park MT Depot, in London, he does not appear to have served overseas before he joined 711 MT Company which was attached to the tanks in July 1916. He was not the original driver for the tank crew; he replaced Private Lee on 15 September. I cannot be certain but he probably fought at Le Sars with the rest of the crew. Ernest served on with the tanks and was Mentioned in Despatches on 15 May 1917, presumably for his actions with D Battalion during the Battle of Arras. In July 1918, he was serving with Capt Heady Head in C Company of 4th Battalion as the NCO in a Mark V tank. After the war, Ernest returned to Weymouth and, in the spring of 1931, married Agnes Churchill who was then 38. They did not have children and lived together in Bradford Road for most of their married life. Agnes died in the summer of 1960; Ernest stayed in Weymouth where he died aged eighty in early 1968.

Tank Crew D19

Captain Stephen Sellick, who commanded all ten tanks tasked to assist the assault on Flers, was born on 6 July 1873 in Kings Lynn, Norfolk. The son of an income tax supervisor, Stephen was educated at the City of London School and then at the University College of North Wales at Bangor. He left England as a young man and worked in the Far East as an engineer. On 23 October 1903, he married Madge Thomas in Hong Kong; sadly she died shortly afterwards. In July 1905, Stephen travelled to Honolulu on holiday; whilst there he met a Californian woman from Benecia named May Wade and they married that same year in Hawaii. They settled in the port of Shanghai where, in 1909, Stephen was commissioned into the Engineer Company of the multi-national Shanghai Volunteer Corps. He returned to the UK in 1916, on leave from his company, and imme-diately volunteered for a commission in the British Army. Transferred into MMGS on 18 March, as one of the more experienced officers, Stephen was appointed to command No 3 Section.

Having become ditched on 15 September, and failing to get into action the next day, Stephen was next tasked to go into action with Heady Head on 24 September but the tanks were not called for. Stephen was wounded in the left leg, two days later near Gueudecourt. This was probably at the same time that Charles Storey earned his DSO by singlehandedly capturing a long stretch of German trench and dozens of prisoners. Stephen's injury was sufficiently serious that he was evacuated to England on 6 October and then sent to the Convalescent Home for Officers, which had been established at Queen Victoria's former residence at Osborne House on the Isle of Wight. After a shell fragment was removed from his left knee, he was sent on leave for a month on 15 October. During this time, Stephen stayed with his wife who had also returned to London. Whilst there, he wrote to Jake Glaister, congratulating him on the award of his Distinguished Conduct Medal. Once fully fit, Stephen was sent to the Foster's factory at Lincoln to learn more about the engineering aspects of tanks. He was then posted to the MGC Training Centre at Bisley, on 14 April 1917 as a staff officer and later appointed Major (Technical training) at the Training Centre at Bovington. After this he served in a variety of technical staff appointments within the Engineer Branch of the Tank Corps, including at the Central Workshops at Erin and the following year with the Inspectorate of Machinery. On 30 September 1918, Stephen joined the Mechanical Warfare Department at the War Office in London. He served on after the Armistice and did not relinquish his commission until 9 November 1920.

Stephen returned to Shanghai and worked throughout the Far East for a further twelve years making periodic trips back to the UK for leave. In October 1923, he arrived from New York with his wife May and, whilst staying in London, claimed his medals. In 1933, the couple settled in London. They initially lived at 27 Roehampton Close, near the Golf course for two years, but then lived at Belvedere Court on the Upper Richmond Road. Stephen died at his home on 14 October 1947; May dying two years later at her sister's home in San Francisco.

Sellick's second in command on 15 September was a Coventry man, Corporal Charles Luck. He was ten years older than most of his crewmates, being born at Rugby in the summer of 1884. Charles was the eldest son of a bricklayer, and he was christened at St Andrew's Church on 17 October 1884. By 1901, the family were living at Earlsdon to west of Coventry and in the summer of 1909, he married Ethel Bromfield who was a year his junior. From his service number, it is likely that Charles originally served in the MMGS. After the first actions, Charles served on with D Battalion and re-trained as a driver. Promoted to the rank of sergeant, Charles fought at the Battle of Arras where he was awarded the Military Medal. This happened whilst serving with No 10 Company, on 23 April, whilst fighting through the Hindenburg Line, when he "drove his tank with great skill and judgment from 4:45 A.M. until 12 noon under severe shell and machine-gun fire, thereby setting a fine example of gallantry and devotion to duty." There were two attacks that day and I have not been able to work out in which section he was serving.

Charles was later selected for officer training and subsequently commissioned into the Tank Corps on 29 March 1918. Returning to France on 8 July with 15th Battalion, he commanded crew O6 in "Omniscient" during the Battle of Amiens in support of the 4th and 5th Australian Divisions. He was awarded the Military Cross "for conspicuous gallantry, good work, and devotion to duty during the operations on August 8 and 9, '18. On August 8, after attaining his objective and dropping his machine-gun personnel on the Blue Line north of Harbonnières, he went almost a mile ahead of the British Line, clearing the ground for the cavalry, who were held up by machine-gun fire, thus enabling them to advance. On August 9, during the attack on the village of Framerville, he handled his tank in such a masterful way that his men were able to inflict many casualties on the enemy and destroy several hostile machine-guns. His skilful manoeuvring and careful watching of enemy shell fire saved his tank from getting hit during the heavy shelling to which he was subjected. On his way back to rallying point, after attaining his objective, on receiving a message that a hostile counter-attack was imminent, he at once returned and patrolled the line for another half hour, engaging the enemy with effect. When 400 yards from our front line on his journey back to rallying point he met a disabled tank. Under direct observation of the enemy and considerable machine-gun and shell fire he got this tank into tow, refilled with petrol, and towed the former back to rallying point. He set a great example to his crew and inspired them with confidence and enthusiasm under very arduous conditions".

Charles fought on with the Battalion during the Final Advance and, shortly after the Armistice, was appointed section commander and promoted captain on 22 November 1918; a role he undertook until 1 February 1919. After that, he returned to Earlsdon and lived there for the rest of his life, becoming a successful building contractor. His daughter Betty was born in 1922. Sadly Ethel died in 1944 at Meriden, at the age of fifty-nine but Charles did not remarry. He died on 17 November 1958, aged seventy-six, at the River Park Nursing Home in Leamington Spa.

I cannot definitely identify Gunner JW Brown but he could well have been John Watson Brown who served in the MMGS, then in the Tank Corps and was later commissioned into the Royal Flying Corps. John was born on 12 September 1896; near West Ashford in Kent and died in Dover in early 1985. Jim Blackmore's service history survived the Blitz and he also appears in print elsewhere. Gunner Jim Blackmore was born at Broadclyst, to the northeast of Exeter, in November 1889. The son of a gardener, he was bought up at Holnicote House near Selworthy. On 1 September 1910 Jim was married, aged only twenty-one, at the Registry Office in Williton to Winifred Ley; their elder daughter, also named Winifred, was born the following year. Later that year, at the time of the census, the three were living with Jim's father in law, a master mariner, at Luccombe near Porlock. Their younger daughter Una was born on 18 February 1913.

On 11 December 1915, when he enlisted, Jim was a motor engineer working in Porlock High Street. He indicated that he wished to serve with Mechanical Transport branch of the ASC; however, he was allocated to the recently formed MGC (Motors). Placed on the Army Reserve for four months, he was mobilised on 22 March. He embarked for France with the final D Company party on 2 September and, after the first actions, was transferred to D Battalion when it formed in November. Granted UK leave in September 1917, which was most unusual, Jim remained throughout the war with same unit (later 4th Battalion) but was never promoted. His records are sparse but there is one entry which shows he was reported absent on leave on 28 September 1918, having been due to return on 21 September. That the Battalion waited for seven days before commencing action reveals that delays were not unusual – if nothing else it was difficult for soldiers to find out where their unit was during the advances through the Hindenburg line. Jim eventually rejoined on 3 October 1918 but there is no record of disciplinary action being taken which indicates that he was not considered to have deliberately delayed his return. Jim returned to the UK on 3 February 1919 for demobilisation at Fovant in Wiltshire and was transferred to Z Class Reserve three days later. After the war, Jim took over the running of the Central Garage at Porlock and also established a cycle shop in the village. He played a full part in local parish life including being a handbell ringer in the church band. He also was a member of the local fire brigade being the senior officer at the beginning of the Second World War. He died aged fifty-two, at Minehead Hospital on 29 May 1942. His wife Winifred then left the village and did not return although Una lived in the village for many years afterwards.

Gunner Henry Chapman was born in York in March 1889. He lived as a young man at East Retford, where he fathered a child in 1908, but did not marry the mother. This was a most unusual occurrence and which resulted in him being taken to court to provide for their child. The following year he married Frances Scott on 27 November at Hatton Parish Church in Lincolnshire. When he was attested on 11 December 1915 at Coleshill, Henry was the head gamekeeper living at The Old Hall in Packington Park in Warwickshire. He was placed on the Army Reserve until 1 May 1915 when he was mobilised; by this time his wife was living at 10 Norris Street in Lincoln. Four months later, Henry left Elveden having received what can only be considered scant training. Two days later he was in France and 12 days later in action. We do not know if Henry fought again in the later actions of 1916 but he stayed with D Company as they prepared for the attacks designed to push the German out of the Beaumont-Hamel area. He was hospitalised, having scalded his left foot on 25 October whilst the company was based at Auchonvillers. In the subsequent report by the Adjutant, Graham Woods, Henry was helping two cooks when a pot of boiling water was tipped on his foot. The wound was considered trivial by the medical officer and he was back with D Company three days later. Henry then served on with D Battalion and certainly fought at the Battle of Cambrai as he was awarded UK leave between 16 and 30 December 1917. Henry re-joined the renamed 4th Battalion Tank Corps and fought with them throughout the Battle of Amiens and the Final Advance, being promoted Corporal on 26 October. Three days later, he was sent on UK leave. This was due to end of 12 November but the leave was extended by one week, presumably because of the Armistice. Back with 4th Battalion, Henry served on until 6 February 1919 when he returned to Grantham for demobilisation, then settled back at Norris Street in Lincoln. Sadly he then is totally lost from sight.

The same is not fortunately true of Gunner John Cameron Tolson. Born in Workington in late 1894, John's father William was an iron turner. John, who was the youngest of three children, became a joiner; he enlisted at Coventry and joined the Armoured Car Section MGC after 1 April 1916. His records show he was wounded twice which he later confirmed to Victor Huffam in1956, one of these must have been in the first tank actions and sufficiently serious to merit his evacuation to England. Whilst at home, he married Christina Barton at Cockermouth. John Senior returned to France and joined No 11 Company of D Battalion. He fought at the 1st Battle of Bullecourt in Captain Field's section, which was destroyed by the German artillery. His oldest son John was born shortly afterwards. He next fought at 3rd Ypres in *Dop Doctor*; his commander was Second Lieutenant GV Butler and their tank was destroyed in the attack on Poelcapelle on 9 October. On 20 November, this time in *Dop Doctor II* and again under command of Lieutenant Butler, John was involved in the attack on Flesquières. The tank was destroyed on the southwest approaches of the village by direct enemy fire. John showed great bravery in the after-action for which he was awarded the Military Medal. The citation states that

> when his tank had been put out of action by two direct hits and three of his crew were wounded, (he) displayed marked gallantry and initiative in organising parties to bring in wounded from several tanks which had been knocked out. On three separate occasions he went back under extremely heavy and practically point-blank machine-gun fire to dress and carry in the wounded. With utter disregard for personal safety, and entirely on his own initiative, he undoubtedly saved several lives.

John was promoted corporal and served with the renamed C Company of the 4th Tank Battalion under Major H S M Baird. John was badly wounded during the Kaiserschlacht when his tank was destroyed, and Wilfred Jaques killed, on the morning of 21 March 1918 near Herdicourt. John was evacuated to England and was being treated at St John's Hospital at Cheltenham when he wrote to Wilfred's widow describing his friend's death. Despite his injuries, John made a full recovery and, after the war, Christina and John had two more sons; William born in the summer of 1920 and Gordon some eighteen months later. The family later settled at Dykelands, 106 Main Road at Seaton. Sadly, their eldest son John died in the Second World War. He was a RASC corporal serving in the Tobruk area and died on 2 February 1941. In 1956, following the BBC TV programme *"Find the Link"* John Senior made contact with Victor Huffam and provided a brief resume of his service which is how we know where and when served. John was one of few D Company crewmen who attended the 50th Anniversary Dinner at Caxton hall, in London, on 15 September 1966. He died the following year, aged seventy-four, and his medals are now held by the Tank Museum.

Pte James Westmacott, who was also a MGC gunner, was born in 1886 at East Knighton, not far from the future home of the Tank Corps at Bovington. The eldest son of a farmer Harry Westmacott and his wife Lucy, James had two elder sisters as well as seven younger siblings. James' father died in 1907 by which time he had started to work in the family business. By 1911, he was running the dairy at Broompound farm near Moreton. James joined the MGC in 1916 and, although his service record has been lost, the local electors' register shows that, by 1918, he was serving with 443 Agricultural Company Labour Corps, which was based at Dorchester, and he was living at nearby Skippet. This change of Corps probably came about because James' ill-health whilst serving from the Tanks and he had been sent home to assist the war effort by improving food production. Shortly after he was demobilised, James was farming at 1919 living at Snelling farm near Tonerspiddle. Eight years later, he was farming at Hurst farm at Moreton; less than three miles from Bovington. James did not marry until 1943, his wife Ida Inkpen was a farmers' daughter and fifty years old when the couple married. Sadly their marriage was not long lived; James died aged fifty eight on 12 March 1945 at the Portway hospital in Weymouth which was only a month after his own mother had died. His wife Ida survived until she was seventy-eight, dying in 1971.

Unusually the service record of the tank's driver has survived. Thomas Hinds was born in Liverpool on 26 February 1896, the oldest son of a cab driver. Thomas had three older sisters and two younger brothers and the family lived in Edge Hill. When he joined up aged nineteen on 15 April 1915, Thomas was already a trained driver. Just five feet two inches tall, he joined the ASC and was sent to the Grove Park MT Depot in London. Within a fortnight, Thomas was posted to 52 Mechanical Transport (MT) Company ASC; this was one of the original six ASC MT companies and had been re-rolled to be a Caterpillar tractor unit. He deployed to France 3 August 1915 and was later transferred to 344 Company ASC. When drivers were required for the tanks, Thomas was sent back to the UK and trained at Elveden as a member of 711 Company. He deployed back to France from Avonmouth on 31 August, accompanying the tanks. After the first actions on 15 September, Thomas stayed with D Company and when the new tank battalions were formed, volunteered to transfer to the MGC Heavy Branch. He was given a new number in common with all the 711 Company men but did not stay with the tanks for a long time.

On 22 June Thomas was posted to the HQ MGC in France as a private soldier where he served for 9 months. He later served with 50th Battalion MGC, which formed on 1 March 1918, and was reported Killed in Action on 27 May. This was opening day of the Battle of the Aisne and the final large-scale German attempt to defeat the Allies before the arrival of the U.S. Army in France. Amongst those defenders were men from 50th Division, who had been sent south from Flanders to recuperate from earlier fighting around Ieper. Fortunately, the initial news that Thomas had been killed in action was untrue but he was seriously injured and had been captured at Roucy, several miles from the front. He let his mother know he was safe using a post card sent from No 1 Camp

Hospital at Germersheim. A subsequent German report sent to the British Authorities confirmed that he had an injury to chest and gunshot wounds to upper left arm. After the Armistice Thomas was released and arrived at Dover on 15 December 1918.

Discharged from the Army five days later, as no longer physically fit for war service, he was awarded a forty per cent disability pension for one year worth eleven shillings a week. He remained in the Liverpool area, marrying Florence Jones on 5 August 1923 at St John the Baptist Church in Tuebrook. Florence and Thomas had three children, May born in 1926; Doris born in 1929 and Thomas on 2 June 1930 and who died aged only fifteen on 10 June 1945. Thomas later moved to Widnes, where he died aged seventy-sex in 1971.

D15

The final tank crew of the central group, D15, successfully crossed no man's land on 15 September but was hit by German artillery as it crossed the German front line. The shell went straight through the front of the tank, wounding the skipper, Lieutenant Jack Bagshaw and the driver, Private Albert Rowe as well as wrecking the steering gear. As its crew abandoned the burning vehicle, the Germans defenders in the Switch Line opened fire. Cyril Coles and Charles Hoban were killed immediately and several others wounded including Tom Wilson died of his wounds seven days later. The tank was never recovered although the guns were salvaged and Cyril Coles and Charles Hoban's bodies were buried close by.

The skipper, Jack Bagshaw was born in Uttoxeter on 3 June 1896. Christened John Lionel, Jack was the youngest child and fourth son of William Bagshaw who was an auctioneer and valuer. Jack's father also owned the Red Lion pub in the Market Place and was later Chairman of Uttoxeter Urban District Council. Jack was educated at Denstone College in Staffordshire and served with the OTC before becoming a clerk with the family firm. Following his enlistment on 20 May 15 at Lichfield, Jack was commissioned into MMGS on 10 October 1915 and initially served with 20 Battery. On 15 September 1916, Jack was wounded in his right elbow and arm and was evacuated back to England; his case was reviewed by a Medical Board at Denmark Hill in early October 16. Granted sick leave until 23 November; his wounds had fully healed by time of a Medical Board convened at Lichfield on 2 December after which he reported for duty at Bovington on 9 December. There he joined E Battalion which was the first unit of twenty-five to be formed, trained and deployed for operations from the newly established tank training centre.

Appointed a section commander, and promoted captain, Bagshaw returned to France on 26 June 1917. Wilfred Bion, the eminent psychoanalyst who served with him in No 14 Company, recorded in his War Memoires. "The section commander was Capt Bagshaw, a very easy-going and hopelessly slack fellow who had been with the original tanks. He was good hearted but weak-minded and incompetent and got in the wrong set". This is an interesting comment by Bion given that Bagshaw was only fifteen months Wilfred's elder. After training at Wailly, they deployed to Hazebrouk arriving on 31 July – the day the Third Battle of Ypres started. We do not have details of their early actions in No 8 Section, but on 20 September, when moving up to their start points, Jack did not lead his section forward, directing Bion to take the lead vehicle whilst he remained in the rear tank. Bion obviously felt this was not what was expected of his section commander and there is no doubt that Bion, who was taking part in his first action, had a point. There is no mention of Jack in the action itself; the tanks did get to the start line despite the thick fog but all ditched either on the way to the objective or on the way back.

One cannot, however, doubt Bagshaw's commitment to his soldiers at the end of the month. On 28 September, he was in action during the assault on Hill 37 east of Douchy Farm. He was commanding his tanks on foot and bought a number of crewmen out of action after their tank *Eileen* had been ditched and their commander fatally wounded. Jack Bagshaw again commanded the section at Cambrai, when it was fighting its way into the village of Flesquières. When the battalion was fighting to hold the Germans back, on 22 March 1918, his section was destroyed and Jack lost his acting rank of captain. Jack was posted to the Reinforcement Depot until he joined No 2 Gun Carrier Company on 27 May, when he took command of A Section which carried out resupply for 7 Tank Battalion. He later served with 2 Field Company and, after a short leave following the Armistice, Jack was posted to 2nd Field Battalion and took part in the battlefield clearances. He then moved to the 6th Tank Carrier Unit and served in the BAOR from 6 April 1919. He relinquished his commission on 19 September 1920. Granted the rank of Captain, Jack returned to Uttoxeter when he joined the family firm. In 1927 Jack became a partner, the same year he married Anne Willeter in Steyning Sussex. Their only daughter Suzanna was born in 1931. Jack worked on as an auctioneer, expanding the family firm which is still operating, until he died on 13 February 1962.

Jack's second in command was Lance Corporal Charley Jung. Born at Parkstone in Dorset in 1889, Charley was the youngest of five children of a Silesian brick maker Friedrich and his English born wife Sarah. The three eldest children were born in Breslau; the eldest children being named Fritz and Friedel. By 1891, the family had moved to Alderholt on the Hampshire Dorset border: twenty years later they were living at Shirley in western Southampton where Friedrich had set up business as a sausage skin maker. Charley's service record has not survived so details about his war service are scant. He joined the MMGS in the first week of April 1916 and was promoted Lance Corporal prior to deployment. He was Mentioned in Despatches in January 1917, one of only eight from C and D Companies but I have been unable to identify why. He served on in the Tank Corps and probably fought at Cambrai as he married Bridget Enright at Alverstoke in Hampshire in early 1918. He reached the rank of Corporal before he was demobilised, according to his medal index card, but no more is recorded. Bridget and Charley had a son, Terence, who was born in the summer of 1920 and a daughter Sheila in 1925. The family sausage skills company expanded during the 1930s and Charley moved to Salisbury to set up an outlet. Terence joined the RAF Volunteer Reserve, at the start of the Second World War, and served as a sergeant pilot. He died on 14 January 1942 near Barnstaple and was buried in the Devizes Road cemetery in Salisbury. In the early 1950s, Charley was still working as a sausage casing manufacturer at 67A Rampart Road in Salisbury whilst the original family firm still in business in Millbrook. Later the family settled at 18 Romsey Road in Eastleigh where Charley died on 3 September 1955. Shortly afterwards, Bridget moved to Exmouth and lived there until her death in 1964.

Charley may have chatted about his early years with Gunner Cyril Coles who was bought up close to Parkstone. Cyril was born on 9 March 1893 and bought up at Creekmoor Mill at Canford where his family had worked for five generations. He was baptised at the Skinner Street Independent Church in Poole on 23 June 1893 where his family had also worshipped for many generations. Cyril worked at the family mill on leaving school but his education did not finish then for he was a member of the pastor's Morning Class until he was at least twenty

Cyril's younger brother, Donald who was a chauffeur, enlisted into the ASC in September 1915 and drove Studebaker ambulances on the Salonika front. Unlike Donald, Cyril's service record has not survived but *The Motor Cycle* confirms he enlisted into the MMGS during the second week of April 1916 whilst living in Wimborne. Cyril was killed by small arms fire, after his tank was hit by German artillery on 15 September, and he tried to make his way back to safety. Initially buried close to the tank, Cyril's body was moved to Bulls Road Cemetery on the eastern outskirts of Flers after the Armistice. He is also commemorated on the War Memorial at Broadstone, at the local parish church and also at the Skinner Street United Reformed Church where his portrait was recently discovered. Cyril's loss was also tangibly commemorated in the family. His younger brother Donald, who survived the war and married Adie Stevens in 1924, named his only son Cyril and the genealogist Caroline Gurney, who is related to Cyril, believes that her father, born in 1921, was given the middle name Cyril in his memory.

The Pastor's Morning Class 1912. (Skinner Street Chapel)

Cyril Coles.
(Skinner Street Chapel)

The other immediate fatality was Charles Hoban. Born at Kenilworth in autumn 1887, he was named after his father who was a valet. Charles had a younger brother Cecil as well as three sisters, Margaret, Mabel and Leila. Bought up in Leamington Spa, Charles was working as a shop assistant in a gentleman's outfitters in 1911 and was boarding at 17 Rosefield Street with a 71 year old widow. The following year, he married Caroline Collins; tragically their only son, Charles, who was born in early 1915, died as an infant. Charles Senior was living at 16 Cherry Street in Warwick, when he enlisted on the same day as Charley Jung but otherwise there is nothing else known about his service. Charles' brother Cecil was killed in action during the Battle of the Somme on 25 July 1916. Cecil was serving with 4th Battalion Seaforth Highlanders and his body is buried at No 2 Cemetery near Serre. Charles must have heard of his brother's death whilst he was training at Elveden before he deployed to France. Charles' own body was buried close by the tank but his grave was later lost. His life is commemorated at the Thiepval memorial and on the war memorial at Warwick.

There was a third fatality from amongst the crew who died of his wounds. Gnr Tom Wilson was born on 17 September 1888 at Loughrigg near Grasmere in the English Lake District. Known as *Tippo*, he was the eldest son of Tom Wilson and his wife Annie Hamblin who ran a family business of joiners, builders, undertakers and haulage contractors. When his younger brother John was born in 1891, *Tippo* was looked after by his grandparents; his grandfather John also being a journeyman joiner. His parents had two further sons, Charles and Maurice. In 1901, *Tippo* was living with his widowed grandmother at 95 Field Side in Grasmere; ten years later, he had joined the family firm and become a joiner. He was involved in the operation of the firm's sawmill and other associated woodworking machinery. These were powered by a system of belts, shafts and pullies driven by a gas oil powered engine which *Tippo* would have maintained and which probably accounts for the ease with which he passed the trade test, on 26 November 1915, required of all those seeking to join the MMGS. After he was wounded on 15 September, *Tippo* was evacuated from the battlefield but not as far as the main hospitals near the coast. This may indicate he was expected to return to return to his unit after treatment. However, he died of his wounds on 22 September at a casualty clearing station near Mericourt-L'Abbe, to the east of Albert. *Tippo* was subsequently buried at Heilly Station Cemetery; his death was announced in the *Westmoreland Gazette* on 30 September and the accompanying photo shows he wore a moustache; this was most unusual amongst the First Tank Crews. His loss was commemorated at St Oswald's Church in Grasmere and he was not only mourned by his family and also Dorothy Harrison, probably his fiancée, who was granted probate in his will.

Sadly, nothing is known of Gunner Arthur Smith, who was also wounded on 15 September, other than he later served in the Tank Corps as a private soldier and survived the war. Gunner Charles Bond, a fellow crewman, died before the war ended. Charles, who was born at Wembdon, near Bridgwater in the autumn of 1888 was the son of a bootmaker. He was baptised on 15 November at the local parish church. As a young man he moved to Cardiff where he worked as a jewelers' assistant and then later moved to Bournemouth where he established a jewellery business. He enlisted in the Army at Southampton on 11 December 1915, with the aim of being a despatch rider in the MMGS. Placed on the Army Reserve, he was mobilised on 10 March and was medically examined at Coventry on 11 March, his record shows that he had green eyes, brown hair and was five feet eight inches tall before. Sent to Bisley for training, he joined D Company on 27 May and deployed to France on 1 September 1916. After his tank was hit on 15 September, Charles was initially reported Missing in Action but five days later, he returned to his unit at Green Dump. Captain Graham Woods' notebook records he had been taken with a New Zealand officer to the Advanced Dressing Station, having been wounded by small arms fire, and was then sent to a hospital near Albert. Charles was soon however sufficiently well to walk back to the D Company forward base which was south west of Longueval. There is no record of his being in action again but, by the middle of October, he was admitted to hospital suffering from trench fever. This was as a result of the wet conditions in which the Tank Companies were living and Charles was so ill he was evacuated to England on 22 October 1916. After a month's treatment at the City of London military hospital, in Lower Clapton, Charles was sent to Eastbourne for a further month's convalescence. He was released on 21 December 1916, having been declared fit for duty, and after Christmas leave, he reported to Bovington where he joined G Battalion on 8 January 1917. Charles made friends with Gunner Leslie Wray who later served with E Battalion and they two men kept in contact when Leslie deployed overseas. Charles was posted to the Depot Battalion on 3 March 1917; this is probably because he was ill. He did not return to active service as, on 23 August 1917, a Medical Board determined he had tuberculosis having previously suffered from measles and recommended that he be treated in a sanatorium. On 13 September 1917, Charles was discharged from the Army as no longer being physically fit for war service. He returned to Wembdon and was awarded the Silver War Badge. He died almost exactly one year later, the *Bridgwater Mercury* reporting on 18 September 1918 that he had been wounded and subsequently died at home of tuberculosis. The link to his service was clearly also seen by his community and, as a result, Charles life is commemorated on the Bridgwater war memorial.

The final member of the crew was the driver Private Albert Rowe. Born on 15 May 1889, in North West Kensington, Albert was the second son of a carpenter. Working as a motor mechanic, in Peckham, Albert had enlisted as an ASC special reservist before the outbreak of war and was called up on 10 August 1914 but unusually did not deploy overseas. He married Mary Bentley on 1 August 1915 at St George's Parish Church in Southwark and their eldest son Albert was born in May 1916. Posted to 711 (MT) Company, Albert deployed to France until 1 September 1916 and, after the first action, was admitted to 11 Stationary Hospital at Rouen suffering from shell shock. He was evacuated back to the UK on 22 September and taken on strength of 621 Company ASC; this being the MT Reception and Discharge Depot at Bulford. Having recovered, Albert was posted to HQ Company Heavy Artillery MT at Bulford on 1 July 1917 when he was appointed acting Corporal. Three weeks later, he returned to France and was attached to I Battalion Tank Corps. Ten days later, Albert was attached to HQ Tank Corps where he served for the next nine months; then he served with HQ 3 Tank Brigade until after the Armistice. On 31 January 1919 Albert was sent to Ireland with 17th Armoured Car Battalion as part of the internal security force. The following month, he caught influenza whilst serving in Dublin with 614 MT Company ASC. Albert was hospitalised but fortunately suffered no long term ill effects. He claimed a war pension whilst serving at Marlborough Barracks in Dublin but this was dismissed as he was in A1 medical condition. Discharged the next month, Albert returned to Peckham where he and Mary bought up another six children. Sadly, Mary died in 1937 but Albert lived for a further 30 years, dying in Hillingdon in 1968.

10

Not too busy for breakfast

Three tanks were allocated to support 41st Division to take the ground to the north and west of Flers. The tanks were known collectively as "F group" and manned by tank crews D7, D16 and D18. D7 became ditched as it made its way towards the German front line and was later recovered; the other two tanks successfully made their way to their final objective (see map 8). This pair got back to their start point with no signification damage although one officer was wounded whilst rescuing a wounded New Zealand infantry officer.

Tank Crew D7

The male tank No 742, manned by Crew D7 and commanded by Lieutenant Alfred Enoch, crossed the British front line and led the other tanks across no man's land. Contemporary accounts of the action say that the tank became stuck as she made her way through the British jumping off trenches; however the skipper of tank crew D16 later wrote that the tank started to spew smoke as she reached the German front line and the crew got out.

The tank was driven back to the Flers Road by the ASC driver Sidney Barnes. From there the 711 Company ASC mechanics, who had positioned themselves in the British front line trenches, recovered it and ensure it was made fit for action. The D7 crew was tasked to support an attack northwards from Flers the next day but the tank became ditched on the way to the start-point and the crew did not get into action. Most of them were however saw plenty of action nine days later north of Martinpuich.

Lieutenant Alfred Enoch was the elder son of a Midlands house finisher Will Enoch who later became a furniture dealer. Born on 25 June 1893 at Willenhall near Wolverhampton, and christened at the parish church on 19 July, Alfred was one of eleven children, seven of whom survived. Before going to university, Alfred studied art at a local college but, following the outbreak of war, he abandoned his engineering degree and enlisted. On 7 April 1915, aged twenty-one, Alfred was commissioned into the Sherwood Foresters and then served with 14th Battalion, at Brocton Camp on Cannock Chase, providing trained soldiers for the other battalions. In January 1916, Alfred married Eva Compston Pile in Sunderland; she was four years older than Alfred and came from Monkwearmouth. Alfred was promoted temporary lieutenant on 18 March 1916, and it was about this time he volunteered to undertake "a secret and dangerous duty". He joined the Heavy Section MGC at Bisley after which he carried out tank training at Elveden. His later told his son William that he was convinced from the start in the tank as a weapon of war.

Having ditched their tank on both 15 and 16 September, Alfred and his crew finally got into action on 25 September, to the north of Martinpuich, supporting an attack by 68th Infantry Brigade on the German trench known as Twenty Sixth Avenue. Two tanks were initially tasked but the second became unserviceable, so Alfred moved forward alone under the cover of darkness on the evening of 24 September. He was in command of the male tank No 743, which had previously been commanded by Second Lieutenant Len Bond at Flers. Alfred and his crew successfully

Tank D7 stopped near the German front line. (Tank Museum)

reached the enemy trench at Twenty Sixth Avenue but German small arms and artillery fire made it impossible for the infantry to consolidate their gains. Alfred therefore returned to the British lines where his tank again became ditched. The tank became a sitting target for the German artillery observers operating from the observation balloons in the region. The crew managed to get back to their own lines but many suffered injuries as well as "bullet splash" resulting from sustained German machine gun fire.

In early October, Alfred accompanied Harold Mortimore to Hébuterne where they established D Company's new tankodrome. They also organised the construction of protective dug-outs for the crews, as well as erecting tents for accommodation and "stables" for the tanks. Alfred did not take part in the abortive attacks later that month as he was tasked to set up a new battle HQ and forward stores dump near Auchonvillers in order to support further attacks to the north of the River Ancre. Here he was joined by Victor Huffam who had recovered from the shell shock and, within a week, they inloaded the stores which were later used for the final attacks near Beaumont –Hamel.

After 14 November, the crews moved to their new home in the Tank Administrative Area at Blangy to the west of St Pol Sur Ternoise. Alfred transferred to the newly formed D Battalion and joined No 12 Company. There is no record of his fighting during attack at Vimy Ridge, during the Battle of Arras, but there were only sufficient tanks for two sections in his company. Nor is there any record that he fought at Bullecourt on 3 May when the Company took heavy losses. However Alfred was in action at least twice during the Third Battle of Ypres. On 22 August, he commanded the female tank *Delysia* near St Julien. He reached his objectives near the Vancouver crossroads, which is now the site of the Brooding Soldier memorial. His crew engaged the enemy despite the tank being hit by artillery shells which nearly pierced the hull, and despite the dreadful ground conditions, and German bombardments, got the tank back to its rally point. On 24 September, Alfred again commanded *Delysia* in support of 51st Highland Division. Owing to the impossible ground conditions, the tanks deployed along the road towards Poelcapelle. The leading tank became ditched and, despite continuous efforts to get past the wreck, *Delysia* driver's was unable to do so. Alfred therefore used his tank's Lewis guns to break up a German counter-attack which was trying to prevent the Highlanders securing the ground they had gained. Having successfully completed his mission, *Delysia* again managed to make its way back to its rallying point in an area which later became a known as the Tank Graveyard.

During the preparations for the Battle of Cambrai, Alfred was appointed to command No 11 Section. On 20 November 1917, again in support of 51st Highland Division, his section took part in the attack on Flesquières. This attack failed due to the deep barbed wire defences which stopped the infantry from moving forward and the German's use of artillery in the anti-tank role. Alfred, who was up with the leading tanks, gathered those which were still serviceable and took them back to the Battalion Rallying point near Ribecourt-La -Tour. In the evening, he led the tanks back up the hill and through the village supporting the Scottish infantry as they cleared the area. Due to the number of tanks destroyed on the first day, No 10 and 12 Companies were merged and Alfred assumed command of No 1 Section. The two composite companies went into action, on 23 November, against the German positions around Bourlon Wood, where every one of the tanks was knocked out, ditched or made unserviceable due to enemy fire.

Having re-equipped and retrained in the early months of 1918, Alfred commanded No 9 Section alongside Heady Head in No 10 Section as they tried to halt the German advance near St Emile on 22 March. Alfred continued to serve with 4th Battalion during the Battle of Amiens and the Final Advance though the Hindenburg Line towards the German frontier. As one of the most experienced tank commanders, Alfred was appointed Liaison Officer to HQ 30th American Division on 8 October 1918 when D Battalion was one of three tank units supporting the American Division's attacks. It was probably during this time that Alfred gained his love for American cars. This was the last action in which D Battalion was to take part and they then withdrew to re-equip and train

Alfred Enoch in Cologne
1919. (William Russell)

for the expected Spring Offensive which would finish the war. On 14 October, as the Battalion was receiving orders to move into its winter base at Bellacourt, near Arras, Alfred was appointed Adjutant. He was the only officer to serve continuously with D Company; D Battalion and 4th Battalion from its deployment to France until the Armistice. He continued to serve with the unit as Adjutant in France and then in Germany on occupation duties. It was here that he gained his love for opera and also where he "acquired" the piano which he managed to recover to England.

Returning to England on 17 March 1919, Alfred was awarded the Military Cross for his sustained service in the Tank Corps, having previously been Mentioned in Despatches on two occasions. On being demobilised, Alfred joined an engineering company in Birmingham which made weights and measures. Relinquishing his commission in the Sherwood Foresters on 20 May 1920, Alfred settled with his wife Eva in Acocks Green although she returned home to Sunderland for the birth of only their son William on 19 September 1924. William, who was named after his grandfather, studied English at Oxford University before becoming an actor in 1949, something which William had always wanted but was not Alfred's plan at all. Under the stage name of William Russell, he became a star on both sides of the Atlantic playing the title role of Sir Lancelot de Lac in the 1950s TV series and then *Ian Chesterton* the companion to the first Doctor Who in the original 1963 series. A regular member of the cast of Coronation Street, he is equally well known for his stage work and is a member of the Royal Shakespeare Company.

Alfred was a hero to his son, who fondly remembers his father's story of the tank action in the Great War as well as his love for keeping pigeons which he ascribes to Alfred's experience of the birds as tank messengers. When William Russell was a boy, Alfred worked for Sheffield Steel Products before eventually joining the metal manufacturing company Orme Evans and company which was close to Alfred's home town of Wednesfield. On the outbreak of the Second World War, Alfred was desperate to rejoin the Tanks but, as general manager of a major metal manu-facturing company whose output was 80% war related, it was decided that he should continue in that role. Sadly, at the end of the 1940s, Alfred was forced to retire due to ill-health. Ten years later, he suffered a stroke and died three days aged sixty-eight, on 22 August 1959. Alfred was buried at St Thomas' Cemetery in Wednesfield but his name lives on through his actor grandson Alfie Enoch. Alfie, who was born in 1988, achieved a large following after playing *Dean Thomas* in the *Harry Potter* films. Having graduated from College Oxford with a degree in Portuguese and Spanish, Alfie is now working on both sides of the Atlantic, currently starring as Wes Gibbins in the American Broadcasting Company legal drama *How to get away with murder.*

Enoch's second in command was Charlie Ironmonger. Born at Clerkenwell, in London, on 5 June 1898 Charlie was the third child of a horseholder. Charlie went to school in Islington and then moved to Southwark where he drove a three-wheeler van for a wet fish shop which says much for his maturity and mechanical ability. Enlisting when he was seventeen, Charlie is the youngest soldier I have thus far identified serving with the First Tank Crews as well as its youngest NCO. After completing initial training at Bisley, Charlie was one of the dozen crewmen who were sent to the Trident Works at Lincoln to assist in the production of the tanks being built by the Foster's company. He was pictured as a corporal on the D Company photo at Canada Farm near Elveden in August 1916; his stature and confident look belie his youth.

On 15 September, after his tank became ditched, Charlie escaped death after he left the safety of the vehicle when a German bullet was stopped by a small notebook in his breast pocket. This notebook, which is now held by the Tank Museum, confirms the names of his tank crew both on 15 September and the follow-up action at Martinpuich ten days later. Charlie had to leave his disabled tank for a second time, on 25 September, and picked up a tin helmet for protection "only to find with the remains of some poor souls head in it". Wounded in chest, knee, face and arm, after he left the tank, Charlie was evacuated from France and arrived at hospital in Bristol on the evening of 30 September. He quickly returned to full fitness and re-badged to the Tank Corps. He later fought

Charlie Ironmonger (seated left) and
two pals 1918. (Tank Museum)

at Cambrai and throughout the battles of 1918. He was photographed with two Tank Corps pals whilst out of the line about this time

After the war, Charlie worked as a driver for Boots the Chemist. He married Louisa Lloyd on Boxing Day 1919, at her parish church – St Michael and All Angels in Southwark. The young couple settled in the Borough and had two sons, Charles born in 1920 and Edward in the spring of 1924. The family which lived at Moulin Street Southwark until 1930, then moved to Lewisham where Louisa died in 1932. Two years later Charlie married Annie Searle in Deptford. The family then settled in Carshalton in Surrey where they lived until 1939. After that, the family disappears from view until Charlie died in February 1976; his wife Annie surviving until September 1992.

Like Charlie Ironmonger, Gunner Alfred Lapthorne was wounded on 25 September during the action at Martinpuich. Indeed he was so badly injured that he was discharged from the Army on 7 May the following year, as he was no longer fit for active service. Gunner Harold Bowen was also discharged but not until after the war. Harold, who was born at Chalford, near Stroud, in early spring 1897, was the son of an engine fitter. Looking for work, he moved his wife Gertrude and his young family to St Budeaux, near Plymouth, where he worked in the Royal Naval dockyard at Devonport. Harold's mother died when he was a boy and he was bought up at 7 Rodney Street by his elder sisters. When he was eighteen Harold enlisted into the MMGS on 1 July 1915. His service records has not survived but the Army medal rolls show that, having transferred to the Tank

Corps, Harold was later promoted corporal. He survived the war but was discharged as a result of sickness sustained whilst overseas on 19 March 1919. Returning to Devon, he married Elsie Pegler in early 1926 probably at her home town of Torpoint. Their only daughter Joan, who was born on 7 March 1928, married Kenneth Hill, who was also born in Plymouth later that year, in the summer of 1952. Harold died aged sixty-seven on 10 March 1965 at his home in St Budeaux. Elsie lived on as a widow, for a further twenty six years in Plymouth where she died in early 1991, having buried both her daughter Joan and son-in-law Kenneth the previous year.

The service record for Gunner George Hume is one of the few to survive the Blitz. Born near Edinburgh on 29 September 1896, George was the son of a lawyer's clerk who later became the assistant clerk of sessions at the highest civil court in Scotland. The family lived at Joppa between Edinburgh and Musselburgh. When he enlisted into the MMGS, one day before his nineteenth birthday, George was working as a lawyers' clerk. He was slight in build, being 5 feet 10 inches in height and just over eight stone in weight. George joined at Bisley, three days later, on 1 October 1915. He was one of the more experienced crewmen who deployed to France on 28 August 1916. Later renumbered as 200775 in the Tank Corps, George later fought at Cambrai with D Battalion at Flesquières and was wounded in the right leg during the attack on Bourlon on 23 November. He was not evacuated from France until 19 December 1917 and then was admitted to Priory Hospital at Cheltenham on Christmas Eve. In addition to his legs wounds, George was also noted as having pneumonia with "an unusual cause". He never recovered and was recommended for discharge from Army on 27 March 1918 by the Special Invaliding Board at Cheltenham. He was awarded the Silver War Badge on 17 April 1918 and was granted a pension for a year. His pension record reveals that, during his service, he had previously suffered from gunshot wounds to his right hand, shoulder and side as well as damage to his lungs. He died less than six months later, of lung cancer, on 7 August 1918 at the Royal Infirmary in Edinburgh.

Another crewman listed in George Ironmonger's notebook was Sydney Thompson from Oldham. Born in October 1889, Sydney was the son of a Scottish whitesmith who later became an electrical engineer. Sydney initially worked as a grocer's assistant but was clearly a capable man, as by the time he married local school teacher Sarah Ward, he had become a grocer's manager at Hattershaw. They married on 21 March 1914 at St Paul's Parish Church in Oldham. Sydney must also have been an experienced motorist as, when he volunteered to join the MMGS in August 1915; he passed the selection tests and was sent immediately sent to Bisley. He was relatively short at 5 feet 2 inches but he was physically well developed with a 38 inch chest. After initial training, Sydney served in 21st Battery MMGS which became a main source of manpower for the embryo tank units. After training at Elveden, he deployed on 28 August 1916 and went into action on 15 September.

Charlie Ironmonger's notebook confirms that Sydney was also in action on 25 September at Martinpuich. Transferred to D Battalion on its formation, in the middle of November, Sydney was soon in trouble for "hesitating to obey an order from the Military Police". This minor offence possibly relates to his being in an out of bounds areas, such as an estiminet which sold alcohol, outside of permitted hours. Sydney was awarded seven days Field Punishment No 2; that is he was placed in handcuffs for two hours a day when he was not undertaking other duties. It was a useful way of preventing those soldiers who had been in trouble from getting into more. It is not recorded whether he took part in any actions in 1917 but, on 11 November, Sydney returned to England and was posted to 10th Battalion. He deployed back to France with his new unit on 20 December with a number of C and D Battalion officers who had been sent back to England to provide the new unit with battle hardened crewmen. Soon after arriving in France, Sydney was injured in an accident at the Mechanical School on 19 January 1918 when his third and fourth fingers on his right hand were badly crushed. They were trapped by a gun sponson door which had not been properly secured. Sydney was holding onto the sponson as it went over a trench, probably to prevent him and his fellow gunner being thrown out of the tank as it was moving. As a result of no longer being able to operate a gun, Sydney was re-trained as a driver. On 10 August, which was the second day of Battle of Amiens, he was wounded – remarkably in the right hand. Evacuated to England three days later, he was treated at the Lichfield Hospital. The wounds were not however serious as he was released after only ten days treatment and sent for convalescence for a further month. He then joined the Tank Corps Depot at Bovington, where he served until he was demobilised on 25 February 1919. It is interesting to note that, despite his injuries, he did not claim for a disability pension when he was discharged in 1919. On 8 January 1920, Sarah gave birth to their only son Eric who followed his mother into the teaching profession. The family stayed in Oldham where Sydney died in Westhulme Hospital on 6 October 1962.

The final member of the crew was Gunner Archie Richards who was the only one of the First Tank Crews who reached his centenary. Born on 7 January 1897, at Linkenthorne in Cornwall, Archie was the third son of a tin miner. His father George became a farmer but Archie worked as a tin miner on leaving school. Joining the MMGS, Archie served as a 6 pdr gunner with Alfred Enoch who, according to his story published in the *Veterans* by Richard Van Emden, called all of his crewmen by the Christian names. Archie's recall of the battle for Flers is quite clear but it is at some variance with the contemporary accounts. He states that his tank managed to get into the middle of the village when his tank was put out of action by a German artillery shell. He then tells how Alfred Enoch took most of the crew back to their lines whilst Archie and a comrade remained near the tank, at one point taking shelter in the cellar of a ruined house until dark when they returned to the tank and stayed there the rest of the night.

Archie did not stay with his comrades when D Battalion was formed but was transferred to C Battalion which was most unusual. Archie fought with them at Arras on 9 April 1917 during 14th Division attack on the Harp position near Beaurains. He later recalled that his tank fought through to its objective and returned to its rallying point; one of the few to do so. His tank was possibly the male tank No 776 which was part of No 8 Company. Archie also fought at Cambrai with C Battalion and reached the rank of acting corporal. The medal roll shows that he returned his British War Medal for amendment in 1923 but I can find more other record of his service. He returned to Cornwall at the end of the war and on 1922 married Florence Howe. The following year Archie travelled to Canada, on his own, in order to work on a farm. He arrived in Quebec on 2 August en route for Manitoba and told the immigration authorizes he planned to stay permanently. Later, he told Richard van Emden, he worked in the United States. Archie returned to Cornwall where he and Florence lived until the mid-1930s, when they moved to London. Initially they lived at 88 Gelatlly Road in Deptford but, after the Second World War, they moved to 101 Northumberland Park in Tottenham where they remained until 1965. Archie later lived with his daughter and son in law in Maidenhead, where he died aged 101, on 10 February 1998.

Dracula and Crew D16

Crew D16 manned a female tank, named *Dracula* by her skipper Lieutenant Arthur Arnold. Having left the Loop around nightfall on 13 September, Dracula and the two other tanks reached the D Company advanced base at Green Dump before dawn. At daybreak, the tank commanders were taken forward to see the ground over which they were to operate. They then returned to Green Dump where the tank's fuel tanks were topped up and additional fuel placed in the box which sat on the tank's rear steering wheels. The crews then rested until the evening. They then left Green Dump at 9.00 p.m. and drove to their start point. The route was through the north-west corner of Delville Wood and it took Dracula and her fellow tanks nine hours to travel to the start point as the driver had to use bottom gear for much of the route to climb in and out of the many large shell holes.

Arriving at the start point around dawn, the three tanks started to make their way across no man's land, following the New Zealand infantry who reached the German front line well before the tanks. Having seen D7 stop, Arthur Arnold pushed on through the German defensive wire to the support trench using her machine guns to disperse the German defenders. Arthur Arnold tried to use his machinegun to dominate the ground but found it had been put out of action by German fire. Having fitted a spare gun, Arthur directed his tank north. On route he observed *Dinnaken* to his east also making its way into the village. By 8.00 a.m. the infantry, supported by the tanks, had cleared the area. As a result, the crews were able to get out of their tanks, get some fresh air and cook breakfast. This calm was interrupted, not by the defenders of the village, but by German artillery fire directed from one of the many observation balloons located to the north of Flers.

The two tanks then moved into the shelter of the woods on the western edge of the village and met up with Graeme Nixon and George Pearsall's tanks. Here they assisted *Die Hard's* crew to put out the fire in Nixon's tank "Dreadnought". In the late morning, Arthur was asked to use his tank's machine guns to disrupt an enemy counter attack which was forming up to the northwest but the location was two miles away. In the afternoon, the tank disrupted another attack and then cruised north towards Factory Corner, however the tank came under fire of a German field gun and Arnold withdrew. On the way back, Arthur Arnold dismounted and started to move a New Zealand casualty into the tank. This was observed by a German soldier who opened fire and hit Arthur in the knee. Seeing his skipper was incapacitated, Gunner Jake Glaister took charge of the tank and maneuvered it so that his skipper could be rescued. Whilst Jake ensured that, despite artillery fire, the tank got back to British lines, Arthur Arnold sent a signal by pigeon to HQ 41st Division confirming his section commander's tank was once again on fire but the other three tanks in the section were returning to Longueval. The three tanks eventually returned to the company forward base at Green Dump by 8:30 p.m.

Dracula's skipper, Arthur Arnold was born at Llandudno on 13 June 1892. Like his company commander, Arthur was the son of a draper who had built up a successful business at the Victorian seaside resort. Arthur was educated at the John Bright Grammar School but, rather than work in the family firm, Arthur and his elder brother Bill trained as engineers. They worked at the Belfast shipbuilders, Harland and Woolf at the same time as three great White Star liners were under construction. Two of these huge ships would be sunk by the end of the decade; the Titanic famously after striking an iceberg and the Britannic which was sunk by a sea mine in the Aegean sea whilst being used as a hospital ship.

Whilst working at the Belfast shipyard, Arthur met his future wife, Marge Todd who lived nearby in Sydenham. Four years later, as war was declared, Arthur was now working at a shipbuilders in Birkenhead. He immediately volunteered with three of his brothers, Bill, Clement and Frank to join the Kings Liverpool Regiment (KLR). However his company was contracted to fit out a vessel to transport horses from Ireland to France. Modifications had to be made when the ship reached Dublin as the ramps were too high to load the animals. Arthur then returned to Birkenhead and enlisted in the KLR on 2 September 1914. He served as private soldier, in the 17th Battalion which has the distinction of being recognised as the first Pals battalion. Although it is not recorded in his service record, his family says he deployed to France in 1915, and having been identified as having officer potential, Alfred was discharged on 31 August 1915 to re-enlist as an officer cadet in the Inns Of Court OTC. He initially joined D Company then served in No 5 and 6 Companies undertaking his training at Berkhamstead and once again reaching the rank of Lance Corporal. He was commissioned into the Welsh Regiment on 20 January 1916 and attached to HS MGC in April 1916.

After he had been wounded at Flers on 15 September, Arthur was evacuated from the Somme and wrote his post-operational report from No 6 Red Cross Hospital at Étaples. He was then transferred back to the Royal Free Hospital in London where he was treated for a further two months.

Arthur Arnold in 1917.
(Ann Burnett)

Whilst he was in hospital, the *London Gazette* announced that Arthur was awarded the Military Cross for his brave action on 15 September. Eventually Arthur was released, and after convalescence at home, was sent to Bovington Camp.

Reporting for duty at the recently established Tank Training Centre on 26 February 1917, he was "claimed" by his former company commander, Frank Summers, who was now commanding the recently formed F Battalion. Also in F Battalion was his older brother Bill, who had joined the tanks, as well as Harold Mortimore and six other officers from D Company. On 12 April 1917, Arthur was appointed acting Captain and a section commander. He returned to France with F Battalion on 20 May. He commanded No 10 Section during their first action on 22 August 1917 travelling in tank F46 *Fay*. The tank was hit; whilst ahead of the infantry near Spree Farm near Wieltje and he directed the crew to evacuate the tank as the Lewis guns were not usable. Arthur was shot though the lung and left arm about one minute after leaving the tank and was taken prisoner. Despite his wounds, he was forced to march a long way to the first rest place at a former monastery. He was then evacuated by rail through Ghent and sent to Paderborn. His left arm healed well but the exit wounds from the chest wound did not. Arthur was treated for his wounds at Limberg, then sent to the Karlsruhe POW camp and later to Freiburg where he was joined by his younger brother Clem. Clem, who had also joined the Tank Corps serving with 6th Battalion, had been captured whilst commanding the hugely successful Whippet tank *Musical Box* at Villers-Brettonaux on 8 August 1918.

Repatriated on 6 December 1918, Arthur went immediately to Belfast to collect Marge. They spent Christmas at Llandudno with his family, including his three soldier brothers, all of whom were to be decorated for war service. Bill, the eldest who initially served with F Battalion, had been awarded the DSO for his service as a tank engineer with 2nd Tank Brigade in 1918; Clem was awarded the DSO for his action whilst commanding *Musical Box* whilst their younger brother Frank was awarded the MC in June 1918 whilst fighting with the Liverpool Scottish. Arthur had developed tuberculosis whilst imprisoned at Freiburg and he was sent to Mundsley Sanatorium, on the Norfolk coast and later to the Swiss resort of Leysin for treatment which was only partially successful. Returning to Wales, he met the Oertel brothers from South Africa who told him that the African climate would aid his health. Arthur emigrated to Mazabuka in Zambia where his elder brother Bill had been granted a farm under the Soldier Settlement scheme. Arthur was also granted a farm and asked Marge to join him. She left Belfast and made her way to Capetown on her own. Marge arrived at 6.00 a.m. on 28 February and married Arthur at 11.30 that same morning. The couple moved to their farm in Zambia but it proved economically unviable. Deciding to move back to South Africa, Arthur looked for other work. He had taught himself book-keeping whilst a POW and he saw an advertisement for a job with the Oertel brothers. He applied for, and got, the job which required him to manage the accounts for a farming syndicate. Moving to Westminster, near Bloemfontein in the Orange Free State, the couple also rented a farm where their only daughter Kathleen was born in 1924. Arthur's sister Nell travelled out to South Africa to help Marge after the birth and settled with the family, Kathleen being known as Nell in her honour. Six years later, Arthur and Marge were able to buy their own farm and, in 1936, purchased Crichton Farm where they lived for the rest of their lives. Arthur built a lot of the farmhouse as well as its furniture. In 1935 he had damaged his back and, whilst recovering, wrote a book on golf putting. Arthur also founded the Senior Golfer Society of the Free State and was later elected its president.

In the 1930s, Arthur identified the potential source of exports to Argentina; he followed this up and his potato export business became highly successful. During the Second World War, Arthur established the local detachment of the South Africa Defence Force at Thabu 'Nchu but he was mainly employed farming; his daughter Nell serving with the coastal artillery. After the war, Arthur guided many ex-soldiers who needed help in establishing themselves as farmers, one of whom Clifford Gilbert married Marge and Arthur's only daughter Nell. The family had made regular trips home to Llandudno in the 1930s but as he got older, Arthur spent less time away from his farm at Westminster.

Clem, who had taken over the running of the family drapery business and commanded the local artillery regiment at the start of the Second World War, and the youngest of the five Arnold brothers, Ted who was only nine of the outbreak of the Great War, visited South Africa in the 1950s Although Arthur did not attend the annual Cambrai celebrations in London, he was still in contact with one of his D Company comrades, Victor Huffam who made regular business visits to South Africa. During one of these visits, in 1963, Victor prompted Arthur to write an account of his actions at Flers which was subsequently published in the *Tank*. They were meet more frequently when Victor settled in Durban and Arthur helped Victor buy some polo ponies. Arthur Arnold died, aged seventy-seven on 25 May 1969, at Westminster in South Africa.

For some unknown reason, Arthur's second in command did not go into action on 15 September. Corporal Ernest White was later commissioned into the HSMGC on 26 June 1917 and later served as a Captain in the Tank Corps from 27 December 1918. When he applied for his medals, on the anniversary of Armistice in 1924, he was staying at a hotel in Berners Street London but that is all I can find about him. The man who assumed his role on 15 September, Gunner Jake Glaister, was used to organising matters as he ran his own building company. Jake was born at Whitehaven in Cumberland on 28 February 1886. His father was also a self-employed builder and contractor and Jake initially worked for his father as a stonemason. In 1910, Jake became engaged to a girl called Isabella Starkey, who he was to court for many years but never married. The story was to make the press twenty years later.

With the introduction of conscription in late 1915, and as a single man over 30, Jake realized he was vulnerable for call-up. The MMGS had stopped recruiting in early 1916, but from March

Jake Glaister.
(Tank Museum)

1916, they looked for large numbers of trained drivers. Jake quickly volunteered and was enlisted at Coventry in the first week of April. Seven months later, Jake was again in action for the second time on 1 October 1916 at Eaucourt L'Abbaye. The D16 crew was again was mounted in *Dracula* but this time commanded by Lieutenant Jefferson Wakley. They attacked the German positions around Eaucourt L'Abbaye working with crew D8, again commanded by Second Lieutenant George Bown. Both tanks got into action, broke through the German front line trenches and were particularly successful in destroying the defensive positions around the Eaucourt farm complex. As they moved towards the German second line positions, both tanks became ditched. Unable to extract themselves, both skippers set light to their tanks and their crews made their escape. Most of the D16 crew got to safety but Jeff Wakley was shot in the leg and it took three days to recover him. We know that several men were injured trying to get him back to the safety of the British lines. Jake, who was one of then, was shot on 2 October; the bullet entered two inches to right of the sternum and exited over left ribs in line with nipple. Fortunately it just missed his heart but it was a bad wound and Jake was stabilised at a series of medical facilities on the Somme before being transferred to 9 General Hospital in Rouen on 11 October. Whilst he was there it was announced that he had been awarded the Distinguished Conduct Medal. Five days later Jake was evacuated to the King George Hospital in London then treated at the Adelaide Hospital in Dublin for two months. It was during this time that Jacob was also awarded the Military Medal for rescuing Arthur Arnold on 15 September.

After post-hospital leave, Jake was posted to the new tank training centre at Bovington. He was not fit to deploy overseas but he was soon employed on instructional duties. On 13 April 1918, Jake was posted to the Tank Corps Depot as acting Sergeant on 13 April 1918 and was then attached to the Cameron Highlanders at Inverness for a fortnight on October 1918. Transferred to Z Class Reserve on 19 February 1919, Jake was granted a twenty per cent disablement pension. He took over his father's building and sculpturing business, and amongst other large projects, built Whitehaven Bus Station which was only the second covered bus station in England when it was built. In 1929, Jake was sued for breach of promise by Isabella Starkey, who considered an engagement of nineteen years was too long. She was successful in her claim and it cost Jake over £1,000 as well as some unwelcome publicity in a number of newspapers. Two years later, at the age of 45, Jake married a teacher Lydia Jackson who was ten years his senior. Jake, whose hobbies remained motoring and motor engineering, died relatively young at 64 in Whitehaven on 23 October 1950. His wife Lydia lived on at Whitehaven almost reaching her century, dying aged ninety-nine on 28 April 1978.

Jake Glaister was not the only member of the crew to be decorated that autumn. 32016 Gnr F J Roberts was awarded the Military Medal for his actions between September and November; but I have been unable to find anything else about him or the reason why he was decorated. I have also been unable to identify Douglas and can find little about Gunner Percy Collett. He was from Erith in Kent and, like Jake Glaister, joined the MMGS in April 1916. Percy, who was the son of a joiner, was born in 1889 at Bromley and worked as a carpenter before joining the Army. He served with the Tank Corps throughout the war and was demobilised as a private. After the war, he settled in Sevenoaks, having married his wife Edith. He died, aged only forty-eight, on 22 March 1937.

The D16 crew was fortunate in that only one crewman did not survive the war. This was John McKenzie, the eldest son of a railway shunter named Francis McKenzie and his wife Mary. John who was born in Carlisle in early 1889, moved with his family to Tranmere in Lancashire in 1891 where, in 1915, John enlisted in the MGC. Following the first actions, he was posted to D Battalion on its formation and later fought in the Battle of Arras. He served on with No 10 Company and took part in the successful attack on the Harp Feature near Beaurains on 9 April. Sadly he died of wounds on 5 August 1917, probably received during No 10 Company's actions on 31 July near Poelcapelle to the northeast of Ieper. He is buried at Lijssenthoek Military Cemetery, the site of the main hospitals near Poperinghe; together with more than 10,000 other casualties, Lijssenthoek being the second largest British military cemetery in Belgium.

The tank's driver, Private Samuel Workman was born in Nailsworth in Gloucestershire in 1892. He was baptised on 9 October, the church records showing that his father was a groom and that the family was living on Chestnut Hill. Samuel, who was named after his father, had three older sisters and originally worked as a labourer for his father who had taken up farming. He learned to drive when he joined the Army in 1915 and, after driving tanks on the Somme, returned to the ASC. After the war, he settled at Cainscross and became a bus driver with the national omnibus company at Stroud. He was twice called as a witness at Stroud magistrates' court following road accidents and near misses for which he was wholly blameless. On 10 September 1928, now aged thirty-six, married Winifred Bird at Cainscross Parish Church and the wedding lines show Samuel was now working as an engineer. Winfred, who was ten years younger than Samuel, gave birth to their only son Jeffrey three years later. The family later moved to Forest Green near Nailsea in Somerset where Samuel died aged forty-nine on 14 February 1941.

The final member of the D16 crew was Gunner Cecil Frost. Born in Tiverton Devon in October 1888, he was the fourth son of a publican named William Frost and his wife Mary. Cecil was one of thirteen children of whom only seven survived. Bought up at the Boar's Head in Tiverton High Street, Cecil was educated at the East Devon County School in Samson Peveril. By 1911, he had moved to Plymouth and was working as a photographer at 71 Fore Street in Devonport. Four years later, when he enlisted into the MGC, he was employed as a theatrical manager in Alma Road. Mobilised on 25 April 1916, he deployed to France on 2 September with the final party of D Company. After the first actions, he was transferred to D Battalion on its formation and moved with them to Blangy in December. He later claimed that, in December, he started to suffer from ill-health and he was hospitalised on 11 January 1917 with tonsillitis. He remained at 12 Stationary Hospital at St Pol for three weeks, before returning to duty. Cecil served with D Battalion throughout 1917. There is no evidence that he went into action at the Battle of Arras but he almost certainly attended the driver training camp at Wailly in May 1917 after which he was selected to serve as a driver. He fought in the Ypres Salient that summer and was classified as a Second Class Tank Mechanist on 1 September 1917. He must also have been in action at the Battle of Cambrai as he was granted home leave from 11 to 25 December returning to the Battalion on 27 December.

Classified as a First Class Tank Machinist on 7 March 1918, he survived the destruction of 4th Battalion during the Kaiserschlacht in March 1918. Cecil was admitted to hospital on 29 May, with influenza but he quickly recovered. He fought with the renamed 4th Battalion throughout the Battle of Amiens and during the Final Advance; the last Battalion action being at the Bellacourt Tunnel. With only eight tanks fit for action, the Battalion formed a composite company which was attached to 1st Battalion. 4th Battalion was removed from the order of battle and a large company was sent to the International Tank School. The remainder of the unit moved to Bellacourt, near Wailly, and started preparations for the expected 1919 advance. Many of the crewmen went sent on courses whilst others, including Cecil were granted UK leave. He left the unit on 29 October and was on his way back to his unit when the Armistice was announced. He stayed with 4th Battalion over the Christmas period and, during his pre-demobilisation medical on 17 February 1919, reported that he was suffering from deafness which he stated resulted from the bad weather and poor accommodation available to D Company two years before. After his demobilisation on 13 March, Cecil tried to obtain a Service pension as a result of "catarrhal deafness"; the subsequent examination found his ears to be heavily waxed and he was unsuccessful in his claim. He returned to Plymouth and the entertainment business. By 1922 he was managing the Theatre De Luxe cinema at 116 Union Street after which I can find no more information.

Crew D18

The third tank in F Group, on the morning of 15 September, was manned by crew D18. This male tank was commanded by Second Lieutenant Len Bond who was born on 11 February 1895 in Gravesend. Len, who was working as a bank clerk, joined the "Shiny" 7th Battalion of the London Regiment on 8 October 1914. He initially deployed to France in March 1915 and probably fought at the Battle of Aubers Ridges and at Loos; he was injured by shrapnel in July 1915 but this was not so severe he was evacuated to England. Commissioned into the Heavy Section MGC on 14 in April 1916, he attended the 6 pdr course at Whale Island before moving to Elveden for tank training. Len had two brothers and he was the last one to arrive on the Somme; Alfred, serving in the RFC, was taking trench photographs in late June and early July and Henry, who was known as Bob, who won a Military Cross on 7 July whilst serving with 6th Battalion the Buffs (East Kent Regiment) and was later wounded at the Battle of Transloy Ridges and Len at Flers-Courcelette. All three brothers were decorated for their actions.

Len was injured on 15 September, suffering splinter wounds to the hand and head as well as shell shock. He was sufficiently badly wounded to be unable to take the tank into action on subsequent attacks. He was awarded the Military Cross "for conspicuous gallantry in action. He fought his Tank with great gallantry, putting a machine gun out of action and capturing the team. Later, he went to the support of a party of infantry, and finally safely brought his Tank out of action". Len was sent back to England and, after he had recovered from his wounds, was "gathered-in" by Frank Summers who was CO of the newly formed F Battalion. Like Arthur Arnold, Len was promoted acting Captain when he was appointed section commander on 12 April 1917 at Bovington. He served in No 17 Company under Major Charles Hawkins, his second in command being Captain Bill Mann with whom he served in D Company. He deployed back to France on 20 May and, having undertaken the standard driver training camp at Wailly and gunnery training at Merlimont, on the French coast, were issued with new tanks and prepared them for action. Len attended the F Battalion dinner on 27 June 17, at which a large number of former C and Company officers were present, before departing for the Ypres Salient on 2 July. Arriving at Oosthoek Wood the following day, the Battalion tankodrome was soon targeted by German long range artillery and the majority of troops were withdrawn to La Lovie. On 25 July, No 17 Company started its journey forward to its forward deployment location and reached Trois Tours, the crews making their way back to La Lovie. Bill Mann was killed at Trois Tours that same evening and his body was taken back to La Lovie and buried at Dozingham British Military Cemetery, a ceremony at which Len would have been present.

Three nights later, Len was wounded by shrapnel in the right lung whilst leading No 7 Section towards the tank bridge at Essex Farm to the north of Ieper. He was so badly injured that he was no longer able to command his section and was evacuated to England. Having recovered sufficiently to undertake home duties, he was posted to 1st (Depot) Battalion at Bovington and took up his first post as an instructor. He decided to remain in the Army after most of his comrades were demobilised, and he was appointed Assistant Instructor at the Tank Driving & Maintenance School on 1 September 1920. Obviously good at the job, he remained at Bovington and was promoted to Assistant Instructor (Class GG) from 14 December 1920.

Len was then employed as an Executive Officer with HQ Tank Corps; that is to say on the staff. After this, he was posted to India, where he met his future wife Muriel, who was known as Monty, and they married at Peshawar. He saw action, as a subaltern, in 10th Armoured Car Company where one of the two section commanders was Billy Sampson, who commanded *Delilah* at High Wood, the other being Archie Holford-Walker who commanded *Clan Leslie* on 15 September 1916. Len then took part in the "Military Aide" provided to the civil authorities in Delhi during the November 1927 disturbances.

In 1928 he transferred to the Royal Indian Army Service Corps (RIASC) with whom he saw active service on the North West Frontier during 1930-31 and in the Mohmand Campaign of 1933. Len qualified in the senior course at the RIASC Training Centre at Chaklala, in December 1934, before being promoted to Major in February 1935. After

Len Bond post war 1918. (TPC)

taking six months leave in England, he took command of No 6 District Supply Company. Nine months later, Len had transferred to the Special Unposted List on which he remained until 1940 when he was attached to the Indian Signals Corps. He then was posted, as an instructor to the RAISC depot at Kakul, close to the British garrison at Abbottabad in Kashmir. It was here that, on 16 December 1942, Len suffered a pontine hemorrhage. He was buried in the Karachi War Cemetery.

There are, as ever, some members of the crew about whom there is little information. Other than Len's second in command, Corporal Paul, being wounded there is no firm evidence about his service. I believe that he was Corporal Arthur Paul, who served in the MMGS and who later lived in College Street in Gloucester. Arthur Wood's notebook also shows one gunner was called Morgan and the driver was Fred Burrows from Liverpool. After the first actions, he rebadged into the MGC then the Tank Corps where he served as a Private. The Tank Corps Book of Honour shows that he died or was killed in action. However this is not confirmed by the Tank Corps Medal Rolls, in the list of Soldiers who died in the Great War, or on the CWGC register.

The Adjutant lists one of the crew as Gunner Sydney Wenmoth. Much older than most Tank Crews, he was born in May 1879 at Launceston in Cornwall. Sydney was the son of an ironmonger named Alfred Wenmoth and his wife Elizabeth who lived with his elder sister Rose May in Broad Street Launceston. By the time he was twenty-one year old, Sydney was boarding at 4 Alma Street in Smethwick, working as a self-employed electrician. Ten years later, in 1911, he was again living with his widowed father Alfred and his sister Rose at Broad Street in Launceston and working on his own account as an electrical and telephone tradesman. Attested at Launceston on 27 November 15, aged thirty-six, Sydney was transferred to the Army Reserve the next day and, after a trade test and further medical test at Coventry on 28 March, was mobilised on 29 March. Sydney joined the Armoured Car Section MGC at Bisley the same day; joined the Heavy Section on 4 May and then was posted to D Company on 27 May. He was not injured in the first action on 15 September. However, after the war, Sydney purchased a book by war correspondent Phillip Gibbs in which he wrote an inscription "Tank Corps. In action at Flers Sept 15th 1916, High Wood Sept 20th 1916 and Thiepval Sept 26th 1916 – wounded in 4 places and lucky to get out of it". There is no other record of tanks being in action at High Wood on 20 September which had been cleared by the 47th London Division – see Chapter 11.

His wounding on 26 September is confirmed by his Service record but I have been unable to identify the tank in which Sydney was fighting. This action on Thiepval Ridge involved six tanks; three from C Company called *Cognac; Crème de Menthe* and *Cordon Rouge* and three from D Company whose crew details are not known. One of these was the female tank no 542, which became ditched at Mouquet farm and assisted in securing it against a German counter-attack; a further tank ditched on the road between Pozières and Thiepval and took no part in the action; the third tank also ditched on the road to the west, as it crossed the Schwaben trench on the eastern edge of Thiepval. It had previously managed to get out of a large crater near the German front line trench called Joseph, and then made its way into the German support trenches. It was hit by German shells three times after it was stuck and set on fire. This is possibly the tank in which Sydney was wounded. After treatment at No 6 General Hospital at Rouen, where his wounds were stabilized, Sydney returned to the United Kingdom on 4 November. He was then sent to Ireland where he was also treated in Cork Hospital for influenza from 7 November to 20 December. He was then granted post hospital leave until 29 December.

Tasked to report to Bovington Camp where new battalions were being formed, Sydney was allocated to No 21 Company of G Battalion on 2 January 1917. At the end of the month, he was posted to E Battalion and deployed back to France on 9 July 1917. He served with the Workshop Company until 18 January 1918 when the sub-unit was disbanded as part of the centralization of repairs. Sydney then served at the Central Workshops at Erin, was posted to the Reinforcement

Depot at Mes-Les- Bains on 8 March 1918 and then to 1st Advanced Workshops on 19 April. Less than a month later, he was posted back to the Central Workshops, which by this time had moved to Teneur. Sydney worked there until 28 October when he was sent to the Engineering School. Posted back to the Central Workshops in France on 24 March 1919, he returned to England on 5 April and was demobilized one month later. Twenty years later, in the summer 1939, Sydney married a Launceston born woman called Gwenllian Rhys in the seaside town of Tenby. The couple settled there and lived together at Queens Parade until Sydney died aged seventy-three on 22 February 1953; Gwenllian died later that year on 24 November 1953.

Gunner Arthur Race, who was born in Barnsley in June 1893, was the youngest of seven children of a clog and boot maker. Arthur was working as a boot repairer when he enlisted into the MGC on 21 January 1916. Mobilised on 29 March, he joined the Armoured Car Section then the Heavy Section on 4 May. Arthur was in the last party to deploy to France arriving on 2 September and less than two weeks later he was in action. Arthur transferred to D Battalion, on its formation, after 18 November. I do not know if he fought at Arras or Ypres but he must have fought at the Battle of Cambrai as he was granted home leave from 11 to 25 December 1917. Still a private soldier he returned to 4th Battalion on 28 December and served with them for the rest of the war. Whilst on leave immediately after the Armistice, he married Jessie Micklethwaite on 21 November 1918 at Salem Chapel in Barnsley. He did not return to his unit until 2 December 1918 and was charged with overstaying leave for six days. The officer who dealt with him was the Adjutant, Arthur Enoch, which means that Arthur Race was probably serving in the Battalion HQ. Given the circumstances, the Adjutant dealt with him very leniently. He admonished his old comrade which meant that Arthur only forfeited six days' pay but was not otherwise punished. Arthur was eventually was able to return to UK on 17 February 1919 for demobilisation at Clipstone. He returned to 69 Honeywell Street in Barnsley where Jessie and he had two children: Stephen in the summer of 1922 and Kathleen four years later. Sadly Arthur did not see his children grow up; he died aged thirty-eight on 2 February 1932.

The final member of the crew was Gunner George Thornton. Enlisted on 12 December 1915, George probably served with the MMGS before he transferred to the Heavy Section MGC. He stayed with D Battalion, after the first tank actions, and served with No 11 Company. He probably fought at the ill-fated action at Bullecourt on 11 April 1917. Transferring to the Tank Corps, he was badly wounded on 9 October 1917. This was during an attack on the village of Poelcapelle, when he was in the crew of *Damon II* with skipper Lieutenant John Coghlan. Coghlan later wrote an article in which he recalled the tank was hit by artillery fire. "The right hand side of my tank was a complete shambles and mangled almost beyond recognition, lay the bodies of my Sergeant and two of my gunners. Skinner who was beside me when we were hit was untouched. My poor driver Thornton, a mere boy but a very gallant one, had his arm practically severed from the shoulder." The tank was hit in the centre of the village, close to the sight of the Tank Memorial at Poelcapelle. Dudley White and Eddie Williams, who also fought in D Company on 15 September, were in the same tank and were killed in action. Coghlan's daughter Mary tells that George retrained as a technician after being invalided out of the Army, on 25 March 1919, and that he made a 10 inch long model of *Damon II* which he gave to John Coghlan at some point after the war.

11

Die Hard at Dawn

The newly formed New Zealand (NZ) Division, who were commanded by a NZ born officer Major General Andrew Russell, undertook their first attack to the west of Flers on 15 September 1916. Their front was narrow, at only 900 yards wide, so the initial assault was undertaken by two battalions; the remainder of the Division being deployed as their advance pushed north into the German held territory. The New Zealanders were supported by four tanks operating in two groups: this first was a single tank manned by the D8 crew which was to move along the Division's western or left flank to Factory Corner, a defensive position to the northwest of Flers. Meanwhile the remaining three tanks, under their section commander Captain Graeme Nixon, were to work together on the NZ centre and right flank, closer to the village (see map 10).

HQ Fourth Army had planned that the tanks should be on the first objective, the Switch Trench, five minutes ahead of the infantry. The aim was for the tanks' machine guns to fire along the trench system, preventing the Germans from firing at the Kiwis as they advanced across no man's land. Thereafter the tanks were to move forward at best speed with the infantry being told not to wait for them. Sadly the four tanks arrived late at their first objective, their approach march being slowed as they worked their way along their route from Green Dump in the dark. Despite this lack of close support, the NZ Division crossed the start line and reached their first objective, the vital Switch Trench which linked the key elements of the German defences, without tank support. They not only captured the trench but, once the tanks caught up, took the remainder of their objectives. As such they were one of the most successful formations who attacked on 15 September.

D8

The D8 crew's tank was damaged as it moved up to the start point, its steering wheels becoming useless. The crew pressed on and caught up with the infantry at their first objective by 07:05 a.m. Fifteen minutes later, the tank continued north as the British artillery barrage resumed its progress. The crew reached their third objective, to the northwest of Flers, and in so doing, not only provided support to the NZ Division but also put pressure on the German units seeking to reinforce High Wood who were well within range of the tank's six pounder gun. As the Germans had a number of observation balloons to the north of Flers, they soon identified the tank to artillery units and the tank became the target of many shells. The tank was hit and the tank's skipper, George Bown and his ASC driver Private Bertram Young were temporarily blinded by glass fragments from the tank's broken periscopes. Despite this, the tank stayed in the open ground to the north-west of Flers, protecting the NZ troops until midafternoon. At 2.50 p.m. the infantry received orders to consolidate on the third objective; forty minutes later, a further order was given for attacks to cease until the following day and for the tanks to return to their base. Accordingly George Bown, who had recovered his vision, ordered that his crew turn for home. They travelled towards the northwest edge of Flers where they linked up with the D16 and D18 crews and the three tanks made their way south, reaching the company advanced base at Green Dump almost five hours later.

George Bown was born on 22 August 1892 at Mudford Manor in Somerset. He was the eldest son of a well-established farmer named Walter Bown and his wife Clara who had twelve children, all of whom survived to adulthood. George was educated at the West Somerset County School in Wellington and then read engineering at Glasgow University where he joined the OTC. Returning to Mudford in January 1914, George joined his younger brother Cyril's Regiment – the West Somerset Yeomanry – one month after the outbreak of war on 5 September. Within four months, George had been promoted to the rank of Sergeant; his military experience from the OTC being recognised. He probably deployed to East Anglia in 1915 with his unit on anti-invasion duties which was the main role of Yeomanry units. George was commissioned on 2 May 1915 but, although the West Somerset Yeomanry was deployed to Gallipoli in October 1915, there is no record that George went with them. In February 1916, George's younger brother Leslie was attested and later that month joined the RAVC at Woolwich. George was attached to the MGC from 16 April 1916 and deployed to France in early September. After the first action on 15 September, George was tasked to support George Mann on 22 September but his tank did not go into action. Three days later, his brother Leslie deployed to France and served as a groom at 23 Veterinary Hospital, being demobilised in 1919.

Promoted Temporary Lieutenant at the end of the month, George and his crew took part in the attack at Eaucourt L'Abbaye on 1 October in concert with the D16 crew which was commanded by Jefferson Wakley. George Bown's tank became ditched once it had got into the middle of the Germans' defences but it allowed the infantry to break into the German position. Knowing it could not be recovered, George ordered that the tank be set on fire to prevent its capture by the Germans in accordance with the direction given to tank commanders. George and his crew then tried to return to their lines but did not get back to the main base at the Loop until 4 October.

Three days later, whilst undertaking a recce prior to the attacks in the Auchonvillers area, George was badly injured by artillery shrapnel and was evacuated back to the UK on 11 October. Shortly afterwards, he was awarded the Military Cross for this action on 15 September 1916. Once he had recovered from his wounds, he was appointed to G Battalion and promoted acting Captain. However his old company commander, Frank Summers claimed him just prior to F Battalion being deployed and George returned to France on 20 May as a section commander in No 16 Company. On 27 June, just before deploying to the Ypres Salient, George met up with many of the original C and D Company tank skippers who were invited the F Battalion dinner night. During the first part of the 3rd Battle of Ypres, he commanded No 2 Section of No 16 Company. His company commander was Arthur Inglis, who had commanded *Crème de Menthe* at Courcelette on 15 September and commanding No 1 Section was Harold Darby who had commanded the female tank No 535 (D10 crew) in support of the New Zealanders on 15 September. On 29 July 1917, most of George's section got beyond the German front line despite having ditched in the swamp-like conditions near St Jean. The battalion was withdrawn from the Salient on 31 August and, on 6 September, No 16 Company was sent by train to Blairville, to the south west of Arras, for driver training. Eight days later, George was admitted to 43 Casualty Clearing Section suffering from scabies but was released on 20 September and returned to his company which had returned to Erin.

Having undertaken further training, the battalion returned to Auchy. On 15 November, whilst the company's tanks were being loaded to trains at the Le Plateau railway sidings before moving forward for the Battle of Cambrai, George suffered a dislocated shoulder after being thrown inside a moving tank. George was sent back to hospital in Harrogate and, as a result, was not present at the Battle of Cambrai when his younger brother Cyril, who had also joined the Tank Corps, was Killed in Action on 30 November. George recovered from his own injuries quickly but was not sent overseas again. He was re-appointed to the rank of captain in October but his service records give no clue as to his employment. He was also not released from Army service until 10 May 1919 after which he moved to Sherborne where his father and mother had relocated shortly after Cyril's death.

Less than two weeks later, George was in Halifax, Nova Scotia, on route to the Mexican province of Tataboyrie. He stayed overseas for two years before returning to Sherborne in Dorset. After three months, George decided to try his hand at sugar planting in Jamaica; on the boat out, he met Gladys, the daughter of the late Sir Walter Menzies and Lady Margaret Menzies of Fintry, and they married the following year. They returned to Sherborne in 1926 where their son Michael was born two years later. By now, George had started a successful farming career near Dorchester and was soon appointed to represent the local Farmer's Union. He participated in many farming shows and also dominated the Dorchester tennis championships from 1929 to 1931. In the 1930s the family moved to the Home Farm on the Bryanston estate, to the north west of Blandford Forum, where it is likely that George regularly met Bill Brannon who had served in D Company headquarters in 1916; Brannon was farming at nearby Tarrant Monkton. In the early 1950s, George sold up and he and Gladys moved to the Mount at St Leonard's Avenue in Blandford. In 1969, George entered the St Audrey's Nursing Home where he died on Boxing Day. His widow Gladys moved to Cambridge to be near her son where she died in early 1987.

George's second in command was James Lindsay. Born on 5 October 1889 at Clarence Street in Edinburgh, James was the third son of a cooperage manager. Bought up in Edinburgh and Liberton, James was, according to his family, a world class sprinter who was expected to represent his country at the Berlin Olympics planned for 1916. However James joined the MMGS in 1915 but did not deploy overseas until he joined D Company. After the first actions, I have been unable to locate James until he was Mentioned in Despatches on 25 May 1917 probably for actions during the Battle of Arras. Later rebadged to the Tank Corps, he was posted to 1st Salvage Company in which unit he was awarded the Military Medal for his work at Hooge during the Third Battle of Ypres. At this time, the Menin road was a mass of enormous shell craters; all full of water and there was no possibilities of any advance. Despite this, the tanks were deployed to assist in the destruction of German defences and many of them sank in the mud. According to the citation for his medal "On the morning of 27th August 1917, a tank was badly ditched and left at Clapham Junction, Sgt Lindsay was in fully view of the enemy and at a place which was constantly shelled. By a remarkable display of perseverance, judgement and devotion to duty, he succeeded in bringing the tank back."

He later returned to 4th Battalion where he was selected for officer training and commissioned into the Tank Corps on 3 March 1919. The following summer, having resigned his commission, James married an actress Agnes Fox, who was known as Jez, at Scarborough. He settled with Jez and their daughter Marjorie, who also became an actress, in Yorkshire and James became a commercial traveller. When war was declared in 1939, James attempted to join the Army but was rejected when his age became known. He died of heart failure aged fifty-nine, on 6 February 1949, at his home in Bessacar near Doncaster.

Sadly two of his crewmates were killed in action during the battles of Passchendaele and at Cambrai. The first, Private Eddie Williams, was born in 1892 in Ferndale in Glamorgan. The son of a colliery engineer, Eddie was educated at Tylerstown Boys School then Ferndale Secondary School before becoming as a school teacher in Ferndale. Eddie later worked as an engineer at the local colliery and was a member of the Sion Calvinistic Methodist Church. After the first tank actions on the Somme, he stayed with D Battalion and served with No 11 Company. He almost certainly fought during the Anglo-Australian assault at Bullecourt on 11 April where the tanks failed to break-though, and was recommended for a bravery award. Appointed lance corporal, he probably served during the early part of the Third Battle of Ypres. On 20 September, his tank *Damon* was swamped when it was hit and two men killed. Eddie was later killed in action, at the age of 25, when *Damon II* was destroyed as it fought its way into the centre of the village of Poelcapelle on 9 October 1917. His tank corporal was Dudley White, who fought at High Wood on 15 September in crew D22 and the men were probably buried alongside the tank hulk close by the site of the new Tank Corps memorial in the village.

The second fatality was the tank's driver, Private Bert Young ASC, who was probably the oldest member of the crew. Born in 1879 at New Hampton in Middlesex, Bert was the eldest son of a licensed victualler John Young and his wife Martha. Bert was christened at St James' Church in Hampton Hill on 6 July that year. Bert worked as a blacksmith's assistant when he was twenty-one but, by the time of the 1911 census, he was working as a motor engineer whilst living with his parents and six of his seven siblings in Wimbledon. He joined the ASC in 1915 but did not deploy overseas before he was attached to the tanks at Elveden. Bert was temporarily blinded during the assault near Flers but recovered and drove the tank back to the rally point. He was awarded the Military Medal for his actions which included driving for ten hours using only the brakes and gears; something which was not considered possible when the tanks were introduced. Bert continued to serve with D Company after the first actions, then to D Battalion having rebadged to the MGC. He almost certainly fought at Arras and at Ypres, before being Killed in Action, aged thirty-eight, on the opening day of the Battle of Cambrai. This was probably whilst D Battalion was attacking the western side of Flesquières on 20 November; the battalion losing nine tanks from defending German artillery which was used in the direct fire role, as the tanks tried to force their way into the village. His grave site is not known, possibly because it was not possible to recover his body from the tank hulk, and he is therefore commemorated at the Louverval memorial. After his death, Bert's pay balance of more £25 was distributed not just to his mother, as next of kin, but unusually to his five remaining siblings on an equal basis. It was his mother Martha who received a war gratuity of £5 10s just over two years after his death on 24 November 1919.

Sadly I have not been able to identify Gunner Clayton although it may have been Sydney Clayton, who later served with F Battalion. Gunner William Pestell was the eldest of five children of a hairdresser Frederick Pestell and his wife Kate. William was born in Fareham in Hampshire on 6 June 1892 and bought up in West Street. As a young man, William worked as a sales assistant on the bookstall at the local railway station, which was very close to the family home. He must also have had experience as a motorcyclist as he originally served with the MMGS. Having served as a gunner in the MMGS, and then in the Tank Corps, he was later transferred to the Royal Engineers and probably served in one of the Tank Signal Units. After the war, he moved to Wimbledon and became a newspaper representative. On 7 July 1928, he married a shorthand typist named Ethel Wilton at St Andrew's Parish Church in Wimbledon. Their only son Michael was born on 14 April 1930 in Northampton but sadly his parents' marriage did not last. According to his grand-daughter Julia, Ethel abandoned the family when her son was only four and later remarried. William moved to Hove from 1939 and lived there until his death, aged ninety, in September 1982; his son Michael having pre-deceased him six years earlier.

Gunner John Tennant was born in January 1895 in Edinburgh, he had an older brother named William and the boys lived with their parents, James and Jemima Tennant at 17 Rossie Place off the Easter Road. James was a house joiner but John gained employment as assistant postman from 1912. The following year he became an assistant postal clerk, in 1913, and was promoted to postal clerk before he enlisted on 13 October 1915 at Edinburgh. After training at Bisley and Elveden, John deployed to France on 27 August. He served on with D Battalion after 18 November 1916 and qualified both as a tank instructor and machine gun instructor. He was appointed acting Lance Corporal on 24 November 1917, presumably as result of losses at Cambrai and then paid for the rank from 29 November 1917. Following the fighting of the Kaiserschlacht, when the renamed 4th Battalion fought hard to hold back the German advance, John was awarded the Military Medal. The citation states

> On 24 Mar 18, at Combles, a runner was required to take important messages forward to his section commander. This NCO volunteered and, in the face of very heavy rifle and machine gun fire, succeeded in delivering the messages. On a subsequent occasion, he volunteered and delivered his messages.

John was again in action, during the British attack at Arras in August 1918. He was reported missing on 10 August 1918 after he had been captured by the Germans at Parvillers-Les-Quesnay as 4th Battalion pushed forward in support of the Canadians. He was imprisoned at Friedrichsfeld near Wesel in Germany, but was released almost immediately after the Armistice. He returned to the UK on 22 November 1918 and was posted as a lance corporal to the Tank Depot. He was promoted corporal and continued to work as an instructor. He had become infected, during his imprisonment, and was admitted to Wareham Military Hospital. He was later transferred to the Royal Victoria Hospital at Netley on 3 March 1919, so that the infection could be investigated. Three months later, he was transferred to the Reserve and was dispersed from Kinross on 5 June 1919. However, he was far from well and, fifteen months later, he was awarded a pension for thirteen months for dermatitis of the neck. Other than returning to work with the post office, as a clerical office, there is no other information I can find about him.

The final member of crew D8 was Gunner Ernest Didcote who was born at Homerton in North London on 8 October 1892. The youngest son of a draper and house-furnisher, Ernest was working as a mechanic and living in Coventry when he enlisted in the MMGS on 3 November 1915. Ernest undertook his initial training at Bisley and was transferred to 21 Battery on 4 March; he then transferred to the Heavy Section MGC on 4 May and posted to D Company on 25 May. Ernest deployed to France on 28 August and stayed with the Company after they fought on the Somme. Soon after being posted to D Battalion, he was admitted sick to 22 Field Ambulance on 28 November but was back with his unit three days later. Renumbered as 200789 in the Tank Corps, Ernest was appointed to lance corporal on 28 August 1917 and then promoted corporal on 12 October, presumably to fill vacancies resulting from casualties sustained in the final actions during the Battle of Ypres. After the Battle of Cambrai, when he was wounded, he was granted leave from 11 to 25 December. Feeling unwell, he admitted himself to St Luke's War Hospital in Bradford where he was found to be suffering from septic poisoning to the legs and foot, presumably from injuries sustained in action. When he failed to return to his unit after Christmas, absentee action commenced but, when the Metropolitan Police visited his mother on 6 January 1918, she stated that she had not seen Ernest for 18 months; that is before he deployed to France.

Coincidently Ernest was discharged from hospital that same day, and two days later, returned to his unit in France where he was immediately promoted acting corporal. Having been involved in the Kaiserschlacht, when D Battalion delayed the advancing German troops, Ernest was posted to the Mechanical School at Bovington as an instructor. He arrived on 17 May 1918 and was immediately promoted to corporal and graded as a Tank Mechanist 1st Class with the appropriate increase in pay. As part of an exchange arrangement put in place to balance the workloads of instructors, he was detached to the Reinforcement Depot at Mers-les-Bains in France for a short while, before returning to the Bovington where he was employed as an assistant instructor at the Driving and Maintenance School. He must have been sent back to the Driving School in France as he was granted home leave from 26 October to 9 November. As a result of the Armistice, courses were reduced in number and Ernest was posted to the Reinforcement Depot on 3 December 1918 which was commanded at that time by Major Victor Smith who had been skipper of *Casa* on 15 September 1916. Ernest was discharged to the Reserve, on 23 March 1919; his new address being shown as 25 York Road at Woking in Surrey. He had met Winifred Plymen, a local girl who was a schoolmaster's daughter and they married at New Malden Parish Church on 18 August 1923. The couple settled at 25 York Road, where Ernest must have been in contact with the crew members of *Champagne* who lived close by. The couple, who had no children, lived at Woking until his death aged fifty four, on 3 August 1947 at St Peter's Hospital in Chertsey. Winifred lived as a widow for eight years dying in 1955 aged sixty-seven.

D12 and *Dreadnought*

The other three tanks operated as a group under their section commander Captain Graeme Nixon. He was in the centre of the NZ Division's advance leading the way. Like George Bown, Graeme's tank *Deadnought* was late getting to the first objective near what is now the site of the New Zealand memorial (see coloured image 12). He led the other three tanks parallel to the Switch Trench and then turned to the north-east. Midway across the NZ frontage, Nixon's tank turned north (see map 10) and went forward until he received a request for help at 09.15 a.m. The message, which was carried by Rifleman JW Dobson, was follows: "From Lieut Butcher to O.C. Tanks. Enemy machine guns appear to be holding infantry in the valley on your right. Can you assist in pushing forward?" Dobson was the target of heavy enemy rifle as he tried to reach *Dreadnought* but eventually got inside the tank and accomplished the first example of infantry – tank target indication. Dobson guided the tank crew to a farm building where the machine guns were located. Rather than use the 6 pdr quick firing guns to destroy the machine guns, Nixon used the tank's weight to collapse the building and the machine gunners scattered in all directions. He then pressed on, heading for the northwest corner of Flers until *Dreadnought* was hit by artillery fire. The tank's steering was damaged so Graeme headed south to return his vehicle back to the British lines. The tank became ditched in a shell hole, where it was once again hit by enemy artillery fire and the crew abandoned the hulk when it caught fire. Although the fire was put out by the other tanks' crews, *Dreadnought* had become totally unusable and was therefore abandoned. When the crew regrouped, Gunner William Debenham was missing and his body was never found. The tank hulk remained where it was and became a playground for the Flers children until the end of the Second World War.

Capt Graeme Nixon was born in May 1894 at West Derby in Lancashire, the third child of headmaster Robert Nixon and his wife Ann; Robert later being appointed as the Assistant Director for Education in Liverpool. Bought up in Fairfield, in the east of the city, Graeme studied Engineering at Liverpool University graduating in 1913. Whilst a student Graeme served as a sapper in the local Royal Engineers Fortress Company based at Aigbirth and, on the outbreak of war, volunteered to join the Kings Liverpool Regiment (KLR). Graeme's elder brother Robert, who had studied medicine at Liverpool, also volunteered for the KLR in August 1914 but was discharged due to ill health in early 1915; he later was commissioned into the RAMC and served in East Africa. Graeme was commissioned into the Royal Inniskilling Fusiliers and served at Gallipoli. Transferring to the MGC (Motors) in April 16, Graham was one of the select group of officers who visited Foster's tank factory at Lincoln in May so that they could develop training for the new crews. Promoted temporary Captain on 12 August, when appointed as a section commander, Graeme appears to have served in the fourth section at Elveden but later commanded No 2 Section. The photograph of D Company officers, on page 115, shows him looking away from the camera, an trait he repeated when the image of the second half of the company was taken shortly afterwards. This trait revealed itself again forty years later in a school photograph.

Although he was not injured during the first attack at Flers on 15 September, Graham Woods' diary shows that Graeme Nixon was wounded on 24 September. No other details of this action are known but his injuries could not have been significant as he was later to command tanks as they tried to capture ground to the north of the River Ancre. On 14 November, he led a section of six tanks from Auchonvillers to Beaucourt Station, crossing no man's land to relieve Morty Mortimore and his section. When the tanks were withdrawn from action, Graeme moved from Acheux to Beaussart on 22 November preparing three tanks for recovery back to the Erin area. He continued to serve as a section commander in D Battalion, probably in No 12 Company, but may not have been involved in the fighting at Thelus or Bullecourt as only two sections were in action fought during the Battle of Arras.

When the Battalion moved to the Ypres Salient, Graeme commanded 12 Section of No 12 Company during their action on 22 August. The St Julien to Winnipeg Road was so badly damaged that none of the six tanks detailed to travel along it made it to their objectives. Three of his tanks did engage the enemy and returned safely although D51 broke down despite having managed to undich. Graeme led the same section during the Battle of Cambrai. He was wounded on the opening day of the battle when two of his three tanks were destroyed by direct fire as they attempted to push into the village of Flesquières from the east by the Chateau wall. Replaced temporarily by Alfred Enoch, Graeme was soon however able to return to duty. He then commanded a company, probably No 12 Company, from 5 to 20 December 17 and was appointed acting major.

In early 1918, Graeme led his company to the Tank Corps Gunnery School, on the coast at Merlimont where they undertook gunnery practice. He was also in command of the company throughout the Kaiserschlacht withdrawal when their tanks were either destroyed or abandoned and the following month during the Battle of Lys, when his company was used in the dismounted role as Lewis gun detachments to hold back the advancing Germans between Armentieres and Ypres. He was awarded the Military Cross for sustained gallantry on 31 May 1918. Around that time, D Battalion was re-equipped with the new Mark V tanks and Graeme commanded a company at the Battle of Amiens in support of 2nd Canadian Brigade. Having taken part in the successful advance, he relinquished command on 6 September and was posted to Bovington where he was assumed command of a company in the newly formed 22nd Battalion Tank Corps. After the Armistice, he served for a while at Bovington, and joined 17th Battalion Tank Corps where he commanded B Company. Because of the shortfall of officers' accommodation, Graeme lived in the village of Owermoigne, between Wool and Dorchester, using a motorcycle to travel to Bovington each day, in July 1919 he was one of several Tankers caught riding without lights presumably late on evening. He was subsequently fined £1.00 for the offence. The following month, he deployed with 17th Battalion to Marlborough Barracks in Dublin, where he commanded B Company who were supporting anti-insurgency operations against the Irish Nationalists during the autumn. Relinquishing his commission later that year, he returned to Liverpool to the family home at Radstock Road in Fairfield. He became a schoolteacher joining the staff of newly established Quarry Bank High School in 1926. There he became great friends with an art teacher Walter Simmons, who taught at the school and Graeme was a witness, and probably best man, at Walter's wedding to Elsie Hall at All Hallow's Church at Allerton on 4 April 1931. Graeme was still regularly visiting Dorset as he was courting Audrey Thomas, the only daughter of Martha Thomas who farmed at Winfrith. On 12 August 1931, he married Audrey at St Mary's Church at East Stoke and they settled in Liverpool where Audrey gave birth to their son Gerald on 8 March 1933 and their daughter Valerie four years later.

After the outbreak of the Second World War, Graeme returned to uniform being commissioned into the KLR as a lieutenant on 27 June 1940 and appears to have reached the rank of colonel by the end of the war. After the war, he continued to teach mathematics at the Quarry Bank High School where he was known by the boys as "Old Nick". One of his pupils was John Lennon whom Graeme noted was likely to fail his end of year exams due to his persistent absence. He also awarded Lennon detention for not completing his homework but in this he was not alone, as Lennon attracted detention from a large number of staff for bad behaviour. When Graeme was contacted by Victor Huffam, after he and Victor Smith had appeared on the BBC TV programme *Find the Link*, Graeme indicated he was saddened by the fact the majority of the Tank Corps had forgotten the efforts of those who fought at Flers-Courcelette. He did however attend the 40th Anniversary celebrations for the Battle of Cambrai the following year.

In May 1957, shortly before Graeme retired, he was again photographed with other members of the staff of Quarry Bank School and, as with the pictures taken at Elveden, he again is looking away from the camera to his left – a remarkable coincidence. Graeme lived at Pinfold Road at

1 From Leuze Wood looking SE showing Purdy's route towards Combles (centre).

2 From Dickens' Cross looking SE showing Arnold's route towards Bouleaux Wood (right).

3 From Dickens' Cross looking north to the Quadrilateral (low trees central on horizon).

4 From south of Ginchy looking ENE showing Henriques, Macpherson and Murphy's route towards Quadrilateral (low trees central on horizon).

5 From the Quadrilateral looking south towards Leuze Wood showing how the position dominates ground.

6 From the Quadrilateral looking south west towards Guillemont and the tanks' approach route.

7 From Ginchy looking NE across the ground crossed by the Guards Division accompanied by Clarke and Smith who reached the wood line (second left breaching the skyline).

8 From the Guards Memorial looking west towards Delville Wood (left) and High Wood (centre).

9 Looking NW toward Delville Wood showing Mortimore's route to eastern edge.

10 From the German artillery position, on the Bulls Road, looking south towards Delville Wood.

11 Sunken lane, used by Blowers to avoid artillery fire, looking north towards Gueudecourt.

12 Flers, looking north from the New Zealand memorial, showing the attack routes.

13 Looking north towards Martinpuich, towards Colle's objective on the east of the village.

14 Drader's route from the SW west towards Martinpuich; he halted on the left by the crops.

15 Looking north from the Sugar Trench to Courcelette (behind trees) and factory (right).

16 Looking south from the Courcelette Sugar factory, showing Inglis' route from Pozieres.

Hunts Cross until his death, aged seventy-one, on 1 September 1966 at John Bagot Hospital in Everton.

It is difficult to track Nixon's second in command, Sgt Reginald Vandenburg as his spelling of his surname changes frequently. The second son of a commercial clerk, he was born on 8 December 1889 in Islington, and was baptized with his two siblings on 9 November 1890 at St Luke's Church West Holloway. When he enlisted on 9 February 1916, Reginald was working a clerk. He was posted to Bisley on 13 March and, despite having no previous military experience, was appointed acting lance corporal on 12 April. A month later, he was promoted corporal on 13 May and then sergeant on 5 August. He was deployed to France on 28 August, as part of the Advance party and probably fought with Graeme Nixon in the actions in September and November. Reginald was posted to D Battalion on formation; I cannot be sure what he did in early 1917 but it is likely he was used as an instructor. He was attached to the Reinforcement Battalion on 13 July then returned to the UK six days later. After ten days home leave, and rebadging to the Tank Corps, he was posted to the School of Instruction at Bovington where he served for four months. Reginald was then posted to the newly formed J Battalion on 1 Dec 1917, deployed overseas twenty days later and served with C Company as Technical Machinist Sergeant from 23 January 1918. He returned to Tank Training Centre at Bovington, as an instructor, on 14 August 1918 which was unusual as his unit was fully committed to the Battle of Amiens. Reginald married Amelia Whitehead on 5 October 1918 at Christchurch in Kensington Liverpool and, on 25 January, was posted to the Central Schools. Unlike many of his former comrades who were with fighting units on the continent, he was not demobilised but was retained. From 16 Apr 1919 served as a Technical Mechanical Sergeant Instructor and managed to get permission to live out, rather than live in the barracks. When he was discharged on 27 September 1919, he moved to Brighton. The family settled in Sussex and their three daughters, born between early 1920 and 1923, were all registered at Steyning. Sadly I can then find nothing else about him until the 1950s when he was living in Paddock Wood in Kent. Reginald died in Brighton, aged eighty-eight, in the summer of 1977.

Gunner Harry Zimmerman died somewhat earlier in his mid-forties. Born at Hull in the summer of 1894, his Warsaw-born father Barnett was a furniture dealer at 164 Hessle Road. Harry became a naturalized British subject, as did the rest of his family, in April 1902. After Barnett died on 14 November 1905, Harry's eldest brother Wolf took over the furniture business on the Hessle road. Harry was educated locally and also attended the Hull Municipal School of Art where, in 1910, he obtained a first class pass in model drawing. Harry initially worked with his brother Wolf in the family furniture business. His service record has not survived but he joined the HS MGC and trained at Elveden from where he obtained compassionate leave to attend the funeral of his mother after her death on 16 August 1916.

It is due to an article in the *Hull Daily Mail* published on 30 November 1916, that we know his tank on 15 September was known as *Dreadnought*. In the report, Harry confirmed he had supported the New Zealanders in the attack and also that the tank entered the Flers village to deal with snipers who were creating difficulties for the British infantry trying to secure the village. This is not recorded elsewhere. Harry also stated that, following the action at Flers, he was forced to spend two days in a British frontline trench, presumably near Flers itself.

Ten days later, on 25 September he was allocated as a 6 pdr gunner to the scratch A Crew attached to the Reserve Army which fought at Thiepval. He was later gassed near Beaumont-Hamel and the newspaper reported that he was in six different hospitals as part of his treatment. After treatment in England, Harry returned to duty and later served in the Tank Corps until the end of the war as a private soldier. After he was demobilised, Harry returned to work in Hull with his brother with whom he built a large property portfolio. Harry also established a wholesale clothing company on Whitefriargate in the centre of the town. Harry never married but settled with his brother on the coast in Withernsea where he was heavily involved in local affairs. Appointed a JP, Harry was also elected to the Urban District Council in 1929, the same year he and Woolf retired from business, and was appointed chairman in 1934. Harry was also instrumental in the establishment of the Withernsea Home for Children in 1931 and was involved with many other charities. Harry became ill in December 1936 and died aged forty-three at the Queen's Hotel at Withernsea on 14 Mar 1937; his obituary stating that gassing during the war may have a contributory factor. He was buried at the Delhi Road Jewish Cemetery and the mourners included Harry Jacobs who probably served as the Company QMS in C Company on the Somme in 1916.

Gunner Mead joined *Dreadnought*'s crew just before they went into action. The Adjutant, Graham Woods, struck through the name of the original 6 pdr gunner in his notebook so that it is impossible to read but the name of his replacement Mead is very clear. Like Harry Zimmerman, Gunner Mead was also listed as a member of the "A" tank crew allocated to support the Reserve Army on 25 September, this being the action near Thiepval. I believe that Gunner Mead was probably John Victor Mead who served on with 4th Battalion and promoted corporal. He was captured during the German advance on 21 March 1918 and his details appear in the index cards of the International Commission of the Red Cross as well as in the Tank Corps medal rolls. He was born in Deptford on 25 December 1893. He was named after his father John and was the eldest of three children. At the age of four, he entered New Road School in Lambeth on 28 November by which time his family were living on the Wandsworth Road. In 1911 he was working as a 17 year old barman at a public house on 119 Bishopgate in London. Following his release from captivity, John married Dorothy Free and their daughter Ruby who was born in 1919. Dorothy died in 1966 after which John lived for a further six years before his death aged seventy nine in the summer 1972 at Havering

The tank's driver Corporal Robert R Murray transferred to the MGC, as did many of the members of 711 (MT) Company in early 1917 but must have found the transition difficult as he later transferred back to the ASC and served with them for the duration of the war. Gunner William Debenham, who was declared missing after his tank was destroyed on the edge of Flers, was born in Berlin on 29 January 1892. His English parents bought him to Canterbury when William was three weeks old. His father subsequently died and his mother married James Appleton who was a professor of music. The family settled in Coventry by 1901. William initially was apprenticed to a pork butcher but later was employed by Robinsons and Sons Ltd, the long established Coventry clockmakers. He enlisted at Coventry on 3 April 1916, at the age of twenty three, but there are no other details of his service until he was reporting missing on 15 September 1916. His body was never located and his life was commemorated at St John's Church in Coventry as well as the Thiepval memorial.

Gnr Horace Allebone was killed in action the following year during the attack on Flesquières. Horace, who was born at Rushden in Northamptonshire on 29 August 1889, was the elder son of a boot manufacturer; shoe and boot making being the major industry in the Nene Valley. Horace was educated at the Alfred Street National School from 1 February 1897 until 26 October 1903. In 1908 his father's firm moved to larger premises in High Street Rushden and, when the business was converted into a limited company in 1913, the management was left in the hands of Horace and his younger brother Arthur. Prior to the Great War, the firm were mainly manufacturing medium class youths' and boys' shoes but, with the outbreak of hostilities, switched to Government work including making boots for the Russian army. In early 1916, Horace appealed against being conscripted on the grounds his work was critical to the war effort. However, whilst the appeal was underway, he enlisted at Rushden on 10 March 1916. Arthur was initially left in sole control although his father came out of retirement later. Horace, who was unmarried, initially trained as a machine gunner. He served with D Battalion, after the first actions and retrained as a tank driver. Whilst serving in No 10 Company, he had his photo taken, probably in France or the rear areas of Belgium given the state of his boots.

Horace was not only a good driver but also a brave and determined man. He was awarded two parchment certificates signed by Brigadier General Hugh Elles: one for gallant and meritorious service in the field for cool and skilful driving of a tank between 9 to 18 April during the Battle of Arras "on the Hindenburg Line" and the second for soldierly conduct under heavy fire on 4 October 1917. This action was in support of an attack on the village of Poelcapelle. Twelve tanks set out and eleven managed to reach the village proper and destroy the German strongpoints. Two sections proceeded through Poelcapelle reducing concrete Mebus emplacements with 6 pdr solid shot and using Lewis guns and 6 pdr case shot to shoot down those Germans who didn't surrender to the accompanying infantry. The strong point at Menuier was similarly dealt with. The reserve tanks, D10 and D12 also moved forward and engaged the enemy. All the tanks returned and rallied except crew D5. Fletcher points out that the only feasible route for the tanks was along the St Julien – Poelcapelle road which was well defended by artillery in an area which became known as the graveyard of the tanks.

Horace was killed on the opening day of the Battle of Cambrai. He was serving in No 2 Section, probably driving the tank *Devil May Care* which was hit during the attack on the western part of Flesquières and burnt out. Capt CR Nichols, the section commander, wrote to his parents

> I deeply regret having to inform you that your son was killed in action on November 20th. However, great the loss is to us, I know it is nothing to be compared with that sustained by yourself. Your son was in my section and was one of the best drivers in the company. However, apart from the loss as a driver, I feel that I have lost a very old friend and I hope you will accept my deepest sympathy. I am sorry I cannot give you full details, but I may say we buried your son near the village of Flesquières.

Horace was commemorated in the Louverval Memorial and at Rushden War Memorial Northants. Augustus and Mathilda were clearly proud of their son as they paid for him to be commemorated in de Ruvigney's Roll Of Honour and he is also commemorated on their gravestone.

The final member of *Dreadnought*'s crew survived the war. Cecil Gloyn was born in Plymouth on 8 March 1897 and baptised on 23 March at Holy Trinity Church. He was the son of a grocer's manager and, on leaving school, Cecil followed his father into the business. Cecil was mobilised and arrived at Bisley on 3 March 1916, undertook initial training and was posted to D Company on 24 May. After only three months training, he moved to France on 28 August. Sadly the details of his service, recorded on the Casualty Form Active Service, are indistinct. Cecil continued to serve with D Battalion, probably in the same company as Horace Allebone, and like him was rebadged into the Tank Corps. Cecil certainly fought at Cambrai as he was granted home leave from 16 to 30 December; getting back to his unit at Meulte despite dreadful weather conditions – 1917 being the worst winter in living memory. Cecil was probably in action during the Kaiserschlacht but his records were destroyed during action on 23 March 1918; D Battalion's equipment being destroyed as the Germans advanced. On 30 July, he was a crewman in the baggage tank No 8164 with 5 Section in B Company under the command of Heady Head. He was later promoted corporal, probably because of losses amongst crewmen during the Battle of Amiens in the following month.

At some time in late 1918, Cecil was sent back to England and served as a corporal in the Tank Corps Officers Training Battalion which had moved from Hazeley Down to Swanage. Cecil was demobilised, as part of early release scheme on 29 January 1919, and returned to his family at 2 Sussex Street in Plymouth. On 26 April 1922, he married Elizabeth Pain at St Andrew's Church in Plymouth but sadly she died within a year and there were no children. Cecil then established himself as a wholesale tobacconist and confectioner at 57 Notte Street in Plymouth. When he was forty-four, he married Ivy Whitaker on 6 November 1941, at Linkinhorne in the Tamar Valley. Cecil continued to work as a wholesale tobacconist in Plymouth but the couple settled at

Callington, which is about 4 miles from Linkinhorne, from 1970. Cecil died aged seventy-six, in the autumn of 1973 and Ivy lived on at Callington until 1984 but later moved to St Germans where she died aged ninety-three in 1996.

D10

The family of Gunner Lionel Britt has a picture of the D10 crew whilst they were training at Elveden. Sadly there are no names on the back so we cannot names to the faces of the crewmen, nor identify Leonard Haygarth who was killed in action at the end of the battle of Cambrai. On 15 September 1916, the crew took a female tank No 535 into action in support of the NZ Division assault to the west of Flers (see map 10). Leaving the RV on the western side of Delville Wood, the tank followed the track up the hill to the British front line, crossing close to the current NZ memorial. It then followed the track north which was also the route of the German communication trench, known as Fish Alley. The original plan was for D10 to veer off towards the northwest edge of Flers, but Harold Darby, its skipper, continued north until he reached the track linking Flers with the rear of High Wood as he had seen that the NZ infantry were held up by a large barbed wire obstacle. As he guided his tank towards it, the tank was hit by an artillery round which shattered the prism glasses which temporarily blinded both Darby and his ASC driver, Ernest Phillips. A second shell hit the tank which smashed one of its tracks and buckled the outer plating, shattering the cast-iron controls inside the tank. As a result, the tank was uncontrollable and Darby and his crew abandoned the vehicle, first taking shelter in the Fish Alley trench and then joining the infantry in the attack, using one of the machine guns from the disabled tank. The tank was abandoned and never recovered from the battlefield.

Harold Darby and his crew at Canada Farm Elveden. Summer 1916. (Brett Seabrook)

   Harold Darby was born in Tottenham, north London on 17 February 1888 but moved with his family as a boy to Ipswich where his father worked as a commercial traveller. Harold initially worked for Messrs Oxwoods Motor Works and then at Mann Egerton as an engineer. He served with the Suffolk Yeomanry from 1908, before moving to Cirencester where he again worked as a motor engineer. On the outbreak of war, he joined the Gloucester Hussars, and deployed to Gallipoli where he was wounded and subsequently evacuated. Having been appointed lance corporal, he was identified as suitable for officer training and commissioned into the Heavy Section MGC on 15 April. Harold, who was wounded in the first action and was taken for a short time to hospital, was awarded the Military Cross "*for conspicuous gallantry in action. He fought his Tank with great courage and determination. Later, with his crew and one gun, he went to support the infantry. He set a fine example.*" Promoted temporary Lieutenant on 1 October, Harold later served with D Battalion before returning to the UK in December 1916 with D Company's commander Frank Summers. He joined F Battalion and was promoted temporary Captain when he was appointed to command a section on 12 April 1917 under Arthur Inglis, who commanded *Crème de Menthe* at Courcelette. Harold deployed with F Battalion on 20 May to France, where it established its base to Auchy-Les-Hesdin. On 1 June he went to the Corps Driving School at Wailly for two weeks, and then to the Corps Gunnery School at Merlimont for live firing. Harold attended the F Battalion dinner night on 27 June 1917, at which several of the original members of C and D Companies were present. He commanded No 1 Section of 16 Company during the action on 31 July, the opening action of the muddy disaster that was the third Battle of Ypres. Harold also fought at Cambrai and through the Kaiserschlacht. Having been with the Battalion as it converted to Whippets, he was sent on leave in UK in early August 1918. Harold was back in action during the Battle of Amiens and was promoted major, from 11 August 18 after Major Alfred Rycroft had been severely injured during the initial action.

Harold Darby 1918.
(Tank Museum)

Harold then commanded B Company during its action in support of 4th Army. Originally based at Le Quesnel, where it undertook repairs and necessary maintenance after its action, his Company was tasked to support the Northumberland Fusiliers on 22 August 1918, during an action on the Albert to Bray Road. The infantry were held up and Harold Darby moved forward to undertake a recce in order to get his section of tanks in action. Whilst doing this, he was severely injured and was evacuated back to the UK. He did not return to action again and relinquished his commission on 23 August 1919.

After the war Harold moved to Leicester to find work as an engineer. On 21 October 1920, at All Saints Church in Marylebone, he married Dorothy Blackwell who came from Leicester. He and Doby, as she was known, had moved to York by 1924, where he represented Rolls Royce motors for many years. He may have sold cars to a former member of C Company crewman, Fenwick Styan, who owned a taxi service in Beverley and had three Roll Royce cars as well as a property in York. In 1930, Doby and Harold's only son Jeremy was born in York. Harold returned to the Army service during the Second World War, serving as a RTR officer in France after D Day and also in Germany. He also served with Fire Service for at least ten years. He was one of the veterans who attended the 40th Anniversary Cambrai dinner on 23 November 1957 and corresponded with Basil Liddell Hart shortly after he wrote the history of the Tank Corps. After his Doby died in 1960, Harold lived alone until he married Sheila Rogers at Hemel Hempstead in 1973. Five years later, Harold died in Littlehampton, aged eighty-nine, on 12 March 1978.

Harold's second in command was Lance Corporal William Hogarth who was born on 6 October 1886 in Galashiels. The youngest son of a master joiner, William was working as a clerk when he enlisted at Galashiels on 9 November 1915. He went to Bisley for training but was must have been granted leave in the New Year as he married Annie Walker of Edinburgh on 17 January 1916; their daughter Janet being born exactly nine months later. William was posted to 21 Battery MGC on 3 March then to Armoured Car Section MGC and was appointed unpaid lance corporal on 10 April. He was promoted lance corporal on 5 May and posted to D Company HS MGC on 27 May. William remained with D Battalion on its formation in November that year, attending a course at 3rd Army Gas School in January 1917 and gunnery training at 6th Corps school in May 1917. Promoted corporal on 17 July 1917, to bring D Battalion to establishment, he fought at Ypres and Cambrai after which he was granted him leave from 11 to 25 December 1917 when he saw his daughter for the first time. Sadly Janet died of tuberculosis and meningitis on 19 February 1918. Apart from a short detachment to 5th Battalion in April 1918, William served with 4th Battalion until he was transferred to the home establishment on 27 September 1918 and then joined the newly formed 22nd Light Battalion at Bovington, where he must have met Graeme Nixon who was serving as a company commander. He served with B Company from 15 October 1918 but was demobilised in January 1919 and returned to Galashiels, where his son William was born in 1920. Sadly, I can find nothing more about him but he probably remained in Galashiels as his son died there on 2 May 2010.

Gunner Lionel Britt, who was Killed in Action in March 1918, was the eldest surviving son of a monumental mason George Britt and his wife Mary. Lionel was born at Hollington near Hastings on 21 March 1892 and bought up at Beauport Cottage on Hollington Street at Leonards-on-Sea. Lionel, who also became a monumental mason, married Ada Marchant in the summer of 1914; their only child Laura being born in the following autumn. Lionel was attested at Hastings and joined the Machine Gun Corps. He fought with D Company as part of the crew of scratch B Crew which was allocated to support the Reserve Army at Thiepval on 25 September. After his commander Harold Darby returned to England for Christmas 1916, he sent a postcard to Ada which shows Lionel in the typical dress of a tank crewman including leather gaiters and the plain leather belt.

Lionel Britt in 1916.
(Brett Seabrook)

Lionel, who originally trained as a Vickers machine gunner, served with D Battalion and probably fought as a tank crewman at the Battles of Arras, Ypres and Cambrai. He was serving with 4th Battalion, during the great German Advance in the spring of 1918 when he was Killed In Action on 21 March 1918; his twenty-sixth birthday. His grave was lost and he is commemorated on the Pozières Memorial to the Missing. His wife and parents commemorated his loss annually in the local newspaper; his widow Ada continued to live in the St Leonards-on-Sea area, dying aged sixty-seven, in early 1960.

Lionel's family received a letter from his tank commander after his death in which he told them that Lionel was in the area of Delville Wood when his tank was hit by German artillery. As the crew abandoned the tank, Lionel received a direct hit which killed him instantly. This is odd as the majority of 4th Battalion tanks were well to the north trying to disrupt the German advance between Cambrai and Tincourt. The other oddity is that Lionel's wallet was found in Trafalgar Square in London about twelve months after the Armistice and his wife Ada often wondered if he had survived but was so disfigured that he felt he could not return home.

Gunner John Ellocott was also allocated to the scratch B tank crew, according to the notebook of Captain Graham Woods. Born on 12 May 1893, at Roath in Cardiff, Horace was the eldest son of an engine maker John Ellocott and his wife Ellen who later gave birth to two daughters, Olwen and Mildred, and a younger son Leonard who was born in 1898. John's mother died in 1904 so he was then bought by his grandmother. By his eighteenth birthday, he was living at 149 Broadway and working as a railway clerk. John enlisted on 9 November 1915 into the MMGS and trained on both Hotchkiss and Vickers machine guns. After the first action on 15 September, the crew must have been split up as John was allocated as a Vickers gunner of the B Crew attached to the Reserve Army on 25 September. John probably served on with D Battalion but was discharged on 2 August 1917, as no longer physically fit for war service which indicates that he had become ill rather than wounded. He was subsequently awarded the Silver War Badge. John married Eva Woodhouse in the autumn of 1925 in Hammersmith; the following year John was appointed, as a civil service clerk, to the Ministry of Health. Eva and John's only son Owen was born in early March 1928 in Peterborough. By 1937, the family settled in the Headlands in Northampton where they lived until John's death aged sixty-six on 3 August 1959.

A third crewman, fighting alongside John Ellocott and Lionel Britt on both 15 and 25 September, was Frank Dale. Born in Uttoxeter in early 1888, Frank was the fourth child of a painter Charles Dale and his dressmaker wife May. Charles died in 1900 and his widow was left to bring up their nine children alone. The family lived in Bridge Street in Uttoxeter and then at 37 Balance Street.

By 1911, all of the children were employed except the eldest daughter and the two youngest boys who were still at school. Frank was employed as a grocer's assistant, a role he was still filling at Messrs Parkman and Co at the Market Stores, when he enlisted into the MGC and reported for duty at Bisley on 25 March 1916. Frank's elder brother Albert had enlisted into the King's Royal Rifle Corps in 1915 and, whilst Frank was undergoing initial training, was serving with 11th Battalion on the Somme as a sergeant. The battalion, which was part of the 20th Light Division, was fighting between Trônes Wood and Guillemont when Albert went missing on 23 August 1916 and his body was not identified. Frank probably found out this news whilst he was on the Somme and before his mother who was not informed of the news until early October.

According to Graham Woods' notebook, it was Frank Dale took his skipper, Harold Darby to hospital after the first tank action on 15 September. Frank took part in the subsequent action on 25 September to capture the village of Thiepval and Mouquet farm; this time it was successful but, according to the local Uttoxeter newspaper, Frank suffered from shellshock as a result of his actions on the Somme. Frank served on with D Battalion and presumably during the Battle of Arras. He probably fought during the early stages of the Third Battle of Ypres but, on 19 August 1917, he was admitted to 3rd Australian General Hospital with trench fever. Despite a month's hospital treatment at Abbeville, he made no progress and was evacuated to Queens Mary Hospital Whalley in Lancashire, arriving on 20 September 1917. His medical records showed that Frank had been wounded in the hands, probably during the Battle of Arras when many of the tanks were hit by German armour-piercing bullets, but the wounds had healed. He was still suffering from pains in legs and Frank was not considered fit to be released, until treatment was completed at the Primrose Band Hospital in Burnley on 2 April 1918. Posted to the Tank Depot, he was again admitted to hospital at Wareham on 16 June 1918 suffering from neck swelling. Frank did not go overseas to fight again but, in October 1918, he was one of a party of four instructors which took a Mark V female tank and four Whippets to provide demonstrations to the Japanese Army at their driving school at Setagaya. On his departure, Frank was presented with the Order of the Rising Sun Eight Class which was an exceptionally rare award as, according to *Statistics of the Military Effort of the British Empire,* only nine such medals were presented to British other ranks throughout the Great War

On his return to England, Frank claimed a disability pension prior to his discharge on 31 January 1919 but the Medical Board did not however approve his claim. Frank returned to Uttoxeter, where he made another claim but this again does not appear to have been granted. Ten years later he married Eveline Walton, who was twenty eight, in the summer of 1930 in Uttoxeter. Eveline and Frank's only son Thomas was born in 1931 but sadly the boy died aged seven. I have been unable to ascertain Frank's employment between the wars, but he and Eveline later lived in Windfield House, a substantial property on Stafford Road in Uttoxeter. Frank died, aged sixty, at Derby City Hospital on 19 September 1958. Evelyn lived as a widow until her ninetieth year when she died in early 1982.

There was a fourth member of the crew, who fought alongside Francis and Horace on 25 September, who was later Killed in Action in one of the last actions of the Battle of Cambrai. Gunner Leonard Haygarth was born in Colne in Lancashire on 3 January 1889 and christened on 27 January. From the census records, it appears that his mother Elizabeth was single and that Leonard and his younger brother Wilfred, who died as an infant, were bought up in his grandparents' house. In the 1890s Colne was the location of more than thirty cotton mills in the 1890s ranging from 30 to more than 2,400 loons. By the age of twelve, Leonard was working part-time as in a cotton warehouse and in 1911 was working as a cotton winder as was his mother and his sixteen year old cousin Rennie . Sadly there is no surviving record of Leonards' military service. He initially joined the Machine Gun Corps, probably in the spring of 1916. In the picture of the D10 tank crew, he is sitting in the front row on the left hand side of the photograph. He transferred to D Battalion on its formation but, as there is no record of his service, it is impossible to say in which company he served. Although the record of Soldiers who Died in the Great War states he was Killed in Action on 30 November 1917, the Register of Soldiers' Effects records that he died of wounds. His body was buried at Grevillers Military Cemetery near Bapaume. His young cousin Rennie did not survive the war either. Serving as a Sapper in the 8th Division Signal Company, Rennie died on 27 May 1918 and is commemorated on Soissons Memorial.

The driver of the tank, Lance Corporal Ernest Phillips, was Killed in Action the following year as the Allied Forces pushed the Germans back during the Great Advance. Ernest was born in Brackley in Northants in the spring 1890; his Welsh-born father James Phillips being employed by the Parish Guardians as a relieving officer whilst his mother Alice ran a tobacconist shop in the High Street. As a young man, Ernest worked as a chauffeur to Lady Brown of Astrop House at Kings Sutton, a village to the west of Brackley, but by 1911 he was living near Hannover Square in London and working as a motor mechanic. In the spring of 1914, Ernest married Helena Rhodes who was born in Kings Sutton. Their only son Leslie was born in the village on 4 December. At the time of his enlistment Ernest was an instructor and lecturer at the Motor Training Institute Ltd in London. He enlisted into the ASC at St John's Wood London and probably trained at the Grove Park MT Depot, before being posted to 711 Coy ASC.

Ernest was wounded in the action at Flers but not seriously. He was one of the original tank drivers who rebadged to the MGC and then to the Tank Corps serving with A Battalion. He served as a corporal during the Third Battle of Ypres which is probably when the photograph was taken. He was Mentioned in Despatches on 21 December. He was later promoted to Sergeant and then to Staff Sergeant where he would have been employed either as assistant to the 1st Battalion's engineer officer or as the senior mechanic within a company. Ernest had been awarded the Belgian Croix de Guerre for an unknown action in 1918 but it is likely to have been awarded for bravery, rather than for long term service in a key position. Ernest was Killed in Action on 29 September 1918; this occurred during the attack on the Hindenburg Line near Bellicourt when 1st Battalion was supporting the American 30th Division. Sadly he has no known grave and he is commemorated on Vis-en-Artois memorial. His widow remarried after the war but their son Leslie was fostered.

During the Second World War, Leslie was commissioned into a Green

Ernest Phillips near Ypres 1917. (John Phillips)

Howards territorial battalion and later served with 2nd Battalion Northamptonshire Yeomanry in Italy. The Regiment entered Normandy through GOLD beach on 18 June 1944 and then acted as the recce regiment for 11th Armoured Division which fought through France, the Netherlands and, after the Rhine Crossing, through northwest Germany finally capturing the Baltic town of Lubeck. After the end of hostilities in Europe, he attended the Army Staff College and eventually retired as an acting Major in 1946. Leslie was one of the first Administrators appointed by Ernest Bevan in 1947 to initiate the new National Health Service. He died on 4 June 1999.

The final member of the crew, Robert Frost, did survive. Born on Boxing Day 1892 in Teignmouth Devon, Robert and his two older sisters lived in 5 Regent Street in East Teignmouth, where his father Frederick was an estate agent and auctioneer. Robert joined his father's firm as a pupil after leaving school and later worked as en estate agent. He joined the MMGS and then started training at Bisley and Elveden. As it became clear that he would soon deploy to France, Robert made arrangement to marry his fiancée Margaret Rowe. Margaret came from West Hartlepool and was a photographer's assistant but they married in Teignmouth on 22 July 1916. Robert's Army service record has not survived but, from his RFC records we know he was deemed fit to be a pilot on 12 October 1917 and joined No 1 Officer Cadet Wing on 8 November. By this time, Margaret had returned to 44 Milton Street in West Hartlepool; the place which Robert recorded as his home address. He was then posted to the School of Military Aeronautics on 3 December 1917 at Reading, where he studied rigging, engines and instruments at Wantage Hall, the recently built university hall of residence which had been commandeered in December 1915. Commissioned into the Royal Flying Corps in January 1918, Robert was posted to No 28 Wing on 9 March and trained as a pilot. He was posted to 12 Squadron, who were based at St Omer, three days before the Armistice. He returned to the UK on 21 April and was demobilised two days later.

The couple returned to Teignmouth where Robert later took over the family business. Margaret and Robert's only son Ian was born in 1933 at Teignmouth, when the couple was in their mid-forties. After that, there is no record of Robert until 1961 when he attended the first meeting of the Devon branch of the Tank Corps Old Comrade Association. He was one of seven members who had served in the Tank Corps but only one of two who fought on 15 September 1916; the other was Morty Mortimore who was commanded the first tank in action *Daredevil*. In 1966, Robert attended the 50th anniversary dinner of the first tank action at Caxton Hall in London on 15 September. The following year, he appeared on Westward TV programme *"Fear Naught"* which interviewed two other First Tank Crews. Robert described his experiences in D Company fifty-one years previously including that, when they went into action, his tank had spare petrol cans attached to the roof. By this time, Margaret and Robert were living at 4 Coombe Vale Road; it was here in Teignmouth that Margaret died aged eighty-eight, on 13 August 1976. Robert however did not live on alone; four months later he married Gladys Alben, who was fourteen years his junior. They lived together until his death aged eighty-six in early 1980.

D11 – Die Hard

Die Hard was the fourth tank supporting the New Zealand Divisional assault and she was manned by crew D11 under their skipper George Pearsall. The name of the male tank was probably taken from the motto of the Middlesex Regiment although there is no obvious link between any of the crew and the regiment. *Die Hard* followed Harold Darby's tank northwards towards their third objective (see map 10) and, realising the leading tank had not cleared the barbed wire defences when it was knocked out, closed up and flattened the wire without difficulty. As a result, the infantry then stormed through the gap and captured 100 Germans at about 08.15 a.m. *Die Hard* then followed the track towards Flers village and assisted two tanks, D16 commanded by Arnold and D18 commanded by Len Bond, as they destroyed the enemy position to the northwest of the village.

Despite being ordered to return to the company base at Green Dump, sometime after 2.30 p.m. George Pearsall remained at Flers at the request of the New Zealanders. It was probably *Die Hard* which supported the 28th Battalion Royal Fusiliers as they advanced north out of Flers on the afternoon of 15 September; there were no other tanks in the area by that time. Fearful of becoming a static target, he ranged across the fields (see map 9) and was spotted, at 6.00 p.m. that evening by a RFC aircraft less than 350 yards south east of Gueudecourt – this was the nearest any tank got to the final objective of the day.

As night fell, *Die Hard* returned to Flers where it continued to protect its defenders. The next morning, at about 09:30 a.m. *Die Hard* broke up a German counter-attack to the north of Flers. The tank then supported the New Zealanders as they continued their advance north towards Factory Corner. Soon after leaving the northern edge of the village, *Die Hard* was hit by artillery shells which damaged the tank's gear box. Pearsall and his crew continued to fire their guns, as the troops advanced, then left the vehicle and supported the attack with dismounted machine guns. The tank however was too badly damaged to recover and was cannibalized for spare parts to sustain the remaining Mark I tanks still in use. The tank hulk was photographed by Captain Billy Sampson two years later after the village of Flers was retaken during the allied advance on 1918.

Die Hard's skipper, Lieutenant George Pearsall, was a grammar school teacher. Born at Smethwick on 17 July 1888 he was the elder son of George and Mary Ellen Pearsall, his father being the clerk of works to the local school board. Although his first name was Herbert, he used the name George like his father. He had an older sister called Lucy and a younger brother named Charles. Bought up in Smethwick, George was educated at Five Ways Grammar School and then at the Smethwick Pupil Teacher's Centre from 1904 to 1906, where he trained to be a teacher. He was then awarded a Toynbee Hall Scholarship to study at Emmanuel College Cambridge, entering during the Michaelmas term in October 1907 and graduating in 1911. The following year, he was appointed as a mathematics master at Batley Grammar School, where he was acknowledged as a thorough and caring teacher as well as an active sportsman.

Die Hard at Flers Summer 1918. (Stuart Sampson)

George joined the MMGS, enlisting on 6 April 1915 at Dewsbury. He was quickly promoted to Sergeant and applied for a commission whilst serving with 22 Battery MMGS at Bisley. Commissioned into MGC on 15 April, George Pearsall was awarded the Military Cross for conspicuous gallantry in action on 16 September 1916. The citation says "He fought his Tank with great gallantry, protecting the flank of the infantry and repulsing an enemy counter-attack. Later, when his Tank was disabled, he fired a machine gun from the trenches, displaying great coolness and initiative." Appointed temporary Lieutenant on 1 October 16, George worked with Heady Head and Stuart Hastie, under the direction of Arthur Inglis at Green Dump. He was not used in the action on 18 October but his crew would have been busy removing parts from irrecoverable tanks; salvage work being vital to keeping the remaining tanks in action. Their own tank was plundered as can be seen in the photograph.

Unusually George was granted ten days home leave before the Christmas period, returning to France on 21 December 1916. George served on with D Battalion and was appointed temporary captain from 12 April 17 which probably means he was in command of a section. Although there is no record of his service during the Battle of Arras or the Third Battle of Ypres, he is known to have served with No 10 Company. He was granted another period of home leave, from 21-31 October, before moving to the training areas in preparation for the Battle of Cambrai. On 20 November 1917, George was second in command of No 10 Company during the attack on the western side of the village at Flesquières. Eleven of the twelve tanks reached their first objective which was a railway line. Here they were joined by tanks from No 12 Company and they started the attack on the second objective, which was on the northern side of the Flesquières ridge. Of the eleven tanks three were knocked out by German 77mm artillery in the direct fire role. By the end of the day, George's company Commander, Maj Edgar Marris had been taken prisoner, and No 12 Company's commander, Maj ROC Ward was fatally wounded, so the remaining crews and serviceable tanks of D Battalion were re-organised. George was appointed second in command of one of the two composite companies who later fought at Bourlon Wood on 23 November. The attack failed as the limited numbers of infantry available could not take the village even though eleven tanks reached their objectives.

As the Battalion was withdrawn to Meulte, at the end of the battle, George was appointed acting Major in command of No 10 Company. He was then transferred to 1st Battalion on 10 January and took command of A Company two days later. He was granted home leave, from 24 February to 3 March 1918. During the Great German Advance, known as the Kaiserschlacht, George commanded A Company whose tanks fought to hold back the advancing Germans for two days. On 26 March, the crews, whose tanks had been destroyed, were formed into eleven Lewis gun teams and these were tasked with men from 4th Battalion to fight a rear guard action with 21st Division. George's men were deployed on the Corbie to Bray road, close to Heady Head's teams, and created significant numbers of casualties amongst the advancing enemy by this time who were confidently marching advancing in close column, much in the 1914 manner, rather than the infiltration tactics earlier in advance.

One month later, on 24 April, one of George's tanks, commanded by Lieutenant Frank Mitchell, took on and defeated three German tanks in the first tank versus tank action near Villers-Brettonaux. George was detached to HQ 5 Tank Brigade on 19 May but returned to 1st Battalion on 11 June. I cannot identify what role he undertook during the Battles of Arras and the Third Battle of the Somme, as the British forces pushed the Germans back towards the Belgian border. However, he must have been exhausted as he was granted home leave from 23 September to 7 October, arriving back with 1st Battalion on 10 October. Immediately after the Armistice, George returned to 4th Battalion and was then detached to the Resettlement Organisation as an education officer. As an early volunteer for enlistment, and a qualified teacher, he was one of the first officers released from his service. He embarked from Le Havre for UK on 20 January and was awarded his

MA eleven days later, just before he returned to teach at Batley Grammar School. Six weeks later, on Wednesday 19 March 1919, he died from Spanish Influenza aged only thirty years. This was not just a dreadful shock to his family and pupils, but also to his comrades. Billy Sampson, with whom he had served since 1916, later commented that his death was unexpected considering his excellent physique. George's body was returned to his family and later buried in the Uplands Cemetery at Smethwick.

George's second in command in *Die Hard* was Lance Corporal Harry Earle Nixon. Born on 10 December 1892 at Grimsby, Harry was the only son of a railway locomotive driver, Henry Nixon and his wife Betsy. The couple also had two daughters, Elsie who was three years older than Harry and Muriel who was five years younger. By 1911, Harry was working as a fishmonger's clerk and the family had settled at 58 Heneage Road. Harry initially served with the MGC, before being joining the tank crews. He was wounded when *Die Hard* was hit and was hospitalised for a short period; he made a full recovery and returned to D Company. His personal kit was destroyed when *Die Hard* was hit by an artillery shell and Harry lost all his possessions with the exception of a single playing card, the Nine of Hearts, which remains in his family's safekeeping

His bravery as a crewman in *Die Hard* was recognised through the award of the Military Medal on 14 November 1916. The following year, he was one of the few members of D Battalion selected for officer training and having completed the course at Pirbright, was commissioned into the Tank Corps, the date being shown in the *London Gazette* as 29 July 1917. However, four days previously, Second Lieutenant Harry Nixon was presented with his Military Medal on 25 July at an investiture held on the Queen's Parade at Aldershot when more than one hundred officers and other ranks were presented with medals by King George V in front of huge crowds.

Second Lieutenant Harry Nixon MM.
(Mike Nixon)

Harry was then sent to Bovington, for tank officer training and, on 23 November, joined the newly formed M Battalion which was then undergoing collective training. He deployed with their main body back to France on 1 February 1918. Seven weeks later, as the Battalion was undertaking driver training, the Germans started their great Spring Offensive on 21 March 1917. Harry's unit, now known as 13th Battalion Tank Corps, was quickly re-roled to become a machine-gun unit and all the crews less drivers, formed into Lewis gun teams. After the main thrust, known as *Michael*, failed to take the strategically vital city of Amiens, the Germans launched another thrust, known as *Georgette*, on 9 April to south of Ypres designed to capture the Channel Port. Harry's battalion was sent north to hold the line near Mont Noir on 10 April and, on the evening of 24 April, B Company took over the front line near Vierstraat from a company from 5th Tank Battalion. According to the 13th Battalion War History, this was achieved "without undue interference" from the Germans but at 2.30 a.m. they started a preparatory bombardment. After three hours, the Germans attacked the British lines. B Company fought until they ran out of ammunition, losing three officer and seventy-three men dead, wounded or missing.

Harry was gassed and buried during this attack and was evacuated back to England suffering from shell-shock. Harry was treated at the Imperial convalescent hospital at St Anne's on the Fylde coast, met Ethel Armstrong who was on the administrative staff. His family remembers that he returned to France again in July 1918 but I cannot identify the unit with which he served. Harry was subsequently attached to the Ministry of Labour and was still suffering from the effects of being gassed and buried alive when he married Ethel, on New Year's Day 1919, near her home in Belfast. Harry relinquished his commission much later than most others, on 1 December 1920, probably because he was involved in war pension work which was a key task for the Ministry of Labour. The couple returned to his home at Heneage Road in Grimsby but later moved to Healing and Harry became a successful fish merchant. He and Ethel had three children, their eldest son Harry joining the Royal Navy as a midshipman and eventually retiring in the rank of rear admiral. Following the outbreak of the Second World War, Harry senior volunteered to join the RAF and was commissioned on 9 July 1940. Serving in the Administration Branch, he was promoted flying officer after a year and then promoted war sub-substantive flight lieutenant on 10 February 1945. After the war Ethel and Harry settled at Montague House in Fairford in Gloucestershire. Harry did not relinquish his commission until 10 February 1954 by which time he had reached the rank of squadron leader in the Volunteer Reserve. Ten years later, aged seventy two, Harry died in October 1964 in Fairford; Ethel dying the following year.

Unusually Graham Woods lists all nine members of the crew including the "reserve". Sadly I have been unable to positively identify Lance Corporal Kettle. Woods shows that Gunner J Lee, who was the reserve crewman, was wounded on 15 September and was evacuated back to a casualty clearing centre. He recovered and reported back to the D Company HQ, at the Loop three days later. He was again wounded on 25 September. He was possibly Gnr James Lee who enlisted on 12 December 1915 and later served in the Tank Corps, remaining with 4th Battalion until his demobilisation. *Die Hard's* driver Frank Still, who was awarded the Military Medal following his actions on 15 September 1916, also served on with D Company. He transferred to the MGC and then the Tank Corps with his comrades in D Battalion. By the summer of 1918, he was serving with No 8 Section of B Company of 4th Battalion. No longer was a driver, Frank now second in command of the male tank 9111 commanded by Lt BG Heath on 30 July 1918. This tank was hit by artillery fire and Knocked Out near Hangard Wood, to the south of Villers-Brettonaux, on 8 August as the British advanced on the opening day of the Battle of Amiens. Frank was seriously injured but recovered and left the Army in 1919. After that, I can find no record of him

Lance Corporal William Moss, who was born in Kendal in 1897, was the son of a school teacher who later managed the Thatched House Hotel in Poulton-le-Fylde. William, who had an elder sister Eleanor and a younger sister Kathleen, was educated at Baines Grammar School before starting work with an accountant in Preston. He enlisted into the Army at Clapham, and after the formation of D Battalion, served with No 10 Company. On 30 July 1918, he was the second in command of tank 9440 which was commanded by Lieutenant Gammie. William was Killed in Action on 10 August 1918 on the third day of the Battle of Amiens. Six out of the tanks committed to the attack were knocked out by anti-tank guns. William's obituary, which was published in the *Fleetwood Express* on 31 August 1918, record that "Cpl Moss was driving his tank into action" The details of his death are given in a letter from his OC [tank skipper] who was probably Albert Gammie. He wrote "on the afternoon of his death I was sitting on the left of your son, when a bullet came through the flap of the tank and hit him through the left side of his neck. He was killed instantly and fell back on his seat without uttering a moan, this gallantly laying down his life for his King and his country. I cannot speak too highly of his fine qualities. Even since he came under my command in May this year, I have held him in the highest esteem and soon became acquainted with his fine capabilities as a man and a soldier. He was most popular with officers and men in this company, and his loss has been greatly felt by all". Following his death, his mother Ann received letters of condolence including several describing her son's burial. William's body was subsequently moved to Bouchoir New British Cemetery.

Gunner Charles Stuart, who was replaced by Gunner Lee, was a journalist from Wigan. Born on 14 October 1888, Charles was the eldest son of James and Mary Ann Stuart. His father was first recorded in the 1891 census as a tobacconist's assistant but twenty years as a tobacconist manager. Before he enlisted, Charles worked for Thomas Watt and Sons on the *Observer* newspaper in Wigan. His medical record shows Charles was a small man being only five feet in height, below standard weight and having very bad teeth. He enlisted on 10 December 1915 and later volunteered for the MMGS being mobilised on 4 February of the following year. Charles initially served with A Company, being transferred to D Company just before deploying to France on 28 August. He continued to serve with D Battalion and then 4th Battalion where he worked as an orderly room clerk as a shorthand typist; this was, according to a employing officer, a task for which he was physically suitable which reveals the nature of tasks being undertaken by tank crewmen.

Granted home leave in January 1918, after the battalion had settled at its new base at Meulte, Charles was admitted to hospital on 5 March 1918 with trench fever. Trench fever was caused by a blood infection resulting from lice and provided difficult to treat in the trenches; it was less usual in the rear areas where the opportunities to disinfect clothing were better Charles did not recover as expected and was evacuated home and treated at the Keightley War Hospital. On 7 May, he was sent to 2nd Western General Hospital in Manchester for further treatment and eventually sent on home leave following his discharge on 29 June. He was then posted to the Tank Depot at Bovington where he continued to work as a clerk and was promoted to paid acting corporal.

Just before he was demobilised from the Army, Charles' bad teeth were removed but he was not fitted with a denture. He suffered from significant infection after the operation and therefore claimed for a pension when he was demobilised in early 1919. He successfully gained a 30% pension. Shortly afterwards, he married Elizabeth Crook in Wigan and they had three children; Gordon, Marjory and James by 1923. Thereafter I can find no record of Charles until his death, aged eighty-three, in Bristol in the summer of 1975.

Gunner George Honour, who also survived, was born in Willesden on 6 October 1897 and christened on 30 January the following year at Holy Trinity Church in Kilburn. His father James was working as a horse keeper when George was a baby but he later became a self-employed bus proprietor. George, who was the oldest of three children, was working as a postman when he enlisted at Kilburn on 18 November 1915. Reporting to the MMGS Depot at Bisley the same day, he was posted to "21" Battery on 5 March 16 then to E Company. He was disciplined for two minor charges of absence before he was posted to D Company on 27 May; shortly after which he was admitted to hospital for three weeks. George deployed to France on 28 August and later rebadged to the Tank Corps. Never promoted he returned to the UK for demobilization on 2 April 19. He returned to work as a postman and married Kate Duffield at Hampstead on 10 March 1923. The couple had two sons James and Aubrey, and a daughter Audrey. The family originally lived at Maygrove Road in Kilburn but later moved to Manor Farm, in Greenford, where they lived with George's father and his younger son Aubrey. In the 1950s, George and the family moved to Stanley Avenue in Wembley, where he died in the spring of 1969.

Gunner Charles Leeming was the final member of the crew. He was the manager of a buckle works when he was attested on 8 December 1915. He was born in Walsall in 1891 where his father John working as an insurance agent. Charles volunteered to join to join the MMGS in December 1915 and as, with many other MMGS recruits, his application was countersigned at Coventry by the editor of *The Motor Cycle* Geoffrey Smith. Charles was placed on the Army Reserve and not mobilised until 20 March 1916. Like George Honour, Charles served first with E Company of the Armoured Car Section and also like George he also was found guilty of overstaying his leave in April.

Captain Wood's notebook records that Charles was wounded in the right knee on 16 September 1916, presumably after the tank had been destroyed, and that he was sent for treatment to the NZ Field Ambulance. Charles recovered but was sent sick on 7 November after which he was treated at the General Hospital at Dannes. On 8 December, Charles returned to his unit, now re-designated D Battalion, with which he served throughout the war. Usually Charles was granted home leave in early November 1917, rejoining his battalion on the first day of the Battle of Cambrai. He does not appear to have gone into action again as he was later employed as a cook. Charles was again granted home leave, just before the Armistice, when he married Nora Cooper at St Peter's Church in Walsall. On his return to the Battalion, he was detached to the Tank Group HQ as a cook and later served with HQ 3 Tank Group in Germany. He did not return to Walsall and civilian life until 13 September 1919. Sadly, as with a number of the First Tank Crewmen, he and Nora had no children. They lived at Walsall for the rest of their lives when Charles died aged only fifty-three years on 11 May 1945.

12

Sampson and *Delilah*

The British Army had been trying to take High Wood since 14 July 1916. Sitting on a saddle on the Bazentin Ridge, High Wood dominates the landscape to the south and was a superb observation point which the Germans used to good effect. They also built strong points, mainly to house machine guns, and also dug a communications trench, known as the Switch Line that ran along the Bazentin Ridge from Courcelette, through the northern part of High Wood, and on to Flers, allowing German troops to deploy safely between defensive locations in the event of an attack.

The wood gained a fearful reputation; *the hell of High Wood* and *The rottenest place on the Western Front* amongst the more printable ones! The first British attack was took place on the evening of 14 July 1916 when the German defences were breached by a mix of infantry and cavalry but the Germans regained the whole of the Wood within two days. The cavalry suffered casualties of 102 men and 130 horses on 15 July; the next day the British infantry also withdrew, having suffered 2,500 casualties. For the next 2 months, the British attacks continued often at short notice and rarely with adequate planning or artillery support. These attacks were always answered by German counter-attacks, often from the Switch Line. Whilst this trench was the key to the German defences, they also dug a series of trenches, as well as many machine gun emplacements, between the Switch Line and the forward British outposts in the southwest quarter of the wood. Shelling by both sides continued unabated on the now shattered wood, flame throwers and mines were used and the levels of casualties rose to levels which were excessive even by Somme standards with many bodies remaining unburied.

On 15 September, the task of capturing High Wood was given to the 47th (2nd London) Division who were to be supported by four tanks. High Wood was far from ideal for tank operations and the tank skippers argued that the numerous shell holes and shattered tree stumps made the Wood impassable to tanks. They appealed to the Divisional Commander, Major General Charles Barter, that the plan was unworkable. After making a personal reconnaissance, accompanied by the commander of 141st Infantry Brigade Robert McDouall, Barter agreed with them. He pressed HQ III Corps to allow him to withdraw his infantry from their forward positions, close to the German front line, so that a proper artillery barrage could precede the attack, and then send the tanks round the flanks of the wood. The commander of III Corps, Lieutenant General Sir William Pulteney, rejected this plan despite objections from Lieutenant Colonel Hugh Elles, who represented the British CinC at a conference on 10 September.

The artillery plan was adjusted to allow for lanes down which the tanks would move through the wood but these lanes meant that parts of the German defences were left undamaged and some heavily protected machine gun positions were not destroyed. 47th Division had three objectives for their attack: firstly, a line just north of High Wood; secondly, the Starfish Lane to the north of the wood 750 yards down the slope which lead towards Eaucourt L'Abbaye and finally, on the right, the strongly defended Flers Line. Finding it difficult to travel across the heavily shelled terrain between their base at Green Dump (see map 11), passing the Calvary at Bazentin le Grand (known

Delilah in High Wood Summer 1918. (Tank Museum)

to the troops as Crucifix Corner and then following a communications trench up the hill to the southern tip of High Wood, the tanks did not arrive at the Wood until 6:52 a.m.. This was thirty minutes after the infantry started their assault. Three of the four tanks were wholly ineffective in their support but the Wood was eventually captured by the Londoners, albeit at great cost.

The C Company tank, *Clan Ruthven*, was a female commanded by Second Lieutenant Andrew Henderson. It reached no further than 200 yards along the south western edge of the Wood before becoming stuck on a tree stump. The two tanks on the right of the wood, male and female commanded by Lieutenants Sharp and Robinson respectively, moved through the wood's southeast edge. Robinson's tank headed off on the right course but became fouled on tree stumps, the ground having wrecked its steering tail. Stranded near the huge double crater of a mine blown on the east of the wood, Robinson's crew kept its guns working in support of the attack. Sharp's tank, *Delphine*, broke the axle of its steering tail after ten minutes trying to force its way through the shattered trees which littered the ground and also finished near the mine crater. Neither however crossed the British front line.

The most effective tank, *Delilah* commanded by Second Lieutenant Billy Sampson, success-fully made its way amongst to the centre of the Wood and crossed the German front line despite German infantry climbing on the tank as it pushed forward. As it reached the centre of the wood, the engine started to falter as the spark plugs became fouled. It was not long afterwards the tank stalled that the German artillery started to hit the tank. The first shell did no real damage but the second penetrated the crew compartment so Billy Sampson ordered his crew out of the tank and set fire to it in accordance with his instructions. Taking cover in the German support trench, the crew was surprised to find more than seventy defenders still in place who quickly surrendered to the tank crew. The eight British soldiers, who had no previous battle experience, were probably wondering how they could control such a large group of potentially dangerous captives when, fortunately, soldiers from the Civil Service Rifles arrived and took care of the situation.

Captain Frank Deverall, the transport officer of the Post Office Rifles wrote after the battle: "the tanks were not worth a damn there and never did anything except to spoil the show. The Boche was not touched there, when the attack took place, and it was hung until Goodes did a wonderful job with his guns". Captain George Goodes was in command of 140th Trench Mortar Battery (TMB) and, after the initial assault failed, Brigadier General McDouall arranged for a further artillery bombardment. This barrage, which started at 11:00 a.m., included 140th TMB firing 750 Stokes mortar rounds in fifteen minutes. The bombardment was such that the Germans began to leave their positions and surrender by the hundred. With five London Regiment battalions now involved in the fighting, High Wood was cleared of the enemy after five hours fighting and, by 1.30 p.m. the German collapse was complete. High Wood, and the Switch Line trench to its north, was at last in British hands. *Delphine* was recovered the following month but *Delilah* was left where she was; immovable.

Crew D13 and *Delilah*

Delilah was the D Company reserve tank which was sent into action with a scratch crew. It is sometimes difficult to work out how a tank obtained its name but in the case of *Delilah* it is obvious – her skipper's name was Billy Sampson. Billy was born on New Year's Day 1890 in Wytheville in Virginia. He was the youngest child of a farmer named Henry Sampson and his wife Ellen who had moved to the United States having purchased farmland as did a number of Cornish families. Billy's elder brothers and sister were also born in Virginia but, within a year of Billy's birth, the

Billy Sampson in Canadian uniform 1915. (Stuart Sampson)

family had returned to England. Initially they settled near Perranporth but later moved to the Treyford Manor Farm Treyford. Billy was educated at Churcher's College at Petersfield where he was a member of the OTC. By 1911, he was boarding at 70 Victoria Road in Finsbury Park and working as a clerk in a bank in London. According to his grandson Stuart, Billy worked in South America for a while but he later moved to Saskatchewan where his eldest brother George who was farming. Billy found work at a bank in Regina and joined the local militia unit, the 95th or Saskatchewan Rifles, where he qualified as a marksman.

When the Great War started, Billy was mobilized for home defence duties. On 23 October, he enlisted in the Canadian Expeditionary Force and joined the 28th Canadian Infantry Battalion. After 6 months initial training at Winnipeg, and deployment with 2nd Canadian Division to England in May 1915, Billy was identified as suitable to be an officer. After training, he was commissioned into the Northumberland Fusiliers on 15 October 1915; the next day he married Hilda Pennycuick at St Paul's Church at Frimley in Surrey. Hilda, who had been born in Madras, was the younger daughter of a Royal Engineer colonel, John Pennycuick who designed and, after mortgaging his home in England, constructed the Periyar dam which is still vital to the lives of those living in Kerula. Billy was gazetted to the MMGS on 21 October 1915 and started training at Bisley. Initially allocated to E Company Heavy Section MGC, he was posted to D Company just before their deployment. During the move to France, Billy was made responsible for taking the first packet of tanks and drivers by rail to Avonmouth and then on SS *Hunston* to Le Havre. When it was decided to use several tanks to support the attack on High Wood, Billy was selected to command the sub-section as well as the scratch crew which manned the Reserve Tank which he named *Delilah*. Billy was wounded on 15 September but not so badly seriously that he needed hospital treatment. His success at High Wood was recognized by the award of the Military Cross for conspicuous gallantry in action. The citation states: "He fought his Tank with great gallantry, enfilading an enemy trench and capturing 15 prisoners".

The file containing Billy's Indian Army reports, which is in the British Library, lists the tank engagements in which he fought over the next two months. Most of these do not appear in the D Company War Diary including an action at Martinpuich on 17 September and at Eaucourt L'Abbaye on 23 September. Promoted temporary Lieutenant on 1 October 1916, Billy's file also shows he was in action on 4 November near Le Sars. It is recorded that a tank was designated to take part in an attack on the Butte de Warlencourt on 28 October but, when the prehistoric monument was eventually taken on 5 November, tanks could not be used because of the impossible ground conditions. The file finally states that Billy was in action at Beaumont-Hamel on 13 November, which is also not recorded elsewhere. On 22 November Billy proceeded to Auchonvillers and controlled the movement of four tanks back to Beaussart before moving to Blangy-sur-Ternoisee when D Battalion had been established. Billy remained with D Company when it formed the backbone of D Battalion, probably joining No 10 Company. On 9 April 1917, the opening day of the Battle of Arras, Billy's section of four tanks which fought their way through on the Harp defensive position at Telegraph Hill near Beaurains. Having been appointed temporary Captain three days later, Billy again led his section into action at Heininel on 12 April. The list of tank actions also includes that he was at Bullecourt on 10 May, which again is unsupported by any other records I have found. During the Third Battle of Ypres, Billy commanded a section at Poelcapelle in August 1917 but later that month, he was directed to return to England and was posted to the Central Driving and Maintenance School at Bovington.

Billy was presented with the Military Cross, by King George V at Windsor Castle, on 6 September. The next month, Billy was selected as one of four tank commanders in the Special Service Company for deployment to Ireland in November. With Len Bates and Tom Murphy, he arrived in Dublin on 9 November but his time in Ireland was short as the tanks were found suitable for anti-insurgency tasks. This failure, which was compounded by the accidental death of

Len Bates on 10 November, must have been most dispiriting to Billy and his comrades who were all involved in the Board of Inquiry which followed Len's funeral. On his return to Bovington, Billy joined L Battalion where he served in No 36 Company with Archie Holford-Walker and John Clarke who had served in C Company on the Somme. By 5 January 1918, Billy was back in France with renamed 12th Tank Battalion and, in March, took part in delaying action during the Kaiserschlacht, commanding a group of Lewis gun teams who had been quickly formed to prevent a wholesale German success. In the summer of 1918, Billy was a witness, and probably best man, at the wedding between Archie Holford-Walker and Nea Grimshaw. The wedding took place, by a special licence, at Holy Trinity Church in Guildford on 17 July and the trip home also allowed Billy to see Hilda who was pregnant with their first child Tony.

On the opening day of the Battle of Amiens, as his battalion was in reserve, Billy was busily involved in the administration of his company holding a pay parade as is shown by Gnr John McDade's paybook. Twelve days later, as the British pushed the Germans back across the old Somme battlefield, Billy was in command of the Mark IV tank *Laverock*, as well as No 11 Section. Billy supported the Guards Division, which advanced through thick miss but with no preparatory bombardment, in an attack at Courcelle-le-Comte. Jack Clarke was also in action at Ervillers commanding No 1 Section as well as the tank *Ladybird*. No 11 Section was again in action on 2 September but it is not recorded if Billy was fighting with them. Nine days later, Billy and Hilda's elder son Tony was born on 11 September 1918 whilst Hilda was living at Bushey.

On 4 October, whilst his company was behind British lines near Masnieres, Billy was wounded in the hand whilst chatting to his CSM. The injury, which was caused by a stray round, was enough to get Billy sent back to England. Having recovered from his wound, Billy was appointed an assistant instructor at the Tank Driving and Maintenance School Bovington on 17 January 1919, a post he relinquished eighteen months later.

In his confidential report for 1920, Billy was described in one line by his CO, Lieutenant Colonel Hugh Woods as "a reliable officer" which was countersigned without further comment by Brigadier General Hugh Elles who was now commanding the Tank Training Centre.

Billy Sampson and his elder son Tony in 1919.
(Stuart Sampson)

Billy decided to make a career in the post war Regular Army and served at Bovington, as a company officer, in 1st (Depot) Battalion of the Tank Corps where he was graded as above average and "having more character than the average subaltern" which is a revealing comment on Billy's peers. Hilda gave birth to their younger son Teddy on 15 February 1921 whilst the couple was living near Bovington but they soon established a family home at Sandgate in Kent. In May 1922, Billy was posted to India where he served as an assistant instructor at the Armoured Motor Centre in Ahmednagar east of Bombay. He was then posted to 10th Armoured Car Company as a section commander in the rank of captain. Billy was one of two captains in the company, the other being his old friend Archie Holford-Walker, whilst another of the company officers was Len Bond who commanded Tank Crew D18 at Flers seven years before. In May 1926, Billy was seconded to the Royal Indian Army Service Corps (RIASC) and attended his first logistic course which he passed comfortably. Appointed Quartermaster of the Mechanical Transport (MT) Depot at Chaklala, on the outskirts of Rawalpindi, Billy's next report noted that he was "a hard worker and very keen with special aptitude for MT work". As a result, he was transferred permanently to the RIASC on 13 August 1927 as a captain with seven years seniority. Previously having served on an unaccompanied basis, Billy was joined by Hilda whilst he served for the next four years as an MT instructor at Chaklala, initially teaching British officers and later Indian officers and NCOs which indicates his proficiency in local languages. In 1931, Billy was placed in charge of a deployable MT section, his report in 1934 showing that he had in support of an Indian Cavalry brigade on operations and that he was "an excellent MT officer, fit for promotion". Billy returned with Hilda to Sandgate in March 1934 where she had named their home *Silourie* after her family home in Camberley. Promoted major on 20 July 1934, Billy returned to India for another two year posting leaving the boys in the guardianship of Dick Haigh, who had served with D Battalion including during the disastrous attack at Bullecourt on 11 April 1917. Returning to England, Billy and Hilda lived in Folkestone until 1939 when he again returned to India.

At the start of the Second World War, Billy was sent back to England and participated in the ill-fated Norwegian campaign in April and May 1940. At this time, Billy's elder son Tony, who had been educated at the Seabrook Lodge School in Hythe and at the King's School in Canterbury, had started officer training. He was commissioned into the Royal Artillery on 24 August shortly after his younger brother Teddy had been commissioned into the Royal Signals on 14 June 1940. Although Billy was above normal retirement age, he was tasked to rejoin the RIASC in India. He travelled on SS *City of Simla*, in a convoy which was attached by the German submarine *U138* on 20 September 1940. The ship was torpedoed fifty miles off Malin Head in Ireland but, fortunately there were only three fatalities. One month later, Billy set off again for India, this time travelling on SS *Britannia*. He reached India safely but the ship was sunk the following year, on 25 March 1941 by the German auxiliary cruiser *Thor* with most of the 500 passengers and crew being killed. Later that year, Billy's elder son Tony was posted to 3rd Heavy Anti-Aircraft Regiment which formed in Singapore in September 1941. The two men met in Singapore when Billy was sent to Burma to command a transport unit whilst his younger son Teddy was posted to Bovington as a signals officer.

On 15 February 1942, on Teddy's twenty-first birthday, his elder brother Tony was Killed in Action defending Singapore against the invading Japanese forces. Billy meantime was further north and took part in the British retreat leaving Rangoon on 7 March 1942 and reaching Kohima three months later. He caught malaria during the retreat and, as a result, was not sent to North Africa as had been planned. The following month, Billy was appointed Commandant of 9 MT Training Centre at Meerut where he was again reported on as "hard-working, efficient and doing well in command of the training centre". Despite his "quiet manner and lack of personality", and the fact that Billy was now 53 years old, it was recommended that he be retained in his appointment. He was subsequently promoted to the rank of lieutenant colonel and served on, despite being well beyond the normal retirement age of fifty, until 24 March 1944.

Retiring to England, Billy and Muriel settled at Sandwich in Kent. Teddy continued to serve in the Royal Signals, spending his forty-second birthday at Bovington where he was Chief Instructor of the RAC Signals School and retiring in the rank of lieutenant-colonel, before becoming a tax inspector. Billy and Hilda continued to live in Hythe until 1971 and then moved to Harwood House at Maidenhead where Billy died in late 1977. Teddy died on 12 October 1984 and Hilda died, the following year, aged ninety-seven, on 28 April 1985.

Billy Sampson in his later years. (Stuart Sampson)

Sadly I have been unable to find out anything about Billy's second in command Corporal JE Harper. Gunner Samuel Pick was injured at High Wood but later served as a corporal in 4th Battalion before being discharged through sickness in September 1918. Frederick Mays, who suffered burns to his eyes, continued to serve with D Battalion and then 4th Battalion, eventually being demobilised with the rank of acting corporal. Also wounded that day was Gunner Frank Divall who was born and brought up at Southborough in Kent. Born in February 1887, Frank was the youngest son of a cricket ball manufacturer. In 1911 he was employed as a fine art dealer but, when he was attested in February 1916, he had become a chauffeur and electrician. Assigned to the MGC, he was mobilised in May and his service in the Heavy Section was authorised at Bisley by Captain Graham Woods on 8 June. After two and half months training, and imminently expecting to deploy to France, Frank arranged to marry Winifred Maybanks at West Ham Register Office which was near her home at 68 Leyton Park Road, on 25 August 1916. Four days later, Frank was deployed to France. Frank obviously wanted to ensure Winifred was financially secure whilst he was overseas so the day before he was went into action he arranged an allotment from his pay. His wounds on 15 September were later described as superficial but they took several months to heal as metal fragments had entered his knee. Evacuated on 22 September, he was initially sent for treatment at Oxford.

Once back in England, Frank wrote a long letter to his sister Edith which described the battle at High Wood but which is somewhat different from other accounts, in that Franks says that Delilah drove back to her starting point. The letter was soon published in a number of newspapers as editors who were desperate to provide details about the tanks whose use had caught the public's imagination.

On 3 October, Frank was sent to a smaller hospital at Chipping Norton but his wounds did not heal. Eventually x-rays were used to identify the location of the medal fragments, which were removed. Frank was not released from hospital until 10 March 1917. Posted to the Tank Depot at Bovington, he retrained as a driver and was later allocated to 12th Battalion which included a number of officers who had served with C and D Companies in September 1916 including Billy Sampson. On the day the Battalion deployed to France, Frank was promoted lance corporal and served in No 3 Company alongside his former skipper. Frank steadily rose through the ranks, being promoted to corporal on 6 August just before the Battalion went into action at Amiens, and then sergeant on 18 October 1918 as the renamed 12th Battalion was pushing back the German beyond the River Selle. Losses of tanks and crews meant that the battalion was becoming less and less effective; C Company was the last of the three companies in action and they were withdrawn on 24 October, having fought their final action at Vertain, less than twenty miles from the Belgian border. The German Army was withdrawing in contact but they were not able to stand against the continuing Allied advance.

Frank returned to England on 4 January 1919 and was demobilised on 12 February. His discharge papers show that he had also been employed as a tank instructor and he gave his correspondence address as Laudhurst, where his sister Edith was living. When Frank later attempted to claim a pension, a letter was sent to his wife Winifred who replied that she did not know where he was. She thought that he had rejoined the Army but he was actually working at the Vine Garage in Rugeley. Their marriage did not survive much longer as, in the latter part of 1923, Frank married Alice Samuel. This probably took place at Rugeley as the marriage was registered at Lichfield. Winifred, who remained in London, married Peter Wingrave the following summer. Alice and Frank's first child Peter was born in 1929 in Chester and, the next year, the family moved to Flaunden in Hertfordshire where Frank took over the village stores. Alice had two more children, their daughter Joan who was born on 10 April 1931 tragically died ten days later but her younger son, Arthur was born two years later, survived. Frank expanded to the business at Flaunden to include a sub post-office and he kept the shop until 7 February 1953 when he died at the West Hertfordshire Hospital.

Another of the crewmen was a gunner called Yates who was almost certainly Harry Ironfield Yates. Harry, who was born in Preston, in early 1885, was the eldest son of an insurance agent Thomas Yates and his wife Elizabeth and was christened on 28 May at St Matthew's Church. Harry's younger sister Lily was born in 1887. In 1891, the family was living at 11 Cave Street in Preston but, by this time, Harry's father had died and Harry's aunt, Ann, was living with the family. Ten years later, the family was living at Peel Street in Preston. His aunt Ann was still living with them, his mother had become a confectioner and Harry was working as a post office telegraph messenger. In 1902, Harry was appointed temporary assistant postman in Preston; he became a permanently employed postman in 1904 and, in August 1909, he moved to work for the Post Office in Blackpool. On 25 June 1913, Harry married Christine Heppenstall at the South Shore Parish Church. According to his wedding lines, Harry was still a postman and his wife was a postal clerk. His service record has not survived but the date he enlisted, 25 March 1916, was recorded in *The Motor Cycle*. Harry retrained as a driver in 1917 and, as a result of his superb skills and courage was awarded two gallantry medals in 1918 whilst serving with 4th Tank Battalion. The first, a Military Medal, resulted from his action on the opening days of the Battle of Amiens. The citation states "on 8 August, he drove his tank continuously with exceptional skill for 15 hours until the final objective was reached. On August 9, he again drove his tank into action and when the tank developed mechanical trouble in full view of the enemy, he repaired it on two occasions, although subjected to heavy machine gun and rifle fire." In September 1918, Harry was serving in No 2 Section of A Company in a Mark V tank commanded by Second Lieutenant George Court. On 27 September, this tank was supporting an attack by 106th US Infantry Regiment, during which Harry drove more than 2 miles against a well prepared set of defences reaching all of its objectives. During the attack, the crew fired 160 rounds of 6 pdr ammunition as well as 500 rounds of machine gun ammunition, however all of his crewmates were injured as the tank was struck by armour piercing bullets. Harry was awarded the Distinguished Conduct Medal for his bravery, the citation stating "During the attack upon the Hindenburg Outpost Positions, east of Ronnsoy, on 27th September 1918, he drove his tank with great skill and determination. Notwithstanding the fact that all his crew were wounded by the fire from anti-tank rifles which pierced the tank, and were incapable of rendering any assistance, he carried out the orders which had been issued to his officer, and it was solely due to his fine-courage, devotion to duty and initiative that his tank reached its objective and was brought back to its rallying point."

Following the Armistice, Harry was granted home leave in Blackpool over Christmas but he failed to return to his unit. Thereafter he completely disappears and, despite extensive research, I can find no other information about this remarkable man or his family.

According to Billy Sampson, *Delilah*'s driver Alfred Bloomfield was a "*diminutive Geordie staff car driver*". Alfred was born in Willington in 1877 which, at thirty years old, made him one of the oldest crewmen to go into action. In 1901, he was working as an apprentice brass finisher at the local engine worker and by 1911 he was working as a domestic chauffeur at Darlington. He joined the ASC in 1915 and saw service in France although the details are not recorded nor are the dates he returned to join 711 (MT) Company. After the first actions, Alfred transferred to the MGC and then was rebadged to the Tank Corps. He served on after the Armistice but died, possibly from pneumonia, on 31 January 1919 whilst serving with the Central Tank Workshops at Erin. He is buried at St Pol Military Cemetery.

The final member of *Delilah*'s crew, Gunner William Chandler, did get safely home. Born in Streatham, South London in 1893, William initially worked as a clerk for his father, a nurseryman from Brixton. Standing over six feet tall, William was a driver in civilian life. On 1 March 1916, William enlisted at the Central London Recruiting Depot at Whitehall, London. Transferred to the Army Reserve, William was not mobilised until 1 May. He was posted to D Company on 27 May and started training at Elveden on 12 June. Only three months later, William was fighting for his life in High Wood. As *Delilah* worked her way through the shambles of what was left of High Wood, one of the sponson doors was lifted off its hinges by a tree stump. Concerned that the German troops, who had surrounded the tank, could fire ammunitions and lob grenades through this entrance, William Chandler got out of the tank and replaced it!

Like the other crew members, William was wounded but did not require hospital treatment. He was awarded the Military Medal for replacing the sponsor door; this was no mean feat given the amount of ammunition being fired at *Delilah* and the difficulty in fitting the heavy armour-plated door back onto a moving tank. William joined D Battalion, as it formed and later served with 4th Battalion. That he was never promoted could have been due to a less than perfect disciplinary record. Whilst serving with No 10 Company, on 1 June 1917, William failed to salute the Recce Officer, Captain the Earl of Rocksavage, and was punished by being Confined to Barracks for seven days. A second entry is entered on his conduct sheet but is too faint to be legible. He was however still committed to the Tanks; he stayed with the Battalion as it fought at Ypres, Cambrai and Amiens. As the battalion fought its way through the Hindenburg line, on 29 September 1918, he was again wounded, with time with burns to his face and hands.

Evacuated back to the UK, he was admitted to Netley Hospital ten days later, and not released from hospital until 20 December. Posted to A Company of the Tank Depot at Bovington, his request for a pension was declined on 14 January 1919 and he was demobilized one month later. His wounds must have still been visible as his discharge certificate shows burns to face and arm. William asked that his Military Medal should be sent to his home in Tulse Hill, rather than being publicly presented; it was sent with his other medals, by post, two months later. William never married; he lived with his parents at Tulse Hill until 1939. Later he lived at 126 Beacon Road in Broadstairs and died aged seventy-two on 3 September 1965 at the Isle of Thanet Hospital at Ramsgate.

Clan Ruthven

Like *Delilah*, *Clan Ruthven* was a reserve tank which was tasked to participate in the assault on High Wood. Just after dawn, on 15 September, the tank headed parallel with High Wood's southwest edge, fouled on a tree stump, and became stuck fast. The crew continued to provide fire support to the attacking infantry but this was dangerously close to *Delilah*. Billy Sampson crossed the wood to identify the problem. He was told by the skipper, Andrew Henderson that he was laying down a protective barrage with the tank's machine guns. Sampson's comments are not recorded but can probably be imagined!

Andrew Henderson was born on 6 July 1892, at the School House, Cherry Bank in Perth where his father was a teacher. He was educated at Perth Academy and later became an engineer. On 6 October 1914 he enlisted as a private soldier in 11th Battalion Royal Scots. Six months later, on 1 April 15, he was claimed by his elder brother who was a major in 18th Battalion Royal Fusiliers. Andrew deployed to France on 14 November but, after the battalion was disbanded, he returned to England on 20 March 16. Andrew was admitted to 4 Officer Cadet Battalion at 9 Alfred Street in Oxford on 24 March, seeking a commission in East Lancashire Regiment. However he was commissioned into the MGC on 24 April and deployed to France on 16 August.

Following the attack at High Wood on 15 September, Andrew was tasked to command tank no 705, during attacks in the Morval, Quadrilateral and the Bouleaux wood area on 25 September – he sprained his ankle during the lead up to the action and was replaced by Len Bates. Andrew stayed with C Battalion on its formation. As there is no record of the section commanders, at the Battle of Arras, I cannot determine in which actions he fought. I believe he commanded the supply tanks on 31 July on the first day of the Third Battle of Ypres, the other section commanders in No 9 Company included Eric Purdy and Len Bates. Andrew was appointed a section commander again on 15 October and also commanded 9 Section of No 9 Company during Battle of Cambrai.

On 20 November his section was part of the second wave, supporting the assault on Le Pave farm, near Bonavis, which was captured quickly and after the section then fought its way through Lateau Wood. On 23 November, Andrew commanded a composite section of three tanks in support of 51st Highland Division at Fontaine Notre Dame with Eric Purdy commanding the other composite section. Andrew travelled in tank C46, known as *Challenger*. The other tanks, C47 and C48, were hit after reaching the village but C46 continued in action, patrolling the road to the south west; the tank only returning to its rally point after it had run out of ammunition. C Battalion then started to prepare to withdraw from the Cambrai battlefield and, on 28 November, new sprockets arrived and were fitted to those tanks which could easily be made ready for action. On 30 November, after the German counter-offensive started, all serviceable tanks from C Battalion deployed to Metz where they were prepared for action so that Gonnelieu, which had fallen to the Germans, could be recovered. Gonnelieu was recaptured the next day by the Guards Division supported by H Battalion tanks, those from C Battalion not being used. That day, orders were received for a small guard to be left to protect the tank at Metz and the remainder of the crews to move by train to Bray sur Somme. Large numbers of crewmen were sent on leave over Christmas and the New Year and these would have included Andrew. By the time he returned, the battalion had been re-designated the 3rd Light Tank Battalion and the first two Whippet tanks arrived from Erin.

In the next three months, based at a camp close by the original C Company location of September 1916, the tanks' crews learned to operate the fearsomely complicated Whippet. When the German Army started to push the British Army back across the old battlefields of Cambrai and the Somme, the worn-out Mark IV tanks could not hold them. On 26 March, the 3rd Light battalion was sent into action for the first time. Operating from a base near Colincamps, C Company's Whippets first located column of marching German troops near Serre and used their mobility and machine guns to break up three separate battalion-sized units of 500 men. Andrew Henderson, who was commanding the tank *Conqueror* and two other tanks in No 9 Section, was again paired with Eric Purdy commanding No 12 Section. Henderson's tanks successfully got behind one of the groups of enemy who surrendered whilst Purdy's tanks pursued another large group of enemy to the outskirts of Auchonvillers, inflicting many casualties and capturing four machine guns. The tanks had secured the line to the north of the River Ancre but the Germans continued to push the British Army back across the old Somme battlefield and were threatening to over-run the 3rd battalion tankodrome. The 3rd Battalion tanks held the enemy back for two more days and then withdrawn west of Albert. The tanks then undertook a series of actions to try to prevent the Germans advance and eventually a line was put in place near Villers-Brettonaux. The tank crews then spent the next three months preparing for the battle to retake the ground lost over the previous month.

During the Battle of Amiens, which started on 8 August, Andrew Henderson and Eric Purdy's sections again fought together. On 8 August Andrew he commanded tank no A253 *Conqueror III* as well as three others; Eric was again in a tank called *Cayenne* and both men were in support of 7th Cavalry Brigade. The cavalry successfully broke through the German front line positions but were then stopped by machine guns well positioned in woods. The Whippets moved forward and suppressed or destroyed the enemy guns until their own guns jammed. Later that afternoon, when the 4th Canadian Division had caught up with the tanks, the Whippets attacked again and, with the infantry, drove the Germans out of the woods enabling the infantry to reach their final objective. Andrew also commanded 9 Section again on 21 August, on an attack near Achiet-le-Grand; the British and Empire troops having recaptured the whole of the all Somme battlefield in less than two weeks. Andrew's own tank broke down during the action but the remainder of the Whippets, using the thick morning mist as cover managed to reach the objectives.

Granted home leave from 31 August, Andrew stayed somewhat longer that planned at his destination of Bein Bhan in Oban as he contracted sinusitis. He returned to France and took part in the Final Advance as the Allied armies pushed through the Hindenburg line. On 29 October 1918, Andrew was appointed company second in command and then moved with the rest of the unit to its winter base. The following year, in May 1919, he was awarded the Military Cross for his sustained service. Initially returning to Craigie in Perthshire, Andrew left London on 5 June 1920 on the SS *Shidzuoka Maru* for Malaya to work as a rubber planter, returning in 1925 to Perth from Port Swettenham in Selangor province. On 22 May 1930, he again travelled to Singapore to take up work as a rubber plantation controller. Following their invasion, Andrew was interned by the Japanese in Borneo during the Second World War. He was released in October 1945 and returned to Perth. On 25 January 1947, he married Jessie Taylor Morris from Tullibardine at the Royal George Hotel in Perth. They lived in Perth until Andrew died on 22 June 1961. Sadly, there are no clues as to the other members of *Clan Ruthven's* crew on 15 September as, unlike for No 1 Section, there are no extant records for C Company.

Delphine

The attack on the eastern side of High Wood, on 15 September, was due to be supported by tanks manned by crews D21 and D22. D21 crewed the tank named *Delphine* which followed the wood's southeast edge where the axle of its steering tail was broken by the tree stumps after ten minutes. The tank became ditched whilst trying to cross a British trench and broke its track. It was so badly stuck that it could not be immediately recovered, despite the effects of a party from 711 MT Company and it remained stuck until late in the autumn.

Like Andrew Henderson, *Delphine*'s skipper Alex Sharp was a Scot. Born at the Dundee Hospital on 26 July 1892, Alex was the son of a machine fitter. He studied engineering at St Andrew's University from 1911 to 1916; the last two years included undertaking research with Professor R H Gibson. He was also a popular singer, particularly of patriotic songs. Alex served with St Andrew's UOTC as Cadet Lance Corporal and Corporal. Whilst undertaking research, he also supervised 200 ASC soldiers undertake engineering training. He applied for commission on 1 November 1915, and having been awarded a Bachelor of Science degree, was attested in Dundee on 18 February 1916. Several of tank crewmen were small but Alex was probably the shortest officer, being only 4 feet 7 inches tall and weighing only eighty seven pounds. He joined 5 Officer Cadet Battalion at Pembroke College in Cambridge on 14 March and was commissioned into the Heavy Section MGC just 31 days later. He was promoted temporary Lieutenant on 1 July 1916 whilst training at Elveden where he was photographed with his section. Having deployed to France on 2 September 1916, and after the fighting at High Wood, Alex was admitted to 4th London Field Ambulance on 24 September. He was not released from medical care until 2 October. He joined D Battalion on its formation but was detached for instructor duties to Headquarters 1st Tank Brigade on 10 March and then granted home leave from 19 to 29 March.

During the build-up to the Battle of Arras, Alex was very severely wounded on 5 April 1917; shell fragments hitting his left upper arm and forearm which caused fractures to all three bones. He was evacuated from France on 10 April and admitted to Yorkhill War Hospital, in Glasgow, two days later. The wounds did not fully heal until late 1918 and, even then, his arm required daily massage treatment to maintain flexibility. Alex was in hospital until 30 November, the final treatment being undertaken at Cawdaw Auxiliary Hospital at Bishopbriggs. He had to relinquish his commission on 9 February this following year as a result of his wounds on 9 February 1919; his war service being commemorated in Rosebank Parish Church.

Alex applied for membership of the Institute of Engineers in 1919 whilst he was at home in Dundee, shortly before he moved to India and joined the Indian Civil Service on 1 October 1919. From 1920, he worked at the Bhatghar Dam near Poona, as an assistant executive engineer and then worked for the Bombay Public Works Department. Billy Sampson notes that he met Sharp whilst serving at Poona but he does not mention meeting his wife Bessie or their daughter Catherine who was born in October 1924, around the time that Alex was promoted to executive engineer. In 1936, Alex was appointed deputy secretary of the Sind public water department, a post he held for two years. Retiring in April 1938, Alex and Bessie returned to Scotland with their three children. During the Second World War, Alex was commissioned into the Royal Engineers and served as Deputy Commander for the Angus area. After the war, he continued work as a civil engineer and the family settled in Dundee. Having retired, Alex applied for the role of assessor at St Andrews University in July 1950 but was not appointed. He lived in Dundee until his death aged seventy five on 18 December 1967.

Alex's second in command was Corporal Harold Wigley. Harold, who was born in late 1887 in Birmingham, was the son of a carpenter. On leaving school, Harold worked for his elder brother, Frank who was a jeweler and he later worked for JJ Woodgate on Coventry Road in Small Heath. After the first actions in 1916, his family provided a picture of the tank crew, taken at Elveden, which was published in *Birmingham Daily Mail* on 26 September, the earliest picture of its type ever published. Harold stayed with D Battalion and fought at the Battle of Arras. On 11 April 1917, possibly during the attack at Bullecourt, Harold was captured by the Germans and remained a POW until the end of the war. Returning to Birmingham, Harold married Violet Stanley in the summer of 1925; their only daughter Violet being born in early 1928. The family later lived in Bromsgrove where Harold worked as a commission agent. He died aged seventy nine, at the General Hospital in Bromsgrove on 8 March 1966. His wife Violet, who was twelve years younger than Harold, died at the Wrekin aged 90 in May 1989.

Sadly two of Delphine's crewmen were killed in action in 1917. The first, Gunner Ernest Shepherd, was born in Birmingham and later moved to Wolston, between Rugby and Coventry. The record of his personal effects record his father as Henry, which could indicate that he was the son of Armina and Henry Shepherd who was a brass finisher living in Sparkbrook. Ernest was a clerk before he enlisted into the Machine Gun Corps at Coventry and after the first actions, served with D Battalion. He probably fought at the Battle of Arras, during the assault near Thelus, on 9 April 1917. He was serving with No 12 Company, at the second Battle of Bullecourt on 3 May 1917, when he was killed in action as the tanks attempted, for the second time, to drive through the German defences and for the second time failed. Sadly that is all that is known about him.

His crewmate Gunner George Foote was killed on the opening day of the Battle of Cambrai as his tank was hit as it travelled through the village of Flesquières. George was born on 3 September 1897 in the Regent's Park area of London, George's father Charles originally being a commercial traveller. George's younger brother Charles was born in 1899 but died in 1902. George was bought up in Tufnell Park road, his father later becoming the commercial manager of Hawkes and Co, the musical instrument makers. They family later moved to Great Missenden in Buckinghamshire, the village being only forty five minutes journey from Marylebone on the Metropolitan railway line and therefor very convenient for businessmen working in London.

George enlisted in late 1914 at Aylesbury and initially served with the Welsh Regiment before joining the MGC. Although injured on 15 September, at High Wood, George was again in action at Eaucourt L'Abbaye on 1 October after which he was awarded the Distinguished Conduct Medal. The description of the action, in the citation, relates to the incident when Lieutenant Jefferson Wakley was badly injured whilst commanding tank D16. It states that George "displayed great courage and determination fighting with his tank. Later he remained for 30 hours with a wounded officer under heavy fire". This was the same incident in which Jake Glaister was awarded the DCM. Having joined D Battalion, George was promoted Lance Corporal. He probably fought at Arras and Ypres and was, according to his skipper, likely to be commissioned. Serving with No 12 Company, on 20 November 1917, George was a crewman in *Deborah* which was put out of action as she fought her way through the German occupied village of Flesquières; one of the few tanks who managed to enter the village. After his death, *Deborah*'s skipper Second Lieutenant Frank Heap wrote to Charles Foote stating George "was killed instantly and painlessly. We buried him two days later where he had fallen". George's body is buried, along with the four other members of *Deborah's* crew, at Flesquières Hill Cemetery. His tank *Deborah* was also buried, as part of the post-war clear up and remained undiscovered until she was located by Philippe Gorczynski. She has since been recovered and *Deborah* is now displayed in a barn in the centre of Flesquières.

Gunner George Moscrop also survived the war. Born in May 1894, at Longtown in Cumberland, George was a bootmaker's driver before he enlisted on 10 December 1915; the boot maker was possibly his future wife's grandfather. Three months later, he was mobilized in March 1916 and first joined for duty with the MMGS at Coventry on 27 March. There he met Arthur Tweddle, who was from the same town and who later served with crew D23 – see chapter 13. Posted to Heavy Section MGC on 4 May, George went absent without leave from the training location at Bullhousen Farm for two days and was later confined to barracks for seven days. Posted to D Company, the day after he was sentenced, he undertook training at Elveden and was part of the final element of D Company to deploy to France. George stayed with D Company, then D Battalion, then C Company of 4th Battalion Tank Corps until after the end of the war. George eventually returned to England on 30 January 1919 and was transferred to Z Reserve, as a tank crewman, in February 1919. After the war, George travelled to Patagonia initially as a sheep farmer but he later became an engineer. He married his wife Alexandrina in 1925; the couple had five children whilst in Chile and they returned to England on the SS *Saxon* star arriving in Liverpool on 19 May 32. The family then returned to Cumberland, George living at Longtown until he died aged seventy five on 19 January 1970.

I have unable to identify any substantial information on the remaining three members of the crew. Gunner John Preston originally served with the MMGS whereas Gunner Hales served with the Machine Gun Corps. He was probably Albert Harry Hales who later served in the Tank Corps as a private and survived the war. The driver, Pte Herbert Ernest Wilson, who joined the ASC on 16 January 1916, rebadged to the MGC as D Battalion formed on 18 November but returned to the ASC on 17 February and survived the war. Thereafter I can find nothing about him.

D22

The final tank used at High Wood, manned by crew D22, was commanded by Lieutenant Eric Robinson. It headed off on the correct course parallel to the wood's south eastern edge but the crew became disoriented and fired on members of the City of London Rifles in Worcester trench who were waiting to advance. Eric Robinson then attempted to get the tank out of the wood to continue the advance but the tank became stuck. After fourteen hours digging, the crew recovered the tank which was again in action on 25 September. Fighting in support of the Canadians near Courcelette, the tank was destroyed to the east of the village.

I have been able to obtain details about most of the crew although I cannot definitely identify Gunner Lawson. The tank's skipper, Eric Robinson was born in Wood Green in East London on 2 October 1892, the eldest son of cable engineer and RN Reserve officer named Frederick Robinson. Eric, who was named after his father Frederick, was called Eric to differentiate between father and son, was apprenticed as an engineer to a shipbuilding company and then worked in the electrical department of the India rubber Company at their East London works at Silvertown; his father working for the company in submarine cable division. A keen motorcyclist, Eric enlisted in the RNAS on 18 November 1914. He served at HMS Pembroke III as a Petty Officer Engineer until 31 March 1915, then with the RNAS Armoured Car Division on 15 August 1915 after which he was released having applied for a commission in the Army. Commissioned directly into the MGC, he embarked from Southampton on 2 September 1916 and arrived at Le Havre the following day. For his actions at High Wood, Eric was awarded the Military Cross "for conspicuous gallantry in action. He fought his Tank with great gallantry. Later, when his

Eric Robinson when wounded 1918.

Tank became ditched, he and his crew dug for 14 hours under heavy fire, eventually getting his tank out and back to the assembly point".

On 26 September, Eric commanded one of two tanks, Harold Cole with D25 commanding the other, during the Canadian Division assault to the east of Courcelette. A German counter barrage caught the attackers in No Man's Land and Eric's tank was destroyed. Eric also commanded one of three tanks tasked to capture German positions to the north of Hamel on 14 November; again his tank was hit by artillery fire and put out of action but Harry Drader supported by Hugh Bell pressed on and captured the garrison. Eric transferred to D Battalion on its formation and, whilst on Christmas leave, married Elsie Mapley at Ilford Parish Church on 27 December 1916. The couple was pictured in *The Motor Cycle* in February 1917 when details of his MC were also published. Eric commanded a section of No 12 Company during the assault on Vimy Ridge on 9 April but all his tanks became ditched due to the poor ground conditions. Appointed temporary captain on 12 April 1917, he again commanded a section at the second Battle of Bullecourt on 3 May 1917 when the tanks were unable, yet again, to lead the infantry to success. I can find no record of his fighting at the Third Battle of Ypres but this is not unusual as the names of section commanders are seldom recorded.

Eric returned to England in September 1917 and was presented with insignia of the MC by King George at Buckingham Palace on 31 October; the same day as Len Bates and Harry Drader who had become a very close friend. The two men were sent to Bovington to serve in the newly formed 10th Battalion, Eric was appointed to command A Company whilst Harry commanded B Company. Eric was wounded on 21 May 1918; his unit was not in action so it was probably as a result of artillery fire. Whatever the cause, his wounds were such that he had to return to England and was granted leave in London to recover. Back in France in time to lead A Company at the Battle of Amiens, Eric was awarded a Bar to the Military Cross for his leadership in battle. The citation states:

> ... near Mallard Wood, on August 8th and 9th,'18, this officer showed conspicuous gallantry and coolness directing his tanks under heavy fire. Owing to the heavy mist on the 8th., a large number of tanks and infantry lost direction. Major Robinson, realising the situation, came forward under shellfire and rallied the tanks and sent them forward again to lead the infantry to their objectives. It was largely due to this officer's personal gallantry and disregard for danger that his Coy was successful in its attack. On Aug. 9th, when the tank commanded by 2/Lt Champeney was disabled in front of our infantry, Major Robinson went forward to obtain information regarding 2/Lt. Champeney and his crew. Throughout these actions his great coolness and courage were a splendid example to all ranks serving under him, and inspired the whole Coy.

Eric continued to fight on through the Final Advance and was killed in Action on 4 November 1918, aged twenty-six, leading the only two sections the battalion could field during the battle for the Mormal Forest. He was the last of the First Tank Crews to be killed in action. The next day, after Eric's body was buried at Cotillon sur Sambe; Harry Drader took command of the composite company with the few tanks left in the Battalion. Eric's remains were later reinterred at the Highland Cemetery at Le Cateau, his name was inscribed on the war memorial at Ilford Town Hall, The Church of St John the Evangelist at Seven Kings and also on the family gravestone at the City of London Cemetery Manor Park London. His widow Elsie settled at Bushey; her elder sister Bessie had a baby boy in February 1919 named Eric who became a Harley Street Ear Nose and Throat surgeon. Elsie who later married the actor Frank Tickle lived in Bushey until her death on 28 November 1961.

Eric's driver, Ernest Howes, was awarded the Military Medal for his actions in September 1916. Born on 10 October in 1892 at Shirehampton, close to the mouth of the Bristol Avon, Ernest was the eldest son of Ernest Henry Howes and Annie Hancock. After her husband's death, Annie became the housekeeper for a widow Mrs Susanne Whitefoord who lived at Springfield in Shirehampton. When his mother died in 1903, Mrs Whitefoord became the guardian to Ernest and his younger sister Emma. As a young man Ernest worked as an apprentice electrical engineer. He joined the Army in 1915 and initially served in the ASC as a mechanical transport driver. After the first tank actions on the Somme, Ernest transferred to the MGC and later fought with the Tank Corps. Just after the Battle of Cambrai, he married Violet Heath in Bristol although I cannot find any record of the couple having children. After the war, Ernest returned to work as an engineer and, whilst his sister Emma settled in Bedminster, by 1938 Ernest was living at Sea Mills. He died aged seventy-seven in Bristol in the summer of 1970.

Eric's second in command was Corporal Dudley White who was killed in action at Poelcapelle during one of the last tank actions in the Ypres Salient. Dudley, who was born in Coventry in early 1897, was the second child and eldest son of a watch manufacturers' manager. The family later moved to Kenilworth where Dudley worked for Eykyns Motor Garage. After his enlistment in 1915, Dudley was appointed lance corporal within two weeks and later selected for service with tanks. At High Wood, he was not quite twenty and yet was still the tank corporal. After the first action, he continued to serve with D Battalion, probably with No 11 Company and almost certainly fought at the first Battle of Bullecourt on 11 April 1917. Later renumbered 200865 in the Tank Corps; Dudley was Killed in Action on 9 October 1917 when a German shell struck his tank *Damon II* as it was fighting its way into the village of Poelcapelle. After Dudley's death, his skipper Lieutenant John Coghlan wrote to the family thus:

> I am very sorry to inform you that your son, finest and bravest boy I have ever met, was KIA on the 9th on this month. He was in my crew and went into action at dawn on the morning against some strong points at Poelcapelle. From the start we were shelled heavily and about 8.30am a shell struck the tank killing your son at his gun, he never uttered a word. He is buried beside his tank and rests in Belgian soil.

His body has never been found but it is presumed that he is buried very close to the site of the recently erected Tank Corps memorial at Poelcapelle.

Gunner James Anderson was born in early June 1993 at South Leith in Scotland. A short man, standing only five feet two inches, he was attested on 29 September 1915 in Edinburgh as a special enlistment. James was described as "a smart, well-educated lad and a very good motor cyclist. Seems in every way to be a suitable recruit for MMGS." Sent to Bisley, he followed the normal training pattern for those who were to join the Heavy Section MGC. After the first actions, James served with No 12 Company. He fought at Vimy Ridge on 9 April 1917; Ewart Doodson of *Daredevil 1* dying on his knee. James then fought at the second Battle of Bullecourt as a gunner in crew D41 in tank no 742. His tank was commanded by Lieutenant CM Knight and driven by Lance Corporal Wateridge. Like Wateridge, Anderson was wounded but he refused to leave his post. He returned with the tank to the south east of the village with a new crew, where again the tank patrolled the German trenches until it virtually ran out of ammunition. James Anderson was subsequently awarded the Distinguished Conduct Medal and the Croix de Guerre. The citation states

> At Bullecourt, May 3. '17. Although wounded and blinded in one eye he continued to work his gun with great determination and kept up a steady fire on the enemy. He asked not to be evacuated until the action was over, and made a second journey into Bullecourt.

James retrained as a driver and transferred to the Tank Corps. He was one of the twelve experienced officers and seventy other ranks, all of who had seen action, who were brought together under the command of Major Byngham to form the 14th Battalion at Bovington. Arriving on 14 November, James may well have been part of the team which took tanks to major towns and cities in support of Government's war bond sales. He was posted to 16th Battalion on 3 January 1918 where he was appointed as 2nd Class Tank Mechanic on 2 March 1918 which provided a daily increase to his pay. Three months later, James was confirmed as 1st Class Tank Mechanic with a further rise in pay. He then caught from influenza, probably the Spanish variant, and was hospitalized until 21 July 1918. James returned to France, when 16th Battalion deployed in early September and was in action from 29 September, serving with C Company, in support of 3rd Australian Division during the Battle for the St Quentin Canal. In the next eighteen days, the battalion was in action on sixth occasions, after which it had to be withdrawn, its men and equipment having been used to exhaustion. It was not until well after the Armistice, on 18 January 1919 that James was appointed Lance Corporal, the first time he was promoted. He held the rank until he returned to the UK on 25 March 1919; James was demobilised 4 days later and returned home to Leith. Thereafter I can find nothing else about him.

Gunner John Applegate was born on 4 January 1892 at Chelsea. The eldest son of a coachman William Applegate and his wife Ann, John was baptized at Christ Church on 16 March 1892. Bought up in Chawton and Alton in Hampshire, he worked as a butcher. John was initially attested on 30 October 1915 whilst living in North Camp at Aldershot. He joined the MMGS two days later and underwent the standard training at Bisley on Lewis and Vickers machine guns. John was posted to "W" Company on 24 May 1916, but then transferred to D Company deploying to France on 2 September 1916. After the initial fighting, he was transferred to D Battalion where he served until almost the end of the war. Having been granted Proficiency Pay as Class 1 soldier on 22 October 1917, John was sent on leave on 10 November and, three days later, married Ada Mansfield at St Michael the Archangel Parish Church in Aldershot.

He returned to duty on 21 November and rejoined his unit for the end of the Battle of Cambrai. He then served with C Company, under Captain Alfred Enoch who commanded D7 at Flers. John and Ada's daughter Elsie was born on 4 August 1918 at Aldershot. John was posted back to the Tank Corps Depot on 17 October 1918 and then to the newly formed 19th Battalion on 13 November. He remained at Bovington until his discharge on 31 March 1920, when he returned to North Town in Aldershot. Eleven months later, whilst working as a storeman, John was asked to join the Army's B Reserve. Agreeing, he was attested at Guildford but he was subsequently discharged as he was suffering from varicose veins. With the onset of the Great Depression, John moved to London in 1927 to find work as a carpenter but was unable to survive without help from one of the YMCA street patrols who assisted those in difficulty. Sadly there is no record of him thereafter until his death, aged seventy one, in Portsmouth in 1963.

Gunner Lawson was possibly William Lawson from Stourport. He joined the MMGS in early 1915 and initially entered France on 10 May 15. Later transferred to the Tanks he was commissioned on 23 October and survived. Gunner Jack Choules was born in December 1897 and was bought up in Maidenhead. Jack's father was a soldier who was recalled to serve during the Second Anglo-Boer war but later became a self-employed "dog doctor". Jack, who was the second of eight children, initially got a job as a learner with the Post Office in 1913, his older brother working as a telegraph messenger. However Jack was working as a builder's clerk, when he was attested at Reading on 18 October 1915. Jack enlisted into the MMGS and transferred to Heavy Section MGC on 4 May 1916 having been trained as a Vickers machine gun and later on the 6 pdr Hotchkiss QF gun. He was posted to D Company on 27 May and preceded to France on 1 September. After the first action, Jack joined D Battalion. He then served with No 12 Company as a gunner and probably served with No 9 Section during the assault from Neuville St Vaast towards Thelus on 9 April 1917.

Like James Anderson, he fought in the attack by No 12 Company at the second Battle of Bullecourt on 3 May. During this action, he suffered gunshot wounds to the scalp which were so bad that he was hospitalised and later evacuated to England. He was discharged from hospital on 16 June 1917 and posted to the Tank Depot at Wareham. His health was considered to be so poor that he was transferred to 3rd (Reserve) Battalion Manchester Regiment on 20 August 1917 which was based at Cleethorpes as part of the defences of the River Humber. Jack as appointed unpaid lance corporal on 19 April 1918 and discharged from the Army, as a lance corporal on 20 March 1919. Although his discharge papers shown Jack was of a A1 medical status, he was subsequently accorded a 40% disability pension due to his scalp wounds and severe headaches. He eventually recovered and married Elsie King in autumn 1921; their daughter Pamela being born the following summer. The family later settled at 436 Broad Oak Court on the Farnham road in Slough where Jack worked as a clerk at an engineering packing factory. He died, aged only fifty two, on 25 April 1950.

The final member of the crew was, like Eric's second in command Dudley White, Killed in Action. Gunner Percy Raworth was born in Knaresborough near Harrogate in June 1890 and was, according to the *Harrogate Herald* newspaper, was "one of our most brilliant footballers and a sportsman through and through". He was the only son of a prominent local builder, William Raworth, who served on Harrogate Council for many years. In 1910, Percy's sister, Ellen, married Hubert Ingle who owned a leather factor's firm at Leicester. When he established an outlet at Rushden, Percy moved there and became a storekeeper. It was at Rushden that he enlisted so he may have known Horace Allebone.

Percy joined the MMGS then transferred to the MGC serving with Eric Robinson from the start. Eric got to know Percy's family as one of his chums recalled seeing a picture of Eric with Percy's mother Mary. Following the action on 15 September, Percy was awarded the Military Medal. Writing to Percy's father, Eric Robinson later recalled. "After our tank had stuck he jumped out and assisted in digging it out for 14 hours under very heavy fire. Your son worked in the most exposed position, thus setting a fine example of pluck and endurance to the remainder of the crew". A letter published in the Harrogate Herald confirmed he was in action with the tanks near Thiepval on 26 September; this was certainly the action near Courcelette where Eric Robinson's tank was destroyed. News of his exploits was published in *The Shoe and Leather and Allied Trades News* on 26 October 1916: I have two budgets of congratulations to offer this week. The first is very heartily to Private Percy Raworth, of the "Tanks," who has received the Military Medal. The son of Councillor W Raworth, of Harrogate, he was storekeeper with Messrs Ingle at their branch in Leicester, and at the outbreak of war came to Rushden, and then enlisted in the Motor Machine Gun Section. He has been in action several times in the "Tanks," and had some very narrow escapes.

Percy remained with D Battalion as it formed and fought with them in action during the Battle of Arras. Renumbered on allocation to Tank Corps, he was in action again during the Battle of Passchendaele. On 23 September 1917, he volunteered to stand guard on the Battalion's animals whilst the unit was in the rear areas. Sadly he was fatally wounded by a bomb, dropped by an aircraft and is buried at Gwalia cemetery near Poperinghe. Eric Robinson, who was in England, received the news from Cecil Howes, an ASC driver who had transferred to the tanks in January 1917. Eric subsequently wrote to William Raworth:

I feel I must write to you, and offer my heartfelt sympathy on hearing of the death of your son Percy, I only heard from France on Saturday. The news came as a terrible shock to me, as your son had been with me ever since he joined up in 15, and we have been through so many bad times together in France. Raworth was the most popular man in the Company with both officers and men, and I could not have wished for a cooler or braver man in action. I am enclosing a letter I have just received from him written just before his death, also letter from one of my old men. Again offering you and family my deepest sympathy.

An enclosed letter gave more details of his death, although the writer is not known.

He was made as comfortable as it was humanly possible under the circumstances, and you will doubtless find some consolation in the knowledge that he did not appear to feel very much pain. I should like to add that in company with all his friends of the battalion – and there are many – I wish to offer my sympathy in your sad loss. You have lost a good son and we have lost a popular chum – one who was always cheerful and ready to help others. Quiet and genuine, those with whom he came in contact quickly learned to respect and like him, and I ask you to accept this as the sincere opinion of myself and all those others on whose behalf I am writing. He and I served together in the MMGS at Bisley, and ever since have been together through the monotony of training, in games and in lecture, whilst when we came out here our experiences of war were gained together. With opportunities like these of weighing up a man, one naturally sees him as he really is, and we were all glad to count Percy as our chum.

13

Percy the tank cat

The village of Martinpuich is located, in a shallow valley, between High Wood and Courcelette. By September 1916, the village was heavily fortified and four tanks were tasked to help the assaulting infantry from 15th and 50th Divisions break through the German defences. The tanks were all from D Company and were under the command of Captain William Mann. Mann split his tanks into pairs; each containing a male and female – one to destroy machine guns and the other to kill the defending Germans in their well-prepared trenches. Two crews, D20 fighting in the male tank *Daphne* and D23 in a female tank whose name is unknown, supported 15th Scottish Division who attacked Martinpuich. The other crews D24 and D25 attacked the eastern side of the village in support of 50th Division (see map 12).

On the move up to the start point, on the evening of 13 September, the tank commanded by George Mann failed and the crew had to return to the administrative area near the Loop railway sidings for a replacement. They then moved to their rendezvous point at the Brigade Headquarters south of Contalmaison. On the evening of 14 September, *Daphne* and the replacement set out for their start points but as they approached the British front line, one of D23's tracks was smashed by German shell fire. There were no spare tanks so that tank could not be repaired so, having removed the locks from the machine guns, George Mann sent his crew back to Contalmaison. George Mann then went forward to make sure that the D20 crew, in *Daphne*, got into action. *Daphne* crossed No Man's Land and got beyond the first objective, reaching the southwest entrance to Martinpuich (see coloured picture `14), but then returned to refuel and re-arm. At 09:47 a.m. following a request from the infantry, George Mann tasked *Daphne*'s skipper, Harry Drader to go back into action but *Daphne* did not deploy as her driver Alfred Bowerman was suffering from shock. At noon, George Mann again tasked Harry Drader to take ammunition forward to form a dump to the southwest of Martinpuich; again Drader was unable so to do which is somewhat surprising given that some of his crew would have sufficient skills to drive the vehicle. Eventually George Mann took *Daphne* forwards himself, having brought forward his own driver Jack Rossiter, from the rendezvous at Contalmaison, to complete the task.

D23

George Mann was the only ex-Regular non-commissioned officer to serve with the First Tank Crews. His father, who was also named George, was serving at the Guards Depot at Caterham when George was born in 1889. He subsequently was promoted to Quartermaster Sergeant and, when he retired, settled his family at Croydon where George attended Archbishop Tenison's school. On 18 September 1906, George enlisted into the oldest British infantry regiment, the Royal Scots, and served for two years with 1st Battalion initially at home and then for five years in Allahabad in India. George had reached the rank of corporal by the time he was discharged on 8 December 1913 joining the Reserve in accordance with his contract. Settling in Croydon, he became a member of the Old England Masonic Lodge on 2 July 1914, when his occupation is shown as a wireless operator.

When war was declared, George was recalled to the Royal Scots and later allocated to 13th Battalion. This service battalion formed at Edinburgh on the outbreak of war but soon moved to Aldershot in September 1914 and then to Bramshott Common, where George would have been extremely useful in training the newly formed unit. However, on 15 December 1914, he transferred to the MMGS and deployed to France with 10th Battery on 22 March 1915 which was attached to the 9th (Scottish) Division. He was subsequently promoted sergeant and possibly saw action at the Battle of Loos in September 1915.

George later served as a Quartermaster Sergeant in the rank of WO2 and, on 8 November, was commissioned into the MMGS "in the field". Sent back to England, probably to assist in training at Bisley, George married Dora Pugh at her local parish church, All Saints Church in Fulham on 12 February 1916. Dora was the youngest daughter of a city missionary named Richard Pugh who had died in 1914, and her brothers Richard and Alexander were witnesses at the wedding. Dora and George settled in Wimbledon. In May 1916, George was selected to command a section in D Company in the rank of captain. Deploying back to France on 2 September, Frank Summers allocated George's section to support III Corps on arrival at the Somme and George attended a Corps conference for instructions on 12 September. Although his own tank was damaged on 15 September before it could get into contact with the enemy, George's other three tanks got well beyond the German front line and one was knocked out as they pressed home their attack. As D Company was re-organised after the losses on 15 September, George was tasked to stay near Contalmaison. The adjutant, Captain Graham Woods visited George on 21 September and the next day, he was allocated another four tanks which had been in action at Flers. The War Diary does not make it clear whether George Mann himself went into action, during the actions known as the Battle of the Ancre but his two of his tanks, commanded by George Bown and William Wakley were destroyed as they fought their way into the farm complex at Eaucourt L'Abbaye on 1 October.

When Captain Graham Woods was detached to set up the Company's winter quarters on 6 November, George Mann was selected to assume the role of Adjutant. However, he did not remain in the company headquarters. On 14 November, George was tasked to establish a route across the British lines and through German positions near Beaucourt station, which was then used by members of his section including Harry Drader for the last tank action of the year. For his actions on the Somme, George was Mentioned in Despatches. He served with D Battalion until 9 March when he was sent back to England and, as a result he was able to see Dora and their infant daughter, Betty, who had been born on 13 February 1917 in Wimbledon. George had been posted to F Battalion, "gathered in" by the recently promoted Lieutenant Colonel Frank Summers, and was appointed second in command of No 17 Company. George deployed with the F Battalion on 20 May to France where it established its base to Auchy-Les-Hesdin. On 1 June the Battalion moved to Wailly, the Tank Corps Driving School, for two weeks and then to the Corps Gunnery School at Merlimont for live firing. Tanks were then drawn from the Central Stores at Erin and taken back to Auchy before deploying to the Ypres Salient on 2 July. Initially based at Oesthoek Wood, the Battalion moved to La Lovie after their tankodrome became a regular target for long range German artillery fire. As part of the preparations for the start of the Third Battle of Ypres, George moved forward to a rendezvous at Trois Tours Chateau on 25 July. Whilst sheltering from artillery fire in a dug out, he and two others were fatally wounded. George was sent to the rear for treatment but he did not survive and is buried at Dozingham British Military Cemetery to the west of Poperinghe.

I have been able to find some information about most of George Mann's crew but cannot positively identify his second in command Sergeant Nicholson. He may have been Sergeant John Gibson Nicholson who later served with the Tank Corps as a colour sergeant. Gunner Parkin was probably William Parkin from Leeds. Known as Eddie, he was born on 28 October 1896 and was the eldest son of a publican, Robert Parkin, who later became a brewer. Bought up in Headingley, where he worked as a groom, Eddie married Lily Annal on 23 March 1916, at St Agnes' Church in Burmantofts, one week before he enlisted in the MMGS. His service record has not survived but the medal rolls shows he served with 4th Battalion throughout the rest of the war, leaving the Army in the rank of corporal. Looking for a better life, after the war, Eddie travelled to Canada in May 1920; Lily being pregnant with their son Eric. He stayed for three years in Toronto before returning to Leeds where his daughter Lily was born in 1926. The family returned to Canada in 1929, Eddie deciding to give up driving and to take up farming but I can find no other details after they had arrived.

Gunner John Starkey, who was the same age as Eddie Parkin, came from Basford which is a northern suburb of Nottingham. He was the only surviving child of a fruiterer also named John Starkey whose wife Sarah Barnes lost her two daughters whilst they were infants. John was baptised on 12 August 1896 at Basford Parish Church. Fifteen year later, John was working for his father who had moved to nearby Bulwell with Sarah. John' service record has not survived but the list of those Soldiers who Died in the Great War records that John enlisted at Nottingham and his MGC service number was issued in early 1916. He transferred to D Battalion after the first actions when it formed in December but later served with F Battalion in No 17 Company whose officers included his former skipper Captain George Mann and Captain Charles Storey who won the DSO near Gueudecourt in September 1916. John was declared Missing in Action after the fighting on 27 November 1917 at Bourlon. This village had originally been attacked on 23 November with some success but the Germans counterattacked the following day, ejecting the small party of British defenders. The second attack was carried out by two brigades from 62 West Riding Division supported by three tanks from C Battalion and seventeen from F Battalion. The tank started their approach march at 6.00 pm on 26 November and reached the assembly point at 12.30 a.m. There was continuous rain and snow overnight and the farmland over which the tanks advanced the next morning was bad. The tanks left the start point on the Arras to Cambrai road at 6.20 a.m. and advanced north, over the Bourlon ridge and into the village. They were ahead of the infantry by the time the tanks reached the village and the crews used their 6 pdr QF guns to destroy the German machine guns. However the Germans were well prepared and seven tanks were knocked out. The attack petered out by 10.00 am and the infantry withdrew.

There were only four tanks from No 17 Company in the action; *Formidable* was damaged by shell fire and did not get into action; *Fearless II* broke into the village and was engaged in a dual with an anti-tank gun which was silenced. The tank then had mechanical problems and withdrew. The other two tanks, Fighting *Mack* or *Flaming Fire*, were knocked out at close range by direct fire as they approached the village. The War History of the Six Tank Battalion simply says that there is no information about what happened to their crews but John Starkey was amongst the twenty eight members of No 17 Company who were later declared missing. Some of these crewmen were captured but, after the Armistice when all surviving prisoners returned home, John was not amongst them. He was presumed dead and, on 18 January, 1919, the balance of John's pay was sent to his father. On 20 November 1919, his family was also paid a war gratuity of seven pounds and ten shillings exactly two years after John and his comrades breached the German defences near La Vacquerie. John is commemorated on the Memorial to the Missing at Louverval. He is also named on the war memorial at his home parish church at Bulwell in Nottinghamshire. He is "not forgotten".

His crewmate, Douglas Tweddle, survived the war. Douglas was born in April 1892 at Longtown in Cumberland. He was a keen motorcyclist and, in 1914 whilst preparing for the Isle of Man Tourist Trophy Races, broke his leg. He therefore could not join the Border Regiment like many of his friends. He recovered from his injury and was able to ride again. Douglas, who worked as an ironmonger, was living at 44 Bridge Street when he was attested on 11 December 1915 at Longtown. Like many other crewmen, he responded to an advertisement in *The Motor Cycle* and travelled to Coventry where successfully passed the MMGS trade test on 21 March. He was mobilized two days later and immediately sent to Bisley camp, where four days later, he was joined by his friend George Moscrop from Longtown. After initial machine gun training at Bisley, Douglas was one of those to be trained at Portsmouth on the 6 pdr QF gun fitted to the male tanks. On 28 May, Douglas was posted to D Company with his friend George Moscrop and, the following moth, travelled to John O'Groats camp at Elveden in Norfolk. There the crews did their limited training on the newly manufactured tanks but Douglas was mainly employed as a despatch rider. He deployed to France on 2 September but I can find nothing about his service immediately after the first actions, other than he was a machine gunner.

Douglas was allocated to No 12 Company when D Battalion was formed but was hospitalized with impetigo on 12 January at St Pol sur Ternoise. He lost all his hair and, despite constant care, failed to recover. As a result, Douglas was sent back to England on 3 March and posted to the Depot Battalion until he was fully fit. He was sent on ten days post-hospital leave on 16 March, to his home in Longtown, and then joined E Company of the Depot battalion at Bovington on 31 March 1917. He did not go overseas again but trained as a driver mechanic; this being recommended by his company commander Major ROC Ward who was later killed at the Battle of Cambrai. Douglas was clearly good as a unit level instructor as he posted to the Driving School on 17 November and immediately appointed a first class tank machinist. He was then selected to participate in a Government Bond fund raising tour, when tanks were used to gain public support. Having undertaken a tour in southwest England, Douglas was appointed acting lance corporal on 1 December 1917 and, on 14 February, was promoted to Corporal Instructor at the School of Instruction at Bovington. He was disappointed to miss further tank tour trips but this was because Douglas was selected the right-winger in the School's football team at weekends – his family say that he was the only amateur in the team. His skills at football were clearly more important that his ability as an instructor as, when in the latter part of 1918 when he was tasked to deploy to Russia with a tank training team, strings were pulled to keep him playing soccer in England.

On 16 January 1919, Douglas married Agnes Rutherford at St Andrew's United Free Church at Longtown. The family finances received a welcome boost when he was promoted sergeant six days later. Douglas was demobilised on 25 April 1919 and he returned to 43 Swan Street at Longtown. His elder son Stanley was born in the following spring and his younger brother Martin was born in autumn 1925. Like many other ex-Tankers, Douglas found work in the motor trade and eventually became a director of Graham & Roberts Ltd of Butchergate in Carlisle. This company was the first distributor of MG cars in the North of England and later became a very large and successful enterprise. He continued his interest in motor sport and became president of the Cumberland Car and Motorcycle club. Following the outbreak of the Second World War, Douglas joined the Local Defence Volunteers, eventually serving as a Platoon Commander in the Carlisle Home Guard, where his instructional skills on the Vickers machine gun were revealed to his son, who served with him, as he supervised his platoons' training. Douglas died, aged only sixty two years old, on 7 October 1954 and was buried in the church yard of Arthuret Parish Church near Longtown; his wife who survived for another thirteen years being later buried beside him.

His crewmate Gunner Henry Tillotson was born at Deptford near London on 17 February 1898 and was one of the youngest of the First Tank Crews. Henry was the youngest son of a pewterer named Albert and his wife Elizabeth Fenton. By 1901 the family was living at 75 St John's Road. Henry attended the nearby Lucas Street School in 1907. Sadly his service records have not survived so little is known of his military career. However, according to an officer's notebook now held at the Tank Museum, on 30 July 1918, Henry was later a crewman in tank 9125 allocated to No 12 section of C Company of 4th Battalion. On the opening day of the Battle of Amiens, 8 August, he is again listed as a member of the crew of tank 9125, which advanced ahead of the infantry and cleared their way through the German defences. It attacked a howitzer battery and forced the crews to flee, before reaching the first objective or Green Line at 8:00 a.m. The tank then crossed the River Luce at Ignacourt and reached the crew's final objective at Cayeux at 10:30am, the infantry eventually reaching the village thirty minutes. The advance stunned the German defenders, not just at the speed of the tanks but the depth of the advance. Henry's tank then towed a broken down tank to its company rally-point at Cerfs Wood. The tank was again in action on the following day and again on 11 August, when it was hit by enemy fire and burnt out. Whether Henry was a crewman on that day, I cannot determine.

After the Armistice, Henry remained with 4th Battalion and then was granted UK leave. Whilst in England, he made the decision not to return to his unit and he deserted on 15 January 1919; no disciplinary action seems to have been taken against him. On Christmas Day 1920, at Acton Parish Church, Henry married 18 year old Christina Hobden and they settled at 47 High St Acton. Their four children were born whilst the couple was living at 5 Mansel Road close by Acton Park. By 1935, the family had moved to a much larger house at 34 Myrtle Road, about five minutes' walk away. After the war, they moved to Brunel Road close by Wormwood Scrubs, and then settled close to their first home at Bromyard Avenue, where they was living when Henry died, aged sixty three, on 15 March 1961.

Generally I have been unable to find much about ASC drivers but I have been fortunate to learn a lot about George Mann's driver "Jack" Rossiter from his grand-daughter Ann. Jack, who was christened Osmond Woodford Rossiter, was born on 10 May 1897 at Marnhull in the Blackmoor Vale. The Blackmoor Vale was immortalised by the novelist Thomas Hardy in the Wessex novels; he used Marnhull or "Marnlot" as the home of *Tess of the D'Urbervilles*. Jack, who was born just two years after the publication of "Tess", was the fifth child of Thomas Rossiter and his second wife 'Bessie' who farmed Moorcourt Farm for many years. Jack joined the ASC in 1915, aged only eighteen, and trained as a motor driver at Grove Park MT Depot in southeast London. He returned to Marnhull in March 1916 for confirmation as a member of the Church of England. The ceremony took place on 27 March; the celebrant was the Bishop of Salisbury – the Right Reverend Frederick Ridgeway.

Although known to his family as Osmond, he was called Jack by his chums in the ASC. Jack was attached to 711 (MT) Company and trained at Elveden before he deployed to France. There are no records that he again went into action after 15 September but Jack was one of the ASC drivers who volunteered to transfer to the Heavy Branch of the MGC and then to serve with the Tank Corps. He continued to serve with D Battalion and was promoted to lance corporal by 1918. Jack was twice injured in action; the second time being 29 September 1918 when his tank was destroyed by a mine and he was rescued by Australian troops – this was at Bellicourt when American, Australian and British units broke through the Hindenburg line. Jack had to be carried from the blown up tank and was evacuated to the UK. He recovered and was posted to the recently formed 19th Battalion at Bovington where Jack served as a sergeant.

After demobilization in 1919, he returned home to Marnhull. Two years later, on 22 January 1921, Jack married a Yorkshire girl named Sarah Daniels at Sturminster Register Office. They had two sons, Harry who was born on 5 August 1921 and John who was born in 1928. Jack set up himself up in business as a butcher at Droop near Hazelbury Bryan, a small village 17 miles south of Marnhull. The butcher shop and slaughterhouse was on a farm owned by his brother-in-law, Captain Graham Burnand who had married Osmond's younger sister Rhoda. Jack delivered the meat to his customers in a Morris Cowley van but, after five years and with the onset of the Depression, business became difficult. The family moved to a much larger village and again he set up as a butcher, obtaining meat from a local slaughterhouse. His vehicle was a Trojan van, which had chain drive and hard rubber tyres. A family story tells that Jack was charged with driving without a license but he didn't have any money so the local policeman paid the fine and Jack paid later him back.

The butchery business eventually failed and Jack moved to Boscombe looking for work. He gained a job driving a brewery lorry but lost it immediately. During the interview, Jack was asked if he was a drinker, to which he replied in the negative. The owner of the brewery then asked Jack if he would like a drink to celebrate his getting the job and not wanting to cause offence, Jack agreed and was told he had lost the job. Fortunately, being a first class mechanic. Jack was able to find work at Hendy's Garage in Boscombe. He sent for Sally and his two sons, and they lived in a flat over Hockey's butcher shop. The job at Hendy's lasted until Ford stopped making the Model T variant and the company bought in new staff. Fortunately, Jack was offered a job working in the butcher shop where he worked until Mr Hockey retired.

Like Douglas Tweddle, Jack joined the Home Guard during the Second World War. He also used to undertake rounds each evening to check that all was safe. His wife Rhoda recalled that he was out one night, after a bombing raid and, as he passed one garden thought he saw a head of cabbage that had been separated from its root. When he got closer, Jack saw that it was the head of a little girl and returned home much shaken by the grisly discovery. His son Harry, who was an electrician, joined the RAF as war broke out and fought with 7 Squadron RAF during the Second World War, initially flying in Sterling bombers and later in Wellingtons as a wireless operator. Despite a number of narrow escapes, Harry survived the war

After the war, Jack again set up his own butchery business. The shop, which was on the Charminster Road at Wimborne, was hard work with long hours and its profits were not helped as Jack's cashier was stealing from him. In his spare time, Jack enjoyed tinkering in his garage but his first love was his garden which was a sight to behold as he was particularly good at growing roses. Jack Rossiter died, aged only sixty six years on 3 November 1963.

Daphne

Daphne was the male tank which was tasked to accompany George Mann's crew into the attack. This tank later attracted worldwide interest because the crew had a mascot – a black kitten named Percy who appeared with the crew in the film "The Battle of the Ancre". This film was made by Geoffrey Malins who was well positioned to photograph *Daphne* as she went into action at Martinpuich on 15 September but, for some unknown reason, he failed to do so. The pictures of *Daphne* and Percy were taken in the rear areas as the tank deployed towards her start point near Bazentin. Percy not only went into action on 15 September but according to the family of *Daphne*'s skipper, on several occasions afterwards. The film was released in Great Britain just after Christmas 1916 and was a smash hit. Daphne's crew became known as the "Black Cat Crew" and Percy was mentioned in newspapers overseas when the film was shown to foreign audiences.

Daphne's skipper, Second Lieutenant Harry Drader, was born on 28 April 1897 in Marthaville in the middle of the Canadian oil fields. Harry was the youngest son of oil drilling specialist Henry Drader and his wife Cora Bell who maintained a diary during the Great War which provides hints to his service. Before Harry's birth, Henry Drader had assisted with the opening up new oilfields in Romania where Harry's elder sister Alice were born. The year after Harry's birth, Henry took the family back to Romania as part of another oil exploration project. However, when the job was over, Henry did not return to Canada but by 1901 settled the family in Dover. Henry then moved the family to Bedford and later moved to Colney Hatch. In 1909, Harry entered Bedford Grammar School where he served with the OTC. In July 1914, having left school, he made his way across Europe to join his father was again working in Romania. Travelling through Berlin, within a few hours of the declaration of war, Harry was able to avoid arrest but two of his school friends, who travelled out to join him were not so lucky.

When he got back to England, the seventeen year old Harry was too young to join the Army so, in January 1915, he travelled to Le Havre to work for the YMCA supporting the troops who

The Black Cat crew at Elveden July 1916: Standing left – Walter Atkins, seated centre Harry Drader and right, Owen Rowe. (David Drader)

travelled through the port. Harry was first used as a driver at Le Havre and then onto worked at Rouen, returning to England by early March. Having failed to join the RNAS, he was advised to join the Army as a Romanian interpreter and also the RAMC. On 26 May 1915, and now eighteen years old, Harry was accepted by the Inns of Court OTC and undertook initial officer training at Berkhamstead. Six weeks later, he was commissioned into 4th Battalion Northumberland Fusiliers and served in France for ten weeks before returning to England. Harry was seconded for duty to the Heavy Section of the MGC on 27 May 1916, which was well after most of the tank skippers arrived at Bisley.

About that time, Harry visited his parents at their home at Colney Hatch where his cousin Eugene Drader, who was serving with 49th Battalion CEF, was present. Eugene wrote that "Harry was back on leave from the front and is to take a course in armoured motors." Eugene was accompanied by a close friend, Stanley Davies, who was later to marry Harry's sister Alice. Harry, who had joined D Company, trained with his crew at Bisley and Elveden before deploying overseas on 2 September. Unlike the rest of his crew, who travelled by train to their final training grounds, Harry led the company's cars and lorries by road from Le Havre to the training ground at Yvrench. It is probably here that Percy joined the crew. Pure black, small and totally fearless, Percy was filmed with Harry and Corporal Owen Rowe, outside the tank as the crew prepared *Daphne* for action. Harry is then shown carefully passing Percy into the tank to where Owen would have been standing, before entering the tank himself. When the film "*the Battle of the Ancre*" was shown in cinemas, the audience cheered the tanks and they especially cheered Percy. Percy was not only famous in Britain as, when Harry's father was working in Mexico in October 1917, the film was shown at a cinema in Tampico and the local papers included a description of Harry and his black cat.

The smiles which would have been raised by the sight of Harry and Percy on film did not soften grief amongst the Drader family. Whilst Harry and his crew were returning to their base on the evening of 15 September, his cousin Eugene Drader and Alice's sweetheart Stanley Davies were attacking the German positions near Courcelette, only two miles to the north of Martinpuich. During the move up that afternoon, Eugene's company commander was injured and Eugene assumed command. He was mortally wounded as he led his troops during the close-fighting with the Germans. His loss affected Harry greatly. Although Harry's actions were modest in comparison with some of his fellow skippers on 15 September, he was awarded the Military Cross. The citation states "He fought his Tank with great gallantry, putting enemy infantry to flight and silencing a machine gun. Later, he carried ammunition to the front line under heavy fire"; the latter part of the citation being patently untrue.

Harry was promoted temporary Lieutenant on 1 October but, although he prepared his crew for action on several occasions that month, the bad weather and shell-damaged ground made the use of tanks impossible. The next month was slightly drier and, on 14 November during the final tank action of 1916, Harry commanded one of three tanks which attacked a German strongpoint in support of 63rd (RN) Division near Hamel. The other tanks were commanded by Hugh Bell and Eric Robinson. The D Company War Diary records at

> 8.00 pm. Orders received to send to two tanks to attack isolated strong-points situated Q17 B7.4. [due north of Hamel]) Lts Drader and Robinson were detailed with Lt Bell in reserve. On journey to starting point, Lt Robinson's tank was hit by shell fire and placed out of action. Infantry guide was picked up and travelled in leading tank [Harry Drader]. At zero (6.00 am) tanks advanced to the attack and at 50 yards range, Lt Drader opened fire with 6 pdr guns. The tanks still advanced and crossed the first line of the strong point, doing good enfilading work. Simultaneously the enemy hoisted the white flag. The tanks at this moment became ditched and an awkward occasion arose, which was handled splendidly by both officers. A machine gunner was ordered to watch for any signs of treachery on the part of the enemy & the officers and crews then left the tanks and entered the German trenches with loaded revolvers, then coaxed the enemy out of their dug-outs and after about an hour, the prisoners who numbered about 400 were despatched to the rear with an infantry escort. When the adverse conditions of the ground are reckoned with, this must be considered a very fine performance and all ranks engaged with the operation are to be congratulated.

Harry was Mentioned in Dispatches for this action. Although Percy the tank cat is not mentioned in any official records, he was mentioned in a letter written by Harry two days later. As revealed in Chapter 2, Harry's soldier servant, Rol Elliott was close friends with Walter Atkins who had been wounded after *Daphne* came out of action on 15 September. Writing to Walter who was in hospital, Harry skated over the details of the action but the impact of Percy on the crew's morale was obvious.

> The crew had another joy ride the day before yesterday at Dawn, and as before behaved splendidly, even better results than the 15th [September]. The black kitten, which is nearly cat size now, seems to being us more and more luck, I don't think the crew would part with it for anything
>
> We've had a few more casualties in the company including Sgt Davies. For the past month we have been attached to Capt Mortimore's section. With the new organization which will probably come into force soon, God knows where the wounded will return to, unless you get back before we get back to strength. How long do you think it will be before you get back? However take my tip and make the most of your leave.

Harry and Percy stayed in France over the winter of 1916 serving with the newly established D Battalion at Blangy. Harry was promoted temporary captain and appointed Section Commander from 12 April 1917 probably as a result of casualties sustained during the opening action of the Battle of Arras. On 23 April 1917, his sub-section was tasked to support an attack near Croisilles on 23 April 1917 but neither tank got into action owing to mechanical failure. Later that year, Harry was sent back to England to act as an instructor and it was at this time that he and Percy were photographed. On 31 October, Harry and Eric Robinson received their MCs from King George V.

Harry and Eric returned to France, with the recently formed 10th Tank Battalion, on 20 December 1917 and probably met many old friends after Christmas as their unit took over the residue of 4th Battalion's tanks – 4th Battalion being the new name of Harry's old unit D Battalion. On 21 March 1918, on the opening day of the German Spring Offensive, Harry was appointed adjutant when the Battalion HQ was shelled and many of the staff were injured. On 4 April, Harry took command of a tank company and they went into action the next day. Sadly the majority of tanks became ditched in old Somme battlefield trenches although, just as on 14 November 1916, his men did capture 60 German infantry. From 10 April, Harry commanded ten tanks positioned to stop the Germans pressing round the British flanks near Sousastre; by 13 April the threat had passed and the unit went back into training.

On 16 July, his family received a letter from Harry in which he told them he had become engaged to a French lady. This however came to nothing. Sadly nothing is also recorded about Percy at this time. In August, during the Battle of Amiens, whilst Eric was commanding A Company, Harry commanded B Company of 10th Battalion. On 9 August, his unit was in action at Morlancourt to the south west of Albert. Twelve days later, Harry's company was in action near Bapaume. This was remarkable progress in two weeks compared to 1916 when the same ground took four months and thousands of lives to capture. Eric Robinson and Harry continued to command companies through the Final Advance but Harry must have been devastated when Eric Robinson was killed on 4 November at Cotillon sur Sambe; the same action in which the poet Wilfred Owen was killed. Having buried his friend, Harry took charge of the consolidated company but only two tanks were deployed the following day and they did not engage the enemy. It was the last day 10th Battalion was in action. The Allied Divisions continued to push the Germans further back towards the Belgian border and the German Government, undermined by civil unrest at home, sued for peace.

After the Armistice, Harry served with the Army of Occupation in Germany. He was demobilised on 14 February 1919 and returned to live at Colney Hatch. Harry then studied at the School of Mines in Kensington for two years. He joined his family in Romania to work as a petroleum engineer but did not stay in Europe for long. The following year, on 13 February 1923, Harry disembarked at New York en route for Los Angeles. There he met and, in 1928, married Peggy Schafer. Harry moved to Trinidad to find work the following year; Peggy accompanied him but they soon returned to Los Angeles where their only daughter Patricia or "Trixie" was born in 1934. When the family was visited by his mother Cora in 1937, family photos reveal Harry as a well-established businessman.

The following year Harry became an American citizen and, by 1940, the family was living in North Highland near the Hollywood Bowl. Trixie was educated at the Hollywood High School and her Year Book reveals she was a member of a service society alongside the comedienne Carol Burnett. Sadly Harry never met Trixie's children; he died aged only fifty nine on 14 November 1956; exactly forty years to the day when he, Hugh Bell and their crews had captured four hundred German soldiers using pistols and a lot of courage.

Corporal Owen Rowe, who was the son of a farmer, was born at Chagford on Dartmoor in the autumn of 1897. He was bought up on Westford Farm near Drewsteignton and educated at the Schoolhouse at Crediton. He enlisted into the MMGS at Coventry in the last week of February 1916 at the same time as Frank Styring and Herbert Statham. Despite being only eighteen, Owen was promoted corporal and appointed second in command of *Daphne*. After the first actions, Owen became an instructor at the Driving and Maintenance School at Wailly where he was promoted

Harry Drader in Los Angeles 1937. (David Drader)

Sergeant. During the Battle of Cambrai, when the Driving Instructors crewed tanks which ripped away German barbed wire to assist the British cavalry, Owen was badly injured. His leg was amputated and Owen sent back to England where he was discharged on 1 November 1918 as he was no longer "fit for service". However, he did not lose contact with his Tank Corps comrades as he moved to Bovington and worked as a taxi driver with fellow-driving instructor Roy Reiffer – one of the gunners in *Dinnaken* which fought its way into the village of Flers on 15 September 1916. Sadly Owen died of tuberculosis in the summer of 1923 at home in Devon.

Although Percy was a lucky cat, not all of the First Tank Crewman survived. Frank Styring, who was killed in action in April 1917, was born on 8 November 1889 at Nether Hallam in the west of Sheffield. Frank, who was the eldest son of an optician Charles Percy and his wife Lily, was educated locally at Kings Edward VII School, before joining his father's firm and training as an optician. He was a member of the Young Men's Society at St Stephen's Church before he enlisted into the MMGS on 28 February. After the first tank actions, Frank was transferred to D Battalion and served with No 10 Company. In 9 April 1917, Frank was fighting as a member of No 2 Section; this section was tasked to assist the capture of the German defensive position known as the Harp near Beaurains. According to a letter, sent by the Battalion chaplain to his parents, Frank "was in the open pointing out the way so that his crew might get along safely." His company commander, Major William Haskett-Smith, wrote that Frank was guiding a tank over the Hindenburg line when he was mortally wounded; this confirms the tank was negotiating the trenches which protected the western side of the German position. Frank was initially buried on the Harp objective but his body is now buried at Beaurains Road Military Cemetery. His parents, who later named their house "Beaurains", erected a fine memorial to their son at the Crookes cemetery in Sheffield and another memorial in St Stephen's Church. Frank was also commemorated with the other seventeen members of the Church Young Men's Society who lost their lives in the Great War.

His crewmate, Gunner Joseph Clark, was also an optician. Born on 5 October 1889, he was the only son of a glass cutter and optician named John Clark and bought up at Elswick in Newcastle-upon-Tyne. Joseph, his parents and two younger sisters Mary and Dorothy, later moved to Corbridge where Joseph later worked for his father. Joseph was attested in December 1915 at Hexham and was immediately transferred to the Army Reserve. He volunteered to join the MMGS and visited Coventry on 3 March 1916, where he was accepted. His medical records show that he was five feet inches tall and nine stone six pounds in weight. Sent to Bisley for machine gun training, Joseph .was posted to D Company on 27 May and deployed with them to France on 1 September. He probably remained with the Black Cat Crew throughout the autumn actions. After he transferred to D Battalion, Joseph was retrained as a tank driver and mechanic and probably fought in the Battle of Arras. He qualified as a second class mechanic just before the Third Battle of Ypres. On 27 September 1917, he was posted to the Tank Corps Central Workshop at Erin on whose strength he remained until de-mobilization in May 1919. Other than two periods of home leave, in October 1917 and October 1918, and six days leave which he took in France in February 1919, his service record reveals little about his time with the tanks. He returned home to Corbridge on Tyne and joined the Z Reserve. Seventy years later Joseph died, in his one hundred year, in Newcastle upon Tyne.

Many of the First Tank Crews included men from Coventry and *Daphne*'s crew included three; Walter Atkins, Rol Elliott and Herbert Statham. Walter Atkins was born on 4 August 1895 at 57 Henley Road in Bell Green. The only son of a coal hewer, Walter became a machinist in the burgeoning bicycle manufacturing industry. He enlisted at Coventry in March 1916 joining the MGC. His service before he deployed overseas is described in Chapter 2. Walter was injured during the action on 15 September, wounded by enemy artillery splinters whilst outside the tank. His wounds were so bad that he was evacuated to the United Kingdom where he was treated at Oswaldtwistle. Walter recovered and, in early 1917, was posted to the new tank training area at Bovington to join one of the new tank battalions. Arriving on 1 February, he was allocated to No 19 Company of G Battalion whose officers including Basil Henriques. Eight days later Walter reported to the Medical Reception Station complaining of severe abdominal pain. The medical officers suspected Walter had appendicitis and he was taken for surgery the next day. Sadly he died during the operation at Bovington Camp on 9 February 1917, aged only twenty-one years of age. His body was sent back to his parents but without any military escort. He was buried at home in Foleshill Congregational Burial Ground. His obituary which was published in *The Motor Cycle* showed a picture of the tank crew, in which it called the Black Cat crew. His grave stone included a cast metal version of the MGC badge; the unit in which he was serving when he died. Sadly the grave marker became damaged and has been recently replaced by the Commonwealth War Graves Commission; the new marker includes the badge of the Tank Corps.

Gnr Rol Elliot, who knew Walter by sight before they arrived at Bisley, was born in Foleshill. He was the son of a mechanic named Robert Elliott and his wife Florrie. Rol was christened at the parish church of St Laurence on 31 January 1897. Robert and his eldest son Arthur worked in the cycle trade, which was a major source of employment in Coventry, but when he left school, Rol first worked as a butcher's assistant. However he soon learned to ride a motorcycle and found work as a motorcycle tester. He was fined for speeding in December 1915 after Rol and two other motor testers were seen riding three abreast along the Stoneleigh Road to the south of Coventry and later passing two ladies cyclist at speed in a built up area. His companions who already had records for speeding were fined £4 and £3 respectively whilst Rol, for whom it was a first offence, was fined £1 which was a significant of money in 1915.

Being a motor tester, Rol easily passed the entrance test for the MMGS at *The Motor Cycle* offices in early April and met up with Walter at Bisley shortly afterwards. He became one of

Harry Drader's crew at Elveden where he also served as his servant at Elveden – he is almost certainly sitting to Harry's left in the crew photo. The Tank Corps medal rolls confirm that Rol eventually left the Tank Corps as a lance corporal. Rol returned to Foleshill and took up work again in the motor trade. In 1921, he participated in the Isle of Man Senior Tourist Trophy riding a Rover motorcycle but failed to finish. Ten year years later, at the age of thirty five, Rol married a local girl called Annie Taylor. They settled at 38 Churchill Avenue, only half a mile from his childhood home. Just before the Second World War, Roland took over the running of a motor garage in St Mary's Road close to the Foleshill Road, which he managed until he retired in 1962. Rol died, aged sixty-eight on 9 July 1965, at the Royal Victoria Hospital in Bournemouth.

The third gunner from Coventry, Herbert Statham, may not have been as fast a rider as Rol but his son Eric represented England in the speedway World Championships before and after the Second World War. Herbert was born in Aston in Birmingham about 15 March 1891. The christening record, which was completed at St Stephen's Church on 13 April, shows that his Coventry born father William was a bicycle builder and he and his wife Elsie Davies were living at 112 Cloudwater Street. Herbert was the eldest surviving son and he and his siblings were bought up in Aston before the family moved back to William's home town of Coventry. William and Herbert then worked in the expanding motor and cycle industry where William built vehicle frames and Herbert was a filer. The family settled at the Jetty at Keresley and, in the summer of 1911, Herbert who had just turned 20, married a Keresley girl named Frances Cliffe. Their only son Eric was born on 30 March 1912 and their elder daughter Phyllis was born the following summer.

Alice Drader and Percy.
(David Drader)

Herbert joined the MMGS in the last week of February 1916 at Coventry at the same time as Owen Rowe and Frank Styring. His service record has not survived so it is impossible to say in which units he fought after the Battle of Flers-Courcelette. He left the Tank Corps as a private soldier and returned to his home at Keresley. He had set up business repairing heavy boots, working at Longfield Road in Foleshill, when his younger daughter Thora was born in 1923. By the time Eric was representing England in the Speedway World Championships in Wembley and Brisbane, Herbert had become a chiropodist and had moved the family to Heathfield Terrace on the Heath at Old Keresley. At his home, Herbert set up a leather goods manufacturing business called *the Leicester Boot and Harness Company* but, after his wife Frances died on 10 February 1949, Herbert was unable to keep the business together and he was declared bankrupt. He was released from his debts in 1953 and later moved to Meriden when he died eight years later, aged seventy-one in 1961.

As for Percy the Tank Cat, he returned to England and lived with the Drader family at Colney Hatch. He was pictured with Harry's sister Alice who is wearing a Military Cross emblem. This was probably bought by her fiancé Stanley Davies to celebrate the award of the gallantry medal for leading a bombing party at Courcelette; the same attack in which Harry and Alice's cousin Eugene was killed. Alice and Stanley married in 1918 and moved back to Canada in March 1921, settling near Calgary. Sadly the family does not know whether Percy went with them or moved to Romania with the rest of the family.

14

Breakthrough at Martinpuich

Whilst George Mann and Harry Drader's crews were tasked to assist the attack of the western side of the village, two more crews attacked the eastern side of Martinpuich in support of assault of 50th Division. Crew D24, commanded by Lieutenant Walter Stones, fought in a male tank whilst the D25 were in a female tank was commanded by Lieutenant Eric Colle. These two moved up on 14 September, without incident, to their start point at Bazentin le Petit Cemetery (see map 12). Their orders were to reach the German front line before the British infantry left their jumping off trenches. The two tanks crossed the British front line at 06:03 a.m., seventeen minutes before the infantry started their attack. The route across no man's land was mainly downhill (see coloured image 13) and the tanks made good progress. At zero hour, as the artillery bombardment lifted and the infantry advanced, Colle and Stones were in their designated positions on the German front line, providing covering fire along the trench lines, as the British infantry crossed the 200 yards of no-man's-lands. They then gave close support to the assault and, once the position had been consolidated shortly after 7:00 a.m. followed the infantry forward to their next objective. D24 got through to the second line of German trenches when it was hit by artillery fire; the skipper, Walter Stones being injured in the head and the driver, Private Wood, in the eyes. The tank was again hit on the right track, which broke, and the tank had to be abandoned. The crew took cover in shell holes and, according to one account, joined in the attack.

Crew D24

Walter Stones was one of the oldest tank skippers. Born on 5 May 1881 in Doncaster, he was one of four children with an elder brother and sister George and Eleanor and a younger sister named Mable. Walter educated at the local Grammar School after which William became a farmer, like his father, working on the family farms and managing others as an agent. Soon after the start of the Great War, he joined 18th Service (Public Schools) Battalion Royal Fusiliers. He deployed with them to France in November 1915 and reached the rank of a corporal. When Walter applied for commission on 3 March 1916, he sought a vacancy in 3/5th Battalion of the Yorkshire and Lancashire Regiment but, having completed training at Pembroke College Cambridge, he was commissioned into the Heavy Section MGC on 14 April 1916.

Walter's head wounds during the attack at Martinpuich were so serious that he was evacuated back to London on 17 September. He was treated at the Royal Free Hospital at Whitechapel in London, at the same time as Arthur Arnold who was injured at Flers, by Mr Gay French. An Army Medical Board on 19 October recorded "when in a tank a bullet hit the end of the periscope and travelling down it hit his face over the right temporal artery close to the ear anteriorly". An aneurism had formed at the site of the wound and this had been excised on 3 October 1916 with the vessels being tied. There was also a blood clot in his right ear and Walter suffered from severe headaches for the rest of his life.

Walter Stones and his crew July 1916; standing left – Fred Rule and right Billy Foster; kneeling centre Walter Stones. (Tank Museum)

Walter was later treated at the Prince of Wales Hospital at Staines from 28 October to 26 January. On being released from hospital Walter was posted to F Battalion, probably as a result of being claimed by Frank Summers. He was not however declared fit for duty until 9 February and reported to Bovington five days later. He was appointed temporary captain on 1 March 17 and at the end of the month, a Medical Board found he was fit for home service. On 28 April, a follow-up board stated he had recovered from his wounds and was fit for general service. Allocated to No 17 Company, Walter deployed with F Battalion on 14 May to France, where it established its base to Auchy-Les-Hesdin. On 1 June the Battalion moved to the tank driving School at Wailly for two week training and then to the Corps Gunnery School at Merlimont for live firing. New tanks were then drawn and taken back to Auchy before deploying to the Ypres Salient on 2 July and making their base at Oosthoek Wood where they were heavily shelled the following day.

Before the initial action on 31 July, No 17 Company took a number of casualties amongst its officers including George Mann Walter's former section commander who was killed and Len Bond who commanded D18 at Flers, who was injured. During its only action in the Salient on 31 July, No 17 Company was fairly successful with eight of the twelve tanks being in action although five later became ditched. Just before the company was withdrawn from the Salient, Walter organized a dinner on 3 September 1917, which was attended by Frank Summers as well as Arthur Inglis who commanded *Crème de Menthe* at Courcelette on 15 September 1916. Walter was a keen race-goer and the event was based around the St Leger classic horse race which takes place at Doncaster each September. During the Battle of Cambrai, Walter served as second in command of No 17 Company; the company again being commanded by Major Charles Hawkins. The company success-fully broke through the German defences at La Vacquerie, on the morning of 20 November and by noon reached the Masnieres canal which could not be crossed. The company took heavy casualties, seven days later, as they attempted to capture the villages of Fontaine Notre Dame and Bourlon.

After the Battalion was withdrew from battle, several officers, including Frank Summers and Charles Hawkins then returned to England. Walter then stayed with No 17 Company and established the new Battalion home, on the Bray to Albert Road, close by D Company's original offloading point at the Somme. The Battalion, which was now designated 6th (Light) Battalion, started to re-role to operate Whippet tanks although most of the unit's energy was put to improving the dilapidated accommodation huts so that they could withstand the severe weather conditions. Walter was granted home leave from 21 to 27 January. Whilst at Doncaster, he was appointed acting Major and within two weeks of returning to France, was ordered to return to Bovington where Frank Summers was now commanding the new formed 15th battalion.

Walter assumed command of B Company of 15 Battalion on 12 February. He was not the only former member of D Company serving in the new unit as Frank Summers had obtained the former Company Sergeant Major, Paddy Walsh, as the RSM. Walter returned to France on 8 July 1918 but, on 6 August just before the company went into action at Amiens, he became sick and his company second in command, Captain Matheson took command for the duration of the battle. Walter officially relinquished command of his company on 26 August when he was posted to Training and Reinforcement at Mers-Les-Bains. He was given the opportunity to recover his heath but, on 18 October 1918; a Medical Board determined he was suffering from debility owing to insomnia and neuralgia resulting from his wounds received two years before at Martinpuich. He was sent back to Britain on light duties and discharged on 22 January 1919 at Clipstone.

Eighteen months later, on 28 July, Walter married Catherine Roe at Sandford Church at Ranelagh in Dublin; the couple probably having met whilst Catherine was working as an auxiliary nurse. In 1921 they moved into 8 Regent Square in Doncaster. When his father died in 1923, Walter developed the family farming and business opportunities further and became financially secure. Sadly Catherine developed Rheumatoid Arthritis soon afterwards and her younger sister Caroline moved to Doncaster to look after her. Like Walter, the two sisters were keen racing fans but they were not successful gamblers. Caroline lived with Walter after her sister's death in 1947 and, according to family members, Walter had to cover her gambling debts. Caroline died on 13 December 1952 and, the following year, Walter retired and moved into 10 Crossways at Wheatley Hills in Doncaster. He died, aged ninety-one on Saturday 1 April 1972 and was buried in same plot as his wife Catherine. Walter left a substantial estate and, having no children, his housekeeper became the main beneficiary of his will.

The soldier standing on the right of the tank crew photograph in the rear rank was Billy Foster. Billy was born on 5 December 1893 at Mansfield in Nottinghamshire. He was the younger son of a miller, also named William, who had set up a grocer's shop on Alma Terrace on the Chesterfield Road. When William died in 1904, Billy's mother Ellen took over the shop which the family ran until after the Second World War. Billy enlisted in the Army at Mansfield on 16 February 1916. At that time, he was five feet eight inches tall but only just over eight stone in weight. He was also of slight build with a twenty-eight inch chest, fair complexion, brown hair and brown eyes; he also wore glasses. Placed on the Army Reserve, he was mobilised the following month and travelled to Coventry to join the MMGS. He passed the trade assessment on 31 March and was sent to Bisley the same day.

Six months later, when his tank left Bazentin le Petit, Billy was manning the left hand 6 pdr gun. He later wrote that the tank got through to the second line of German trenches when it was first hit by artillery fire. The tank was struck on the right hand track and had to be abandoned; the crew taking cover in shell holes. Billy continued to serve with D Company then with D Battalion and qualified as a Lewis Gunner. He then qualified as a first aider and served on with 4th Battalion as an MT driver. Throughout his service, Billy took a number of photos which are now available on the Oxford University Poetry Society website. On 30 July 1918, Billy was a crewman in tank 9421 under the command of Sergeant William McNicoll, who was a crewman in D3 on 15 September 1916, and his section commander was Alfred Enoch.

On 10 August 1918, on the second day of the Battle of Amiens, Billy was wounded in his lower left arm and abdomen by an artillery shell; he was also gassed. The Battalion war history shows that, on approaching Aubercourt, the crew was told the infantry were held up by machine-gun fire. The tank went forward and discovered the machine gun fire was coming from an old quarry. The tank neutralised the quarry whilst the infantry came forward and the quarry's occupants surrendered. The tank then went through Innaucourt and attacked Cayeux where it was hit and knocked out, the tank skipper and four crewmen being wounded. Billy's wounds were so bad that he was evacuated to 3 Australian General Hospital at Abbeville. Having been stabilised, Billy was then sent on 29 August to the Military Hospital in Endell Street in London, later being treated at Albert House Auxiliary Hospital near Stockport. Billy was never well enough to return to active duty and was discharged from the Army Hospital at Sheffield on 11 April 1919.

Declared unfit to undertake further military service, Billy was awarded a 30% pension and, on 21 May 1919, was awarded the Silver War Badge. Billy was subsequently examined in January 1921 and on February 1922 when further pensions were awarded. On 4 June 1923, Billy married Winifred Morris at Mansfield Parish Church by which time he was working as a clerk. He later became a transport manager and, on 15 September 1966, attended the 50th anniversary dinner at Caxton Hall in London. Billy later moved to Rearsby in Leicestershire where he lived with his nephew Ronald. Billy Foster died aged ninety one, on 11 May 1984 at the Leicester General Hospital.

The D24 crew included Gunner Robert Coffey who was born on 21 November 1881 in Bradford. Robert was the youngest son of an Irish Presbyterian minister, after whom he was named, and who published a well-regarded pamphlet on the life of Thomas Carlyle the year after his son's birth. Bought up in Manningham, a northern suburb of Bradford, Robert later became a merchant seaman who sailed to Australia and must have regularly visited Ireland as he was married in Dublin in the summer of 1913 although I have not been able to identify the name of his wife. Robert, who was at thirty four, was one of the older members of the First Tank Crews when he volunteered to join the MMGS. After the first actions, he was transferred to D Battalion and was allocated to No 12 Company. He probably fought near Thelus, on 9 April 1917, during the capture of Vimy Ridge. On 3 May 1917, during the second Battle of Bullecourt, he was wounded in the right shoulder and forearm as his tank was destroyed as it attempted to break through the enemy defences. He was captured by the Germans and, after initial treatment at Minden, was transferred to the prison camp at Dulmen on 8 June 1917. He remained in German custody until the Armistice. Having been released at the end of the war, he became a wool-buyer and regularly travelled to Australia and South Africa. He later moved to Sydney where he died, aged fifty one, in 1931.

I have also been unable to positively identify Gunner Reeve although Roy Reiffer mentions that Les Reeve died of his wounds received on 24 April 1917 whilst driving the tank *Diana*. From this, I believe Les was the son of a publican Arthur Reeve and his wife Alice from Small Heath near Birmingham. Born in the summer of 1891, Leslie moved with his family to Bickenham where his father ran a public house on the Coventry Road. He later lived with his parents at Sheldon. By the time he was twenty, Leslie was working as motor accessories salesman at Dorridge, some fourteen miles to the south. Leslie joined the MGC in 1916 and appears to have been uninjured during the first tank actions. He transferred to D Battalion. He was probably in action at the Harps feature, near Beaurains on 9 April, during the successful opening operation. Two weeks later, still serving with No 10 Company, he was fatally burned; his tank skipper Lieutenant Rankin and Gunner James Miller being burnt to death as they attacked the German defences near Wancourt on 23 April. Leslie was evacuated but died the next day and is buried at the Warlincourt Halte British Cemetery at Saulty. He is remembered on Sheldon's First World War Memorial.

Another crewman, Gunner John Wells was killed in action eleven months later. John, who was born at Harpurhey near Manchester on 6 November 1892, was the eldest son of wire-drawers' labourer. His father John had married his mother Hannah after she was widowed with three daughters. On 28 November, John Junior was christened at St John's Church in Colleyhurst where his parents had married on 23 January that year. John, his three step-sisters and four siblings were bought up in Bradford, which is a suburb of Manchester. By 1911, John was working as a commercial clerk at a company of wire drawers, probably the same one which employed his father. John enlisted at Coventry, into the MMGS, in the spring of 1916 and later served as a private in 4th Battalion Tank Corps. He was killed in action aged twenty-five on 22 March 1918 as the battalion tried to prevent the Germans retaking the ground between Cambrai and Peronne. John's body was never identified and he is commemorated on the Pozières memorial.

Walter Stones' right hand man at Martinpuich was his driver Private Fred Wood, who was wounded in the eyes during action. We know of Fred's injuries owing to the diary kept by Gunner Billy Foster. Fred transferred from the ASC to the tanks in early 1917 and served with them for the duration of the war, first re-badging to the MGC and then to Tank Corps. The other Fred in the crew, Gunner Fred Rule who is pictured standing on the left in the rear rank of the crew photograph, was from Ford, a Borders village about thirteen miles from Berwick upon Tweed. The youngest son of a slater and plasterer, Fred was three years younger than Billy Foster, being born on 9 July 1890. Fred's family had run a plasterer's business since the 1780s and, on leaving school, Fred naturally joined the firm too. Fred was a keen cyclist, enjoying road races, and was also a keen motorcyclist.

On 7 June 1913, Fred married Jane Athey at Alnwick and their daughter Elizabeth was born on 25 August of the following year at Wooler. In common with most of the First tank Crewmen, Fred did not immediately volunteer to join up but waited until 9 December 1915 when he was attested at Wooler, probably as a result of the recently introduced conscription act.

Fred Rule on his racing cycle. (Clare Rule)

Deciding to join the MMGS, Fred rode his Swift motorbike from Ford to Coventry, which is almost 300 miles in distance. He attended one of the selection events on 5 April 1916 and was medically examined the same day. He was just one pound under ten stone in weight and five feet, five and a half inches tall. His company conduct sheet was not signed by his section commander but rather by Alfred Enoch. It was however a form which was never used. By the time he was photographed with the other members of his crew, at Elveden (see page 210, standing in the rear rank on the left hand side). He had grown a very military looking moustache, something which survived his return to civilian life. Fred proceeded overseas on 1 September with D Company by which time Jane, who was six months pregnant, had settled on Green Batt in the centre of Alnwick. Their son Eric was born on 15 October 1916.

Fred served with No 10 Company and was probably in action near Beaurains on 9 April 1917. He was burned during the attacks on 23 April, near Fontaine-Les –Croiselles, when his and Len Reeve's tanks in B Section caught fire as they fought their way through the Hindenburg line. Fred was treated at the Stationary Hospital at Rouen but was sufficiently well to be released to the MGC Depot at Dannes-Camiers near Étaples by 11 May. By the time he returned to his unit on 10 June he had retrained as a driver and was graded as a second class tank mechanic on 8 August 1917. He probably fought with No 10 Company at Poelcapelle on 10 October and he was certainly in action at Cambrai as he was wounded on 24 November. No 10 Company was not in action that day Fred's injuries may have resulting from harassing fire. He was not fit to be granted home leave until 10 January 1918, which was the first time Fred saw his son Eric.

Fred then served with C Company in the renamed 4th Tank Battalion, being graded as a first class tank mechanic on 13 February 1918, As a driver he did not fight during the Kaiserschlacht, when his unit was employed in the machine-gun role. However, after the unit was equipped with Mark V tanks, Fred was selected to drive the male tank 9029. He was serving with C Company which was under command of Captain Heady Head, whom he had known since Elveden. On the first day of the battle of Amiens, his tank became lost and broke down but Fred managed to repair it and the tank got to its rallying point the following day. In the next two months, as his unit suffered casualties amongst its junior NCOs, Fred was promoted eventually reaching the rank of corporal by 18 October 1918. As 4th Battalion was being pulled out of action to prepare for the expected 1919 campaign, Fred was sent back to Britain and posted to Wareham where he served as a corporal in 25th Officer Cadet Battalion. After the Armistice, Fred was quickly released from active service and sent to Duddingston, near Edinburgh, for dispersal on 22 January1919. Fred returned to Ford Forge, near the battlefield of Flodden, and took over the running of the family slating business. He also continued to ride a motorcycle from many years.

During the Second World War, his son Eric joined the Royal Army Medical Corps. He served in North Africa as a Lance Corporal, driving ambulances, and took part in the Battle of El Alamein. Eric, who was Mentioned on Despatches in January 1944, was later captured by the Germans and held as a POW in Muhlberg from 1942. The family later moved to Alnwick where Fred died, aged sixty-nine, on 6 November 1959. His widow Jane, who was five years older than Fred died three year later; their son Eric having taken over the running of the family firm, which operates to this day.

Crew D25

The final tank of the four attacking Martinpuich was a male tank manned by crew D25. When Walter Stones' tank was hit by artillery and the track was smashed, the tank which was commanded by Lieutenant Eric Colle pressed on across the ridge towards Martinpuich, covering the infantry to the south east and then moved along the eastern edge of the village where the tank crew put three machine guns out of action. D25 pushed on again reaching the final objective, before returning to her rally point. She fully achieved her mission, albeit with some repairs required to the tail gear and steering pump and with several of her crew wounded. Although the names of the crew were recorded in Graham Woods' notebook, it has been difficult identify some of them. It is impossible to identify any of them in the crew photograph which is held by the Imperial War Museum and I cannot find anything about Gunner Bell, who Colle reported as slightly wounded, nor firmly identify Gunner Garner as there are three early Tankers who are possible fits.

However the service record has survived for Colle's second in command. Corporal Henry Reynolds, who was born on 15 December 1884 at Plymstock St Mary in Devon, was the eldest son of watchmaker James Reynolds and his wife Clara. The family operated a jewellery business from their home at 76 Ridgeway. On 9 August 1911, Henry married Ellen Clarke in Tonbridge and their elder daughter Molly was born on 16 May the following year in Exeter. Eighteen months later, the couple' son Bruce was born on 8 January 1914. Henry was, by now, working as a commercial traveller for the Oxo Company whilst the family lived at Trelake Cottage at Ide. Henry volunteered to join the Army Service Corps under the Derby Scheme on 12 December 1915. He was not mobilised until 28 April 1916 but was then posted to the MGC Depot at Bisley. He was appointed acting Lance Corporal two weeks later. Posted to D Company, he was promoted Corporal on 5 August whilst training at Elveden. Henry deployed to France arriving in Le Havre on 3 September; Ellen being in the late stages of her third pregnancy. Promoted to sergeant "in the field" on 12 October, whilst D Company was preparing for actions both on the Somme and north of the Ancre, Henry would have been relieved to learn of the safe arrival of his younger daughter Margery who was born on 22 October at Tonbridge.

After the end of the first actions, he was transferred to D Battalion on 18 November and, unusually was granted home-leave from 1 to 11 January 1917. Henry also received the welcome news, on 1 April that he had been awarded 6 pence additional pay per day backdated to the formation of D Battalion; this is probably because he was employed as a Company Quartermaster Sergeant. Henry was involved in the preparations, support and recovery of tanks during the Battle of Arras and for the move to the Ypres Salient. Being employed in administrative duties was, however, no guarantee of safety for anyone in the Salient; on 22 August 1917, Henry was appointed Battalion Technical Quartermaster Sergeant (TQMS), and promoted WO2; after the death in action of WO2 Harrison McCloy the previous day. Henry was in this role during the Battle of Cambrai, which included moving spare parts and equipment well forward to enable battle damaged tanks to be repaired and returned to action. After the battle Henry moved with the recovered and damaged tanks back to the Battalion's new base at Meulte, close by the original tank offloading point for the Battle of the Somme. He was then granted home leave and was lucky to spend both Christmas and New Year with his family in Kent. Henry served with the renamed 4th Battalion Tank Corps for the remainder of the war; the unit was equipped with new tanks and the associated equipment early in 1918 to replace the lost and damaged equipment lost at Flesquières on the opening day of the Battle of Cambrai. These tanks were lost during the Kaiserschlacht, in late March 1918, and replacement Mark IV tanks issued to enable 4th battalion to rebuff the Germans in April 1918. Further replacements, this time the new and improved Mark V tanks, were issued for the Battle of Amiens and replacement equipment for subsequent losses during the100 day advance.

In late October, 4th Battalion was withdrawn to its winter base to the south of Arras. Once the decision had been made not to send the Battalion to undertake occupation duties in Germany, Henry was again granted home. Ellen and their children were staying at her parent's home in Tonbridge which gave Henry ready access to London. He had much to organise as his mother had died earlier that year and the estate needed resolution. As he was planning to move the family to America, Henry sought and was granted an extension of leave using the time to claim backdated ASC rates of pay for the whole of his service in the QMS role starting from 18

November 1916. He also made contact with his former company and he was offered re-employment as a commercial traveller when released by the Army. He therefore abandoned his plans to emigrate and sought local discharge which was granted. Initially working from Tunbridge Wells, Henry was soon able to move the family back to Alphington Road at Exeter which is where, in 1922, he claimed his medals. In the 1940s, presumably after their children had left home, Ellen and Henry moved back to their pre-war home at Barton Hill. Henry died aged seventy-three, in Exeter on 18 December 1957.

Service records have also survived for a number of the gunners in the D25 crew. Gnr James Petrie was, like his skipper, a shipping clerk. Born on 1 March 1895 in Markinch in Fyfe, James was attested on 9 December 1915 at Perth. Placed on the Army Reserve, he was not mobilized until 1 May 1916 and exactly four months later, he deployed to France. He was wounded on 15 September and sent to 22 General Hospital at Dannes-Camiers on 19 September but was back with D Company by 10 October. Like Fred Rule, who served in D24, James was also wounded on 23 April 1917 but these injuries were minor. Although admitted to 99th Field Ambulance with gunshot wounds to his left thigh and to his hands, he was able to rejoin his unit on same day. He served with D Battalion for the duration of the war but was never promoted. He almost certainly fought during the Battle of Cambrai as he was granted home leave over Christmas 1917. When the battle was redesignated 4th Battalion, James served with A Company but there is no record of the further actions in which actions he fought. He was sent on leave over the New Year 1919 but, rather than return to his unit, reported to the Duddingstone depot and gained his discharge on 13 January 1919. Sadly that is the last record available until his death in 1972 at Auchtermuchty.

Gnr Herbert Routledge was one of several men from Cumberland who served in the First Tank Crews. Born on 23 May 1892 at Abbey Town, Herbert was the son of a carpenter Robert Routledge and his wife Emmaline who was a school teacher. As a young man Herbert worked as a farm labourer on Hagginstone Holm at Brackenhill, ten miles to the east of Longtown. Herbert later got a job as a milk recorder for the Board of Agriculture and lived with his mother at the School House in Sowerby Row. When he was attested on the same day as James Petrie, on 9 December at Penrith, Herbert asked to be posted to the Motor Transport section of the Army Service Corps. However, when he was called up from Army Reserve on 28 April, he was directed to report to Bisley and join the MGC. Herbert was not injured during the first actions on the Somme and Ancre but, on 25 November, he was admitted to hospital with boils. Boils had been a common complaint for soldiers across the centuries due to the poor diet available whilst on operations. Herbert was released from hospital on 4 December and joined the newly formed D Battalion at Blangy two days later.

Herbert was probably present at the battles of Arras and later in the Ypres Salient. He was serving with No 10 Company, when he was wounded on 20 November at Flesquières; a machine gun bullet passing though the left arm. This could well be because he was serving as a driver. He was evacuated from France on 11 December and treated at No 3 Southern General Hospital at Oxford for ten days followed by a month's convalescence at the Barton Court Auxiliary Hospital at Maidenhead. Herbert returned to Oxford for two days then was granted leave from 18 to 28 January. At the Tank Corps Depot, he was posted to BEF non-technical staff, arriving back in France on 27 April. Unusually, when Herbert was sent back to the Field Army, he did not return to 4th Battalion but rather he was posted to 5th Battalion on 9 May 1918. It was not initially a happy time as, on 26 June, he was charged with causing damage to tank equipment and using improper words to a NCO. On 4 August, he was admitted to hospital with impetigo for six days but he recovered and returned to 5th Battalion. He was obviously a competent crewman as he was graded 1st Class Tank Mechanic on 3 October 1918. He returned to the UK on 19 January 1919 for discharge; he initially settled at his mother's address at the School House in Southwaite near Carlisle but sadly thereafter he disappears until his death, aged seventy five, in Carlisle.

I am also not sure about the identity of one of the crewmen named Wilkie who was wounded on 15 September. It was probably Gnr John Thomson Wilkie who later served with the Tank Corps. As for the driver, Pte John Maude the details are limited. Graham Woods' notebook shows John was wounded during the action and his medal index card shows he continued to serve with the Tanks Corps which he left, still a private soldier, at the end of the war. In comparison with this limited information, there is plenty on the skipper as his service record survives as do details of his service in the Second World War; the documents having been lodged with the Imperial War Museum.

Edward Colle was born on 12 February 1893 at Llanishen near Cardiff. He was the eldest son of a well-known Cardiff tailor. After attending Penarth County School, Edward worked as a chartering clerk for the shipping firm of Lysberg Limited at Cardiff Docks and was also a member of the Penarth Yacht Club close by the family home on the Green. On 14 August 1914, ten days after war was declared, Edward enlisted as a trooper in the Glamorganshire Yeomanry. He later joined its Machine Gun Section and was eventually promoted to sergeant major. He does not however appear to have served overseas with the Yeomanry, as they were undertaking home defence tasks. He later was selected for officer training and, in common with many of the first tank skippers, was trained at No 2 Officer Cadet Battalion in Cambridge for six weeks.

On 15 April 1916, Edward was commissioned into the Heavy Section of the MGC and then undertook training at Bisley and then Thetford, where the photograph of the crew was taken. For his actions on 15 September, Edward was awarded the Military Cross. The citation *states* "He fought his Tank with great gallantry, reaching the third objective. Later, on several occasions he went to the assistance of the infantry, and finally brought his Tank safely out of action". Colle was wounded in the arms and chest, probably 26 September when D25 was deployed with Eric Robinson. The tanks were in support of the 2nd Canadian Division's attack to the northeast of Courcelette. Sadly Colle's tank became ditched as it moved through Pozières and, although Robinson's tank caused the Germans to withdraw, it was later destroyed by their artillery and to be abandoned. Edward Colle was evacuated home and was treated at the Northumberland Hospital in Gosforth. Promoted temporary Lieutenant on 1 October 1916, he was presented with the Military Cross at Buckingham Palace on 14 February 1917. He did not return to serve again with the tanks in France but was employed at the Ministry of Shipping from March 1917 until he relinquished his commission on 29 January 1919.

That autumn, he married Lucie Leak at Capel en le Frith in Derbyshire and their only child Pamela was born in the Spring of June 1921. After the war Edward became a Chartered Shipbroker initially living in Llanishen in Cardiff then at Pen y lan and then from 1933 settling in Cheltenham. Following the outbreak of the Second World War, Edward was granted an emergency commission in the RTR. Serving from 22 April 1940, and initially employed as a records officer at GHQ 2nd Echelon, Edward was attached to the Pioneer Corps on 6 July and was employed as the Adjutant of 26 Pioneer Coy at Caister on Sea. Edward then deployed to Deolali in India for 4 months before returning to the UK, stopping over in Melbourne where he took part in a parade and then in South Africa.

Resuming the role of Adjutant of 26 Pioneer Company, which had been re-located to London, Edward then served with 35 Company for 11 months at Rusilip. From February 1942, he served in North Africa as a salvage officer clearing the battlefields. Whilst he was overseas, his daughter Pamela, who was serving as WAAF officer, married an RCAF navigator, Flying Officer Edwin Higgins, at Cheltenham Parish Church. Edward returned to the UK in May 1944 and was attached to the Intelligence Corps. In December 1944 he returned to India and was posted first to the Calcutta Censor station and then to Simla as the OC of the Censor Detachment. In August 1945, he applied to transfer to the Corps of Military Police but this was not taken up as he was sent to Malaya to undertake censor duties. However the end of the war meant that he never reached

Malaya. Rather than return to the UK, he volunteered to serve on in the Far East. Edward was employed as Officer Commanding Embarked Troops, in the rank of major, on the troop transport SS *Pulshere*. From January 1946 until 7 October 1947 he travelled between India and the ports in Burma and Singapore travelling with parties of troops who had been fighting or were stationed in Malaya. Returning to the UK, he settled in London where he died, aged eighty-three, in early 1978; his wife Lucie dying eleven years later in Cheltenham.

15

Cocktails at Courcelette

On the left flank of the British assault, on 15 September 1916, 2nd Canadian Division was tasked to capture the village of Courcelette and a large beet processing plant to its south east known as the Sugar Factory. This was the first stage of an attack which was designed to remove the Germans from the area to the north and west of Pozières. It also included the clearance of Mouquet Farm and Thiepval village; areas which had been thorns in the British side since the start of the Somme campaign. The fighting in this area in September 1916 lasted for eight days and caused more than 4,000 casualties amongst the Canadians alone. To their north, 11th (Northern) Division attacked Mouquet farm and the village of Thiepval on 15 September but the attack was only partially successful and this part of the ridge was not cleared until 26 September when tanks were deployed in support of 18th (Eastern) Division under their innovative commander, Major General Ivor Maxse.

All the tanks, which supported the Canadian attack on 15 September, were from No 1 Section of C Company. They were all named after French drinks with the initial letter "C"; *Champagne, Cognac, Chablis, Chartreuse, Crème de Menthe* and *Cordon Rouge*. The section was commanded by Captain Arthur Inglis of the Gloucestershire Regiment who was one of only two Regular Army officers in the company; the other being his company commander Major Allen Holford-Walker. Holford-Walker had detached No 1 Section, under Arthur Inglis as an independent command, to the Reserve Army which was operating on the northern part of the Somme battlefield. Later Inglis had ten tanks under command and, given his leadership at Courcelette, Holford-Walker clearly made the right choice when he selected Arthur Inglis for the task.

The records for C Company are generally less detailed than those of D Company. However, in the case of the Cocktail crewmen, we know the details of every crewman as Arthur Inglis listed them in his post action report which survives in the Canadian archives. His section's six tanks arrived on the Happy Valley rail siding on 8 September and, over the next two days, having been refitted with their sponsons, loaded the tanks with the huge amount of stores needed for action. On Monday 11 September, the section started their drive to their section base or "tankodrome" near Aveluy, which was to the north of Albert. They stopped at Meulte overnight and stopped for breakfast on the outskirt of Albert. According to a diary maintained by Victor Archard, who was a crewman in *Cognac*, they were observed by David Lloyd George, the recently appointed secretary of State for War who stopped and spoke to the crews. The crews reached their new base that afternoon and were soon inundated with visitors. On 13 and 14 September, the tanks were cleaned and prepared for action, At 7:00 p.m. as dusk started, the six tanks followed the line of the main Albert to Bapaume road to a dressing station just south of Pozières where there is now a large Memorial and military cemetery. Here the tank crews refuelled their tanks using petrol-filled water cans. According to *Crème de Menthe* crewman Lionel McAdam, it was difficult for the crews to distinguish between two in the dark. The main fuel tanks on a Mark I tank were fitted either side of the command and driver's positions so each petrol can had to be passed through from the doors in the sponsons and then emptied in pitch darkness. The crews became very tired as a result.

Having eaten some Army biscuits, eased down with cocoa, the crews made their final preparations and moved to their two start-points. Following discussions with the 2nd Canadian Division staff, Inglis had split his section into two groups; three were to support an attack on Courcelette village whilst Inglis would lead the other three along the Bapaume road to capture the Sugar Factory then turn south towards Martinpuich (see map 13). The Germans were aware that an attack was imminent as the British had been bombarding their positions for three days. As a result German artillery put down harassing fire throughout the night behind the Canadian lines. The northern tank group, consisting of *Champagne, Cognac* and *Cordon Rouge* made their way to the starting points to the north of Pozières and, although *Champagne*'s steering wheels and *Cognac*'s stub axle was damaged by artillery fire, all three reached their start points on time.

Champagne

Champagne led the three northern tanks. She was the only male tank and her main armament, the 6 pdr quick-firing gun, was designed to destroy enemy machine guns and fortifications. Despite her damaged steering gear, *Champagne* pressed on and crossed the start line albeit after the infantry had departed. The tank was to follow a German communications trench but, in the dark, the tank travelled too far north on her approach route and then followed the wrong one. The ground conditions were awful, with shell holes up to nine feet deep, but *Champagne* managed to get across no man's land and Sugar Trench, its first objective, successfully. The tank then drove parallel to the German communications trench towards the village of Courcelette but her driver, Private Horace Brotherwood had difficulty in controlling the tank and it slipped into the trench at about 7:00 a.m. and stuck fast. Brotherwood was unable to drive the tank out of the trench, the crew then tried to dig out *Champagne* for four hours during which time the tank was the target of constant German artillery fire. The tank's skipper, Lieutenant Alfred Wheeler, was just about the order that the tank should be abandoned when her driver was killed by German shrapnel. The reminder of the crew returned safely to their own lines bringing Horace Brotherwood's body with them but *Champagne* was never recovered.

HMLS *Champagne* – Courcelette 1917. (Tank Museum)

Alfred Wheeler was born in Coventry on 19 October 1889. He was the third son of James Wheeler who owned a large drapery shop in the Broadgate. Alfred was educated at Wolverhampton and became an Associate of Arts of Oxford University, passing examinations in Mechanics and Hydrostatics; and Heat. Despite his interest in mechanics, Alfred joined the family firm which opened a branch at Waterloo House on the Epsom High Street in 1913. Alfred, who was one of the many men from Coventry who joined the MMGS, enlisted in March 1915 and was soon in action in Flanders with No 10 Battery. Commissioned "in the field" on 26 August 1915, Alfred returned to the MMGS Depot at Bisley the following day and formed part of the Depot training staff. Alfred was later selected to join the Armoured Car Section which was the embryo of the first tank unit in April 1916. Like a number of the original tank skippers, Alfred was tall at almost six feet tall. He joined the newly formed C Company of the Heavy Section of MGC the following month and, after training at Elveden, deployed back to France with the C Company advance party on 16 August. There are no records of Alfred Wheeler being in action on the Somme after 15 September and, in November 1916, he was one of two C Company officers who transferred to the newly formed B Battalion; the other being John Allan who commanded *Cordon Rouge* at Courcelette.

Alfred served with John in No 6 Company and, on 12 April, both men were appointed to command sections and promoted acting captain. Alfred commanded No 11 Section which provided the two supply tanks at the Battle of Messines on 7 June 1916; the tanks successfully replenishing the fighting tanks who acted as protection for the Empire troops who had captured German positions. Less than two months later, Alfred was in command of four fighting tanks ready for the start of Third Battle of Ypres. On the move-up on 30 July, two tanks were damaged when his section was hit by artillery fire as they passed Valley Cottages to the east of Zillebeke. It is likely that Alfred suffered from gas poisoning as this was mixed with the artillery bombardment and caused casualties amongst the commanders who were leading their tanks. Alfred however recovered and commanded the same section during the Battle of Cambrai. This time, the tanks were involved in the break-in battle in support of 16th Infantry Brigade on either side of the Villers-Plouich to Marcoing railway line. Alfred may have been in action again of 23 November, when the remaining tanks of his battalion supported the attack on Fontaine Notre Dame.

Alfred was granted home leave after the battle and, returning to France, stayed with B Battalion until 25 February 1918 when he was posted to the Training and Reinforcement Depot at Le Tréport as an Assistant Instructor. He remained at the Depot until 4 July 1919, later working under Victor Smith who had also served in C Company in 1916. After he was demobilised, Alfred returned to the family drapery business, initially working at Coventry and later managing the Epsom branch. In his spare time, Alfred was a keen tennis player and, in 1921, played at the Drive Hard Tournament at Fulham. Two years later, on 8 May 1923, he married Gladys Webb at Leatherhead Parish Church and they settled at Waterloo House in Epsom. Sadly they had no children. After the Second World War, they moved south to Kingswood from 1946 until 1959 before settling in Horsham. Late in life, the couple retired to the New Forest, where Alfred died aged eighty nine in 1968; Gladys surviving him for a further ten years.

Remarkably three of *Champagne*'s crew came from the same town – Woking. The tank's second in command Fred Saker was the youngest son of an agricultural labourer. Fred was born on 3 September 1890 near Esher and, with his two elder brothers and five sisters, was bought up at Claremont. This was one of the first landscape gardens in Great Britain and, at the time of Fred's birth, was part of the Crown estate. Fred went into the grocery trade, initially working in Queens Road in Aldershot. He later became the branch manager of the Cooperative store at Knaphill between Woking and Bisley, which was the location of the MMGS Depot. Fred enlisted into the MMGS on 8 October 1915 and, within two months, he was appointed acting bombardier. Promoted paid corporal in April, and then unpaid sergeant in June, Fred deployed to France on 16 August 1916.

In November 1916, whilst his skipper moved to B Battalion, Fred remained with C Battalion and was promoted substantive sergeant. Serving with No 8 Company, Fred fought at the Battle of Arras in April 1917. On 9 April, he was probably serving in Lieutenant Henry Johnston's tank which ditched before it could cross the British Lines. The tank was recovered and, on 11 April, was again in action. The tank advanced into the village of Monchy Le Preux and neutralized several German machine guns. The tank then effectively captured the village on its own as the Germans abandoned it. The tank's engine however seized and had to be abandoned but the crew handed over their machine guns to the supporting infantry. Fred was awarded the Military Medal for conspicuous gallantry and devotion to duty during this action. "During the capture of Monchy-le-Preux, on April 11, '17, this NCO served his gun with the greatest coolness and effect. When his tank broke down under a very severe artillery barrage, he remained with it, using every effort to get it moving again. When the tank had to be abandoned, he showed great courage and resource in consolidating a trench under heavy fire."

Fred served on with C Battalion and almost certainly fought at the Third Battle of Ypres. He must have fought at the Battle of Cambrai as he was granted home leave in December 1917. On 11 December, he married his fiancée Lizzie Edwards at Old Woking Parish Church. Returning to his unit, which was converting to operate Whippet tanks, Fred was admitted to hospital in the middle of March, suffering from what became known as Spanish flu. As a result, he did not participate in the fighting withdrawal by the British troops against the German Forces in their advance which re-took all of the ground captured during the battles of the Somme and Cambrai. Fred remained in hospital for a month then after a week's convalescence, was sent back to 3rd Battalion on 27 April where he served with B Company. He was not promoted sergeant again until 24 September when he appointed Company QM Sergeant. After the Armistice, he was again granted home leave and was demobilised in February 1919, settling at his wife's home at 125 High Street in Old Woking.

Their only daughter Myrtle was born 5 May 1920 and Fred became the buyer for fourteen Co-op shops in the Woking area. In the 1930s, the family later lived at 7 St Martha's Avenue in Westfield. Myrtle served in the WAAF during the Second World War.

Lizzie and Fred Saker in 1917.
(Les Crow)

Lizzie and Fred Saker enjoying their retirement.
(Les Crow)

In the 1950 and early 60s, the family lived at 42 High Street in Teddington but, when Lizzie died in late 1967, Fred moved north to join his daughter in Nottinghamshire. He died aged eighty-eight, on 5 November 1978, at Radcliffe on Trent.

Gunner George Lloyd was born in Woking on 1 October 1896 and returned there after he was demobilised where he must have seen Fred Saker as they both lived in Old Woking. George was the third son of a domestic gardener and, on leaving school, became as a motor mechanic and worked at the Mount Hermon Garage. George enlisted into the MMGS on 15 November 1915 at Bisley. He was, at the age of nineteen years, five feet eight inches tall. George transferred to the MGC on 1 December, then to the Armoured Car Section on 1 April which was renamed to Heavy Section MGC on 4 May. Posted to C Company on 27 May, he trained at Elveden before deploying to France on 16 August 1916. Although George got safely back from the action on 15 September, he was admitted to 4th Canadian Hospital two days later suffering from diarrhoea. He soon recovered and returned to duty after a week.

George joined C Battalion on its formation and served with the unit for most of the war. On 5 April 1917, he was admitted to hospital, suffering from a dental abscess which took almost a month to cure, and therefore did not participate in the Battle of Arras. After treatment at Boulogne, and time at the Base Depot and the Reinforcement Depot at Le Tréport, George returned C Battalion on 12 June and served with them during the opening actions of the Third Battle of Ypres. Two months later, on 12 September, he was posted back to the Reinforcement Depot to be transferred to the infantry. However, this did not take place and he stayed with the Tank Corps. Oddly, he was sent on home leave at the time of the Battle of Cambrai, and then served with the Reinforcement Depot until 21 February 1918 when George returned to what was now known as 3rd Light Battalion. When the Battalion was converted to operate Whippet medium tanks, he was employed as 1st Driver within B Company and, on 1 June 1918, was classified as a 1st Class tank mechanist.

George fought through the Battle of Amiens and during the Final Advance, was wounded on 8 October 1918 near Cambrai. Suffering from wounds to the upper right arm and right leg, George was evacuated to the UK where he was treated at St Luke's War Hospital in Halifax. After his discharge from hospital, he was demobilised on 20 March 1919 and returned to 12 Kingfield in Old Woking. The 3rd Battalion Old Comrades Membership Lists show he was still there is 1925 but, thereafter, his life story is uncertain. It is likely that he married Gwendoline Gascoigne, a publican's daughter on 24 August 1935, near her home in Stoke next Guildford, and they lived to the south of Woking between Mayford and Brookwood. George was shown working as an engineer but I cannot find any records of the couple having children. He died, aged only fifty seven on 10 June 1953 at the Victoria Hospital Woking, Gwendoline living as a widow until her death, aged eighty six, in the spring of 1995.

The third and youngest member of the crew from Woking was *Champagne*'s driver, Pte Horace Brotherwood. Born on 20 May 1898 at Yewtree Villa, in Old Woking, Horace was the youngest son of a journeyman carpenter and builder George Brotherwood. His wife Laura had four children, Horace's elder brother Frederick was born in 1889 but her next two children who died in infancy. Horace enlisted into the ASC at Guildford when he was just seventeen years old and, after initial driver training at the Grove Park MT Depot in south London, served in France from 26 September 1915. I have been unable to identify when he returned to England but he must have joined 711 (MT) Company which provided the drivers for the tanks at Elveden in June 1916. Horace was only eighteen when he was Killed in Action when his jugular vein was severed by enemy shrapnel as the crew tried to extract *Champagne* from the German communication trench. His crewmates recovered his body and his remains are now buried at the Pozières British Cemetery, the site of the dressing station where the tanks had rendezvous before the attack. The *Woking News and Mail* recorded his sad death on 6 October 1916 "Mr and Mrs Brotherwood of 1 Elm View Villas Goldsworth Road have received news of the death, in action in France, of their son Pte H Brotherwood of the HS Machine Gun Corps. It is understood that Pte Brotherwood has been engaged with the famous tanks". There is, however, no memorial to Horace in his home town.

The rest of the crew survived the war although Herbert Rothera was badly injured at the Battle of Arras. Herbert, who was the elder son of a pork butcher from Bolton, was born in 1896 and baptised on 22 March 1896 at St George's Church at Bolton-Le-Moors. His father was James Isherwood Rothera and his mother Louise Broughton and Herbert had two older sisters, Lily and Clara and a younger brother named Thomas. By 1911, the family was living at 63 Bitchburn Road in Bolton but, by the time Herbert enlisted on 11 December 1915, they had moved to 53 Blackburn Road. At his medical examination on 29 December 1915 Herbert was five feet six inches tall. He was mobilised on 6 January and his recruit pass reveals he had grey eyes and auburn hair. After training at Bisley and Elveden, he deployed to France on 16 August 1916.

After the first battles, Herbert was transferred to C Battalion and admitted sick to 12 Stationary Hospital at St Pol on 10 December but returned to unit on 16 December. Herbert was burnt in the legs during the Battle of Arras, but returned to duty after treatment by an American doctor. Herbert continued to serve with C Battalion through the battles of Ypres and Cambrai and, after the unit was re-equipped with Whippet light tanks, he was serving with A Company. Usually he was granted home leave on 18 June 1918 after which his mother Louisa sought indefinite leave for her son on the grounds of her ill health and that she needed Herbert to run the butchery business. Herbert's CO recommended that he be granted a compassionate discharge but this was not approved. Herbert served on with 3rd Battalion beyond the Armistice but, after another request from his mother, was posted to the Tank Corps Depot at Wareham on 4 December 1918. Demobilised in February, he did not claim an army pension for his injuries but later required daily treatment with oil to his leg. Herbert took over the family business when his father died in 1922. Three years later, Herbert married a local girl named Annie Slater and their only daughter Margaret was born in the town in the summer of 1929. Herbert and his family was still living at 53 Blackburn Road in 1933 and he died there aged fifty-two in the autumn of 1948.

His crewmate Gunner Fred Stone was born at Belper on 17 October 1896. He was one of twin sons of a railway signalman William Stone and his wife Annie Orbiston who had three older sons. Fred was baptised on 6 February 1897. On leaving school Fred worked as an errand boy for Boots the Chemists whilst his twin brother Charles was a telegram messenger for the Post Office. Charles joined the MMGS first, Fred who was by then working as a clerk, enlisted into the MMGS on 13 December 1915 and moved to Bisley for training the following day. He later served with No 9 Company of C Battalion at Arras, Ypres and Cambrai. Fred was wounded on 15 April 1918; the Battalion war history says that the unit was not in action that day but they were in position to repel a German attack. It is possible he was injured by German artillery fire. He soon returned to duty and fought through the Battle of Amiens.

On 5 September 1918, Fred returned to England as a candidate for a commission in the RAF. He trained with No 8 RAF Cadet Wing at Sandling Camp West Shorncliffe in Kent from 28 October and later served at No 5 Cadet Wing which was also at Shorncliffe. With the end of the war, and reduction in the size of the Air Force, training ceased and Fred was returned to the Tank Depot at Wareham on 10 January 1919 and demobilised two weeks later. His brother Charles, who had remained in the MMGS, left as a temporary sergeant. Fred married a local farmer's daughter, named Margaret Howarth, the following summer in Belper and their son Douglas was born in early 1928. Sadly that is all I can find about his later life but his medals left the family and are now held by Simon Payne.

Gunner William Smith, who was born in May 1884 in Edinburgh, was the oldest member of the crew. William enlisted into the MMGS on 24 November 1915 at Glasgow when he was thirty one years old. An insurance superintendent, with blue eyes and brown hair, who lived at 14 Frankfort

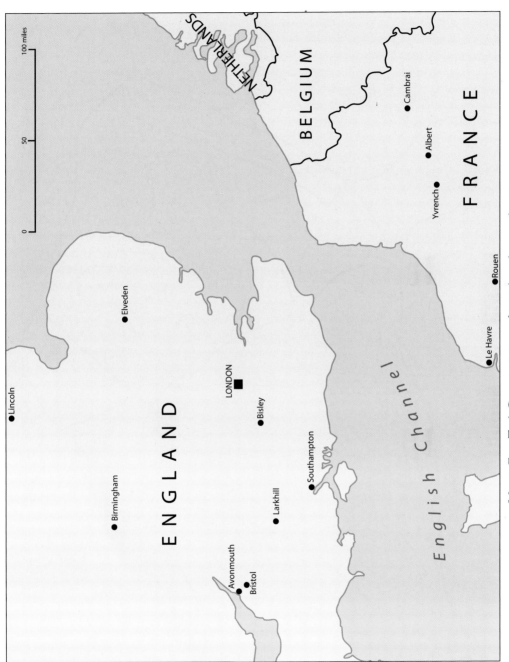

Map 1 First Tank Crews training and initial employment locations.

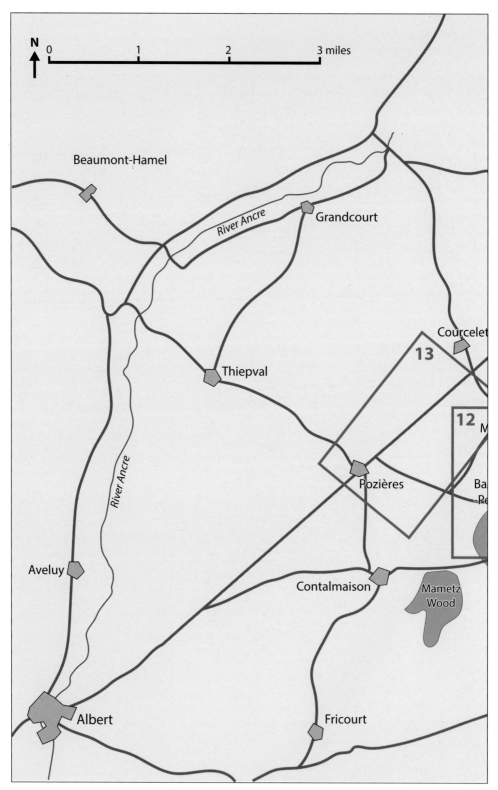

N

0   1   2   3 miles

Beaumont-Hamel

River Ancre

Grandcourt

Courcelet

13

Thiepval

12 M

Pozières

Ba
-Pe

Aveluy

River Ancre

Contalmaison

Mametz
Wood

Albert

Fricourt

Map 2 The Flers-Courcelette battlefield western features.

ii

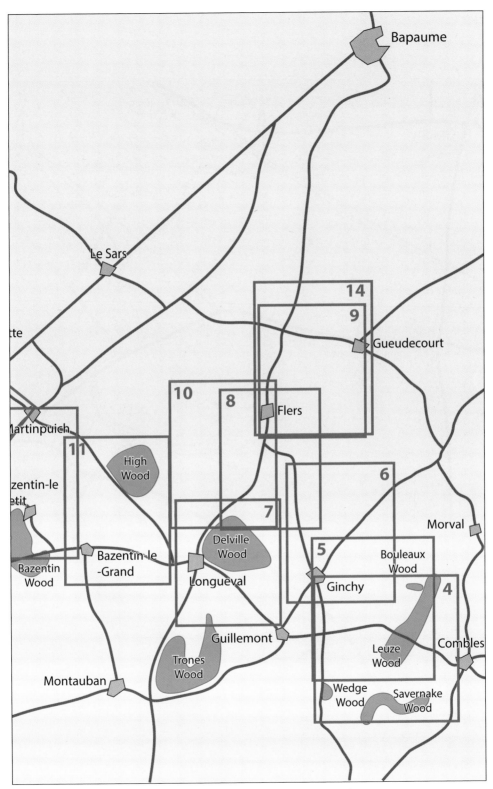

Map 3 The Flers-Courcelette battlefield eastern features.

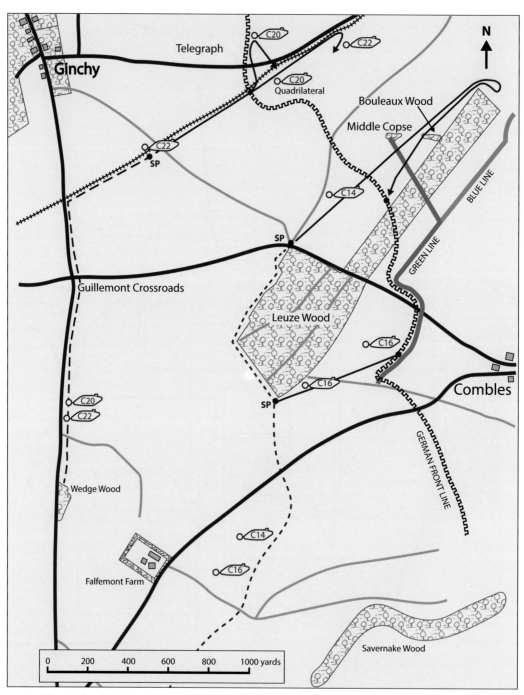

Map 4 Combles, Leuze Wood, Bouleaux Wood and the Quadrilateral – 15 September 1916.

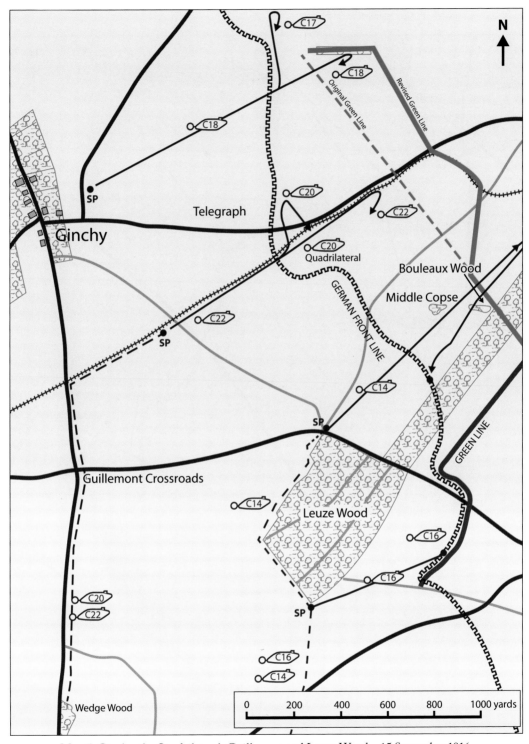

Map 5 Ginchy, the Quadrilateral, Guillemont and Leuze Wood – 15 September 1916.

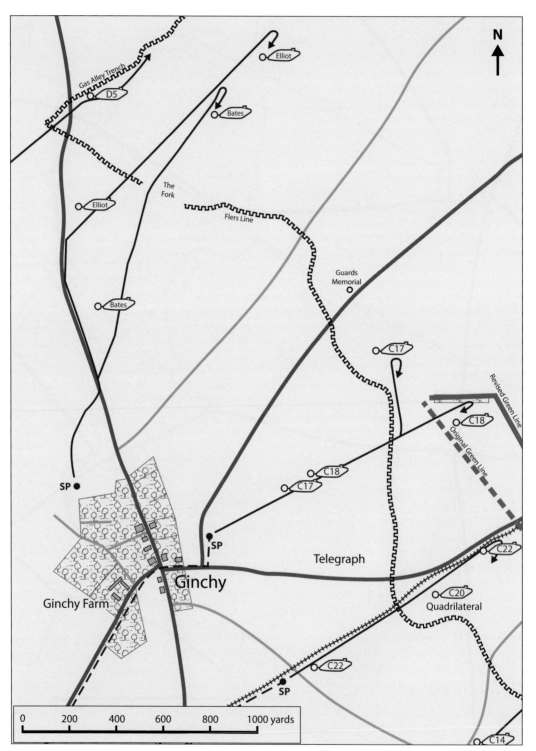

Map 6 Ginchy, the Quadrilateral and the ground to the northeast – 15 September 1916.

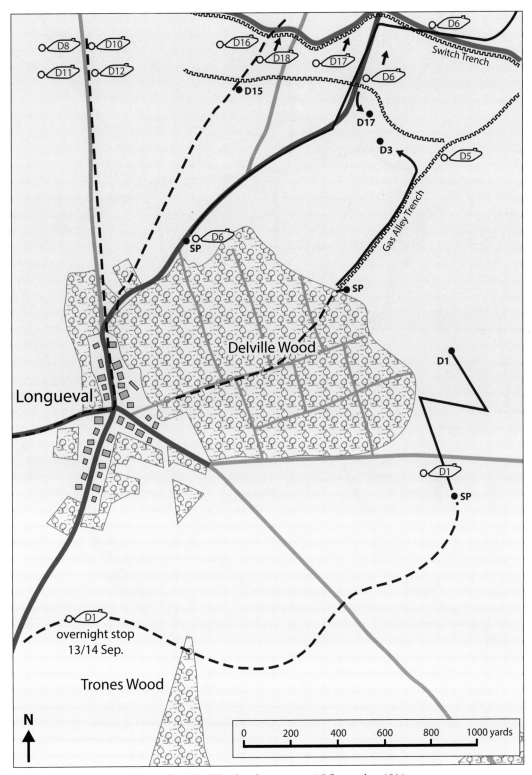

Map 7 Delville Wood and environs – 15 September 1916.

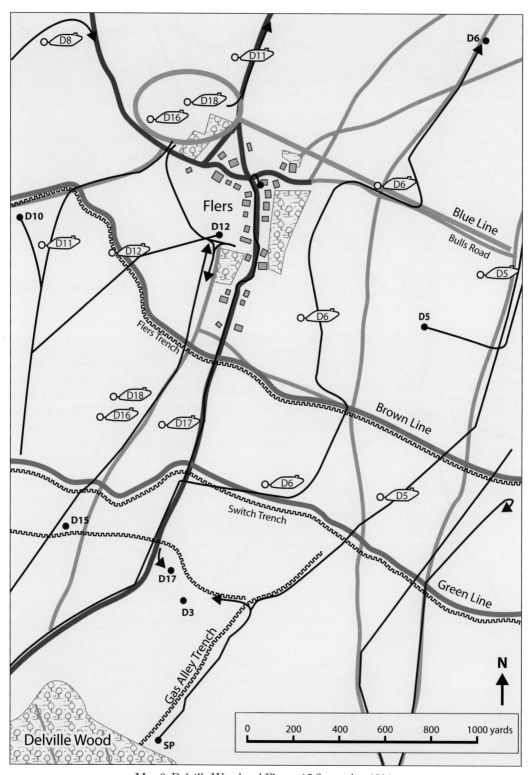

Map 8 Delville Wood and Flers – 15 September 1916.

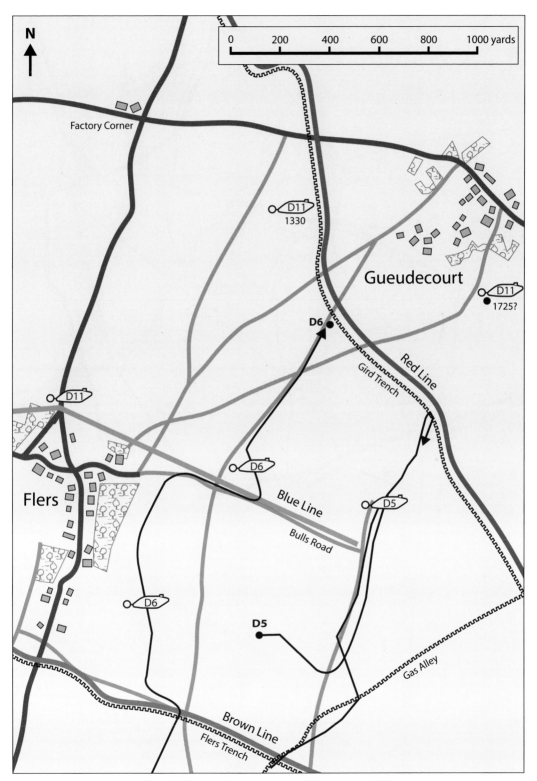

Map 9 Flers and Gueudecourt – 15 September 1916.

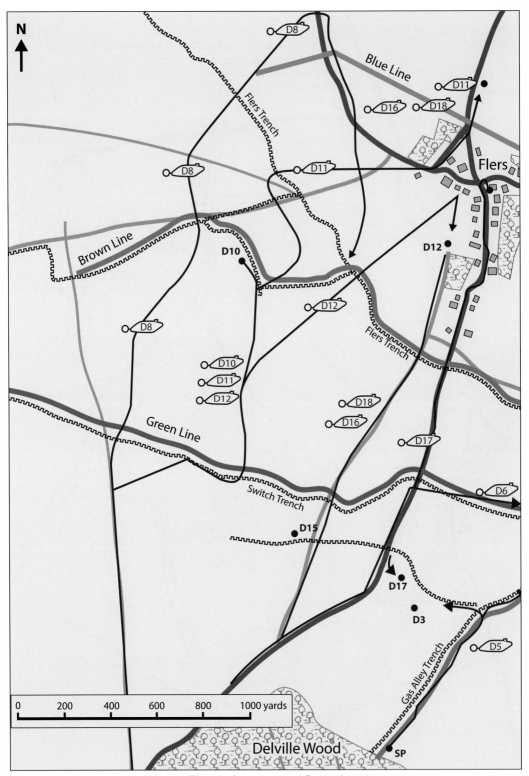

Map 10 Flers and the west – 15 September 1916.

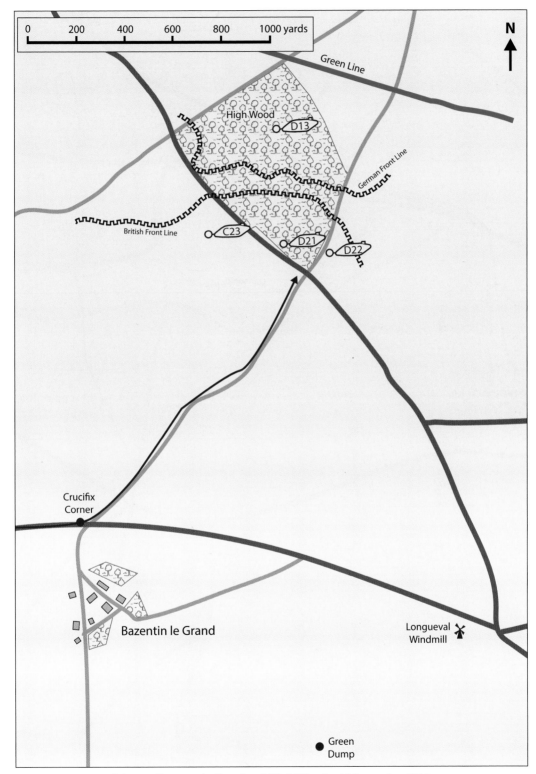

Map 11 Bazentin le Grand and High Wood – 15 September 1916.

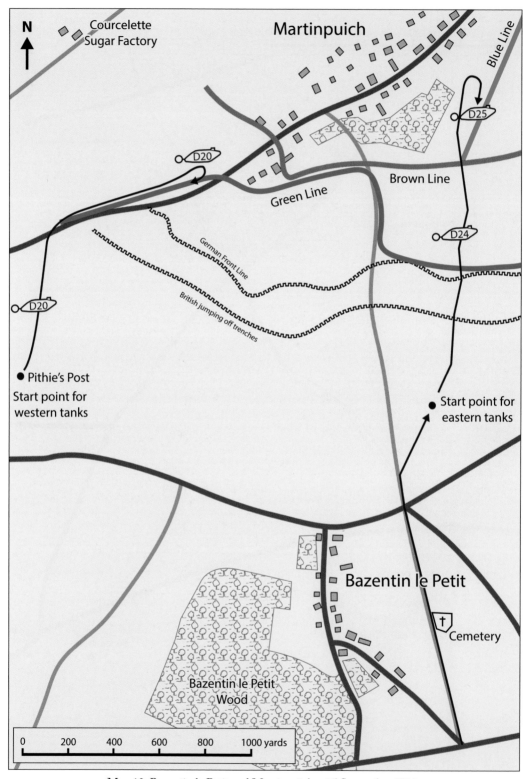

N

Courcelette
Sugar Factory

Martinpuich

Blue Line

D25

D20

Brown Line

Green Line

German Front Line

British Jumping off trenches

D24

Pithie's Post
Start point for
western tanks

D20

Start point for
eastern tanks

Bazentin le Petit

Cemetery

Bazentin le Petit
Wood

0   200   400   600   800   1000 yards

Map 12 Bazentin le Petit and Martinpuich – 15 September 1916.

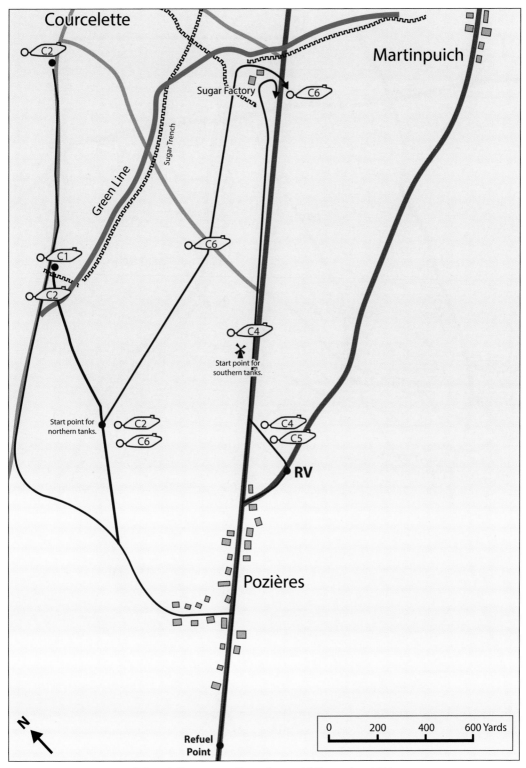

Courcelette

C2

Martinpuich

Sugar Factory

C6

Sugar Trench

Green Line

C1

C2

C6

C4

Start point for
southern tanks.

Start point for
northern tanks.

C2

C6

C4

C5

RV

Pozières

N

0   200   400   600 Yards

Refuel
Point

Map 13 Pozieres to Courcelette – 15 September 1916.

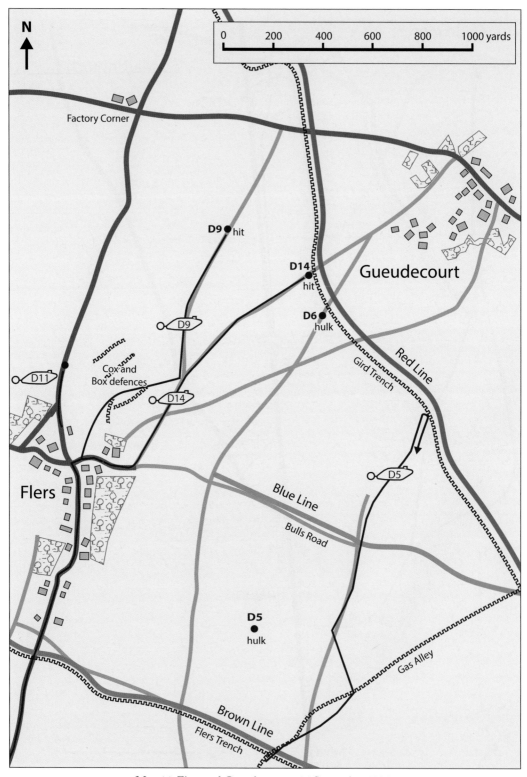

N

| 0 | 200 | 400 | 600 | 800 | 1000 yards |

Factory Corner

D9 hit

D14 hit

Gueudecourt

D6 hulk

D9

Red Line

Cox and Box defences

D11

D14

Gird Trench

D5

Blue Line

Flers

Bulls Road

D5 hulk

Gas Alley

Brown Line

Flers Trench

Map 14 Flers and Gueudecourt – 16 September 1916.

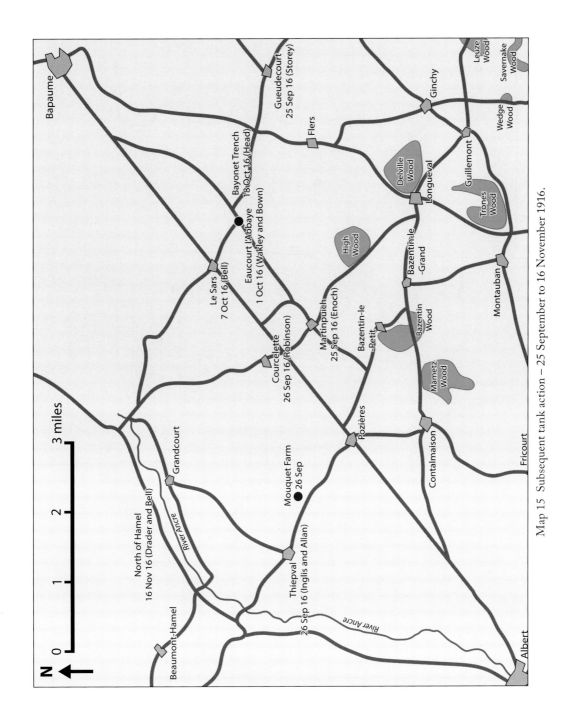

N

0   1   2   3 miles

Bapaume

Gueudecourt
25 Sep 16 (Storey)

Flers

Ginchy

Leuze
Wood

Savernake
Wood

Wedge
Wood

Guillemont

Bayonet Trench
18 Oct 16 (Head)

Delville
Wood

Longueval

Trones
Wood

Eaucourt l'Abbaye
1 Oct 16 (Wakley and Bown)

High
Wood

Le Sars
7 Oct 16 (Bell)

Bazentin-le
-Grand

Montauban

Martinpuich
25 Sep 16 (Enoch)

Bazentin-le
-Petit

Bazentin
Wood

Courcelette
26 Sep 16 (Robinson)

Mametz
Wood

Grandcourt

North of Hamel
16 Nov 16 (Drader and Bell)

River Ancre

Pozières

Contalmaison

Fricourt

Mouquet Farm
26 Sep

Thiepval
26 Sep 16 (Inglis and Allan)

Beaumont-Hamel

River Ancre

Albert

Map 15 Subsequent tank action – 25 September to 16 November 1916.

XV

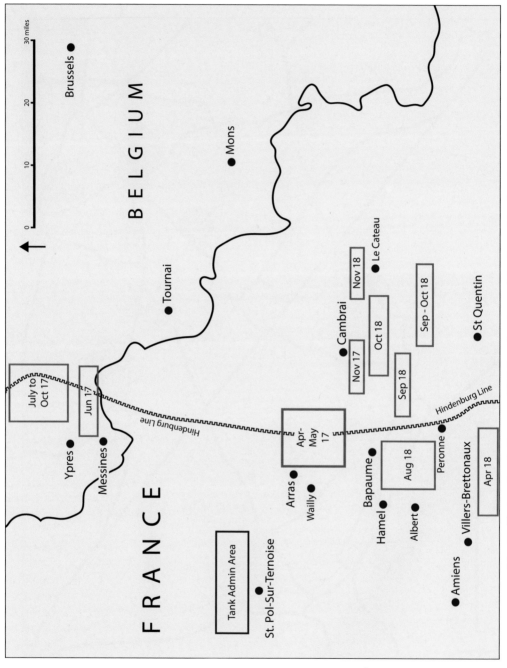

Map 16 Tank actions in France and Belgium showing tank battles and key locations in 1917–18.

Street Glasgow; William's family were farmers at Auchinleck in Ayrshire. William was awarded the Military Medal for bravery in the field on 14 November 1916 but there is no record as to what he did to be honoured. He was appointed lance corporal, as C Battalion formed, and later promoted corporal to bring the Battalion to full establishment on 18 May 1917 – this was as a result of the high level of casualties suffered during the Battle of Arras. William later transferred to the Tank Corps and was somewhat usually granted home leave in September 1917 just after the Battalion ceased action in the Ypres Salient. He probably fought at Cambrai.

Willie served on with the renamed 3rd Battalion in whippet tanks before being attached to 7th Battalion from 2 to 10 September 1918 and then granted home leave for three weeks which was unusual as the norm amongst the other crewmen was ten days. Soon afterwards, the Tank Corps Record Office received a letter from "his intended" Catherine J Wilson was seeking his whereabouts but the relationship does not appear to have lasted. William was promoted to colour-sergeant in 3rd Battalion on 17 October 1918, when Arthur Milliken who fought in *Cognac* on 15 September, left for England. William served on as a Company QM Sergeant until he returned to Scotland on 4 February 1919 for demobilisation. When he was transferred to Z Reserve on 11 March 1919; his home address was given as 4 Manse Road in Cumnock. He returned to work in insurance and, on 27 April 1923, married Mary Reid at the Johnston United Reform Church in Glasgow. He eventually became a district manager for his insurance company and the couple settled at 133 Wilton Street in North Kelvinside. He died at home of a heart attack, aged seventy-two, just after midnight on Boxing Day 1956.

Gunner Ernest Bax was not only awarded the Military Medal for bravery in November 1916 and was later decorated for services during the Second World War. Born on 2 January 1893; and christened on 26 February 1893 at St Michael's Church in Wood Green, Ernest was the younger son of book-keeper Harry and Sarah Bax. The family later moved to 97 Westbrook Road which was in a newly built garden suburb called Noel Park. Ernest's father later became a company secretary and Ernest worked as a financial journalist. Ernest initially enlisted in the Wiltshire Regiment and fought in Salonika from 14 July 1915. Returning to the UK, he joined the MGC as a gunner and deployed to France on 16 August 1916. As a result of his bravery in the first tank actions, Ernest was awarded the Military Medal and identified as being suitable for officer training.

Commissioned into the Tank Corps on 27 July 1917, he married Phyllis Sanderson at Edmonton shortly afterwards and their first daughter Mary being born the following summer. Ernest was appointed as an Equipment Officer from 1 September 1918 and served as an acting Captain at HQ Tank Corps at Bermicourt from 26 October 1918. He was a great friend of Bill Boylin, who fought in *Chablis* on 15 September 1916, and was a witness at Bill's wedding on 24 February 1919. Ernest served on after the Armistice in England until 1 September 1921 and he and Phyllis had a further two daughters: Joan in early 1920 and Betty in the summer of 1921. Ernest left the Army, having spent his last few months in the Labour Corps and settled in Wood Green in London. A fourth daughter, Nancy, was born in the Spring of June 1925. Returning to Army service during The Second World War, Ernest was commissioned into the RAOC on 1 May 1940 and, within two years, had been appointed a temporary Major. He was awarded the MBE on 5 June 1942. Phyllis died in September 1944 and the following year, Ernest married Elizabeth Sedgewick on 22 May at St Pancras. Their eldest daughter Shelagh was born the following year, and a younger daughter Wendy was born in 1949. Ernest and Elizabeth continued to live in Wood Green until his death on 31 January 1968.

C2 – Cognac

Cognac, which was a female tank, followed the same route into action as *Champagne*. Despite being damaged whilst travelling through Pozières on route to start line, the C2 crew reached their start point and, after the crew tightened the tracks, crossed the start line on time. *Cognac* also ditched in the German communications, not far away from *Champagne*'s resting point, but her driver Herbert Ledger managed to drive it out and continue towards Courcelette. *Cognac* then ditched again, within 200 yards of the village, and the crew started to dig the tank out at about 7:00 a.m. They eventually abandoned the task, fifteen hours later at 10:00 p.m. After removing the machine gun locks so that they could not be used should the German retake the hulk, they wearily returned to their own lines.

Cognac was recovered and went into action again near Thiepval on 26 September in support of the 18th Division attack. With a second tank, which cannot be identified, she left from Authille Wood on 25 September and made their way to a quarry near the Nab, At 12:35 p.m. the tanks went north towards Thiepval but the tank became ditched, after a shell exploded in its path whilst negotiating a large shell hole, well before she got amongst the German positions. The crew however used their machines to good effect as the infantry stormed the German defences. *Cognac* was again recovered the next day and returned to its advance base at Le Chemin Blanc. The tank was allocated to Charles Ambrose on 23 October but, owing to the dreadful ground and weather conditions, the planned attacks were cancelled.

On 15 September, *Cognac*'s skipper was Lieutenant Will Bluemel. He had been born on 6 June 1889 on the Mile End Road in East London. Will's father Frank was originally an umbrella stick maker but he and his brothers soon realised that they could use their skills in the rapidly developing bicycle business and set up their first works in Stepney. In 1901, whilst Will was living with his grandmother in Newbury; the family moved their successful manufacturing business to an old artificial silk works, at Wolston, to cater for Coventry's fast developing cycle and motoring industry. From a small start with 150 employees, the company's products were mouldings first made of cellulose and then from the recently discovered natural plastic Bakelite. Later they built spark plugs, steering wheels, pumps, and later bicycle mudguards and gear cases. Within nine years, the family firm had become a public company and Will was working for them.

Following the outbreak of the Great War, Will joined the Civil Service Rifles as a private soldier in November 1914 whilst his cousins Neville and Roland joined the Honourable Artillery Company. After completing training with the unit at Maidstone and Watford, he applied for a commission on 27 July 1915. It was probably due to his links to the motorcycle industry in Coventry, that Will was commissioned into the MMGS on 9 September 1915. Twelve days later, both of his cousins were badly wounded by shell-fire at Hooge, near Ypres. Both were evacuated by ambulance train, Neville dying of his wounds at Abbeville two days later and Roland, who survived, was transferred to Reserve and was attached for service with the family firm just after Will commanded *Cognac* at Pozières and later at Thiepval on 26 September.

Will was later attached to the newly arrived A Company in October, and then became part of a composite section of six tanks under command of Morty Mortimore. These tanks supported the Royal Naval Division in their attack on 14 November near Beaumont-Hamel. After his tank became stuck in the shell-hole, Will was severely wounded by a German "whiz bang" as he attempted to get to safety. This shell was probably from a 77mm artillery piece used for close defence of the German positions. The shrapnel caused Will's right elbow to be shattered and a huge lump of flesh removed from his left buttock. His right forearm and right thigh were also hit and he was evacuated to Boulogne. Will was so seriously hurt that he was not evacuated back to England until 3 December. Initially treated in London at Queen Alexandra's Military Hospital, on the Millbank in Westminster, Will later recovered at an Auxiliary Hospital which had been established by the Hon Mrs Beckett at her Mayfair home in 34 Grosvenor Street.

Will was not sufficiently well to be released from hospital until 22 July 1917 although, even then, he could not extend his elbow beyond 90 degrees. As he was convalescing, Will realised he would not return to active service with the tanks and sought alternative work with the Ministry of Supply. This arrangement was approved by HQ Tank Corps and he was transferred to the Army General

List on 10 August 1917. He then served with the Ministry of Munitions, in London, for the rest of the war; for the latter part in the Department of Aero Supplies in the Kings Road Chelsea where Will must have been in contact with Victor Huffam as they were working in the same sector. Will slowly recovered from his injuries although the damage to his elbow and buttocks remained a problem such that he was awarded a wound pension for five years. He relinquished his commission on 31 May 1919 and he returned to his home in Cannon Hill on the outskirts of Coventry.

Will again took up employment with the family company and, on 16 September 1922, married Katie Nichol at Hatch End in northwest London. He later took charge of the family engineering firm based in Coventry and they became famous not just for manufacturing cycle accessories but also for steering wheels used by the MG Car Company. Will, who developed and patented many of their products, became Chairman of the Company in July 1945. He also served as Vice President of the Coventry Branch of the Tank Regiment Old Comrades Association. He died aged seventy two on 29 August 1961.

Will's second in command was Sergeant Arthur Milliken. Born in June 1886, Arthur was the ninth of twelve children born to an Antrim born commercial traveller named James Milliken and his wife Mary. The family lived at 146 Anfield Road at Walton on the Hill and, on leaving school, Arthur started work as a clerk at the Bank of Liverpool. He enlisted into the MMGS on 24 November 1915 at Coventry. He was posted to Bisley and having been attached to the Armoured Car Section from 1 April 1916, was appointed unpaid Lance Corporal on 10 April and paid Corporal on 8 May. Arthur joined C Company on 25 May and was promoted Sergeant on 24 August, the same day he deployed to France. After the first tank actions, he remained with C Battalion and, serving with No 7 Company, retrained as a driver. He fought with No 1 Section at the Battle of Arras in April 1917 although on 9 April, his tank became stuck owing to the sodden ground. On 23 April, Arthur was a crewman in tank C4 commanded by 2Lt Charles Le Clair which one of two tasked to assist the capture of Gavrelle to the north of the River Scarpe. The left drive chain of the other tank (C1) broke soon after leaving its starting point but the tank pressed on. Five of the C4 crew were wounded by armoured piercing bullets and Arthur was awarded the Military Medal for conspicuous gallantry and devotion to duty. The citation stated "This NCO has shown great coolness and gallantry in action, notably during the attack on Gavrelle on April 23, '17. Owing to his skill and coolness he drove his tank through a heavy barrage to his objective, where it was of the greatest assistance to the infantry, until put out of action by armour-piercing bullets.

Arthur continued to serve with C Battalion and then with 3rd Light Battalion, when the unit was re-equipped with Whippets. Still serving with A Company, he had reached the rank of colour sergeant and was serving as Company QM Sergeant when he married Marjorie Constantine in the summer of 1918 at Birkenhead. On 18 October 1918 Arthur was transferred from 3rd Battalion back to England – he was replaced by William Smith who had served alongside him in *Champagne* during the attack on Courcelette. Arthur was posted to the newly formed 22nd Light Tank Battalion, based at Bovington, where he served with A Company as the Technical QMS. When he was discharged on 24 January 1919 Arthur's home address was shown as Huntley Bank at 33 Penkett Road in Liscard. In common with many of his comrades, he asked that his Military Medal be sent to his home address rather than to be presented.

Arthur and Marjorie's only son Christopher was born in 1919. Arthur returned to banking and later worked for Martin's Bank, which had been purchased by the Bank of Liverpool, in 1918, at their head office at 4 Water Street. Arthur eventually rose to become head of the Foreign Branch and then retired in 1945. Arthur, who was also a member of the C Battalion Old Comrades Association, lived at Bidston on the Wirral from 1925 until his death in the spring of 1964. He died at St Catherine's Hospital, in Liverpool, on 6 March 1964, aged eighty, and was buried in St Oswald's Churchyard in Bidston.

Gunner Donald Thompson was also a Liverpudlian albeit four years older than Arthur Milliken, and the oldest member of the crew. Born in late 1882, Donald was the second son of a grocer, named Robert Thompson, and was baptised at St Simon's Church on 4 February 1893. The family lived in Halewood, but, before his marriage Donald was living at Allerton Road in Mossley Hill. On 6 July 1910, Donald married Eliza Williams and they settled in Tranmere, on the Wirral, where Donald was working as a grocer according to the 1911 Census. The couple had three sons, Robert born in 1912, Jeffrey in 1913 and Rodger in 1915. By the time he was attested at Liverpool in December 1915, Donald was working as a provisions merchant. He was mobilised three months later, having volunteered to join the MMGS at Coventry, trained at Bisley as a machine gunner and then at Elveden before deploying to France on 24 August 1916. Donald remained with C Battalion, fought at Arras then trained as a 6 pdr QF gunner and fought at Passchendaele. Appointed lance corporal on 13 November 1917, he later fought at Cambrai. Admitted to hospital in early December, to have a fish bone removed from his throat, Donald Thompson was granted home-leave over Christmas.

He returned to serve with C Battalion, in its new role as 3rd Light Battalion on Whippets and must have retrained as a driver at some point as he was appointed 1st Class Tank Mechanic on 1 May 1918. On 15 September 1918 Donald returned to UK for selection as RAF aircrew. Two weeks later, he joined No 8 RAF Cadet Wing at Shorncliffe and was found fit to be employed either a pilot or observer. His RAF training was brought to an abrupt end with the signing of the Armistice, and he was posted to the Tank Depot at Wareham. Demobilized on 26 February 1919, Donald returned to Liverpool and was living at Hunts Cross in 1925. He therefore probably knew Graeme Nixon, who commanded tank D12 during the first action on 15 September 1916, who lived close by. Sadly Donald died on 8 April 1932, aged only forty-nine years, and was buried on 11 April 1932 at St Nicholas' Church in Halewood.

There were a number of teachers amongst the First Tank Crews including Gunner Victor Archard. Victor was one of twins, born near Melksham in the autumn of 1892. Bought up in at Bradford upon Avon and then Trowbridge, he became a teacher, first at Bradford and then in Winchester before the outbreak of war. He was a keen organist who played at his local church; he was also a keen motorcyclist which is why he joined the MMGS in November 1915. He spent Christmas in an auxiliary hospital at Woking. Deploying to France on 16 August 1916, on the SS *France*, Victor kept a diary for the first six months of the deployment and a copy is held in the Tank Museum archives.

After taking part in the actions at Courcelette and Thiepval, he was mainly employed on routine and salvage duties at Acheux and then at the Loop and did not go into action again that year, the weather and ground conditions being such that the tanks could not deploy.

When C Battalion was formed, Victor was posted to No 7 Company which was initially commanded by Major Allen Holford-Walker. During the winter, at the company location of Tilly Capelle in the Ternoise valley, Victor developed his schoolboy French by making friends with a local French family, and was often used as an interpreter by the Battalion staff. He was well regarded in the Battalion HQ and, in February 1917, was offered the post of unit telephonist which he declined as he wished to remain as a tank crewman. Victor served in No 1 Section of No 7 Company and was a crewman in Tank C4 on the opening day of the Battle of Arras, 9 April 1917, when he received gunshot wounds to the scalp. At the time, he was out of his tank, looking how to recover another which had ditched, when he was hit by enemy machine gun fire. The bullet entered his helmet four inches above the rear brim, passed across his head and exited through the front. Victor was later admitted to No 10 General Hospital at Dannes-Camiers and then, on 17 April, was evacuated on the SS *Donegal* as a walking casualty back to England. En route, the *Donegal* and a hospital ship *Lanfranc* was torpedoed by the German submarine U21. Twelve crewman and twenty-nine wounded men were drowned but Victor was amongst those rescued by HMS *Jackal* and taken to Southampton. Victor was initially treated at B Division Clearing Hospital at Eastleigh in Hampshire. Although his scalp wounds healed, he was not well enough to go overseas again. He was posted to Bovington where he became an instructor and was promoted to the rank of sergeant. Whilst at Bovington, he met Winifred Bugby who was the daughter of the national schoolmaster living in Bere Regis.

Victor was discharged from the Army on 20 June 1918 as a result of poor health. He returned to teaching in Winchester, living in the parish of Weeke. Two years later, on 4 August 1920, Victor married Winifred at Bere Regis Parish Church and they had later two sons. Their elder boy, Eric was born in Winchester in December 1921, whilst Mellis was born in Whitchurch five years later. Victor later became the headteacher at the Senior Elementary School in Whitchurch and was also the choirmaster and organist at the Parish Church for many years. At the end of the Phoney War, when the threat of a German invasion of Britain became real, Victor joined the Local Defence Volunteers. Owing a lack of military equipment, at first the men wore civilian clothes and a LDV brassard. In a photograph taken at the time, he wore the drab green overalls issued to the Home Guard.

From a studio photograph, taken at the time, it is just possible to see two stripes on his epaulettes which denote that he was the company commander. When the Home Guard was subsumed into the Army in 1942, he transferred to the Second (Whitchurch Battalion) of the Hampshire Regiment Home Guard. Sadly, Victor died, aged only fifty-one, on 9 November 1943 after a minor operation at the Royal County Hospital in Winchester, and is buried in the grounds of Whitchurch Parish Church.

Gnr Robert Caldicott also started his military service in the MMGS. He was born on 28 January 1890 and baptised, seven days later at St James the Less Church at Ashted in Birmingham. The eldest son of an iron caster who was in the bicycle manufacturing trade, Robert originally trained as a carpenter and joiner. He was attested on 17 November 1915 and medically checked at Coventry

Victor Archard at Bovington 1917.
(Graham Archard)

Victor Archard in LDV uniform 1940.
(Graham Archard)

the same day. A physically small man, at only five feet two inches tall, he reported for training at Bisley on 25 November 1915. He followed the standard pattern of transferring the Heavy Section MGC on 4 May 1916 and then to C Company on 27 May. Robert deployed to France on 24 August, which was later than most of his section, and presumably fought at Thiepval as well as at Courcelette. He stayed with C Battalion on its formation and continued with the unit eventually serving with 3rd Light Battalion until after the Armistice. He attended a 6 pdr gunnery course in early 1917, probably at the new tank ranges at Merlimont Plage, and then fought during the battles of Arras and Ypres as a tank NCO. He must also have fought at Cambrai as he was granted home leave from 8 to 22 December 1917, and was then appointed acting sergeant on 19 January 1918.

Promoted substantive sergeant on 16 April 1918, after the crew losses during the German "Kaiserschlacht" advance, Robert was promoted mechanical staff sergeant on 13 August 1918, probably as a result of wounds sustained by the key equipment NCO during the opening days of the Battle of Amiens. He fought with the Battalion throughout the Final Advance and, after the Armistice, was again granted home leave. Robert returned to the Battalion which then deployed into Germany and undertook occupation duties in the Rhineland. He returned to England on 23 March 1919 for demobilization; Robert returning back to the family home in Birmingham. In the spring of 1920, aged thirty, he married Margaret Wilson but the couple do not appear to have been blessed with children. They settled at Duddeston at 117 Great Lister Street, where they lived with Robert's father. From 1935 to 1945, they were living at 178a Aston Road in Duddeston. After that, I cannot find any information until Robert's death in Birmingham, aged eighty four, in the spring of 1974.

Gunner Alfred Hemington, who was much older than most of Cognac's crew, was a draper's assistant from Sheffield. Born on 28 June 1885 at Sheepbridge near Whittington Moors in Derbyshire, Alfred was the oldest surviving son of an elementary schoolteacher. The family had moved north to Eccleshall by 1891 but by 1911, Alfred was working as a draper's shop assistant whilst living at Cobnar Road in Woodseats near Sheffield. Aged thirty, Alfred enlisted into the MMGS at Coventry on 24 November 1915. He was five feet four inches tall and therefore ideal for serving as a tank gunner. After the first actions, Alfred transferred to C Battalion in November 1916. Rebadged into the Tank Corps, he continued to serve with C Battalion then 3rd Light Battalion operating Whippets tanks until demobilised. He was appointed acting (unpaid) lance corporal on 3 October 1918 and was made substantive 6 days later, probably as a result of the heavy casualties sustained by the Battalion during the Final Advance. He continued to serve on, after the Armistice, and undertook occupation duties in the Rhineland. When he was granted a fortnight's home leave in 1919, he immediately found a job and was demobilised on 15 January 1919; his home address being given as 40 Pinner Road at Hunters Bar. He later became a tobacconist, in 1925, working at 141 London Road but sadly the business failed. He continued to live in Sheffield, as a bachelor, where he died aged eighty-one, in the spring of 1967.

Gunner Harold Teft joined the MMGS on the same day as Alfred Hemington. Born near Gainsborough in Lincolnshire on 15 June 1894, Harold was the son of machine fitter Edwin Teft and his wife Kate whose family were publicans. He was educated at the local Grammar School and was a useful boxer as a boy. Harold was working as a clerk, at the engineering company Rose Brothers of Gainsborough, until he enlisted in the MMGS on 24 November 1915 where met several others who would later serve with No 1 Section. Harold deployed to France exactly nine months later and, after the action at Courcelette, took part in the salvaging of tasks. This was an essential task as there were very few spare parts taken to France and cannibalization of hulks was essential to keeping the remaining tanks fit for operations.

I cannot be sure if he took part in any actions north of the Ancre but he obtained a German bayonet around this time, probably whilst the Company was near the old German front line. Harold marked the scabbard with his service number and name, as well as his section and company details, and later took it back to England. At some time, it became lost to the family until 2010

Harold Teft (second left) autumn 1916. (Phillip Teft)

Harold Teft in 1918. (Phillip Teft)

when a collector placed a photo on the First Tank Crews website – as a result the bayonet is now with Harold's grandson Philip.

Harold joined C Battalion on its formation in November 1916 and, whilst serving with No 7 Company as an unpaid acting sergeant, applied for a commission on 19 February 1917. His records state he was at the Battle of Arras near Roclincourt, in April 1917 and he undertook driver training at Wailly from 11 to 16 June before returning to England on 25 June 1917. Harold trained at No 2 MGC Officer Cadet Battalion at Grantham, before being commissioned into the Tank Corps on 19 December 1917.

Having competed tank officer training at Bovington, Harold remained at Worgret Camp, near Wareham, until he deployed back to France with 18th Battalion on 2 October 1918. The unit never saw action and Harold was detached to 1st Tank Brigade for 5 days then back to 18th Light Battalion. He turned to the UK on 7 February 1919 and was released from service having grown two inches since he first enlisted. He first settled at 158 Trinity Street at Gainsborough and then at Saundby nearby. Harold married Doris Mawer at Gainsborough early in 1920 and their only son Gerald was born in early 1925. By this time, Harold was a shopkeeper and beer retailer living at 9 Bridge Road. He was also employed by his mother who still was a licensee, using his pugilistic skills where necessary when customers became over-boisterous. When she died in 1936, Harold is recorded as a merchant's clerk. He died at the John Coupland Hospital on 29 May 1945 and is buried in Gainsborough Parish churchyard; Doris survived until she was ninety.

There is no information on the remaining crewman, Gunner Alfred Sims, other than he served on in the Tank Corps as a private soldier and survived the war. Unusually the service record of the ASC driver, Private Herbert Ledger, has survived. Herbert was the elder son of agricultural labourer George Ledger and his wife. Emma. He was born on 23 March 1885 at Leeds in Kent and bought up in nearby Langley. Herbert joined the ASC in 1915 and, after the first tank actions, transferred to the MGC and was later rebadged into the Tank Corps. Unusually he was transferred to D Battalion, rather than staying with his original unit which may have been because he was badly injured and evacuated back to the UK. Herbert fought at the Battle of St Julien, which was part of the Third Battle of Ypres as a result of which he was awarded the Military Medal. This was for his actions during the attack in the swamp-like conditions on the Poelcapelle Road where so many tanks came to grief. Herbert was driving tank D44 *Dracula* – this was a male Mark IV tank commanded by Lt CL Symonds and was part of 9 Section in No 12 Company. *Dracula* proceeded up the Poelcapelle Road and, despite being ditched and unditched four times, almost reached its objective at Delta House before breaking down with engine trouble. The citation states: "on September 20, '17, at Delta House, north of St Julien, he left his tank on four separate occasions under heavy shell fire when it had become ditched and collected material to make ramps, and enabled his tank to reach firm ground. When his engine finally gave out, within 50 yards of the enemy's line, he worked unceasingly for over two hours, until everything had been tried to rectify it without avail". Herbert served on with the tanks, and was employed as an instructor for the rest of the war reaching the rank of acting corporal. After the war he returned to Kent and worked as an engine fitter, for over 25 years, with the Maidstone and District Motor Services. He also was a member of the St John Ambulance Service from 1930 to 1943 and he was awarded the Defence medal for his service in the Second World War. By this time Herbert was living at 2 Pheasant Cottages in Sutton Road. He never married and, when he died of a heart attack aged eighty-nine on 1 October 1974, his body being found at his cottage by his younger sister Leah.

Cordon Rouge

The three northern tanks were tasked to support the attack on the village of Courcelette but the skipper of *Cordon Rouge*, John Allan, did not follow his orders, choosing to support the attack on the Sugar Factory. His female tank, which was fitted with Vickers machine guns, took a totally different route to the others, towards the Sugar trench, which ran across the middle of the Canadian area. When the tank reached this this point (coloured image 15) she was about two hundred yards from *Crème de Menthe* which was driving parallel to Pozières – Le Sars road. According to the 6th Canadian Brigade War Diary *Cordon Rouge* "fired on and silenced several machine guns and thus proved of much assistance in enabling our troops to advance." In his post operation report, John does not describe the reason for his change of plan but it is more than likely that he saw that *Créme de Menthe* had lost her two companion tanks and was taking on the main German strong point alone. He would have seen *Champagne* and *Chablis* had successfully crossed no man's land and so, as later recorded by Lionel McAdam, *Cordon Rouge* took up a parallel course with *Créme de Menthe* towards the Sugar Factory. Approaching the factory, from the north-west, John Allan positioned his tank to stop the enemy's withdrawal from the strongpoint. Having seen that the factory had been secured, the tank crew then waited until *Crème de Menthe* had completed its exploitation task, before they both returned to the rally point by the site at Pozières Windmill. Several crewmen were injured in the action but none sufficiently seriously to be evacuated back to England. The tank was later photographed as she made her way back down the Albert Road with her crew sitting on the outside of the vehicle. As she approached the tankodrome, near Aveluy, soldiers were arranged to cheer her return and this photograph later appeared in many newspapers as a stock image.

Eleven days later *Cordon Rouge* was again paired with Crème de Menthe for the attack on Thiepval. She almost reached the main German positions, before becoming ditched to the north-west of the site of the Thiepval memorial.

The C6 crew was a high quality team. Sadly two were later killed through enemy action, but three others were commissioned and the remainder survived. Their skipper, Lieutenant John Allan, was born in 1887 in Aberdeen. His father George was the Governor of Aberdeen Poor House. John was educated locally at Robert Gordons' Technical College and then later moved to South America where he worked as a shipping manager for the Anglo-Chilean Nitrate and Railway Company. On the outbreak of war, John returned from Callao in Chile on *SS Oriana* docking at Liverpool on 28

HMLS *Cordon Rouge* returning from action – 15 September 1916. (Tank Museum)

January 1915. On 10 March, he enlisted at Hampton Court as a trooper in King Edward's Own Horse, a Special Reserve unit which had traditionally only recruited men who had lived overseas. Just under six feet tall, John served with 2nd Regiment which deployed to France on 15 July and was appointed lance corporal three months later. Later selected for officer training, John returned to England and was commissioned into the MGC on 14 April 1916. After training at Bisley and Elveden, John deployed back to France on 24 August.

John was slightly injured during the attack on the Sugar Factory on 15 September and sent to the 4th Canadian Field Ambulance but returned to duty the same day. Having taken part in the attack on Thiepval, he was detached to D Company under Arthur Inglis' command, in the area around Flers, but rejoined C Company on 28 October 1916. On 14 November, the *London Gazette* announced he had been awarded the Military Cross for conspicuous gallantry in action. He maneuvered his Tank with great skill under heavy shell fire over difficult and unknown ground, and brought it into a good position for enfilading the enemy trenches, which he succeeded in doing with good effect."

John transferred to B Battalion on its formation on 18 November and moved back to their winter base near St Pol sur Ternoise at Sautricourt. Unusually John was granted home leave from 15 to 25 December. He then worked as an assistant instructor and, having trained crews with the new battalion, he was promoted captain on 12 April 1917 and continued in the instructional role until 28 April. Six weeks later, he commanded No 10 Section of 6 Company during the Battle of Messines. Only one of his tanks managed to get beyond the German font line on 7 June but the others later moved forward. On the following afternoon, John went to check that his tanks were in good order and was mortally wounded as he returned to the British lines. Having sustained bullet wounds in his back, John was sent to No 2 Casualty Clearing Station where he died of his wounds the following day. His body is buried at Ballieul Communal Cemetery Extension.

The other fatality from amongst the crew of *Cordon Rouge* was Clarence Kilminster. Born in Cardiff on 23 March 1893, Clarence was the only son and youngest of thirteen children of a joiner named George Kilminster and his wife Alice Bailey who came from Gloucester. Unusually Clarence was not baptised until 24 February 1899 when he was nearly six and living at Grangetown in Cardiff. By 1901, the family had moved to Scotland and was living at St James' Place in Leith. Although his rest of family then moved to Liverpool, just before the war, Clarence remained in Leith, having gained a pupilage. Living at Pilrig Street, Clarence was attested at Edinburgh and joined the MMGS in February 1916. Deploying to France on 16 August 1916, he remained with C Company, after the first actions, and transferred to C Battalion as it was formed. In April 1917, he took part in the Battle of Arras when he was injured and evacuated to 8th Casualty Clearing Station. He died of his wounds, aged only twenty-four, on 3 May 1917 and was buried at Duissans Military Cemetery to the west of Arras. His mother had died the previous day In Ellesmere Port and it was therefore a double shock for his family when they sought compassionate leave for their only son to return for her funeral. Although Clarence was born an Englishman, who was bought up in Wales, he is commemorated in the Scottish National War Memorial at Edinburgh Castle because he was a resident of Leith. He is not forgotten.

John Allan's second in command was an actor named Frank Vyvyan who was awarded both the Military Medal and Distinguished Conduct Medal, a rare feat amongst tankers. Born at Croydon on 25 February 1891, Frank was the third son of an actor Herbert Vyvyan and his wife Alice. Frank enlisted into the MMGS and, after the usual training regime, deployed to France on 24 August 1916. As a result of his actions at Courcelette, he was awarded the Military Medal. Frank remained with C Battalion on its formation and became a regular performer as a member of the *Willies*, the C Battalion concert party. He fought at the Battle of Arras, receiving the Distinguished Conduct Medal for conspicuous gallantry and devotion to duty. The citation states that "During the opening of the offensive on April 9 '17, when the officer had been killed, he took charge of his tank and continued to fight it with the greatest boldness and skill. When he could not reach the enemy with his Lewis gun inside the tank, although under heavy fire, he fixed up a Lewis gun on top of the tank, and fired it from there. He thereby greatly assisted the infantry to advance." This action was probably on the Fampaux Road; the tank becoming ditched and the officer, Lieutenant William Tarbet killed whilst reconnoitering ahead of the ditched tank.

Rebadged to the Tank Corps, Frank was promoted sergeant and served with C Battalion almost until the end of the war. He was selected for officer training and, on 22 March 1919, was commissioned into the Tank Corps. After the war, Frank returned to his parent's home in Brixton and, in 1920, married an actress named Olive Emerton. Olive's brother had lived in Canada before the war and, in 1913, she had visited his home at Field in British Columbia. The couple decided to emigrate and left London on 5 March 1924 planning to settle in Seattle. When he arrived at Nova Scotia, Frank stated he wanted to work on the land but, for the next three years, the couple was employed by the Allen Players, a theatre company touring Canadian cities. Olive and Frank eventually settled in Vancouver, where they were joined by Frank's father, mother and sister Ruby who was also an actress, dancer and later a broadcaster. Frank's father died within months of settling in West Vancouver and Frank's first wife Olive died on 15 January 1931. Less than six months later, on 22 July 1931, Frank married Olive's sister, Phyllis, and they had two daughters. Although Frank was mainly a stage actor, he was also as a set designer and radio actor. His second marriage failed in 1940 and he married again, this time to an English woman called Gladys Simmonds who had emigrated to Vancouver from Birmingham. Unusually the wedding, which was held on 10 May 1941, took place in Whatcom in Washington State. Gladys was a scriptwriter, a role Frank also undertook as well as being a sound effects specialist. He appeared in a number of films made in Vancouver and, in the late 1950s, Frank appeared in the first children's TV series, produced by CBC Vancouver, called *Cariboo County*. He later appeared in *Tidewater Tramp*, another CBC children's series from 1959 to 1962 filmed at Vancouver. Frank died, just before his seventy sixth birthday on 22 February 1967 in Vancouver.

Of *Cordon Rouge's* crew, the least is known about the tank's driver Private Joseph Barton ASC. He started his service in the Horse Transport trade of the ASC, before retraining to drive vehicles. He rebadged to the MGC in early January 1917 and later served with Tank Corps as a private soldier. Gunner Harry Bedford was born on 24 November 1896 in Sidmouth in Devon. Before he enlisted into the MMGS, aged nineteen, he was a greyhound trainer living at Walton on Thames with his parents who ran the Ashley Arms public house. He was posted to Heavy Armoured Car Section on 1 April 1916, at Bisley, and then to C Company on 4 May 1916, deploying to France with the main body on 24 August. Harry was recorded as being wounded on 15 September but not sufficiently seriously to require evacuation to the UK. Having been treated in France, Harry returned to C Company on 28 October and was transferred to C Battalion on its formation the following month. On 25 February 1917. Harry was injured whilst playing football at the Tank Corps Central Stores at Erin. His leg was placed in a splint for five weeks after which he was returned to the UK. Medically downgraded in May 1917, he sought to be discharged but this was denied. He served the rest of his service as a mechanic at Bovington and Wareham with the Tank Depot. He was discharged in March 1919 having injured himself again in August 1918, whilst on leave, which required that his cartilage be removed. He settled at his mother's address, the New Inn Hotel at Littlehampton and later went into the hotel business at Newquay. He died in 1974.

There is a connection in film-making between Frank Vyvyan and one of other gunners Ernie Hunt although it would not be apparent until the late 1950s. Ernie also enlisted in the MMGS then transferred to MGC as the Heavy Section was formed. He was born on 18 May 1896 at 170 Little Green Lane at Aston near Birmingham where his father Edward was a foreman in an ice factory. The youngest of four children, Ernie was something of a tearaway according to his younger daughter Molly. Skipping school whenever he had a mind to pop back home for coffee, Ernie thought nothing of tying neighbours' front doors together – before knocking on both! However, he was also capable of leading boy scout parades with controlled displays of both baton twirling and the rhythmic banging of big bass drums. A bright inventive youngster, Ernie was educated at Waverley Road Secondary School in Birmingham. Prior to enlistment, whilst working as a motor-cycle mechanic in Acocks Green Ernie was only nineteen when he became involved with Alice Bailey who became pregnant.

It was shortly after their liaison that Ernie passed the MMGS trade test and enlisted at Coventry on 17 November 1915. According to his family, Ernie was present at the trial of the prototype tank *Mother* at Hatfield House, when her capabilities were demonstrated to the War Office staff on 29 January 1916. Ernie often told the story that, whilst taking part at this trial, one crewman suggested the name Tank. "When we were testing *Mother* the top brass lined us up. They said: "Look men! We've got a transportation problem… How are we going to escape detection en route to the railheads? Any suggestions?" One bright spark stepped forward… He said: "Well, why try and disguise it at all?" The top brass replied: "Don't you know this is a secret weapon?" "No, Sir!" the man from the ranks persisted. "With respect, you misunderstand me. Why not hide it in full view, after first stripping away its armaments, so that if anyone asks – "What the bloody hell is that great monstrosity" – you can say that it's just a water-carrying tank for re-supplying front line troops!"

According to his family, Ernie also served at the Foster's factory at Lincoln prior to move of tanks to Elveden. His elder daughter Belinda was born on 14 July 1916 and Ernie deployed to France on 26 August. Having fought at Courcelette on 15 September and at Thiepval eleven days later, Ernie was pictured in *Birmingham Daily Mail* on 6 October and the accompanying report recorded he had taken part in a third action as a driver. It was also around this time that Alice sought help from Ernie's parents in supporting Belinda. They were not prepared to assist her so she sought mainte-nance through the courts and was awarded five shillings a month. Ernie was awarded the Military Medal in November 1916, for his service at Courcelette and his family state that whenever he recalled the attack on the Sugar Factory, he was terribly affected by its memory. Whilst scavenging amongst the former German positions, in October 1916, Ernie acquired a number of German helmets known as *pickelhaubes* as trophies which he later took back to Birmingham. His father later threw them in a local canal which created a major disagreement in the family. It is also interesting to note that Ernie's Military Medal was never displayed in the family home.

Ernie transferred to C Battalion in November 1916 and was serving in No 9 Company when he applied for a commission on 26 January. His application was supported by Arthur Inglis, who was by now commanding a company in F Battalion at Bovington. Ernie was selected for a commission on 11 March and returned to England four days later. Ernie later told his family that, during the Battle of Arras, he was again in action and that, for his bravery, he was offered either another medal or a commission. Deciding to accept the commission, he was removed from his unit at short notice much to the angst of his tank commander who was extremely upset that Ernie could not accom-pany him into action and fearing for his safety, burst into tears. Ernie also recalled that the officer and his replacement driver were both killed in the following action.

Ernie initially trained as an officer with No 35 Depot Company MGC at Belton Park near Grantham but, from 1 May, he served with No 2 MGC Officer Cadet Battalion at Pirbright. Copies of maps marked by Ernie, which are in his daughter's care, show that he took part in field exercises which were linked to his being trained for service as a MGC officer. On completion of his initial training, Ernie was commissioned into Tank Corps on 28 July 1917 after which he was sent to Bovington to learn to be a tank commander, Ernie usually was not sent to France as part of a formed unit. Instead, on 7 January, Ernie was posted to the Training and Reinforcement Depot, where he spent two months before being posted to 7th Battalion in France on 3 March. He failed to let Alice Bailey know of his whereabouts and she had to write to the War Office to regain contact after he again failed to pay for Belinda's maintenance; Ernie's record shows this incident did not occur a second time.

In early July 1918 Ernie was admitted to hospital for dental treatment and he did not return to his unit for nine days. The following month, he fought with 7th Battalion during the Battle of Albert when the British recaptured the ground lost during the Kaiserschlacht. Unusually Ernie granted home leave in early September but was back in action at the Battle of the Hindenburg Line when, two year after he had supported the Canadians at Thiepval, Ernie again fought alongside them as they re-captured Bourlon Wood on 27 September 1918. Unlike the majority of tank units, 7th Battalion was equipped with Mark IV tanks. These were again a magnet for German machine gun fire and, where his hand gripped the Hotchkiss machine guns provided for tank commanders, Ernie's left hand was badly scarred by bullet "splash". He also recalled having to remove metal fragments from his face as a result of being wounded whilst looking through a periscope. In the latter part of the war, he had to intervene to prevent the killing of German prisoners who were being machine gunned by one of his crew. His intervention was quick and effective as he knocked the man out with his fists.

On 18 October, after 7th Battalion was withdrawn from action, Ernie was sent back to England. Along with several other members of the First Tank Crews, he was posted to the newly formed 19th Battalion but, following the Armistice, it was disbanded. Promoted Temporary Lieutenant on 28 February 1919, Ernie was posted to the Central Schools and commanded the tank *Birmingham* at the Royal Tournament at the Olympia exhibition hall in London from 26 June 1919. Here he was photographed with Lieutenant Colonel Francis Fernie, under whom he had served in 7th Battalion, and other members of the tank display team in front of *Birmingham*. During the Royal Command Performance, his was the only tank to balance on the fulcrum which was directly in front on King George V which proved his crew must have been well practiced. Ernie also took

Ernie Hunt (centre right) at Olympia in July 1919. (Cosmo Corfield)

part in the Peace Parade, commanding *Birmingham* as one of the four tanks which drove through Westminster on 19 July 1919. On 31 March 1920, Ernie relinquished his commission on completion of service and returned to Small Heath in Birmingham. There, in 1922, he married Violet Ware and their only daughter Molly was born in 1928. Sadly the marriage did not last but, after a chance meeting in a Birmingham pub with Alice Bailey in 1935, Ernie met his older daughter Belinda for the first time. He became a successful business man, initially running a cycle shop in Ward End which he expanded into a radio shop and then relocated to Weoley Castle where he named his business College Radio. Family life was good but strawberry jam was never on the table as the smell reminded Ernie of the sweet smell of burning oil and human flesh, which bought back vivid memories of his service as a tank commander

On the outbreak of war, Ernie applied to rejoin the Army but, when not selected, handed over the running of his shop and moved to Gloucestershire where he worked in a munitions factory, living on his boat at Tewkesbury. At the time of evacuation of the British Forces from France, he volunteered to take the boat to Dunkirk but his offer was declined on the grounds that his boat was too small. Must to his angst, Belinda joined the ATS in 1940 and, three years later, was commissioned shortly before Ernest decided to return back to his business. He was far from well and was worn out by fighting a one man battle against pilfering at the factory. Belinda managed to get a posting to Edgbaston close to his home and the business, which had declined because Ernie was unable to get payments from customers now serving in the Armed Forces, became a success after the war. He spent every weekend on his boat at Tewkesbury and was a keen golfer. He also became a prize winning amateur film maker.

Ernie Hunt receives the IAC Award for Best Fiction Film from Petula Clark 1959. (Cosmo Corfield)

When he retired, Ernie moved to Redditch, where he selected the house on basis of converting double garage into a film studio and uprooting the orchard in order to practise his golf swing. In 1959, his film *The Mind of Dr Furber was awarded the* Institute of Amateur Cinematographers (IAC) Award for Best Fiction Film and he was presented with an award, by the singing star Petula Clarke. This was the first amateur film to successfully achieve lip-synching which Ernie achieved by spooling the film around empty beer bottles. His film *A House in the Country (*1968) won the John Player Trophy at the 1970 Midlands Amateur Cine Association film festival. The following year, it was also placed third in the Melbourne International Amateur Film Festival. Ernest followed the example of Alfred Hitchcock by appearing in his own films. However, despite berating his amateur cast for sometimes looking at the camera, his own cameo performances always required multiple takes!

Ernie was, for many years, a chain smoker perhaps due to the wartime habit amongst tank commanders of guiding their drivers during light approach marches using a lighted cigarette held behind their back. He had however given up smoking by the time he won the John Player award when he noted that, despite a smoked filled room and availability of free cocktail cigarettes none of the tobacco company were smoking. Ernie's daughter Molly believes that part of the reason he gave up smoking was due to damage caused to his lungs from poisoned gas used during the Great War. Despite this Ernie survived until just before his eighty-fourth birthday, dying on 9 April 1980.

Gunner Arthur Jakins, who was the oldest member of the crew of *Cordon Rouge*, was born on 27 December 1886 in Deptford. The son of a carman, Arthur became a telegraph messenger on leaving school and then worked for the Post Office in a variety of roles before joining the Civil Service. Arthur deployed to France, with the main body, on 24 August. Wounded on 15 September, during the attack on Courcelette, he remained with C Company and then was transferred to C Battalion. He had a brush with Army discipline when he was awarded 10 days Field Punishment for being absent for one hour on 8 January 1917 and also for being in a French bar during prohibited hours, which was a far from unusual occurrence. On the opening day of the Battle of Arras, on 9 April 1917, Arthur was again wounded in action and, according to William Piper's diary, suffered a nervous breakdown. Six weeks later Arthur caught influenza and was hospitalised in France until 8 July. He became so ill that he had to be evacuated to the UK and sent to the Eastern Command General Hospital in Cambridge. After being granted post-sick leave in early August 1917, he was posted to Command Depot at Alnwick, serving with 17 Company MGC before being sent to Bovington to join the newly forming L Battalion. Appointed lance corporal on 31 December 1917, he embarked with the renamed 12th Battalion Tank Corps five days later for France. On 16 March he reverted to the rank of gunner at his own request. On 20 May Arthur was admitted to hospital and then to the Medical huts at the Central Stores at Erin, for convalescence, before returning to his unit on 5 July. Promoted acting Corporal, he fought with 12th Battalion at the Battle of Amiens and throughout the Final Advance. Arthur's elder brother Charles died of his wounds on 24 August which he received whilst serving with the New Zealand Division during the fighting to take back the ground to the north of the 1916 Somme battlefield. Charles, who worked at a freezing plant before he joined the Canterbury Regiment, embarked from Wellington on 16 November 1917. His body was buried at the Bagneux British Cemetery at Gezaincourt.

Arthur was also wounded on 8 October, as 12th Battalion fought its way through the German Hindenburg line and against German manned Mark IV tanks, which had been captured at Cambrai and converted for use against the British armoured units. Having recovered from his injuries he was sent back to England and posted to 24th Officer Cadet Training Battalion. On 13 November 1918, he was appointed the Technical MT Sergeant, serving with C Company. During his Christmas leave, he looked for civilian employment, and on 6 February 1919, he accepted an appointment with the Post Master General. Demobilised and transferred to the Z Reserve one month later when he returned to 207 High Road in Lee South East London. He lived with his father at Lee until 1926, after which, he lived his brother Charles and sister Patience in Lewisham until 1939. As far as I can identify, he never married but he lived until the age of seventy-eight; his death in early 1972 being registered in Eastbourne.

The final member of Cordon Rouge's crew, Victor Newby came from Yorkshire. Born on 11 December 1897, Victor was the younger son of solicitor named John Newby and his wife Pauline. The couple had married at Bradford Parish Church, at what is now the local cathedral, on 13 March 1893. Pauline was two years older than her husband and was also the daughter of a solicitor. John Newby died, aged only thirty-six, on 11 June 1903 and Victor was therefore educated, as a scholar orphan, at the Crossley and Porter Orphan Home & School in Halifax. When he enlisted into the MMGS on 17 November 1915 at Coventry; Victor was studying engineering. Like a number of other volunteers, he lied about his year of birth, adding a further two years to his age. He was however able to pass the trade test and was sent to Bisley for training the following day. Having transferred into the Heavy Section MGC, he deployed to France on 24 August 1916. Victor was slightly wounded during the attack on Courcelette on 15 September and admitted to 4th Canadian Field Ambulance before returning to duty the same day. He was probably in action at Thiepval eleven days later. He stayed with C Battalion and served with it during the Battles of Arras, Third Ypres and Cambrai. He was granted home leave, after the battle, returning to his unit on 24 December just in time to join in the Christmas festivities. In early 1918, Victor retrained onto Whippets and then served with C Company of the renamed 3rd Light Battalion. He fought at the Battle of Amiens and during the Final Advance. He was promoted acting Corporal on 14 September 1918, as a result of the large number of casualties taken by the Battalion, but was transferred back to the UK on 17 October 1918.

Like Arthur Jakins, he was posted to 24 Officer Cadet Training Battalion and promoted acting Corporal on 4 January, before being transferred to Z Reserve on 12 February 1919. Like his elder brother George, who served as a sergeant in the York and Lancaster Regiment, Victor returned to Bradford to live with his widowed mother and, in 1925, was a member of the C Battalion Old Comrades Association. On 12 June 1930, he married Margaret Slater in Bradford. He later re-trained as an agriculturist, which required that he and Margaret had to travel overseas particularly to South America. They remained living in Bradford until 1958 when they travelled to Valparaiso in Chile and then settled in Buenos Aires. Victor died there in 1972; Margaret who was ten years his junior died four years later in Barcelona.

16

Crème de Menthe – the model tank

In the early hours of 15 September 1916, the three tanks tasked to assist 2nd Canadian Division take the Sugar Factory at Courcelette, made their way to a rendezvous point to the east of Pozières (see map 13). *Chablis* was equipped with four Vickers machine guns which would assist the Canadians break through the German trench lines whilst the other two, *Chartreuse* and *Crème de Menthe* were equipped with quick firing (QF) guns which fired 6 pound shells, capable of penetrating the machine gun emplacements which the Germans had constructed within the fortified complex. Once this first task had been completed, *Champagne* was to assist the Canadian troops exploit their success and defeat any counter-attacks whilst *Chartreuse* and *Chablis* were to head downhill towards Martinpuich and assist in the capture of the northwest of the village by supporting Bill Mann and his four tanks from D Company.

The Germans were aware that the attack was imminent and used artillery fire on likely approaches to disrupt the Canadians as they moved to their attacking positions. Although the tanks' rendezvous and approaches were hidden by both terrain and darkness, the artillery rounds found their targets and damaged two of the three tanks as they moved up for the assault. *Chablis* was also slowed on her approach because her tracks were slipping. The driver Private Daniel Cronin, assisted by Corporal Charles Harrison, attempted to tighten the tracks before they joined the assault but they soon worked loose again and one track fell off completely. *Chablis* skipper, Lt Geordie Campbell, decided to abandon the attack and, having removed the commander's machine-gun, sent his crew back to safety. He then joined his section commander Captain Arthur Inglis in *Crème de Menthe* for her lone assault on the Sugar Factory. *Chartreuse*'s steering was damaged by artillery fire between rendezvous and start point and, as a result the tank ditched at zero hours, close to the Pozières Windmill, in a shell hole which was filled with logs. Despite the crew working for three hours to extract the tank, the engine seized as *Chartreuse* was stuck at an angle and the oil could not provide sufficient lubrication.

Chablis

Chablis' skipper Geordie Campbell could trace his family line back to Charlemagne. Born on 11 January 1896, he was the younger son of Lieutenant Colonel Colin Campbell and Lady Ileene Hastings who was the second daughter of the 14th Earl of Huntingdon. Geordie was born at Clumber Castle near Worksop which was the family home of the Dukes of Newcastle; Geordie's grandmother being a daughter of the fourth duke. Geordie was bought up at his father's home, Stonefield castle in Argyllshire and then educated at Wellington School. When he was fifteen, he travelled to New York with his elder brother Colin and their uncle the Duke of Newcastle where they stayed at the Metropolitan Club on Fifth Avenue in December 1911.

Nine months after war was declared, the nineteen year old Geordie was commissioned into 3rd Battalion the Royal Sussex Regiment on 10 March 1915. He joined the Heavy Section MGC on 17 April 1916 and was awarded the Military Cross for his conduct on 15 September. The citation states

HMLS *Chablis* near Pozières September 1916. (Tank Museum)

"when his Tank broke down he sent the crew back and removed all his guns to his Commander's Tank, remaining with him throughout the entire operation and personally taking charge of one of the guns." Transferring to C Battalion in November 1916, Geordie was appointed assistant Adjutant on 28 March 1917. He assumed the role of Adjutant one month later and stayed in this post for the remainder of the war. As such, he was the only officer in C Company who served with the unit and its successors throughout the war.

Resigning his commission, Geordie married Jessie Mackie, who was the elder daughter of Sir Peter Mackie, the founder of White Horse Distillers. The wedding was held on 20 January 1921 at the Holy Trinity Church in Ayr and it was celebrated by the Bishop of Glasgow. Geordie took his wife's family name on marriage and the couple had three children; their only son Peter later serving in the Rifle Brigade during the Second World War. The family initially lived at Monkton, near Ayr, which was close to Jessie's father's estate in South Ayrshire. Geordie joined his father in-law's company and, in this role, regularly met Stuart Hastie, who had commanded *Dinnaken* on 15 September 1916 and had become a manager at the Mackie Distillery laboratory at Campbeltown in 1920. Later both men were to act as chairman of the rival distillery companies. Geordie's family later lived on their estate at Tarbet, in the Scottish Highlands, where Geordie took up farming between the wars. He returned to active service on the outbreak of war, being commissioned on 8 September 1939 and served throughout the war with the RTR. In 1951 he was appointed deputy Lord Lieutenant of Ayr, whilst living near Troon, and died at Monkton on 28 December 1956.

Sadly I have been able to find very little about one of *Chablis*' crewmen even though he was decorated towards the end of the war. Geordie's second in command, Norman Harrison, was later selected to act as a tank driving instructor under Stuart Hastie, firstly at Wailly and then at Aveluy in the rank of sergeant. In June 1918, Charles was awarded a Belgian decoration in June 1918; the citation for the Medaille d'Honneur avec Glaives en Argent stating "This NCO has been with the Mechanical School since its formation and has done exceptionally good work as assistant instructor throughout." Using the Ancestry database, I believe Norman was born in London in 1891 and was the only son of a grocer, his mother Rosa was French dressmaker named Vageneur. By 1911, Rosa had been widowed and she and Norman, who was working as a junior bank clerk, lived with his mother and grandmother in Putney. In 1915, Charles married Winifred Thom but the marriage did not survive as Norman divorced her two years later. After the war, he returned to banking and, in 1921, married Charlotte Young who was the daughter of a buyer's merchant and eight years younger than her husband. I can find little trace of Norman after his marriage. In 1927, the couple travelled to Marseilles by boat, at which time Norman was still a bank cashier but, by 1951 when his mother died, he had retired having worked as a bank accountant.

Gunner John Makin, who was born in Bolton in 1897, was decorated with the Military Medal "for conspicuous gallantry and devotion to duty. During the Battle of Arras on April 9th 1917 this man displayed the greatest gallantry in climbing out on top of his tank to remove a burning tarpaulin, although the tank was being subjected to heavy fire at the time at close range. Later when his tank was put out of action, he displayed great coolness in removing the Lewis guns to a place of safety. Throughout the action, he displayed the greatest courage and resource." Owing to the lack of detail in the unit's War Diary, it is not possible to identify where this brave act took place. John had been born the year after the marriage of his father Thomas Makin, then in his mid-twenties, to a 39 year old lady's maid named Ruth Hattin. Thomas Makin died when James was only ten but his mother lived on in Bolton until her death in 1943. The C Company landing record confirms that James arrived in France on 24 August 1916 with the second party of tank crewmen. He served with C Company, then C Battalion and then 3rd Battalion, serving on for almost 18 months after the Armistice when he was discharged as a result of sickness on 15 April 1920. He returned to Bolton and married Alice Harfield in the summer of 1921. The couple then moved to Liverpool where their daughter Sheila was born in 1924. James maintained contact with his former

Reg Acock's shop, Cheltenham, ('John Aycock').

comrades as he is listed in the 3rd Battalion Old Comrades Association in 1925, which shows he was living at 41 Knocklaid Road on Club Moor near Liverpool. The last record I can find relates to his mother's death in 1943 when James was appointed executor whilst working as a branch manager for an insurance company.

Fortunately there is more information on most of the other crewmen. For example Gunner Reg Acock was born on 30 March 1890 at Leckhampton, near Cheltenham in Gloucestershire. He was the son of a master grocer named James Acock and his wife Annie. After leaving school, Reg was an apprentice at an engineering works in Cheltenham then worked as an assistant at the Oxford branch of the Halford Cycle Company. He went on to open his own cycle shops in Tewkesbury and Cheltenham and he became very interested in motorcycling. Reg left his shop in Cheltenham to volunteer for the Motor Machine Gun Corps.

He was attested at Cheltenham on 8 February 1916 and joined for duty at Bisley on 25 March. Having been trained on machine guns, Reg joined C Company on 27 May and, less than a month later, was sent to Elveden for tank training. Reg deployed to France on 24 August and, after the first actions, was posted to C Battalion. He fought at the Battle of Arras and at Ypres, after which he was decorated with the Military Medal for conspicuous gallantry and devotion to duty. The citation states "During the 3rd Battle of Ypres, on 31st July, '17, this man, with a Lewis gun kept up covering fire from a shell hole, to enable his tank to be unditched. Later, when a 6 pdr gunner became a casualty, he took his place and put out of action several enemy machine guns. Finally, when his tank was put out of action, he worked under heavy fire to get his guns up to the infantry". Reg served with C Battalion at Cambrai and, during the Kaiserschlacht when the German Army pushed the British and French back to beyond Albert. Retrained to drive Whippets, he was appointed lance corporal on the opening day of the Battle of Amiens, 8 August 1918. Reg then fought with 3rd Battalion until the Armistice, being promoted to corporal on 3 October and Sergeant Mechanist on 26 October; this reveals the level of casualties being experienced by his battalion during the Final Advance. After the Armistice, Reg deployed with 3rd Battalion in Germany and, on 22 March 1919 he was transferred, as a sergeant, to 12th Battalion. Reg served with that unit as part of the British Army of the Rhine and was a crewman of tank L8 which formed part of the guard of honour provided at Koln for the visit of French Field Marshall Petain on 19 July 1919.

Reg remained in Germany until 18 September 1919, before he returned to England. Seven days later, he was transferred to the Z Reserve, which had been formed against the possibility that the Germans would renege on the Armistice. Reg settled in Cheltenham and, on 3 August 1920, married Anne Clark at the local Parish Church; they later had two sons Peter and Reginald. Reg was appointed manager of the Halford's Cycle shop at Hereford from 1920 to 1926. He remained working with Halfords, managing a shop in Birmingham 1926 to February 1931 and finally the shop in Gloucester until his retirement in 1956. Reg was one of the last surviving members of the First Tank Crews, becoming a great grandfather. Like many of his ilk, Reg did not discuss his wartime experiences and achievements with his family in any detail although he did talk about his time in Germany and his pals. He was however happy in his life, still enjoying a smoke and a drink until his old age. He died in his hometown of Cheltenham, aged ninety eight, on 21 December 1988; his wife of sixty-eight years marriage Anne living for another eleven years until she died aged 103.

Gunner Bill Boylin was one of the Empire men who returned to England to join the Army. Born on 1 October 1886, and christened on 7 November 1886 at Holy Trinity Church in Stroud Green. Parish records show he was the son of a teacher William Boylin and his wife Alice from Harringay. Bill was educated at Dalston but the family later moved to South Africa. Initially Bill worked with the Gresham Life Assurance Company and then as the chief clerk and cashier of the Sun Life Assurance Company of Canada. He lived with his family at Green Point near Capetown and was a keen motorcyclist. For three years, Bill was the secretary of the Cape Peninsula Motor Cycle Club,

Reg Acock (second right)
returning from Germany.
(John Aycock)

Bill Eastoe (left) Roy Garlick (centre) and Bill Boylin (right) during OTC training
(Motoring in South Africa 1 Sep 1917).

known as the CPMCC. Another club member was Roy Garlick who was to serve with him both in No 1 Section of C Company and, after they had been commissioned, as officers in 11th Battalion.

Bill joined the Motor Cycle Volunteer Corps, a militia unit, at Capetown in January 1915 and was appointed corporal on 10 December 1915. Shortly afterwards, he resigned to join the British Army and arrived in London on 6 January, enlisting in the MMGS at Coventry four days later. Bill must have felt frustrated by the failure of *Chablis* to get into action on 15 September, and was no doubt concerned for his friend Roy Garlick who had gone forward in *Crème de Menthe*. Although

Bill escaped unscathed during the attack on the Sugar Factory, he was soon in action again and was slightly injured during the action at Thiepval. As his original tank was not in action, it is not possible to say in which tank Bill fought on that day although it may have been *Crème de Menthe*. He remained in France until 13 March 1917 when he returned to the UK.

Bill and Roy Garlick had applied for commissions in the London Regiment and trained together at No 1 Officer Cadet Battalion at Newton Ferrers with their friend Bill Eastoe, who was also a member of the Cape Province Motor Cycle Club. All were commissioned into 7th Londons on 26 September 1917; Bill Boylin and Roy were seconded to the Tank Corps whilst Bill Eastoe joined the Royal Flying Corps. Bill returned to France on Christmas Eve 1917 with 11th Battalion whose officers included Roy Garlick as well as Henry Hiscocks. His record does not mention in what role he served but it was probably as an equipment officer, in which role he appointed to HQ Tank Corps on 2 October. He remained in France until 26 December 1918 when he was sent on home leave and, having returned to France, he was sent back to the UK for demobilisation on 21 January 1919.

Five weeks later, on 24 February, Bill married Bertha Mitchell at St Martin's Parish Church in Epsom who was nine years his junior. His best man was Ernest Bax, who fought with *Champagne* on 15 September and who had also been commissioned as a tank equipment officer. Bill was promoted substantive lieutenant on 26 March 1919. On demobilisation, Bill took up his old employment as a cashier but remained in the strength of the London Regiment, eventually relinquishing his commission on 30 September 1921. Soon afterwards, Bill took Bertha back to Capetown where he worked in insurance. In 1924, he was appointed to the Reserve of Officers of the Union of South Africa and reached the rank of major. He was successful in insurance, quickly becoming a manager but he regularly returning to England with Bertha. He had retired by 1938 and in November 1952, the couple moved back to England and settled in Suffolk. Sadly Bill died the following year, aged only sixty-three on 2 December 1950 at Wolfhound Cottage at Martlesham. He is buried at All Saints' Church Cemetery at Kesgrave in Suffolk.

Gunner Frank Pickworth, who was born on 29 June 1897 at Donington near Spalding, was also in insurance. He was the eldest son of a farmer at Harringworth, in Nottinghamshire, until his retirement when the family moved to Nottingham where Frank was educated. Frank, who was living at nearby Bingham in 1915, worked for the Fine Art and General Insurance Company prior to joining the Army. He volunteered to join the MMGS on 24 November 1915, as did several others in his section, and deployed to France with the C Company advance party on 16 August 1916. When C Battalion was formed, in November 1916, Frank was posted to No 8 Company with whom he fought through the Battle of Arras. Following his action during the Third Battle of Ypres, Frank was awarded the Military Medal for conspicuous gallantry. The citation states "on August 22, '17. When most of the crew of his tank had been severely wounded near Pommern Redoubt this man displayed great courage and self-sacrifice in several times passing through an intense artillery barrage in his efforts to obtain stretcher-bearers."

Frank's service record did not survive the Blitz so there is little information about the rest of his Army service. However the medal rolls confirm he continued to serve with the Tank Corps for the rest of the war. He was never promoted but, according to a Nottingham newspaper article, Frank was wounded on three occasions. The article also described how, on 18 January 1919, Frank was presented with the Military Medal, by the Mayor of Nottingham Alderman JE Pendleton. On leaving the Army, he returned home to Scarrington and to work in insurance. Frank became a broker and, in the summer of 1930, married Phoebe Parry. They settled at Rancliffe Lodge at Keyworth but sadly Phoebe died, when she was only forty, on 6 December 1942. Frank lived on at Keyworth until 1958 when at the age of sixty-one, he married Margaret Laurence. The couple settled at the White House in Hickling, near Melton Mowbray, but later moved to Trinity Road in Scarborough where Frank died, aged eighty, on 2 April 1978.

Gunner Bill Cheadle, who was born in Salford on 15 January 1889, was the youngest son of a butcher James Cheadle and his wife Sarah Ann. The youngest of nine children, six of whom survived, Bill lived with his widowed father until the latter's death in April 1913 by which time Bill was working, in his own right, as a meat and cattle salesman. Despite the fact that he was running a company, employing a number of staff, Bill volunteered to join the MMGS in November 1915. Bill was injured during the Battle of the Ancre but, as with Bill Boylin, there are no details as to when or in which tank he was fighting. After the first actions, he served on with the tanks but later was transferred from the MGC to the Labour Corps as a result of illness. In 1921, having settled in Exeter, he married Lilian Sercombe and they lived at 32 Cross Park Terrace. I have been unable to find any children. Bill, who worked as a commission agent, became one of the founder members of the Devon Branch of the Tank Corps Old Comrade Association in 1958 when Harold Mortimore was appointed deputy chairman. Bill lived in Exeter until 1974, when he died aged eighty five.

Charles Kidd, who was slightly younger than Bill, was born on 10 October 1891 in Brixton south London. His father Arthur was a decorator and Charles had six siblings, of whom only three survived childhood. Charles became a pencil maker and, in 1911, was living at 35 Linden Road at Hampton on Thames. On 23 November 1914, he enlisted at Wembley into 1st Battery MMGS RFA. He was the earliest member of the MMGS to serve in the First Tank Crews having been allocated the Regimental number 88. Charles served with J Battery MMGS from 1 May 1915 and deployed to France the following month, when he was posted to No 5 Battery MMGS which was supporting the Lahore Division. Within a month, he was admitted to No 4 General Hospital at Versailles with internal damage to his knee joint. Evacuated to the UK, Charles was treated at the Voluntary Aid Hospital at Cheltenham for six months – the problem being a nipped cartilage to the left knee. After post hospital leave, at the end of January 1916, he was posted to Bisley and later joined C Company on 27 May. After training at Elveden, Charles deployed to France on 24 August; he later transferred to C Battalion and, almost certainly, fought at the Battle of Arras. On 3 July 1917 he was again admitted to the hospital at Étaples for a month, and after a short detachment to A Battalion, was back with C Battalion on 1 September.

After the Battle of Cambrai, Charles was granted Christmas leave at home after which he rejoined the newly renamed 3rd Battalion. On 19 April 1918 he was posted to HQ 3 Tank Brigade where he served, in France and in German on occupation duties until 4 March 1919, when he was returned for demobilization at Wimbledon. In total he served 4 years and 132 days' service, the longest of any Other Ranks in the First Tank Crews. On 7 August 1920, Charles married Nellie Gerrard at St Giles' Church in Gunnersbury and the couple initially lived in South Tooting where their daughter Joyce was born in 1925. Charles stayed in the pencil making industry but later became an analytical chemist with The Royal Sovereign Pencil Company. The family moved west to Harrow in 1927, then to Hillingdon and subsequently to Ruislip. Sadly Charles separated from his wife in 1947 and his fortunes waned. He died on 20 February 1963 at Margate in Kent and is buried in an unmarked shared grave.

The final member of the crew, the driver Pte Daniel Cronin was born on 6 December 1890 at Bawnatoumple near Ballingeary in Co Cork. A farmer's son, he was the eldest of nine children. Daniel joined the ASC late in 1915. After the first actions, he continued to serve with C Company and then transferred to the MGC and later to the Tank Corps. Daniel retrained as a gunner and fought at the battles of Arras, Passchendaele and at Cambrai where, as a lance corporal, he was awarded with the Military Medal. The citation reads. "During the attack on Lateau Wood and Pam-Pam Farm, on November 20, '17, this NCO displayed the greatest gallantry in firing on the enemy with his Lewis gun, although his tank had been pierced by armour-piercing bullets. Throughout the action he showed a magnificent example of courage and cheerfulness. This NCO has been previously brought to notice for conspicuous gallantry both at Arras in April, '17, and again at Ypres on July 31, '17"

The Cork Examiner reported, on 11 October 1918, that Daniel had become an instructor in England and promoted to sergeant, having received four certificates of merit for bravery in action. Will Dawson, who served with him in C Battalion and could well have met him again at Wareham, described him as "an interesting character" which is a remarkable but impenetrable comment. After demobilisation, Daniel settled in England rather than return back to County Cork where there was the great unrest due to the Anglo-Irish War of Independence. Daniel's younger brothers were all recorded as members of the local IRA Company at the time of the truce in 1921 but, whilst there is mention of a Dan Cronin in later records, his grand-daughter Ann is convinced he was not a member. In 1924 he was living in Kent; he returned to Ireland the following year but he was back in England in 1926. Daniel married his wife Mary in the UK and the couple had a daughter. They settled at Stanhope Road in Reading and Daniel died aged sixty-three, at the Prospect Hospital in Tilehurst on 29 September 1953.

Chartreuse

It is difficult to positively identify how far *Chartreuse* reached before she became ditched. Based on the image below, and a map of the area produced in early 1917, I believe that her driver, Private Alfred Boult almost reached the Canadian front line and the tank failed close to the site of the Pozières windmill. The crew worked for three hours to try to extract her but were unable to do so. Subsequent attempts also failed despite the large number of men, based on the shovels in the picture, given the task. It is however possible that the tank's engine had seized given the position in which the tank came to rest and the lack of a pressurised lubrication which would soon have resulted in "lock-up"

Chartreuse's skipper was Stanley Clarke who was born in East Preston near Arundel on 13 October 1888. The son of a bank manager, Stanley was educated at Lancing College after which he trained as an engineer and, for a while, lived at Woolston near Southampton where there were large numbers of engineering firms. He joined the Army soon after war was declared and was

HMLS *Chartreuse* ditched close to the Pozières Windmill. (Tank Museum)

selected for officer training. Completing a short course at Pembroke College in Oxford, Stanley was commissioned in the Royal Fusiliers on 26 March 1915 and allocated to 15th Battalion, where he undertook home defence duties. He volunteered for the "secret and dangerous mission" in early 1916, was interviewed by Colonel Swinton and attached to the Heavy Section MGC on 17 April 1916.

After the first action, Stanley was detached from Inglis' section and attached to D Company. He commanded Tank No 740 during the assault by 5th Division on 26 September. On the way from Trônes Wood and Guillemont, the tank ditched at 5.30 a.m. but the crew managed to get the "bus" out and onto the start point by 3:00 p.m. when Stanley was ordered to halt and therefore took no part in the attack. He was also held in reserve for the attack on 27 September. Stanley joined C Battalion on its formation and was appointed temporary lieutenant on 1 July 1917. On 27 August 1917, he was appointed an Assistant Instructor at the School of Gunnery and was then attached from 26 September at Hotchkiss and Revolver School. On 17 December, Stanley was attached to Central Workshops and then posted to Reinforcement Depot on 1 January 1918. Granted home leave from 14 to 28 March 1918, Stanley remained at the Reinforcement Depot, probably as an instructor until 9 October 1918, when he conducted a draft of soldiers back to the United Kingdom and granted fourteen days' leave. At the end of the war, on 26 October, Stanley was in command of a company as an acting captain and is pictured at a railhead loading after the war, possibly in Germany. Stanley was then detached to Rouxmesnil, near Dieppe, for instructor duties on 17 March 1919 after which he has granted UK leave from 26 March to 18 April 1919. He did not return to the United Kingdom for demobilization until 28 June 1919.

Stanley settled at Barnet in Hertfordshire and was later employed by North Metropolitan electric supply company. In the summer of 1928, he married Frances Eade at Bournemouth; they had three sons and a daughter and settled in Harpenden. Stanley died in 12 September 1954 whilst Frances died in 1966.

Chartreuse's second in command was Corporal Reginald Shaw. Born on 29 March 1892 in Tixall, in Staffordshire, Reg was the only son of Frank Napoleon Shaw, a farmer who died when Frank was only eight years old. The following year, Reg was living with his widowed mother Helen and younger sister at Castle Church near Stafford. Having been educated at the local grammar school, Reg became an auctioneer's pupil and later became a valuer and auctioneer in his own right. He joined the MMGS on 11 November 1915 and became firm friends with Bill Stockdale. He was promoted corporal on 27 June whilst his unit was training at Elveden where he was known as Tubby. He deployed to France with the C Company advance party on 14 August 1916.

After the first actions, Reg was recommended for officer training and was commissioned into the Tank Corps on 29 August 1917. He was posted to L Battalion, which had formed at Bovington the previous month, and deployed to France on 4 January 1918 together with Captain Archie Holford-Walker and Lieutenant Jack Clarke with whom he had served in C Company. The Battalion moved to a camp near Meulte, where they were issued Mark IV tanks which had fought at the Battle of Cambrai and had received no maintenance since being withdrawn. The crewmen put them back in working order, despite the fact that twenty sevens had frozen radiators and eight needed new engines. In March, the renamed 12th Battalion moved to the north of Vimy Ridge in order to counter the expected German spring advance and was positioned so that it could retake the ground between La Bassee and Loos where the British Army had been holding the line since 1914. By April, it was clear the Germans were not to attack this area so the battalion was relocated to Arras to undertake a similar task but again did not go into action.

In May, the battalion was told it would be re-equipped with Mark V tanks but this plan was altered so that 12th Battalion would be equipped with Whippet tanks. In August, the unit commenced training at Merlimont but, after less than two weeks, the crews were taken back to Bermicourt where they were again equipped with Mark IV tanks, many of whom had seen action at Ypres twelve months before. The battalion went into action seven days later on 21 August. Reg, who was commanding the tan*k Leader*, formed part of the A Company reserve but he was soon in action and destroyed a number of machine gun posts. The battalion was also in action four times between 23 August and 3 September although Reg's name is not listed amongst the tank commanders. After the unit was withdrawn, on 8 September, to get replacement Mark IV tanks, Reg was granted two weeks home leave returning to France on 25 September. Sent back into action to the south of Cambrai, 12th Battalion was in action on 8 October, assisting the advance and destroying a number of German tanks which had been built from Mark IV hulks which had been captured the previous year. The unit was last in action on 23 October, the Mark IV tanks being worn out, and was withdrawn on 29 October to winter quarters and, two weeks later, the Armistice was declared.

Reg was granted home leave over the New Year and returned to 12th Battalion where he was promoted lieutenant on 25 February. There, he volunteered to join the Military Mission to South Russia, a training team, which consisting of eleven officers, fifty-five Other Ranks and six tanks. He sailed from France on 1 March 1919, landing at Butami in what is now Georgia. Shortly afterwards, he was sent to Novorissick where he supervised the unloading of the eleven Whippet tanks and eighteen 18 Mark V heavy tanks which were to be used as a training fleet. Having been appointed as an instructor, Reg was promoted acting captain on 16 March and made responsible for Whippet driver training and unit battle practice. The training team moved north to Ekaterinodr, now known as Krasnodar, where a tank school was established for the White Russian Forces. Training however was not complete by the time the White Russian general Deniken commenced operations in May 1919 who used members of the training team to lead the Russian crews into action. Reg meantime moved to Tarangog, where a battle practice ground school was established. Whilst Reg continued his task, the small number of British-crewed tanks was used to break through the Bolshevik defences around Tsaritsin (now Volgograd) which lead to the city's capture in June 1919. General Deniken's advance almost reached Moscow in October but he was soon forced to withdraw. In December, the British cabinet decided to abandon their support to the White Russian and the bulk of British forces were ordered to return to the United Kingdom, although some elements stayed until the spring of 1920. Reg was awarded two Russian medals for his service including the orders of St Anna and St Vladimir, presented for exemplary service to the Czar.

Reg was also awarded the MBE for his service in Russia. He arrived by boat at London on New Year's Day 1920 and, twenty days later, he was discharged from the Army, on the grounds of ill-health, and was granted the rank of captain. Reg was suffering from colitis and received a 20% disability pension. His medal record card shows he settled at Iron Hill near Byfield in Northamptonshire and, according to Pat Trevor who has researched Reg's later life, married but his wife subsequently died in childbirth. By 1922, Reg moved to Eccleshall in Staffordshire, where he worked for a draper and insurance firm called Garlick in the town. He never remarried but lodged at Ivy Mount on the High Street, until his death. Reg was principally involved in farm insurance work but his firm was also the focus for fire insurance in the area. The local brigade captain has been Harry Garlick from 1890 until 1920 and Reg took over the role in the interwar years. On the formation of the National Fire Service in 1941, he became the Station officer and was pictured with his prize winning team in the local paper wearing their steel helmets. He lived at Eccleshall until his death, aged sixty-one on 9 June 1953 and is buried in the local churchyard.

Many of the tank crewmen were associated with drapery and clothing including Gunner Ernest Edwards. Born on 4 November 1892 at Haverhill, Ernest was the only son of a tailor's cutter named William and his wife Elizabeth. Ernest followed his father into the clothing business and moved with the family to Newhaven in Sussex. He enlisted, at the age of twenty three, into the MMGS at Coventry on 24 November 1915. Having joined the Armoured Car Section on 1 April, Ernest was posted to C Company on 25 May and deployed to France on 16 August. There is no record of his actions after 15 September until he was posted to C Battalion on its formation. He was

Reg Shaw wearing British and Russian medal ribbons on his uniform as captain of Eccleshall Fire Brigade. (Staffordshire Archives and Heritage)

Eccleshall National Fire Brigade during the Second World War. (Staffordshire Archives and Heritage)

appointed paid acting lance corporal on 20 February 1917 as the Battalion reached its full strength. Just after the Battle of Arras, he was sent to the 17th Corps Lewis Gun School and then sent as an instructor, for three weeks, to 2nd Tank Brigade's gunnery school. Immediately afterwards, he was sent to the driving school at Wailly for a driving course where he showed sufficient skill to be re-assigned to the role of driver. Serving with C Battalion throughout the Third Battle of Ypres, he was graded as Tank Mechanist 1st Class and promoted corporal on 6 November 1917 as the Battalion was preparing for the Battle of Cambrai. After the battle, he was granted home leave from 6 to 16 December, returning to his unit for Christmas. He remained with 3rd Battalion when it re-roled to light tanks and served through the Battle of Amiens. He returned to England on 24 September 1918 and was posted to the Tank Depot. He was promoted sergeant on 6 November and, like Arthur Milliken, was posted to 22nd Light Tank Battalion where Ernest served as a Mechanist with C Company. He was transferred to Z Reserve on 23 February 1919 and returned to Newhaven, where he was still living in 1925.

Gunner Alex Garden was born on 8 October 1895 in Aberdeen. Alex was working as a clerk for a produce merchant named AR Gray on the Upper Quay, when he enlisted at his hometown on 17 November 1915. He was unusual in that he did not enlist at Coventry but was sent directly to the MMGS Depot at Bisley arriving the following day. Having deployed to France on 16 August, with the main body, and been uninjured during the first actions, Alex remained with C Battalion on its formation. During the follow-up training, he was admitted with tonsillitis to 12 Stationary Hospital at St Pol. After the Battle of Arras, he attended gunnery training in May and then a driving course at Wailly in June. Having fought with C Battalion through the Third Battle of Ypres and Cambrai, Alex was granted two weeks home leave before rejoining before Christmas. He was detached to the Mechanical School in early 1918 but his duties are not specified. He must however have maintained his skills as a driver and undertaken a conversion course to drive the new Whippet tanks.

Whilst Alex was at the Mechanical School, 3rd Battalion was heavily in action during the Battle of Amiens and the advance towards the Belgian border. In early October, he was sent back to his old unit to replace one of the many casualties. Alex arrived on 3 October 1918 and was sent into battle that same day as the Battalion was supporting the attack of XIII Corps on the Hindenburg line.

Alex was allocated to A Company and was the driver of the tank *Casa III*, the name originally being borne by Victor Smith's tank in 1916. His time away from the unit had not reduced his fighting spirit but enhanced it. Although *Casa* was hit, and all three of the crewmen were wounded, Alex determinedly drove on. To quote from the Military Medal citation "near Estrees his tank was hit by antitank rifle fire and the crew wounded, although wounded himself brought the Whippet out of action and conveyed the badly-wounded personnel to a dressing station. After having his own wound dressed he remained at duty, and endeavored to drive his whippet to a rallying point through heavily shelled area. His great coolness and presence of mind showed a high sense of duty and he remained with his whippet until relieved by his company commander."

Alex's wounds were so bad that he was evacuated back to the UK on 18 October 1918. Whilst he was being treated, the award of the Military Medal was announced in the local newspaper, the *Aberdeen Evening Express*, on 15 November. Alex was not well enough to return to his duties until after the New Year when he was posted to 24th Battalion, the officer cadet training unit, on 4 January 1919. He was immediately promoted to corporal and tank mechanist. He had looked for work, during the Christmas leave and rejoined his former employer Grays on 17 January 1919. Demobilised from the Army one month later, he returned to Aberdeen after which I can find nothing more about him.

Gunner George Stonehouse was also a Scotsman and a clerk. Born on 4 October 1894 at Edinburgh, he was the son of a licensed grocer who lived at Clark Street. On 11 November 1915, he enlisted at Edinburgh and was training at Bisley within a fortnight. He was quite a small man, only

5 feet 3 inches tall, but this would have had been of an advantage to George as well as his fellow tank crewmen, given the limited height in the fighting compartment of a tank. George deployed to France on 16 Aug 1916 and, like his fellow crewmen, transferred to C Battalion on formation. He almost certainly fought at the Battle of Arras, probably as a machine gunner. The next month, he attended a 6 pounder gunnery training course, at the 2nd Tank Brigade School, followed by a driving course at Wailly from 11 to 19 June.

Rebadged to the Tank Corps, George fell foul of military discipline on 11 August, when he was sentenced to be Confined to Barracks for 5 days as his revolver was not properly maintained. Having fought during the Battle of Cambrai, he was granted home leave from 5 to 19 December. George stayed with 3rd Battalion as it re-roled to Whippets and re-trained as driver. He fought right through to the end of the war, being granted home leave after the Armistice from 27 November to 11 December 1918 – sadly he delayed his return by one day and forfeited one days' pay – however George was not otherwise punished. Never promoted, George did not leave A Company of 3rd Battalion until 15 February 1919 and was demobilised from Duddingston camp, close by his home in Edinburgh, on 15 March 1919. In 1942, George married Alice and they established a licensed grocery business initially at 37 Marionville Road and then they opened a second shop at 2 Dalkeith Road. George died in Edinburgh on 28 March 1958 but the company continued to operate until 1975.

Gunner Alf Simpson probably learned about the MMGS whilst visiting his parents as their home at Brookwood is about fifteen minutes' walk from the MMGS depot. Born in London on 7 December 1892, Alf was the second son of a newsagent after whom he was named, and his wife Bertha Finnis. They were living at 416 Northampton Buildings in Clerkenwell when Alf was christened on 27 January 1893 at St James's Church. Alf, who was bought up in Islington, worked on the London Evening Standard circulation staff from 1909. His family had settled at Brookwood before the war but Alf was living at 15 Magland Street in Highbury, and working as a newspaper cyclist, when he enlisted in the MMGS in early December 1915. His parents must have been extremely anxious as Alf's elder brother Arthur had been Killed in Action on 13 May 15 whilst serving with 3rd Battalions Middlesex Regiment in the Ypres Salient. His grave was lost and he was later commemorated on Menin gate

Alf was a tall man, just short of six feet, and with a well-developed chest measuring thirty-eight inches. After training at Bisley and Elveden, Alf deployed to France on 16 August. Although he did not get into action on 15 September, he fought with D Company at Beaumont-Hamel on 14 November with either Harry Drader or Hugh Bell as he recalls being in a tank stuck in the mud yet convincing large numbers of Germans to surrender. Alf continued to serve with C Battalion on its formation. He was injured at the Battle of Arras but soon returned to the Battalion. He fought at the 3rd Battle of Ypres and awarded a Tank Corps Card of Honour for fighting his tank for thirteen hours.

Alf was also at Cambrai, as a driver, and was in a section fighting towards Bleak House, on the eastern side of the battlefield on 20 November. After the lead tank was hit, Alf's tank became stuck in the third barbed wire entanglements and one crewman was shot in the ankle as the crew cut themselves out. Alf's tank was also hit by direct fire by German 5.9 inch gun from Lateau Wood but fortunately only one crewman was injured. From his description Alf's tank could well have been *Comet II* commanded by 2Lt P D T Powell. Alf returned to the rally point on foot and later drove a salvaged tank in later actions during the battle. He also took part in the grisly removing the remains of dead crewmen from E Battalion's burnt out hulks at Flesquières.

Alf stayed with C Battalion and fought through to the Armistice operating Whippets. On demobilization, he returned to employment with London Evening Standard and became an early member of the Fleet Street branch of the British Legion. On 10 June 1923, he married Elizabeth Garwood and their son Alfred Bernard Simpson was born in Willesden in the spring of 1925.

Alfred junior followed his father into the newspaper distribution business. Following the Find the Link TV programme on 3 September 1956, which featured Victor Smith and Victor Huffam, he corresponded with Basil Liddell Hart in September 1957, providing lots of details about the first tank action. He was also interviewed by John Foley, who has incorporated his memories of training at Elveden and on the Somme, in the "Boilerplate War" which was published shortly after Alf's death on New Year Eve 1962; his wife Elisabeth dying in 1971.

Only one of the service records for a number of *Chartreuse* crewmen did not survive the Blitz and that was for Gunner Charles Phillips who deployed to France on 16 August 1916. *The Motor Cycle* records he came from New Malden in Surrey and joined the MMGS on 24 November 1915, the same day as Lionel McAdam and Roy Garlick. The Medal Rolls confirm that he was posted to G Battalion and was later promoted acting corporal in the Tank Corps. Although he survived the war; I can find nothing else about him. In comparison, and most unusually, a lot is known about the tank's driver, Pte Alfred Boult ASC. The oldest member of the crew, Alfred was born near Scarborough at the turn of 1880. He was the son of a gardener and bought up in Stocksley but, by 1901, Alfred was working an ironmonger's assistant in Leamington Spa. He then moved back to Yorkshire and married, on 22 August 1904, Jane Miles at Brompton Wesleyan Methodist Church. Their only daughter Kathleen was born at Leeds on 28 December 1904. By 1911, Alf was an ironmonger in his own right, living in 65 Lorne Terrace on the south bank of the river Tees in Middleborough.

Alf volunteered to join the Army in early 1915. Now aged thirty-five, his medical records shows he was in good health although he had to wear glasses. As a special enlistment, with no previous military service, he was required to undertake a MT trade test on 5 January 1915 which showed him to be a skilled driver and mechanic. Attested two weeks later at York, he joined the ASC at Grove Park MT Reserve Depot in London at the end of the month.

Alf was initially posted to Norwood and then deployed to Boulogne, arriving on 11 March 1915. He was posted to No 16 Siege Battery as part of 272 Company ASC and then, unusually for an ASC driver, to 54 Brigade Artillery Ammunition Column. On 10 May 1916 Alf was posted to 363 MT Company which supported V Corps Heavy Artillery but then was sent back to the UK on 12 June "for the New Armies." He deployed with 711 MT Company on 16 August from Avonmouth to Le Havre; arriving on 22 August with the tanks. The following day, Alf created delays to the tank deployment, when he left a train without permission, being absent when the train was about to leave from Le Havre. On 28 August he was awarded fourteen days Confined to Barracks for the offence. Other than his action on 15 September, little is known of his service with the tanks. In January 1917 Alf was on C Battalion's held strength, employed as a driver, when his general ability was assessed as "fair but unsuitable for the Heavy Branch". As a result, in 27 January 1917 he was sent to No 1 MT Base Depot and, on 7 February, he was posted to No 5 Auxiliary Company ASC where served as a caterpillar driver. Alf served in France for another eleven months but his health was not good. On 9 April 1918, he was admitted to hospital with an ulcer on his left leg which took two months to cure, before he returned to 5 Auxiliary Company ASC. On 24 November he was again admitted to No 2 Stationary Hospital, this time suffering from scabies but he was back with his unit on 5 December 1917. He celebrated News Year Day 1918 by being admitted to hospital at Abbeville, this time due to knee problems, where he and remained until 5 February 1918. On 18 March he was again admitted to hospital and evacuated back to England on 27 March 1918 where he was recorded as suffering from boils. He was eventually discharged from the Central Military Hospital at Chatham and, after leave at Knaresborough, was examined at the Royal Military Hospital Woolwich as his eyesight had become poor. Classified as fit for duty on 2 July, he was posted to the Tractor Depot at Avonmouth until 17 September when he deployed to Italy. In October 1918, he was fined 28 days' pay for being "in the unlawful possession of the property of the Italian Railways". He stayed on in Italy, after the Armistice serving at the MT Evacuation

Depot in Milan, extracting vehicles used in the Italian campaign until 19 July 1919. Returning to the UK, he was transferred to the Z Reserve on 28 August 1919 when his home address was given as Kilmore Grange, Felixkirk near Thirsk. Thereafter he disappears from view until his death in West Yorkshire in 1961.

Crème de Menthe

Crème de Menthe was, for many years, the best known of all the tanks which fought in the first action. Her picture was the first ever published in the United Kingdom on 14 November 1916 when the *Daily Mirror* obtained a copy of which was originally published in Canada. She was also used as the model for ceramic tanks sold at towns across the United Kingdom to celebrate the invention and success of the tanks.

Crème de Menthe was the only one of the three tanks, tasked to 2nd Canadian Division attack on the Courcelette Sugar Factory, which actually engaged the Germans. According to Lionel McAdam, who described the action in an article published in Toronto in August 1919, the rear of *Crème de Menthe* was hit by two German shells as she waited to go into the attack at her start point near the site of the Pozières windmill. The result was the tank was lifted onto her nose and then dropped back which shook the crew pretty thoroughly and blew half of the steering tail away. The tank started her advance just as dawn was breaking and whilst there was a little ground mist. The tank's route was along the line of the Pozières to Bapaume road was a morass of shell holes; some of which were nine feet deep. The Canadian infantry had been halted by the Germans defenders, and their heads were down. Private Donald Fraser, who was serving with 31st Canadian Battalion, recorded the impact of the tank's appearance.

> As the attack subsided and not a soul moved in No Man's Land save the wounded twisting and moaning in their agony, it dawned upon me that the assault was a failure and now we were at the mercy of the enemy. It was suicide to venture back and our only hope lay in waiting until darkness set in and then trying to win our way back. During this period of waiting, I expected we would be deluged by bombs, shrapnel and shell fire, and when darkness set in, ravaged by machine-gun fire, altogether a hopeless outlook, especially for our lot, who were lying up against his trench. The situation seemed critical and the chances of withdrawal to safety nigh

Crème de Menthe in action on 15 September 1916.

impossible. So many things had happened, so many lives were snuffed out since I left the comparative safety of our front line, that I lost completely all idea of time.

Lying low in the shell hole contemplating events with now and then a side glance at my sandy-moustached comrade, lying dead beside me, his mess tin shining and scintillating on his back, a strange and curious sight appeared. Away to my left rear, a huge gray object reared itself into view, and slowly, very slowly, it crawled along like a gigantic toad, feeling its way across the shell-stricken field. It was a tank, the "*Créme de Menthe*," the latest invention of destruction and the first of its kind to be employed in the Great War. I watched it coming towards our direction.

How painfully slow it travelled. Down and up the shell holes it clambered, a weird, ungainly monster, moving relentlessly forward. Suddenly men from the ground looked up, rose as if from the dead, and running from the flanks to behind it, followed in the rear as if to be in on the kill. The last I saw of it, it was wending its way to the Sugar Refinery. It crossed Fritz's trenches, a few yards from me, with hardly a jolt.

When first observed it gave new life and vigour to our men. Seeing away behind men getting up, and no one falling, I looked up and there met the gaze of some of my comrades in the shell holes. Instinctively I jumped up and quickly, though warily, ran to where I could see into Fritz's trench, with bayonet pointing and finger on the trigger. Running my eyes up and down his trench, ready to shoot if I saw any signs of hostility, and equally on the alert to jump out of view if I saw a rifle pointing at me, it was a tense and exciting moment but I felt marvelously fit and wits extremely acute, for any encounter. I expected opposition and was ready for danger, but a swift glance, and to my amazement, not a German was staring at me, far less being defiant. Down the trench about a hundred yards, several Huns, minus rifles and equipment, got out of their trench and were beating it back over the open, terrified at the approach of the tank.

Crème de Menthe's progress was indeed "painfully slow". Having no suspension, and with the crew being badly shaken every inch she travelled across the battlefield, *Crème de Menthe* plunged down into the shell craters, dragged her way out the other side and slowly straddled the shell-torn trench lines arriving at the Sugar Factory after the first of the Canadian infantry. Her progress was also slowed by the large numbers of German infantrymen who tried to surrender. However, the tank's arrival at the Factory was timely for, as she arrived, a Canadian infantry officer bought a message stating that the attack had been held up. The tank's 6 pdr guns enabled the factory wall to be breached and, as Crème de Menthe entered into the factory, resistance weakened and broke. As the Canadian infantry organised their defence, the tank pushed forward about fifteen hundred yards and patrolled the area against the expected counter-attack. When this did not occur, *Crème de Menthe* returned to the factory and then retraced her route towards Pozières. Some newspaper accounts state that the tank carried a German colonel, who had commanded the defences of the Factory, and that he was furious at the use of tanks, however Lionel McAdam however states this incident involved one of the northern group of tanks which attacked Courcelette village.

On her way back, the tank deployed an armoured cable to provide communications between the former Canadian front line positions and their new outpost. Sadly a German artillery shell destroyed the cable drum, which was attached to *Crème de Menthe's* hull, just as she approached her rally point which is now the site of the Tank Corps Memorial at Pozières Windmill. The Germans shells also caused one of the tank tracks to crack but *Crème de Menthe's* driver George Shepherd managed to drive the tank out of the firing zone at which point one of the tracks fell off. A guard party was then bought up and the crew, who had been in action for fourteen hours, was able to walk back to their camp.

Crème de Menthe went into action again on 26 September, accompanied by *Cordon Rouge*, in support of the 18th Division attack on Thiepval. She was delayed in crossing no man's land from

HMLS *Crème de Menthe* near Thiepval Chateau – October 1916. (Tank Museum)

Thiepval Wood but arrived in time to crush the resistance of the German machine gun teams around the chateau. This allowed the infantry, who had been stopped by those machine guns, to take the position. *Crème de Menthe* then moved forward but became ditched across a trench just yards north of the Chateau's ruins. Owing to the state of the ground, it was not possible to recover *Crème de Menthe* and the hulk was use for a while as an oil lamp signaling station and store whilst the southern side of the river Ancre was cleared of German troops in October 1916.

Crème de Menthe's driver Corporal George Shepherd was awarded the Distinguished Conduct Medal for his actions on 15 September which was the first ever such award to a tank crewman. The citation states this medal was "for conspicuous gallantry and skill in driving the Tank of his Section Commander throughout an action. It was entirely due to Pte Shepherd's skill and courage that it reached its objective, and was successfully withdrawn." George was born in Warrington in Cheshire on 3 August 1892 and was the eldest son of a successful butcher and shopkeeper after whom he was named. George had three younger sisters, Lila, Elsie and Annie and a younger brother named Fred who, like George worked for their father in the family business in Orford Road. He joined the Territorial Force on 9 December 1912 and served, as a butcher, in the West Lancashire Division Transport and Supply Column which was based in Warrington. At the time of his enlistment, George was five feet ten inches tall and weighed just under fourteen stone. Initially serving with No 3 Company, he attended the unit annual camp in Denbigh in August 1913.

With the outbreak of year, George achieved rapid promotion as second corporal, corporal and then sergeant on three successive days between 4 and 6 August 1914. The division was sent to Sussex and on 4 January 1915, George volunteered for overseas service. Four months later, George was discharged on 24 May 1915, having been "convicted of an offence by the civil powers" but his record does not reveal the nature of the offence. Given however that he was a senior NCO, aged only twenty-two years of age, the offence must have been grave. Shortly afterwards, George joined the ASC again this time as a learner driver and was later allocated to 711 MT Company. Given his previous experience, it is not surprising that he was quickly appointed acting sergeant. When the new tank battalions were formed in France, in early 1917, George rebadged to the MGC and later to the Tank Corps. Promoted to sergeant, he served at the Mechanical School as an instructor on 15 August 1917. Later he served as a staff sergeant and, according to a local Liverpool paper, as a sergeant-major although I can find no other evidence of this.

After he was demobilised, George returned to Liverpool and took over the management of a motor garage in Anfield. He lived with his wife Catherine, who had previously worked as a conductress on the Portabello trams in Scotland, in the Manningham road together with his cousin Phyllis Baldry who lodged with the couple. In the early hours of 29 November 1919, Phyllis found George's body in the kitchen and Catherine's body was discovered in the vestibule of their home. The inquest heard that George had attempted to cut his throat in the kitchen but was initially prevented from killing himself by Catherine who threw her arms around him. George then shot his wife, twice, using a revolver and then killed himself with the razor. Catherine meanwhile attempted to seek help but collapsed on the way to the front door as a result of fatal injuries. The court heard evidence from one witness that Phyllis and George had been sweethearts, prior to his marriage to Catherine, but Phyllis denied this. The jury concluded that George had committed suicide and, in the process, had killed his wife. There was however no evidence to show his state of mind had been affected; a verdict which today would be unlikely given what is known about post-traumatic stress disorder.

The crew's second in command was a South African named Roy Garlick. Born on 1 May 1892 in Cape Town, he was the youngest son of John Garlick and Ellen Miller. John was the founder of the Garlick's department store, in Cape Town, unusual for those days in that it had a thriving type-writer agency that offered typing schools and also a cycle supply store that grew into the Garlick's Motor and Cycle Supply importing the first cars for resale into South Africa with a brisk trade in motorcycles. Roy's father later became a noted philanthropist who supported the foundation of a sanatorium for the relief of tuberculosis at Nelspoort as well as the University of Capetown. Roy, who was christened Ronald Roderick Garlick, and his older brother Archie were educated in England, initially at West House School in Edgbaston and then at Tonbridge School from 1906 to 1908 where Roy served in the OTC.

During school holidays, Roy and his brothers were in the care of Frederic Mason Matthews, a partner in the firm Hollingsworth and Matthews who were John Garlick's agent in London. In 1907 Archie was commissioned into the Royal Navy whereas Roy was articled to the firm of the chartered accountants Josolyne, Miles & Co, from 1910. He lodged with Ellen Huggett at Forest Hill in southeast London and part of his training was as a law student. His studies over, he returned to Capetown and joined the family business working as a clerk.

It was around this time that Roy joined the Cape Peninsula Motor Cycle Club and there first met Bill Boylin. In November 1915, Roy returned to England to join the Army. His family was kept informed of his progress in letters and cables sent between the Garlick's offices in London and Cape Town. To a letter written by F M Matthews, on 12 November 1915, there was a postscript: "Roy looked in the office on Thursday. He was then going to find out what was best to join". A week later, there was another message "Roy has not fixed up anything. They don't appear to be wanting men, except for the Infantry and for that branch unlimited numbers are needed". It is interesting that Roy did not try to join the Royal Navy, in which his brother was serving, but rather joined the MMGS on 24 November 1915. In early 1916, Roy met his first wife, Grace Greaves who was the daughter of a civil servant from Battersea. It is fairly clear that Roy did not let his family know he was serving with the tanks. In a letter of 23 September 1916, Frederick Matthews wrote "I have posted two copies of the Daily Chronicle, in which are details of the doings of the armoured cars, which I thought might interest you, as I think it certain Roy was in one of them".

Roy served on with C Battalion until he obtained a commission with Bill Boylin in the "Shiny" 7th Battalion London Regiment, the CO being a fellow South African from Cape Town, Sir

Pieter Stewart-Bam. The two men undertook their pre-commissioning training at No 1 Officer Cadet Battalion at Newton Ferrers in Devon and were commissioned on 27 September 1917. Roy soon found infantry life "less desirable" and on 3 December was seconded to the Tank Corps. He returned to Wareham that same day but his service record gives no details of his time as a tank officer. His family were also in the dark for, as late as 31 December 1918, cables were sent from Cape Town to ascertain his whereabouts; "We are very anxious indeed to know how he is getting along and shall be glad if you would cable us regularly until he is quite out of danger." What we do know is that he was awarded the Croix de Guerre on 3 June 1919, for his service with 11th Battalion. This means he served with his friend, Bill Boylin as well as Herbert Elliot, Herbert Hiscocks and Hugh Bell who was killed in action in September 1918 whilst serving with the Battalion.

Roy did not relinquish his commission until 1 September 1921. Earlier that year, on 12 February, Roy had married Grace Greaves, who was living in Lower Sloane Street in Chelsea. Their twin daughters, Isobel and Pamela were born on 22 October 1922 but the marriage did not last and Roy returned to Cape Town. He worked in Garlick's Head Office, where he had responsibility for the firm's buildings and fabric. He later managed the company's car and motorcycle sales department. On 21 April 1927, he married Gladys Faure and they visited the UK the following year. Nine years later, on 1 July 1936, Gladys died from malaria whilst the couple was in Mozambique. Roy's third wife was Flora Burmeister. Lolie, as she was known was eighteen years Roy's junior and they had two children Gillian and Ronald, who was known as Rory.

Roy Garlick in the 1920s. (Gill Doddington)

Roy Garlick and his daughter Gill in the 1940s. (Gill Doddington)

During the Second World War, Roy was commissioned into the South Africa Defence Force, serving in Pretoria and then at the Dynamite Factory at Somerset West to the south of Cape Town. In the 1940s, the family settled at the Homestead, at St James, on the False Bay coast which is an idyllic spot. In 1953 Roy returned for two months to England but he soon returned home to Cape Town where he died on 24 February 1960.

The left male gunner, Lionel McAdam, was unique amongst the First Tank Crews that he was a Canadian citizen who paid his own way to England to join the British Army. *Mac*, as he was known, was born on 17 April 1891 at South River in Ontario. He was the youngest of five children of Samuel and Sarah Rebecca Bond who was known as Becky. Lionel was also a nephew of a Canadian politician William Templeman who later became Minister for Inland Revenue in the Federal Government. Lionel's father died in 1898 in Buffalo, New York, during a confrontation with a business partner who was accused of embezzling funds from their sawmill operation in South River. Becky, who was left to raise the five children, moved the family to Toronto and became a school teacher. Mac left school early to help support the family but he had difficulty gaining a job. Eventually, in 1905, he found work with the Toronto Railway Street Company, which operated electrically powered tramcars along a grid of roads.

In September 1914, at the start of the war, Mac tried to enlist in the Canadian Expeditionary Force but, as he was only five feet one inch tall, he was rejected. Deciding to join the Royal Flying Corps, he gained permission from his employers to travel to England. Mac saved for several months before sailing from Montréal to London at his own expense arriving in England on 30 August 1915. Unable to join the RFC, due to oversubscription, Mac enlisted in the MMGS on 22 November 1915 and reported to Bisley the next day. After initial machine gun training, which Mac is seen undertaking in image (page 15), and a short course on the 6 pdr gun, he moved with C Company to Elveden in May. There Mac undertook plenty of gunnery practice, including using the 6 pdr gun to destroy a cottage. Mac deployed to France, with the first main body, on 16 August 1916 and thereafter fought with C Company for the rest of the year. His family recalls a story told by Mac that one of his crewmates, who was much taller than Mac, was badly wounded when a German shell hit the door of the tank causing the leg to be crushed and ultimately amputated. Mac joined C Battalion on its formation and moved with it to the new Tank Administrative Area near St Pol. He must have been sent back to the front line, probably on salvage work, as on 25 January, Mac was admitted to hospital with shrapnel wounds to the legs. His injuries were so severe that he was not expected to be able to return to C Battalion and he was evacuated to the UK and treated at No 2 Western Hospital in Manchester. His injuries were later reported in the *Toronto Star*. Mac however made a full recovery and he was posted to the Depot Battalion at Bovington on 13 April 1917.

Less than six weeks later, he deployed back to France with F Battalion's Workshop Company. He later told his family, when repairing a damaged tank, that he came face to face with a very young German soldier. They stood and stared at each other for a moment but Mac realised he was in danger and shot first. He told them that this was the first time that he killed a man on a one to one basis, rather than shoot at enemy with a machine gun, and it haunted him. This tragic event probably took place south of St Julian on 1 August when F Battalion's Workshop Company deployed to recover sixteen tanks which had ditched in the swamp-like conditions which 16 and 18 Companies encountered on 31 July 1917.

The first two weeks of August were spent trying to get more tanks back into action. On 25 September, Mac was hospitalised for a month. He rejoined F Battalion and again served with the Workshop Company during the Battle of Cambrai in the latter part of November. After tank repair was centralized, and the workshop companies disbanded on 11 January, Mac was posted to the Central Stores at Erin and, then granted leave in the United Kingdom in February 1918. He returned to No 1 Tank Stores and served with that unit for the next twelve until he demobilised on

Lionel McAdam whilst serving with the Central Stores. (Sue Handley)

7 March 1919. During his service, he was wounded a second time although his medical records do not reveal when this occured.

Mac returned to Canada, on 22 May 1919, where he rejoined the Toronto Street Railway Company. He wrote three articles on his initial service with the tanks, under the pen name of Gunner, which were published in the July, August and September editions of the local Motor magazine. Mac was subsequently awarded an enhanced war pension by the Canadian Government as the British pension was less than that paid to those who fought with the Canadian forces. In 1921, Mac's company was amalgamated with the Toronto Transit Commission and, on 28 September 1922 Mac married Leila Charlton at York near Toronto. Leila was an accomplished dance teacher at the Amy Sternberg studios and she had two sons named Charlton and David. The couple had a cottage at Wasaga beach on Lake Simcoe, which is about two hours travel from Toronto where Mac took his whole family, teaching his boys to swim and enjoying time away from his work. Mac continued to work with the Transit Commission becoming an electrical engineer. At work, he became known as "Doc" as he initiated the fitting of first aid kits to the tram-cars for use in accidents.

During the Second World War, Mac served in 2 Field Park Company of the Royal Canadian Engineers based at York near Toronto. His son Charlton who joined the unit at the age of sixteen in 1942, later trained as a parachutist at the Canadian Forces Base at Shilo. His unit was in Halifax, waiting for a troopship to take them to Europe in 1945 when Germany surrendered.

Lionel and Charlton McAdam in 1942. (Sue Handley)

Mac, meantime, continued to work as an electrical engineer for the Toronto Transit Company. He retired in 1957 from having completed fifty years of continuous employment. His grandchildren remember Mac as "as a warm-hearted man with a puckish sense of humour", keen to teach them cribbage and always delighted by their company. They also tell that his favorite breakfast was bacon, eggs and toast with piccalilli and Mac carried a copy of Fitzgerald's translation of the "Rubiyat of Omar Khayyam" throughout the war, reading being his passion from the age of three. Mac retired to the Blythwood Road where he died aged eighty two on 31 May 1973.

Someone who would not be expected to join the Army, little alone be prepared to fight in *Crème de Menthe*, was Gunner Laurie Rowntree. Laurie, who was a Quaker, was the grandson of the social reformer Joseph Rowntree. At the time conscription was introduced in 1916, many Quakers in York became conscientious objectors but Laurie was not amongst them – he joined the Machine Gun Corps. Laurie, who was born on 4 March 1895, was the only son of John Rowntree, a chocolate factory director, and his wife Constance Naish who built their home at Low Hall at Scalby near Scarborough. Laurie's father died in New York in 1905 at the age of 36. Laurie, who had three sisters, was educated at Bootham School – the Quaker boarding school in York from 1905 to 1912 where he played in the first XI football team and was captain of the school fire brigade. He was also keen on running and riding, swimming and lifesaving as well as a motorcyclist enthusiast. On leaving school, Laurie visited America before entering King College Cambridge in October 1913 to study medicine.

On the outbreak of war, he joined the Friends Ambulance Unit (FAU) and, with some other sixty young Quakers, undertook pre-deployment training consisting of first aid, stretcher drill, field cookery, sanitation and hygiene at Jordan's, the Quaker centre in Buckinghamshire. Towards the end of October, the FAU was asked to assist the plight of the Belgian Army and they deployed to Dunkirk. Laurie was given his grandfather's Rolls Royce car which he had modified to transport medical supplies. He initially made daily trips from Dunkirk to Poperinghe, and then between Poperinghe and Ypres and the villages to the south and east. Although a non-combatant, he was regularly under enemy fire but, after Christmas 1914 when his car became unusable, Laurie acted as a hospital orderly. As the Army Medical Services expanded, the role of the FAU switched to caring for Belgian civilians. Laurie was near Ypres when the Germans used poison gas for the first time and the FAU was asked to assist the British forces in the Salient. In August 1915, after ten months overseas, Laurie felt he was no longer making a useful contribution and returned to York where he worked at the Haxby Road Military Hospital. As conscription was being introduced, he

Lawrie Rowntree wearing the uniform of the Friends Ambulance Unit. (Rowntree Society)

volunteered to join the MMGS. He was enlisted by Geoffrey Smith at Coventry on 16 May and, as an experienced motorcyclist, approved for the MMGS. A record of a medical examination undertaken that same day confirms he was just short of five feet nine inches, weighed eleven stone nine pounds and had a thirty six-inch chest. Lawrie was accepted for service at Bullhouse Farm Camp neat Bisley on 23 May 16 and allocated to C Company five days later. After completing tank training at Elveden, he deployed to France with C Company on 16 August 1916.

Laurie was injured during the first action on 15 September although this is not recorded by Arthur Inglis in his post action report or in Laurie's service record. On 27 September, The *York Press* newspaper reported he had been shot by a sniper and evacuated back to the UK, being hospitalised in Edinburgh. I believe that Laurie's wounds were actually caused by German shrapnel just before the tank went into action in an incident described by Lionel McAdam in his article published in August 1919. Having recovered from his wounds, Laurie was posted to Bovington. He was recommended for a commission by the former York MP, Sir Frederick Milner, and reported to the Royal Artillery Cadet School at Topsham Barracks in Exeter on 5 January 1917. Having completed initial officer training he was commissioned on 12 April into the Royal Field Artillery (RFA). Following more training at Bordon, in Hampshire, Laurie returned to the Western Front on 15 July 17. He served with A Battery 26 Brigade RFA, during the Third Battle of Ypres otherwise known as the Battle of Passchendaele. After three months, he was granted home leave but shortly after he returned to the Salient, was Killed in Action on 25 November 1917. He is buried at the Commonwealth War Graves Commission Cemetery at Vlamertinghe.

A number of those who served with C Company later served with the Royal Air Force and one such was Gunner Ronald Gibson. Born on 13 November 1888 in Earlestown, to the west of Newton-le-Willows, Ronald was the youngest son of John and Lydia Gibson. By 1911, he was working as an estate agent and living with his parents at Bootle where he married Marjorie Wood on 5 August 1914. Ronald did not volunteer for service until 1916; this may have been because he was quite short being only five feet one inch tall. He was employed as an under-manager in wood-working company when he was attested on 22 March 1916. His wife was pregnant and their daughter Marjorie was born just before he deployed to France. Ronald served with C Battalion then 3rd Light Tank Battalion until 18 July when he returned to England to join the RAF as a learner pilot. He attended No 1 School of Aeronautics at Reading and graduated as Observer cadet on 1 November 1918. However, following the Armistice, those who were not fully trained were discharged; Ronald being awarded the honorary rank of second lieutenant on 20 March 1919. He returned to Bootle and sadly that is all I can find out about him.

Gunner Will Stockdale was also to be commissioned but remained with the Tank Corps. Born in the summer of 1896 at Walthamstow, Will was the only son of a baker named William Stockdale and his wife Alice Buffam who also had a younger daughter named Phyllis. By 1901, the family had moved to 42-44 High Street in East Grinstead where they lived with Will's grandmother. Will's father owned a bakery in the town and Will was educated locally.

Having joined the MMGS, he made great friends with Reg "Tubby" Shaw. After he had fought at Courcelette, Will was identified as being suitable for officer training. Returning to the UK, he was commissioned on 28 July 1917 with Harry Nixon just as the Tank Corps was being formed. Three months later, on 27 September, he was present at the wedding of C Company's adjutant, Richard Williams in Wallasey to Lilian Wallis; Will being one of the witnesses. He later served at Bovington and was appointed an Assistant Instructor on 1 September 1918. Will was still serving in the Tank Corps when he married Dorothy Edwards in the summer of 1919. Their daughter Joan was born in East Grinstead the following summer and, on 3 May 1922, their son William was born. Uncle Tubby Shaw regularly visited the children and Will kept in contact with his crewmates by joining the C Battalion Old Comrades' Association. In the 1930s, he and the family moved to the Hampshire / Wiltshire borders where they settled southeast of Salisbury in the village of East Grimstead. It is somewhat remarkable that they should choose such a similarly named village for their new home. From 1938 to 1953 Dorothy and Will were living at Brookmead at East Grimstead and from 1955 at Withymere. Will's son followed his father's early career by serving as an officer in the Royal Hampshire Regiment and was awarded the MBE in 1968. It was he who was assigned probate after his father's death at East Grimstead on 11 May 1964.

The final gunner in *Crème de Menthe* was Joseph Shepherd who manned the right hand 6 pdr QF gun. Born on 18 September 1894 at his mother Emma's home in Marksbury near Keynsham, Joseph was named after his father who was a railway guard. He later

Bill Stockdale. (Caroline Peake)

moved to London with his parents and younger siblings Ada and Albert where, in 1901, they were living at 13 Raglan Street in Kentish Town. Joseph senior was now working for the London and North Western Railway and, on 1 June 1910, his son Joseph joined the company as an apprentice. He first worked at the London Road and then became a parcels clerk at Euston station. Joseph enlisted at St Pancras on 24 November 1915, under the Derby Scheme which meant his mobilisation was deferred. On 18 January, he joined the MMGS, his medical records showing he was a tall man at just under six feet. He deployed to France on 16 August 1916 and, given that he was not wounded during the attack at Courcelette, was probably in action again at Thiepval. Shortly after he joined C Battalion, Joseph was admitted to 12 Stationary Hospital at St Pol sur Ternoise on 10 December. He was discharged and sent back to C Battalion eight days later, Joseph's service record has survived but it provides very little detail information about his time with the tanks.

It is likely that he served with No 12 Company at Thelus and during the attack at Bullecourt on 3 May 1917. He then attended the driver training camp at Wailly from 11 – 19 June and successfully qualified as a driver. Transferring to the Tank Corps, Joseph later fought with C Company of 3rd Battalion as a Whippet crewman. He was granted home leave from 28 November to 12 December 1918. He did not claim a pension prior to his discharge and he returned to the UK on 22 February and demobilised two days later from Wimbledon. Thereafter I can find nothing else about him.

Crème de Menthe's skipper was probably the most experienced officer in all of C Company. Captain Arthur Inglis was born at 9:00 p.m. on 14 July 1884 at the Caledonian Hotel in Inverness. He was the younger son of Lionel Inglis, a merchant who was once the British Resident at Chota Nagpur in Bengal, and Agnes Murrell whom he had married in Tewkesbury on 21 October 1868. Arthur had an elder brother, also named Lionel, and the two boys were bought up in Prestbury and educated at the nearby Cheltenham College. Agnes divorced her husband in 1899 after Lionel, who had an affair on the way back from a trip to the East, threatened Agnes with violence on a

Courcelette Sugar Factory c 1916. (TPC)

number of occasions. Lionel subsequently married his lover, Maud Hemmingway, at Wandsworth Register Office on 2 August 1900.

Possibly trying to escape the situation at home, or perhaps looking for adventure, Arthur was commissioned, aged seventeen, into 3rd (Militia) Battalion the Wiltshire Regiment on 2 November 1901. He was soon serving overseas guarding the 5,000 Boer Prisoners of War held on the South Atlantic island of St Helena. Returning to the UK, Arthur transferred to the Regular Army in May 1906 and joined 2nd Battalion of his county regiment, the Glosters. Promoted Lieutenant on 7 April 1908, he was serving at Verdala Barracks in Malta in 1911 where he almost certainly met his future company commander as Allen Holford-Walker was serving only ten miles away at Intarfa Barracks. Garrison duties palled and Arthur sought an overseas secondment. On 6 December 1911, Arthur was appointed ADC to Sir Henry Galway, the Governor and Commander in Chief of the Gambia on 6 December 1911. In August 1912, he returned to the UK but soon back in Africa, this time serving as a subaltern with the Gambia Company of the West Africa Frontier Force (WAFF). This unit consisted on 130 locally recruited soldiers with five British officers and NCOs.

As war broke out in Europe, Arthur was serving at the capital of the Gambia, Bathurst, which was situated on the Atlantic coast. On 14 September 1914, Arthur and the company signalers left for the German colony of Cameroon to join the advance party of the British force which was tasked to capture the colony under Sir Charles Dobell. Dobell was later selected to command an Anglo-French force of 20,000 men. The campaign was successful although it was poorly equipped to deal with the terrain and it lost more than one fifth of its strength from disease. Arthur, who commanded the base which supported the field force, returned to the UK in May 1916 and then, probably at the suggestion of Lieutenant Colonel John Brough with whom he had served in Africa, joined the HS MGC on 12 July. Within a month, he had been appointed to command a section of tanks and had deployed to France.

As the most experienced captain in C Company, he was given independent command of a section working in support of the Canadian Division. He was also awarded an immediate DSO, the first ever for action in a tank, for conspicuous gallantry in action on 15 September 1916. The citation, which was published on 20 October, states "He brought his 'Tanks" forward over very difficult ground. Although one of the wheels of his own "Tank" was blown off early by a shell he succeeded in reaching his objective and manoeuvring throughout the whole operation."

Following the attack at Thiepval, on 26 September, Arthur was detached to D Company and took command of all the tanks that did not go north of the river Ancre to Hébuterne. Based at Green Dump, those under his command included Head, Hastie and Pearsall who went into action again on 18 October at Bayonet Trench. On 23 October Arthur was placed in command of a group of seven male and three female tanks, north of the River Ancre, but they never got into action because of the appallingly wet conditions which combined with the shell-smashed ground, made movement impossible. On the formation of D Battalion, in November 1916, Arthur commanded a company for short while before he was appointed to command No 6 Company of B Battalion. Just before Christmas, he returned to England and on 29 December, took command of a company in the newly formed F Battalion at Bovington; the CO of the unit being Frank Summers. Arthur was presented with the DSO at Buckingham Palace on 6 February and, having bought his company up to deployment standard, returned to France in May 1917. He commanded No 16 Company during the Third Battle of Ypres.

After F Battalion was withdrawn from the Salient, on 3 September, Arthur took No 16 Company to Blairville, near Arras, where the tanks were overhauled and then undertook driver training at nearby Wailly. During this programme, he was photographed with his Highland terrier Jock. In November, he commanded No 16 Company throughout during the Battle of Cambrai, where the battalion was successful during the break-in battle and the advance to the Masnieres Bridge although their actions at Bourlon and Fontaine were unsuccessful owing to a lack of infantry able

Arthur Inglis and his dog Jock on 20 October 1917. (Tank Museum)

to secure and hold the ground. On 1 December, the Battalion started to withdrawn to Bray and Frank Summers with many of the experienced officers were sent back to England to newly formed battalions. Arthur however remained with the now renamed 6th Battalion, in command of A Company. In January 1918, training commenced on the new Whippet tanks at Bray although the battalion was also equipped with twenty-four Mark IV tanks against emergencies. In February, most of the original members of the Battalion were sent on leave whilst at the same time, being tasked to proceed to Wailly in case the Germans made an attack on Arras. The Battalion was in position by 28 February and was warned to stay for a month after which it would be withdrawn. On 22 March, when the German advance started, Arthur was ordered to provide support to a Guards Brigade to take St Leger; the attack did not come off but one section of A Company later helped the Welsh Regiment take the village. The tanks then withdrew by night onto a new position near La Cauchie; they stayed until 9 April by which time the German advance had halted. The tanks then were moved to new battle positions near Fonque-Villiers and the gunners formed into Lewis gun section. F Battalion was ready for action throughout May with constant reconnaissance being undertaken by officers, NCOs and first drivers. It was not until 30 May when the first party of officers and other ranks were able to entrain for Merlimont, on the coast, to form the training staff and commence a programme to re-role onto the new double-engined Whippet tank with its three man crews.

Two months later, the newly re-equipped F Battalion moved to Amiens to take part in the huge attack planned for early August. Having given his final orders to the B and C Companies at 8.00 a.m. on 8 August, Lieutenant Colonel Charles Truman DSO who was now commanding F Battalion, moved to Marcelcave to where A Company, under Arthur Inglis, was awaiting orders. Satisfied that the battle was progressing satisfactorily, he directed Arthur to send his tanks towards

Caix. At about 9.15 a.m., as his tanks deployed, Arthur was standing alongside his CO when a passing Whippet ran over an unexploded shell. Both men were severely wounded and Arthur was evacuated to the UK. Arthur did recover from his wounds but did return to his Battalion in France. After the Armistice, Arthur was appointed Railway Transport Officer for Eastern District and lived in London. He was however far from well and was allowed to return home to Prestbury. Arthur Inglis died of his wounds, on 12 May 1919 and was buried by his family in the south east corner of St Mary's Churchyard. Over the years his grave marker deteriorated and, in 2009, it was replaced by the CWGC. The gravestone bears the badge of the Glosters which he wore throughout his service with the Tanks. He was unique amongst the First Tank Crews as also wore the Sphinx badge "back badge" recalling the battle honour awarded to the Glosters after they fought "back to back", against the attacking French infantry, at the Battle of Alexandria in 1801. The back-badge is worn today by the descendants of the Glosters who now serve with the Rifles Regiment.

17

The Chain of Command

When you examine the men who fought in the tanks at Flers-Courcelette, you can identify a series of patterns: Empiremen who returned to Great Britain take their place in the Army; keen motor-cyclists who were recruited into the MMGS through the offices of Geoffrey Smith at Coventry; tradesmen with an engineering background; sons of drapers and public schoolboys who were commissioned six months before they went into action as tank skippers. There is one obvious group missing amongst those forming the Chain of Command – that is professional soldiers.

There was only one former Regular Army NCO and only one Sandhurst commissioned officer in either C or D Company. The former NCO was George Mann who commanded No 4 Section of D Company – see chapter 13 – and the officer was Allen Holford-Walker who commanded C Company. Allen was born on 3 January 1890 near Southend; probably at Shoeburyness. He was the second son of a Royal Artillery officer Edgar Holford Walker and his second wife Maria Cumming. Edgar's first wife Rosabelle had died on 19 February 1887 – their four children tragically dying from diphtheria eight years earlier when Edgar was stationed in Nova Scotia. Allen and his younger brother Archie were educated at Cheltenham College, after which Allen followed his father into the Regular Army. Edgar died aged sixty, just before Allen was commissioned into the Argyll & Sutherland Highlanders on 6 November 1909.

Allen probably met Arthur Inglis who was to command *Crème de Menthe*, whilst the two men were serving in Malta, after which he deployed to India with the 1st Battalion in 1912. On the outbreak of war, his battalion was recalled to England, arriving on 17 November 1914. During his disembarkation leave, Allen married Joan Moody at Tilford on 14 December 1914 "quietly due to the war". He was posted to the recently formed 10th (Service) Battalion of the Argylls, joining them at Alresford in January 1917. The battalion then undertook field training at Bramshott in Surrey where Allen met another of his future section commanders, Sir John Dashwood, who was serving in 10th battalion. Deploying to Flanders on 15 May 1915, Allen was badly injured and was returned to the UK. Allen and Joan's elder daughter Alleyne was born in early 1916 and her younger sister Joan the following year. Allen was attached to the HS MGC on 3 May 1916, just after his brother Archie, and was the first major to command C Company. He deployed to France with the Advanced Party on 16 August 1916 and, after training at Yvrench, moved to the Loop on 7 September. Allen provided advice to both corps and divisional commanders prior to the attack on 15 September but sadly they paid little attention on how his tanks could best be used.

In the early hours of the morning of 15 September, Allen brought his Sunbeam staff car from his Company's forward operating base at a brick works to the south of Bernafay Wood along the traffic packed roads, bringing petrol cans to refuel Basil Henriques' tank. He commanded his unit from the Briqueterie for the remainder of September and then moved north for the Battle of the Ancre, until the British attacks on the Somme ceased in November 1916. Allen then joined C Battalion, on its formation, as OC No 7 Company. Awarded the Military Cross for his sustained services in command of C Company, he departed the new battalion shortly before Christmas. He did not however forget his soldiers, and his wife Joan sent members of C Company tobacco, cigarettes,

Allen Holford-Walker.
(TPC)

Allen Holford-Walker during the Second
World War. (TPC)

cake and chocolates as gifts. Allen was then appointed the first commander of No 20 Company of G Battalion and trained them at Bovington. He deployed back to France on 24 May 1917 and moved with them to Flanders for their first action during the Third Battle of Ypres. However, he had to leave G Battalion in early August 1917, owing to ill-health, and returned to England where he served for the rest of the war until 19 June 1919.

Allen then relinquished the rank of temporary major and reverted, as did all Regular officers, to their substantive rank which, in Allen's case, was captain. Fourteen months later, he was appointed Adjutant 10th Battalion Kings Liverpool Regiment and afterwards Adjutant of 9th Battalion of the Argylls from 15 March 1921 for three years. His son Alan, known as Fionn, was born on 5 February 1922. The same year Allen decided to retire from the Army and farm in Africa. On 27 November 1922, Allen left England with his family for Mombasa. They settled on the Killean Estates at Nanyuki near Mount Kenya where Allen became a cattle breeder. He was appointed an official game warden on 21 February 1929 and his Ayrshire Bull won prizes at the Nairobi show in December 1933. Two years later, the family returned to England, boarding at Lorenzo Marques in Mozambique and arriving at Southampton on 15 July 1935. Whilst in England, Allen provided notes on the first tank action, including pen pictures of those who served with him, to the authors of the official history of the Great War. Many of the more illuminating comments were not published, especially his comments on the attitude of Hugh Elles to the first company commanders which were far from favourable.

Recalled to active service on 19 September 1939 as a Staff Captain, Allen returned to home and was later to organise the ground-based air-defence in Scotland whilst living on the outskirts of Arbroath. With the end of the war in Europe, his employment ceased on 23 May 1945 and he was granted the honorary rank of Lieutenant Colonel. Joan and he then returned to Kenya where Allen died at Killean on 22 April 1949.

Allen's counterpart in D Company was Major Frank Summers. Although he was not a Regular officer, Frank had significant military experience. Frank was born on 28 October 1872 in Redhill, the youngest son of a draper who established a highly successful business in Redhill and later became mayor. Initially educated at Brighton, where his mother had a house on the Steyne, Frank attended the Merchant Taylor's School in London. As a young man, Frank would have been aware of the opportunities becoming available in Southern Africa, so he decided to seek his fortune. He left Southampton on 6 March 1891, travelling to Capetown on SS *Mexican*. By now Frank was almost six feet tall and a robust young man. In 1893, Frank served as a trooper in the Victoria Column of Cecil Rhodes Chartered Police during the expedition which broke the Matabele rebellion. Frank remained in the newly established colony of Southern Zambesia, working both as a correspondent for Reuters and editing a newspaper in Bulawayo. He is reported to have spent some time prospecting for gold and also became a good friend of Cecil Rhodes.

Returning to England, Frank gained a law degree at the University of London and later practiced at the Middle Temple. In September 1898, Frank married Marjorie Pryor and their only son Cyril was born on 18 April 1899 at Leighton Buzzard. Following the outbreak of the Second Anglo-Boer War, Frank volunteered to join the Imperial Yeomanry. Commissioned on 2 February 1900, he initially served in 14th (East Kent) Battalion in South Africa. He later served with 53rd Squadron of Imperial Yeomanry, commanding a section of Mounted Infantry, and was Mentioned in Despatches for the first time. When his year-long contract ended, Frank returned to England and resigned his commission on 19 September 1900. In 1901, around the time of the census, the family was living at 17 Holland Park Avenue in Kensington. Frank became Secretary to the Imperial Service Club from its foundation in 30 September 1901 until its failure in 1905, after which he became secretary of the Cosmopolitan Club in London. Marjorie and he travelled to Durban in 1909 and he invested in the Shalo Copper Mines in East Sweden, a venture which lead ultimately to financial failure and Frank's bankruptcy in 1913.

At the outbreak of the Great War, Frank was one of the Gentlemen Chauffeurs who volunteered to drive their own cars in support of the Royal Naval Division (RND). He was later commissioned into the Royal Marine Light Infantry and, at Dunkirk, was appointed Adjutant of the RND Transport Company on 21 September 1914. Frank then served with the Transport Company during the Antwerp action and, after the unit deployed to Flanders, was present during the First Battle of Ypres in November 1914, the Second Battle when the Germans used gas for the first time, and at Neuve Chappelle. At this time his son Cyril, who was serving as midshipman on HMS *London*, was supporting the landings at Gallipoli. Frank was also sent to the Dardanelles from September 1915 where he was attached to the Royal Naval Air Service (RNAS) as a staff captain serving under Colonel Frederick Sykes. Frank later served with No 3 Wing RNAS from December 1915 to March 1916.

Whilst in the Dardanelles, Frank was Mentioned in Despatches for the second time and on 31 December 1915 was awarded the DSC "for services with the RND Motor Transport Company in France". This was a remarkable occurrence and reflects highly on his leadership. Returning to England Frank relinquished his commission in the RMLI on 23 March 1916, at the request of the War Office, and was immediately transferred to the MGC as a Captain. On 19 April, Frank was presented with the DSC by King George V at Buckingham Palace and appointed temporary major on 4 May as D Company was formed.

On 31 May 1916, Frank's seventeen year old son Cyril was killed when his ship HMS *Indefatigable* was sunk at the Battle of Jutland. Frank was fully occupied training his new company but he felt the loss of his child keenly. The pictures of Frank, taken with his officers and men before he deployed to France, clearly show him wearing a mourning band.

Frank Summers wearing Royal
Marine uniform. (*War History of
the Sixth Tank Battalion*)

Frank deployed to France with the company advance party arriving on 29 August 1916. Having undertaken final training at Yvrench and attended various briefings of Corps HQ staff, Frank established his forward HQ at the Green Dump on 13 September, and remained there until 29 September. Green Dump was about half a mile south west of Longueval and was well placed to enable Frank to exercise command of his company. He lived in the box-bodied car which acted as the Company HQ office. His demeanor in the build-up to the first attack was such that Graham Woods, his Adjutant, abandoned his plans to sleep in the office and found a bed space between the horns of one of the tanks. Frank clearly briefed his skippers, prior to their deployment, on the afternoon of 13 September, and was forward near the action on 15 September. He made it very clear to those tank commanders who failed to get into action that day they were to do better in future. When orders were received to push on the attack the next morning, he walked up to Flers to brief the tank commanders who were to attack Gueudecourt. Being told that the main infantry attack had been postponed, Frank directed the tanks to advance and they provided support as the New Zealand units advanced towards the Factory Corner on 16 September.

He continued to command D Company, during the follow-up actions known during the Battle of the Ancre, until 18 November 1916 when his company formed the basis of D Battalion. Just before Christmas, Frank was sent back to Bovington to establish one of the newly formed tank battalions. Awarded the DSO in the New Year's Honours list, Frank was promoted acting lieutenant colonel on 11 January 1917 and took command of F Battalion on 26 January 1917. He trained and then deployed the Battalion to France on 20 May and, after driver training at Wailly then live firing at the Corps Gunnery School at Merlimont, tanks were then drawn from the Central Stores and taken back to Auchy. Before deploying to the Ypres Salient, he organised a dinner attended by officers from the Tank HQ as well as many of the original tank skippers from C and D Companies. Frank commanded F Battalion during the Third Battle of Ypres, where it was badly mauled, and at Cambrai where it achieved significant success. On 13 December 1917, he handed- over command and returned to England to form another battalion. One month later, he was appointed CO of

15th Battalion but did not accompany them to France. Rather he was selected to travel to the United States, accompanied by Major Philip Hamond who been in command of No 18 Company at Cambrai. Arriving in New York on 11 July 1918, they gave a series of lectures in Washington and also briefed the US War College. They later visited Camp Colt at Gettysberg where the US Army had established its tank school. Frank was photographed, still wearing the mourning armband, with Hamond, Colonel William Clapton and a young US tank training officer, Captain later President Dwight D Eisenhower. Frank returned to England just before the Armistice and served in the Air Ministry until he relinquished his commission. After the war, Frank and Marjorie lived near Marble Arch but the marriage was on shaky ground. In February 1919, Frank sued Marjorie for divorce on the grounds of her adultery; her daughter Bettina being born later that year. In November 1919 Frank attended the first Cambrai dinner which continues each year to this day. On 24 February 1920 he was appointed Deputy Controller Appointments Department, Ministry of Labour and Director for London District, tasked with finding work for some of the 14,000 former officers who were unemployed after the end of the war. When he retired two years later, Frank was given a dinner at the Prince's Restaurant in Piccadilly. Thereafter he served as Honorary Secretary of the RAC Club and was on the organising committee of the Empire Fellowship Ball at Bognor in July 1928. He attended the 50th Matabeland and Mashonaland Campaign reunion in November 1933 which was presided over by Robert Baden-Powell and again ten years later. Just before the outbreak of the Second World War Frank was hurt in a road traffic accident which prevented him attending the funeral of the Hon Philip Henderson on Friday 24 March 1939. Henderson had served as a tank engineer during the Great War and served under Frank Summers in F Battalion. On the outbreak of war, he was a prime mover with Ernest Swinton in the foundation of the Royal Armoured Club., Frank becoming the Honorary Secretary. He died in Chelsea, on 14 February 1948 aged seventy-five years. He was buried privately on 20 February 1948 and his obituary written by Ernest Swinton was published in the London Times on the following day.

The man who has provided much of the First Tank Crews information was Frank Summers' adjutant, Graham Woods. He maintained detailed records in the D Company's War Diary of each tank's achievements during September 1916, and also kept a diary and notebook which are now in the care of the Tank Museum. The notebook includes the surname of every crewman who deployed on 15 September 1916 as well as members of the ASC who were attached to D Company. Arthur Graham Woods was the son of a clergyman Graham Woods and his wife Jane. Born on 28 August 1886, he was known as Graham, to distinguish him from his father. Graham was educated at the North London Collegiate School, the Belmont House School at Blackheath and finally the King's College School. Graham had a passion for engineering and worked as an apprentice at three locations: Bouverie Street in London from 1902-04, then the Midlands Railway locomotive works at Derby where he worked as a pupil railway clerk at Derby but was called upon to resign in 1906 due to indifferent timekeeping. He then worked at Manchester with Charles Churchill and Co for two years. In 1908, he was working in Darlington with John Patterson doing experimental work, then from 1909-1910, he was a foreman at Headingley in Leeds. Later that year, aged twenty-nine, he established his own company Woods' Garage Ltd in Selby close to where his parents were living in the nearby Haddlesey rectory. Three years later, he closed the company and moved to Sunderland to work for the auto engineering and coach-building firm owned by Charles Grimshaw.

Following the outbreak of war, Graham was commissioned into 11th Battalion Yorkshire and Lancashire Regiment on 14 December 1914. He married Evelyn Day, who he called Evie, on 15 March 1915 at St Mark's Church in Harrogate, and was appointed temporary Captain in the MGC on 29 March 1915, the same day that he reported for duty at the MMGS Depot. Graham served at Bisley until June 1916 when he deployed to Elveden. Unlike most MMGS officers, he was fully aware of the tank's developments and, in April 1916, visited the Foster's factory in Lincoln for more than a fortnight. On 5 May 1916, Graham counter-signed an attestation form on behalf of the Adjutant 1st Battalion Heavy Section MGC, but the new unit was soon to disappear. On 9 June he assumed the post of Adjutant of D Company and moved to Norfolk on 22 June. He deployed to France on 1 September 1916 and ran the Company HQ at Green Dump where he slept on several occasions between the horns of a tank. Graham then moved north with the Company HQ during the Battle of the Ancre, maintaining the War Diary throughout.

On 11 November 1916, he led a small party to establish the Company's winter base at Blangy-sur-Ternoise which became the base for D Battalion on its formation. Graham, who became D Battalion's first adjutant, was Mentioned in Despatches in January 1917. On the formation of the 2nd Tank Brigade, he was appointed Staff Captain in which role he was later awarded the Military Cross. Graham next served with Headquarters 1st Tank Group as the senior personnel and logistics staff officer until 14 Oct 1919, his efforts being recognised with the award of a Distinguished Service Order on 31 December 1918. Graham was given home leave in January 1919 and visited his widowed mother in Selby. Finally he served as the senior staff personnel officer, in the rank of lieutenant colonel at the Tank Corps HQ at Bermicourt where one of his final tasks was to attend the presentation of a tank to the town of Mers-les-Bains 9 – see page 64. Graham Woods is standing slightly left of centre and towers above most of those present. The officer standing on the step, making the presentation, is Major Victor Smith who commanded *Casa* on 15 September 1916.

When he returned to England, at the end of his service, Graham was presented with the DSO and MC by King George V on 20 February 1920. Three days later, he wrote to the editor of the Tank Journal stating he had planned to go overseas to the West Indies but his doctor would not permit it. He therefore found work as general manager with a firm of auto engineers and body manufacturers at Sunderland. Graham and Evie lived in Whitburn in County Durham for five years after which they settled at Disley in Cheshire. Graham started the Manchester and District branch of the Tank Corps OCA and was later became its president attending the 1928, 1936 and 1938 RTR annual dinners. With the outbreak of the Second World War, Graham was commissioned into the Auxiliary Military Pioneer Corps as a subaltern on 9 July 1940 but was soon employed undertaking experiments on waterproofing vehicles for wading. Promoted war substantive major in the newly-formed REME on 26 July 1943, Graham was intimately involved in the preparation of vehicles for the D Day assault across the Normandy beaches.

Graham Woods did not relinquish his commission until 12 July 1946 when he was granted honorary rank of Lieutenant Colonel. After the war he worked as a sub area secretary with the Northwest Electricity Board and after his retirement, continued as civil defence advisor to the Board. Graham was also busy in local affairs, being a member of the local British Legion branch, a Rural District Councilor, lay-reader, churchwarden, editor of the Parish Magazine and Secretary of the Parish Council. Evie and Graham lived at Disley until 1958 when they moved south to Sussex where Graham died in the summer of 1964.

C Company's adjutant, Richard Williams, had served in the Territorial Force as an NCO before the outbreak of the Great War. He was born at New Brighton on the Wirral in the autumn of 1889, the fifth child and eldest son of a shipowner's freight clerk after whom he was named. Richard became a commercial clerk and, according to his family, married Nettie Bowyer in the summer of 1914 and later had three sons. Commissioned into MMGS on 22 September 1915, he deployed to France on 16 August 1916 and was later appointed as Adjutant of C Battalion in March 1917. Richard later transferred to the Tank Corps and was awarded the MC for service with 3rd Light Tank Battalion in June 1918. Whilst on home leave, after the Battalion's involvement in the Third Battle of Ypres, Richard married Lillian Wallis on 26 September 1917 at Wallasey Parish Church. The marriage certificate shows that Lieutenant William Stockdale, who had been a crewman in *Crème de Menthe*, was a witness. The couple's only son Richard was born on 4 December 1918 by which time Richard had transferred From the Tank Corps to the General List. After the war, he returned to Merseyside and in 1925 was living in Wallasey. Richard re-joined the Territorial

Army and served with the Duke of Lancaster's Own Yeomanry. His medal index card shows he was awarded TF War Medal in 1927 and TA Efficiency Medal in 1928 whilst serving as a WO2. In 1931, whilst living in Manchester and working as a fruit broker's assistant, Richard was sued for divorce by Lilian following his adultery with "Mrs Williams" at the Mitre guest house on the Isle of Man. The judge found in Lillian's favour and she was awarded a divorce and custody of their son. His family then says Richard died in 1953, aged sixty-five, and Nettie, his first wife died in 1976.

The two companies shared a quartermaster who was responsible for unit equipment. This was Charles Weaver-Price who was born at Brecon in South Wales in 1876. Charles' father was initially employed as a railway station manager and his mother a music teacher, but his father established himself as a coal merchant in Brecon where he became very successful. He also served in a volunteer battalion of the South West Borderers (SWB). Charles was educated as a day boy at Christ's College Brecon and later joined his father's firm initially working as a clerk. Like his father he also joined the SWB as a Territorial Force soldier. In 1906, Charles married Rhianedd Jones, who was four years his junior, in her home town of Pontypridd. They settled in Brecon where he took over the running of his father's coal merchant business. Charles was also well known as a bee-keeper and, to facilitate this hobby, Charles and Rhianedd moved to a large house called Ashgrove at Llansypiddid. It was here that their only son Charles, who was known as David, was born on 27 Jul 1913.

When war was declared, Charles re-enlisted in the SWB on 6 September and was immediately appointed corporal. Initially charged with improving the drill of recruits at Brecon, eight days later he was sent with the newly formed 7th (Service) Battalion to Seaford and the following day was promoted sergeant; a further four days later Company QM Sergeant and on 25 September as Battalion QM Sergeant. When the Motor Machine Gun Service was formed, Charles volunteered to join the ranks and was immediately appointed Battalion QM Sergeant. In early February 1915, Charles managed to obtain fifty pairs of socks from the stocks of warm clothing knitted by the women of Brecon. He initially deployed to France on 12 July 1915 and was appointed Battery Sergeant Major in the field. Whilst in France, his interest in bees did not leave him and, in a letter to his parents, in early September, detailed how he came across an Apis Melifica or British honey bee, which was trying to create a cone, a discovery which took place whilst sheltering from German bullets. Charles saw action in the Ypres Salient and then during the Battle of Loos in September and October 1915. On 9 December 1915, Charles was commissioned "in the field" and later returned to England to take up his new role as Quartermaster of C Company. The Brecon papers reported that he was on leave in July 1916; this was prior to his return to France on 16 August 1916. The local papers also reported, in late September, that he was serving with the tanks and that "I am having the time of my life now. Much more exhilarating than "Wipers". In early October 1916, whilst his soldiers were out of battle and needing distraction, he wrote to the editors of three Welsh newspapers seeking books and other reading material as his soldiers were too far forward to be able to visit the institutes available to those out of the front line. He asked that the books be sent to his mother who was a leading light amongst the supporters of the YMCA. The diligence Charles showed to all his duties during the first tank actions were reflected through the award of the Military Cross in the 1917 New Year's Honours List.

Charles was then appointed the Equipment Officer of HQ 1st Tank Brigade in early 1917 where his pre-eminence as a beekeeper was noted by Boney Fuller. Later Charles became the Staff Captain Quartermaster at HQ Tank Corps at Bermicourt in which role he planned and supervised the loading of all 400 tanks used in the Battle of Cambrai. Once battle was joined, Charles led a packet of replenishment vehicles forward on 20 and 21 November, making sure that his vehicles got well beyond the Hindenburg Line to ensure rapid restocking of key equipment. Granted leave at Brecon in the New Year, he was later appointed substantive captain on 16 April 1918 with eighteen months seniority. He also managed to get some leave in July 1918, just before all tanks were deployed during the Battle of Amiens. He was promoted to major on 25 October and appointed Chief Equipment Officer at HQ Tank Corps. Finally he was promoted lieutenant colonel in the Equipment Branch in which role he was also awarded the OBE on 3 June 1919. Charles served on well after the armistice, not relinquishing his commission until 17 February 1920.

He returned to Rhianedd at Ashgrove where sadly she died, aged on 39 later that year. Charles then established the Welsh Bee Gardens at Ashgrove and, in 1922 and 1923, made a number of BBC radio broadcasts on beekeeping. The following year Charles married Eva Barley in Bath and they settled at Ashgrove. Charles was not called up for the second world war as he was over 60. His son David, who had been commissioned in the RAF in 1936, was however soon in action against German U-boats and was Mentioned in Despatches. Serving on 269 Squadron RAF, as part of Coastal Command, David was killed whilst piloting a Hudson Bomber which collided with a Hawker Hurricane whilst taking off from RAF Wick. The aircraft caught fire and the bomb load exploded killing all four crewmen. His body was returned to his father who buried his son in the local churchyard. Charles Weaver-Price died aged sixty seven on 27 August 1943 and is buried alongside his son and his first wife at St Cattwg's Church in Llansypiddid.

Each of the companies had Park Officers responsible for the tanks when not issued to crews. Sir John Dashwood first undertook this role for C Company before he took command of No 3 Section. D Company's Park Officer, Lieutenant Jefferson Wakley, was born in London on 21 September 1893 and christened on 15 October at St Stephen's Church in Paddington. The son of an engineer, Jeff was educated at St Paul's School in London and, from 1908, served a 4 year apprenticeship with the Northam Iron Works in Southampton. He subsequently studied at University College London. He was living in Birmingham at the outbreak of war, when he enlisted into 15th (Service) Battalion of the Royal Warwickshire Regiment on 14 September 1914. Commissioned on 10 March 1915 into 6th Battalion, Jeff was attached to the Heavy Section MGC on 17 April 1916. Promoted temporary Lieutenant on 1 July that year, he departed Thetford on 25 August 1916 with the first thirteen tanks to deploy to France. He accompanied them on the SS *Hunsden* which left Avonmouth on 28 August 1916 and arrived on 1 September at Le Havre. On arrival at Yvrench, Jeff was tasked to deploy with ten men, on 5 September, to Le Havre to receive eight spare tanks which he brought to the Loop railhead by 05:00 a.m. on 11 September 1916. It was these tanks which provided replacements for those which broke down on their initial deployment on 13 and 14 September.

Jeff was not in action on 15 September but, on 1 October, he commanded one of two tanks supporting the attack on Eaucourt L'Abbaye. The tanks broke through the German defences but then became ditched. As the infantry could not hold their gains and withdrew, the tanks were abandoned and set on fire. As the crews made for British lines, Jeff was wounded in his left leg by a shell fragment which lodged four inches above the knee. He also sustained a compound fracture of the leg. Billy Sampson reported that Jeff could not be recovered from no man's land for three days and nights, which is corroborated by Captain Graham Woods' diary, and that several men lost their lives trying to rescue him. Jeff was taken initially to Becourt field hospital where the shell fragments were removed and he was evacuated to England on 17 October. He was then taken to Princess Henry of Battenberg's hospital in London where his septic leg continued to give concern. The leg was eventually amputated at the hip in January 1917 and in May 1917 he was fitted with an artificial leg.

Jeff was promoted substantive lieutenant on 1 July 1917 and was employed at the War Office from August that year. He was later employed by Directorate SD7 on what was described as "highly technical work – checking drawings related to design and to prepare diagrammatical sketches of ideas submitted." Placed on the retired list on account of ill health caused by his wounds on 14 February 1919, Jeff was awarded a Silver War Badge on 30 April 1919. On 21 November 1921, Jeff married Evelyn La Touche. Her previous marriage to a Regular Army officer had failed in 1913 but despite this, her husband failed to release her and the couple had to go through the embarrassment of a divorce case. Jeff later worked for the Drewry Railcar Company and, from 1936 to 1939, and patented a series of improvements to self-propelled railway vehicles built by the company. On 26 February 1931, he was elected as a member of the Institute of Mechanical Engineers and he kept in close contact with fellow engineers from the Great War. He represented his company at the funeral of Philip Henderson who died in 1939 but, owing to the traffic accident, was unable to be joined by Frank Summers. Jeff and Evelyn were unable to have children and so adopted a daughter called Susan who married in 1940. From 1926 to 1958, the couple lived at Molewood House in Hertford and later in Knightsbridge. Jeff Wakley died, aged eighty-five on 22 June 1978.

There was also a reserve crew in each company headquarters; D Company's "spare skipper" was Billy Sampson who fought at High Wood on 15 September whilst Second Lieutenant Robert Aitken filled this role in C Company. Robert was born on 1 September 1894 at Guildford and christened on 10 October at St Mary's Church. His Scottish father Thomas was a colliery agent and Robert was educated at Brighton after which he served as an articled clerk to an auctioneer and estate agent. When he enlisted on 5 September 1914 into 19th Battalion Royal Fusiliers, Robert stated he was engaged in poultry farming although, when he applied for a commission, he changed this employment to estate agent. He was a tall man standing six feet two inches and weighing ten stone ten pounds. His unit deployed to France in November 1915 but was disbanded the following spring after many of its soldiers were selected for officer training in England. Robert returned from France on 20 March 1916, was posted to No 4 Officer Cadet Battalion on 25 March and commissioned into the HS MGC on 14 April 16, with many other tank skippers who served with the Public Schools' Battalions.

When Robert took a tank into action at Thiepval on 26 September, his tank was hit and the first and second fingers of his right hand injured. Robert reported sick on 8 October, suffering from headaches, sickness and rigors and was sent back to England on 21 October 1916. He was treated at Guy's Hospital in London, until 14 November. Examined by a RAMC doctor on 26 March 1917, his general health was good but he complained of attacks of vertigo. Robert suffered from neuralgia for rest of service and did not return to active duty although he was employed at the Tank Depot. He relinquished his commission on account of ill-health contracted on active service, and was granted the honorary rank of Lieutenant on 25 August 1918. He did not however move far away from Bovington as, 7 December, he was living at the Ranch at Owermoigne near Dorchester, possibly with Graeme Nixon. Robert returned to poultry farming, settling in Stoke Ferry in Norfolk, which is only 15 miles north of Elveden. He later married and had two children. He tried his luck in Australia in the early 1920s but returned to Stoke Ferry in 1926. The family later moved to Taverham, in the early 1940s where Robert lived until his death in 1971.

C Company's Sergeant Major was Joseph Hackett from West Bridgford in Nottinghamshire. Born in Blackheath in Staffordshire, Joseph was a butterman. He later became the first RSM in C Battalion and was commissioned on 15 March 1917 into the Northumberland Fusiliers. Unusually for a commissioned warrant officer, he was not employed as an equipment officer but commanded a section of tanks at the end of the war until April 1919. D Company's Sergeant Major was Thomas "Paddy" Walsh. He initially served in 5th Dragoon Guards, arriving in France in 21 September 1915. I cannot identify when he joined D Company but he was certainly at Elveden by 11 August 1916 as his name is recorded on a soldier's conduct record from that time. Like Joseph Hackett, he was appointed RSM of the newly formed D Battalion on its formation and was Mentioned in Despatches in January 1917. Paddy later served with 15th Battalion as RSM, with Frank Summers, and was later injured by mustard gas on 21 August 1918 at Ayette, during the advance after the Battle of Amiens. According to a letter he sent to Billy Foster, he was badly burned and was blind for about 10 days. He was evacuated to the US hospital at Boulogne and then home but, by 15 December 1918 was back with 15th Battalion at Auchy-Les-Hesdin. He was by this time married with children and had been offered a job at Newcastle. However Paddy did not stay a civilian for long as he volunteered to join the North Russian Relief Force, which replaced British units sent to assist the White Russians take back control of Russian from the Bolsheviks. He served as RSM of the 20th Battalion MGC, which was part of the 2nd Brigade and was initially successful in their deployment south of Archangel. The expedition however ultimately failed and was withdrawn; Paddy returning to England where he was transferred to the Army Reserve in January 1920.

Each of the Company also had a sergeant responsible for the unit stores; the role was known as the Company Quartermaster Sergeant or CQMS. The C Company CQMS was Harry Jacobs who was born on 7 June 1895 in Bristol. He was the youngest son of a Polish born Russian Jew named Isaac Mouat Jacobs and his wife Blema who later became known as Rosalie. The couple emigrated to Abertillery where Isaac worked as a tailor and then moved to Lydney in Gloucestershire. By Harry's birth, Isaac had become a successful boot factor. Harry was educated at Merchant Venturers Technical College after which he became an accountant. In 1915, recognizing he was likely to be conscripted, Harry joined the Bristol University Officer Training Corps on 28 November and served with them until he was attested into the MGC on 22 March. He was then appointed CQMS and deployed to France on 16 August. When C Battalion was formed following the first actions, Harry was selected for the post of Battalion QMS and promoted to the rank of WO2. The increased number of tank units was accompanied by the formation of a Central Workshops and Central Stores at Erin. Harry was identified as being suitable for the role of Equipment officer and, when he was recommended for commissioning, Brigadier General Hugh Elles requested Harry take up his post immediately at Central Workshops without attending the usual officer cadet course in England.

Commissioned on 15 February 1917, Harry was replaced in C Battalion by Gordon Bainbridge. Harry was promoted to lieutenant on 17 June and later then acting captain. He lost this rank by a most unusual set of circumstances. During the Battle of Cambrai, on 22 November, he was sent forward to assume the role of Battalion Equipment Officer, which was a subaltern's post so Harry lost his acting rank. He was not granted home leave after the battle but, on 6 January 1918, he was appointed a Senior Equipment Officer at the Central Stores in the substantive rank of captain. He did however get a short break in February when he was granted three days leave in Paris which may have offered more fun than a trip back to Bristol. Harry served in the vital but unglamorous role at Erin for which he was Mentioned in Despatches in May 1918. On 10 September, as the tank battalions were fighting their way east as part of the Final Advance, Harry was again appointed Battalion Equipment Officer with 4th Battalion who still retained a number of the original members of D Company from 1916. This time he did not lose his rank but served with 4th Battalion through the Battle of St Quentin and was not released until 18 October. He was then sent back to England to serve with 24 Officer Cadet Battalion near Winchester.

After the war, Harry returned to Bristol and settled in Redland. He became a merchant dealing with South American companies; his first trip to Argentina being in 1922 and he returned regularly over the next thirty years. Harry married Olga Rosen on 4 July 1929 and their son Charles was born the following year. Charles joined his father's business travelling with his parents to Buenos Aires in 1945. Harry and Olga seem to have made their last trip in 1952 after which no further records can be found until Harry's death in 1971 at Sutton in south west London.

Sergeant Gordon Bainbridge, who replaced Harry Wolfe in February 1917, was another Empire man who returned to the mother country to enlist after the outbreak of war. Born in Edinburgh 12 March 1889, Gordon was the only son of a printer named Andrew Bainbridge and his wife Ellen. Gordon initially followed his father trade but also served, from 1903 to 1907, as a trooper in Lothian and Borders' Horse. This was a yeomanry unit which would have provided him with an enhanced social life as well as the chance to learn new skills. In 1908, Gordon travelled to Toronto in Canada but returned the same year. By 1911 he had moved with the rest of the family had moved to Forest Hill in South East London. He must have found new employment on settling in London as, on 20 August 1913, he sailed on SS *Abasso* to work as a merchant in Accra.

He returned to Liverpool on 7 June 1915 having travelled from Sekundi to Plymouth. As he enlisted at Coventry on 21 June 1915, he must have made his decision to join the MMGS either before or immediately on his return. Gordon was a tall man, at just over 6 feet, and with his yeomanry experience would have been a useful asset to the Chain of Command. He was appointed paid bombardier on 31 July 1915 and promoted acting Sergeant on 20 August which is remarkably quick even by the MMGS standards. He was not however without fault as his records show he appeared before a District Court Martial for drunkenness on 18 March 1916. Fined £1 and reduced to the ranks, Gordon soon recovered his good name and was appointed QM sergeant of C Company by 1 June 1916.

Following the formation of C Battalion, Gordon was appointed Battalion QMS on 13 February 1917 replacing Harry Jacobs. Gordon served in this role throughout the battles of Arras and Third Ypres. On 17 September 1917, he was commissioned and transferred to HQ Tank Corps at Bermicourt.

During Battle of Cambrai, Gordon bought forward a packet of trucks carrying machine guns and others spares parts joining up with Charles Weaver-Price well forward in the newly captured territory despite massive traffic hold-ups and smashed roads. He was later promoted captain and, on 26 October 1918, appointed acting major while employed as an Equipment Officer at HQ Tank Corps. Like Charles Weaver-Price, he did not relinquish his commission until well after the armistice on 26 February 1920 and was granted the rank of major. Gordon did not remain in England as he soon returned to Africa and settled in Kenya. It was there that he died on 16 August 1927, aged thirty-eight, and was buried in the Forest Road cemetery in Nairobi.

Quartermaster Sergeant Victor Williams was born in Dalston London between in early 1887. Victor was the eldest child of a bootmaker who later became a shoe manufacturer. His father Ernest, after whom he was named, and mother Lydia who were both from St Helier Jersey, had another eight children of whom seven survived. Victor worked as an auctioneer's clerk and, when he was twenty eight years old, married Ethel Newman on 14 August 1915 at St Peters Church in Hornsey. Ernest's service record has not survived but the medal rolls confirms that he initially joined the MGC. He was rapidly promoted and served as a QM sergeant in C Company. He stayed with the Tanks throughout the war and eventually reached the rank of WO2.

After the war, Victor and Ethel lived with Ethel's parents in Enfield. They had two sons, Eric was born in 1921 and Kenneth was born in early 1923. Victor became an auctioneer and the family settled in Palmers Green. Following the outbreak of war, Eric was joined the RAF Volunteer Reserve, and trained as a wireless operator and gunner. According to his gravestone, he was killed on active serving on 19 June 1941 whilst flying and was buried in Southgate Cemetery. Unusually he is not recorded in the Commonwealth War Graves records. In the 1950s, Victor and Ethel retired to Holland on Sea in Essex. Victor's younger son Kenneth married Doreen and settled at Winchmore Hill. However Ernest also had to bury his younger son Kenneth who died aged only thirty five whilst visiting his parents on 28 December 1958. Ethel died, less than two years later, aged seventy-one on 25 March 1960 and was buried in the same plot as her sons at Southgate. Victor himself died at Holland on Sea aged seventy five, on 19 January 1962.

Sergeant Edwin Levey also initially served as the QM sergeant with C Company. Edwin was born on 16 March 1893 in Charlton as his father worked as a saddlery surveyor at the Royal Arsenal at Woolwich. On leaving school Edwin initially worked as a draper and then joined the Army Reserve. He later became a Government inspector of woolen clothing, probably at the Arsenal whose roles had expanded greatly on the outbreak of war. Edwin was not mobilised until March 1916. When he joined the MMGS, he was five feet six inches tall but with a narrow thirty-three inch chest. Reporting to Bisley on 30 March 1916, his Government employment marked him out for quartermaster employment and he was soon promoted sergeant. His service records do not give any details of his service other than he remained serving with C Battalion for the bulk of the war. He later was posted to the 2nd Tank Carrier Company and served with that unit in Germany as a colour sergeant in the quartermaster role. He was not demobilised from the Rhine Army until September 1919. After he left the service, he became a commercial traveller and on 3 March 1922, changed his surname to Lawrence. He married Evelyn Pett at Greenwich later that summer and they had two sons; Brian who was born in June 1923 and Peter two years later. Edwin died aged seventy-seven in Dartford Kent in late 1971.

The final member of Companies HQ staffs was Sgt Frederick Howe who, like Edwin Levey, lived near Woolwich. He was born on 11 August 1889 in Charlton as the fourth son of a commercial clerk Walter Howe and his wife Frances. Frederick was baptised on 8 September 1889 at St Mary Magdalene Church in Woolwich. By 1911, he was working as an electrical instrument maker and living at 67 Little Heath in Old Charlton which was close by the Royal Artillery Barracks. When Frederick joined the Army, he was allocated to the Army Ordnance Corps and trained as an armourer. Whilst with the tanks, he would have carried out the repairs to the various weapons although the tank crews maintained the equipment. He served on in the armourer role after 1916 and eventually was discharged at the end of the war, having reached the rank of staff sergeant. Frederick did not marry until late in life. In the autumn of 1935, aged forty-six, he married Elizabeth Tinker at Greenwich where their elder daughter Frances was born in the autumn of 1936. Twelve years later, when Fredrick was fifty-eight, the couple's younger daughter Patricia was born. Sadly Frederick did not see Patricia grow to be a woman as he died aged sixty five, on 11 February 1955 at the Miller Hospital in Greenwich.

The list of C Company personnel extracted from the Landing Records at Le Havre mention a number of NCOs who did not serve in the headquarters. They were section sergeants, one of whom was to be commissioned before the end of the war whilst the other died in Burma in 1942, having taken part in the three month retreat from Rangoon to Imphal. Londoner Albert Bedford had been a key player in the training of C Company as he was a machine gun instructor. Born on 31 July 1893 in Lewisham, Albert was the elder son of a wholesale tobacconist and cigar importer. Albert's mother Louisa, who was seven years older than her husband, gave birth to Albert's younger brother Frederick the following year. The two boys were educated at Lewisham Bridge School but by 1901, the family had to 13 High Road in Lee where Albert's father, who continued to worked as a tobacconist. Ten years later, Albert Senior had set up as a cycle maker. Albert assisted his father as a tobacconist whilst Fred worked with bicycles. By the time he joined the MMGS on 11 August 1915, Albert had found work as a mechanic whilst his hobby was shooting with the London Volunteers. He was only five feet three inches tall but had just the skills required to become a machine gun instructor. Appointed acting lance corporal on 13 April 1916 and acting corporal one month later, he was promoted to acting sergeant on 27 June. He deployed to France with the first part of C Company on 14 August, so probably fought with No 2 Section. Certainly he was wounded during the first tank actions but not severely, he joined C Battalion as it formed and appointed as a section sergeant. Allocated to No 9 Company, he served under Major Edmond Forestier-Walker, who described Albert as one of his best section commanders. Albert contracted pleurisy in early March 1917 and, having been admitted to No 12 Stationary Hospital at St Pol Sur Ternoise on 18 March, was evacuated back to England at the end of the month.

Albert was initially treated at the Bradford War Hospital until 10 May when he was sent to convalesce at Ashton in Makerfield near Wigan where he heard about the new Tank crew arm badge and commented about it favourably in *The Motor Cycle*, his views being published on 7 June 1917. Two weeks later Albert was released from hospital and after nine days home leave, reported to Bovington where he served for two months. In September 1917, he was sent to the MGC Depot at Grantham where he served with No 36 Company. During his time at Bovington Albert was identified as having officer potential and on 10 November, he commenced officer training, first at Pirbright and then at Hazeley Down near Winchester.

Albert was commissioned in the Tank Corps on 29 March 1918 and then undertook further training at Wareham. On 10 July, at St Mary's Church in Lewisham, he married Lucie Brown, the twenty five year old daughter of a butcher Charles Robert Brown of 75 Ellerdale Road. Albert was now serving with 18th Battalion alongside Harold Teft, who had also been commissioned, as well as Charles Malpress and Robert Read who served in the ranks. They deployed back to France on 2 October but did not see action again. Albert returned to England on 31 January and was released from military duties on 29 March. Initially he lived with Lucie at her parents' house in Lewisham. Albert relinquished his commission on 1 September 1921 but never moved from Lewisham. Lucie and Albert's only son Michael was born in 1928 and was still living at home with his parents in 1959. Albert died aged seventy-nine, in Lewisham in early 1973

Sergeant Jimmie Anderson was more than twelve years older than Albert. He was born at Bridgend House in Musselburgh in Scotland, on 28 December 1881 and was the elder son of a regular soldier, Sergeant George Anderson of the 7th Dragoon Guards. In 1882, after a rebellion by Egyptian officers, 7th Dragoons were sent as part of 30,000 strong British and Indian Army force under Sir Garnet Wolseley, to protect British interests. The Egyptian took the attack to the British force at Kassassin on 10 September, catching them by surprise but the prompt action by the recently arrived Highland Brigade and 7th Dragoons forced the Egyptians to retreat. Three days later, George Anderson was again in action at the Battle of Tel El Kebir where the Egyptians lost more than 2,000 men against British fatalities of fifty-seven. George was later awarded a campaign medal for the action as well as a clasp for the Battle of Tel El Kebir. George later returned to Musselburgh where he and his wife Margaret had three more children, daughters Euphemia and Agnes and a son George. In 1893, Jimmie and his sisters were orphaned when his parents and younger brother George died.

On leaving school, Jimmie trained as a plumber and lived initially with his younger sister Agnes. He later retrained as an engineer and found work with the Oriental Telegraph Company in Rangoon where on 18 June 1913, he married Jeanni Federico. Their eldest son Dennis was born the following year. On 17 May 1915, Jimmie arrived at Liverpool from Rangoon and, after arranging for Jeanni to live at Markethall in Musselburgh, joined the MMGS. His service record has not survived but he was serving as a sergeant when C Company deployed to France on 16 August. His second son George, possibly named after his younger brother, was born on 6 July 1917. Jimmie was later transferred to the Royal Engineers, probably serving with one of the Tank Brigade Signal Companies

Jimmy Anderson and his sister Euphemia wearing a Motor Machine Gun Service sweetheart brooch. (Pattiann Nordgren)

where his professional expertise as a telegraph engineer would have made him extremely valuable. He later served as a company quartermaster sergeant.

After the Armistice, Jimmie returned to Scotland where Jeanni gave birth to their only daughter Helen on 18 July 1920 and their youngest son Francis on 22 November 1922. The following year Jimmie returned to Rangoon where, despite the fact that he was over 40, joined the locally raised British militia unit. He served with them throughout the 1930s and was company sergeant major when the Japanese invasion of Burma commenced. His unit included a battery of 18 pdr guns which were used in the anti-tank role as the British withdrew from Rangoon. The battery was in support of the 46th Indian Brigade on the east bank of the Sittang River before the railway bridge was blown and many men and most equipment lost. Some men, including Jimmy, managed to cross the 600 yard wide river and he eventually reached Imphal, on the Indian border, where the British established defensive positions to protect the entrance into India. He died, aged sixty, on or about 4 May 1942 and is buried at the Imphal War cemetery.

18

Crewmen casualties

Tanks were designed to reduce casualties amongst the British infantry by breaking through German barbed wire and destroying machine gun positions. The crewmen knew that their vehicle's armour was not proof against every bullet or shell and they expected to take casualties. Surprisingly, of the 390 men who went into action on 15 September 1916, only fifty-three were killed or died of their wounds as a result of their service in tanks. Some received injuries which affected them for the rest of their lives; some however were lucky and recovered to full health.

The Battle of Flers-Courcelette

Sergeant Alfred Howard, despite receiving gunshot wounds to the head on 15 September 1916, was one of the lucky ones. The son of a cashier, Alfred was born in Manchester on 10 April 1884 and baptised on 18 May at St Jude's Church in Ancoats, some 2½ miles from the family home at Lyme Grove. By the time he was sixteen Alfred was working as a commercial clerk and living on the Bradford Road with his uncle who was the vicar of St Philip's Church. The following year, Alfred married the nineteen year old Elizabeth Mills at St Thomas' Church, Ardwick on 24 March 1902. The couple were living at 12 Spring Street in Longsight when their eldest son Percy was baptised on 13 August at St Chrysostom's Church. Percy's brother Claude was born four years later on 10 March 1906. By 1911, the family had moved to Wilmslow in Cheshire, where they lived at Woodbine Cottage in Simpson Street. Alfred was, by now, working as a shipping clerk's manager and his sister Annie was living with them.

When Alfred joined the Army at Wilmslow on 8 December 1915, he was working as a correspondent and also a commercial traveller. He was thirty one years old, five feet six inches tall and ten stones three pounds and therefore better physically developed that many of the crewmen. Mobilised on 15 December 1915, Alfred joined the MMGS and was approved at their Bisley training centre on 28 December. He was transferred to the Armoured Car Section on 1 April 16 then to the Heavy Section of the MGC on 4 May. He was appointed lance corporal four days later and posted to C Company on 25 May 1916. Just over a month later, he was appointed paid acting sergeant and after training at Elveden, deployed to France with the main body of the company arriving at Le Havre on 24 August.

There is no record of the tank in which Alfred fought on 15 September but, given that he suffered head wounds, he must have been forced to leave the tank and was probably trying to make his way back to the British lines when he was wounded. He was initially treated at 34 Casualty Clearing Section at Grove Town near Meaulte, then sent by train to 11 General Hospital on the coast at Dannes-Camiers, arriving three days later. He was evacuated to the UK on the Hospital Ship *Asturias* on 27 September and would have been assessed by a casualty clearing centre, such as the one at Eastleigh, on arrival in the UK. Wherever possible, wounded men were allocated to hospitals near their families and Alfred was treated at 2nd Western General Hospital at Manchester. His wounds had healed by 21 November but, as Alfred had developed influenza, he was not released from hospital until 4 February 1917.

After nine days home leave, he was posted to the Depot Battalion at Bovington on 20 February. On arrival his wounds were assessed and Alfred was designated category C3 that is fit for service in garrisons at home. He was re-categorized to B1 on 12 July 17, which was a major improvement in his condition but he was still not fit for active service. He was therefore employed as an instructor, at Bovington, for the rest of the war. He was able to get regular leave and returned home. Towards the end of his service, he was employed at the Tank Corps Reserve unit at Swanage. His youngest daughter Ethel was born on 10 February 1919, just before Alfred was demobilised. Transferred to the Army Reserve on 26 March 1919, Alfred was awarded two medals: the British War Medal and the Victory Medal. Thereafter he totally disappears.

One of the D Company crewmen, who did not return from France, was thirty year old Gunner Meurig Jones from Llangadfan. He was born in the spring of 1886 at Llanfair Caereinion, a market town eight miles west of Welshpool. Meurig was the only son of John Jones, a woollens manufacturer; and the family lived on the Pool Road, the main road to Welshpool which is now the A458. By the time Meurig was fifteen, his father had become the proprietor of an hotel located in Llanfair High Street. Ten years later, the family had taken over the historic Cann Office Hotel at Llangadfan. Meurig assisted his father who also had five members of staff living in. In 1916, Meurig enlisted in the MGC at Welshpool. He made his will before deploying overseas with D Company, leaving his estate to his sister. I cannot identify in which tank he served on 15 September but he soon became very ill. This is not surprising as the tank crews had little protection against the elements and pictures show their bell tents and clothing being soaked by the foul October weather. Meurig was evacuated to 24th General Hospital at Étaples where he died on 2 November 1916. He is buried amongst the 10,000 who succumbed to wounds and sickness whilst at Étaples, making its military cemetery the largest CWGC site in France.

Just as there is no complete list of the members of C and D Companies, there is no full list of those who were killed or died as a result of their service with tanks. The Tank Corps Book of Honour, first published in 1919, attempted to list all fatalities but there are omissions amongst who served before 1 January 1917. Amongst them is Fred Horrocks, who was killed in action on 25 September 1916 as he was recovering tank D4 from the centre of Delville Wood. Fred was initially identified by Simon Payne, who has collected tank medals for many years and has developed a large database of those who served between 1916 and 1919. Having bought Fred's medal in 2009, he was intrigued by the lack of information about Fred's service and many friends helped in his search. I was able to find a mention of "Pte Horrocks" in the notebook of D Company's adjutant which is how we know his unit as the date of death was shown in Capt Woods' diary. His death was also mentioned in Eric Blake's letter and Simon's researches provided more information about his family.

Fred, who was born in summer 1885 at Tottington near Bury in Lancashire, was the eldest son of calico machine printer named Jeptha Horrocks and his wife Alice. Fred had three younger sisters, Mary who was born in 1888, May who was born three years later and Edith in 1897. As a young man, Fred joined the Refuge Assurance Company and worked at their local office in Bacup as a clerk. According to the 1911 census, Fred was working as a secretary in an insurance company at Tottington whilst his younger brother Frank was an articled clerk to an accountant. A contemporary photograph shows him to be an intelligent and smart young man.

By the time he enlisted into the Machine Gun Corps in 1916, the family had moved thirty miles away to Woodland View on the northern outskirts of Bacup. All the family were members of the Bacup Natural History society and Fred was employed by the Refuge Assurance Company as the cashier at their Burnley office which was seven miles to the north of his home. He joined the Army in March 1916 and, as he was a keen motor cyclist and had technical knowledge, he was assigned

Fred Horrocks. (Bacup Natural History Museum)

to the MMGS for training at Bisley and later to the Heavy Section MGC. There is no mention of him in the crew lists for 15 September so he was possibly a spare crewman for one of the female tanks. According to Graham Woods' notebook, Fred was designated as a Vickers gunner of the C tank crew allocated to the Reserve Army on 25 September. It was that same day when, aged thirty-one, he was killed. A local newspaper, The Rossendale Express, reported on 4 October 1916 that Fred had been killed in action whilst the Bacup History Society records that Fred was killed by a bursting shell having just finished writing a letter to his brother Frank who was serving as an assistant paymaster in the Royal Navy. A letter, written at the end of September by Eric Blake who fought in the tank *Dinnaken* on 15 September 1916, reveals that Fred was killed whilst trying to extract a tank from Delville Wood. Harassing fire by artillery on the rear areas was a constant threat to soldiers and, as well as killing Fred, the German shells injured three other crewmen. Fred's body was recovered and buried to the northeast of Green Dump which was the forward headquarters of D Company, located to the south west of Longueval by a track leading to Montauban. After the war, bodies located in the smaller burials grounds were concentrated and Fred's remains were moved to the Quarry cemetery near Montauban. Fred's life was commemorated at the Refuge Assurance Company War Memorial in the grounds of Fulshaw Hall at Wilmslow and at Christ Church in Bacup. Also on that brass memorial is the name of his younger brother Frank who drowned after his ship HMS *Redbreast* was sunk, by a U-boat, in the Aegean Sea on 15 July 1917 whilst on passage from Skyros to the Doro Channel. Both Frank and Fred were also commemorated at the Bacup Natural History Museum where their photographs were on display for many years; the image being recently located by the Museum staff.

Gunner Charles Bull, of C Company, died of wounds the following day. The younger son of a painter, Charles was born in Pokesdown near Bournemouth in February 1891 and was christened at St James' Parish Church on 3 May 1891. By the age of ten, Charles had moved north to live with his uncle Richard Bull in Tenbury Wells in Worcestershire. Richard was a postman and the family lived at Tene Street in the centre of the small spa town. Ten years later, Charles was living in Preston in Lancashire, where he worked as an ironmonger's assistant. By the time he enlisted in 1915, however, he had returned to the south of England and was living at Bridport. His service numbers indicates he must have joined the MGC in early 1916 and after training at Bisley, joined C Company. Deploying to France on 16 August 1916; he was badly injured, possibly whilst forward during a tank attack. He died aged twenty-five, on 28 September at a Casualty Clearing Station to the south of Meaulte and his body is buried at the Grove Town Cemetery.

Charles Johnson was wounded on 12 November 1916 whilst he was working at Euston Dump, a field storage area to the west of Serre. The British had been fighting in the area since 1 July 1916 and C Company's tanks were sent there in October to finally break through the German defences but were unable to do so due to the state of the ground. Charles was born in March 1886 at Great Munden in Hertfordshire and baptised on 8 December 1886. He was the youngest of seven children of Thomas and Helen Johnson; Thomas working as a farm manager. Charles became a carpenter and joiner and, from 1906, was employed by Messrs Ekins at Ware eventually becoming a foreman. By the time, he enlisted at Coventry into the MGC (Motors) on 15 May 1916 at the age of thirty, Charles had moved with his father in South Kensington. Just three months later, Charles deployed to France on 16 August with C Company but I can find no records of his tank crew. On 12 November 1916, Charles was wounded in the right elbow whilst working at Euston Dump. He was evacuated via Étaples where it was decided to treat the compound fracture in England and he was sent to the Norfolk War Hospital in Thorpe. Despite eight months treatment, his elbow could not flex and Charles had no feeling in his little finger. As a result it was decided he was unfit for further service. Awarded the Silver War Badge, Charles was discharged from the Army on 16 June 1917. He returned to the family home at High Cross Farm near Ware and, being unable to work as a carpenter, became a farmer. In 1919, he married a local farmer's daughter named Elsie Vigus who was nine years junior and they had two children Winifred, who was born on 24 April 1920 and Allan who also became a farmer. Charles originally worked for his father in law at Suter's farm but, by 1929, he was running both Rennesley and High Cross farms on his own. Elsie died in early 1942 but Charles survived eight years more. When he died, aged seventy-four, on 21 July 1950, he left an estate worth £20,847.

Not all wounds were physical and many tank crewmen suffered from shell shock. The cause of this illness was not well understood by the medical staff or chain of command but its effects were obvious to see. One such casualty was Gunner Willie Shire. Born on 1 September 1894, in Taunton, he was the eldest son of a postman Charles Shire and his wife Elizabeth. Willie and his two sisters were bought up in Rowbarton, first at 4 Gladstone Street, then at 27 Salisbury Street. Willie did not leave school at the normal age of fourteen but was still in education two years later which enabled him to gain work as a clerk. When he enlisted at Taunton on 9 December 1915, he volunteered to join the MMGS but he was not mobilised until 9 March 1916 when he was ordered to report to Bisley. He joined C Company on 27 May 16 and deployed to France on 16 August. I cannot identify the tank actions in which he fought in September 1916 but, given his later illness, he must have been affected by the sights, sounds and smells of close combat.

He was posted to C Battalion on 18 November 1916, returned to the Tank Depot on 18 March 1917 and then admitted to the Military Hospital at Woking ten days later with enlarged tonsils. He was released after they had been removed on 18 April 1917. Although Willie rebadged to the Tank Corps in July, he did not return to active service. He was obviously seriously ill with neurasthenia as, on 3 September, he was admitted to the Abram Peel War Hospital in Bradford. This hospital had become a recognised centre of treatment for shell-shock victims. After ten weeks, it was decided he was not fit for further military service but he was fit to return to his civilian occupation. Discharged from the Army on 13 December as "no longer physically fit for war service due to sickness" he was awarded the Silver War Badge and returned to Taunton. He recovered from his illness and in the autumn of 1921, he married a local girl, Gladys Penny who was from Bradford on Tone. Their daughter Kathleen was born in Taunton three years later. Despite having left the Army as a result of shell-shock, Willie obviously retained fond memories and did not lose touch with all of his fellow crewmen as, in 1925; he is recorded as a member of the C Battalion Old Comrades Association. He lived in Taunton for the rest of his life, his daughter Kathleen marrying in 1957. He died in 1974 in his eightieth year; his widow surviving until 1993.

The Battle of Arras

Sergeant Robert Hillhouse was injured even before the first tanks went into action on the Somme. On 11 September, as C Company's tanks were being prepared for action near the Loop railway siding, a fire broke out inside a tank and a crewman was trapped. Robert, together with Gunner John Callaghan, rescued the soldier, John Callaghan receiving burns to his face and hands. Robert, who was also injured, was the eldest son of John and Isabella Hillhouse. He was born on 10 October 1886 in Kilpatrick in Dunbartonshire and, as a fifteen year old, he was employed as a railway clerk. Ten years later, he was living next to his parents in a bothy at Stoneywood to the west of Denny and was working as a carter with his father. On 27 December 1912, Robert married Janet Dunn and the couple had two daughters. Although Robert was a carter by trade, he was also an experienced driver as he passed the MMGS trade test at Coventry. He rose rapidly through the ranks, reaching the rank of Sergeant before he deployed to France on 16 August 1916. For his bravery in rescuing the crewman from the burning tank on 11 September, Robert was Mentioned in Despatches.

After the first actions, Robert was allocated to No 8 Company in the newly formed C Battalion. On the opening day of the Battle of Arras, this Company was in action near Beaurains, assisting 14th Division in their successful assault of the defensive position known as the Harp. Two days later Robert was killed as tanks attacked the village of Monchy-le-Preux. Only three tanks got into the village but they managed to suppress the enemy machine guns until the attacking infantry took control of the village. The unarmoured Mark II tanks were easily penetrated by German armour piercing bullets and the defenders were also not afraid to take on the tanks at close quarters. None of the tanks returned to their rallying point and several crewmen were killed including Robert. As his gravesite is unknown, he was commemorated on the Arras memorial to the missing and at Denny and Dunipace cemetery.

Another C Company crewman who lost his life during the Battle of Arras was Gunner Maurice Voile. Born on 11 January 1893, in Cheltenham, Maurice was the younger son of a coal merchant George Voile and his wife Ellen Carter who was from Geelong in Australia. His father died when Maurice was only eleven years old after which he was educated at Cheltenham Grammar School. He later moved, with his mother and elder sister Edith, to Herne Hill in South London where he trained as a surveyor. Maurice visited Canada for a short while before returning to the UK, via New York on 11 January 1914. On 2 September 1914, aged twenty-one, Maurice married his childhood sweetheart Winifred in Cheltenham. They bought Ivy Home Farm, a poultry farm between Tonbridge and Royal Tunbridge Wells, where their daughter Joan was born on 3 July 1915.

Maurice Voile and his
daughter Joan 1916.
(Oliver Davey)

Prior to enlisting in the Army, Maurice moved his wife and daughter back to Cheltenham. His MGC number is one of the series issued to the MGC Cavalry but it is likely he served with the MMGS as he is pictured wearing leather gaiters when visiting his family home in 1916 (above). Maurice deployed to France on 16 August 1916 probably with No 2 Section, and was probably a spare crewman at the Battle of Flers-Courcelette. Like most of those in C Company, Maurice transferred to C Battalion on its formation and, like Robert Hillhouse, served with No 8 Company. He retrained as a driver over the winter months and served in a section commanded by Lieutenant Charles Elliot, who had commanded a male tank in support of the Guards near Ginchy on 15 September 1916. On 9 April 1917, the opening day of the Battle of Arras, Maurice was the driver of the female tank C39, commanded by James Cameron, whose crew also included Corporal Charles Spurgeon and Gunner John Newell. As they fought their way through the Harp position, the tank was hit from the front by direct fire as it reached an enemy strongpoint. David Fletcher in his book "Tanks and Trenches" states: "2nd Lieutenant Cameron found a gap in the attack where the infantry had lost touch. He engaged the enemy with Lewis gun fire until the infantry had time to come up and consolidate. During this time he routed an enemy machine gun crew and captured their gun. A little later the tank received a direct hit, killing one and wounding three of the crew. After attending to the wounded, Lieutenant Cameron handed five of his Lewis guns and ammunition to the infantry. The man killed was Maurice Voile and his comrades buried him near where he fell".

This burial spot, known as the Harp Redoubt Cemetery, was close to a German strongpoint on the south side of village of Tilloy. Maurice's death was reported in the local Cheltenham paper; the obituary on 28 April added the information that the shell which killed Maurice was from a long range gun. Maurice's life was commemorated at Cheltenham Grammar school; on his father's gravestone in Cheltenham Cemetery and on the Cheltenham Borough war Memorial. His widow Winifred settled at Cleeve Hill and brought up their daughter Joan. She died, after forty-six year widowhood, in 1963. Joan never married and she died in Bristol in 1996.

Gunner David Haywood was sent back to England, during the Battle of Arras, on 20 April 17 and was later discharged from the Army because he was no longer fit for war service. Henry David Haywood, to use his full name, was born on 7 September 1888 at Church Lench, a small village 5 miles to the north of Evesham. His father, also known as Henry, was fifty-six when his eldest son was born, his wife Alice Greening being almost half his age when they married in 1886. Alice and Henry had three more children, Ernest, Leonard and Miriam who was born in 1899. Henry must have died soon after as, by 1891, Alice had moved to Evesham where she worked as a charwoman. Sadly Ernest is recorded, the next year, as being a permanent inmate at the newly constructed infirmary of Evesham Union Poorhouse.

David later became a mechanic and, in 1911, was boarding at 23 North Road at Bengeworth where he was working as a cycle and motor repairer. On 16 November 1912, at the age of twenty-four, he married Henrietta Bearcroft at the Evesham Wesleyan Methodist Chapel. The couple's elder son Henry was being born at 3 Kings Road in Evesham on 27 November 1913. When David enlisted into the Army, on 18 November 1915, he tried to join the Royal Engineers possibly as a dispatch rider. He was not however mobilised until 16 March 1916 and was then allocated to the MGC. He was authorised at Bisley on 11 April and deployed to France on 24 August which means he served in either No 3 or No 4 Section on the right flank of the British attack on 15 September between Ginchy and Combles. In November 1916, he was transferred to C Battalion but was returned to the UK on 20 April 1917 but sadly his pension record gives no clue as to the reason. He was discharged on 3 October 1917 and returned to Evesham. Henrietta and David's son Raymond was born on Boxing Day 1918. Despite his injuries, David survived and lived at Evesham until his death, at the General Hospital in Cheltenham, on 6 December 1944. His widow Henrietta lived in Evesham until her death, aged eighty-one, in 1970.

Sergeant James MacGregor was, like Meurig Jones, the son of an hotelier. He was born on 15 June 1896 at Fetteresso which is a small village near the Aberdeenshire coast. By the time James was five, his father George was running the hotel at Muchalls, five miles north of Stonehaven. George and his wife Angela had four children of whom James was the third. After leaving school, James started work with the Northern Cooperative Society in Aberdeen and trained as a chemist's assistant whilst boarding in Crown Street. He was an extremely slim young man; his chest measurement was only 33 inches. He enlisted into the MMGS on 13 August 1915 and, three days later, was at Bisley. After initial training, he joined No 27 Battery and then, on 1 April 1916, was transferred to the Armoured Car Section. He was appointed acting lance corporal on 13 April and acting corporal on 15 May before joining C Company on 27 May. Despite the fact he was only twenty years old, and had no military experience, he was appointed acting sergeant on 27 June. His service record does not reveal much about his operational service other than he was posted to C Battalion on 18 October. He served with No 9 Company and retrained as a driver. On 31 July, as his section attempted to cross the swamp-like conditions of the Ypres Salient, he was driving the tank *Coquette* which he managed to get to her objective at Frezenberg. The tank eventually bellied but its crew continued beating off a German counter-attack. According to the Company war history, James was wounded but this could not have been serious as it is not mentioned in the Brigade list of casualties.

James was appointed 1st Class tank machinist on 6 August 1917, which indicates that he was a senior driver. James was again wounded on 20 November, the opening day of the Battle of Cambrai, whilst his tank was attacking the objective at Le Pave Farm. Again this was not sufficiently serious for him to be evacuated from the unit. After Christmas leave, James stayed with the now redesignated 3rd Light Tank Battalion as it re-equipped with Whippet tanks and served with them through the loss of British captured ground in March 1918 and as the Allies advanced in August and September 1918. After the Battalion's final action, at the second Battle of Cambrai on 8 October, James was sent back to the UK and joined the Tank Depot. Here he was allocated to one of the nearest formed units, 22nd Light Tank Battalion which had a number of Flers-Courcelette veterans amongst its ranks. He served on, after the Armistice, at Bovington until he was discharged on 23 March 1919. Returning home to Aberdeen, he tried to get his old job back with the Northern Cooperative Society but he was not in good health. He suffered from Disordered Action of the Heart; a condition known to affect veterans since the American Civil War and which is nowadays known as neuro-circulatory asthenia. The symptoms were susceptibility to fatigue, shortness of breath, rapid pulse, chest pains and anxiety. He was granted a pension until April 1920 and then made a further claim which was being actioned in September 1920. Thereafter, he disappears from view, one of the many whose war service caused not physical damage but who suffered greatly from stress as a result of their experiences.

The Third Battle of Ypres known as the Battle of Passchendaele

Gunner Philip Evans, who was born at Chester in early 1896, was killed shortly after C Battalion arrived in the Ypres Salient in July 1917. He was the son of the Upton schoolmaster, John Evans and his wife Annie. Philip was working in London when he enlisted into the MMGS at Coventry. He deployed to France on 16 August 1916 and, after the first actions, served with C Battalion as a clerk. Philip was promoted to corporal and worked in the battalion headquarters. During the build-up to the Third Battle of Ypres, the tanks of C and F Battalions were offloaded between Poperinghe and Ypres and then moved into Oosthoek Wood. The activity was spotted by the Germans and, on the night of 3 July, the wood was targeted using long range artillery. The shells hit C Battalion Headquarters and Philip was badly wounded. He died of his wounds the following day and is buried, with three other members of the battalion headquarters at the Gwalia Military

Cemetery. Philip is also commemorated on the parish war memorial at Upton and the local record shows he was awarded the Military Medal. I have been unable to find this either in the Tank Corps Book of Honour or in the *London Gazette*.

During the Third Battle of Ypres, which started twenty-eight days later and lasted four months, the attacking British Empire forces suffered over 300,000 casualties. The ground conditions are unimaginable and contemporary photographs do not adequately show the ghastly devastation between Ypres and the high ground around Poelcapelle. The farmland had been pulverized by shell fire, woods had been reduced to fragments and the ditches and streams which were essential to drain the former marshland were destroyed. Heavy rain had saturated the ground for several weeks and it was almost impossible to survive the elements, let alone reduce the well organised German defences. Well sited concrete bunkers, equipped with machine guns, had clear fields of fire over attacking troops and, when tanks deployed to help the "Poor Bloody Infantry", the ponderous vehicles were unable to cope with the conditions. Many were swamped and the area became known as "The Graveyard of the Tanks". The battle was eventually won by the Australian, British, Canadian and New Zealand formations as they pushed the Germans back to the top of the ridge which dominated the city of Ypres. The remains of the small village of Passchendaele were captured on 6 November but Victory was however short lived. When the Germans attacked again the following spring, most of the ground was recaptured.

One of the earliest tank casualties in the Ypres Salient was Gunner Lionel Griffin. He was the eldest of four sons born to a Bristolian named Joseph Griffin and his Welsh wife Ellen Ryan who came from Merthyr Tydfil. Lionel was christened on 6 September 1886 at the Catholic Church of St Nicholas of Tolentino in Easton and bought up in the Montpelier area of the city. His father was originally a commercial traveller but, by 1901, he had no work. Ellen had become a boarding house keeper and Lionel a pupil teacher to sustain the family. Lionel later moved to Scotland and, from 1911 to 1914, joined the teaching staff on the Training Ships *Mars*, which was moored on the River Tay off Woodhaven opposite Dundee. He then joined the staff of the Dens Road School in Dundee where he enlisted into the Army. As he deployed to France on 24 August, he must have been a member of either No 3 or 4 Section. He continued to serve with C Battalion after its formation in November 1916 and, having retrained as a driver, was killed in action on 31 July 17 during the Battle of Pilkim Ridge. Whether he was serving with No 7 or No 9 Company is not recorded, nor are the details of his tank. Moreover, either his body was not recovered or his gravesite was lost, as he is commemorated on Panel 56 of the Menin Gate Memorial at Ieper. His life is also remembered at St Joseph's Roman Catholic Church in Wilkies Lane Dundee and on the Scottish National Memorial at Edinburgh Castle.

Gunner John Newell, who also served with C Battalion, was fatally wounded the same day. However he did not die until four months later. Born in Bradford, West Yorkshire, on 8 February 1893, John was the only son of cabinet maker and shopkeeper John Newell. He was baptised on 19 March at St Matthew's Church Bankfoot close to the family home st 75 Manchester Road. John had two younger sisters, Emma and Suzy. The family firm expanded and they lived above their furniture premises on 822-4 Manchester Road. The firm must have been successful as, at the time of the 1901 census, John was a visitor to the Hydropathic Hospital at Southport which was a favoured resort for cures. By 1911, Haigh had moved the family business to Morecombe Bay but John remained at Bankfoot working as a pawnbroker's assistant. John enlisted into the MGC at Bradford and, after the normal machine gun training at the Heavy Section Centre at the Siberia Ranges near Bisley, moved with the main body of C company to Elveden and then on to France on 16 August. After the first actions, he was transferred to C Battalion and served with No 8 Company.

On 9 April 1917, the first day of the Battle of Arras, John was a crewman in the female tank 599; she was commanded by Lieutenant James Cameron and amongst her crew were Charles Spurgeon and Maurice Voile. The C Battalion War Diary states:

The objective of this company (No 8) on the BLUE LINE was that formidable work known as the Harp which, owing to the width of the trenches and number and form of the traverses, was a most difficult proposition for tanks to tackle. It was afterwards found that the ground on the top of the plateau was waterlogged and much blown to pieces by shell fire. In spite of these difficulties half of the company succeeded in fighting their way as far as the String of the Harp before becoming "bellied". The tank then received the direct hit which killed Maurice Voile.

Later renumbered as 205475 in the Tank Corps, John was transferred to No 7 Company and served in No 4 Section under Captain Wilfred Gates MC. On the opening day of the Third Battle of Ypres, John was wounded whilst serving in the female tank *Cuidich'n Rich* which commanded by Lieutenant Evelyn O'Conor. The tank, named after the motto of the Seaforth Highlanders, bellied near Wild Wood but was successfully unditched by the crew who then supported the infantry attack. The tank crew engaged German snipers and enemy machine guns which were dug into the German defensive position. The tank then went forward but bellied halfway between the defensive locations called Potsdam and Frezenberg. It was hit by a large calibre German shell, which wrecked the engine and four out of five Lewis Guns. All of the crew but one was wounded and John was so badly hurt that he was evacuated to the United Kingdom. He died of his wounds in Glasgow, three months later, on 13 November 1917 and was buried three days later, by his parents in St Matthew's Churchyard at Bankfoot.

Getting bellied tanks back into action was not without risk as crewmen from the tank battalions and specialists from the Salvage Company worked to extract swamped and damaged tanks often under enemy fire. As a result there were casualties amongst the tank crewmen including Charles Malpress. Charles who served with No 8 Company knew only too well about the dangers of being in the Salient. His older brother Edward had been killed on 2 August 1917 whilst serving with 197 Siege Battery near Voormezeele. Charles and Edward, who were sons of a chimney sweep from Sydenham in South London, had both enlisted on 7 February 1916. Charles, who was born on 14 April 1889, was educated at Holy Trinity School in Lewisham. Whilst most of the family later worked for their father, Charles worked in a laundry; he also moved away from the family home at Willow Walk in Sydenham and lived in Raynes Park. He was running his own business when he enlisted into the Army. Unusually, Charles and Edward did not serve together as Edward was sent to an artillery unit in Plymouth for training whilst Charles was sent to the MMGS Training Centre at Bisley.

Having been posted to C Company in late May, he moved to New Farm Camp in Elveden for tank training. Charles was granted pre-deployment leave in early August but delayed his return by two days; as a result he was charged with absence and was awarded seven days No 2 punishment and two days stoppages of pay. This was his first and last brush with formal military discipline. Charles deployed to France on 24 August and, after the first tank actions, was posted to C Battalion. It is likely that Charles served with No 8 Company during the Battle of Arras although no crew lists exist. Charles then attended courses at the Tank Driving School at Wailly between 19 – 25 May and then again from 11-19 June and qualified as a driver.

No 8 Company was not in action on 29 July, the first day of the Battle of Passchendaele, being held for future tasks, but Charles was wounded on 10 August. He was hit in the head, whether by a bullet or a piece of shell-fragment is unknown. He was evacuated straight back to 1 Canadian General Hospital at Étaples on 11 August; this is a remarkably long journey for a wounded man and quite out of the normal run of things. Charles stayed at Étaples until 4 October 1917, when he was posted to the Tank Reinforcements Depot at nearby Dannes-Camiers. Four days later, he was sent to rejoin C Battalion which was back at the Tank Corps Administrative area near St Pol sur Ternoise. On 3 November, Charles left for the Plateau railhead, which was the same location as the Loop railhead where he had arrived with C Company in early September 1916. Then he moved forward, with his company by rail to the tank concentration areas near Villers-Guislan in preparation for the Battle of Cambrai.

Charles was wounded again, on 20 November on the opening day of the battle; this time receiving a gunshot wound to the hip; the bullet travelling down into his thigh. This is an odd wound for a driver so it is likely that he received it after his tank had been hit; both tanks in his section being destroyed. The wound was sufficiently serious for Charles to be evacuated to England where he was first treated at the West Bridgford Military Hospital and then, from 29 December, at the Pavilion Auxiliary Hospital at Chorley Wood. Although it is clear the bullet had not been removed, the wound had healed and he was released from hospital on 9 January. Granted local leave until 18 January, he was posted to the Command Depot at Catterick on 25 January 18. On 6 February, Charles was admitted to the local Military Hospital suffering from tetanus. He was seriously ill but responded well to treatment and was released on 23 March. Charles was then posted to Tank Corps Receiving Depot at Worgret Camp near Wareham on 20 April. It took four months before he was fully fit for active service. On 17 August 1918, Charles married Alice Poyton at All Saint's Church in Hampton upon Thames. The Allied advance had begun earlier that month with the striking success of the Battle of Amiens and new tank units were being prepared for deployment. Charles was posted to 18th Battalion at Bovington on 13 September and embarked for France on 2 October. As it was, the German Government sued for armistice before the new unit could get into action.

Charles was then posted to 16th Battalion which was sent to Germany as part of the British Army of the Rhine. Promoted to corporal on 27 March 1919, his duties were not onerous and Charles was granted home-leave in April. He did not however return to England for de-mobilisation until 5 September 1919. Remarkably Charles did not seek a war pension as he was discharged. He was fully fit (A1) and presumably felt he was lucky to be unscathed despite his wounds. Charles and Alice settled at Hampton upon Thames and had three sons; the eldest Edward being born in early 1922 – he was named after Charles' dead brother. James was born in 1930 and Thomas in 1935. In January 1950, Charles and Alice accompanied their eldest son Edward to New South Wales. Charles' younger sister had settled at Murwillumbah near Richmond; Alice and Charles settled close by. Charles planned to be a farmer and in 1954 he set up a dairy herd at Kunghur. He stayed there until 1963 when he retired. He had a well-deserved retirement and died aged seventy-nine, in Liverpool NSW; Alice lived until she was eighty-five, dying in 1980 at Green Valley.

Not all of the First Tank Crews stayed with their original units; two were posted to the MGC Infantry branch and lost their lives on successive days albeit many miles apart. Gunner George Wootley was the first casualty. Born in September 1888 at Welling in Kent, George was the son of a general labourer named Henry Wootley and his wife Emily. In 1891 the family was living at 27 Francis Street in Plumstead. Sadly, Henry lost his father when he was young and his mother, having remarried in 1895, was again widowed ten years later. The family moved to Tottenham where George worked as a printers' machine minder. When he enlisted on 16 November 1915, he joined the Royal Artillery and served with 43 Battery and then 45 Battery RFA at Plymouth. Posted to U Motor Battery on 19 March, he was transferred to C Company on 24 May. Having fought with C Company on the Somme and served for a short while with C Battalion, he was posted to the MGC Base Depot on 21 January. He was hospitalized from 9 to 20 February whilst at Dannes-Camiers but did not return to serve with the tanks. On 22 June, he was transferred from the Heavy Branch to Infantry Branch and on 7 July 1917, was posted to 149 Company MGC, which was supporting 50th (Northumberland) Division. This formation was not initially engaged in the Third Battle of Ypres but held the line near Arras. George was killed in action, on 15 August 1917, and his body buried at Heninel Communal Cemetery Extension, ten miles to the south east of Arras and sixty miles from where the British were trying to push back the Germans near Ypres.

Gunner Alfred Williams was killed the following day in the Salient. He was born on 22 September 1888 in Great Sutton near Ellesmere Port. His father Richard was the manager of an oil cake mill which produced fertilizer, and was also a farmer. Alfred was one of ten children; two of whom died. His brothers were also involved in the oil cake business but, in 1911, Alfred was a clerk in a soap works. He later moved to Rusholme which was part of Manchester and where he enlisted into the MGC. Like George Wootley, he did not stay with the tanks after their early actions but was posted to 25 Machine Gun Company, which was part of 8th Infantry Division. He was killed on 16 August, during the ongoing British attacks in the Ypres Salient, but the location of his death and grave is unknown. As a result, he is commemorated, together with more than 34,500 others whose graves are unknown, at the Tyne Cot Memorial to the Missing. After the war, his balance of pay and a small war gratuity was paid to his widow Hannah; sadly I have been unable to ascertain when they were married or if they had children.

The Third Battle of Ypres lasted almost four months. Although No 8 Company was not committed to the initial attacks on 31 July, it was deployed, with 18 Company of F Battalion, to support the follow-up assault on 22 August. The rain had not ceased and the tanks had to approach across ground which was covered with large shell holes full of water. Many ditched and, despite the urgent efforts of crewmen using the new unditching beam and material found on the battlefield, some tanks became stuck before they reach the British front line Crews were killed and injured as they tried to get their tanks forward to support the infantry or, if the tank was immovable, to return on foot to safety. One of those killed was Gunner William Hudson who was born in Aston in Birmingham about 1897. William was the tenth of eleven children born to Alfred Hudson and his wife Sarah Dolby. William was brought up at 35 Fisher Street in the Bishop Ryder area, which is now the site of Aston University. His service record has not survived but he enlisted at Coventry into the MMGS in late 1915. He deployed to France on 16 August 1916 with No 2 Section of C Company and, one month later aged only nineteen, took part in the first tank actions. Sadly his tank is not recorded but he was probably fighting in support of the Guards Division. In November 1916, he joined C Battalion and was posted to No 8 Company which mainly consisted of veterans from C Company. He fought through the Battle of Arras unscathed but was killed, aged only twenty years old, during the action near Frezenberg on 22 August. Unusually his body was recovered and it is now buried at the specially made concentration cemetery called New Irish Farm to the north of Sint Jan.

According to the C Battalion war history, Gunner William Wood was also serving with No 8 Company when he was seriously wounded on 22 August 1917. He had enlisted into the MMGS on 22 November and deployed with C Company in August 1916. He was seriously wounded in the Gallipoli Farm area, which sat on Hill 35, about 4 miles from Ypres on the Roeselare road. William was evacuated back to England and, just over one year later, was discharged due to his wounds. He was awarded the Silver War Badge on 26 August 1918 but did not lose contact with his comrades, He was still alive in 1925, according to the 3rd Light Tank Battalion Old Comrades Association but sadly his address was unknown.

A third crewman who was injured on 22 August, and evacuated back to England, was Private Stanley Conder who suffered gunshot wounds to his right thigh during the attack near Hill 35. Stanley was born on 28 June 1892 at Chesterton in Cambridgeshire. He was the eldest son of John Conder, a horticultural builder, and his wife Edith, who later moved to Cherry Hinton. John was a prominent local councilor and a member of Cambridge Corporation with a particular interest in education. On 28 February 1910, aged only seventeen, Stanley was appointed, after open competition, as a second division clerk in the Register General's office. He initially worked locally but then was appointed as a second class clerk to the India Office. Despite being in a good position, and presumably eligible to join one of the London Regiment battalions, Stanley decided to enlist into the MMGS on 14 July 1915. He was sent to Bisley the same day and was therefore one of the more experienced soldiers who volunteered to join the Armoured Car Section in April 1916. Stanley was eventually allocated to C Company and, given that he embarked for France on 24 August 1916, he probably served with No 3 or 4 Sections.

There is no official record of the tank in which he fought either at the Battle of Flers-Courcelette or during the Battle of Arras when he was served in No 8 Company. However, a letter sent to his parents in late April 1917, which was published in a local paper, confirms that Stanley was in action both on 9 and 23 April. "I was in action again last Monday and I believe we did very well. It was the hottest time I have ever had, so hot that we used every round of ammunition we carried. About 100 Fritzes gave themselves up to us eventually but it took us a couple of hour's hard work to persuade them to do so. They showed a great deal more fight that they did a fortnight previously." It is often difficult to link an individual report to battalion records but, from his description, I believe that Stanley was a crewman in the male tank no 776, commanded by Sergeant Jimmy Noel who was awarded the Distinguished Conduct Medal for the actions near the Chemical Works at Roeux. Stanley's letter also provided details of a more domestic nature describing his failure to separate his handkerchiefs whilst washing with the obvious result that his white handkerchief was no longer white and his concern that his attempts to repair a rent in his trousers would be equally unsuccessful.

Stanley then attended a 6 pdr gunnery course at No 2 Tank Brigade school from 14 to 19 May 17 before attending a driving course at Wailly from 16 to 23 June 17. Deploying to the Ypres Salient, he was next in action on 22 August when he was wounded, probably as he tried to get back to safety after his tank had become bellied in the dreadful ground conditions between Ypres and Frezenberg. Stanley made a full recovery and rejoined C Battalion on 27 December 1917. Having retrained as a driver, he was detached to 13th Battalion as an instructor on 4 March and was graded 1st Class Tank Mechanic nine days later. Stanley returned to 3rd Light Battalion on 4 May 1918 and was promoted lance corporal on 11 August 1918 to replace one of the NCOs injured on the opening days of the Battle of Amiens. On 19 October, after 3rd Battalion was in action for the last time, Stanley was transferred to the Home Establishment and sent back to England, possibly to serve in one of the new Battalions. This was unnecessary, following the Armistice, and Stanley was released to return to the Civil Service. During his demobilisation leave, on 29 December 1918, Stanley admitted himself to No 4 London General (Kings College) Hospital, where two weeks later, part of a bullet was removed from his right thigh.

Stanley was discharged from the Army on 23 January 1919 and settled near Clapham Common. On 17 February 1921, Stanley married a domestic economy instructor named Margaret Bailey at his local church, St Barnabas'. Margaret was originally from St Johns' near Woking so it is possible that they met whilst Stanley was training at Bisley. The couple moved to Baldock in Hertfordshire where Stanley would have had good rail links to his work in London and also to his family in Cambridge. The couple settled in a newly built house on Mons Avenue but sadly Margaret died in early 1924. He returned to London and remarried in 1926, his bride Dorothy Baylis being the thirty-one year old daughter of a fellow civil servant. The couple, who settled in Carshalton, had two daughters, Jean born in 1927 and Ann two years later. Sadly Dorothy died on 4 November 1943. Stanley remained in Carshalton and married a third time in early 1946, his wife Winifred Gant having worked as civil servant in the India office in 1926. The couple lived at Carshalton until Stanley's death aged sixty-three, on 15 January 1956.

The Battle of Cambrai

Every fit tank was withdrawn from the Ypres Salient by early October although the fighting in the area did not cease for another six weeks. Despite the sustained efforts of the Salvage Company, few of those tanks which were swamped could be extracted and stayed in the Flanders mud until the rivers and drains were reinstated, the hulks were then blown up as part of the battlefield clearances. The large losses near Ypres confirmed that tanks needed good going if they were to be useful in the attack and an opportunity presented itself at the southern limits of the British Line near Cambrai. Almost 400 tanks, both new and repaired, were sent there in November 1917 where they successfully broke through the German defences. It was the largest British advance of the Great War to that date but there were insufficient infantry available to defend the captured positions and the British were soon evicted from much of the ground they had taken.

By comparison with some tank units at Cambrai, C Battalion escaped relatively lightly in terms of tank and crew losses. The unit was initially tasked to work on the eastern edge of the attack between La Vacquerie and Banteux. The Battalion managed to break through the German defences although No 8 Company, which had most of the First Tank Crews in its ranks, lost two tanks to direct fire and one crewman casualty was Gunner Harry Tiffin. Harry, who was born in Kirkoswald in Cumberland, was the eldest son of a draper and bank agent called John Tiffin. Baptised at Kirkoswald on 14 February 1892, Harry had five surviving siblings, two brothers called Maurice and Edmund and three sisters; Elsie, Ena and Florence. On leaving school, Harry worked in his father's drapery shop. His service record has not survived but *The Motor Cycle* confirms that he enlisted into the MMGS at Coventry on 24 November 1915. He was later joined by his younger brother Maurice who served with the Tanks in E Company. Maurice fought with the Middle East Detachment at the Second Battle of Gaza in His Majesty's Landship *Tiger*.

Harry Tiffin served with No 9 Company of C Battalion at the Battle of Cambrai. He was a member of Captain Eric Purdy's section and his tank commander was Lieutenant Palgrove Powell of the Welsh Regiment. On 20 November, his tank *Comet II* formed part of the second wave and was one of five tanks tasked to support the attack on Pam-Pam Farm. This strong point was

Gunner Harry Tiffin.
(David Storey)

the location of four German bunkers which dominated the road junction between Peronne, St Quentin and Cambrai. Its garrison put up a remarkable fight and eventually ten tanks were needed to suppress the defenders before it could be captured by infantry from the Royal West Kent and the Suffolk Regiments. *Comet II* then drove north to capture Le Quennel Farm, another complex which dominated the St Quentin to Cambrai road. Accompanied by the tank *Cayenne, Comet II* captured the farm building without opposition and then continued north. It was then knocked out by a German artillery piece and set on fire. Harry's body was not recovered and he is commemorated on the Cambrai memorial to the missing at Louverval.

Two other crewmen, who originally served with C Company, were so badly wounded on 20 November that they had to be sent back to England; one was Gunner Charles Hewitt and the other Gunner Robert Read. Charles Hewitt was born 6 February 1897 at Winterbourne near Bristol. The eldest son of an engine fitter, Charles left Winterbourne as a young man and, when he enlisted into the MMGS, at Coventry on 18 August 1915, he was working as a mining engineer living in Maeshyref in Monmouthshire. After initial training at Bisley, he was posted to 27th Battery MMGS on 1 December 1915 then to the Armoured Car Company on 1 April 1916. Charles' military record tells us nothing about his service after he deployed to France on 16 August as a gunner. He probably joined No 7 Company when C Battalion was formed and, after the Battle of Arras, attended the driving course at Wailly on 11 – 19 June 1917. Charles' tank must have either have ditched or been knocked out on 20 November. A shell burst near him, whilst he was unprotected by his tank's armour and he suffered wounds to the shoulder, right arms, buttocks and both thighs. He was sent back to the Base Hospital at Étaples where a shrapnel ball was removed from his neck on 1 December. Evacuated to London five days later, Charles was treated at Hornsey Auxiliary Military Hospital where more matter was removed from his right thigh. He was sent to convalescent hospital on 26 January and then released.

Six months later, he was admitted to Central Military Hospital at Eastbourne on 25 June when an abscess was found in his right thigh. The abscess was caused by metal fragments remaining in his body and the subsequent treatment was protracted. Charles was readmitted to hospital twice more before he was sent to the Summertown Convalescent Hospital on 20 September 1918. Here he would have met a man with an interest in his story as Captain Harold Mortimore, who commanded the first tank to go into action on 15 September 1916, was adjutant at the hospital. A Medical Board later declared Charles was no longer fit to serve in the Army and he was discharged on 28 November 1918. He was awarded a Silver War Badge on discharge but more importantly, a pension for six months. Although his home address was given as the Grove at Penmaen in Monmouthshire, Charles did not stay in Wales for long. In early 1920, he married Vera Carrell at Blaby near Leicester and they had two daughters, Vera who was born in the spring of June 1921 and her younger sister Sylvia was born in the autumn of the following year. The committee of 3rd Light Battalion tried to get in contact with him in 1925 but they probably failed as his address is shown as Winterbourne Down. However, he did not lose touch entirely and Charles attended the 50th anniversary dinner night at Caxton Hall in London on 15 September 1966. Vera and Charles moved to Somerset for their retirement; Vera died at Weston Super Mare in 1986 and Charles died two years later aged ninety one.

Gunner Robert Read was born at Evercreech, between Shepton Mallet and Bruton in Somerset, on 15 November 1885. The son of grocer Charles Read and his wife Ellen, Robert worked for the family business before he enlisted at Bristol on 17 December 1915. He sought a MMGS vacancy at Coventry on 13 March, was mobilised two days later and joined the Armoured Car Section as it was formed on 1 April 1916 at Bisley. Robert's service record does not reveal much about the actions in which he fought. After the Battle of Arras, he went with other members of C Battalion to Wailly from 11 to 19 June 1917 for driver training. During the Battle of Cambrai, Robert served with 5 Section of No 8 Company. He fought as a gunner and third driver, that is to say he also operated the secondary gears which were fitted at the rear of the tank. Robert was injured on 20 November, suffering from gunshot wounds to the right shoulder. After initial treatment locally, Robert was treated at Rouen and returned to England on 25 November. He was sent to the 3rd Western General Hospital, which had been established at the Cardiff Royal Infirmary, and stayed there until the end of January. He was declared fully fit for duty then granted home leave until 8 February 1918. Posted to Depot Battalion ten days later, he joined B Company of the Tank Reserve Unit although his role is unknown. He was posted to 18th Battalion, as it formed, on 22 August and was allocated to C Company. He returned to France on 3 October but did not see action again as the Germans sued for peace before the unit could take to the field. When he undertook the pre-discharge procedure, at Le Tréport on 27 January 1919, he declined to claim a war pension. He dispersed from the centre at Fovant on 10 February and returned to his parents' house on the Weymouth Road in Evercreech. After he claimed his medals in 1921, he disappears completely from public view until his death, aged seventy five near Salisbury in 1970.

Hugh Montgomery was serving with No 8 Company when he was wounded on 20 November 1917. The second youngest of eight children, Hugh was born at Stevenston in Ayrshire in 1898. Stevenston was the site of a major industrial site, developed by the Nobel Company at Ardheer, for the manufacture of explosives. Hugh's father Robert had worked there as a nitric acid foreman and Hugh worked there as an apprentice engineer. On 29 October 1915, Hugh enlisted at the Unionist Club in Stevenston, aged just eighteen. Hugh was relatively tall and well-built for his age being five feet ten inches tall and weighing exactly eleven stones He was living with his widowed mother Ann in a company property called 21 Nobel's Villa which had been built to house the factory's labourers. Hugh passed the MMGS trade test at Coventry and was sent to the Depot at Bisley for initial training where he was approved on 18 November. Hugh's service record does not reveal the number of his original battery but he was attached to the Armoured Car Company posted on 1 April 1916. Posted to C Company on 27 May, he was allocated to No 2 Section and deployed to France on 16 August 1916.

Hugh probably fought with No 2 Section near Ginchy on 15 September and was then transferred to C Battalion in November 1916. Hugh was admitted to 12 Stationary Hospital at St Pol on 22 December suffering from influenza. He was released back to C Battalion on 2 January and probably fought during the Battle of Arras. He then trained as a driver at Wailly in June 1917 after which he was transferred to the Tank Corps. Hugh then served as a driver with No 7 Section and was wounded in the right thigh on 20 November 1917 during the attack on Bleak House to the east of Gonnelieu.

He was later evacuated to England and, on 2 January, was treated at 1st Western Hospital at Fazakerley Hospital in Liverpool. Hugh's wounds took more than two months to heal and he was eventually granted home leave from 16 to 25 March. He was then placed on the strength of the Catterick Depot until 12 June and then to the Tank Corps Depot where he served with the Reserve Unit. He was later graded A1 for fitness and did not claim a pension when he was demobilised through No 1 Dispersal Unit at Georgetown near Paisley. Thereafter I cannot find any further information about him

Gunner James Walton, who was a grocer's son, was wounded on 23 November as C Battalion tried to capture the village of Fontaine Notre Dame. He was born in Bradford on 21 February 1897 and baptised on 11 April at St Andrew's Church in Livesey. On leaving school, James initially worked as a cotton weaver which was the main employment in the area. Later, however, he worked for his father Jacob. He enlisted on 11 December 1915 at Blackburn and was immediately transferred to the Army Reserve. When he was mobilised on 22 March 1916, he was recorded as being only 5 feet 3 inches tall although this was an advantage when later serving in tanks. He was deployed to France, with No 2 Section of C Company on 16 August and was one of the youngest crewmen on the Somme being only eighteen years old. He transferred to C Battalion on its formation. There are no details about his wounding near Cambrai other than the date and that he was posted to the Tank Corps Depot the following day.

James remained in England for the remainder of the war eventually being promoted acting lance corporal. He was transferred to the Z Reserve on 25 February: this Reserve had been formed against the possibility that Germany might rescind the Armistice and the British Government wanted to ensure it could easily respond to any hostilities Despite being placed in the Reserve, James was granted an immediate pension due to rheumatism, Valvular Disease of the Heart and neurasthenia also known as shell shock. As the pension came to an end, James married Mona Morris on 15 September 1919 at St Andrew's Church in Livesey. The couple lived on the area but did not appear to have children. The 1924 *Kelly's Directory* shows that James was a grocer living at 96 Livesey Road but in the 1930s, the couple moved to Brooklands at Langho. Brooklands was a newly built five-bedroom house some five miles from Bradford and its purchase would indicate that James had become a successful businessman in his own right. James then disappears but Mona regularly appears on immigration records as she visited her sister in the USA after the Second World War, travelling cabin class on the RMS *Queen Elizabeth* and first class on the *Queen of Bermuda*.

The Great German Advance

The Great German Advance in the spring of 1918, during which they recovered all of the territory captured in the previous eighteen months, was no surprise to the Allies. The Germans were no longer fighting the Russians on the Eastern Front, after a cease fire in December 1917, and they wished defeat the British and French Armies before the American Army arrived in strength. The Germans identified the juncture of the French and British Forces at Peronne as a weak point for the break-in which was to be followed by an attack towards Arras. Both the Allied Armies were weak in this area and an appeal for reinforcements by the British Commander in Chief, Field Marshal Haig, had been rebuffed by David Lloyd George, the British Prime Minister. Kaiser Wilhelm recognised the importance of the advance succeeding and he visited the divisions which were to take part. As a result the German advance became known as the Kaiserschlacht or Kaiser's Battle. The attack which started on 21 March forced the British and French Armies backwards despite desperate fighting, tanks being of little assistance in their counter-attack role.

One of those Tankers who went missing was Gunner Wilfred Jaques of 4th Tank Battalion. Wilfred, who was born in Cirencester in the autumn of 1891, was the youngest son of a bacon curer named John Jaques and his wife Rhoda and was a member of the local Church Lad's Brigade. Twenty years later, John had become a dairyman and Wilfred was working for him. On 24 June 1915, Wilfred married a grocer's daughter named Gertrude Williams at Cirencester Parish Church and their daughter Betty was born the following year. By this time, Wilfred had joined the MGC. He served with D Company on the Somme during the opening actions where he is listed, in the Adjutant's note book, as a Vickers machine gunner. He is also shown as a member of B Crew attached to the Reserve Army, on 25 September which links him to the 18th Division attack at Thiepval.

There are no further official records until he was declared missing on 21 March 1918 whilst he was serving with 4th Battalion. However some of his service and how he was killed was reported later in the local Cirencester newspaper, the Wiltshire and Gloucestershire Standard. This shows that his wife Gertrude had received a letter from Corporal John Tolson, who had been a member of the D19 crew at the Battle of Flers, and was now a patient at St John's Hospital in nearby Cheltenham. Tolson reported that he and Wilfred had been in the same crew in early 1917 and were both wounded which would indicate that they both served in No 11 Company during the battle of Bullecourt. They would have been part of the crew of Dop Doctor which had been knocked out on

20 November 1917, between the first and second objective during the attack on Flesquières. Tolson told Gertrude that, after Wilfred was released from hospital, he and John were again in the same crew and he had been wounded by the same shell that had killed Wilfred, near Herdicourt on the morning of 21 March.

Unusually there is no mention of Wilfred amongst the record of the effects of dead soldiers. He is however commemorated at Pozières Memorial to the Missing, at the St John the Baptist Parish Church War memorial and on the Roll of Honour at Cirencester Memorial Hospital. Gertrude did not remarry and she died, aged seventy, in her home town of Cirencester.

Another grocer's son was lost by 4th Battalion in the delaying action when he was captured by the Germans. Gunner Sam Cotton, who came from Loughborough, was born on 19 November 1896 and had an elder brother William who was named after their father. He was educated at the Grammar School in Market Bosworth as a boarder and, after his father died in 1904, the family moved to Leicester where Sam worked as a clerk. He joined the Army just after his nineteenth birthday when he was attested at Leicester on 1 December 1915. Nine days later he enlisted into the MMGS at Coventry. Sam was placed on the Army Reserve and not mobilised until 3 March 1916. As well as the usual machine training at Bisley, he was trained to fire the naval 6 pdr QF gun at Whale Island. He later joined D Company and deployed to France on 28 August in either No 1 or 2 Section. Sam is not listed amongst those who fought on 15 September 1916 so he was probably a spare crewman. He was allocated, as 6 pdr gunner, to Crew A which was allocated to the Reserve Army on 25 September.

He continued to serve with D Battalion in November 1916. There is no record of his actions for the majority of 1917 but he was awarded 1st class proficiency pay on 9 December 1917.

Sam was then granted home leave from 21 December 1917 to 4 January which indicates he fought with D Battalion during the Battle of Cambrai. He returned to his unit by 7 January despite the appalling weather in France at that time. Sam continued to serve with 4th Tank Battalion until he was captured by the advancing Germans on 23 March 1918. The tank crews continued to fight when possible but the tanks were in very poor condition and many broke down, or ran out of fuel as they pulled back, across the old Somme battlefield. According to POW records held by the International Committee of the Red Cross, Sam was eventually held at Gustrow in Mecklenburg in northeast Germany and repatriated after the Armistice arriving in England on 1 December 1918. Surprisingly, Sam was compulsorily retained and not transferred to Z Reserve until 17 July 1919. Although his Army correspondence address was Loughborough, Sam found work in London and by 1921, he was living in Bayswater and working near Euston. In 1934 he was living in West Kensington; thereafter there are no other records until his death at Hastings in the summer 1975.

Even though the British were outnumbered, and tanks were not suited for defending ground, their crews did not give in. Commanders and drivers, whose tanks had been lost, were withdrawn and the gunners were formed into ad-hoc infantry support units using their tank's Lewis machine guns. One of these gunners was Private Walter Gammon who was born in Upacombe in Devon in early 1886. Walter was the ninth child of William and Hilda Gammon. William was a hairdresser and, by the time Walter was five years old, the family had moved to the High Street at Ilfracombe. The family paid for Walter's education at the Wallingbrook School at Chumleigh in the middle of Exmoor. Walter followed his father's profession but did not stay in Devon. By 1911, he was working at Balsall Heath with Frederick Price and boarding with his family at 156 Ombersley Road in Sparkbrook. He did not settle in Birmingham as, by the time he joined the MMGS in 1916, Walter was living at 51 North Street in Exeter. After the first actions, Walter was transferred to D Battalion and served with No 10 Company with which he would have fought at Beaurains, Ypres and Cambrai. When the majority of tanks had been lost to the German advance, by 23 March 1918, the now renamed 4th Battalion was tasked to organize the machine gunners into twenty Lewis Gun teams. They were placed under command of Captain Heady Head who was the skipper of crew D2 on 15 September 1916. Heady was tasked to place twenty teams along the Bray to Albert Road where he was supported by two of the remaining tanks which had made their way back from Saulcourt. This road was just behind what had been the British front line on 1 July 1916; the German advance had been so great as to completely wipe out all the British gains in 1916 and 1917 in just four days. Ordered to hold the left flank, the Lewis gun teams did so for six hours until they were outflanked by the advancing Germans. Their resistance was not however without loss and Walter Gammon was one of those killed. His body was buried on the battlefield, near where he was killed but later buried at Bray Hill Cemetery. Walter's loss is commemorated on the Roll of Honour at St George's Church in Exeter.

May 1918

The German advance on the Somme did not achieve the necessary breakthrough and the line stabilised. Soon the Allies were sought to gain the initiative from the German defenders. The Australian Army Corps, under General John Monish, undertook a series of small attacks near Villers-Brettoneux designed to capture prisoners, create uncertainty and create the conditions for long term success. On 3 May 18, during the second of these attacks, the Australians were supported by two tanks from 1st Tank Battalion; the Australian captured 21 prisoners and then retired when the German brought up reinforcements. The male tank commanded by Lieutenant Donnelly used case shot to good effect and rallied; the other commanded by Lieutenant Arthur Hume fell into an old trench from which it could not be extracted; it was then heavily bombarded by the Germans and the crew, including Sergeant Clement Tinker were captured. Lieutenant Hume died of his wounds on 21 May 1918 and he was buried by the Germans at Le Quesnoy communal cemetery.

Clement Tinker, who was born in Cardiff on 16 March 1893, was bought up in London. The younger son of a clothing outfitter, Clement started school on 16 Oct 1896, aged only three, attending Buckingham Street School whilst living at 153 Caledonian Road. In 1902 the family moved south of the River Thames and Clement continued his education at the Honeywell Road School in Wandsworth. According to the 1911 census, he was working as a shipbrokers clerk, living in Clapham with his parents, brother and sister in law and their daughter Clare. When John Tinker died, Clement moved with his mother to the western side of Clapham Common. He had become an insurance broker and the family was quite well-off. On 22 October, he enlisted into the MMGS and later was allocated to C Company. He was appointed lance corporal on 26 June 16 and then promoted corporal on 7 July, deploying to France with No 2 Section on 16 August. Following the end of the 1916 fighting season, he was posted to the newly formed A Battalion and promoted sergeant on 22 December to bring the unit to its full establishment. He stayed with A Battalion throughout 1917 but there are no details of the roles he undertook. However, the fact that he was not granted home leave until 25 January, well after most of those who fought at the Battle of Cambrai may indicate that he was a section NCO and he made sure his men went home first.

His role must have changed after the Kaiserschlacht as his capture as a member of a tank crew in May confirms. He was not repatriated from Germany until 11 December 1918. He was demobilised on 23 March 1919 and returned to his employment as an insurance broker. In early 1920, Clement married Gertrude Russell in Wandsworth and their only son Hugh was born on 27 July 1921 in Rochford. Hugh Tinker served with the Indian Army during the Second World War and became a distinguished historian and academic whose works on South East Asia have been extensively published. Clement did not lose contact with his C Company friends as his address at Westcliffe on Sea was included in the list of members of 3rd Light Tank Battalion Old Comrades Association. He continued his career in insurance, eventually becoming a broker. He retired to Sheppey House in Marlow just after the birth of his grandson David in 1957. Hugh died aged seventy, on 12 July 1963; his grandson later served as a logistics officer in the Royal Navy and was killed in action whilst serving in *HMS Glamorgan* off the Falkland Islands on 12 June1982.

Another of the First Tank Crews captured in May 1918 was Gunner Percy Fordham. He was born in Ipswich Suffolk in May 1896 and the sixth child and youngest son of Robert and Sarah Ann Fordham. Percy moved to London as a young man and worked as a tailor and cutter employed by Coborn and Co which was a wholesale clothiers and bespoke tailors in Bishopsgate. He was attested on 21 November whilst living at 28 Union Square in Islington. Percy initially served with the Royal Garrison Artillery, first with 42 Company and then with 45 Company from 17 February 1916. One month later, he was transferred to the MGC on 18 March; posted to C Company on 27 May and deployed, with Hugh Tinker, to France on 16 August with No 2 Section. Once C Company had completed its actions in November, Percy was transferred to C Battalion but did not stay with them for long. On 24 January, he was sent to the Base Depot at Lamilliers and was transferred to Infantry Branch MGC on 22 June. On 8 July, Percy joined 149 Company MGC, which was part of 50th Northumberland Division and serving in the Ypres Salient. His unit then took part in the whole of the 3rd Battle of Ypres including the final attack known as the Second Battle of Passchendaele. He was granted home leave for Christmas 1917 but was late back, having not left England until 29 December. He re-joined 149 Company on 5 January and was fined three days' pay and awarded two weeks' Field Punishment.

The Division remained in the Ypres area and, when the Germans launched the second part of the German Spring Offensive, known as Georgette, to the south of Ypres, his Division was thrown into the line and with French and other troops, fought them to a standstill. His Division which was sent to a quiet area on the Chemin des Dames to rest and reform, was unlucky as it was holding the line as the third element of the Spring Offensive, known as Blucher, commenced on 27 May 1918. Percy was captured on the first day and later held at the Kassel POW camp. He was not repatriated until 22 January 1919. He was offered, and accepted, reemployment by Coborn and Co that the same month. On 7 August 1920, Percy married Kate Stebbings at St Saviour's Church in Wood Green but the couple was not blessed with children. He did not claim his medals until four years later. In his later years, he moved to West Yorkshire where he died aged seventy-six in 1971

The Battle of Amiens

Having absorbed the German Spring Offensives, and reconstituted their units, the British and Empire Forces were launched against the German forces on 8 August. The attacking troops included seven infantry divisions with 580 tanks, the majority equipped with the Mark V variants which were much improved over their predecessors. The initial assault was wholly successful to the extent that the German commander Field Marshall Erich von Ludendorff described the event as "the black day for the German Army". In fact the Germans never recovered and the Battle of Amiens was the precursor to the Allied Victory four months later. The German Army did not however give up without a fight and many infantry and tank crewmen were killed and injured almost to the end of the war.

One of those killed on the first day of the Battle of Amiens was Herbert Pryce. He was born at Leavesden in Hertfordshire on 10 June 1897 and was the only son of a Welsh domestic gardener Charles Pryce and his wife Mary who also had two daughters named Florence and Jessie. Christened on 30 July 1897, Herbert moved with his family to Garston near Watford as a young child. It was at Watford that he enlisted into the MGC. He served with C Company in the autumn of 1916 and then transferred to C Battalion. He fought with them throughout 1917 and, after they had re-roled to operate Whippet tanks, continued with them serving in 7 Section of B Company under Captain H W Johnson. On 8 August, his tank *Crab III* was destroyed during the attack by the attack by the Canadian Cavalry Brigade. His section was on the right in supporting the Canadian cavalry unit Lord Strathcona's Horse which was the only unit to break-through the German defences at Cambrai. 3rd Battalion's Whippet tanks crossed the River Luce at Ignaucourt and then moved quickly eastwards following the river. As the cavalry advanced, they were targeted by German machine guns which were hidden in woods; the cavalry took cover in a convenient sunken road and the tanks went forward and eliminated the guns and dispersed the crews. In the follow-up Herbert's tank was hit by enemy fire and caught fire near Cayeau en Santerre. All three crewmen were killed and Herbert is buried at Le Quesnel Communal Cemetery alongside his skipper Lieutenant Harry Newsam and Private Harold Walker who had joined C Battalion as it formed at Christmas 1916. Herbert's loss is commemorated on the Leavesden memorial but also in a more human form; his sister Florence named her eldest child, who was born on 30 March 1920, after her brother.

The last 100 days

The advance towards the German Border was characterised by hard fighting. The combined arms tactics initially used at Cambrai, rehearsed at Hamel and proven at Amiens were used time and again to defeat German defences and units. Tank battalions were wholly integrated in the plans, sometimes taking the lead and sometimes fighting in support. The crewmen and tanks were destroyed or worn out but the unrelenting pressure lead to the defeat of the German Army in the field. The attacks at the St Quentin Canal on 29 September 1918 were routine for most tank units but for the recently arrived 16th battalion, it was to be their debut. Although most Tankers had not seen action before, they did have a few experienced men such as Jethro Tull and Corporal William Lock who had both served with C Company at Flers-Courcelette.

William Lock was born c 9 April 1893 in Dawlish and was the second son of John Lock and May Slocombe, who owned and operated the Strand Mill on the Dawlish water. William worked for his father on leaving school; the mill was only one of two flour mills in the area William was attested at Exeter on 3 December 1915 and immediately placed on the Army reserve. He volunteered to join the Army Service Corps but, when he was mobilised on 2 May, he was allocated into the MGC (Motors). He joined C Company HSMGC on 27 May 16 and deployed to France with No 2 Section on 16 August. William followed the standard pattern of joining C Battalion on its formation and attended a driving course at Wailly from 10 to 17 June. However, the following month he was detached to HQ Depot. It is possible that this was to enable him to take part in the training for Operation HUSH in which the British were to attack the Belgian coast around Middelkerk following the opening of the Third Battle of Ypres. Whilst training was undertaken at the tank gunnery range at Merlimont, the operation never took place.

Later transferred to the Tank Corps, William was returned to the UK for special duties on 6 November 1917. This was at the time that four tank crews were sent to Ireland, several others from that party also being attached to N Battalion at Bovington. The deployment was unsuccessful and the crews returned to Dorset. William was posted to 16th Battalion on 13 January 18, being appointed acting lance corporal albeit unpaid one week later. He was promoted corporal on the day he returned to France. Only twenty days later 16th Battalion was in action at the St Quentin Canal. William was wounded that day, receiving injuries to the head, thighs and hands. He was firstly evacuated to hospital in Le Havre then onto Reading for treatment at No 1 War Hospital. On 7 October, a procedure was used to remove fragments from his thigh and William remained at Reading until 1 February 1919. He was then sent to the Dispersal Hospital at Devonport so that he could be closer to home. He claimed a pension for his injuries but a Medical Board, held at Devonport on 4 February, confirmed that he was not suffering from any disability and that his medical status was A1. He was discharged from the Army the following day and gave his address as the new family home, a large detached house named Brookdale on Barton Hill in Dawlish. However he does not seem to have returned. In his service file, there is a letter dated 20 August

1919 from John Lock seeking his son's discharge but I have not found any record of him after that date.

Gunner Roderick Woods was wounded on the same day whilst serving in Whippet tanks with 3rd Light Tank Battalion. Born on 2 February 1892, near Ipswich, Roderick was the eldest son of a boot and shoemaker named Donald Woods and his wife Edith. By the time Roderick was nine, the family was living in 70 Stanhope Road a6 St Chads in Derby. As a young man Roderick followed his father's lead, working as a boot repairer but working on his own account at 33 Bakewell Street. His service records did not survive the Blitz but the medal rolls reveal key information about his time with the tanks. He enlisted on 18 December 1915 and deployed to France on 16 August 1916 which indicates he was serving with No 2 Section.

Roderick served on with C Battalion, on its formation, fighting with them throughout 1917 and then rerolled on to Whippets. After he was wounded, during the attack near the St Quentin Canal on 29 September 1919, he was so badly wounded that he was evacuated to England and treated in hospital at Bristol. He was discharged from the Army on 24 January as a result of his injuries but was sufficiently recovered to marry his fiancée Mary O'Neill in Derby later that spring. Their daughter Dorothy was born the following year. Roderick kept in contact with his comrades as his address of 80 Portland St Derby is recorded in the Old Comrades Association membership list in 1925. Mary and Roderick had a son, also known as Roderick in 1931, and they continued to live in Derby where Roderick senior died, following a road accident, on 3 January 1953.

Another man wounded on 29 September 1918 was Gunner Percy Sargeant but the cause is somewhat unusual. Percy, who was born on 12 July 1888 at Turvey in Bedfordshire, was the fifth child of an agricultural labourer. A gardener by trade, Percy married Lottie Williams on7 November 1909 in Wellingborough. The couple had three children, Amy born 30 January 1910 and two sons Ronald and Harry who were born in subsequent years during which the family moved to Great Billings near Northampton. Percy enlisted into the Army on 3 November 15 at Northampton. His medical record shows he needed dental work but was otherwise fit. He was initially trained at No 4 Depot Royal Garrison Artillery at Ripon but was then transferred to the MGC and deployed to France with C Company on 16 August 1916.

Having been transferred to C Battalion, Percy was posted to MGC Base Depot for dental treatment in February 1917. After the Battle of Arras, he was sent to the 2nd Tank Brigade Gunnery School between 19 and 26 May to train as a 6 pdr QF gunner and was detached to the School as a batman until 2 June 1917. Having returned to C Battalion, Percy later attended a driving course at Wailly Camp from 11 to 19 June. He must have fought through the Third Battle of Ypres and Cambrai as he was granted home leave in early December rejoining his unit on 22 December 1917. Percy and Lottie's daughter Marguerite was born on 15 September 1918.

Percy stayed with the 3rd Light Tank battalion as it re-roled onto Whippet tanks and he fought with them until his injury on 29 September 1918. The wounds were the result of mustard gas on his left and right buttocks which leads one to ask exactly how a soldier could be injured in this way. Percy was admitted to No 3 Stationary Hospital at Rouen on 2 October then evacuated on HS *Guildford* on 4 October. Having been treated at Reading War Hospital, he was posted to Tank Corps Depot at Wareham on 21 October and then four months later, he was transferred to the Z Reserve. The following year, due to pain in his right thigh, Percy made a post-service claim for pension; 1% disablement agreed and a final payment of £25 plus £7/10/-was made on 13 March in respect of three year's war service. Like Roderick Woods, Percy was a member of the Old Comrades Association in 1925. He continued to live in Great Billings until his death, aged eighty eight years on 31 August 1976.

One of his comrades' wounds were fatal. Gunner Arnold Peace died in Rouen on 8 October and was buried at the Saint Sever communal cemetery. This cemetery was used by the many hospitals at Rouen which was a supply major base for the British Army during the Great War and there are more almost 9,000 casualties buried at St Sever alone. Arnold was the son of a coal miner from Basford near Nottingham. Born in late 1893, he was the elder son of Joseph and Elizabeth Peace. In 1911, Arnold was living with his parents in Doncaster, working as a builder's clerk but, by the time enlisted into the MMGS, he was living in Coventry. His service file has not survived the Blitz so information on his time with the tanks is almost not existent. He joined C Company in England and deployed with them on 16 August which indicates he served in No 2 Section.

Arnold must have served with C Battalion at the Battle of Cambrai as he granted home leave immediately afterwards. He quickly arranged to marry his fiancée, May Parks at the Grantham Wesleyan Chapel in Finkin Street on Saturday 8 December 1917. According to the reports in the local paper, the bride was dressed "in ivory crepe de chine with a veil and orange blossom and she was attended by the sister of the bridegroom, Florence, who wore a brown dress trimmed with fawn and opossum fur. The reception was afterwards held in Messrs Caitlin's in the High Street. The couple subsequently then departed for a honeymoon in Skegness." Arnold returned to serve with 3rd Light Battalion and gained his injuries in the later stage of the war which lead to his death on 8 October 1918 at Rouen. Gertrude remarried in 1921 but she ensured that her first husband was not forgotten as she added her details to the list of those inscribed in the war graves records.

8 October 1918 was also the day that 3rd Light Tank Battalion fought its last action. Ten Whippet tanks from A and B Companies went into action that morning, seeking enemy position and units around Serain and Elincourt to the south of Cambrai, and where possible destroying them. Although the tanks pressed home their attacks, the German used their field guns to good effect and five tanks were destroyed by direct fire. Four crewmen were killed including Gunner Wilfred Bolingbroke who was the last of the First Tank Crews to be killed in action.

Wilfred was the youngest son of Alfred Bolingbroke who was a monumental engraver. He and his wife Sarah had ten children of whom seven survived. Wilfred was born in 1896 and brought up in West Norwood as his father worked at the nearby cemetery which had been established in 1837. By the time Wilfred was fifteen, the family had moved to Brookwood as his father was working for the nearby Necropolis Company. Wilfred joined the Motor Machine Gun Service in October 1915 after he was no doubt attracted by the soldiers he met from their Training Centre. He lived within 100 yards of Brookwood Railway station at 142 Connaught Road which was the most direct access to their Bisley camp. He deployed with C Company on 16 August and then disappears from public record until his death, 2 years later on 8 October. This was the last action in which 3rd Battalion fought and, although it is described in detail in the War History, it is not possible to determine exactly the tank in which Wilfred was fighting. Several tanks were engaged by a German artillery battery as they assisted that the infantry forward near Serain. One tank was hit, whilst its commander was liaising with the infantry, and its two crewmen burnt to death. The other was hit by the German battery after its pair had also been hit; the tank gunner was killed and the other two crewmen wounded. The crew was initially buried close to where they were killed but Wilfred's body was subsequently moved and re-interred in the Busigny Communal Cemetery extension. Wilfred is commemorated on Woking town memorial and at the Brookwood Memorial Hall, which was built on land donated by the London Necropolis Company in memory of those who lost their lives in the Great War.

19

Honours and Awards

Both of the companies, who fought at Flers-Courcelette on 15 September 1916, had a number of crewmen whose tanks are not identified but who later awarded gallantry medals or who were commissioned which provides an insight into their lives before or after their Army service.

Commissioned from the ranks

Corporal Leonard Groutage, who was a tank NCO on 15 September 1916, was one of the first crewmen to be commissioned and was also honoured for his bravery in battle. Born on 29 September 1896 at Aston Manor in Birmingham, Leonard was the eldest son of a pattern maker and plasterer called Charles Groutage and his wife Edith. Leonard was baptised when he was only eighteen days old at St Peter and St Paul's Church in Aston. The family later moved to Erdington and, when Leonard left school at fourteen, he started work as a brass chaser. By the time he enlisted in the MMGS at Coventry on 24 November 1915, he had become an electrician. Leonard was sent to Bisley the same day and was later pictured in *The Motor Cycle* undergoing machine gun training. Allocated to C Company he was promoted acting corporal on 24 July and substantive corporal two weeks later which says much about the maturity of this nineteen year old. He embarked for France on 16 August, which means that he probably served in No 2 Section, and was in action at the Somme one month later.

When C Battalion was formed, he was posted to No 9 Company. The British Commander in Chief, Douglas Haig, sincerely believed that tanks could save lives and achieve success so eight new tank battalions were to be formed and they needed officers. Many came from training units but C Company provided twelve from amongst the First Tank Crews. Leonard, who applied for a commission on 14 January 1917, was accepted as an officer candidate only sixteen days later and was sent back to England on 12 February. He completed officer training at No 2 MGC Cadet Battalion at Pirbright from 14 April and was commissioned into the Tank Corps on 27 July 1917. Leonard was then posted to F Battalion in France where many of the First Tank Crews were serving under Lieutenant Colonel Frank Summers. In 1918, Leonard was serving under command of Major Arthur Inglis who had commanded *Crème de Menthe* in September 1916. The day after Leonard was allocated to B Company of the renamed 6th Battalion which was re-equipped with Whippet tanks in early 1918.

During the Battle of Amiens, 6th Battalion was tasked to support the Cavalry clear either side of the railway leading from Villers-Brettoneux to Chaulnes. With B Company to the north and C Company to the south, the tanks pushed the German defenders back from Bayonvillers and cleared the ground as far as Harbonnières before every rallied successfully. The following day, 9 August 1918, at approximately 5:45 p.m. Leonard led a section of three tanks to take and hold a German trench 2,000 yards to the northwest of Fouquescourt. According to the citation for the Military Cross with was later awarded, "near Mehacourt, though under heavy anti-tank gun fire, he worked his way continually up and down a trench strongly held by the enemy infantry and machine-guns.

On his tank receiving a direct hit from an anti-tank gun, which jammed the door, he climbed out with his guns through the roof and came into action on the ground, though under heavy machine-gun and anti-tank gun fire. His example had a very inspiriting effect on his men" whom he led to safety.

In early 1919, Leonard was posted to Ireland with 17th Armoured Car Battalion to support anti-independence actions. Whilst in Ireland, he met Lucy Davenport whom he later married. Lucy was the only daughter and surviving child of a Royal Naval captain Edmund Davenport. Her brother Edmund had been Killed in Action after being shot down on 3 January 1918 whilst on a bombing mission near Masnieres. Leonard was demobilised on 5 July 1919 and married Lucy in 13 January 1920 at St Patrick's Church in Cork. He relinquished his commission, on completion of service on 1 December 1921, and established a motor repair business named The Cork Installation Company.

The Irish Independent newspaper reported that, on 21 June 1929, Lucy had won a prize at a dog show – she won another prize two months later. The *1933 Cork Trade Directory* shows that 17 Parnell Place was the location of Leonards' company. Sadly the same year, on 9 June, the local newspaper published a report of Leonard's death. According to the testimony given at the inquest he was under medical treatment as a result of his war service and had been prescribed a powerful narcotic called *Bromidia*. Lucy Groutage gave evidence that Leonard had been particularly unwell prior to Saturday 3 June and had worked briefly on a customer's car and finished at 2:00 pm. That evening, they had travelled to Crosshaven for a meal and returned home after 2:00 am. Lucy Groutage informed the inquest that her husband then retired to bed and she followed shortly afterwards. When she entered the room, he complained of feeling very ill. The doctor was called but Leonard died shortly afterwards. The coroner said there was no evidence to suggest, although the drug was highly addictive, that Leonard deliberately took an overdose. However the jury found that the death was due to an overdose, resulting in cardiac failure. He was buried in the Catholic Cemetery at Douglas. Lucy lived in Cork until her death in the 1970s.

This volume contains the stories of many men whose exploits have not been published. The exception is Neville Tattersfield who was commissioned in 1917 and whose story is told in the book, *A Village Goes to War* written by the Western Front Association development officer David Tattersfield. Neville was born on 7 April 1892 in Dewsbury. The youngest of seven sons born to Louisa and Moses Tattersfield, Neville was educated at Heckmondwike Grammar School after which he joined his eldest brother, John, working in the dyeing laboratory at Jas Smith and Sons in Ravensthorpe. Neville who owned his own motorcycle, joined the MMGS on 18 August 1915. On 1 January 1916 he was posted to the 27th Battery MMGS and then to Armoured Car Section. He was one of the crewmen selected to fire 6 pdr guns which were to be fitted to male tanks and, on 21 July, went to Whale Island for live firing training.

Given Neville was sent to France with the first draft of C Company, he probably served in No 2 Section. David Tattersfield believes that he served in Charles Ambrose's crew on 15 September which makes sense. Neville was transferred to C Battalion as the tanks were withdrawn in November, after which he was recommended for officer training. Unusually Neville was sent on home-leave at the end of March 1917, arriving back just three days before the start of the Battle of Arras. He was then sent straight back to England and, like several others, commenced training at Grantham before completing the course at Pirbright. Commissioned into the Tank Corps on 4 November, Neville undertook tank commander training at Bovington before being sent as an individual reinforcement to France arriving on 13 March 1918. Allocated to 2nd Battalion, Neville arrived at Haplincourt on 21 March, where the unit was in reserve, arriving on the same day as the start of the German offensive known as the Kaiserschlacht. That evening, the wood in which the tanks were located was shelled but there were no casualties. All three companies deployed to Beugny the following day and, in a series of small engagements, slowed the German advance with the loss of eight tanks. The next day the surviving fourteen fighting tanks, with six supply tanks, withdrew to Aveluy, where the Tank Driving School was now located. Those crews who had lost their tanks were formed into a Lewis gun teams.

Neville was next in action on 8 August 1918, which was the opening day of the Battle of Amiens. He commanded tank no 9004, a male tank, which was part of C Company supporting the 2nd Australian Division. The tank reached its first objective and probably reached Bayonvillers after which the tank ran out of fuel. The next day, Neville was again in action, this time supporting the 1st Australian Division. Many of the tanks were destroyed by German artillery operating in the direct fire role. Neville survived, despite receiving machine gun wounds to the arm and buttocks which occurred as he tried to unditch his vehicle; his life being saved by a spirit flask which stopped one of the bullets.

Neville was evacuated to England and, after his wounds were treated, was sent home to recuperate. This successfully achieved, Neville rode his motorcycle to Scotland to visit a cousin and in the process, exacerbated a cold. He reported, as ordered, to Bovington on 3 November where he subsequently contracted influenza. He was admitted to the local military hospital on Armistice Day but, despite treatment, did not recover. Neville died on 20 November 1918, his brothers at his bedside, and was buried in Wareham Parish Churchyard two days later.

Another C Company crewman who was commissioned was John Thomas. Born on 11 February 1887 in London, John's Danish father died shortly after his son's birth. His mother Frances remarried and the family moved to Coventry where John worked for an ironmonger. John did not enlist into the MGC until 14 June 1916, just three months before his unit went into action, and given that his company conduct sheet was signed by Herbert Hiscocks, John probably served with No 3 Section. He was a tall for a tank crewman at just under six feet tall. After the first actions, John served with No 8 Company of C Battalion and was accepted as a candidate for commissioning on 1 April 1917. Despite the fact that his unit was preparing for the Battle of Arras, he returned to England just eight days later. He did not start officer training at No 2 MGC Cadet Battalion on 1 June 1917 and was commissioned into the Tank Corps on 3 November 1917.

John did not however return to France until 13 March 1918 when he was posted back to 3rd Battalion who were now equipped with Whippet light tanks. John served with A Company during the Battle of Amiens. On 8 August he commanded *Comme ca*, which was part of No 2 Section. His tank was again in action the following day and later on 21 August as they cleared the villages near Achiet-le-Petit in support of the New Zealand Division. John was then granted home leave in England between 7 and 21 September 1918 before rejoining his unit on 26 September. He served with 3rd Battalion until after the Armistice and was granted further home leave from 29 December until 12 January. Whilst in England, John found employment and asked for his leave to be extended until he was demobilised on 28 January 1919. He initially lived with his mother in 4 Albany Road but thereafter I can find no sign of him. He became a member of the C Battalion Old Comrades Association where their membership list for 1925, shows him living in Earlsdon Street.

One of the older members of the First Tank Crews was a thirty-four year old literary agent named John Farquharson. Born in Aberdeen on 20 February 1882, John attended the Robert Gordon College and then University of Aberdeen between 1900 and 1902 where he studied art. Moving to London, John worked in Red Lion Square in Bloomsbury which was the location of many literary agents. John did not volunteer for MMGS service but was attested 1 May 1916 in London. Sent to Bisley, John was one of those in C Company who were selected to train as a 6 pdr gunner which included training at Whale Island and on a Royal Naval warship in the Channel. Deployed to France on 16 August 1916, John's commissioning application shows that he mainly worked in the QM's Department as a clerk. He joined C Battalion in December 1916 but, on 20 February, was admitted to hospital with influenza. Five weeks later, having not recovered, he was evacuated to the UK on 27 March and then given two months convalescence. He was then posted to Wareham, where he was allocated to the newly formed L Battalion on 26 July and promoted corporal on 17 August.

Now a member of the Tank Corps, John applied for a commission on 14 November. In early 1918, he commenced the standard training package but was not commissioned until 20 October 1918 when he was sent to France to join 12th Battalion. There he served alongside a number of former members of C Company including Archie Holford-Walker who was commanding B Company.

After demobilisation in early 1919, John returned to London and set up his own literary agency. One of his first clients was the children's author E Nesbitt, and he later attracted a series of successful authors including David Niven, John Le Carre and George Macdonald Fraser. In 1928 John married Margaret Adams, their son John being born in 1930 and their daughter Margaret in the spring of 1933. Shortly afterwards, John moved the family from 9 Upper Gloucester Place, near Regent's Park, to North Gate at Pachesham Park in Leatherhead. His literary business went from strength and he was able to retire, in the late 1950s to Eden Lodge Tilford near Farnham. He died, in 1976, aged ninety four.

Londoner Frank Short had joined the MMGS before John Farquharson and was already a lance corporal by the time C Company was sent to Elveden. Born on 3 February 1888, in Old Ford Essex, Frank's mother's name was Ellen and his father, after whom he was named, was a decorator. As a young man, Frank worked in the Inland Revenue Valuation Section at Stratford East and then trained as a surveyor. He was living at 36 Campbell Road in Bow East when he was attested on 19 November 1915. Promoted corporal on 27 June 1916, he was present at Elveden on 8 August, when he was called as a witness to a minor offence. As he deployed to France on 24 August, he probably served with either No 3 or 4 Sections on 15 September. After the first actions, he transferred to C Battalion and served with No 8 Company. He attended an instructor's course at 3rd Anti-Gas school from 21 to 30 January 1917. He then applied for a commission which was accepted on 1 April 17. During the build-up to the Battle of Arras, he was working alongside Robert Hillhouse and John Newell, clearing an iron works which was presumably being prepared to act as a forward operating location. He did not however go into action with C Battalion as he was sent back to England for officer training at the same time as John Thomas.

Frank was unusual in that he did not commission into the Tank Corps but, on 17 December 1917, joined the Rifle Brigade which was an infantry unit. He was allocated to 5th Battalion, a training battalion on the Isle of Sheppey, where he was asked to provide information about the disappearance of Corporal Hillhouse. Eventually Frank served with 11th Battalion Rifle Brigade, which was part of 20th (Light) Division, and took part in the Final Advance towards the Belgian border. After demobilisation, he returned home and lived with his mother and younger brother Charles. In 1923, he applied for a post as a tax clerk and did not claim his medals until June 1930. He never married and lived in Bow until after the end of the Second World War. He died aged ninety-one near Kingston upon Thames.

Another C Company machine-gunner who was later commissioned was Maurice Shelton. He was born at Headington to the east of Oxford on 19 December 1887 and was therefore, one of the older crewmen. Maurice was the eldest son of Henry and Annie Shelton, Henry being a book-binder. Maurice was educated at the Wesleyan Higher Grade School in Oxford and then trained as an upholsterer. He volunteered to join the MMGS later than many and possibly did so to avoid conscription into the Infantry. By the time he was attested on 11 February 1916, Maurice was working as a foreman upholsterer. He enlisted on 17 February and mobilised just over one month later. He deployed to France on 16 August 1916, possibly as part of No 2 Section, but his service record gives no clues as to the tank in which he fought in September during the Battle of Flers-Courcelette. Posted to C Battalion on 18 November, he was then allocated to No 7 Company. For the next three months, Maurice suffered from ill health. On 13 December, he was admitted to hospital but he was back with his unit within three days. He was again admitted to hospital on 15

February 1917 suffering from pneumonia. This may have the Spanish influenza which was starting to appear on the Western Front or it could have been the result of the poor conditions in which the soldiers were living. Maurice was transferred to a base hospital on 14 March and returned to the England two weeks later suffering from trench fever. Admitted to the War Hospital at Bradford on 26 March, he was not discharged until 1 May having also recovered from a bout of tonsillitis whilst in hospital.

Maurice was then posted to Bovington where he served with the School of Instruction from 28 July 1917 where he applied for a commission. Maurice left the School of Instruction on 20 October prior to entry into the officer cadet unit. He was transferred to 24 Officer Cadet Battalion at Pirbright on 18 December 17 which moved, whilst he was still under training, to Hazeley Down near Winchester. He was eventually commissioned on 30 April 1918, into the Tank Corps, but did not deploy back to France until 11 September. Unusually this was not part of a formed unit but as an individual reinforcement. Maurice stayed at the Depot at Mers-Les-Bains for five weeks when he would have met Victor Smith who was commanding the Officer's Company. On 17 October 1918, Maurice was posted to 9th Battalion, which had been in action for much of the previous two months and had been withdrawn to recover, replenish its reserves and integrate new crewmen for the expected actions which were to take place in 1919. Maurice joined A Company and settled into the autumn training regime. However the Germans sued for peace and the Tank Corps started to prepare to reduce in size. Maurice was sent on leave at the New Year. Whilst at home, Maurice found a job as a salesman and was demobilised. He moved to London and married Ethel Ship at St Mary's Church in Kilburn on 21 July 1919. Their only son John was born in Oxford in early 1921. The family lived in Oxford until 1961 when they moved to Brighton. Maurice died, on 24 February 1963, aged seventy-five at his home at 78 Wayland Avenue. Ethel, who was seven years younger than her husband, lived until she was seventy-nine and died ten years later, in Hove, in 1973.

There were two gunners named Rennison serving in C Company. Billy Rennison was badly wounded at the Battle of Cambrai and was discharged from the Army in 1918 about the time Francis started to learn to fly. Francis, who was a year younger than Billy was born on 15 September 1896 in Stretford, the son of a rubber works manager. Francis, who had an elder sister, was the eldest of three boys, lost his father whilst he was still at school, his widowed settling with her young family in Levenshulme. Francis joined the MMGS in later 1915 and served with C Company and then C Battalion through 1917. His Army service record has not survived and the details in his Royal Air Force record are scant. Francis was transferred to the RAF, from 3rd Battalion, on 7 June 1918 and, after initial training at Reading, was commissioned on 28 October. Following the Armistice, the requirement for air crew dramatically reduced. Francis' training continued for a further two months but he was released, informally in April 1919.

Francis returned to Lancashire and, using the expertise gained during his service, became an engineer. On 14 August 1929, Francis married Ida at the Congregational Church in Withington. Ida was the daughter of a science teacher from nearby Rusholme. After the local trade directory showed Francis was working as a draughtsman, he is recorded on the wedding certificate as an engineer. In the1930s, he used his engineering knowledge to good effect. In 1936 he patented improvement to the road markings and two years later patented designs for machines used to grinding floor and road surfaces. As far as I can establish, Francis and Ida did not have children. They later moved to London where Francis died in 1979, aged eighty-one in Hammersmith

The Battle of Arras

The first crewman to be so honoured during the Battle of Arras was Lance Corporal Charles Spurgeon. He was not only awarded the Military Medal for bravery but he was later commissioned. Born on 11 November 1892 in Clerkenwell, Charles was the son of an iron foundry labourer Robert

Spurgeon and his wife Sarah. The family later moved west to 3 York Road in Brentford and Charles was educated locally at St Paul's School. He initially worked as a grocers' assistant but later was employed as an assistant inspector for the local gas supply. He therefore probably knew Harold Mortimore, who commanded *Daredevil* on 15 September 1916, who was working as a clerk at the company. Charles enlisted into the MMGS at Bisley on 6 December 1915 and was posted to C Company on 25 May. He was promoted acting Lance Corporal at Elveden on 13 July and deployed to France on 16 August. On 24 August 1916, he made his will leaving all his effects to his widowed mother Sarah, who had emigrated to Oakland in California that same month.

After C Company was withdrawn from action in November, Charles was transferred to C Battalion and was posted to No 8 Company. He was promoted to substantive lance corporal on 17 February 1917 and corporal on 2 April 1917. On 9 April 1917, the opening day of the Battle of Arras, Charles was the NCO in tank C39, which was commanded by Lieutenant James Cameron and whose crew included Maurice Voile and James Newell. The Battalion War History records:

> The objective of this company was that formidable work known as The Harp which, owing to the width of the trenches and number and form of the traverses, was a most difficult proposition for tanks to tackle. It was afterwards found that the ground on the top of the plateau was waterlogged and much blown to pieces by shell fire. In spite of these difficulties half of the company succeeded in fighting their way as far as the String of the Harp before becoming bellied.

The crew routed an enemy machine gun crew and captured their gun. A little later the tank received a direct hit, by German artillery fire, which killed Maurice Voile and wounded three other crewmen. Charles "showed great devotion to duty in extracting wounded comrades from a wrecked tank, attending to their wounds under heavy fire" and, for his conspicuous gallantry, was awarded the Military Medal.

The following month, Charles attended the 2nd Tank Brigade School to train to use the 6 pdr quick firing gun fitted to male tanks. He had initially applied for a commission on 16 February 1917 but this application was not approved until 6 June when he returned from the coastal training range. Presumably after an interview, the application was countersigned by his CO Lieutenant Corporal Sydney Charrington who would also have approved the recommendation for the Military Medal. Charles then attended the driving training camp at Wailly from 11 to 19 June and was then posted to MGC Depot at Merlimont on 2 July. Eighteen days later, he was directed to report to No 2 MGC Officer Battalion at Pirbright and was commissioned into the Tank Corps on 20 December 1917. He was then posted to the Tank Depot near Wareham and was subsequently allocated to No 5 Tank Supply Company which formed in February. Charles received his Military Medal on 26 February.

The tank supply companies all included a number of veterans, many of whom were decorated. Charles returned to France on 19 June and was promoted lieutenant one week later. During the Battle of Amiens, Charles commanded a two tank sub-section on 8 and 10 August. On 14 August, he was in command of a section near Heilly and on 29 August he was in command a single supply tank replenishing 10th Tank Battalion supporting the New Zealand Division near Achiet-le-Petit. The supply tanks were a key asset as the British forces advanced, allowing for the quick replenishment of ammunition to both infantry and tank units. The pace of the advance could not have been sustained without them and they were a force multiplier. On 21 September, Charles was tasked to remain at Achiet-le-Grand with eleven tanks which were unserviceable. He therefore was in command of almost fifty men which would normally have been a demanding role for a junior officer and which is probably why he was selected for this role. Just over a month later, he rejoined the Company on 26 October, which was now at Bois de Gurlu near Peronne. It remained there until the Armistice. Charles was the sent to the Training and Reinforcement Depot at Mers-les-Bains for a training course on 23 November and rejoined Company on 9 December after it has relocated to the Tank Administrative Area at Humeroeuille. He was sent on home leave from 29 December until 14 January 1919 and then stayed with the Company until 15 February 1919. He then returned to London for demobilization and looked for work.

With most of his family now in the USA, Charles decided to follow them to California. He settled in Sacramento and became a US citizen in 1925. By 1929, he had established the Motor Inn Garage whilst living at 3733 Pacific Avenue. The following year he married Gladys Randal, a divorcee who worked for the State Department of Agriculture. Sadly they had no children and Gladys continued her employment as a stenographer. In 1942 Charles was required to register for the US military draft but was not called up. He ran the Motor Inn until 1949. Life in Sacramento was good for the couple and Charles lived until he was seventy-seven dying on 18 July 1970. Gladys, who was twelve years younger, lived in Sacramento until her death aged eighty-two on 22 January 1987.

Gunner Willie Illingworth, who came from Middlesborough, had enlisted into the MMGS on 24 November 1915 and deployed to France, with the C Company main body on 24 August 1916. After the first actions, when he probably served in either No 3 or 4 Section, he was transferred to C Battalion and, like Charles Surgeon, served with No 8 Company at the Battle of Arras. He almost certainly took part in the fighting near Beaurains on 9 April and, as a gearsman, was awarded the Military medal for conspicuous gallantry and devotion to duty during the follow-up action at Monchy Le Preux two days later. The citation for the Military Medal states that "during the capture of Monchy-le-Preux, although badly wounded, this gunner carried out his duties by supplying ammunition to Lewis guns, and thus enabling a continuous fire to be maintained from his tank. He showed a fine example to the rest of his crew."

He was evacuated back to England for treatment and, on 25 September 1917, was presented with the Military Medal by Lieutenant General Sir John Maxwell at the Sunderland War Hospital. Returning to duty, Willie was posted to 7th Battalion in France which contained a number of soldiers who had previously served in C and D Companies. Willie was however far from well and he was then discharged, as a result of his wounds, on 17 December 1918 and was awarded the Silver War Badge. He however survived until he was eighty.

Following the initial fighting on 9–11 April 1917, in which large numbers of tanks were destroyed, both C and D Company reformed their tanks into a number of small sub-sections each consisting of two tanks. They were sent into action on 23 April 1917 as a result of which three corporals from C Company were awarded the Military Medal.

The first of the three NCOs, Tom Lowe, was born on 2 August 1894 and was brought up, with his five younger siblings, on the Moor Pool garden estate in Harborne near Birmingham. Tom, who was a grocer, enlisted into the MMGS at Coventry just after his twenty-first birthday on 18 August 1915 and reported to the MMGS Training Centre at Bisley the same day. After completed his initial training, Tom was posted firstly to 27th Machine Gun Battery on 1 January 1916 and then joined the Armoured Car Section on 1 April. Appointed acting lance corporal on 13 April, he was posted to C Company on 27 May. Tom was promoted corporal on 7 August whilst at the tank training ground at Elveden. After he had been transferred to C Battalion in November 1916, Tom retrained as a driver. He was in action during the Battle of Arras and "during the action on April 23, 17, when his officer had been temporarily blinded by splinters, and several of the crew wounded, and the Lewis guns disabled, this NCO displayed conspicuous courage and coolness, and managed to drive his tank back to its starting point".

From 11 to 19 June, Tom deployed with the rest of his unit to the Wailly driver training school. Two months later, despite his battalion being in action at the Ypres Salient, Tom was posted back to Wailly on 6 August to join the Mechanical School as an instructor. There is no documentary evidence that Tom fought at the Battle of Cambrai, however the driving instructors from Wailly were allocated to fighting battalions to drive training tanks and pull away the German barbed wire entanglements on 20 November. Given that Tom was granted home leave from 25 November to 9 December I believe that he was amongst those instructors.

The Tank Corps regularly arranged for its instructors to move between the various training schools and, from 15 February 1918 just after the Tank Driving School moved from Wailly to Aveluy, Tom joined the Tank Corps Training Centre at Bovington. On 30 March 1918, his Military Medal was issued and would have been presented publicly. Having been promoted to acting sergeant on 15 May, Tom joined the Mechanical School in France as an NCO assistant instructor. However, within seven days, he reverted to corporal after Mechanist Sergeant George Shepherd, who drove *Crème de Menthe* on 15 September 1916 at Courcelette, joined the school. Tom stayed as an assistant instructor later being promoted staff-sergeant on 18 December as the Driving and Maintenance School was formed. In the latter stages of the war, the Spanish influenza epidemic became prevalent and the Army suffered a number of fatalities. In January 1919 Tom was admitted to the 2nd Canadian General Hospital at Le Tréport suffering from influenza. He was sent back to England on 8 February and released on 26 February and granted leave until 7 March when Tom was posted back to the Tank Corps Reinforcement Depot at Mers les Bains as an instructor. Ten days later, Tom returned to the Tank Corps Depot at Bovington on 17 March but only to complete his discharge as he was sent to Fovant Camp the following day for dispersal. Tom was transferred to the Z Reserve on 15 April against the need to expand the British Army should the German government renege on its appeal for peace.

Tom returned home to live with his parents and younger brother Charles at 14 Moor Pool Avenue. He found work as a commercial traveler and, on 23 May 1923, married Ilse Fielding at Harborne Parish Church. Ilse, who was the eldest daughter of a Regular Army colour sergeant, was known as "Pep" perhaps because her name sounded German. Tom and "Pep" continued to live with his parents at Harborne where they had two children, Colin in 1924 and June who was born three years later. Deciding to move to Australia, In January 1929, the family departed for Freemantle on SS *Borda* and settled in Perth at 131 Ninth Avenue. Tom continued work as a commercial traveller and in 1936 they moved to the Subiaco area. By the 1940s, Tom had become a manager and the couple had moved to the Wembley park area of Freemantle. They lived in the delightfully named Floreat Park in 1945. Tom died in Perth, aged only sixty, on 15 April 1955; Ilse dying eight years later.

The second recipient of the Military Medal for his action on 23 April was one of the founding members of the Professional Golfers' Association (PGA). Jimmy Dodd was born on 3 February 1888 at Hoylake in Cheshire and he was the eldest of eleven siblings. He became as a groundsman at the Leek Golf Club in the early 1900s and was sufficiently well paid to marry Mary Bestwick at All Saints Church in Leek on 9 March 1909. Jimmy was elected to the PGA on 9 September the following year, just one day before his elder daughter Eileen was born. Jimmy did not join the Army until the last week of March 1916 when he volunteered to join the MMGS at Coventry. His former employers paid him 12/6d a week to supplement his army pay, which indicates the regard in which he was held by the club. Like Charles Rowe, Jimmy served with No 8 Company of C Battalion during the Battle of Arras and would have taken part in the attack on the Harp near Beaurains on 9 April. Two weeks later, at Roeux, "During the action on April 23, 17, he did great execution with his Lewis gun. When his tank came under very heavy hostile machine-gun and artillery fire, although wounded, he continued to carry on and fire his gun with great effect."

Jimmy was awarded a Card of Honour by the Tank Corps HQ which also records his deliberate and straight shooting, and later awarded received the Military Medal for his actions. Jimmy was promoted to sergeant shortly afterwards and fought with C Battalion during the Third Battle of Ypres. On 22 August, whilst serving in the tank *Curiosity* with 2Lt HF Nicholson, he was wounded during an attack on the Pommern Redoubt to the south-east of the village of Wieltje. The tanks were due to lead the infantry into the attack but the ground was so bad that Jimmy's tank ditched shortly after crossing the Steenbeke River. Pulled clear by the tank *Celerity*, Jimmy's tank ditched again whilst making its final approach to the British front line and Jimmy was wounded as the crew made their way to safety.

Jimmy was sent back to England for treatment and, on 25 September 1917, was presented with the Military Medal by Lieutenant General Sir John Maxwell at the Sunderland War Hospital. Willie Illingworth received his medal at the same ceremony. Jimmy retained the rank of sergeant and was photographed with Mary once he had recovered. He served on in the Tank Corps, until he was demobilised in January 1919, after which he returned to work at the Leek Golf Club. In 1923, Mary and Jimmy had a second daughter Marjorie, who was born on 29 June. Two years later, Jimmy was presented with a gold Albert watch and chain and £10 for his dedicated work at the Leek Golf Club where he had been pivotal to the extension of the course to eighteen holes.

After Mary died in 1933, Jimmy moved to Sweden to work as the professional at Djursholm Golf Club in Stockholm. He was appointed the Club Professional at the Saltsjobadens Golf Klubb in 1934 and he stayed there until 1948 when he appears to have joined the Djursholm Golf Klubb. The PGA record card suggests that he was made an Honorary Member of one or both of the Klubbs at that time. In his later years, when he played golf, he wore a beret with 2 badges – a style started by General Montgomery in the Western Desert and like Monty one of the badges was that of the Tank Corps. Jimmy lived until he was eighty-seven, dying in Sweden, on 26 October 1973.

Corporal George Kennedy's Military Medal was awarded for ensuring his crewmates were safe after his tank was destroyed on 23 April 1917. George was the son of a railway locomotive driver named Andrew Kennedy and his wife Mary whom he had married in Belfast on 25 November 1877. George was born on 25 July 1884 in Greenock but soon afterwards the family moved to Glasgow. When he left school George became a clerk, initially living at 396 Mathieson Street in Hutchesontown and later in the Pollock Buildings in Cockerhill. Like Tom Lowe, he was an early member of the MMGS, being attested at Glasgow on 10 August 1915. George was transferred to the MGC on 1 December and posted 27th Battery one month later. He was then transferred to Armoured Car Company at Pirbright on 1 April and appointed unpaid acting lance corporal on 13 April 1917. He was posted to C Company on 25 May and promoted paid corporal on 7 August, nine days before he deployed to France.

Based on this latter date, George probably served with No 2 Section in support of the Guards on 15 September. George was injured during the actions on the Ancre, between 25 September and 2 October but not so seriously as to require him to leave C Company. He was then posted to No 9 Company when C Battalion was formed in December. On the opening day of the Battle of Arras, his tank was tasked to support 12th Division in their attack along the Arras to Cambrai Road with their objective being the north western side of Tilloy village. However, his tank was one of five which became stuck in a morass during the approach march in a low lying valley to the west of the Crinchon River; they were all eventually recovered but none were in time to take part in the attack.

On 23 April, his tank was one of two tasked to support 17th Division whose final objective being the village of Pelves on the south of the river Scarpe. The tanks were to be kept in reserve to assist in the final assault but George's tank was destroyed as it made its way forward near Monchy Le Preux. As the tank approached a wood to the northwest of the village, it was hit by an artillery barrage and George was wounded. One of the rounds penetrated the radiator and the tank had to stop. The crew was able to take cover in shell holes but three were injured. To quote the citation for his Military Medal "after his tank had received two direct hits and several of the crew wounded, this NCO although wounded himself in the face, insisted on looking after the other wounded men and dressing their wounds under intense shell fire, before being attended to himself. Whilst he was attending to one of the men he was again wounded in the leg."

His service record states that, on 21 May, George was posted to a Base Depot but there are no other details afterwards. This would indicate that his wounds were sufficiently serious for him to be evacuated to a major hospital on the French coast. Granted home leave, George married Isabella Donnelly on 28 August 1917 – Isabella was a neighbour who also lived in the Pollock Buildings. He recovered and later rejoined C Battalion in time to take part in the Battle of Cambrai. He was promoted sergeant on 21 November, presumably after another NCO had been wounded. His record is not clear but it appears he lost his third stripe when the NCO returned to duty. However, George was again serving as a sergeant by early August 1918 as he commanded the Whippet tank *Cynic* in action on the opening day of the Battle of Amiens. His section commander was Captain Eric Purdy who had commanded Tank Crew C16 at Combles on 15 September 1916. He managed to remain unwounded for the rest of the war and was demobilised in February 1919.

When George was contacted shortly afterwards, about the award of his Military Medal, he declined to have the Medal presented publicly and asked that it be sent to him by post. After the war Isabella and George had a son and he continued to work as a clerk. The family moved to the newly built estates near Renfrew and it was there at Second Avenue that George died of a heart attack, aged sixty, on 21 November 1944, his death being registered by his daughter in law Ida. Isabella stayed at Second Avenue until 1964 when she was in contact with the Army Records staff but sadly there is no record of her death.

The Third Battle of Ypres

Gunner Joseph Walker was from the spa town of Matlock. He was born on 31 May 1893 at Ashover in Derbyshire and his father Sam had an independent income as did his grandmother Sarah who lived in Wellfield House at Matlock Bank, a Regency house which had been turned into a hydropathic centre in the 1870s but later returned to being a private residence. Sadly Joseph's father died while he was young but his mother then married George Else who acted as overseer to Joseph's grandmother's estate. George also had a number of children and there was a large family at Wellfield House. When Joseph joined the MMGS in 1915, he was working as a wireman. He deployed to France with No 2 Section on 16 August 1916 and initially served as a machine gunner with C Company. After he transferred to C Battalion, he retrained as a driver and it was in this role that he won his gallantry award. To quote the citation: "During the Battle of Ypres, on July 31, 1917, this man continued to drive his tank although one of his arms had been rendered useless and only gave in when in a fainting condition."

Joseph recovered from his injury and, in 1918, joined the Royal Air Force as a potential pilot. His RAF records show he was only five feet four inches tall but this did not prevent him from being successful in training. He graded as flight cadet on 5 October 1918 and a learner pilot on 19 March 1919. However, with the reduction of the Armed Forces, Joseph was transferred to the G Reserve on 1919 and he returned to Wellfield House. He did not however forget his comrades in C Battalion and joined their Old Comrades Association. He is listed on their 1925 membership still living in Matlock Bank but thereafter, I can find nothing about him.

The Battle of Cambrai

Many of those who fought at Flers-Courcelette in September 1916 were also in action when the tanks smashed through the Hindenburg defensive position near Cambrai. Private Clifford Ridout, who was a member of C Company, was awarded the Military Medal for his bravery on the opening day of the Battle of Cambrai. Born on 9 November 1898 in King's Norton Birmingham, he was the second son of a builder named Alfred Ridout and his wife Emma. After leaving school, Clifford became an engineer's clerk and he enlisted into the MMGS just after his seventeenth birthday on 22 November 1915. Having passed the pre-employment test at Coventry, he was given a railway ticket and sent to the MMGS Training Centre at Bisley arriving the following day.

Having deployed to France on 24 August 1916, Clifford was still only seventeen when the tanks first went into action. It is therefore possible that he was kept out of battle; the company commander Allen Holford-Walker having had one "underage" soldier being removed from his company just before they deployed to France. Having joined C Battalion in November 1916, Clifford almost certainly fought at the Battle of Arras the following spring. He then attended the driver training camp at Wailly from 11 to 17 June and retrained as a driver. There are no records of his service during the Battle of Ypres but it is unlikely that his unit would not have employed a battle-hardened soldier during this part of the campaign.

It was in the driving role that Clifford fought on 20 November 1917 and was wounded in the face. The medal citation reveals that: "during the attack on the Gonnelieu Ridge, this man displayed the greatest gallantry. Although severely wounded, he insisted on driving to the final objective, which he reached before collapsing from a loss of blood". Evacuated from the battlefield, Clifford was admitted to 8 General Hospital at Rouen and later moved to 5 General Hospital. Sent to the Reinforcement Depot on 9 December, he did not rejoin C Battalion but was posted to the recently arrived J Battalion on 29 December. He was then sent on home leave from 15 to 29 January 1918. He was appointed 1st class tank mechanic on 23 January and served with the redesignated 10th Battalion as they fought to limit the German success during the Great Advance in March 1918. He also took part in the Battle of Amiens in August.

On 15 September, Clifford was admitted to hospital with influenza but was soon back with 10th Battalion, having undergone crew refresher training at the Training and Reinforcement Depot at Mers-les-Bains. On 4 October, he was sent on a one month course at the Depot and returned to 10th Battalion three days before the Armistice. Now serving in B Company, Clifford was promoted corporal on Christmas Day 1918. On 30 December, he was offered employment as a technical engineer by James Scott and Co in Birmingham. Having been granted home leave from 8 January 1919, he immediately sought his release and gained his discharged by post, rather than have to travel to one of the demobilisation centres. In common with most decorated soldiers, he decided to have his Military Medal sent by post, rather than being presented by a local dignitary, but the medal had to be returned and re-struck as the number was incorrectly inscribed. Within three years, Clifford had set himself up in the motor manufacturing business at 388 Park Road and was sufficiently financially secure to marry Nellie Lovell at Edgbaston Parish Church on 24 March 1926. Nellie was three years older than her husband who was now working as a motor fabricator. Their son Bert was born the following year. During the 1930s, Clifford's business interests changed and he became an electrical contractor working from the Dudley Road. He later expanded the scope of the company even further and moved into TV and radio sales and repairs. Clifford and Nellie stayed in Birmingham after he retired. After Clifford died in 1969, Nellie moved to join their son Bert who was living at Kingswoodford where she died aged ninety-seven in October 1993.

Battle of Amiens

The first day of the Battle of Amiens, on 8 August 1918, was a black day for the German Army, owing to the numbers of soldiers killed, wounded, and most importantly captured. It was also the start of the Allied advance which could not be stopped by the German forces. Amongst those fighting at Amiens was Wilfred Edwards who was a tank corporal at the Battle of Flers-Courcelette serving in either No 3 or No 4 Section of C Company. Like several of those in the MMGS, he worked in the motor parts industry at Coventry. He was born in the city on 26 January 1896; the youngest son of a machinist called John Edwards and his wife Maria. Wilfred was baptised at the St John the Baptist Church in Coventry on 8 April 1896 whilst the family was closeby living at 8 Trafalgar Street.

Leaving school at 14 years, Wilfred started work making gear-cases but, by the time he enlisted on 1 December 1915, he had become a metal and celluloid glass case maker. He was not mobilised until 20 March 1916 but, within two months, had been appointed acting lance corporal. He was posted to C Company on 27 May and promoted to corporal exactly one month later. This was about the time that C Company moved to Elveden for tank crew training. There he was admitted to Bury St Edmunds Hospital for ten days with tonsillitis, returning to Elveden on 15 August. Nine days later, he deployed to France and probably fought with No 3 or 4 Section on the right flank of the British Attack between Ginchy and Combles. Having served with C Company throughout the first tank actions, Wilfred was transferred to C Battalion on 18 November. Like Maurice Shelton, he was hospitalised on 31 January. Whilst in hospital, his rank of corporal was lost but he regained it when returning to duty. He almost certainly fought throughout at the Battle of Arras. In May 1917, Wilfred attended the same 6 pdr gunner's course at 2 Bde Tank School as Charles Spurgeon. He then fought with C Battalion during the Third Battle of Ypres and also the Battle of Cambrai after which he was granted home leave from 5 to 19 December 1917. With other members of the Battalion, now rebadged as 3rd Light Battalion, Wilfred retrained to operate Whippet light tanks and was in action with B Company during the Battle of Amiens.

On 21 August 1918, during the fighting near Achiet-le-Grand, Wilfred was the driver of the tank *Cynic* which was commanded by Corporal Budd. "After their tank had been knocked out by a direct hit from enemy artillery, he (and Gunner S L Clark) displayed most conspicuous gallantry by rescuing many injured infantry who were lying out in the open exposed to intense artillery and machine gun fire. They carried many to a place of safety and showed the greatest contempt of danger" for which both men were awarded the Military Medal. Wilfred was wounded in the right knee during this action, probably whilst helping the injured, but was not immediately taken to hospital. Two days later, he was evacuated to a Casualty Clearing Station and then to the hospital in Dannes-Camiers before being sent to Convalescent Depots at Étaples and Trouville. Wilfred was released on 21 September and, after a week at the Tank Corps Reinforcement Depot at Mers-les-Bains, he returned to 3rd Battalion on 26 September. His company had been in action the previous day and a composite company was in action on 8 October. Whilst there is no record of him being in action, Wilfred was promoted Machinist Sergeant on 18 October. He stayed with 3rd Battalion until 13 February, when he returned to Chiseldon for demobilization on 17 February 19. His Military Medal was sent to home address on 23 August 1919, Wilfred having declined to have it presented. He lived in Coventry for the rest of his life, dying aged seventy three in the summer of 1969.

Distinguished Conduct Medal

One of the greatest dangers for crewmen has always been fire breaking out inside a tank; a lesson learned by C Company even before they went into action at Flers-Courcelette. During the preparations for battle, near the Loop railway offloading area, a fire broke out in a tank which caused second degree burns to the face and hands of Gunner John Callaghan as he assisted Sergeant Robert Hillhouse rescue another crewman. John was born in Glossop, Derbyshire on 17 November 1893 and was the youngest child of a proof reader William Callaghan and his wife Mary. John was working as a dairyman and shop manager for Sherry's dairy when he enlisted on 7 December but he was not called up until 18 May 1916; only three months later he deployed to France. After he was burned on 11 September, John was initially sent for treatment to the 1st Canadian General

Hospital at Étaples. He was evacuated to England on HS *Brighton* on 15 September and admitted to Graylingwell War Hospital near Chichester. He was discharged just under two months later and, after ten days home leave, was posted to the Tank Depot on 21 November 1916. Joining the newly formed H Battalion, John retrained as a driver and was appointed lance corporal on 17 May 17. He deployed back to France, on 22 August 1917, with No 22 Company. The battalion served in the Ypres Salient but John probably did not see action.

On the first day of the Battle of Cambrai, John drove the tank *Harrier*, carrying the section commander Captain Percy Batten, through the German defences to the Hindenburg support line between Ribecourt and Masnieres. As *Harrier* and two other tanks attempted to cross the wide trenches, they were engaged and knocked out by the German field guns sited on the high ground to the east side of Flesquières. On 29 November, when waiting to be entrained at what was perceived to be the end of the battle, John and his tank's skipper, Lieutenant Joseph Hassell were amongst the crews tasked by HQ 2 Tank Brigade to deploy against the German counter–attack. The following day, John drove one of three tanks in support of the Grenadier Guards' assault on a trench system near Gauche Wood. His tank then led the section towards Villers-Guislan where the tanks separated. Pushing on alone, John's tank charged a battery of German artillery which was preparing to move. Using the tank's Lewis guns, they inflicted casualties before the guns got away. Joseph Hassell then used his tank to rescue Lieutenant Scott and his crew whose tank had been disabled. Hassell's tank then advanced towards the Germans again but became ditched in a trench when its engine failed. After seven minutes, John Callaghan managed to repair the magneto, which was full of oil, and get the engine started. He then drove the tank out and, despite the fact that it was impossible to change gears, or change direction, coaxed the tank back to the rallying point at Gauche Wood.

As a result of the need to replace crewmen lost during the Battle of Cambrai, John was promoted acting corporal on 2 December 1917 but was then reduced to lance corporal in April 1918; this was probably due to the return of a wounded NCO from Great Britain. Two months later, whilst undertaking training at the tank gunnery school as Merlimont, John became seriously ill with Spanish flu. He was admitted to 20 General Hospital at Dannes-Camiers, near Étaples, on 11 July. Despite being away from his unit, John recovered the rank of corporal on 24 July 1918 and appointed sergeant on the same day. The next day he was evacuated to the UK on SS *Cambria* and admitted to 1/5 Northern General Hospital at Leicester where he was treated for two months. John was discharged on 27 September and granted leave until 4 October. He was then posted to the Royal Artillery and Tank Corps Command Depot at Catterick and classified medical state B2 on Armistice Day.

Being medically downgraded, John could not return to 8th Battalion but was posted to the Tank Corps Depot on 3 December 1918. Re-classified as a 1st class tank mechanist, John was awarded the Distinguished Conduct Medal in the 1919 New Year's Honours List. The citation stated: He has done admirable work in many tank actions, both before operations by his devotion to duty in keeping his tank fit, and during operations, by his extreme coolness and skillful driving under heavy fire. His conduct was of the highest order and he has set a fine example to all." His old tank skipper, Captain Joseph Hassell who was by then the adjutant of 8th Battalion, wrote to John noting that he had 'been put in for a decoration more than once...I am very pleased that they have seen fit to recognise your good work at last". John was transferred to the Army's Z Reserve on 23 February 1919 and returned to live at St Mary's Rectory in Glossop. He lived in his home town for the rest of his life, working as a provision dealer and in 1941, was working at 45 West Street which had been the location of a grocer's shop for the previous forty years. He kept in contact with his old comrades and, in 1957, at the time of the 40th Anniversary of the Battle of Cambrai was recorded as living at Woodview on the Sheffield Road in Glossop. John Callaghan died in Glossop, aged seventy-seven in 1970.

Bravery in Russia

One of the last Tank Crewmen to be honoured was for his service in the Baltic States after the Great War had ended. Alexander Lawson was born in October 1893 in Darvel in Ayrshire. He was the youngest son of a lace weaver, also called Alexander, and his wife Margaret. The family originally lived at 62-64 Main Street but, when Alexander Senior died, they moved to 70 East St Main. Alexander was a newsagent working for his mother when he enlisted into the MMGS. He was mobilised on 15 March 1916 and the following day reported for duty at Bisley. His record reveals little about his life in the Tanks until 1919. He was transferred to Armoured Car Section on 1 April then to Heavy Section MGC on 4 May. Posted to C Company on 27 May, Alexander deployed to France on 24 August 1916 which means he served with No 3 or No 4 Section. He joined to C Battalion on 18 November, and having rebadged to the Tank Corps, he was sent to the Tank Reinforcement Depot on 12 April 1918 and returned to 3rd Battalion seven days later. As he has no illnesses recorded on his record, this probably means that Alexander undertook a training course.

Having fought with his unit though the Battles of Arras, Ypres, Cambrai, the Kaiserschlacht and Amiens, Alexander was sent back to the UK on 14 September 1918 arriving at Bovington two days later. He was not however allocated to a new unit, the 22nd Light Battalion, until 10 January 1919 when he was posted to the Depot and then to 20th Battalion on 31 March 1919. Perhaps because of the lack of jobs at home in Darvel, Alexander did not press for demobilization. Indeed when the British Government decided to send three tank training teams to Russia in the summer of 1919, Alexander volunteered to go with them. The three tank detachments were required to train the White Russian units who were seeking to overthrow the Bolshevik Government. One was sent to North Russia, one to the Black Sea and Alexander's party was sent to assist the conquest of the area around St Petersburg. On 28 July, the advance party left the Port of London to serve with General Yudenitch's forces in the Baltic. In total the detachment, under the command of Lieutenant Corporal Ernest Hope-Carson, consisted of twenty-two officers, twenty-six other ranks and six Mark V tanks

The advance party disembarked on 5 August 1919 at Talinn in Estonia and later moved to Narva. Here a base was established and training began with a new White Russian infantry unit known as the Tank Push battalion. All six tanks arrived had arrived by the first week of September and the first three tanks were deployed. The tanks were used in a series of attacks including an advance on St Petersburg in October. Although the Mark V tanks were generally crewed by Russian troops, they could not be maintained by them. The tanks crewmen must therefore have deployed forward as Alexander was one of four crewmen who were awarded the Military Medal for bravery in the field. The tanks successfully reached the location of the former imperial palace at Tsarskoye Selo, about fifteen miles from the centre of St Petersburg. However, the White Russians could not hold the ground against the advancing Red Army. All six tanks were successfully withdrawn to Narva, although some had mechanical problems, and the training team then returned to England arriving on 23 November 1919. Alexander was demobilised on 10 February 1920 but later received not only the Military Medal but also a Russian decoration, the Cross of St George 4th Class.

Returning to his home in Darvel, three years later, he married a Madras weaver named Jenny Morton. Madras cloth was a specialist industry in the Darvel area which, despite the downturn in the fabric sales, remains in production. Like Alexander, Jenny's father was a lace maker – the Morton family having brought lace making to Darvel in the 1870s. The couple married after banns "according to the rights of the Church of Scotland" in the Cooperative Hall on 20 February 1926. The location is to say the least unusual as the Church of Scotland has a fine parish church in Darvel which is directly opposite the Cooperative Hall. Jenny was twenty three at the time of her marriage, ten years younger than Alexander who had by then set up business as a motor hirer. Thereafter I can find no more information about them although a young man called Alexander Lawson was born in Darvel in 1931.

20

Nil Sine Labore

Nil Sine Labore [Nothing in achieved without effort] was the motto of The Army Service Corps (ASC). The ASC provided the whole range of logistic support to the British Army, wherever it was sent, reaching at its peak strength 10,547 officers and 315,334 other ranks as well as thousands of locally employed men in all theatres of war. Amongst this vast organisation was a specially formed Mechanical Transport (MT) unit, 711 Company, which not only provided the first tanks' drivers but also the mechanics and maintenance support to both C and D Companies. The names of some of those ASC men who supported C Company are included in an extract from the landing records held by the Tank Museum whilst the names of those attached to D Company are listed in the notebook kept by the Adjutant Captain Graham Woods which is also held at Bovington. Sadly neither list is fully complete as there are a number of drivers from C Company who are not recorded. This chapter gives details of those officers and soldiers who were not recorded as being assigned to tank crews in either C or D Company.

One of the original section commanders in C Company was an ASC officer. Captain Richard Trevithick, who was the great-grandson of the Cornish locomotive pioneer, was born in Carlisle on 7 October 1891. Richard was bought up near Nantwich in Cheshire and was educated at Bilton Grange Preparatory School near Rugby from 1901 until 1905 and afterwards at Cheltenham College. He then worked as an apprentice at the London and North Western Railway workshops at Crewe from 1909 for five years, living at 96 Nelson Street, after which he departed for New York on 24 February 1914 to study mechanical engineering. Richard returned in May 1914 to join the London based firm of Dewrance where he gained expertise on high pressure valves and associated equipment.

Following the outbreak of war, Richard was commissioned into the ASC on 12 October 1914 and deployed to France two weeks later. He served with a MT company, that is a company equipped with lorries, and was the engineering officer responsible for 120 vehicles. When 711 MT Company was established in June 1916, Richard was tasked to instruct tank crews on driving and maintenance at Elveden and then was placed in command of No 3 Section. Richard deployed with the first group of tanks to France. He travelled with them by rail to Avonmouth and thence to Le Havre where he managed the offloading whilst commanding twenty-five ASC men. The names of these are not listed in either the 711 Company War Diary or in the C Company diary which is why it is difficult to identify many of the first tank drivers. Richard then travelled to the training area at Yvrench during which time he injured his knee.

Replaced as section commander by Sir John Dashwood, Richard remained in France until December 1916. On his return to England, Richard was employed with the Ministry of Munitions and appointed the resident engineer for the southwest of England. Richard lived in Bristol close to the College Green and then lived at Great Dover Street in Southwark, when he worked at the main Ministry offices in Whitehall. In February 1919, Richard was demobilised and returned to work for Dewrance as an assistant manager. He married Marie Miller at St Margaret's Church in Westminster on 19 June 1919 and their only daughter Noel was born in 1926. Richard continued work in Pall Mall as a chartered engineer whilst his family lived in Chislehurst. He travelled extensively both between the wars and in the 1950s. Eventually Marie and Richard eventually settled at Cheddington in Dorset, where he died aged eighty-two on 10 April 1973.

Richard was not the only ASC officer to have worked in New York before the outbreak of war. Second Lieutenant Theodore Wenger, who was the technical officer for C Company, was employed by the Edison Company in New York. Theodore had been born on 21 February 1890 in Newcastle under Lyne, the fourth son of a French-Swiss named Albert Wenger who ran a successful chemical and ceramic colour manufacturing company. Theodore was educated at Newcastle High School and then attended Birmingham University where he studied Electrical and Mechanical Engineering. He moved to New York in 1910 and worked for Edisons for four years. In August 1915 he returned to assist with the manufacturing of munitions. However, he soon enlisted as a private soldier into 28th Battalion London Regiment, also known as the Artists' Rifles, at Romford. The Artists' Rifles was an officer training unit. Theodore's engineering skills marked him out for employment with the ASC and he was commissioned as a temporary second lieutenant on 15 May 1916.

Theodore initially served at Grove Park MT Depot and was then soon posted to 711 MT Coy at Elveden. He deployed to France on 16 August at the same time as the C Company advance party. Throughout the first actions, Theodore was constantly on call to repair individual tanks –indeed he was mentioned in one of the first messages, sent by pigeon, from Victor Smith commanding *Casa* after he had nursed his tank back from across no man's land on 15 September 1916. Theodore transferred to the newly formed Heavy Branch MGC on 18 November and was promoted temporary lieutenant on 1 December 1916.

Having been appointed to the B Battalion Workshops Company, and supporting their attack at Messines in June 1917, he joined No 2 Field Company on 23 July 1917 and was appointed second in command three days later. After the Third Battle of Ypres, Theodore was awarded the MC "for conspicuous gallantry and devotion to duty in repairing a badly damaged tank under heavy shell fire and in full view of the enemy and driving it back to safety. He has consistently displayed a very high standard of determined courage and ability when engaged in salvage work, and has set a very fine example to all ranks." He undertook a similar task during the Battle of Cambrai and later throughout the rest of the war. Theodore was first appointed acting major while he was employed as a Mechanical Engineer at HQ Tank Field Battalion on 26 October 1918 and then acting lieutenant colonel after he took command of 2nd Field Battalion on 23 March 1919. He was responsible for the clearance of the tank hulks from the battlefields during 1919 which included removing *Crème de Menthe* from Thiepval and destroying D6 near Gueudecourt. At the end of the year Theodore was sent to visit the Tank Training Team, supporting the White Russians against the Bolsheviks in Ukraine, in December 1919 and January 1920. He relinquished his commission on completion of service on 3 June 1920 and returned home to Newcastle under Lyme where he continued work as an engineer. He later became a director of the family company. Theodore was a keen huntsman and was a regular organiser of the North Staffordshire Hunt Ball. He also attended a ball organised by his brother who was commanding 5th Battalion Staffordshire Regiment in the 1930s. He did not lose touch with his Tank Corps comrades, attending the 1936 Cambrai dinner. In 1938, he travelled to Australia where he contracted bacterial encarditus and died on 1 May 1939 at Mount St Evins Hospital in Melbourne.

The tank companies' transport officer was Lieutenant Bill Brannon who had previously seen service in Namibia. His full name was Allan Cuthbert Brannon and he was the youngest of four children. Born on 25 August 1890, in Forest Gate, Bill's father was a shipping agent from Wootton on the Isle of Wight who died by the time Bill was ten. His Scottish mother Mary had to run a boarding house to sustain her young family. In 1912, Bill moved to South Africa and worked on a farm. When the British declared war on Germany, the South Africans decided to invade German South East Africa. Bill joined up on 9 September 1914 and soon reached the rank of sergeant. He was then commissioned in the field and reached the rank of captain. At the conclusion of the South West African campaign, Bill left Cape Town on 17 November 1915 for England. He was commissioned into the ASC on 29 May 1916 and shortly after joined 711 Company.

Deploying to France with the unit transport, he led the majority of D Company vehicles from Le Havre to the training area at Yvrench. Five days later, Bill then commanded the move of the entire MT to the Loop railhead, leaving Yvrench at 7:30 a.m. on 9 September and arriving early the following morning. There is no record of his activities after the first actions but, a year later, Bill was appointed as an acting captain and an assistant instructor although it is unclear is this was in France or at Bovington. He appears to have stayed in the instructional role for the rest of the war. After the war, whilst nominally serving in the Middlesex Regiment, Bill served as an assistant instructor at the Tank Corps Driving and Maintenance School at Bovington. From 1920 to 1923, Bill served at the Royal Tank Corps training school in Ahmednagar, probably as an instructor. At this time, the Tank Corps was primarily employed on internal securities amongst the tribal areas of the North West Frontier. He then returned to Bovington and again served as an instructor at the Central Schools. Bill then returned to India, serving with 11th Armoured Car Company, in 1926 and 1927, in Waziristan serving at Razmuk and then Razani. Returning to England, he was appointed Adjutant of Tank Gunnery School at Lulworth Cove on 27 May 1931. Bill held this post for three years and then retired on 29 June 1935. In the summer of 1938, he married Gertrude Laird at Kensington, the couple having met whilst Bill was living in Bournemouth. When war was declared, Bill was appointed Brevet Major in the RTR; he was appointed a driving examiner in 1940 and served throughout the war eventually retiring as a Lieutenant Colonel. He returned to his first life as a farmer, living at Bay Farm at Tarrant Monkton from 1951 and almost certainly meeting up with George Bown, who served with him in D Company in 1916, who was now farming at Blandford Forum. Bill died in his ninetieth year on New Year's Day 1981 and is buried in Tarrant Monkton churchyard.

The majority of those who supported the tanks in France remained with ASC for the rest of the war. Corporal Herbert Lane, who was attached with D Company, later reached rank of sergeant. Three other ASC men who served with D Company but who did not change their capbadge were George Roylance, M Wicks and Thomas Wigley, none of whom were promoted. Remaining in the ASC was no guarantee, however, of being safe from enemy fire. For example Private James Storey was discharged from the Woolwich ASC Depot on 31 October 1917 due to wounds. James was born on 10 February 1891 in Longwitton in Northumberland and baptised six weeks later at nearby Hartburn on 22 March. He was the youngest son of a coal miner, John Storey and his mother Ellen Leighton had two other children, his elder sister Ann and his elder brother Joseph who became an apprentice joiner. By the age of twenty, James was working as a farm labourer living with his uncle at Roughlees Farm near Ewesley Station which is close to Morpeth. In July 1914, James married Kate Hall in Belford Northumberland and they had a son Jack who died as an infant on 15 July 1915. James enlisted into the ASC as a driver on 24 Nov 1915 and was attached to D Company. After his discharge he returned to Roughlees and continued farming. He died there, aged forty-five on 7 May 32. He was buried in the Beednell Cemetery, having left more than £1,200 to his wife. Kate Storey died, aged 62, on 14 March 1954 and was buried with James and her son at Beednell.

Whilst Pte Sydney Precious continued to serve with ASC, Pte Edward Lord transferred to the Tank Corps in the summer of 1917 and served with them until the end of the war; unfortunately I had been unable to get any information about either man. There was one ASC driver from D Company who rebadged to the MGC and who definitely served as a tank driver. Private Jim Luxon was born 22 February 1892 at Clayhidon near Wellington in Somerset. Jim's father Ephraim was an agricultural worker and Jim was his eldest son. He left home as a youngster and, in 1911, was working for his uncle as a farm labourer at Gladhayes at Clayhidon. Jim joined the ASC, as a trainee MT driver in 1915 but did not deploy overseas before he was allocated to

711 Company. After the first tank actions, he transferred to the MGC in early 1917 and joined D Battalion where he was allocated to No 10 Company. He retrained as a tank driver and, on the opening day of the Battle of Arras, fought at Neuville Vitasse in the tank *Diana*. The tank's skipper was Second Lieutenant Arch Nelson who named his tank after his finance. The tank was delayed on her way into action, as a result of a broken engine fan belt, and once repairs were complete, the crew went into action as rapidly as the ground conditions would allow. The ground was covered with snow but the interior of the tank was hot as there was no possibility of opening the vision flaps more than a fraction as they were being targeted by enemy machine gun fire. The crew apparently was cursing Jim as his officer told to press on, Jim having to be coaxed to drive over bodies that were in the way of the tank. *Diana* became ditched as she crossed no man's land just before the German front line however Jim managed to get the tank back into action. *Diana* caught up with 12th Battalion London Regiment, known as the Rangers, who were unable to break through a German barbed-wire entanglement which was covered by a German machine gun. *Diana* flattened the wire and, whilst her crew suppressed the machine gun, the Rangers broke through and the tank followed up. The tank became ditched again but Jim managed to get *Diana* moving and back the rallying point.

Diana was again in action on 11 April. This time she got forward, ahead of the infantry, suppressed the defending German trenches whilst the infantry took the position and then remained on the position, at Heinel, for four and a half hours to prevent the expected counter attack, before returning to the rallying point. The next time *Diana* went into action was on 23 April – this time she had a new commander and it is not clear if Jim was her driver. Jim transferred to the Tank Corps in July 1917 and served with them as a private soldier until the end of the war. Returning to Somerset, in 1921, he married Florence Bright who was living in his home village. They had four children; his daughters and youngest son were born in Somerset but his eldest son Hubert was born in Weston in Hertfordshire. The family later moved to Hoddesden where Jim was interviewed by Jonathan Nicholls for his book Cheerful Sacrifice. Florence died in 1977 but Jim lived on another 12 years, dying aged ninety-seven, one of the last tank crewmen to die.

Private Edwin Reekie, who was also older than most of the ASC drivers, was the son of a Scottish commercial traveller who settled in Lancashire. Edwin was born in Chorlton on Medlock in the spring of 1881 but the family moved to Manchester. By the time he was twenty Edwin was working as a grocer's clerk and living at Stretford with his widowed mother. He later became an insurance agent and moved to Sale in Cheshire. In early 1907, he married Mildred Cotton, the couple both being twenty-six years old. Their daughter Beatrice was born later that year and the family settled at 7 Eaton Road in Sale. In 1913, the couple's son James was born but he did not survive infancy. Edwin is listed in Graham Woods' notebook as serving with D Company on the Somme but he gives no other details. Edwin did not transfer to the tanks but continued to serve with ASC and RASC. After the war, Edwin returned to Sale and Mildred gave birth to their second son Ian on 16 December 1920. The family later moved to Plymouth where Mildred died, aged fifty-six, in 1936. In late 1940, Edwin married Hilda Tremelling and they later lived at 14 Corporation Flats on Vicarage Road. Edwin died aged sixty-seven, at the City Hospital in Plymouth on 12 August 1947.

Augustus Brotherton, who served with D Company, was born in Edmonton, North London in early 1892. Gus was the fourth son of a draper's clerk Walter Brotherton and his wife Florence. As a young man, Gus worked as a hotel porter living at 27 Canonbury Grove in North Islington. He joined the ASC at motor driver in 1915 and continued to serve with RASC until the end of the war. Whilst in the Army, Gus learned about electrics and, when he married Louise Kirby on 15 May 1921 at St Michael at Bowes Church in Wood Green, Gus was working as an electrical fitter. Their eldest daughter Joan was born later that summer and her sister Marjorie in 1923. Gus and Louise lived at 3 White Hart Lane from 1924 until 1931, their youngest daughter Patricia being born in the summer of 1929 and their only son Roy in the autumn of 1931. The following year Gus and Louise left their home at 3 White Hart Lane in Wood Green. They later moved to Kent; Gus dying in Hastings in early 1968 and Louise in Gravesend in 1986.

Few of the ASC drivers had served overseas before they accompanied the tanks to France but Vincent Gale was an exception. He joined as a military specialist in September 1914 and, because he was a trained driver, was in France with the British Expeditionary Force within weeks, Vincent was born near St Pancras on 3 September 1885 and was baptised seventeen days later at St Bartholomew's Church. Vincent was the eldest son of a mail driver Vincent Gale and his wife Emma who lived at 6 Gough Street in Clerkenwell. Educated at the Halford Road and then Arkmar Road Schools in Parsons Green, Vincent married Edith Nora Smith on 3 July 1910 at St Mary Magdalene Church in the Holloway Road in Islington. Unusually the wedding was witnessed by the rector and verger rather than by the couple's relatives. At the time of the 1911 census Vincent was employed as a domestic chauffeur and the couple was living in three rooms at 7 Brading Road in Tulse Hill in South London. Edith gave birth to her elder daughter, Edith Rosemary on 21 November 1911 and her sister Dorice on 31 October 1912.

On the outbreak of the Great War, Vincent was working as a motor lorry driver. When he enlisted on 4 September, he was recorded as having a fresh complexion with blue eyes and brown hair. He was nine stone twelve pounds in weight, sixty-eight inches tall and had a hammer toe on his right foot. He joined the ASC at Aldershot on 6 September and was allocated to the 2nd Indian Cavalry Supply Column. He deployed to France on 21 September and remained there until 20 December 1915 when he was posted back to the UK. He deployed back to France on 28 August 1916 with 711 Company by which time his wife Edith was pregnant with their third child. Vincent, who was a light car driver, was attached to D Company but soon fell ill and, on 17 November 16, was admitted to hospital in England. In common with all of those sent home as a result of illness or wounds, Vincent's officers provided a character reference which records him as being intelligent, sober and reliable; a lack of sobriety being a major issue for the Army. Whilst Vincent was in hospital, Edith gave birth to his third daughter was a named Winifred.

Vincent was released from hospital on 20 December and granted ten days leave, His health was assessed as fit for duty at home but not likely to be fit for service overseas. On 12 January 1917, the baby Winifred died of whooping cough and convulsions. On being released from hospital, Vincent was posted to the Grove Park MT Depot. He took leave for two days without getting permission, presumably to care for his family, and was charged for the offence. The charge was heard by his company commander on 27 January. Vincent was found guilty and he was admonished which was the least possible sentence. Vincent was however required to forfeit four day's pay which would indicate that he was missing from Grove Park for twice as long as that for which he was officially absent.

On 13 March 1917, Vincent was posted overseas again, this time to serve in Mesopotamia. His service record shows that he became a casualty but it does not give the date or the cause. The wound must have been minor and the treatment prompt as the levels of death through sickness in the Iraqi area were amongst the highest in the Great War. Posted to Egypt, Vincent next served at the Middle East Force Base MT Depot, as a MT fitter. On 15 May 18, he was charged with stating a falsehood and insolence to two sergeants and was awarded seven days Field Punishment No 2. Vincent returned to England as a result of sickness and was treated at Bath. He was transferred to the Reserve on 18 February and returned to his family at Myddleton Square in Clerkenwell. He later moved to Lavender garden in Enfield where, in January 1925, he claimed an Army pension for malaria and neurasalthea. Both of these claims were not accepted although a future claim for hemorrhoids was not discounted. Vincent lived in 18 Lavender Gardens until 1950 after which he lived with his daughter Dorice. He died in Enfield, aged seventy-six years, on 29 July 1962, Edith having pre-deceased him.

William Nightingale, who was attached to C Company, was born in one month earlier than Vincent in August 1885. He enlisted as a learner MT driver on 13 December 1915 and deployed to France on 16 August 1916. Although he did not join the tanks, he was obviously a capable soldier as he was serving as an acting corporal when he was discharged, due to sickness, on 19 October 1917. Unfortunately I have been unable to find no other information about him. On the other hand, Private John Tetlow's service record exists as do a number of family trees on the Ancestry website. John was the younger son of a merchant seaman from Bootle; his father and mother, Elizabeth married on & May 1887. John, who was born in Kirkdale in December 1893, married Agnes Hinton on 25 September 1905. Before the war, the couple had six children; the youngest of whom Phyllis was born on 21 June 1914. John, who was a self-employed taxi driver, voluntarily enlisted into the ASC on 10 April 1915. He was posted to Grove Park MT Depot London the following day and, because he was already trained, sent to Ireland on driving duties from May 15 to May 16. Allocated to 711 (MT) Company, John was then sent to Elveden and, after a final visit home, deployed to France on 16 August 1916 with C Company. On 15 September, whilst the tanks were in action, John suffered an inguinal hernia possibly as a result of heavy lifting. He was evacuated from France to the Castle Hospital at Dublin, arriving on 7 October. Following a successful operation, he remained in Dublin until 22 October and was then transferred to Bray, where he recovered at the Princess Patricia hospital which had been established in the International Hotel. He was discharged to "furlough" or home-leave on 17 November 1916. In January 1917, he was posted to No 4 Company MT sub-depot at Larkhill on the south of Salisbury Plain. On 23 April, John was sent to Egypt and served with 904 Company ASC, which was in support of two heavy artillery batteries, until 30 July 1917. Whilst there, Agnes gave birth to their seventh child on 21 June who she named after her husband. John Senior then served with Expeditionary Force in Iraq from October 1917 for twelve months after which he served in Persia until February 1919. On his way back to England, John served in Salonika with 61 Heavy Brigade Royal Garrison Artillery for two months before returning to Woolwich after which he was transferred to Z Reserve on 25 June 1919. Whilst he was at Woolwich, before he was demobilised, John made a claim for a pension claiming he had injured his left shoulder by "falling against a gun in September 1916" – his claim was, not surprisingly unsuccessful. Thereafter John returned to Merseyside where he died, aged seventy, on 29 March 1954 in Bootle.

21

Remembrance

Both C and D Companies' records include men who served in tanks from September 1916 but cannot be otherwise identified. This chapter lists those who are not remembered elsewhere in this book.

Four corporals were listed as serving with C Company as they arrived in France, three of whom deployed with the advance party on 16 August 1916. The first was Corporal W Clare who started service with the MMGS but whom I cannot identify in any way. There were also two who with very similar surnames. Tom Hamer enlisted at Coventry in August 1915, later served in the Tank Corps and was discharged in March 1918 whilst Charles Harmer who was one of four MGC soldiers who were transferred to 2nd Battalion the Royal Inniskilling Fusiliers. These include Lionel Worrall, who was born on 7 October 1894 at Finsbury Park. Lionel was the son of a feather merchant named Thomas Worrall and his second wife Mary Palethorpe who lived in Halifax. Lionel's father died in the later 1890s and his widowed mother first moved the children to South Weald, near Billericay and then to Halifax where Lionel was apprenticed to a toolmaker. Having survived the war, Lionel returned to engineering and in 1923, travelled to India and in December 1924, he returned from Bombay to Plymouth on SS *Moldava*. He went overseas again and on 12 April 1946, returned to UK from Bombay on SS *Britannic*, shown as an engineer using the address C/O Mrs Duchesne of 46 Porchester Square London W2. By 1948, he was living at 7 Holland Park Road and three year later, living at 31 Argyll Rd in Kensington with Frances Duchesne living in the same address. He died, aged on sixty-two years old, in Hampstead in 1956.

The fourth C Company NCO, who deployed with the Advance Party, was Corporal James Battell whose service record survived the Blitz. Born on 4 December 1889 in Walthamstow, James was the eldest son of an insurance supervisor named William Battell and his wife Hannah. James, who had three younger brothers and a sister, worked as a clerk for the Pianola Company. Joining the MGC in 1915, he quickly rose to the rank of acting corporal. C Company's landing records reveal that he deployed to France on 24 August 1916 yet, strangely, his name is also found on Army forms in other soldiers' records signed at Elveden the following month. In 1917, James' health must have become poor as he was transferred to the Labour Corps. He later served in the Army Pay Corps where his civilian skills would have been used to good effect. After he was demobilised, James became a tax-valuation clerk and married Florence Vandersluis in Hampstead in 1922. Their son William was born on 23 October 1923 and his younger sister Margaret five years later. Originally the family lived in a flat at the Gondar Gardens near Hampstead cemetery but, in 1934, moved to a masionette above a newly built parade of shops in Wembley. The couple lived there until Florence's death on 8 August 1962, James dying eight years later aged seventy-one.

The service history for Lance Corporal Robert Carruthers not only provides little information about his service life but also hides his exceptional career as a geologist. Born at Ashby de la Zouch in Leicestershire on 1 September 1880, Robert was one of three brothers who were each to carve out solid professional careers. Robert's twin brother Walter became a doctor whilst their younger brother Roland became an accountant. Robert initially studied chemistry at Birmingham

Robert Carruthers.
(British Geological Survey)

University but later studied geology. In 1903, Robert joined the British Geological Survey, moved to Scotland and soon came to prominence through studies of the impact of geology on Scottish economics. He wrote a series of critically acclaimed papers over the next twelve years. As the war broke out, Robert's main area of study – economic geology –became even more important to the British economy as the demands for rare materials increased. Robert's work, on the identification of carboniferous deposit, was essential to the maximization of coal as well as identification of shales which provided fertilizers as a by-product of oil production. Robert's twin brother Walter volunteered for service with the RAMC and deployed to France in September 1915. Robert was attested six months later, enlisting into the Machine Gun Corps (Motors) on 27 April 1916 at Edinburgh.

At just under six feet tall and almost twelve stone in weight, his maturity and intellect made him stand out and, after less than three weeks service, he was appointed local (i.e. unpaid) lance corporal. Posted to C Company on its formation on 27 May, Robert deployed to France where he initially served as a gunner. In February 1917, Robert was awarded the biennial Bigby Medal awarded by the British Geographical Society for outstanding scholarship. He was not able to return to London to receive the medal as C Battalion was preparing new tanks and crews for operations at Arras. However Robert's carefully crafted response, which was delivered in his absence at the presentation, was a model of self-deprecation stating that his award was due to the tremendous support and encouragement of those with whom he worked.

Robert's records show he later retrained as a tank mechanic. Although it is not clear whether he drove a tank into battle, as Robert was granted home leave from 15 to 31 December, he was clearly in action in some role during the Battle of Cambrai. On 1 March 1918, he was classified as Second Class Tank Mechanic as a draughtsman where his graphical skills must have been of great use to his company reconnaissance officers. Robert served with 3rd Battalion until the end of the war and was sent on a second period of home leave on 15 December 1918 by which time he had reached the rank of corporal. Whilst on leave, he was obtained a post with the Geological Survey at Edinburgh and was locally discharged at Duddingston. When he was sent his medals, he refused to accept them which is an unique occurrence amongst the First Tank Crews He did not however forget his former comrades, as in 1925 when he was working at the Geological Museum at Jermyn Street in London, he became a member of the C Battalion Old Comrades Association (OCA).

Robert later moved from London to Stocksfield in Northumberland and, in 1930, published a study of the geology of Alnwick area. In the summer of 1933, Robert married Lucy Askew and they had two children, Sarah and Robert. Lucy, who was twenty-three years younger than her husband, died shortly after her son's birth in 1936. Robert then married Janie Angus the following year at Keighley in Yorkshire. He continued his illustrious career after they returned to Stocksfield and, in the 1950s, lived at High Barn. Janie died in 1962 and Robert died at Stocksfield, aged eighty-four on 24 March 1965.

Scotland

There were four other men from Scotland in C Company. George Bissett, who was born on 19 December 1888 in Dundee, was the son of a photographer. The family lived at Rosefield Road on the western side of the town. George, who was an organ builder, joined the MMGS at Coventry on 16 March 1916 and immediately went to Bisley for training. His service record shows that he did not deploy until 24 August, which would indicate he served in either No 3 or No 4 Sections. He then served with C Battalion, retrained as a driver and, at the end of the war, was serving with B Company of 3rd Light Battalion. Like Robert Carruthers, he did not lose touch with his comrades after he was demobilised in January 1919 as he became a member of the OCA. He became a commercial traveller, later living at 6 Tulloch Crescent in Dundee but does not appear to have married. He died of bronchopneumonia, aged sixty-two, on 5 March 1949 at Maryhill Hospital in Glasgow.

Gunner James Candlish, who also originally served with the MMGS, was born in 1892 at Helensburgh. Named after his father, who was a corn factor, James was attested on 8 August 1915 in Paisley whilst working as a clerk at Bridge of Weir. According to his medical history, James was five feet eight inches tall with a thirty-four inch chest; he also suffered from a stammer. Having completed training at the MMGS depot at Bisley, James joined 27 Battery on 1 January 16. He was transferred to the HS MGC on 4 May and was posted to C Company three weeks later. He deployed to France on 16 August 16 and therefore probably served with No 2 Section during the Battle of Flers-Courcelette.

Three months later he was transferred to C Battalion. James' service record is mostly illegible, due to the water damage following the Blitz, but it confirms James was as both a machine gunner and 6 pdr QF gunner. At the end of the war, on 16 November, he was posted to HQ Tank Corps to work with the Chief Mechanical Engineer and, four days later, was appointed Lance Corporal Clerk when he joined the Tank Inspectorate. Finally James served with the Central Workshops at Erin until 22 May 1919 when he was dispersed through North Camp at Ripon. His dispersal certificate shows James was a corn-factor and left the Army to live at 55 Langside Road in Newlands, Glasgow. Like George Bissett, James Candlish did not marry but continued to work as a corn factor. He moved to Garrowhill and lived, in his sixties at 99 Maxwell Drive. James died of a heart attack, aged sixty-six at the Victoria Infirmary in Glasgow on 20 June 1959; his death being registered by his sister, May.

The last of the Scottish quartet, Private Darnley McCaig was born on 4 May 1891 at Ladhope near Galashiels. He was the youngest son of a tweed manufacturer and wool merchant named Joseph McCaig. Joseph and his second wife Jane Darnley were fifty-two and forty-two at the time of Darnley's birth. Darnley had one elder brother and eight half-siblings. Joseph, who had business links to London, died in 1912 by which time Darnley had joined the family firm. C Company's landing records confirm that Darnley originally served in the MMGS, which means he must have been an experienced motorcycle rider. His medal card confirms that he later transferred to the Tank Corps and he was still a private soldier at the end of the war. Darnley returned to Galashiels on his discharge where he continued to work for the family firm. He also continued motorcycling although not without incident. He was fined £5 in August 1922 for driving his motorcycle at Kelso in such a negligent fashion so that he collided with an excise officer riding a motorcycle combination. On 22 March 1924, Darnley married a local girl Jessie Sheldrake in Edinburgh and they had two children. Darnley became a partner in the family firm and regularly travelled to London to attend wool sales. Like his father, it was during one of these visits that Darnley died on 31 January 1930, whilst staying at the Kingsley Hotel in Bloomsbury.

Lancashire

Lancashire also provided a large number of tank crewmen; one of whom was Gunner James Booth who was born in St Helens in March 1890. He was the only son of bricklayers' labourer Isaiah Booth and his wife Harriet, who also had a daughter named Esther who was three years younger than James. In 1901 the family had moved to 3 Colcloughgate in Milnerow, which is now part of Rochdale. Isaiah died in the early 1900s so Harriet worked as a cotton weaver to support her family James and Esther also working in the industry. On 9 November 1912, James married nineteen year old Beatrice Goss at her parish church St Clement's in Spotland. Their son Harry was born the following year but he did not survive infancy. When James was attested on 10 December 1915, he was still working as a cotton weaver. He was then placed on the Army Reserve and mobilised in March 1916.

James had volunteered to join the MMGS and was examined in Coventry on 21 March. He was a small man, only five feet three inches tall and just over seven stones in weight. He also had a slight curvature of the spine but this condition was not sufficiently serious to prevent him from being declared fit for service either overseas or at home. James enlisted on 23 March 1916 and was sent to Bisley the same day. Having undertaken basic training, on the Siberia ranges, James was posted to C Company on 27 May and probably serving in No 2 Section when he deployed to France on 16 August/ At this time his wife Beatrice was five months pregnant. There is no record of which actions he fought between September and November but he was posted to C Battalion as his company was withdrawn from the Somme. Beatrice gave birth to their son Kenneth on 3 December but, in common with the majority of the soldiers who deployed in August, James did not get home at Christmas to see his family.

The following year, as the number of tank battalions increased, they were formed into brigades and James was attached to the Headquarters of the newly formed 3rd Tank Brigade for nine days in May 1917. He was soon back with C Battalion and redesignated with a new service number 200631 on formation of the Tank Corps. James was not granted home leave immediately after the end of the Battle of Cambrai but was able to spend Christmas with Beatrice and Kenneth. James served with the newly redesignated 3rd Light battalion as they re-roled onto Whippet tanks and served with them, throughout the battles of Amiens and as they lead the Great Advance. When the Battalion was withdrawn from action in early November 1918, James was attached to HQ 1 Tank Group which was formed to undertake occupation duties in Germany. He was permanently posted to the HQ on 24 December 18 and later served in Germany with 1st Tank Carrier Company. He returned to England for demobilisation on 11 February and returned home to Rochdale. His medals were sent to him on 25 June 1921 after which the family is lost to view until Beatrice's death at Littleborough in 1961. James survived until he was ninety one when he died in Rochdale.

Reg Whalley was one of several pawnbrokers who served with the tanks. Born in July 1897 at Walkden, a small town about six miles northwest of Salford, Reg was the only child of Emily and Joseph Whalley who was also a pawnbroker. Reg was enlisted at Atherton near Wigan in 5 February 1916 and was allocated to the MGC. When he passed the Army medical examination on 27 April, he was five feet eight inches tall with brown hair, hazel eyes and a fresh complexion. Having deployed to France on 16 August, with No 2 Section, he joined C Battalion in November

1916. His service record shows he attended the Tank Driving Camp at Wailly from 11-19 June 1917 and, after the Battle of Cambrai, was granted home leave from 27 December to 10 January 1918. Returning to service with B Company of 3rd Light Battalion, he was posted to Paris from 8 to 28 April which is the only such attachment of this type I have identified.

Reg did not leave the Army, as did most tank crewmen in early 1919, rather he was only granted home leave in late February 1919 whilst working in the Central Tank Stores in Erin. Whilst at home, he caught bronchitis and was treated at Townley's Auxiliary Hospital until 18 March 1919. Returning to the Tank Stores on 23 March 1919, he served in Germany for a further six months. Returning to the family home in Walkden, Reg became a tailor. He married Hilda Rigby, a twenty-one year old seamstress, on 18 March 1925 at St Barnabas' Parish Church at Bolton Le Moors. According to the C Battalion OCA Address list published in 1925, Reg was living in 171 Bolton Road in Walkden. Reg moved his shop to 150 Bolton Road where it remained until the late 1950s. Thereafter, the couple moved to Blackpool where Hilda died in 1968. Sadly I have been unable to find any records of Reg after 1965.

Gunner Ralph Baker was born in Bristol in the spring of 1881 in Bristol. He was the son of a grocer and beer retailer John Baker and his wife Alice who, by the time he was ten years old, had moved to Beswick with Bradford in Manchester. By the time he was twenty, Ralph had married and was living with his wife Sarah as a coachman in Altrincham. Ten years later, Ralph had retrained and was working as a domestic chauffeur in Bowden, some six miles to the northeast. His service record has not survived but, from his service number, it is likely he joined the MGC in early 1916. Ralph deployed with C Company on 16 August with Reg Whalley and later was promoted to corporal. He served with the Tank Corps until the end of the war when he returned to Bowden where, according to *Kelly's Directory*, he was still working as a chauffeur in 1929. Thereafter I can find no other records of the couple.

Norfolk

Few of the First Tank Crews came from East Anglia but one who did was Gunner Raymond Bothway. Raymond was born and brought at Ashwellthorpe in Norfolk in early 1896. Baptised on 1 April, at Wreningham, he was the only son and youngest child of a farmer named William Bothway and his wife Annie. Raymond, who had two elder sisters, was educated locally and joined the MGC in 1916. He deployed to France on 24 August 1916 and, although his service record has not survived, it is clear that he remained with the tanks for the rest of the war, eventually being discharged from the Tank Corps as a corporal.

Returning to Ashwellthorpe, in the spring of 1920, Raymond married a local woman named Beatrice Attoe who came from Wreningham and was three years his senior. Raymond, who lived in a substantial property named Canal House, must have kept on contact with his former comrades as he was shown as living in Ashwellthorpe in 1925 edition of the C Battalion OCA membership list. Sadly, two year later, Raymond died at the age of thirty-one on 11 July 1927. His name was added to the war memorial in Wreningham so it is clear that the locals believed Raymond died as a result of his war service. Beatrice remarried three years later in 1930 to Gylby Hairsine who had served as a Royal Navy Volunteer Reserve officer in the Great War. Beatrice died at Norwich aged ninety-one in 1985.

Warwickshire

Birmingham and Coventry provided more of the tank crewmen than any other cities in Britain. Not all were born locally but some were drawn there by the work available through the cycle industry. William Higgs on other hand was a piano tuner who appears to have little in common with most of the Tankers. He had been born in September 1885 in Barnstable where his father Thomas was a draper and his mother Martha a milliner. On 13 July 1908, William married eighteen year old Lilian Ingerson at Holy Trinity Church Barnstable but the couple soon moved to Hinkley. Their eldest children, Ruby and Leonard were born in the town where William had established a drapery and outfitter's partnership. The firm failed in January 1911 and, when the census was taken four months later, he was working as a draper's traveller. By the time their younger son Gordon was born, on 21 March 1914, Lilian and William had moved to 10 Kensington Road in Coventry and William was employed as a piano merchant.

Following the introduction of conscription, William was attested on 11 December 1915 and transferred to the Army Reserve. Now thirty-five years old, he was physically a small man, only five feet three inches tall, less than nine stones in weight and his chest was only thirty-three inches when fully expanded. As he was a married man, with three children, William was not mobilised until 9 May 1916 by which time Lillian was again pregnant. By joining for the MMGS, he avoided serving in the infantry but, according to the locally published *Motor Cycle*, voluntarily transferred to the Heavy Section on 18 May. He was posted to C Company four days later and was immediately appointed lance corporal. Nine days later, William was posted to E Company but reverted to the rank of gunner at his own request. On 22 June, he was transferred back to C Company whilst they were training at Elveden and deployed to France on 16 August. Just as William was moving back from the battle zone, at the end of the first tank actions, their younger daughter Doris was born on 17 November 1916. Two days later, William was transferred to C Battalion and joined the Quartermaster's department. When Lillian wrote to claim an extra allowance in the birth of her fourth child, she was living at 149 Foleshill Road.

William was again appointed acting lance corporal on 20 January although this was not accompanied by an increase in pay. He was detached from C Battalion between 7 to 14 April 1917 when the two tank units were preparing for the Battle of Arras. After he transferred to Tank Corps in August 1917, William remained with C Battalion and then joined 3rd Light Battalion. He was not granted home leave until 6 January 1918, which would indicate he was still serving in the battalion stores rather than as tank crewman. The next entry on his service record did not take place until well after the Armistice when he was again granted home leave on 13 January 1919. He became seriously ill whilst on his way back to join his unit in France and was admitted to the Rochester Row military hospital in London. He was placed on posted strength of Tank Depot at Wareham on 28 January 1919 but was not discharged from hospital on 14 April when he was sent to the Tank Stores at Bovington. He was demobilised on 18 June, having returned to full health and having been transferred to the Army Z Reserve. Other than a mention as a member of the C Battalion OCA, William then disappears until the early 1950s by which time he had moved south to Hounslow. He had established a wholesale millinery manufacturer company which ceased trading in 1951, which was the same year he married Marion Coles at the age of seventy-three. Four years later, William died aged seventy-seven in early 1957.

I have been unable to find as much information about Harold Adams about his life in Coventry after the Great War. Harold was the youngest of nine children of watchmaker William Adams and his wife Eliza. Born on 15 February 1896, and baptised on 5 April, he became a builders' clerk. He enlisted into the MMGS in 1915 and deployed to France on 16 August 1916. Later he served as a sapper in the RE possibly in one of the tank brigade signals companies. He did not, however, lose contact with his former comrades in C Battalion as he was also a member of the OCA and his address is given as Howell's building firm in Coventry. He died, aged eighty-six, in March 1982 in Coventry

Staffordshire

The areas around Stoke and Uttoxeter was also a major recruiting area for the MMGS. One such gunner was Vincent Greaves who was born on 3 January 1884 in Hanley. He was the eldest son and second child of a draper named Edwin Greaves and his wife Martha. Vincent did not follow his father's profession but became a pottery "modeller and designer" which was amongst the most prestigious amongst those in the pottery industry. A single man, Vincent enlisted on 11 November 1915. Like Joseph Higgs, he was only five feet three inches tall. His medical records showing he had a thirty-four inch chest, brown hair, brown eyes and a fresh complexion. He joined at Bisley one week later and was posted to C Company on 27 May. His Company Conduct sheet was signed by Captain Herbert Hiscocks which would indicate that he was serving with No 2 Section when he deployed to France on 18 August. Eight days later, Vincent was hospitalized with PUO or Spanish flu on 26 August. He returned to C Company on 10 September and, after the first actions, transferred to C Battalion, probably serving in No 8 Company. In August 1917, he was sent to hospital as a batman for three days which would indicate that he was still part of the fighting strength. This is reinforced by the fact that Vincent was granted home leave after the Battle of Cambrai from 18 December 1917.

He served on with the renamed 3rd Light Battalion and, as his unit's tanks were supporting the Allied Advance after the Battle of Amiens, Vincent was detached to the Inter Allied School at Fontainebleau on 16 September. He only rejoined 3rd Battalion on 26 October 1918 after they were pulled out of the order of battle. Vincent was again granted Christmas leave in the UK, this time from 13 to 26 December, but returned promptly to B Company of 3rd Battalion. On 2 February 1919, Vincent returned to the UK but did not claim a pension. Transferred to the Z Reserve six days later, Vincent returned home to Bank House in Chamberlain Avenue. By 1924, he had moved to Percy Street in Hanley where he was again successfully employed as a modeler. Vincent did not marry until the spring of 1938, his wife being May Goodhall. The couple did not move from Stoke and Vincent died, at the fine age of ninety-four years, in the autumn of 1978.

Another small man was Gunner Harry Broster who was born in Tamworth in early 1895. The son of a railway signalman John Broster and his wife Hannah, by 1901 Harry was living at 23 Shrewsbury Road in Stafford with four elder siblings. Ten years later he was still living there and working as a switchboard fitter. Harry volunteered to join the MMGS and was attested on 3 December 1915 in Stafford. By now he was working as a chauffeur. On his enlistment, Harry was recorded as the same height as Vincent Greaves and Joseph Higgs. Harry was sent immediately to Bisley and was approved on 5 December at the MMGS Depot. Posted to C Battalion on its formation on 18 November 1916, he served the unit until the Armistice having been promoted corporal on 26 October 1918. Harry returned to Stoke and married Edith Baugh in the summer of 1923 and they had four children: Mabel in early 1925; Ronald in early 1927; Mary three years later and finally Margaret who was born in the spring of 1931. In his later years Harry moved to Stafford where he died aged seventy-one in late 1966.

Gunner Daniel Dean was born in Ladywood Birmingham in early 1897. Daniel was the eldest son of a Bristol-born baker, after whom he was named. His mother Clara was also Bristolian as was his older sister Minnie. By the time he was fourteen the two Daniels had moved to Stafford and were boarding at 12 Rowley Street. Daniel senior was still working as a baker and his son was an engineer at a local cycle factory. By the time he was eighteen, Daniel had become a motor driver. He enlisted on 10 December 1915 at Stafford recruiting office, his medical record showing him to be only five feet two inches tall. He served with C Company then C Battalion and then 3rd Light Battalion but there are no details of the action in which he fought until the last four months of the war.

On 24 August 1918, during the latter stages of the Battle of Amiens , he was serving in a Whippet tank B28 in support of the New Zealand Division, when he injured by shrapnel in the right leg near Bapaume. Two days later, he was admitted to Chester Auxiliary Hospital where he was treated for a month. Granted home leave from hospital between 28 September and 4 October, Daniel was then placed on strength of the Royal Artillery and Tank Corps Depot at Catterick where he served until he was fully fit for Garrison service. He was then posted to the 24th Officer Cadet Battalion, which had by that time moved to Wareham. After he took two days' leave at New Year without permission, he was only admonished as it was his only offence during three years' service. He was detached to Bovington for two weeks training in January and then discharged on 15 February 1919 after which he returned to 26 Cooperative Street in Stafford and disappears from all records.

Somerset and Gloucestershire

Charles Hewitt, who was born on 6 February 1897 at Winterbourne in South Gloucestershire, was the eldest son of an engine fitter John Henry Hewitt and his wife Sarah Jane. Charles was bought up at 4 Winterbourne Mill but by 1911, the family had moved to Crumlin where Charles worked alongside his father in the mines as a coal hewer. By the time he enlisted into the MMGS, at Coventry on 18 August 1915, he was working as a mining engineer at Maeshyref. After initial training at Bisley, Charles was posted to 27th Battery MMGS on 1 December 1915 before volunteering to join the Armoured Car Company MGC on 1 April. He joined C Company on 27 May and deployed to France on 16 August 1916, presumably with No 2 Section, as a gunner. There is no evidence as to which tank Charles fought in at Flers-Courcelette or any other unit until the Battle of Cambrai although it is recorded that he attended a driving course at Wailly on 11 – 19 June 1917.

On 20 November, whilst serving with No 7 Company on the right flank of the British attack, Charles was seriously injured when a shell burst near him. His wounds would indicate that he was outside of a tank but I cannot identify where the tank was halted. Charles received wounds to his shoulder, right arms, buttocks and both thighs. He was initially admitted to 21 Casualty Clearing Section and then sent back to a base hospital at Étaples where a shrapnel ball was removed from his neck on 1 December. Evacuated to England on 5 December, Charles was initially treated at the Hornsey Auxiliary Military Hospital, in North London where he underwent an operation to remove matter from his right thigh. Sent to a convalescent hospital on 26 January, possibly in Eastbourne, he was later admitted to Central Military Hospital at Eastbourne on 25 June when an abscess was found in his right thigh. This was the result of metal fragments which had been found remaining in his body. He was re-admitted on a further two occasions and then sent to Summertown Convalescent Hospital on 20 September where he would have met Captain Harold Mortimore, the commander of *Daredevil* on 16 September, who was serving as the adjutant. Charles was discharged from the Army on 28 November 1918, due to his wounds, and was granted a twenty per cent disability pension for six months. He was also awarded the Silver War Badge. Returning to the Grove at Penmaen in Monmouthshire, Charles soon moved to Blaby in Leicestershire where he married Vera Carrell in early 1920. Charles and Vera had two daughters, Vera who was born in the spring of 1921 and Sylvia who was born the following autumn. Although I can find little about Charles for the next forty years, he kept in contact with his comrades and was one of those Tankers who attended the 50th anniversary dinner night at Caxton Hall on 15 September 1966. He and Vera later moved to Somerset and settled at Weston Super Mare where Vera died in 1986, Charles surviving another two years before he died, aged ninety-one in March 1988.

Charles was not the only tankman from the West Country who was wounded on 20 November 1917. Gunner Robert Read, who was injured in the right shoulder whilst serving either in the tank *Crusty* or *Cumudgeon*, was born at Evercreech near Shepton Mallet on 15 November 1885.

He was the son of a general store owner Charles Read and his wife Ellen who lived at Sunnybank in the Weymouth Road. On leaving school, Charles worked as a grocers' apprentice as did his siblings. On 17 December, one month after his thirtieth birthday, Robert enlisted into the Army. Now grocer, but still working for his father, Robert joined the MMGS at Coventry on 13 March 1916, was mobilised two days later and joined the Armoured Car Section as it formed on1 April. Like Charles Hewitt, there are no details of Robert's part in the Battle of Flers-Courcelette or at Arras in 1917. He also undertook driver training at Wailly between 11 and 19 June 1917 and the C battalion records reveal that Robert was serving with 5 Section No 8 Company in C Battalion as a gunner and Third Driver.

On 20 November, as the tanks fought their way towards Cambrai, Robert was wounded in the right shoulder, probably whilst serving in either *Crusty* or *Cumudgeon*. He was initially treated at Rouen and returned to UK on 25 November. After a protracted stay at the 3rd Western General Hospital in Cardiff, he was granted leave at Sunnybank from 30 January to 8 February having been classed as fit for duty. Posted to the Depot Battalion at Wareham on 18 February, he joined B Company of the Reserve Unit before being posted to 18th Battalion on 22 August. He joined C Company and returned to France on 3 October. His battalion did not see action although Robert, who remained a private throughout his service, was granted 1st Class Proficiency Pay on 4 November. In the New Year, Robert was sent to the Tank Corps depot near Mers-Les-Bains where on 27 January 1919, he started the administrative procedures associated with demobilisation. Despite his earlier wounds, he did not claim a pension and was dispersed through Fovant on 10 February and transferred to the Z Reserve on 10 March. Other than his medals being received on 28 June 1921, Robert then disappears without trace until his death in Salisbury in 1968.

The third gunner from the West Country was also in the grocery trade. Gunner Edward Appleby, who was born in Castle Cary on 17 May 1896, was the son of house painter but, when he left school, he worked as a grocer's apprentice. He enlisted into the MMGS at Coventry on 24 November 1915 by which time he was working as a grocer's traveller. He immediately travelled to Bisley for basic training. The details on his records are sparse but, after the standard training at Bisley and Elveden, he deployed to France on 16 August 1916 which indicates he served in No 2 Section. He transferred to C Battalion on 18 November, joining No 9 Company. After the Battle of Arras, he undertook training at Wailly but, as this for only three days between 16 and 19 June 1917, he probably was still serving as a gunner.

He fought with C Battalion in the Ypres Salient and then at Cambrai after which he was granted home leave in December 1917. He then served with C Company of the designated 3rd Light Battalion until the Armistice and was granted home leave at Christmas in 1918. He served on with 3rd Battalion until 13 February and transferred to Z Reserve on 16 March. He left the Army with a blank conduct sheet and did not claim a pension although this is not necessarily a sign that he had not been wounded. A member of the C Battalion OCA, he married Kathleen Wyatt in 1928 and their only son Alan was born in the autumn of 1931. Edward continued to live in the Market Place in Castle Cary, where he probably owned his own business. He was comfortably off when he died on 5 July 1953 at 8 Harewood Avenue in Pokesdown, his estate of £4098 being jointly granted to his widow and son Adam who was a grocer's assistant.

There was also one tank crewman from Somerset who served in both C and D Companies. Francis Dyer was wounded on 25 September 1916 as the tanks supported the attack on Morval. He was born in Curry Rivel on 21 April 1880 and was the second son of plumber and glazier. He built on his father's business and, by 1911, Francis was running a house building company. Francis enlisted on 10 December 1915 and first joined for duty at Coventry on 13 March 1916. He embarked with C Company on 16 August 16 but was then attached to D Company after the first action. Francis was also wounded in the right buttock but was not evacuated to England until 13 October. Treated at Liverpool until 25 November, he joined G Battalion which was then forming at Bovington. Francis was admitted to the nearby Wool Hospital with bronchitis in February 1917. On 24 May, he embarked from Southampton for France with G Battalion but, on 4 June, joined the 1st Tank Brigade Signals Company. Twelve days later, Francis was posted to Wireless Depot Company.

On 27 July, Francis transferred to the Royal Engineers and exactly one month later, he joined 2nd Tank Brigade Signal Company as a telegraph operator. At this time, the tanks were fully committed to the 3rd Battle of Ypres and the Signal units were well forward. After they withdrew from the Salient, they soon started preparing for the attack at Cambrai. During this time, on 16 November 1917, Francis was absent from a parade and fined two day's pay – this was a harsh punishment and would indicate that his absence created a major problem for his unit. Francis was not granted home leave, after the Battle of Cambrai, but had to wait until 29 January 1918 before he was granted fourteen days leave. Despite he was older than most of his comrades, Frances was not appointed acting lance corporal until 23 June 1918 when he was thirty-eight years of age, Three days later Francis was graded as a Telegraph Operator B and then appointed substantive (and therefore paid) lance corporal on1 July. After the Armistice, he was granted two weeks home leave from 24 November 1918. His Brigade was based at Malmedy, which was then part of Germany, in February 1919. It was here that Francis claimed an Army pension for being "hit by a shell on shoulder and for piles" – the pension was not awarded. He was then posted to the HQ Tank Signal Company on 23 March and later served with Signal Depot in Cologne, returning to 2nd Tank Brigade Signal Company on 18 June 1919. Francis was granted a further fourteen days home-leave on 6 July after which he returned to occupation duties with the British Army of the Rhine. He was not discharged until 2 September 1919. Returning to Curry Rivel, he again took up running his building firm. Francis married Olive Watts in 1922 and they had five children. Francis lived in Curry Rivel until his death aged eighty-seven on 4 May 1958.

Lincolnshire

The first tanks were designed and built in Lincoln and three of the First Tank Crews also came from the county. One lived in the City of Lincoln itself although he was actually born in Doncaster. Thomas Keightley, who was the son of a Primitive Methodist minister, was born on 20 November 1884 and, as a young man, moved to Scunthorpe where he worked as an ironmonger's assistant. On 19 July 1911, he married Florrie Horton at the Porton Place Memorial Church in Lincoln and the couple had two daughters, Gladys who was born in January 1913 and Dorothy who was born in December 1914. By the time, the family was living outside the city centre at Hamilton Road. Thomas' service record has not survived but the C Company landing records show he deployed to France on 24 August 1916 so he must have served with either No 3 or 4 Section. His medal index card shows he continued to serve with the Tank Corps until the end of the war, when he discharged in the rank of corporal. He returned to Lincoln but, within a couple of years, had moved to the centre of the city and lived at 31 Monks Road to the south of the cathedral. Later he moved to a house named Mowcop on Ancaster Avenue. He died aged fifty-eight, in Lincoln on 5 December 1944. He must have been a very successful businessman by this time as Florrie was granted probate for an estate work worth almost £11,000.

Joseph Wressell lived, in the north of the county, at Scawby. A farmer's son, he was born in early July 1894 and on leaving school, worked for his father at Moor Farm. He enlisted, aged twenty-two, on 9 December but did not join for duty until 20 April. Hs application to serve with the MGC was approved by Capt Graham Woods on 4 May whilst he was in Lincoln visiting the Foster's factory. Joseph, who served with C Company, deployed to France on 16 August 1916, transferred to C Battalion on its formation and was posted to No 9 Company. He probably fought with the Battalion during the Battle of Arras but there is no record of his actions. Joseph was detached to the

2nd Tank Brigade Signal School from 24 to 29 May. A most unusual offence is recorded on Joseph's record sheet on 5 October 1917. He was found guilty of speeding and fined five days' pay which is a truly large fine and the offence must have been considered extremely serious. Joseph served with C Battalion during the Battle of Cambrai and was granted home leave from 20 December to 3 January 1918 which was remarkable as he was allowed to spend both Christmas and New Year with his family.

Joseph returned to serve with the redesignated 3rd Battalion until after the Armistice. Joseph was again granted home leave for Christmas and New Year, during which time he managed to arrange his demobilisation. Later that summer, he married Lucy Spilman who was seven years his senior. Their only daughter Rosemary was born in the spring of 1922 but sadly the little girl did not survive infancy. The couple was still living at Moor Farm at Scawby, Joseph having joined the C Battalion OCA whose membership list for 1925 confirms his address. After the Second World War, the couple moved to The Cottage at Claxby where Joseph died, aged fifty-nine, on 24 April 1953, Lucy dying the following year.

The third Lincolnshire tanker was born in London but his parents and siblings were all born in the county and he soon moved there too. Gunner Wilfred Giddins was born on 6 March 1897 at Nunhead in South East London. His father was Thomas Giddins, an iron founder's commercial traveller and his mother was Annie Ashton – both of whom were registered at birth in Boston. Wilfred was baptised on 16 May 1897 at Waverley Park Mission but, by 1901, he was living at East Street in Crowland. His father died in February 1908 by which time the family having moved back to his father's home town of Boston. Three years later, Wilfred was living at Fydell Crescent at Boston with his widowed mother and his elder brother Frank who was working as an apprentice in the family ironmonger's ship opposite the famous Trinity Bridge in Crowland. On the outbreak of war, Frank joined the Northamptonshire Regiment and served with 5th Battalion as a pioneer until he was discharged as a result of sickness in May 1918. When Wilfred was attested, on 10 December 1915 at Lincoln, he was five feet six inches tall but only had a twenty-nine inch chest. He had moved to Crowland and was mobilized in 26 April the following year, posted to C Company on 27 May and deployed to France on 16 August. Although there are no details of which actions he fought in during September 1916, whilst a member of No 3 Section, Wilfred was also far from out of danger the following month. On 15 October 1916, he wrote a letter to neighbours named Lawson who lived in East Street, near to the Giddins shop in Crowland. Wilfred reported that, he had recently escaped death or series injury when three German shells landed within 5 yards of where he was standing as he entered C Company camp. This is far from the only report of its type and Wilfred may have been saved by the extremely soft ground conditions to the north of the River Ancre after a considerable amount of rain earlier that month; weather which would prevent planned attacks being postponed.

Wilfred joined C Battalion on its formation; he probably fought at the Battle of Arras in April and attended the battalion driving camp at Wailly from 10 to 19 June 1917. He also probably fought in the Ypres salient during July and August. It is certain he fought with C Battalion at the Battle of Cambrai, as he was granted home leave from 10 and 24 December, travelling across the English Channel on Christmas day and rejoining his unit on Boxing Day.

Wilfred then served with 3rd (Light) Battalion during its re-role to Whippets and throughout the Battle of Amiens and the 100 day advance to the Belgian border. He was again granted home leave between 12 and 26 December 1918, rejoining his unit two days later. Returning for England for demobilization on 5 February 1919, Wilfred did not make a claim for a disability pension and left the Army on 12 March 1919. His medals were issued in June 1921 by which time he was living in Bridge House on East Street in Crowland. The following year Wilfred married Kate Annible whose family owned the local bakers shop in East Street, and their only son Geoffrey was born in the summer of 1926. Forty years later, Wilfred attended the 50th anniversary dinner night at

Caxton Hall on 15 September and later presented his Tank Corps ID discs to the Tank Museum. Wilfred died in 1972, aged seventy-five, his wife Kate dying later that same year.

Surrey

Woking provided three men for the crew of *Champagne*, the first tank in C Company. It was also the home of Gunner Walter Hamilton who was born on 2 October 1898. Walter was the fifth child and youngest son of Harry Hamilton, a chimney sweep, and his wife Minnie. By 1901, the family was living to the rear of Pondhu house in Knaphill near Woking. On 23 August 1915, whilst living at Primrose Cottage in Knaphill, and working as a carman, Walter was attested at Bisley despite the fact that he was only seventeen. He joined the MMGS on 25 August at Bisley and soon learned that not all pleasures were free from pain. He was admitted to the Duke of Connaught Hospital in Aldershot from 8 to 13 December, suffering from gonorrhea. He made a full recovery but it was far his last visit to a military hospital. Walter as posted to C Company on 25 May and deployed overseas on 16 August with No 3 or No 4 Section despite the fact that he was still under eighteen. He was posted to C Battalion on its formation and. The weather at that time was appalling and the accommodation in which the new units were living was freezing, which might account for the fact that, on 11 January 1917, was awarded seven days No 2 Field Punishment for misappropriating rations.

Walter was attached to the Reinforcement Depot from 20 March to 17 May, whilst his battalion was taking part in the Battle of Arras, after which when he rejoined C Battalion. The following month, he attended the 3rd Tank Brigade Reconnaissance course and, having survived the early stages of the Third Battle of Ypres, Walter returned to the Reinforcement Depot on 2 September. He was sent on home leave in early November, prior to being posted on 25 November to the Gun Carrying Section. However, before he could join his new unit in France, Walter admitted himself to Woking War Hospital where he was diagnosed with gastritis and then bronchitis. After treatment, which lasted until 5 January 1918, he was sent to the Convalescent Hospital at Eastbourne until the end of the month. Walter was then sent to the Tank Depot at Wareham, before returning to France on 4 February and serving in the Reinforcement Depot.

3rd Light Battalion needed to be returned to full strength after the losses of the Kaiserschlacht. As a result, Walter was sent back to his parent unit on 10 April as they were trying to hold back the advancing German troops near Arras. Walter was later admitted to hospital at Étaples, this time with mild psychosis and, on 14 June 1918, he was admitted to 25 General Hospital with impetigo. He then returned to the Reinforcement Depot on 3 August and then rejoined 3rd Battalion on 10 August 1918 as they were engaged in the early part of the Battle of Amiens. Walter served with the Battalion through the Final Advance and whilst they undertook occupation duties. He returned to England on 20 February 1919 and was transferred to the Z Reserve three days later. He initially settled at Anchor Hill View in Knaphill and in July 1919, he applied to join the Metropolitan Police but was unsuccessful. He was awarded the Victory Medal and the British War Medal. He possibly married Dorothy Rutland at Godstone in 1922. Three years later he was living at 4 High Street at Horsell which is to the north of Woking according to the list of members of the C Company OCA which Wilfred had joined. Walter possibly died in Worthing in 1974.

Gunner Fred Laming, who was from Wimbledon, was born on 11 November 1891 but was not christened for eighteen months. Fred's father James, who was a labourer, died when Fred was only eight years old after which his mother Elizabeth married William Duffin in 1906. Fred, who was a bricklayer's labourer, lived his mother and stepfather at 17 Undine Street in Tooting. On 22 May 1915, when Fred was twenty-two years old, he married Jane Peddie at Tooting Parish Church and the couple settled with his parents. There is no record of Fred's service but his MGC number, which was usually allocated to those serving in the Cavalry branch, would indicate he did not join up until mid-1916. He deployed to France on 16 August 1916 and later was promoted to the rank of corporal in the Tank Corps. When his wife died on 11 December 1919, they were still living at Undine Street in Tooting. Indeed Fred lived there until the start of the Second World War. He died, when only fifty-three, in early 1946 in southwest Essex.

Devonshire

Two crewmen came from Devon. Gunner William Lock was born c 9 April 1893 in Dawlish, he was the eldest son of a butcher John Edwin Lock and Mary Jane Slocombe who had married the previous year. The family later moved to Strand Mills where William ran the mill and employed his son. William was attested at Exeter on 3 December 1915 and placed on the Army reserve until he was mobilised four months later. Approved at Bisley on 5 May 1916, by Graham Woods, William joined C Company 27 May and deployed to France on 16 August. He continued to serve with C Battalion on its formation and attended the Battalion driving course at Wailly in June and which he was immediately he was detached to the HQ Depot. He was returned to the UK for special duties on 6 November and was attached to 14th Battalion at Bovington from 8 November. It is possible that he also deployed to Ireland that month.

On 13 January 1918, he joined 16th Battalion with James Anderson, another NCO from C Company, and was appointed a Lance Corporal nine days later. He served as a tank driver and was promoted corporal from 9 September, the same day he redeployed to France. His battalion was immediately launched into battle and William was wounded on 29 September 1918, during the Battle of Saint Quentin Canal, receiving injuries to the head, thighs and hands. He was promptly evacuated to a hospital in Le Havre then sent back to Reading for treatment at No 1 War Hospital and then No 2 Battle Hospital. Operated on 7 October to remove fragments from thigh, he remained at Reading until 1 February 1919 when he was sent to the Dispersal Hospital at Devonport. A Medical Board at Devonport on 4 February confirmed that William had no long term disability and his medical status as A1. His discharge address given as Brookdale, at Barton Hill Dawlish but there is an odd letter dated 20 August 1919 from John Lock seeking his son's discharge. The letter is remarkable as William had been de-mobilised on 4 February of that year.

Gunner Arthur Till is, as far as I can ascertain, unique amongst the first Tank Crews as he served in all three of the British Armed Forces. Born on 30 Oct 1888 at Otterton in Devon, Arthur's father Edward was originally in service and married his first wife, Elizabeth when he was only twenty-one. The couple had nine children and, after Elizabeth died in 1885, Edward married another domestic servant Ann Woodrow. Their daughter Blanche was born in 1886 and Arthur, the oldest of three more sons, was born in 1888. Ann was widowed when Arthur was twelve years old. He went into service as a young man and, when he enlisted into the Royal Navy in 1910, was working as a footman. He was assigned to *HMS Vivid*, the Devonport depot shop as an officer's servant on 25 May 1910 until 14 June where it was found he suffered from persistent sea sickness. He was assigned to the Royal Naval Reserve headquarters in London in which he served until discharge on 30 August.

Returning to domestic service, Arthur had risen to the post of butler by the time he enlisted into the MMGS on 24 November 1915. His army service record has not survived but the C Company landing sheets show he deployed to France on 16 August 1916 which means he probably served in No 2 Section. Arthur must have fought at the Battle of Cambrai as he was granted home leave shortly afterwards and, on 17 December 1917, he married Rose Parkins who was a mother of two children at Otterton. In 1918, Arthur transferred to the Royal Air Force as a Private. Demobilised on 13 February 1919, he rejoined on 7 August 1919 as an officer's batman. Arthur was allocated to 29 Squadron Group and joined them in the Orkneys within a week. Despite his previous experience in the Royal Navy, he was assigned to the aircraft carrier, *HMS Furious* on 30 October 1919 whose aircraft crews were provided by the RFC. Appointed unpaid lance corporal on 11 October 1920 and Aircraftman Class 1 on 22 November, Rose and Arthur's son Ronald born at Eastbourne on 25 February 1921. Arthur was however still stationed in Scotland with HMS *Furious*. He was admitted to a fever hospital in Dunfermline on 8 October 1921 where he died, aged thirty two, seven days later.

Nottinghamshire and Derbyshire

Gunner John Loving was the son of an ironmonger. Named after his father, John was born on 5 March 1896. He was the second of three boys who were born and brought up in Belper. The family initially lived in the High Street and later at *Belper House* in the Market Square, their ironmonger's shop being equipped with a telephone by 1908. All three boys joined their father's business with John working as a clerk. On the outbreak of war, his elder brother William joined the infantry and deployed to France with 10th Battalion Sherwood Foresters. John enlisted into the MMGS at Coventry on 7 November 1915. On 2 to 4 July 1916, whilst John was undertaking tank training in Elveden, his brother was fighting on the Somme near Fricourt. His battalion was later to fight past Trônes wood and in early August was fighting in Delville Wood. John deployed to France on 16 August but probably did not see his brother before he fought in the Battle of Flers-Courcelette. He continued to serve with C Battalion on its formation, serving with No 9 Company during the Battle of Arras and, in the summer, was attached to the 3 Tank Brigade Signals Company when the tanks moved to the Ypres Salient. On 12 October, John's brother William was killed near Ypres, whilst serving as a stretcher bearer during a German counter attack on Friday 12 October, his grave being subsequently lost.

John was granted home leave after the Battle of the Cambrai from 5 to 19 December but did not get back to C Battalion, which was near Albert, until Boxing Day. He continued to serve as a gunner in C Company of 3rd Battalion until 8 April 1918 when he contracted rheumatic fever. He was admitted to No 8 Stationary Hospital at Wimereax on the French coast near Boulogne the following day. Diagnosed with myalgia, John returned to England on 12 April on the Hospital Ship *Brighton* and was treated at the Heavy Woollen Hospital in Dewsbury until 4 May. He recovered but because he was not fit to return to active service, he was attached to the Derbyshire based 411 Agricultural Company Labour Corps on 9 September 1918. John was not released from service until February 1919 but he was however granted a 30% pension, worth 18/3d per week from 6 April 1919, and married Mabel Abbott later that year in Derby. Their son John, who was born in Belper in 1924, later married Margaret and the two families later moved to Dorset. Sadly John Junior died, aged only forty, on 28 March 1964 at Frampton near Dorchester. Mabel died thirteen years later aged seventy-six whilst John Senior survived for a further twelve years until his death aged ninety-four in 1989.

Sadly I have been unable to definitely identify when Gunner Robert Pritchard died. He was born in Manchester on 7 April 1882 and was the elder son of a Welshman from Rhyl Robert Morris Pritchard and his wife Susanna. Robert junior was christened at Nottingham on 3 July 1883 and in 1911 living with his father mother and younger brother Roger at 4 Navigation Square on Canal Street. Robert junior was working as an accountant's clerk whilst his father was working as a goods guard, when he was attested on 24 March 1916. He joined at Bisley shortly afterwards and he deployed to France with the C Company main body and did not return to England until 5 – 29 December 1917 which would indicate he fought through the Battle of Cambrai. His medical records show no illness or wounds and his conduct records are equally blank.

He served with C Battalion then 3rd Battalion being granted Christmas leave in 1918 from 15 to 29 December. He returned to Great Britain on 8 February 1919 and was demobilised at Clipstone in north Nottinghamshire. Returning to 8 New Thorp Street in Nottingham, Robert married

Gertrude Rowe who was five years his junior in the summer of 1922 and their only daughter Joan was born in 1924. Sadly, I cannot find when Robert died but his medals are now held by Simon Payne.

London

London provided a large number of tank crewmen including Gunner Reginald Pinnock. Born on 14 July 1895 at Hammersmith and registered at Fulham, Reg was the younger son of a Wiltshire born bricklayer Henry Pinnock and his wife Emilie Costello. Reg was christened on 29 September at St John the Evangelist's church at Hammersmith whilst the family living at 6 Burfield Street. On 14 January 1916, when he enlisted into the MGC, Reg was still living at 6 Burfield Street with his parents and working as a chief ledger clerk. He was shortage than the average crewmen at only 5 feet 3 ½ inches tall. Reg was not mobilised until 1 May, transferred on 4 May to HS MGC and authorised for service by Capt Graham Woods on 10 May. During his training at Elveden with tanks, Reg was hospitalised at Bury St Edmunds from 11 to 18 July with round worm and treated with saline solution. His service records do not show much detail for the first two years.

Deploying to France on 16 August 16, Reg transferred to C Battalion on 18 November 16 and more than a year later, was granted home leave from 2 to 16 December 1917; this would have reflected his fighting at the Battle of Cambrai. Victor Smith, who fought with the tank *Casa* on 15 September and appealed for his soldiers to be released on leave after the Battle of Cambrai, was posted to the Reinforcement Depot and Reg went with him as a servant from 29 April to 16 June 1918. Reg then served with A Company of 3rd (Light) Battalion. On 8 July he was detached to HQ Tank Corps then posted back to the Tank Reinforcement Depot on 25 July 1918. Reg was granted further UK leave in late September 1918. He returned to the Depot on 5 October and was still serving with Officers' Company under Major Victor Smith on 23 January 1919. Five days later, he returned to England and was demobilised the following day at Wimbledon. In late 1922, Reg married Dorothy Churchill in Hammersmith, their elder daughter Doreen was in early 1927 and the younger, Jane, in 1930 at Marylebone. They lived at 6 Burfield Street until at least 1954, indeed when he died, aged sixty, on 15 February 1963 at St Luke's Hospital in Bayswater, this was the address on his will.

Gunner Charles Malpress was born six years earlier than Reg, in May 1889, at Sydenham in southeast London. The third son and sixth child of James and Agnes Malpress, James was a chimney sweep and Reg's elder brother Edward worked with his father. Charles was working as a laundryman, and working at 36 Russell Road Wimbledon, when he enlisted on 7 February 1916. He was living at 460 Kingston Road in Raynes Park when he was mobilised two months later. Whilst in his last few days training at New Farm Camp in Elveden, and Charles was charged with absence on 4 and 5 August and was awarded 7 days No 2 punishment and 2 days stoppages of pay which probably means he was late from returning from pre-deployment leave. He went to France on 24 August which means that he probably served with No 3 or 4 Sections. As with almost every C Company crewmen, he was transferred to C Battalion on its formation. He attended a course at the 6 pdr gunnery school between 19-25 May and then, with the rest of his battalion, the driver training school at Wailly between 11-19 June.

In preparation for the next British attack at Ypres, C Battalion then moved up to their base at Oosthoek Wood to the northeast of Ypres in early July. On 29 July, 24 tanks from No 7 and No 9 Poperinghe supported an attack near Frezenberg but they were unable to cope with the soaked and shelled ground conditions. On 2 August, Charles' brother Edward was Killed in Action whilst serving as a gunner with 197 Siege Battery Royal Garrison Artillery– he was buried at the Voormezeele burial ground to the south of Ypres. On 10 August, Charles received gunshot wounds to his head. As none of the tanks were forward, it is likely that he was hit by shrapnel from German guns which were trying to interdict the British base areas. It is even possible he was visiting his brother's grave.

He was treated at No 1 Canadian General Hospital at Étaples, after which he was sent to the Reinforcements Depot and then back to C Battalion arriving at Blairville Camp near Wailly on 8 October. Having returned to Blangy-sur-Ternoise, C Battalion was tasked to deploy to the Loop near Bray sur Somme, where C Company had offloaded its tanks prior to the Battle of Flers-Courcelette 14 months before. On 15 November, the tank were loaded to trains and sent forward towards their lying up area at Villers-Guislain.

On 20 November, whilst serving as a tank driver in No 5 Section of 8 Company, Charles was again wounded. All three tanks of his section broke through the German's advance line and 1st trench system, *Cynic* and *Curmudgeon* being knocked out as they assisted the infantry assault through the Gonnelieu spur. Given that Charles was wounded in the right hip and thigh, it is likely that he was shot as he tried to get away from the tank hulk. He was admitted No 5 Casualty Clearing Section at Tincourt and then by train to 12 General Hospital at Rouen arriving the next day. Six days later he was evacuated to UK on HS *Woulda* and treated at West Bridgford Military Hospital in Nottinghamshire. He was then transferred to the Pavilion Auxiliary Hospital at Trent Bridge from 29 December. Released from hospital on 9 January, and granted leave until 18 January, he was transferred to Command Depot Catterick on 25 Jan 18. Twelve days later, he was admitted to Catterick Military hospital suffering from tetanus. He was seriously ill and was treated at Catterick Military Hospital for fifty-seven days. Discharged on 23 March, Charles was posted to the Receiving Depot at Worgret Camp on 20 April and then to Reserve unit at Wareham on 3 August. Expecting to be sent back to France, Charles married Alice Poynton on 17 August 1918 at All Saint's Church at Hampton on the River Thames. He was then posted to 18 Battalion at Bovington on 13 September and three weeks later, returned to France. By this time, the Final Advance was in its closing stages as the British and Empire divisions pushed the German Army back to the Belgian Border. As a result, 18th Battalion was not deployed in action but its soldiers undertook occupation duties. On 18 March 1919, Charles was posted to 16th Battalion and promoted acting corporal on 27 March. He did get some home leave in the summer (the dates are not clear in his record) and on 5 September, he was returned to the UK for demobilisation. Despite his earlier injuries, Charles did not make a claim for a disability pension and he was transferred to Z Reserve on 9 October. His son Edward, who was named after his elder brother, was born in Hampton in early 1922, James was born in early 1930 and Alice and his youngest son Thomas born in 1935. After the Second World War, Charles decided to become a farmer and moved, with Alice and Thomas, to Australia. Arriving at Sydney on 10 January 1950, the family moved to Murwillumbah near Richmond and lived at Kunghur, near the Queensland border for the next ten years. Thomas married Edna Martin in 1954 but sadly he died in 1968, his father Charles dying two years later at Liverpool New South Wales.

John Armistead's father was a farmer from West Yorkshire but John became a teacher in London. Born on 1 November 1884 in Kirkheaton, near Huddersfield, he was christened on 24 May 1885 at St Thomas' Church, Bradley whilst the family was living in Colne Bridge. By 1901, the family was living at Mirfield. Ten years later John was working as a London Education Authority school-master and living at 9 Temple Fortune Hill in Golders Green. On 20 March 1913 he married Barbara Steel, who was the daughter of a lithographer, at St Ninian's Presbyterian Church which was very close to Barbara's home in Golders Green. Barbara was thirty-nine when she married and the couple's only child, John Anderson Armistead, was born on 23 January 1915. John Senior enlisted on 27 November 1915 in London and was attested on 4 April 16 into the MMGS. He was relatively short at five feet four inches tall but he had good chest development. After the first tank actions, John remained with the majority of his mates when C Company was expanded to become C Battalion and he probably fought at the Battle of Arras. On 14 May 1917 John was posted, as a cook, to the 2nd Tank Brigade 6 pdr Gun School and then, having returned for 2 days to C Battalion, on 16 June was posted to HQ Tank Corps at Bermicourt. On 20 July, he was posted to the Reinforcement Depot in France and was granted ten days home leave in London in August 1917 which was most unusual. John then returned to the Tank Corps HQ where he was again employed as a cook in the Officers' Mess where he would have fed Brigadier General Hugh Elles and the small team commanding the tank brigades and the administrative units which kept them in action.

On 11 January 1918, John was admitted with an abscess on his thumb to 56th Casualty Clearing Section and was sent to one of the military hospitals at Abbeville two days later. Despite a month's treatment, the wound remained septic and John was sent back to Chatham on 12 February 1918. When sent back to England for treatment, the soldier's unit had to complete a certificate about his employment. In John Armistead's case, the form was signed off by Captain Graham Woods, the former adjutant of D Battalion who was now serving as a personnel staff officer at the Tank Corps HQ. Woods described John as "sober, reliable, intelligent, educated" and, most intriguingly, "quite a good cook". It took three months treatment before he was considered fit to be discharged from hospital which indicates just how difficult it was to rid wounds of infection before the availability of antibiotics. John was granted post-hospital leave from 10 to 19 May before returning to duty on 22 May 1918. Appointed acting Lance Corporal on 31 August, he remained in England for the remainder of the war firstly serving at Wareham and later, at Swanage, where he served with B Company of the Tank Depot. He was transferred to the Z Reserve on 16 January 1919 and returned to his family in Golders Green. John's service is recorded in the London County Council Record of War service. From 1920 to 1936, the family lived at 15 Willifield Way in Hampstead with Barbara's father. After his death on 6 January 1937, they moved to East Grinstead where Barbara died in 1956 aged eighty. John died two years later, aged seventy-eight, at the Queen Victoria Hospital on 3 January 1962.

Unlike John Armistead, Gunner Ernest Sandwich was actually born and was brought up in London. Born in 1886, he was the eldest son of a stockbroker's clerk and entered Lyndhurst Grove School in Southwark on 30 May 1892. By 1901, the family lived at 7 Holmewood Road in Streatham and by 1911, Ernest was working as a clerk at a gramophone company. He enlisted into the MMGS on 25 November 1915 and, just before he deployed to France, married Winifred Morehead, who was the daughter of the manager of an iron foundry from Tynemouth. Their daughter Betty was born the following spring. Ernest's service record has not survived but the medal rolls show that he was discharged from the Amy on 18 July 1918 as a result of sickness. Ernest then became an accountant and, after the Second World War, was appointed a Fellow of British Association of Accountants and Auditors. The family lived at 406 Chertsey Road in Twickenham from 1946 until his death on 23 May 1957, Winifred living as a widow for a further twenty years.

Sussex

Gunner Walter Newington was born at Wadhurst in East Sussex on 26 September 1890. He was the third child and second son of a grocer and newsagent Thomas Newington and Emily Lucretia Wright. The family business was firmly established in the High Street but Walter became a sign writer. He did not volunteer to join the Army until 1916; this is possibly because his mother had been widowed and need help running the business. He enlisted on 29 February 1916 at Wadhurst and placed on the Army reserve the following day. Mobilized on 15 March, he was sent to the MMG Depot at Bisley. He was posted to the Armoured Car Section on 1 April and was transferred to the Heavy Section MGC on 4 May. He continued to serve with C Battalion on its formation (18 November) and, after the Battle of Arras, attended the 2 Brigade 6 pdr school for a firing course from 26 May to 2 June. His conduct record shows a most unusual occurrence shortly afterwards, on 16 June 17, he went absent without leave and was confined to barracks for 2 days. He served with C Battalion throughout their actions in the Ypres Salient and, after the Battle of Cambrai, was being granted home UK leave over Christmas. Walter continued to serve with 3rd Light Battalion as they took the light Whippet tanks into action for the duration of the war and he was promoted corporal on 1 October 1918 as the Battalion fought its way through the Hindenburg line for the second occasion. However the German Government sued for peace, he was granted home leave from 1 to 25 January 1919, this being extended and he was demobilised on 5 February 1919 and returned to Wadhurst.

Six years later, on 7 February 1925, Walter married Kitty Smith at the parish church of St Peter and St Paul in Wadhurst High Street. He also remained in contact with his fellow Tankers through his membership of the C Battalion OCA. By 1930, Walter had turned the shop into a newsagents shop and there remains a newsagency in the High Street named Newington to this day. Sadly Walter died, aged only forty three, on 6 July 1933 at the Clarence Nursing Home in Tunbridge Wells.

Northumberland

Being a keen motorcyclist was not unusual amongst those who fought with the tanks and Gunner Billy Rennison was also almost too keen. Billy was so keen that he rode his brother's motorcycle without a driving licence on 28 September 1913 which resulted in his being fined 10 shillings. William Pallister Rennison, to use his full name, was the fourth son of a colliery master mason named Richard Rennison and his wife Ellen. Billy was born in 1895 at Seaton Delaval in Northumberland and as a young man worked as a clerk at one of the local coal mines. According to *The Motor Cycle*, Billy was well known as a motorcyclist prior to the outbreak of war. He enlisted into the Army on 22 October 1915 and served in the MGC, His service number was in the series of those who initially were allocated to the Cavalry section. Later transferring to C Company, Billy deployed to France on 16 August.

His service record has not survived but, according to *The Motor Cycle* magazine, Billy served as a dispatch rider with the Tank Corps headquarters and was badly wounded at Cambrai. He was later treated at No 1 Hospital at Etretat which was located on the coast to the north of Le Havre. On 7 February 1918, two telegrams were sent to his family, the first stating that Billy was seriously ill; the second stating that he was how dangerously ill and that he could be visited by his family. This latter telegram would have only been sent if there was an expectation would not survive and the War Office arranged for families to visit their sons in hospital in France. Billy survived but was not fit for active service and he was discharged from the Army on 25 May 1918. Although he was awarded the Silver War badge on 4 June 1918, I can find no record of an Army pension being awarded. Billy did not marry until the spring of 1930, his bride being Elsie Read. The couple lived at the East Farm House in Backworth from 1940 until Billy's death on 7 March 1952. Elsie lived, as a widow, for a further twenty five years until her death in 1987 aged eighty six years old.

Kent

From his family background, Gunner Jack Robson should have been an engineer. He was borne in 1895 at River, a small village to the north of Dover and was the son of an agricultural engineer. Jack was from a family of agricultural engineers, his father John and two uncles lived side by side in three houses at Crabble Hill. Jack, who was an only son with four elder sisters, was working as a surveyor's pupil when he enlisted at Coventry on 17 November 1915, 24 days after his 20th birthday. He must, however, have been an experienced motorcyclist as he was immediately selected for training and arrived at the MMGS Depot at Bisley the following day. Jack deployed to France with C Company on 16 August 1916 and, after the first tanks actions, served with No 8 Company under Major William Kyngdon. The conditions in which the tank companies during the winter of 1916 were awful. However this could not excuse Jack from being charged with being found dirty during an inspection on 23 January 1917 and he was awarded a punishment of three days Confined to Barracks.

Following the Battle of Arras, Jack undertook driver training at Wailly from 11 to 17 June and was one of the few selected to be reclassified as a driver. After he had been transferred to the Tank Corps, Jack was appointed 1st Class Tank Mechanic on 6 August 1917. He was wounded during the attack by No 8 Company on the Ieper to Zonnebeke Road on 22 August 1917. Eight out of the ten tanks ditched or broke down and Jack, like many crewmen had to walk to safety. Despite his wounds, he was not evacuated to a Casualty Clearing Section but, after being treated locally, was remained at duty. Jack must have fought at Cambrai as he was granted home leave from 4 to 18 December. Jack continued to serve with B Company of 3rd Battalion as it re-rolled onto Whippet tanks. On 15 May, he was admitted to 24 General Hospital at Étaples suffering from Pneumonia of Unknown Origin which was the term used to describe Spanish influenza which was becoming of epidemic proportions. After a month's treatment, he was released back to duty with C Battalion without being sent to the Reinforcement Depot. There is no record of when Jack was promoted to lance corporal but he was promoted corporal on 29 September 1918 in place of Ernest Edwards who was a crewman in *Chablis* on 16 September and who had returned to England. After the Armistice, Jack was granted home leave from 23 November until 7 December and returned to his unit the following day. As demobilisation got under way, Jack managed to return home on 4 February and dispersed from Wimbledon two days later. Amongst his family Jack was known as the "General". He trained work as an architect and moved to Kingston where he married in early 1924, his son John being born the same year. Thereafter, Jack and his family lived near Newbury and from 1943, closeby at Burghclere. In the early 1960s, the couple moved in Gidea Park in Essex where Jack died, aged eighty three in 1979.

Gunner George Joseph Rogers was born in January 1888 near Bristol. George was the youngest son of a nursery gardener Joseph Rogers and his wife Elizabeth who lived off the Whiteladies' Road near Clifton Downs railway station. George initially worked as a stationer's clerk and by 1914 was sufficiently financially secure to get married. His bride was Elsie Gingell who lived in Bedminster, the ceremony taking place on Boxing Day at St Paul's Parish Church. George moved in with Elsie's family and, just under one year later, enlisted in the Army. By now, working as a commercial clerk, George was 5 feet 10¾ inches tall and a chest measuring 32 ½ inches. Examined at Coventry on 21 March 1916, he was mobilized the following day, he was authorised at Bisley on 29 March. Two months later, he was appointed and paid as an acting lance corporal and deployed to France on 16 August 1916.

George was posted to C Battalion on its formation and was promoted acting Corporal, George remained with the unit until he was demobilised. He was promoted substantive Corporal on 18 January 1918 and Sergeant on the following New Year's Eve. The stress of combat took its toll of George and, he was admitted to 12 Stationary Hospital at St Pol with neurasthenia. After treatment he was released on 8 January and returned to unit after some time with the Training and Reinforcement Depot which was located at the seaside resort of Mers-les-Bains. He did not however make any claim for a war pension and was demobilised two months later from Chiseldon. After the war, George joined the C Battalion Old Comrades Association and their membership list in 1925 shows him living at 10 North Street Bedminster. Thereafter he disappears from site until his death, aged seventy-nine, in early 1967 in Bathavon

Cheshire

We are lucky that a picture of Gunner John Bowker has survived. John was born in late April 1896 at Burwardsley, near Tatton Hall in Cheshire. He was the only son of a farmer, after whom he was named and his second wife Mary Ann. John and Mary had married on 27 January 1896 at the time John Senior who was farming nine acres in the local area, was 65 years old. Mary, who was a widow with 6 children, was 48 when she gave birth to her youngest child John Jnr. When John left school, he became a domestic groom but five years later, when he enlisted at Chester on 26 April 1916, he had become a Cycle Shop manager. Unsurprisingly, he volunteered to join the MMGS at Coventry on 2 May and was soon sent to Bisley for machine gun training.

His service record reveals little of his service other he deployed to France on 16 August with C Company and that he had been transferred to C Battalion in November 1916. From 16 to 23 June 1917, John attended a driving course at Wailly, after which he was admitted to 12th Stationary Hospital at St Pol suffering from influenza. Released to Reinforcement Depot on 17 July, ten days later, John was detached to G Battalion and then posted to their strength on 29 July. At the end of the month, he was transferred to the Tank Corps and classified as a 2nd class Tank Mechanic on 6 August 1917. Unusually he was not granted Home leave after the Battle of Cambrai, indeed he did not return to the UK until 27 January which may mean he was involved in getting the tanks repaired on their withdrawal from combat. After a fortnight's home leave, he rejoined the renamed 7th Battalion on 11 February 1918. Three weeks later, he was classified as a Class 1 tradesman and then appointed lance corporal in August 1918, presumably to replace one of the casualties suffered by his Battalion during the Battle of Amiens. In the final weeks of the Great advance, whilst serving with A Company, he was promoted to corporal on 26 October 1918. As the battalion

John Bowker. (Della)

started to move to its winter location, John fell ill and, on 24 November, he was sent back to St Pol for treatment of influenza. He recovered and rejoined 7th Battalion on 7 December and was granted home leave from 6 to 20 January 1919. John was not able immediately to find employment and managed to gain an extension to his leave until 10 February. He was demobilised at Oswestry and returned to Church Street Burwardsley on 29 January. His earlier bouts of influenza did not however protect John from the epidemic which killed so many civilians. He died, just before his twenty-fourth birthday, on 17 April 1920 and was buried at St John the Divine Churchyard in Burwardsley with his father, his mother being buried in the same plot when she died 13 years later. He is listed amongst those who died as a result of the Great War on the CWGC website although not in the Tank Corps Book of Honour. John's extended family remembers him to this day, his grave is tended and a photograph has been placed at Burwardsley Church by his great-niece Della.

Yorkshire

Gunner Cecil Kaye, who was a close friend of Will Dawson, came from Sheffield. The two men travelled by motorcycle for pre-deployment leave managing to obtain fuel by acting as despatch riders. Cecil deployed to France on 16 August 1916, with C Company and according to the Sheffield Daily Independent, was wounded during the tank actions by shrapnel behind the ear on 25 September 1916. Cecil later joined the Royal Engineers and probably served in a Tank Brigade signal company. Cecil, who was the only son of Enos and Lucy Kaye, was born in 19 February 1897 in Sheffield. His father was one of three brothers who were fruiterers at Castle Folds market in the 1900s. Enos had set up his business in 1895 and built up his company such that, when he died in 1964, his estate was worth more than £100,000. The family originally lived at Park and Cecil was educated at the local Norfolk College after which he worked for his father. Cecil later took over the wholesale company in Castlefield Market which only ceased operating in 2014. On 14 June 1922, Cecil married a teacher named Irene Foster. The couple initially lived on Dobbin Hill and had two daughters; Jean who was born on 8 March 1924 and Lorna who was born five years later.

During December 1940, Sheffield was heavily bombed by the Luftwaffe to disrupt the steel-making, mining and other industries vital to the British war effort. For example the Vickers factory contained the only drop hammer capable of forging crankshafts for the Rolls Royce Merlin engine which powered both the Spitfire fighter aircraft and the Lancaster bomber. As well as industry, thousands of houses were damaged by the incendiary bombs and it may have been this that caused Cecil and Irene to settle on Haugh Lane in the Western outskirts of Sheffield the following year. In 1950, Cecil was elected president of the Sheffield and District Wholesale Fruit and Potato Merchants' Association. He used the occasion of their white tie 60th Anniversary Dinner, held at the Royal Victoria Hotel, to call for more new shops as part of the rebuilding of Sheffield to prevent local people having to travel to Leeds, Manchester and Birmingham. In 1955, Irene and Cecil travelled to Canada and the United States for seven weeks, eventually returning from Montréal on the RMS *Ivernia*, the newly completed Cunard liner which was undertaking her maiden Atlantic crossing. Irene, who was eighteen months older than Cecil, died in 1970; he died seven years later in the spring 1977.

Having survived his service with the tanks, Hubert Savage set up his own business as an under-taker. According to the record of his church in Hunslet, Hubert was born 1 July 1889. He was the son of a joiner George Savage and his wife Mary Ann Savidge and was baptised when he was two weeks old at the Wesleyan Methodist Chapel in Hunslet. Until he joined up in 1915, he lived with his family at 30 Anchor Terrace in Hunslet and worked as a joiner like his father. He volunteered to join the MMGS and was enlisted 24 November 1915. Hubert deployed to France with C Company on 16 August 1916 and remained with C Battalion on its formation, serving with No 8 Company. His unit fought at the Harp on 9 April 1917 and then in the Ypres Salient. On

6 October 1917 Hubert was admitted to 20 Casualty Clearing Section at Boisleux au Mont with myalgia or muscle pain in back and knee, the sort of illness easily effecting crewmen operating in the cramped interior of an early tank. He was then sent by train to 5 General Hospital at Rouen on 7 October. After about two weeks, it was decided Hubert should be treated in England and he was evacuated, via the Military Hospital at Eastleigh, and then onto 2nd Western General Hospital in Manchester.

Hubert was posted onto depot strength on 27 October 19 17 when he was admitted to hospital and, as well as treatment for myalgia also received dental treatment. Hubert was not released from hospital until 8 March 1918 when he was granted 10 days home leave in Hunslet. Posted to Tank Corps depot at Wareham, he eventually was sent back to France on 7 August 1918, ten months after he left C Battalion. After completing the standard crewman refresher training package, Hubert rejoined the renamed 3rd Light Battalion on 24 August and served with the unit, through the Final Advance and then on occupation duties. He was not demobilised until 17 February 1919 and returned to his original employment as a joiner.

On 8 September 1922, Hubert married Daisy Inns at Christchurch in Mortlake in Surrey. Daisy, who came from East Sheen, was the daughter of a gardener and she married Hubert two days before her thirty-third birthday. The couple settled in Hunslet and had two children, Stella born on 11 May1925 and James born on 20 March two years later. Hubert kept in touch with his old comrades from C Battalion as he is listed in their membership list published in 1925. By now Hubert had however changed his business and in 1926 was working as an undertaker. Three years later, he had moved to Stainbeck and in the 1930s north to Moortown where he established himself on the Harrogate Road. He was also running an undertaker's company on Gledhill Park Road and may have been in contact with Denton Winter who was living in the same area. By 1939, Hubert was well founded as he also repaired property, owned a taxi business as well as a china shop. He remained in Moortown until 1950 when the couple moved to the Yorkshire resort of Filey before settling Knaresborough where Hubert did nine years later, aged eighty. Daisy later moved to Worthing where she died aged ninety-two in 1981.

Another Yorkshireman had an equally successfully business career. Gunner Fenwick Styan was born on 22 February 1888 at Clifton near York. Fenwick was the son of market gardener Fred Styan, and his wife, Frances Isabel Halliday, Fred becoming a self-employed florist. Fenwick learned to drive at any early age and started working as a chauffeur before the war for Clive Wilson who lived near Beverly. Clive Wilson was the son of Arthur Wilson, the shipping company owner and manufacturer who owned Tranby Croft near Anlaby. Arthur Wilson had hosted the house party in 1890 which was the scene of a Baccarat scandal which resulted in the future Edward VII appearing in court as a witness. Fenwick joined the MGC on 24 May 16 and deployed to France on 16 August 1916. According to his family, as he was one of the few people who could drive, Fenwick became one of the first to drive a tank and took part in the first demonstration in front of Churchill: this is however unlikely. Fenwick later transferred to the Tank Corps. He married Doris Shipley in the spring of 1918 in Driffield. This could have been after he had been released from hospital following a wounding or sickness which ultimately led to his discharge from the Army on 3 August 1919.

After the war, Fenwick returned to work for Clive Wilson who, according to Fenwick's family, sent the family a case of champagne when Fenwick and Doris' daughter Margaret was born in 1921. Clive Wilson, who died that same year, also left a bequest which enabled Fenwick to establish his taxi business and buy a garage just outside the North Bar in Beverley. Their only son Clifford was born in 1926 by which time the business prospered sufficiently to include three Rolls-Royce cars. His vehicles would have been in particular demand during the annual Beverley horse-racing meetings. Given that the local Rolls-Royce agency was in York, it is possible that Fenwick met up with Harold Darby who commanded tank crew D10 on 15 September and was now their main

Frederick Styan in Home Guard uniform. (Martin Styan)

agent. The family weathered the 1928 depression due to another inheritance, this time from Doris' father. She used the £500 to buy a row of houses in York. The family however stayed in Beverley through the 1930s and the Second World War during which Fenwick served in the Home Guard. Fenwick sold his taxi business in 1952 and moved to Scarborough, where Clifford met his future wife Beryl Butterfield. For a few years in the 60s, Fenwick and Doris lived in Bournemouth but after Clifford died of stomach cancer in 1967, Beryl decided to return to Scarborough to live near her mother. Fenwick and Doris also moved close to the seaside resort, living in a bungalow at Irton, which is about 4 miles south-west of the town. After Doris died on 21 February 1969, Fenwick lived in two old people's homes in Scarborough before moving to York where he died on 15 April 1971. His funeral was held in St Wilfred's Roman Catholic Church in York.

Remembrance

Remembrance is the theme of this book as is the task of Commonwealth War Graves Commission (CWGC) cemeteries. Since the 1990s, Harkness nurseries have supplied the CWGC with a poppy-red patio rose named *Remembrance*. This rose is used around the world as its low height and hardy nature making the rose perfect as it does not obscure the special words, chosen by families of the dead at the foot of each grave marker.

There is a direct link between that the First Tank Crews and the *Remembrance* Rose through Bill Harkness. Bill was born at Leeming Bar in North Yorkshire on 27 April 1888. He was the eldest son of Robert and Sarah Harkness, Robert being was a partner in the nursery firm of Harkness and Sons which was at Bedale. When Bill was seven, the family moved to Hitchen to open a new nursery specialising in roses. Bill, however, was sent back to Yorkshire and was educated at

Bill Harkness. (Peter Harkness)

Hipperholme School near Halifax. By the age of twenty Bill staged his first major exhibition at Hitchen. He married first wife, Edith Cooper, the daughter of a Hitchen innkeeper, on 2 April 13 and their daughter Mary Elizabeth was born on 23 April 1914. On 16 May 1916, Bill passed the MMGS assessment and joined the Heavy Section, and initially served with the MGC, his number being given to those allocated to the Machine Gun Corps (Cavalry). According to his cousin Peter Harkness, who now runs the Harkness company, "the family story has it that Bill enlisted in 15 and found himself in France as a Private in the Cavalry before joining 'C' Company – one of the four original companies of the Tank Corps – on the principle, he said, that it was better to ride than walk." Bill escaped serious injury in action although he was nearly badly burnt whilst washing down the outside of a tank with petrol whilst smoking a cigarette. Bill later transferred from the MGC to the Labour Corps in the summer of 1917. According to Peter Harkness, "Subsequent bouts of pleurisy and pneumonia led to his being invalided to Devon, where he helped man a Government Depot of Agricultural Horses to enable the local farmers to plough up their permanent pastures and go arable." On June 1918, the lease of Oakfield Farm Nursery expired and, although he was still serving in the Labour Corps, Bill bought the goodwill and customer mailing list. He was back in the rose-growing business before he was demobilised. On release, he found he needed extra money to support the business and took over the Raven Inn at Hexton. Within four years he was sufficiently successful as a rose grower to move to new grounds at Walsworth. Sadly in 1921, his wife Edith died but three years later, Bill remarried and he and his second wife Peggy had a daughter Jane in 1929. In 1932, Bill won the National Rose Championship which was the first time the Harkness Company had won the award for 25 years. Peter Harkness believes that "Bill was modest to the point of being self-effacing, but a very determined and methodical perfectionist in achieving his chosen goals – hence his haul of 22 National Rose Championships out of 26 entries during his years in charge of the nursery."

Probably due to his modesty, Bill was an attractive man and, after the death of his second wife from pneumonia, married his third wife Ena in 1939. During the war, Bill's nurseries were largely turned over to agriculture, in particular growing root crops, but he managed to maintain success in rose competitions. He commanded the Hitchen Platoon of the Home Guard during the war and may well have met Harold Mortimore who was commanding the platoon at Sawbridgeworth. In 1946, the company's new rose, named *Ena Harkness* lead the firm's post war revival. In 1954, having been a prominent role in rose growing associations for many years, Bill was awarded the Dean Hole Medal which is the premier award made to growers by the Royal National Rose Society. Sadly after a few years, his health started to deteriorate and Bill died on 1 December 1959.

Appendix A

First Tank Crew Deaths 1916-1920

KIA = Killed in Action
DOW = Died of Wounds
Crew number reflects the original crew on 15 September 1916

15 September 1916
Horace Brotherwood (C1) – KIA aged 18 near Pozières.
Bertie Giles (C14) – KIA aged 18 at Bouleaux Wood.
Gerald Pattinson (C14) – KIA aged 30 at Bouleaux Wood.
George Macpherson (C20) – DOW aged 20 at Grovetown.
Edgar Barnsby (D5) – KIA aged 25 near Flers.
Leslie Gutsell (D5) – KIA aged 20 near Flers.
Fred Bardsley (D6) – KIA aged 24 near Gueudecourt.
George Cook (D6) – KIA aged 29 near Gueudecourt.
John Garner (D6) – KIA aged 25 near Gueudecourt.
William Debenham (D12) – KIA aged 24 on 15 Sep 1916 near Flers.
Cyril Coles (D15) – KIA aged 23 near Flers.
Charles Hoban (D15) – KIA aged 29 near Flers.

16 September 1916
Reginald Legge (D6) – DOW aged 24 at Gueudecourt.
Alfred Andrew (D9) – KIA aged 29 near Flers.
Ronald Chapple (D9) – KIA aged 19 near Flers.
William Barber (D14) – KIA aged 25 near Gueudecourt.
Gordon Court (D14) – KIA aged 23 near Gueudecourt.
Thomas Cromack (D14) – KIA aged 36 near Gueudecourt.
Joseph Crowe (D14) – KIA aged 24 near Gueudecourt.
Andrew Lawson (D14) – KIA aged 21 near Gueudecourt.
George Mann (D14) – KIA aged 24 near Gueudecourt.
Robert Pebody (D14) – DOW aged 20 near Gueudecourt.
Lawrence Upton (D14) – DOW aged 34 near Gueudecourt.

22 September 1916
Tom Wilson (D15) – DOW aged 28 at Mericourt.

26 September 1916
Fred Horrocks (D Coy) – KIA aged 34 at Delville Wood.

28 September 1916
Frank Bull (C Coy) – DOW at Grovetown.

4 November 1916
Arthur Ritchie (C14) – DOW aged 21 at Abbeville.

9 February 1917
Walter Atkins (D20) – died aged 21 during an appendectomy at Wareham Military Hospital.

9 April 1917
Ewart Doodson (D1) – DOW aged 18 near Thelus whilst serving with No 12 Coy D Bn HB MGC.
Frank Styring (D20) – KIA aged 27 whilst attacking the Harp Feature near Beaurains whilst serving with No 10 Coy of D Bn HB MGC.
Maurice Voile (C Coy) – KIA aged 24 at the Harp Feature near Beaurains whilst serving with C Bn HB MGC.

11 April 1917
Robert Hillhouse (C Coy) – KIA aged 31 near Arras whilst serving with C Bn HB MGC.
Harry Leat (D1) – KIA aged 22 at Bullecourt whilst serving with No 11 Coy D Bn HB MGC.

15 April 1917
Herbert Thacker MM (D6) – drowned when SS *Arcadian* was sunk by a U-boat near Milos.

24 April 1917
Leslie Reeve (D24) – DOW received whilst driving *Diana* in No 10 Coy D Bn HB MGC.

3 May 1917
Oswald Clayton (D4) – KIA aged 35 at Bullecourt whilst serving with No 12 Coy of D Bn HB MGC.
Clarence Kilminster (C Coy) – DOW aged 24 at Duisens whilst serving with C Bn HB MGC.
George Thomas (D5) – KIA aged 26 at Bullecourt whilst serving with No 12 Coy of D Bn HB MGC.

9 June 1917
John Allen MC (C6) – DOW aged 30 at Ballieul whilst serving with B Bn HS MGC.

4 July 1917
Philip Evans (C Coy) – KIA aged 21 at Oosthoek Wood whilst serving with C Bn HB MGC.

31 July 1917
Lionel Griffin (C Coy) – KIA aged 31 near Ypres whilst serving with C Bn Tank Corps.

15 August 1917
George Wootley – KIA aged 29 near Ypres with serving with 149 Inf Coy MGC.

16 August 1917
Alfred Williams – KIA aged 29 near Ypres whilst serving with 25 Inf Coy MGC.

22 August 1917
William Hudson – KIA aged 20 near Ypres whilst serving with C Bn Tank Corps.

23 September 1917
Percy Raworth MM (D22) – DOW aged 27 near Ypres whilst serving with D Bn Tank Corps.

9 October 1917
Eddie Williams MM (D8) – KIA aged 25 at Poelcapelle whilst serving in *Damon II* in No 11 Coy
    D Bn Tank Corps

10 November 1917
Len Bates (C Coy) – died aged 32 of injuries following a tank detraining accident at Dublin.

13 November 1917
John Newell (C Coy) – DOW aged 24 in hospital in Glasgow following wounds received on 31 July
    1917 whilst serving with No 7 Coy C Bn Tank Corps.

20 November 1917
Horace Allebone (D12) – KIA aged 28 at Flesquières whilst serving with No 10 Coy D Bn Tank
    Corps.
George Foot DCM (D21) – KIA age 20 whilst fighting in *Deborah* at Flesquières.
Harry Tiffin (C Coy) – KIA aged 25 near Le Quennet Farm whilst fighting in *Comet II* whilst
    serving with No 12 Coy C Bn Tank Corps.

25 November 1917
Lawrence Rowntree (C5) – KIA aged 22 near Ypres whilst serving with 26 Bde RFA.

27 November 1917
John Starkey (D23) – KIA aged 21 near Fontaine Notre Dame whilst serving with No 17 Coy of
    F Bn Tank Corps.

30 November 1917
Leonard Haygarth (D10) – DOW aged 27 received whilst serving with D Bn Tank Corps.

1918

21 March 1918
Lionel Britt (D10) – KIA on his 26th birthday whilst serving with 4th Bn Tank Corps.
Wilfred Jaques (D6) – KIA aged 37 whilst serving with C Coy 4th Bn Tank Corps.

22 March 1918
John Wells (D24) – KIA age 25 whilst serving with 4th Bn Tank Corps.

23 March 1918
Walter Gammon (D Coy) – KIA aged 32 near Bray sur Somme whilst serving with C Coy 4th Bn
    Tank Corps.

8 August 1918
Herbert Pryce (C Coy) – KIA aged 21 near Le Quesnel whilst fighting in *Crab III* with B Coy 3rd
    Light Bn Tank Corps.

10 August 1918
William Moss (D11) – KIA aged 21 near Bouchoir whilst serving with 4th Bn Tank Corps.

2 September 1918
George Caffrey (C18) – KIA aged 23 near Beugny whilst serving with 7th Bn Tank Corps.

3 September 1918
Hugh Bell (D2) – KIA aged 39 at Haucourt whilst serving with 11th Bn Tank Corps.

4 September 1918
Charles Bond (D15) – died, aged 26, of tuberculosis at Wembdon.

29 September 1918
Ernest Phillips (D10) – KIA aged 28 near Bellicourt whilst serving with 1st Bn Tank Corps.

8 October 1918
Wilfred Bolingbroke (C Coy) – KIA aged 22 near Serain whilst serving with 3rd Light Bn Tank Corps.
Arnold Ross Peace (C Coy) – DOW aged 25 at Rouen.

4 November 1918
Eric Robinson (D22) – KIA aged 26 at Cotillon sur Sambe whilst serving 10th Bn Tank Corps.

20 November 1918
Neville Tattersfield (No 2 Sect of C Coy) – died from influenza at Wareham Military Hospital.

1919

31 January 1919
Alfred Bloomfield (D13) – died aged 32 whilst serving with the Central Tank Workshops at Erin.

12 May 1919
Arthur Inglis DSO (C5) – DoW aged 34 at his home at Prestbury.

29 November 1919
George Shepherd DCM (C5) – died aged 27 at Liverpool killing his wife in the process.

Appendix B

Tank Crews and Their Companies

To operate a tank took a crew of eight men. The commander, usually known as the skipper, was a junior officer who directed the driver to each objective, operated the brakes and indicated enemy positions to the gunners. There were four gunners, two on each side of the tank. The gunners either operated a 6 pdr quick firing (QF) Hotchkiss cannon fitted to the "male" tanks or a machine gun, initially an armoured Vickers water-cooled medium machine gun and later Lewis air-cooled light machine gun fitted to "female" tanks. The gunners were supported by two gearsmen who supplied ammunition and also assisted the driver by controlling the secondary gears. All were needed to starting the engine using a huge crank handle which was integral to the transmission. Some gearsmen were also trained as second drivers and were able to take over if the Army Service Corps (ASC) driver was injured.

From the list of names recorded in Graham Woods' notebook, it appears that each crew contained seven gunners including a spare man so that there was always a trained replacement in the event of illness or injury. This is supported by photographs taken of the crews at Elveden before they deployed to France. On 15 September 1916, when the tanks first went into action, a number of these spare gunners went too including those who had recently been trained to send signals from observation balloons behind the British front lines.

In September 1916, there were twenty-five tanks in each company. Each company was divided into four sections of six crews with each section was commanded by a captain who also commanded a tank. The company was commanded by a major with a captain as adjutant who maintained the company records and War Diary. Discipline was the responsibility of the company sergeant major although former members of the MMGS had a reputation for being "over-officered and under-disciplined." An MGC lieutenant was appointed as quartermaster responsible for the stores and equipment and he was supported by a staff sergeant and two sergeants. The spare tanks were initially managed by a tank park officer but this role disappeared after both captains took command of a section of tanks following injuries to the original commanders. The company headquarters included a fifth section with a spare tank commander, a number of spare crewmen and an Army Ordnance Corps armourer who repaired the weapons of each company.

Each company was provided with a Sunbeam car for the company commander and a number of small vans for the carriage of equipment. The cars were also generally driven by the ASC soldiers who were attached to each company headquarters which moved as required between locations by roads whereas the tanks and crewmen moved by rail. The tanks and their weapons were maintained by the gunners and drivers; major mechanical repairs and recovery were initially undertaken by ASC officers and soldiers from 711 (Mechanical Transport) Company which also provided a mobile workshop. There were initially very few spare parts and insufficient tools for maintenance. Just after he arrived in France in August 1916, Major Allen Holford-Walker had to write to his wife Joan to buy spanners in England and sent a soldier back to collect them so that basic maintenance and repairs to be completed. Whilst the workshop equipment included a number of lathes, there was no equipment capable of recovering a broken-down tank or transport major spare parts

354

to the scene of a breakdown. As a result, an ASC mechanist staff sergeant and four men had to manhandle spare track links from the forward base at Green Dump across the battlefield to High Wood to extract the tank *Delphine* after she became ditched on 15 September.

Despite these early shortcomings, the First Tank Crews gave the British Army at the Battle of Flers-Courcelette an edge over their German opponents which General Haig was keen to exploit. On 17 September 1916, he met Colonel Ernest Swinton and congratulated him on the success of the tanks. Having discussed their future usage, he immediately asked for 1,000 more tanks to be delivered by 1 March 1917 but sadly industry could not provide such a number. Establishing the new tank battalions and preparing them for battle took more than an order, it took time and organisation. In December 1916, the first four tank battalions were formed from the first four companies which had deployed to France. Four more were formed at Bovington and deployed to France within eight months; experienced officers taken from the units which had fought in France providing vitally needed command and control. Lessons learned from the first actions were also implemented. Stuart Hastie led a team of experienced skippers and drivers who trained the volunteers who flocked to join the new battalions in France; Basil Henriques gave lectures to the new tank commanders, being trained at Bovington, on the realities of "fighting" a tank. Both C and D Companies recommended NCOs for officer training and many were commanding tanks within 12 months.

From 1917, battalion were established which consisted of thirty-six tanks formed into three companies. The number of tanks in each company was reduced from twenty-five to twelve tanks and the number of tanks per section from six to three or four. The Tank Headquarters established a scheme of training which was mandated across all units. A captain was appointed as a reconnaissance officer in each battalion with each company being allocated a further officer for reconnaissance duties. Each section commander was supported by an orderly who was picked from amongst the best of the junior NCOs. Tom Bernard was one such orderly and he captured his role in a story which is published for the first time in Annex C. Each company also gained a second in command whilst section commanders lost the responsibility for commanding a tank – they were however made responsible for tactical control of the section on the battlefield. Initially each battalion also contained a workshops company and drivers were no longer attached from 711 Company ASC; they were transferred onto the strength of the tank battalions.

In December 1916, a tank administrative area was also set up to the west of St Pol sur Ternoise with villages becoming the base for each battalion when it was out of battle. A Central Stores and a Workshops which were established in February 1917 at Erin and driving and gunnery schools were established both in France and in England. The instructors were mainly drawn from experienced crewmen and many of the First Tank Crews served in these roles. Tank battalions were grouped into brigades and a Headquarters was formed at Bermicourt under Brigadier General Hugh Elles, who extracted experienced officers and crewmen as well as staff officers from other formations to work here as well.

The problem of recovering ditched and damaged tanks was given to a newly formed salvage company which quickly won a reputation for getting tanks back into action in the teeth of enemy fire. Within two years of C Company arriving in France, eighteen tank battalions had deployed to France. Each of the five tank brigades supported by a signal company and a tank supply company – the section commanders often being tank officers who were decorated following the early battles of 1917. In 1918, two salvage companies and five advanced repair units were also in place. In all more than 20,000 men wore the Tank arm badge but less than 600 were professional soldiers.

Tanks were often key to successful infantry attacks from the spring of 1917, the British and Empire Divisions using combined operations using infantry, artillery, tanks and aircraft which the Germans could not withstand. The breakthrough at Cambrai proved the effectiveness of massed armoured vehicles. After the German Army fought back with a series of the advances in early 1918, the British, Empire and French forces recoiled and, from August 1918, defeated the Germany Army, time and again, forcing them back to their own borders. The Germans attempted to use tanks, captured after the Battle of Cambrai, to slow the advance but they were beaten back by the British crews who outmanoeuvred and out-shot them. By October 1918, Allied victory was complete and the German government sought an Armistice. It is a matter of history that the first unit to cross the border, and then the River Rhine, was 17th Armoured Car Battalion which included in its ranks several crewmen who fought at Flers-Courcelette.

Appendix C

"We Improve Our Line" by "Tankard"
(Newspaper article written by Tom Bernard)

"Brown, the Section Commander wants to see you at once" and the Section Sergeant passed on.

I had just finished up writing up my tank logs for the Section and, being Sunday incidentally a quiet day as far as the war was concerned and withal sweltering hot, I had anticipated a quiet afternoon. I put on my tunic and made my way through the wood to the tent in which my Section Commander lived, dined, slept and used as an office. As I approached I saw him standing at the tent entrance, carefully studying a map, and wondered what was in the wind. Were we going into action or had the section be ordered to another area? My doubts were soon put at rest and my chances of a quiet afternoon faded away.

"Brown, you will fall in at 3.00 p.m. with the tank commanders and drivers for reconnaissance. Just look at this map. When you arrive at point 014 B5, the officers will leave you to come back alone. As we may be going over this sector, I want you to take careful note of all the land marks. You will then come back through the Bois de ….. , you should be back by 7 p.m. This will give you sufficient time to look at the map and memorize these road, and tracks, their conditions and compass bearings" and he traced certain marks on the map with his finger. "Report to me at 9 o'clock."

I took the map and saluted. Shortly after 3 p.m. we were moving out of the wood, a party of twenty, each man equipped with steel helmet, gas mask and map. We moved on in a crowd, there was very little talking, each man was intently scanning the surrounding country or standing for a moment to gaze at his map, or perhaps make a pencil mark, all the time mentally photographing prominent landmarks. From this point we could distinctly see the massive tower of Amiens well above that grand city, at 3 o'clock (clock reference). Church towers were always good landmarks and their position in relation to your course should always be carefully noted.

On arriving at our point 014 B5, we sit on a bank, an officer passes round cigarettes and we smoke whilst comparing notes on the country we have just passed over. The cigarette finished, we get up and spilt into parties of twos and threes, each party moving off in a different direction. I look round to take note of a few scattered and well shelled villages, and then wend my way back to the wood, feeling quite fit for the tea that is awaiting me. I spend another hour at the map, make a few notes, and by that time, I feel I should have no difficulty in finding my way to any point in that area.

The following day (Monday) passes as usual but at 9 p.m. receive orders to have all tanks ready to leave and in fighting order by 10 p.m. I pack my precious logs and send them down to the Company office for safe keeping. At 10 p.m. prompt, I am at the side of my Section Commander in fighting equipment, Section flag and gas mask at the alert, awaiting orders.

Presently tanks come into view from the trees around, swinging into position of line ahead on the track leading through the wood. When all tanks are reported present and in position, they slowly move ahead being guided by the Company Reconnaissance Officer to their new position. I keep with the Section Commander as he moves from tank to tank, assuring himself that they are running perfectly smoothly.

At 3 a.m. we arrive at our resting place in a small copse by the side of a marshy lake and, where a high bank affords us good cover from the inquisitive eyes of the enemy airman. The tanks are camouflaged and the crews supplied with hot cocoa by the cooks who have preceded us, and at 4 a.m. I lay down to sleep within calling distance of the Section Commander. At 9 a.m. I am wakened and receive orders to be ready to proceed on reconnaissance with the Section Officer at 10.30.

This time we have 6 hours walking and, all the time, receive a lot of attention from Fritz by the way of shells. However, they do nothing more than plow up the ground so we arrive quite safely at our reserve line of trenches which are situated jut behind the crest of a ridge. From here, we get an excellent view of the ground over which the tanks have to pass and the wood that has to be taken. The grounds beyond the wood we cannot see but aeroplane photographs give us an excellent idea of the ground here. As we make our way back to our temporary Tankodrome, the Section Commander gives more details of the coming attack. I learn we are in support of the Australian and American infantry tomorrow morning. We will advance 2,000 yards, two tanks will go to the left of the wood, two round the right of the wood and two will go right through and cleat the wood. The objective is 800 yards beyond the wood and there the tanks will meet and offer protection to the infantry whilst they dig in. After that we will pick certain positions in the captured wood and await the expected counter attack by the enemy.

This was the programme in brief and the Section Commander looks forward to the counter attack, hoping that he might have an opportunity to find a weak point in the enemy's tanks, should he use them. A Section Commander usually confides quite a lot of confidential information and information to his orderly as he requires him to jog his memory should he, during the preparation or excitement of the action, forget anything.

We arrive at the tanks at 6 p.m. and, after having tea, pull on our overcoats and sleep again. The tank crews, whilst we were away, have oiled and greased up their engines and were ready to proceed. Four hours we sleep this time and wake up quite refreshed and get to it again. By 11 p.m. we are moving out again, all tanks in a single line ahead. At about 1 a.m. an enemy 'plane dropped a very bright flare to see if there was any movement taking place but evidently we were not seen as we reached our several places of deployment at 2.15 a.m. This left us 40 minutes to make our final preparations, engines were oiled and machine guns cleaned and loaded. The tank commanders proceeded to brigade headquarters to have their watches synchronised.

3.05 "Start-up" and all the engines start together. The Section Commander and I get into the leading tank and away over the crest we go. At 2.30 a terrific bombardment has been put down on the enemy trenches by our artillery so now the noise is deafening. The effect of the artillery is beyond description. There never was a firework display that could compare with it and behind it all was the knowledge that men are being torn to pieces with flying pieces of iron.

It is usually left to the discretion of the Section Commander to guide his tanks into action in the manner most convenient to himself, and they usually prefer to go with the infantrymen where they can see if the infantry are having any trouble as often it happens that the Boche puts up a fight if he has one of his machine guns in a strong point. He then guides his tanks to that point and that seldom fails to clear the way and so this time, we had just passed over our front line when "Right ho! Brown" and the door is opened and out we jump. We climb onto the back of the tank and ride a few more yards until we come in line with the infantry. We then get off and guide the tanks into position. We are now close behind our own barrage and, having had such dry weather, the dust thrown up by the bursting shells rolls towards us like a gas cloud , making us extremely thirsty. The din is so terrific that it is only with difficulty that we can hear ourselves speak. Presently the barrage settles for three minutes on a sunken road and, as it lifts, the infantry advance with their rifles at the ready but our barrage has done its work well and only two machine guns are left in action. Our Australian and American comrades would like to rush them but their officers hold them back.

"Keep steady, lads," shouts our Section Commander as, with a movement of his hand, his guides a tank to the place of trouble. This is sufficient for the Boche, thirteen men suddenly appear running, a dozen rifle crack and the machine guns from the tanks splutter and the men fall from sight in the long grass. The two other tanks of the section debouch to the right and left and some men come out of their shell holes with their hands upheld, shouting "Camerade". Some of our men are told to search them fir weapons and knives which are removed; they are then sent back under escort. We are now at our objective and other sections of tank re-join us and line up or take short cruises to cover the infantrymen as they dig in.

After twenty minutes of hard digging, our men are well entrenched on our new line. Our services are no longer required and so we swing round and make our way back to our temporary resting place. For 48 hours we "stand by" but, contrary to his usual tactics, the Boche does not counter our attack so we receive orders to return to our old camp in the wood. After five hours steaming, we arrive at our destination and it is like home after such a stiff piece of work. The crews are baked and I am weary with walking and lack of sleep. The tanks are well camouflaged and we return to our old billets and sleep for a further 9 hours.

Later we are interested to read in the paper how the Australians and Americans assisted by the tanks carried out a successful attack on a front of 3,000 yards, penetrating the enemy's lines to a depth of two miles, taking more than 2,000 prisoners and some machine guns.

Appendix D

Order of Battle

C COMPANY

Company Headquarters
T/Maj Allen Holford-Walker
Capt Richard Earl Williams
Capt Richard Ewart Trevithick
2Lt Theodore Lateriner Wenger
Lt Charles Weaver-Price
2Lt Robert John Aitken
CSM Joseph Hackett
Sgt Gordon Ferguson Bainbridge
SQMS Harry Wolfe Jacobs
Armr Sgt Harry Taylor

No 1 Section
Commander – Captain Arthur Inglis

C1 *Champagne* (No 721 Male)
Lt Alfred George Clark Wheeler
Sgt Frederick John "Fred" Saker
Gnr Ernest Hubert Bax
Gnr George Lloyd
Gnr Herbert Rothera
Gnr William Neilson Smith
Gnr Frederick Cecil Stone
Pte Horace Brotherwood (driver)

C2 *Cognac* (No 522 female)
Lt Frank William Bluemel
Sgt Arthur Jennings Osborne Milliken
LCpl Harold Edwin Teft
Gnr Victor Stanley Archard
Gnr Robert Thomas Caldicott
Gnr Alfred Ernest Hemington
Gnr A Sims
Gnr Donald James Thompson
Pte Herbert Ledger (driver)

C3 *Chartreuse* (No 701 Male)
Lt Stanley Darrell Houghton Clarke
Cpl Reginald Frank Shaw
Gnr Ernest John Edwards
Gnr Alexander James Garden
Gnr Charles Frederick Phillips
Gnr Alfred Bernard Simpson
Gnr George Kidd Stonehouse
Pte Alfred Boult (driver)

C4 *Chablis* (No 503 Female)
2Lt George Osmond Lorne "Geordie" Campbell
Cpl Charles Norman Harrison
Gnr Reginald James Acock
Gnr William Francis "Bill" Boylin
Gnr William Cheadle
Gnr Charles Augustus Arthur Kidd
Gnr John Warmington Makin
Gnr Frank Richard Pickworth
Pte Daniel D Cronin (driver)

C5 *Crème de Menthe* (No 721 Male)
Capt Arthur Maculloch Inglis
Cpl Ronald Roderick "Roy" Garlick
Gnr Robert Gibson
Gnr Lionel Hemsworth McAdam
Gnr Laurence William Rowntree
Gnr Joseph Shepherd
Gnr William Hughes Stockdale
Cpl George Bentley Shepherd (driver)

C6 *Cordon Rouge* (No 504 Female)
Lt John Allan
A/Cpl Francis George Vyvyan
Gnr Henry James Bedford
Gnr Ernest Albert Hunt
Gnr Arthur Frederick Jakins
Gnr William Jones MGC
Gnr Clarence George Kilminster
Gnr Victor Cecil Newby
Pte Joseph Barton (driver)

No 2 Section
Commander – Capt Herbert Henry Hiscocks

No 507 Female
Capt Herbert Henry Hiscocks

No 722 Male
2Lt Alec Leslie Arnaud

No 513 Female
2Lt Thomas Frederick Murphy

No 714 Male
Lt Leonard John Bates

No 760 Male
Lt Herbert Benbow Elliot

No 554 Female
2Lt Charles Frederick Nelson Ambrose

No 3 Section
Commander – Lt Sir John Lindsay Dashwood

C13 (No 716 male)
Lt Sir John Lindsay Dashwood

C14 (No 509 female)
Lt Francis James Arnold
Cpl Gerald Edmonds Pattinson
Gnr Thomas Herbert Firth Bernard
Gnr Bertie Arthur Garnett "BAG" Giles
Gnr Arthur James Ritchie
Gnr William Williams
Gnr Denton Joseph Winter
Pte Owen Alfred Sleath (driver)

C15 (No 741 male)
Jethro Edward Tull

C16 *Corunna?* **(No 510 female)**
2Lt Eric Layton Purdy
Gnr William H Piper

C17 *Campania* **(No 746 male)**
Lt John Peard "Jack" Clarke
Pte George Leonard Marlow Viner (driver)

C18 *Casa* **(No 508 female)**
2Lt Louis Victor "Victor" Smith
Cpl Douglas James Gardiner
Gnr George Arthur Caffrey
Gnr Harry Greenberg
Gnr William Scott
Gnr John Webby

Gnr John Alfred Witty
Pte Stewart (driver)

No 4 Section
Commander – Capt Archie Holford-Walker

C19 *Clan Leslie* **(No 705 male)**
Capt (Bruce) Archie Holford-Walker
Gnr Robert S Tate

C20 (No 523 female)
Lt George Macpherson
Gnr William Taylor Dawson

C21 (No 740 male)
Lt Harold Hubert Vincent

C22 (No 533 female)
2Lt Basil Lucas Quixano Henriques
Cpl Roger Paterson
Gnr Reginald Harry Fisher
Gnr Frank Raynor

C23 *Clan Ruthven* **(Male)**
2Lt Andrew Morris Henderson

C24 *Clan Cameron* **(No 512? – Female)**
Lt Harold Ralph Clements Cole

Other crewmen

These crewmen were serving with C Company as they landed in France but their allocation to individual tanks is unknown

Sgt James David Smith "Jimmie" Anderson
Sgt Albert William Bedford
Sgt Robert Hillhouse
Sgt Alfred Edward Howard
Sgt James Albert John Macgregor
Sgt James "Jimmy" Noel
Sgt Edgar Parry Williams
A/Cpl James William Battell
Cpl W Clare
Cpl Wilfred Clarence Edwards
Cpl Leonard Charles "Len" Groutage
Cpl Charles Hamer
Cpl Tom Hamer
Cpl George Thomson Kennedy
Cpl Charles Thomas "Tom" Lowe

Cpl Frank Short
Cpl William Smith RAMC
Cpl Clement Hugh Tinker
LCpl Robert George Carruthers
LCpl John Charles Adam Farquharson
Pte George Henry Marchant
LCpl Charles Ernest Spurgeon
Gnr Harold George Adams
Gnr Edward Lawrence Appleby
Gnr John Armistead
Gnr William H Armstrong
Gnr RC Bailey
Gnr Ralph William Baker
Gnr H Barraclough
Gnr William Benson
Gnr Sydney Binks
Gnr Sampson James Birch
Gnr George Hugh Bissett
Gnr Leonard Blackshaw
Gnr Wilfred Bolingbroke
Gnr James Alfred Booth
Gnr Raymond Edwin Bothway
Gnr John Joseph Bowker
Gnr Harry Broster
Gnr Charles Frank Bull
Gnr John Bernard Callaghan
Gnr James Candlish
Gnr OJ Clarke
Gnr Frederick William Cole
Gnr A Collie
Gnr Stanley John Conder
Pte Arthur Corlett
Gnr James Culshaw
Gnr George William Frederick Currie
Gnr Daniel James Dean
Gnr George Ernest Dean
Gnr James Henry Dodd
Gnr Francis John Dyer
Gnr Philip John Evans
Gnr Percy John Fordham
Gnr Adam Gibson
Gnr Wilfred Vernon Giddins
Gnr Vincent George Harold Greaves
Gnr Lionel Ignatius Leslie Griffin
Gnr Frank Halford
Gnr Walter Robert Hamilton
Gnr William Ernest Harkness
Gnr J Heath
Gnr Charles Henry Wallace Hewitt

Gnr William John Thomas Higgs
Gnr Joseph Hill
Gnr JH Hobbs
Gnr William Hudson
Gnr Willie Illingworth
Gnr Frederick Charles James
Gnr Gordon Jennings
Gnr George G Jones
Gnr Charles R Johnson
Gnr Walter Nicholas Johnson
Gnr Cecil Kaye
Gnr Thomas Marmaduke Keightley
Gnr Howard F King
Pte Bertie Augustus Kirk
Gnr Henry Walter Kirk
Gnr Frederick Thomas Paul Laming
Gnr Alexander Lawson
Gnr Cecil Laycock
Gnr William Henry Lock
Gnr Henry "Harry" Lodge
Gnr John Loving
Gnr Charles Thomas Malpress
Gnr Albert Edward Martin
Gnr D Martin
Gnr Darnley McCaig
Gnr James MacDonald
Gnr R Macintosh
Gnr Herbert G Masters
Gnr John Finlay Meldrum
Gnr John Philip Merry
Gnr John Monk
Gnr Hugh Montgomery
Gnr Walter Newington
Pte William John Nightingale ASC
Gnr John Joseph Parsons
Gnr Arnold Ross Peace
Gnr Thomas John Phillips
Gnr Reginald Ernest Pinnock
Gnr Robert John Pritchard
Gnr Herbert Charles Pryce
Gnr Arthur Thomas Prout
Gnr Robert Sainsbury Read
Gnr Francis Aubrey Rennison
Gnr William Pallister Rennison
Gnr Clifford Charles Ridout
Gnr G Roberts
Gnr John "Jack" Edward Bottle Robson
Gnr George Joseph Rogers
Gnr Arthur Max Rose

Gnr Ernest William Sandwich
Gnr Percy Tysoe Sargeant
Gnr Harry G Sanders
Gnr Hubert Savage
Gnr Albert George Selby
Gnr Maurice Hubert Shelton
Gnr Charles William Shire
Gnr George Alfred Smith
Gnr Willie Smith
Gnr Ernest Ramsden Spink
Gnr Fenwick William Styan
Gnr John Walter Sutherland.
Gnr Neville Tattersfield
Pte John Alfred Tetlow
Gnr John Thomas
Gnr Horace Thornhill
Gnr Henry James "Harry" Tiffin
Gnr Arthur Edward Till
Gnr Victor Toombs
Gnr William A Tyrer
Gnr Maurice Carter Voile
Gnr Joseph William Walker
Gnr Eddie Walton
Gnr James Walton
Gnr William Weatherill
Gnr Reginald Whalley
Gnr Alfred Edward Williams
Gnr A Wood
Gnr William Henry Wood
Gnr James Woodcock
Gnr Roderick Donald Woods
Gnr George Albert Wootley
Gnr Lionel Horace Worrall
Gnr Joseph Edward Wressell

D Company

Headquarters and attached personnel
Maj Francis James "Frank" Summers DSC
Capt Arthur Graham Woods
Lt William Jefferson "Jeff" Wakley
Lt Allan Cuthbert "Bill" Brannon
WO2 (CSM) Thomas "Paddy" Walsh
SSgt QMS Ernest Edward Victor Williams
Sgt Edwin Arthur Levey
Sgt Frederick Victor Osbourn Howe
Cpl Herbert Lane
Gnr Charles Wyld Parkes Aggis
Gnr A Barrett

Pte Augustus Frederick Brotherton
Gnr John Joseph Coles
Gnr Samuel Ernest Cotton
Gnr Cressy
Gnr Wilfred Harold Dyer
Gnr Reginald Eric Forward
Pte Vincent Thomas Gale
Gnr Walter Player Gammon
Gnr Claude Godfrey
Gnr Fred Horrocks
Gnr Wilfred Jaques
Gnr Horace Stanley Jeffrey
Gnr Meurig Gordon Jones
Gnr J Johnson
Gnr Bernard Harry Kingham
Gnr Alfred Lawrence Kitching
Pte James Luxon
Pte Edward Lord
Gnr Francis Norman Moysey
Gnr James McPartlin
Gnr Arthur Nichol
Gnr Arthur James Adams Pearce
Pte Sydney Precious
Gnr Frank Puddicombe
Pte Edwin James Reekie
Pte George Roylance
Gnr Stennett
Charles Samuel Smedley
Pte James Isaac Storey
Gnr Louis William Vince
Pte M Wicks
Pte Thomas William Wigley
Gnr Ernest George Wyatt

No 1 Section
Commander – Capt Harold Mortimore

D1 *Daredevil 1?* **(No 765 – Male)**
Capt Harold William "Morty" Mortimore
Sgt H Davies
Gnr Arthur Day
Gnr Ewart Doodson
Gnr Frederick C Hobson
Gnr Henry "Harry" Leat
Gnr Albert Smith
Pte Albert Sidney Wateridge (driver)

D2 *Daredevil 2* **(No 539 – Female)**
Lt Hugh Reginald Bell

Cpl William L Walden
Gilbert James Adamson
Pte Walter Leslie Bell
Gnr Arthur William James Branfield
Gnr James Blackwood Brunton
Gnr John Frank Letts
A/Cpl Ernest Henry Keats (driver)

D3 (No 728 male)
2Lt Harold George Head
Cpl William McNicoll
Pte William Sinclair Barrie
Pte William Thomas Bentley
Gnr Cecil Sydney Chalfont
Gnr William George "Willie" Shelton
Pte William Fritz Steer
Pte George Allen Simpson (driver)

D4 (No 516 female)
2Lt Charles Ernest Storey
LCpl Hawker
Gnr Beardmore
Gnr Oswald Clayton
Gnr Clement John Heath
Gnr Edward Cecil Merrison
Gnr Pte F J Roberts?
Pte William James Shortland (driver)

D5 *Dolphin* (No 540 female)
Lt Arthur Herbert Blowers
Cpl Edward (Ted) Foden
Gnr Edgar Robert Barnsby
Gnr Leslie Robert Gutsell
Gnr William John Hodgson
L/Cpl Frank Rodel Plant
Gnr Faraday Mendelssohn Sladdin
Pte George Henry Thomas (driver)

D6 (No 747 male)
Lt Reginald Charles Legge
LCpl Wilfred da Cuhna Brooks
Gnr Robert Percy Beesley
Gnr Fred Bardsley
Gnr Herbert Harvey Clears
Gnr George Goodwin Cook
Gnr John Harry Garner
A/Sgt Herbert Lane Thacker (driver)

No 2 Section
Commander – Capt Graeme Nixon

D7 (No 742 male)
Lt Alfred James Enoch
Cpl Charles Albert Ironmonger
Gnr Harold R Bowen
Gnr George Kenneth Hume
Gnr Alfred Lapthorne
Gnr Archibald Lee "Archie" Richards
Pte Sydney Thompson?
Pte Sydney G Barnes (driver)

D8 (No 720 male)
2Lt Herbert George Feaver "George" Bown
Cpl James Mather "Jimmy" Lindsay
Gnr Clayton
Gnr Ernest Alfred Page Didcote
Gnr William Frederick Pestell
Gnr John Morris Tennant
Pte Edward George "Eddie" Williams
Pte Bertram John Young (driver)

D9 *Dolly* (No 546 female)
2Lt Victor Huffam
LCpl Arthur Archer
LCpl Harold Sanders
Gnr Alfred William Andrew
Gnr Ronald Charles Eric Chapple
Gnr Reginald Ninian "Reg" Laverty
Gnr D Martin
Gnr Ernest John Powell
LCpl George Arthur Sanders (driver)

D10 (No 535 female)
2Lt Harold Darby
LCpl William Lauder Hogarth
Gnr Lionel George Harry Britt
Gnr Francis James "Frank" Dale
Gnr Horace John Ellocott
Gnr Robert William Frederick Cornish Frost
Gnr Leonard Haygarth
LCpl Ernest James Phillips (driver)

D11 *Die Hard* (No 547 female)
Lt Herbert George Pearsall
LCpl Harry Earle Nixon
Pte William Moss,
Pte James George Daniel Honour

ALCpl Kettle
Gnr Joseph Rowell Lee
Gnr Charles Henry Leeming
Gnr Charles Platt Stuart
Pte Frank Still (driver)

D12 *Dreadnought* (No 719 male)
Capt Graeme Nixon
Sgt Reginald John Vandenberg
Gnr Horace Augustus Allebone
Gnr William Bertram Debenham
Gnr Cecil Frederick Gloyn
Gnr John Victor Mead
Gnr Harry Zimmerman
Cpl Robert R Murray (driver)

D13 *Delilah* (No 548 female)
2Lt William Henry "Billy" Sampson
Cpl Harper
Gnr William Phipps Chandler
Gnr William Frank "Frank" Dival
Gnr Frederick Charles Mays
Gnr Samuel Pick
Gnr Harry Ironfield Yates
LCpl Alfred Philip Bloomfield (driver)

No 3 Section
Commander – Capt Stephen Sellick

D14 (No 534 female)
2Lt Gordon Frederick Court
Sgt Robert Baden Pebody
Gnr William Robert Henty Barber
LCpl Thomas Cromack
Gnr Joseph Elliot Crowe
Gnr Andrew Charles Lawson
Gnr George Monro Mann
LCpl Lawrence William Upton (driver)

D15 (No 537 female)
Lt John Lionel "Jack" Bagshaw
LCpl Charley Frederick Jung
Gnr Charles Edward Bond
Gnr Cyril William Coles
Gnr Charles William Hoban
Gnr Arthur Smith
Gnr Tom Fleming "Tippo" Wilson
Pte Albert Rowe (driver)

D16 *Dracula* **(No 538 female)**
Lt Arthur Edmund Arnold
Cpl E A White
Gnr Collett
Gnr Douglas
Gnr Cecil Frost
Gnr Jacob "Jake" Glaister
Gnr McKenzie
Gnr F J Roberts
Pte Samuel Henry Robert Workman (driver)

D17 *Dinnaken* **(No 759 male)**
Lt Stuart Henderson Hastie
Cpl Edward J Sheldon
Gnr Eric Pauncefort Blake
Gnr Percy Boult
Gnr Frederick "Fred" Gomersall
Gnr Alfred Henry Roy Reiffer
Gnr William Frederick Sugden
Pte Charles Albert Wescomb (driver)

D18 (No 743 male)
2Lt Leonard Charles "Len" Bond
Cpl Paul
Gnr Morgan
Gnr Perkins
Gnr Arthur Race
Gnr Thornton
Gnr Sydney Philip Wenmoth
Pte Frederick Burrows (driver)

D19 (No 753 male)
Capt Stephen Scott Sellick
Cpl Charles Walter Luck
Gnr James Anthony "Jim" Blackmore
Gnr JW Brown
Gnr Henry Chapman
Gnr John Cameron Tolson
Gnr James Westmacott
Pte Thomas Hinds (driver)

No 4 Section
Commander – Capt George Mann

D20 *Daphne* **(No 744 male)**
2Lt Harry Cecil Frank Drader
Cpl Owen Frank W Rowe
Gnr Walter William Atkins
Gnr Joseph William Clark

Gnr Roland George "Rol" Elliott
Gnr Ernest Herbert "Herbert" Statham
Pte Frank Rusby Styring
Pte Alfred James Bowerman (driver)

D21 Delphine (No 512? female)
Lt Alexander Easson Sharp
Cpl Harold Bertram Wigley
Gnr George Charles Foote
Gnr Albert Harry Hales
Gnr George Moscrop
Gnr John Preston
Gnr Shepherd
Pte Herbert Ernest Wilson (driver)

D22 (No 756 male)
Lt Frederick Andrew "Eric" Robinson
Cpl Dudley Nevill White
Gnr James Anderson
Gnr John William Applegate
Gnr Jack Choules
Gnr Lawson
Gnr Percy Raworth
Pte Ernest Cecil Howes (driver)

D23 (No 528 female)
Capt George William Mann
Sgt Nicholson
Gnr Little
Gnr Parkin
Gnr John Barnes Starkey
Gnr Henry Clifford Tillotson
Gnr Douglas Benson Tweddle
Pte Osmond Woodford "Jack" Rossiter (driver)

D24 (751 male)
Lt Walter Stones
Sgt Meyrick
Gnr Robert Steele Coffey
Gnr William Ernest "Billy" Foster
Gnr Hardy
Gnr Leslie Richard Reeve
Gnr Frederick Joseph Rule
Gnr John Thomas Wells
Pte Frederick George Wood (driver)

D25 (No 511 female)
2Lt Edward Carl Kestell Colle
Cpl Henry Thomas Frederick Reynolds

Gnr Bell
Gnr Garner
Gnr James Brunton Petrie
Gnr Herbert Routledge
Gnr Wilkie
Pte John Maude (driver)

Appendix E

The Naming of Tanks

Tanks were often named by their crews, the initial letter usually being the same as the name of the company. In 1916, all of C company tanks used the letter C as the initial letter; likewise D company's tanks names started with D. These names were often re-used as tanks were either destroyed in action or replaced by newer variants in service with C Battalion or D Battalion or later with 3rd Light Battalion and 4th Battalion Tank Corps.

   This annex only records the names of those used in September 1916 or those of tanks identified later which probably fought at Flers – Courcelette. The original names sometimes had a personal link to the commander or his family but the derivation of others is not known

C Company

Name and derivation (where known)	Commander's Name	Crew and Section	Remarks
Campania – named after a region in southern Italy.	2Lt Jack Clarke	C17 of No 3 Section	A picture of a Male Mark 1 tank, with the number C17 and the name HMLS Campania on the glacis, is held by the Victoria Museum in Australia. Her name is also recorded in the diaries of two Australian soldiers who saw the hulk in late 1916 and spring 1917.
Canada	Unknown	Unknown	Female tank 521, with the name HMLS Canada was at Rollencourt in May 1917.
Casa – named after the Smith's family home in Reading	2Lt Victor Smith	C18 of No 3 Section	Name was regularly used by C Battalion for replacement tanks
Chablis	2Lt Geordie Campbell	C5 of No 1 Section	All No 1 Section's tanks were named after French drinks
Champagne	Lt Alfred Wheeler	C1 of No 1 Section	See Chablis
Chartreuse	2Lt Stanley Clarke	C3 of No 1 Section	See Chablis
Clan Leslie – named after the skipper's mother's clan	Capt Archie Holford-Walker	C19 of No 4 Section	

Name and derivation (where known)	Commander's Name	Crew and Section	Remarks
Clan Ruthven – derivation unknown. The name means Clan Chief	2Lt Andrew Henderson	C23 of No 4 Section	Henderson was a Scot from Perthshire.
Cognac	Lt Bill Bluemel	C2 of No 1 Section	See Chablis
Cordon Rouge	2Lt John Allen	C6 of No 1 Section	See Chablis
Corunna – unknown	2Lt Eric Purdy	C16 of No 3 Section?	Corunna was the site of a major British delaying action in 1809 during the Napoleonic war
Créme de Menthe	Capt Arthur Inglis	C5 of No 1 Section	See Chablis

D Company

Name and derivation (where known)	Commander's Name	Crew and Section	Remarks
Daphne	Lt Harry Drader	D20 of No 3 Section	Tank name identified in the film the Battle of Ancre and by war correspondents reporting on the action at Eaucourt L'Abbaye on 1 October 1916
Daredevil 1 – derivation unknown	Capt Harold Mortimore	D1 of No 1 Section	
Daredevil II	2Lt Hugh Bell	D2 of No 1 Section	
Delilah – named after biblical character married to Samson	2Lt Billy Sampson	D13 – reserve tank	
Delphine – derivation unknown	2Lt Alex Sharp	D21 of No 4 section	
Delysia – probably named after the popular French actress Irene Delysia	Unknown	Unknown	This tank was identified by war correspondents reporting on the action at Eaucourt L'Abbaye. A replacement tank named Delysia was commanded by Lt Alfred Enoch in the Ypres Salient
Die-Hard – possibly named after the motto of the Middlesex Regiment	2Lt George Pearsall	D11 of No 2 Section	
Dinnaken – Scottish idiolect term for "I do not know".	2Lt Stuart Hastie	D17 of No 3 Section	According to Hastie's step-daughter, the tank was not named until after the first action; the name was given in response to a question by a reporter.
Dodo	Unknown	Unknown	See Daphne

Name and derivation (where known)	Commander's Name	Crew and Section	Remarks
Dolly – Huffam's fiancée was called Dorothy	2Lt Victor Huffam	D9 of No 2 Section	
Dolphin	2Lt Arthurs Blowers	D5 of No 1 Section	Derivation unknown
Donner und Blitzen			From the German "Thunder and Lightning"
Dracula	Lt Arthur Arnold	D16 of No 3 Section	Derivation unknown
Dragonfly	Unknown	Unknown	A picture of the crew of Dragonfly II, with their skipper Herbert Chick and including Willie Shelton was taken in summer 1917 probably near Ypres. Given that she is the third tank of the name, it is almost certain that a predecessor fought with D Company in 1916
Dreadnought – from the name of the British battleship	Capt Graeme Nixon	D12 of No 2 Section	

A Note on Sources

Piecing together the lives of the First Tank Crews has been a fascinating but sometime frustrating challenge. I have used a mix of official records, newspaper articles, regimental histories and specialist websites but the most illuminating information has come from the soldiers' families.

When I started my search for the crewmen in 2003, I was unaware of the book which would become my lodestone: Trevor Pidgeon's magnum opus *The Tanks at Flers* (TAF). I came across Trevor's impressively researched work through his website but getting hold of a copy of the book proved a challenge. Copies are rarely for sale but I found one in the Tank Museum's Archives (TMA) from which I obtained the names of the majority of those in C and D Companies. Three years later, when I met Trevor and showed him my early research, he encouraged me to press on. After his untimely death in 2011, his widow Marion urged me to continue and donated Trevor's initial notes. To this day, I return to these whenever I discover a new and puzzling piece of information. The TMA also held a copy of the landing lists (LL) of C Company officers and other ranks who landed in France on 14 and 26 August 1916. However, this list is not complete as it omits the members of C Company and 711 Company who travelled with the tanks. The TMA however holds the original notebook (GWNB) maintained by the Adjutant of D Company Graham Woods and his pocket diary, both of which provide the surnames of tank crews and detailed information on the attached ASC personnel.

Undertaking original research relies on finding accurate sources. Official documents, such as the record of Soldiers who died in the Great War (SDGW), provide only limited details of the soldiers surname, service number, place of enlistment and date of death. Whilst this source, especially the volume relating to the Machine Gun Corps (MGC) and Tank Corps, is limited, it becomes more effective when linked with the records held by the Commonwealth War Graves Commission (CWGC) although here, again, the names of next of kin are not always published. The C Company War Diary (WD) is generally less detailed that that of D Company but, after the war, the officers established an Old Comrades Association (OCA) which, in 1925, published a list of members and in most cases, their addresses. Ten years later C Company's commander, Allen Holford-Walker also provided information on the formation and training of his company to the editor of the British official history of the Great War, Military Operations: France and Belgium, 1916 Volume 2, which provides remarkably clear and concise comments on the difficulties faced by his officers during their first action.

Medal Index Cards (MIC), saved from destruction by the Western Front Association (WFA), together with lists of awards of the Silver War Badge (SWB) and Medal Rolls published by the National Archives at Kew (NAK), have been invaluable. NAK also holds the Burnt Records (SBR) i.e. those soldiers' personal files which were not destroyed during the Blitz and which are now available on the *Ancestry* and *Find My Past* websites. The *Ancestry* website has also recently published the Army Register of Soldiers Effects (ARSE) which can be cross-referenced to the CWGC and SDGW. I have also accessed those officers' records in the War Office (WO) file series WO 339 and WO 364 although most of those who served after 1919 are not available to the public. I have also accessed the post war records of those officers who later served in the Indian Army (IA) and Indian Civil Service (ICS) which are held by the British Library as well as correspondence between B.H.

Liddell-Hart (L-H) and several of the First Tank Crews in preparation of his history of the Royal Tank Regiment held in the Liddell-Hart archive at King's College London.

The *London Gazette* (LG) website has provided details of promotion and citations for officers' gallantry medals whilst the Tank Corps Book of Honour (TCBH) provided similar details relating to other ranks. Registration dates of birth (BR), marriage (MR) and death (DR) have been obtained from the indexes held by General Register Office (GRO) and National Records of Scotland Office whilst the LG has provided Probate Records (PRs). The digital *London Times* (LT) and *British Newspaper Archive* (BNF) website have revealed details from family announcements as have local Christening Records (CR) and Burial Records (BR). Many of the First Tank Crews were recruited through *The Motor Cycle*; a weekly newspaper published in Coventry whose editor Geoffrey Smith was authorised to select suitable experienced mechanics, drivers and motorcyclist for service in mechanised units. *The Motor Cycle* published the names of successful applicants which enables the dates of enlistment to be determined. Local newspapers, accessed through the *British Newspaper Archive*, have also provided details of death, wounding and decorations, as well as letters by soldiers to their families and later printed. The Imperial War Museum (IWM) holds one such the letter from Leonard Viner, and I thank the Reading Room staff for their assistance in viewing this, the information relating to Edward Colle and the transcriptions of BBC interviews undertaken with Roy Reiffer and Victor Smith in the 1960s

A major source of information is the *Great War Forum* (GWF) whose members readily share information, advice and experiences good and bad. One of the first I lessons I was taught was "Never trust a caption on a photograph"; the second was "Sharing information pays dividends" and these lessons still apply. Guides and mentors on the GWF have included Steve Beeby, Gwyn Evans, Alwyn Killingworth, Vince McGarry, Gerald Moore and John Taylor. It was through the GWF that I met Simon Payne and Geoffrey Churcher, collectors of early Tanker's medals, who have not only shared their research but have accompanied me on visits to the battlefields over which the Tankers fought in France. I also met two specialists on the tank actions in Belgium through the GWF. Chris Lock, who was the driving force behind the erection of the Tank Memorial in the Ypres Salient (TMYS), and Jan Vanbeselaere who has built a superb replica Mark IV tank, have offered guidance and information about the Tankers who fought in the Ypres Salient in 1917.

Many of those Tankers who fought at the Battle of Flers-Courcelette went on to serve, four-teen months later, at Cambrai. For the many, including most journalists and even some soldiers, Cambrai was the first time that tanks were used in action. As a result I have often been contacted for information about Tank Corps soldiers who fought in November 1917. Several books have been written about this key action, which I have used as references, but the seminal work is *Following The Tanks* (FTT) by Jean-Luc Gibot and Philippe Gorczynski. As a boy, Philippe was bought up on the battlefield and heard stories of tanks which had been buried after the Armistice. After years of diligent research, Phillip located and excavated one such tank near Flesquières. The tank was identified by David Fletcher who has been, for many years, the historian at the Tank Museum at Bovington. Philippe has guided many relatives and other enthusiasts and made them welcome at the *Hotel Beatus* in Cambrai. He has also been wholly supportive of my research as has David Fletcher whose knowledge of tanks is unequalled. Finally, I must acknowledge the huge value of the help provided by Rob Martin as well as his unequalled research into tank actions from 1916-1918 which is available to all through his website *Google Landships*.

Sharing information through the internet is seen by some as a double-edged sword but, from my first tentative steps on *Genes Reunited* and later the *Ancestry* websites, I have provided information about tank crewmen which was unknown to relatives and they have responded by sharing family details. In 2009, when I started to publish original research through the *First Tank Crew* website, I took the risk that its content could be plagiarised. However, whilst this material is often "refer-enced" by other researchers, the website has not been published. More importantly, through the website, I have made contact with several families whose relatives served with C and D Companies and thereby gained otherwise unpublished material or photographs.

In pulling together individual details from such a wide ranging set of sources, I have identified a number of discrepancies and contradictions, some of which I have been unable to resolve. Whilst the information in this book is as accurate as possible, it is not at all complete as I have been unable to identify all the crewmen and I have inadvertently made errors which I will happily amend. I would also welcome information from other families, whose relatives I have been unable to identify in any great detail, to contact me though FirstTankCrews.com, so that I can add the missing information and let their story be commemorated and celebrated.

C COMPANY PERSONNEL

Company Headquarters
Maj Allen Holford-Walker; BC, BR, 1891, 1901 and 1911 census, LG (various dates), MC, MR, MIC, LT (various dates), Kenyan Gazette 1929 and 1937, PR.

Capt Richard Earl Williams: BR; 1891, 1901 and 1911 census, LG (various dates), LL, MR, MC, MIC, Medal Roll, OCA 1925, Divorce Record (NAK) and DR, Family information from John Taylor.

Capt Richard Ewart Trevithick: BR, 1891, 1901 and 1911 census, LG (various dates), WO339 /10620, MR (1917), MC, PR.

2Lt Theodore Lateriner Wenger: BR, 1891, 1901 and 1911 census, LG (various dates), WO 339 / 61414, LT various dates, PR.

Lt Charles Weaver-Price: BR, 1891, 1901 and 1911 census, *Brecon and Radnor Express* (various dates 1914 – 1916), LG (various dates), LT (various dates), MR 1906, MR 1925, CWGC and PR. *Tanks and Trenches* page 70-72 (ed Fletcher) quoting "Q reminiscences" by Charles Weaver-Price first published in the Tank Journal in 1921.

2Lt Robert John Aitken: BC, CR, 1901 and 1911 census, LG (various dates), WO339 / 58819, SWB and DR.

CSM Joseph Hackett: LL, LG (various dates), Army List 1919, *Tank* Journal 1955.

Sgt Gordon Ferguson Bainbridge: BC, 1901 and 1911 census, WO339 / 120996, LG (various dates), OCA 1925 and further information from eamemorials707@gmail,com

SQMS Harry Wolfe Jacobs: 1911 census, WO339 / 91984, LG (various dates), MIC, MR.

Sgt James David Smith Anderson: BC, 1901 census, MR, MIC and OCA 1925. Family information from Peter Anderson and Patti Ann Nordgren; Burma Army information from Stephen Rothwell.

Sgt Albert William Bedford: BR, 1901 and 1911 census, LL, *The Motor Cycle* dated 7 June 1917, WO339 / 122866, MC, London Electoral Rolls 1920 and 1928 – 1963 and DR.

Sgt Robert Hillhouse: BC, 1901 and 1911 census, MC, LL, LG (6 Jan 1917), MICs x 2, CWGC, *Denny and Dunipace Roll of Honour* page 55.

Sgt Alfred Edward Howard: CR, MC, 1901 and 1911 census, LL, SBR and Medal Roll.

Sgt James Albert John MacGregor: BR, 1901 and 1911 census, LL and SBR.

Sgt James Noel: LL, LG (various dates), OCA 1925, Tank Magazine 1919 and 1966.

Sgt Edgar Parry Williams: BC, 1911 census and SBR.

NO 1 SECTION

C1 Champagne (No 721 male)
Lt Alfred George Clark Wheeler: 1901 and 1911 census, WO339 / 40734, LG (various dates), LT (various dates), MC, telephone directories 1946-1959 and DR.

Sgt Frederick John Saker, BC, 1891, 1901 and 1911 census, LL, SBR, LG, MC, telephone direc-
tories (various dates) and DC, Family information provided by nephews Les Crow and Keith
Wickham.
Gnr Ernest Hubert Bax: CR, 1901 and 1911 census, LL, LG (various dates), MC, London elec-
toral rolls and PR.
Gnr George Lloyd: BR, 1901 and 1911 census, LL, SBR, MC and DR.
Gnr Herbert Rothera: BR, 1911 census, SBR, LL, MR, telephone directories (various dates), PR.
Family information from Trevor Guest.
Gnr William Neilson Smith: LL, LG (14 November 1916), SBR, MC and OCA 1925.
Gnr Frederick Cecil Stone: BR, CR, 1911 census, LL, SBR, MR, Belper telephone directories
(various dates).
Pte Horace Brotherwood, BC, 1901 and 1911 census, MIC, SDGW, CWGC, ARSE 247668 and
Woking News and Mail 6 October 1916. Family information provided by Colin Charman.

C2 Cognac (No 522 female)
2Lt Frank William Bluemel: CR, 1891, 1901 and 1911 census, LG (various dates), WO339 /
42105, MC, Bluemel, Company records (various dates), Tank Magazine 1957 and PR.
Sgt Arthur Jennings Osborne Milliken: BC, 1891, 1901 and 1911 census, SBR, LG dated 9 July
1917, TCBH, MR, DR and BR. *Tank* journal dated February 1955 pp 159 – 160. Family information provided by Mrs M Milliken, his daughter in law.
LCpl Harold Edwin Teft: BR, 1901 and 1911 census, LL, WO339 / 112606, MR, MIC, Kelly's
directory for Lincolnshire 1926 and mother's PR. Family information provided by Philip and
Michael Teft (grandson and great-grandson).
Gnr Victor Stanley Archard: BR, 1901 and 1911 census, LL, SBR, Diary and letters held by the
TMA, SWB, MIC, MC and PR, telephone directory 1939 and DR. Family information
provided by his grandson Graham Archard.
Gnr Robert Thomas Caldicott: CR, 1891 census, SBR, MR, Kelly's directories for Birmingham
1930 and 1935-1945 and DR.
Gnr Alfred Ernest Hemington: BR, 1891, 1901 and 1911 census, SBR, LL, Kelly's directory for
Sheffield 1923-1925 and DR.
Gnr A Sims: *The Motor Cycle* dated 31 March 1916 and LL.
Gnr Donald James Thompson: BR, MC, 1911 census, LL, SBR, OCA 1915, Burial Record and
PR.
Pte Herbert Ledger, BR, 1991 and 1901 census, TCBH and DR. Medal information from Howard
Williamson.

C3 "Chartreuse" (No 701 male)
2Lt Stanley Darrell Houghton Clarke, BR: 1901 and 1911 census, WO339 / 31579, MC and PR.
Cpl Reginald Frank Shaw: BR, 1911 census, LL, WO 339 / 85535, LG (various dates), Tank
Journal 1919 and PR. Eccleshall information provided by Pat Trevor.
Gnr Ernest John Edwards: BR, 1901 and 1911 census, LL, SBR and OCA 1925.
Gnr Alexander James Garden: LL, SBR, LG, TCBH, *Aberdeen Evening Express* dated 15 November
1918 and Edinburgh Gazette dated May 1919.
Gnr Charles Frederick Phillips: *The Motor Cycle* dated 28 November 1915, LL and Medal Roll.
Gnr Alfred Bernard Simpson: CR, 1901 and 1911 census, LL, SBR, LG dated 14 November 1916,
correspondence with Liddell-Hart 1957, *The Boilerplate War* – John Foley and PR.
Gnr George Kidd Stonehouse: BR, SBR, LL, Edinburgh telephone directories 1950s and PR.
Pte Alfred Boult: 1881, 1891, 1901 and 1911 census, SBR, LL and PR.

C4 "Chablis" (No 503 female)

2Lt George Osmond Lorne Campbell (later Mackie-Campbell): BR, Burke's Peerage, LG (Various dates), LT (various dates), Company records (various dates) and PR.

Cpl Charles Norman Harrison: LL, TCBH, LG (January 1919) and MC.

Gnr Reginald James Acock: BR, 1891, 1901 and 1911 census, LL, SBR, LG (2 November 1917), MC and DR. Family information and photographs provided by grandson John Aycock.

Gnr William Francis Boylin: BR, LL, WO374/8295 LG (various dates), MC, PR. South African motorcycle information and image provided by Derek Stuart-Findlay.

Gnr William Cheadle: CR, 1891, 1901 and 1911 census, Father's PR. LL, MR, Exeter telephone directories 1927 – 32, Undated 1961 *Herald Express* cutting provided by Mrs Mary Mortimore and DR.

Gnr Charles Augustus Arthur Kidd: BC, 1901 and 1991 census, LL, SBR, MIC, MC, London elector's register from 1921 to 1947 and DR. Family information provided by his grand-daughter Catherine Jenner, medals held by Geoffrey Churcher.

Gnr John Warmington Makin: BR, 1901 census, *The Motor Cycle* dated 28 November 1915, LL, TCBH, SWB, MIC, Medal Rolls, OCA 1925 and mother's PR.

Gnr Frank Richard Pickworth: BC, 1911 census, LL, TCBH, *Nottingham Evening Post* dated 18 January 1919, Aviva Roll of Honour, MR and PR.

Pte Daniel Cronin: BR and LG dated 19 March 1918, Family information provided by his Granddaughter Ann.

C5 "Crème de Menthe" (No 721 male)

Capt Arthur Maculloch Inglis: BC, Parent's divorce papers (NAK), 1901 and 1911 census, LL, GWNB, LG (various dates), WO 339 / 5602, TCBH, *War History of the Sixth Tank Battalion*, CWGC and ARSE 53542.

Cpl Ronald Roderick Garlick: 1911 census, *The Motor Cycle* dated 28 November 1915, LL, MC, TCBH, LG (various dates). Family information and Garlick company correspondence provided by his daughter Gill Doddington and his great-niece Sherry Garlick Stanton. South African motorcycle information provided by Derek Stuart-Findlay.

Gnr Ronald Gibson: BR, 1911 census record, LL, RFC service record.

Gnr Lionel Hemsworth McAdam: Landing record at London 30 Aug 15, SBR and LL. Family information, *The Motorcycle (Toronto)* dated July and August 1919 and photographs provided by Sue Handley, Peter McAdam and Barbara Slate – grandchildren of Lionel McAdam.

Gnr Laurence Edmund Rowntree: WO339 / 81977, CWGC, SDGW, ARSE 35055, *Gunfire* No 10 – A J Peacock – Northern Branch WFA.

Gnr Joseph Shepherd: BR, 1901 and 1911 census, SBR, LL.

Gnr William Hughes Stockdale, BR, 1901 and 1911 census, LL, WO339/93710, LG (various dates), MR, OCA 1925, Various dates Telephone Directories 1938 to 1953 and then 1955 to 1964, PR. Photograph provided by his grand-daughter Caroline Peake.

ACpl George Bentley Shepherd, BR, 1901 and 1911 census, SBR, LG dated 14 November 1916 and *Western Gazette* dated 5 December 1919.

C6 "Cordon Rouge" (No 504 female)

Lt John Allan: WO 339 / 59888, LG (various dates), SDGW and CWGC.

A/Cpl Francis George Vyvyan: BR, 1901 and 1911 census, LL, LG (Various dates), OCA 1925, MC x 2, Canadian Immigration Record dated 18 March 1924, Canadian census record 1940 and CBC Vancouver BC Entertainment Hall of Hall.

Gnr Henry James Bedford: SBR and LL.

Gnr Ernest Albert Hunt: BR, 1901 and 1911 census, WO 339 / 93706, LG (Various). Family information and photographs by his grandson Cosmo Corfield.

Gnr Arthur Frederick Jakins: CR, 1901 and 1911 census, LG, SBR, LL, London electoral rolls 1922-1939 and DR.

Gnr William Jones: MIC.

Gnr Clarence George Kilminster: CR, 1901 and 1911 census, SDGW, CWGC, Scottish National War Memorial and *Gloucestershire Chronicle* 19 May 1917.

Gnr Victor Cecil Newby: CR, 1901 census, SBR, LL, MR, immigration records 1936 and 1958.

Pte Joseph Barton: MIC.

NO 2 SECTION

No 507 female
Capt Herbert Henry Hiscocks: CR, 1911 census, LG (various dates), MIC, LL, WO 339 / 34592, MC and PR.

No 722 male
2Lt Alec Leslie Arnaud: 1901 and 1911 census, LG (various dates), MR, OCA 1915, various telephone directories and DR.

No 513 female
2Lt Thomas Frederick Murphy: 1891, 1901 and 1911 census, WO 339 / 65057, MIC, ICRC POW record, London UOTC Roll of Honour and PR.

No 714 male
2Lt Leonard John Bates: 1891 and 1901 census, SS *Lusitania* passenger record 12 December 1914, LG (various dates), LL, LT 1 Nov 16, *Irish Independent* dated 12 November 1917, Court of Inquiry Report 13 November 1917, WO 339 / 60304, MIC, Information on Birkenhead School provided by Stephen Roberts.

No 760 male
Lt Herbert Benbow Elliot: 1911 census, MC, *The Motor Cycle* dated 22 June 1916, WO 339 / 22861, LT (various dates), OCA 1925 and DR.

No 554 female
2Lt Charles Frederick Nelson Ambrose, BR, 1901 census, LG (various dates), WO339 / 31566, London telephone directories 1927-34, MC and PR. Family information provided by his daughter Rosalind.

NO 3 SECTION

C13 (No 716 male)
Lt Sir John Lindsay Dashwood BT: Burke's Peerage, WO 339/13517, LG (various dates), *Tank* journal dated February 1955 pp 159 – 160. Menu of 2nd Annual Reunion of C Battalion 29 Jan 1921, MC, and PR. Image of christening by National Portrait Gallery.

C14 (No 509 female)
Lt Francis James Arnold: CR, 1901 and 1911 census, MIC, LL, LG (various dates), OCA 1925, MR, Son's BC, PR. Medals held by Geoffrey Churcher.

Cpl Gerald Edmonds Pattinson: BR, 1891 and 1911 census, CWGC, SDGW, ARSE 396518 and Allen Holford-Walker papers (NAM).

Gnr Thomas Herbert Firth Bernard: BR, 1901 census, LL, MR, LG (various dates), DR. Family information provided by his son Tom Bernard. Individual photographs courtesy of his son Tom Bernard.

Gnr Bertie Arthur Garnett Giles: BC, 1901 and 1911 census, LL, MIC, CWGC, SDGW and ARSE 398356.

Gnr Arthur James Ritchie: BC, CR, 1901 and 1911 census, LL, MIC, CWGC, SDGW, ARSE 400846 and PR.

Gnr William Williams: LL and LG (14 November 1916).

Gnr Denton Joseph Winter: BR, 1891, 1901 and 1911 census, SBR, LL MC, Leeds telephone directories 1945 to 1971, PR. Family information provided by ScotsMarie of Romsey.

Pte Owen Alfred Sleath ASC: CR, 1911 census, MR and PR.

C15 (No 741 male)

2Lt Jethro Edward Tull: BR, 1901 census, WO 339 / 42309, UK passenger landing lists for 19 September 1938, 17 October 1938 and 14 August 1945, wife's PR and PR.

C16 "Corunna?" (No 510 female)

2Lt Eric Layton Purdy: MIC, War Diary 1st Battalion Northampton 13 Oct 15, LL, LG (various dates), Willies Concert Party programme 1917, MR, Menu of 2nd Annual Reunion of C Battalion 29 Jan 1921 (TMA), London electoral roll 1921 to 1925, 1929, OCA 1925, 1930 RTR Dinner lists 1938, Northants Regt service information provided by Steve Beeby, BR.

Gnr William Harcourt Piper: BR, 1881, 1901 and 1901 census, SBR, SWB, Scrap book held by TMA.

C17 (No 745 male)

Lt John Peard "Jack" Clarke: BR, 1901 census, WO 339 / 16430, LG (various dates), Taunton *Courier* dated 4 September 1918, Yorkshire Ramblers Club membership lists, passenger list SS *Watusi* dated 8 November 1934, *Kenyan Gazette* Nov 1936 and Dec 1938 plus BR.

Pte George Leonard Marlow Viner, BR, CR, 1901 and 1911 census, MR, Letter dated 18 September 1918 held by IWM, MIC, Medal Roll, Son's MC, PR. Family information provided by grandson Mark Viner.

C18 "Casa" (No 508 female)

2Lt Louis Victor Smith: BR, 1901 census, WO 339 / 31764, letter to sister Vera on Wed 22 March 1916, LT (Various dates), MR, *Reading Standard* dated 30 April 1921, OCA 1925, Huntley, Boorne and Stevens' company reports (various dates), *Reading Standard* dated 5 June 1953 and DR, family information and photograph provided by Mrs Paddi Lilley (daughter).

Cpl Douglas James Gardiner: BR, 1901 and 1911 census, LL SBR, MR, 50th anniversary dinner night at Caxton hall on 15 September 1966 and DR.

Gnr George Arthur Caffrey: BR, 1901 and 1911 census, LL, TCBH, CWGC, *Cambrian Times* articles dated 27 August 1915, 29 September 1916, 13 October 1915, 10 November 1916, 11 May 1916 and 20 September 1918, associated family information provided by Richard Williams.

Gnr Harry Greenberg: LL, MIC.

Gnr William Scott: BC, 1901 and 1911 census, LL, SBR, OCA 1925, photograph provided by Geoffrey Churcher.

Gnr John Pierce Webby: BR, 1891 and 1901 census, LL, SBR, MC and DR.

Gnr John Alfred Witty: BR, 1891 and 1911 census, LL, SBR, TCBH, LG dated 24 Jan 1919, DR.

NO 4 SECTION

C19 "Clan Leslie" (No 705 male)
Capt (Bruce) Archie Holford-Walker: BC, LG (various dates), LL, Willies Concert Party
Programme, F Battalion dinner menu for 27 June 17, 12 Bn Tank Corps War History, 3 Bn
RTC history, Army lists 1916-21, various telephone directories, Indian Army Staff lists 1927
– 32 and PR.
Gnr Robert S (Bob) Tate: BR, 1901 census, SBR, LL, MC, Oral history Interview in 1974
(University of Leeds tape record 1677/444).

C20 (No 523 –female)
Lt George Macpherson: WO 339/41602, BC, 1901 census, SDGW, *Huntly Express* October 1916
and 1921, http://www.winchestercollegeatwar.com/archive/george-macpherson. *Rewriting
history* by Colin Hardy in Stand To Number 89 August / September 2010.
Gnr William Taylor Dawson: BR, 1901 census, WO 339/136333, Family information and
photographs from Audrey Mitchell, Sybil Robilliard (daughters) and Rosemary Mitchell
(granddaughter).

C21 (No 740 – male)
Lt Harold Hubert Vincent: LL, LG (various dates) MIC, LT (various dates), *Straits Times of
Singapore* 21 September 1932, London Electoral Rolls, DR.

C22 (no 533 – female)
2Lt Basil Lucas Quixano Henriques: BR, census 1901 and 1911, MR, LG (various dates), LT
(various dates) and PR. *Tanks and Trenches* (ed David Fletcher) pp 12- 14. *Indiscretions of a
Warden* – Henriques; *Basil Henriques – a portrait based on his diaries, letters and speeches as collated
by his widow*, Loewe. *Henriques papers 1894-1970s* – Southampton University Library special
collection. Photographs from Jewish Museum of London.
Cpl Roger Paterson: BR, LL, SBR.
Gnr Reginald Harry Fisher: BR, 1901 and 1911 census, LL, SBR, MR, OCA 1925, PR.
Gnr Frank Edwin Raynor: BR, 1901 census, LL, MIC.

C23 "Clan Ruthven" (male tank number unknown)
2Lt Andrew Morris Henderson: BC, 1901 census, WO 339/58862, LG (various dates), MIC,
OCA 1925, Passenger lists for 5 June 1920 and 20 March 1930, MR, DR.

C24 "Clan Cameron" (No 512? – female)
Lt Harold Ralph Clement Cole: BC, MC, 1891, 1901 and 1911 census, LL, WO 339/51919, LG
(Various dates), MIC, PR.

The following crewmen were recorded as serving with C Company but their allocation to individual tanks is unknown

Corporals
A/Cpl James William Battell: BR, 1901 and 1911 census, LL, MIC, MR, London Electoral Roll
1934, DR.
Cpl W Clare: *The Motor Cycle* dated 28 November 1915 and LL.
Cpl Wilfred Clarence Edwards: CR, 1911 census, LL, SBR, *Coventry Evening Telegraph* dated 7
December 1918, LG dated 24 January 1919, MIC and DR.

Cpl Leonard Charles Groutage: BR, CR, 1901 and 1911 census, LL, WO 339/88168, LG (various dates), MC, *Irish Independent* 9 June 1933, additional information provided by Pat Gallagher.

Cpl Charles Harmer: LL, MIC.

Cpl T Hamer: LL, MIC.

Cpl George Thomson Kennedy: BC, 1891 and 1911 census, LL, SBR, TCBH, MIC, MR, DR.

Cpl Charles Thomas Lowe: DR, LL, SBR, TCBH, Birmingham electoral roll 1922, MR, passenger list SS *Borda* January 1929, family information by Pauline Rowe and Sylvia Wills.

Cpl Frank Short: BR, LL, WO339 / 101386, MIC, London Electoral Roll 1932, 1935 and 1945.

Cpl William C Smith RAMC: LL, MIC.

Cpl Clement Hugh Tinker: BR, London school records for 1896 and 1902, 1911 census, LL, SBR, IRCR POW record, Battersea absent voters lists 1918 and 1919, MR, OCA 1925, Passenger records for July 1955, 1958 and 1960, Various dates telephone directories, PR.

Lance Corporals

LCpl Robert George Carruthers: BR, LL, SBR, MIC (refused to accept his medals), OCA, British Geological Society (BGS) records, family details provided by his son Robert Carruthers, image courtesy of BGS.

LCpl John Charles Adam Farquharson: BR, 1911 census, LL, WO 374/ 23640, Aberdeen University Roll of Honour, MR, Various dates telephone directories, DR.

LCpl George Henry Marchant: LL, MIC.

LCpl Charles Ernest Spurgeon: BR, 1901 and 1911 census, LL, WO 374/64620, LG(Various dates), 3rd Light Battalion tank Corps Way History, 5 Tank Supply Company War Diary, US naturalization records 1925, MC, DR.

Gunners

Gnr Harold George Adams: BR, CR, 1911 census, LL, MIC, OCA 1925, DR.

Gnr Edward Lawrence Appleby: BR, 1911 census, LL, SBR, OCA 1925, MR, PR, family information provided by Peter Kay.

Gnr John Armistead: BR, CR, 1901 census, MR, LL, SBR, MIC, *LCC Record of War service,* London electoral roll 1920 to 1936 and PR.

Gnr Ralph William Baker: BR, 1891 and 1911 census, LL, MIC, OCA 1925, Kelly's directory for Bowden 1929.

Gnr George Hugh Bissett: BR, 1891 and 1901 census, LL, SBR, OCA 1925, DR.

Gnr Wilfred E Bolingbroke: BR, 1901 and 1911 census, LL, SDGW, CWGC, ARSE 810893.

Gnr James Alfred Booth: BR, 1901 census, MR, LL and SBR, MIC.

Gnr Raymond Bothway: CR, 1901 census, MIC, MC and DR.

Gnr John Joseph Bowker: BR, LL, SBR, DR, photograph provided by Simon Gildea from location of grave maintained by John's great niece Delia.

Gnr Harry Broster: BR, 1901 and 1911 census, LL, SBR, OCA 1925, DR.

Gnr Charles Frank Bull: MGC, CR, 1891, 1901 and 1911 census, LL, C Coy HS MGC War Diary, SDGW, CWGC, ARSE 379876.

Gnr John Bernard Callaghan: BR, 1901 and 1911 census, LL, SBR, TCBH, DR, *The Boilerplate War* pp 140 and 166 to 169 – John Foley 1963.

Gnr James Candlish BR: 1911 census, LL, SBR, MR.

Gnr Stanley John Conder: BR, 1901 and 1911 census LL, SBR, *Cambridge Daily News* dated 10 May 1917, MC, London Electoral Roll, MC, OCA 1925, PR, family information from Bernard Andrews.

Gnr Daniel James Dean: BR, 1901 and 1911 census, LL, SBR and OCA 1925.

Gnr James Henry Dodd: BC, 1901 and 1911 census, LL, 3rd Light Battalion War History, *Newcastle Journal* dated 24 September 1917, TCBH, MIC, OCA 1925, Family and golfing history provided by Lizzie Radcliffe wife of grandson.

Gnr Francis John Dyer: BR, 1911 census, LL, SBR, MIC, MR, PR. Family information provided by Roslyn Falvey.

Gnr Philip John Evans: BR, 1901 and 1911 census, LL, SDGW, CWGC, ARSE 532004, PR.

Gnr Percy John Fordham: BR, 1901 and 1911 census, LL, SBR, ICRC POW record, MC and BR. Additional family details provided by Liz Parkin.

Gnr Wilfred Vernon Giddins: BR, CR, 1901 and 1911 census, LL, SBR, MR, Record of attendees of 50th anniversary dinner night at Caxton hall on 15 September 1966, Additional information provided by Sue Heil, based on a letter written to her family by Wilfred on 15 October 1916.

Gnr Vincent George Harold Greaves: BR, 1901 census, LL, SBR, DR.

Gnr Lionel Ignatius Leslie Griffin: BR, CR 1901 census, training ship records, LL, CWGC, SDGW, ARSE 662003.

Gnr Walter Robert Hamilton: BR, 1901 census, LL, SBR, MIC, OCA 1925.

Gnr William Ernest (Bill) Harkness: BR, LL, MIC, MRs, DR, detailed family information and photograph provided by Peter Harkness.

Gnr Henry David Haywood: BR, 1891 and 1901 census, MC, LL, SBR, SWB, PR.

Gnr Charles Henry Wallace Hewitt: BR, 1901 census, LL, SBR, SWB, MR, OCA 1925, Record of attendees of 50th anniversary dinner night at Caxton hall on 15 September 1966 and PR.

Gnr William John Thomas Higgs: BR, MC, 1911 census, LL, SBR Medal Roll, OCA 1925; LG, DR.

Gnr William Hudson: BR, 1901 census, LL, SBR, SDGW, CWGC, ARSE 574073.

Gnr Willie Illingworth: LL, LG dated 26 May 1917, *Newcastle Journal* dated 24 September 1917 and SWB.

Gnr Charles Romer Johnson: BR, CR, LL, SBR, SWB, MR, *Kelly's Directory for Hertfordshire* (1926 onwards) and PR.

Gnr Cecil Kaye: BR, 1911 census, LL, MIC, MR, DR. Daughter's details provided by Bruce Milner

Gnr Thomas Marmaduke Keightley: BC, 1891, 1901, MC, LL, MIC, PR.

Gnr Frederick Thomas Paul Laming: BR, CR, 1911 census, MC, London Electoral Roll 1919-1938, DR.

Gnr Alexander Lawson: DR, 1901 and 1911 census, LL, SBR, LG dated 3 February 1920, MR.

Gnr William Henry Lock: BR, 1901 census, SBR, LL, MIC.

Gnr John Loving: 1901 census, LL, MIC.

Gnr Charles Thomas Malpress: BR, 1891 census, LL, SBR, London Electoral Roll 1950, DR, Family information provided by Andrew Malpress.

Gnr Darnley McCaig: BR, 1901 and 1911 census, LL, MIC, Medal Roll, PR.

Gnr Hugh Montgomery: 1911 census, LL and SBR.

Gnr John John Newell: BR, 1901 and 1911 census, LL, C Battalion War History, SDGW, BR, John's picture is included in a War Memorial Souvenir booklet was published in 1922 by The War Memorial Committee of St Matthews Church, Bankfoot and complied by J W Firth. Detailed information provided by Mary Twentyman of South Bradford Local History Society.

Gnr Walter Newington: BC, 1911 census, LL, SBR, MR and OCA 1925.

Pte William John Nightingale ASC: SWB, MIC.

Gnr Arnold Ross Peace: BR, 1901 and 1911 census, LL, SBR, MR, *Grantham Journal* 15 December 1917, SDGW, CWGC, ARSE 810582.

Gnr Thomas John Phillips: BR, LL and SBR.

Gnr Reginald Ernest Pinnock: BR, CR, 1901 census, LL, SBR, MR, London Electoral roll from 1925 to 1957, DR and PR.

Gnr Robert John Pritchard: DR, CR, LL, SBR, MIC. Information provided by Simon Payne.

Gnr Herbert Charles Pryce; CR, 1901 census, LL, MIC, SDGW, CWGC and ARSE 773406.

Gnr Robert Sainsbury Read: BR, LL and SBR.

Gnr F Renson: BR, 1911 census, RFC records (NAK), MC, DR and PR.

Gnr William Pallister Rennison: BR, 1911 census, MIC, *The Motor Cycle* dated January 1918, SWB, MR, Telephone Directories, 1940-1952, PR.

Gnr Clifford Charles Ridout: BR, 1901 census, LL, SBR, LG dated 28 January and 4 February 1918, Birmingham Kelly's Directories for 1922, 1938-9 and 1946, DR.

Gnr John Edward Bottle "Jack" Robson: BR, 1901 and 1911 census, LL, SBR, MR, Telephone directories (various dates) and DR.

Gnr George Joseph Rogers: BC, 1891, 1901 and 1911 census, MR, SBR, LL, MIC, OCA 2015 and DR.

Gnr Arthur Max Rose: BR, LL, SBR, OCA 1925.

Gnr Ernest William Sandwich: LL, SBR, London telephone directories 1926-57, PR.

Gnr Percy Tysoe Sargeant: 1911 census, SBR, OCA 1925, DR.

Gnr Harry G Sanders: LL and MIC.

Gnr Hubert Savage: 1901 and 1911 census, LL, SBR, OCA 1925 and DR.

Gnr Albert George Selby: BR, LL, 1901 and 1911 census and DR.

Gnr Maurice Hubert Shelton: BR, 1891 and 1901 census, LL, WO 374/61890, MC, PR.

Gnr Charles William Shire: BR, 190 and 1911 census, SBR, LL, SWB, MR and, DR.

Gnr George Alfred Smith: LL, MIC and OCA 1925.

Gnr Willie Smith: LL and MIC.

Gnr Ernest Ramsden Spink: BR, CR, 1911 census, LL, SBR, MR Ancestry family tree

Gnr Fenwick William Styan: BR, 1891, 1901 and 1911 census, LL, Post card sent to fiancée, MR, MIC, DR, Family information and photograph provided by grand-son Martin Styan.

Gnr John Walter Sutherland: BR, 1901 and 1911 census, SBR, LL, OCA 1925, London Electoral Roll and MR.

Gnr Neville Tattersfield: WO 339 / 101387 with family information provided by David Tattersfield.

Pte John Alfred Tetlow: BR, SBR and DR.

Gnr John Thomas: WO339/ 101388, LL and OCA 1925.

Gnr Horace Thornhill: LL and MIC.

Gnr Henry James (Harry) Tiffin: BR, CR, 1901 and 1911 census, LL, CWGC, SDGW, ARSE 606610, family information and photographs provided by great nephews David Storey, Richard Tiffin and great-niece Sarah Tiffin.

Gnr Arthur Edward Till: LL, RFC records and PR.

Gnr Victor Toombs: BR, 1901 census, SBR, LL, ICRC POW record, MR and PR.

Gnr Maurice Carter Voile: BC, 1911 census, MC, MR, SGDW, CWGC, LT (death notice), ARSE 473975, *Tanks and trenches* David Fletcher, family information and photographs provided by grandson Oliver Davey.

Gnr Joseph William Walker: BR, LG, RFC records and OCA 1925.

Gnr Eddie Walton: BC, 1901 and 1911 census, SBR, LL and PR.

Gnr James Walton: BC, CR, 1901 and 1911 census, LL, SBR, Kelly's Directory 1924, various telephone directories.

Gnr Reginald Whalley: BR, 1901 and 1911 census, SBR, MC, OCA 1925.

Gnr Alfred Edward Williams: BR, LL, SDGW, CWGC, ARSE 574008.

Gnr William Henry Wood: *The Motor Cycle* dated 22 November 1915, LL, *3rd Light Battalion War History* and SWB.

Gnr James Woodcock: LL and MIC.

Gnr Roderick Donald Woods: BR, 1901 and 1911 census, LL, *Derby Daily Telegraph* dated 23 October 1918, SWB, MR, OCA 1925, L-H correspondence August 1957 and PR.

Gnr George Albert Wootley: BR, 1891 and 1911 census, CWGC, SDGW, ARSE 574281.

Gnr Lionel Horace Worrall: BR, CR, 1901 census, LL, Medal Rolls, Various passenger lists, and DR.

Gnr Joseph Edward Wressell: BR, 1901 and 1911 census, SBR, MR, OCA 1925, Kelly's Lincolnshire directory 1926 to 1930 and 1948 to 1952 and PR.

D COMPANY

D Company Headquarters

Maj Francis James Summers: BR, 1881 and 1901 census, passenger list SS *Mexican* 6 March 1891, MR, LT (various), LG (various), bankruptcy proceedings 1911, divorce proceedings 1920, 1st Tank Corps Reunion Dinner 20 November 1920 and subsequent dinners in 1935 and 1937, DR and PR.

Capt Arthur Graham Woods: CR, 1901 and 1911 census. LG (various), MC, GWNB, list of attendees 1st Tank Corps Dinner on 20 November 1919, various telephone directories, Correspondence with Liddell-Hart in 1957, Tank magazine 1959 and DR.

Lt William Jefferson Wakley: BR, CR, 1911 census, LG (various), WO 339/45302, SWB, MC, Patent applications 1936 – 1939 whilst working for Dewry Railcar and DR.

Lt Allan Cuthbert Brannon: BR, 1901 census. Passenger list 17 November 1915, LG (various), LT (various), MIC, various telephone directories, MR and burial record.

CSM Thomas "Paddy" Walsh: MIC, LG dated January 1917, letter to Billy Foster 15 Dec 1918 (http://www.oucs.ox.ac.uk/ww1lit/gwa/document/8989).

QMS Ernest Edward Victor Williams: BR, 1891 and 1911 census, MC, MIC, London electoral register (various), CWGC and PR.

Sgt Edwin Arthur Levey: BC, 1901 and 1911 census, SBR, MIC, LG dated 17 March 1922 page 2287, MR and DR.

Armr Sgt Frederick Victor Osbourn Howe AOC: BR, CR, 1891 and 1911 census, MR and PR.

Cpl Herbert Lane ASC: MIC.

Charles Wyld Parkes Aggio a.k.a. Aggis: BR, 1901 and 1911 census. SBR, MR, various telephone directories and PR. Note: Aggio does not appear in list of crewmen identified in TAF.

Pte Augustus Frederick Brotherton: BR, 1901 and 1911census, MIC, MR, London electoral rolls 1924 – 31 and PR.

Gnr Samuel Ernest Cotton: 1911 census, SBR, ICRC POW records, London electoral roll 1934 and DR.

Gnr Wilfred Harold Dyer: BR, 1901 and 1911 census, SBR, LG dated 25 May 1917, TCBH, *Cleveden Mercury and Courier* dated 12 April 1919. Cleveden telephone directory 1938 – 42 and manuscript by his son in law AH Bell (TMA).

Pte Vincent Thomas Gale ASC: CR, London schools register, 1911 census, SBR, Enfield electoral roll 1925 and 1950 and PR.

Gnr Walter Player Gammon: BR, 1891, 1901 and 1911 census, SBR, SDGW, CWGC, ARSE 661809 and PR.

Gnr Fred Horrocks MGC: BR, 1901 census, SBR, GWNB, SDGW, CWGC, *Rossendale Express 4 October 1916*, ARSE 396510 and PR. Additional family information and photograph provided by Bacup Natural History Society.

Gnr Wilfred Jaques MGC: BR, 1901 and 1911 census, SBR, CWGC, SDGW, *Wiltshire and Gloucester Standard* 4 May 1918.

Gnr Horace Stanley Jeffrey: BR, 1891 and 1901, MR and SBR.

Gnr Meyrick (Meurig) Gordon Jones: BR, SDGW, CWGC, ARSE 379444 and PR.

Gnr Bernard Harry Kingham: BR, 1911 census, SBR, Birmingham electoral rolls 1918 – 22, MIC, MC, LG (various) and DR.

Pte James Luxon: BC, 1901 and 1911 census, MR, page 118 of *Cheerful Sacrifice* Jonathan Nichols London 1990.

Pte Edwin James Reekie ASC: BR, 1891 and 1901 census, MR, GWNB, MIC, MC and PR.

Pte George Roylance ASC: MIC.

Pte James Isaac Storey ASC: BR, CR, 1901 and 1911 census, MR, SWB, MIC, PR. Family details recovered from grave at Beednell cemetery.

Pte Thomas William Wigley: MIC and RASC Medal Roll.

NO 1 SECTION

D1 "Daredevil 1" (No 765 male)

Capt Harold William Mortimore: BC, 1901 and 1911 census, ADM 273/7/99, ADM 273/30/146, AIR 76/359/219 and WO 339/61901 (NAK). LG (Various), D Company HS MGC War Diary September to December 1916, *War History of the Sixth Tank Battalion* (1919), MC, Anthony Mortimore BC, MIC, Divorce papers J77/3804/5871, company accounts for HA and D Taylor, *The Boilerplate War* – Foley (1963) and DR. Correspondence between Mrs Mary Mortimore (widow) and Trevor Pidgeon 1994; further information provided by Dr Tilly Mortimore (daughter) together with photograph.

Gnr Arthur Day: BR, 1901 and 1911 census. MIC, Letter *Lancashire Daily Post* 8 October 1927 and Tank Journal November 1957.

Gnr Ewart Doodson: 1911 census, SBR, SDGW, CWGC, ARSE 474039 and medal Roll. Letters published in *Dewsbury Reporter* in September 1916, October 1916 and 27 April 1917 plus additional information provided by David Tattersfield.

Gnr Frederick Charles Hobson: SWB

Gnr Henry (Harry) Leat: BR, 1901 and 1911 census, SDGW, CWGC, ARSE 533243, *Aldershot News* 15 June 1917. Family information and photographs provided by Sue Chifney (cousin)

Gnr Albert Smith: BR, 1891, 1901 and 1911 census, SBR, LG dated 14 November 1916. Pictured with Victor Huffam in *Lancashire Evening Post* 26 July 1957; letter to Victor Huffam dated 6 September 1967 (TMA)

Pte Albert Sidney Wateridge ASC: BR, 1891 and 1911 census, MC, TCBH, SWB and DC.

D2 (No 539 – Female)

Lt Hugh Reginald Bell: BR, 1881 census, LG (various), WO 374 / 5511, SDGW, CWGC, ARSE 47026, MIC, detailed information on his academic record provided by Prof Richard Sheppard and Dr Robin Darwell-Smith, college archivist and members of Magdalen College Oxford 29 November 2013.

Cpl William Loxton Walden: CR, 1911 census, Medal Roll, Banns 1920, MR and PR.

Gnr Gilbert James Adamson: BC, SBR, ICRC POW card, Canadian immigration document dated 1 July 1923, US census records for 1930, 1935 and 1940, Ventura CA Local trade directory from 1926 to 1946 and DR.

Pte Walter Leslie Bell: BR, CR, 1901 and 1911 census, SBR, Birmingham electoral rolls and DR.

Gnr Arthur William James Branfield: BR, CR, 1901 and 1911 census, MC, SBR, Divorce proceedings 1926, MC, Luton telephone directory 1951-54 and PR.

Gnr James Blackwood Brunton: BC, 1901 census, SBR, MIC and DR.

Gnr John Frank Letts: BR, SBR, TCBH (2 entries), MR and PR.

A/Cpl Ernest Henry Keats ASC: BR, CR,1891,1901 and 1911 census records, MIC, LG dated 15 May 17, Weymouth Absent Voter's List 1919, MR, Weymouth telephone directory 1937, DC, Family information provided by Teresa Jones and Dave Hounsell.

D3 (No 728 male)

2Lt Harold George Head. BR, CR, 1901 and 1911, MR, LG (various), TCBH, MIC, listed as attending 50th anniversary dinner night on 15 September 1966 and DC. *Tanks and Trenches* (ed David Fletcher) page 8, extracts from the *Bournemouthian* and school information provided by Will Pyke of Bournemouth School, family information provided by in-pensioner Tony Head of the Royal Hospital Chelsea and from correspondence between Trevor Pidgeon and Christopher Head August – October 1997. Photographs from Tony Head.

Cpl William McNicoll: BR, 1901 census, University of St Andrews Roll of Honour, 4th Battalion Tank Corps crew lists August 1918, Dundee Courier 29 October 1918, TCBH, MC, PR and Law Society Journal December 1961.

Pte William Sinclair Barrie: BC, 1901 census, SBR, MC, MR and DR.

Pte William Thomas Bentley: MIC, *Chelmsford Chronicle* 26 October 1917 and ICRC POW card.

Gnr Cecil Sydney Chalfont: BR, CR, 1901 and 1911 census, SBR, MR, London electoral rolls 1938 and 1939, PR.

Gnr William George Shelton: BR, 1891 and 1911 census, MC, SBR, LG dated 13 June 19. TCBH, PR. Family information provided by great grandson Tim Kelly and great great- grandson Ken Leese.

Pte William Fritz Steer: BR, 1901 and 1911 census, SBR, MIC, MR, Sittingbourne telephone directory 1955-60 and DR.

Pte George Allen Simpson: MIC.

D4 (No 516 female)

2Lt Charles Ernest Storey: BR, CR, 1891 census, medal rolls (various), LG (various), WO 339/58946, SWB, MC, *War History of the Sixth Tank Battalion* 1919, *Who Was Who Volume IV*, 1941-1950, PR.

Cpl Thomas George Beardmore: Edinburgh Gazette May 1919.

Pte Oswald Clayton: BR, 1901 and 1911 census, MR, SDGW, CWGC, TCBH

Gnr Edward Cecil Merrison: BR, 1901 and 1911 census, *The Motor Cycle* 29 March 1916 and MR.

Pte William James Shortland ASC: MIC and RASC Medal Roll.

D5 "Dolphin" (No 540 female)

Lt Arthur Herbert Blowers: BR, 1901 and 1911 census, WO 339/59889, LG (various). Correspondence with L-H September 1957, Obituary *Ipswich Evening Star*, 14 Jan 1980. Family information provided by his son, Roger Blowers and great nephew Colin Blowers who provided the photographs.

Cpl Edward (Ted) Foden: BR, 1901 and 1911 census, SBR, LG dated 9 December 1916. MR, Correspondence between his son Ted Foden and Trevor Pidgeon on 29 August 1993. Additional information provided by grandson Clive Foden.

Gnr Edgar Robert Barnsby: BC, 1901 census, MC, CWGC, SDGW and *Birmingham Roll of Honour 1914-1918*

Gnr Leslie Robert Gutsell: BR, 1901 census, *Coventry Evening Telegraph* dated 4 November 1915, *Western Gazette* dated 6 October 1916, SDGW, CWGC and ARSE 364168.

Gnr William John Hodgson: SWB.

Pte Frank Rodel Plant: DR, 1911 census, MIC, 2 Tank Fd Coy War Diary dated 21 August 1917, MR and PR. Additional information provided by Simon Payne who holds his medals.

Gnr Faraday Mendelssohn Sladdin: BR, 1911 census, MR, telephone directory (various) and PR.

Pte George Henry Thomas: BR, CR, 1911 census, MC, Edinburgh Gazette dated 16 December 1916, CWGC, SDGW, ARSE 662154 and page 37 of *The Royston War Memorial* – Royston Local History society.

D6 (No 747 – Male)

Lt Reginald Charles Legge: BR, CR, 1901 census, passenger list for SS Karina dated 6 January, WO 339/56072, CWGC, SDGW, ARSE 28576, PR and LT (various).

LCpl Wilfred da Cunha Brooks: BR, 1891, 1901 and 1911 census, SBR, Edinburgh Gazette 12 December 1916, DR, Manchester University Roll of Service, ARSE 662082 and *Altrincham Guardian* dated 8 February 1918.

Gnr Robert Percy Beesley: BR, 1891 census, SBR, LG dated 23 July 1919, TCBH, MR and PR.

Gnr Fred Bardsley: CR, 1901 and 1911 census, SDGW, CWGC and ARSE 401055.

Gnr Herbert Harvey Clears: CR, 1901 and 1911 census, ICRC POW card, London electoral roll 1919, Surrey electoral roll 1932 and DR.

Gnr George Goodwin Cook: BR, 1891 census, SDGW, CWGC and ARSE 400630.

Gnr John Harry Garner: BR, CR, 1901 and 1911 census, SDGW, CWGC, ARSE 398787 and PR.

A/Sgt Herbert Lane Thacker: BR, 1901 census, WO 339/86079, Edinburgh Gazette 16 December 1916, SDGW, CWGC, ARSE 31086 and PR.

NO 2 SECTION

D7 (No 742 male)

Lt Alfred James Enoch: BR, CR, 1901 and 1911 census, WO 374/22861, LG (various), MR, MIC and PR., Family information and photograph provided by William Russell (son) and Vince McGarry.

Cpl Charles Albert Ironmonger: BR, 1901 and 1911 census, MIC, MR, London electoral rolls 1921 – 29 and DR. Family information provided by Frank Daley, who also presented notebook and photograph to TMA.

Gnr Harold Rhys Bowen: BR, 1901 and 1911 census, SBR, SWB, medal rolls, MR and PR.

Gnr George Kenneth Hume: SBR, SWB and DC.

Gnr Alfred Lapthorne: MIC and MR.

Gnr Archibald "Archie" Lee Richards: BR, 1901 and 1911 census, MR, Canadian immigration records dated 8 August 1923, London electoral roll 1937 and 1946 to 1965 and DR. *Veterans* – Van Emden and Humphries (2005).

Pte Sydney Thompson: BR, MR, SBR and PR.

Pte Sydney George Barnes: MIC and RASC Medal Roll.

D8 (No 720 – male)

2Lt Herbert George Feaver Bown: BR, 1901 census, WO 339/60023, LG (various), F Battalion dinner night menu 27 June 1917, Canadian immigration record 25 May 1919, passenger landing record Bristol 27 July 1924, Kelly's Directories for Dorset (various), telephone directories (various) and DR.

Cpl James Mather "Jimmy" Lindsay: BC, LG (various), MIC, Electoral roll 1938-29, Doncaster telephone directory DC and PR. Family information provided by Kay Potts.

Gnr Ernest Alfred Page Didcote: DR, 1901 census, SBR, MC and PR.

Gnr William Frederick Pestell: BR, 1911 census, MIC, MR and telephone directory. Family information provided by Julia Pestell-Hassall.

Gnr John Morris Tennant: BR, 1901 census, SBR, LG 16 July 1918, TCBH, ICRC POW record card, 1921 postal employment records.

Pte Edward George (Eddie) Williams: BR, 1901 and 1911, SDGW, CWGC and ARSE 606349. Obituary provided by JvB.

Pte Bertram John Young ASC: BR, CR, 1881, 1891, 1901 and 1911 census, LG 14 November 1916, SDGW, CWGC, ARSE 593801 and PR.

D9 "Dolly" (No 546 female)

2Lt Victor Huffam: BR, WO339/59981, MC, Army Lists 1918, Institute of Mechanical Engineers, letter to L-H Liddell-Hart including an eight page account of first tank action dated 3 May 1957 with associated correspondence. DR.

LCpl Arthur Archer: BR, 1901 census, SBR, SWB,

LCpl Harold Sanders: SWB, letter to L-H including first-hand account of actions: 1 September 1957.

Gnr Alfred William Andrew: BR, 1901 and 1911 census, MR, SDGW, CWGC and ARSE 396594.

Gnr Charles Eric Ronald "Ronald" Chapple: BR, 1901 census, SDGW, CWGC and ARSE 400636.

Gnr Reginald "Reg" Ninian Laverty: BR, 1901 and 1911 census, SBR and DC. Additional family information provided by Sue Lee and Ingrid Turner.

Gnr Ernest John (Ernie) Powell: BR, 1901 and 1911 census, SBR, MC and PR. Additional family and photograph provided by Graham Powell (son).

Pte George William Mullis: GWNB, MIC.

LCpl George Arthur Sanders: RASC Medal Roll.

D10 (No 535 – female)

2Lt Harold Darby: CR. 1891, 1901 and 1911 census, MIC, LG (Various), *War History of the Sixth Tank Battalion* – 1919, SWB, MC, attended the 40th Anniversary Cambrai dinner on 23 Nov 1957, MC, medals and images presented by Mrs J Greenwood to TMA.

LCpl William Lauder Hogarth MMGS: BC, 1901 census. SBR, Son's BC.

Gnr Lionel George Harry Britt: BR, MR, GWNB, SDGW, CWGC, ARSE 661618 and PR, Hastings *and St Leonards' Observer* dated 25 March 1922. Family information and photographs provided by Brett Seabrook (great nephew).

Pte Francis James Dale. BR, 1891 and 1901 census, SBR, LG, MR and PR

Pte Horace John Ellocott: BR, 1901 and 1911 census, GWNB, SWB, MR and PR.

Gnr Robert William Frederick Cornish Frost: BR, 1901 and 1911 census, RFC records, local telephone directories, LG (various) relating to his work as a liquidator, MR, attended 50th anniversary dinner night on 15 September 1966; 2nd MR and DR

Gnr Leonard Haygarth: BR, 1901 and 1911 census, GWNB, SDGW, CWGC and ARSE 606028

LCpl Ernest James Phillips ASC: BR, 1891, 1901 and 1911 census, MR, LG dated 21 December 1917 and 12 July 1918. SDGW, CWGC and ARSE 814601. Family information and photoographs provded by grandson John Phillips and great niece Linda Hobbs.

D11 "Die Hard" (No 547 male)

Lt Herbert George Pearsall: BR, 1901 and 1911 census, WO 339 / 56080, *Birmingham Mail* dated 16 November 1916. LG various, Batley Grammar School magazine dated April 1919 and PR.

LCpl Harry Earle Nixon: BR, 1901 and 1911, LG (various), Army List 1919, MR, family information provided by grandson Mike Nixon.

Pte William Moss: BR, 1901 and 1911 census. 4th Battalion crew lists dated 30 July 1918, CWGC, SDGW and ARSE 7775431. Obituary in *Fleetwood Express* dated 31 August 1918 and associated local information provided by Eric Curbishley.

Pte James George Daniel Honour: BR, CR, 1911 census. SBR, MR, 1967 electoral roll and DR. Identified by Simon Payne.

Gnr Joseph Rowell Lee: BC, 1911 census, SWB and DR.

Gnr Charles Henry Leeming: BR, SBR, Walsall Observer 19 October 1918, MIC, Burial Record and PR.

Pte Frank Still ASC: Edinburgh Gazette dated 16 December 1916, 4th Battalion crew list dated 30 July 1918 and MIC.

Gnr Charles Platt Stuart: BR, 1891, 1901 and 1911 census, SBR, MR and DR.

D12 (Tank No 719 male)

Capt Graeme Nixon: BR, CR, 1901 and 1911 census, LG (various). *Liverpool Daily Post* 14 June 1918, MC, 40th Anniversary Dinner night MC, Quarry Bank School (QBS) records for 1955 – http://kenwoodlennon.blogspot.co.uk/2013/11/quarry-bank-that-lennons-detention.html and PR. Additional information on QBS provided by Tony Howard

Sgt Reginald John Vandenbergh (note that spelling of his surname is not coherent): BR, CR, SBR and DR.

Gnr Horace Augustus Allebone: BR, 1901 census, SDGW, CWGC, ARSE 606014, de Ruvigney's Roll Of Honour and PR and the Rushden Heritage Group website.

Gnr William Bertram Debenham: BR, 1901 and 1911 census confirming German birth, CWGC and SDGW.

Gnr Cecil Frederick Gloyn: BR, 1901 and 1911 census, SBR, two MRs, Plymouth telephone directory 1940-73 and DR.

Gnr Harry Zimmerman: BR, 1901 and 1911 census, *Hull Daily Mail* (various), GWNB and PR.

Cpl Robert R Murray ASC: MIC and GWNB.

Reserve Tank D13 "Delilah" (No 548 female)

2Lt William Henry (Billy) Sampson MGC: BR, 1891, 1901 and 1911 census, Canadian Army enlistment records, LT dated 15 October 1915, MR, LG (various), WO 339/60304 containing information on deployment to Dublin, Indian Army personal file and staff lists 1922 – 1936 (British library), telephone directory Maidenhead 1977 and DR.

Correspondence between Stuart Sampson and Trevor Pidgeon 1991-1992. Additional family information from Karen Price Patrick concerning Sampson family in Wytheville and Stuart Sampson on family life; photographs courtesy of Stuart Sampson.

Gnr William Phipps Chandler: BR, CR, SBR, LG dated 21 December 1916, London electoral rolls 1932-39 and PR.

Gnr Edwin Frank Dival: SBR, 1891, 1901 and 1911 census, SBR, MR, *Kent and Sussex Courier* 30 March 1917, 2nd MR. telephone directory 1930-1953 and PR.

Pte Harry Ironfield Yates: BR, CR, 1891, 1901 and 1911 census, LG (various), MC,

LCpl Alfred Philip Bloomfield ASC; BR, 1901 and 1911 census, MIC and CWGC.

NO 3 SECTION

D14 (No 534 female)

2Lt Gordon Frederick Court: BR, 1901 census, WO339/56054, SDGW, CWGC, ARSE serials 28146 and 58670, and PR.

Sgt Robert Baden Pebody: 1901 and 1911 census, CWGC

Gnr William Henty Barber: BC, CR, 1891, 1901 and 1911 census, SDGW, CWGC and ARSE
557509.

LCpl Thomas Cromack: BR, CR, 1881, 1891, 1901 and 1911 census, SDGW, CWGC and ARSE
52259.

Gnr Joseph Elliot Crowe: BR, 1901 and 1911 census, SDGW, CWGC and ARSE 558640.

Pte Andrew Charles Lawson. BR, 1901 and 1911 census, SDGW, CWGC and ARSE 557883.

Pte George Monro Mann: BC, 1901 census, *Ross-shire Journal* dated 15 May 1916 and Glasgow
University Roll of Honour, SDGW, CWGC and ARSE 577612. Photograph courtesy of the
TMA.

LCpl Laurence William Upton ASC. BC, 1901 and 1911 census, MC, *Doncaster Gazette* dated 1
December 1916, SDGW, CWGC and ARSE 558336.

D15 (No 537 female)

John Lionel "Jack" Bagshaw:. BR, CR, 1901 and 1911 census, WO 339/43877, LG (various); *War
Memoirs 1917-1919* – Bion, Kelly's Directory of Staffordshire, 1932, 1936 and 1940, PR.

LCpl Charles Frederick "Charley" Jung: BR, 1891, 1901 and 1911 census, MR, MIC, telephone
directories (various), CWGC, DC and PR.

Gnr Charles Edward Bond: BR, CR, 11901 and 1911 census, SBR, GWNB, SWB, *Bridgwater
Mercury* dated September 1918.

Gnr Cyril William Coles: BR, CR, 1901 and 1911 census, *The Motor Cycle* dated 15 April 1916,
SDGW, CWGC and ARSE 396431. Family information and 1911 voters list provided by
Caroline Gurney. Photographs courtesy of the Skinner Street United Reformed Church in
Poole, arranged by Sarah Lambert, exhibitions officer at the Tank Museum in Bovington.

Gnr Charles William Hoban: BR, CR, 1891, 1901 and 1911 census. MR, SDGW, CWGC, ARSE
364502 and PR, *Leamington Spa Courier* dated 6 October 1916.

Gnr Tom "Tippo" Fleming Wilson: BC, 1891, 1901 and 1911 census, SDGW, CWGC, ARSE
383572 and PR. *Westmoreland Gazette* dated 30 September 1916. Family information provided
by John Wilson (nephew) and Hilda Preston (great niece).

Pte Albert George Rowe ASC: BC, 1901 census, SBR and London electoral roll 1921 to 1925.

D16 "Dracula" (No 538 female)

Lt Arthur Edmund Arnold: BR, 1901 census, WO 339/53827, LG (Various), ICRC POW cards,
SWB, SS *Ceramic* passenger list dated 17 May 1927. Post operation report dated 19 September
1916 and *The First Tank Engagement:* The Tank edition 529 May 1963 pp 183-184 and pp
200-201. Family information provided by Ann Burnett (daughter), Mike Arnold (nephew) and
Nell Gilbert (daughter) who also provided the photographs.

Cpl Ernest A White: WO339/98874 and MIC

Gnr Percy George: BR, 1911 census and PR.

Pte Cecil Frost: BR, 1891 and 1911 census, SBR and MIC.

Gnr Jacob Glaister: BR, 1891, 1901 and 1911 census, SBR, LG dated 14 November 1916, Salt *Lake
Tribune* dated 30 June 1929, MR and PR. *Whitehaven News* dated 26 October 1950. Family
information provided by Freda Glaister and Shaun Corkery, photograph courtesy of the TMA.

Gnr John Mackenzie: BR, 1901 census, SDGW, CWGC and ARSE No 558332.

Pte Samuel Henry Robert Workman ASC: CR, 1911 census, MC, DE and PR. Family information provided by great nephew Brian Partridge.

D17 Dinnaken (No 759 male)

Stuart Henderson Hastie: BC, MC, WO 339/4618, LG (various), G Battalion archives (TMA),
Scottish Malt Distillers Ltd company results 1935 to 1955, Correspondence with J Wilfred

Staddon Nov 1963 (L-H archives), BBC interviews 1964 held by IWM, second MC and DC. Family information from correspondence between Trevor Pidgeon and Kathleen Youle (daughter) and Katherine Hastie (daughter in law) in February 1994. Photograph from TPC.

Gnr Eric Pauncefort Blake: BR, CR, 1901 and 1911 census, MC, letter dated 28 September later published in *Letters from the Front* Volume One pp 28-30 and war service record in Volume 2 page 41, Royal Tank Corps enlistment records, *Tank* Journal No 425 September 1954 page 444-445 and PR.

Gnr Percy Boult: BC, 1911 census, MIC, *London Gazette* (various), LT dated 24 September 1954 and DR.

Gnr Frederick "Fred" Gomersall: CR, 1901 and 1911 census, SBR, *Dewsbury Reporter* dated 7 October 1916 and DR.

Gnr Alfred Henry Roy Reiffer, BR, SBR, Edinburgh Gazette dated 12 December 1916. London electoral roll 1918 – 1922. 1920 Kelly's directory for Dorset. 1951 to 1961 telephone directory for South Wales, Weymouth telephone directory and DR. Letter to Victor Huffam dated 1 October 1956 (L-H Archive). First-hand account of first tank action by Reiffer dated 9 September 1957 sent to L-H and associated undated report on removal of weapons from D9 – Dolly (L-H Archive). Letters to L-H dated 9 September 1957 and 6 December 1959 (L-H Archive), BBC interview 1963 (audio held at IWM), letter to the Sunday Telegraph dated 30 June 1963 and letter to Stuart Hastie dated 8 November 1963. Description of Reiffer's activities at the time of the death of T.E. Lawrence drawn from Another *life* by Andrew RB Simpson (2008) pp 38-39, 227, 229, 245 and 262. Family information from grand-daughter Jane Smith and photograph courtesy of Edward H. Metcalf at The Huntington Library, San Marino, CA.

Gnr William Frederick Sudgen: MIC.

Pte Charles A Wescomb: MIC, BC, CR, 1901 and 1911 census, MIC, MR and PR.

D18 (No 743 male)

2Lt Leonard Charles "Len" Bond: BR, 1901 and 1911 census, LG (various), MR, Indian Army List April 1926, British Library file IOR/L/MIL/14/8820, Indian Army lists 1936, 1940 and 1942, DC and CWGC. Correspondence between Anthony Bond and Trevor Pidgeon 1999 – 2000 with additional military information provided by Geoffrey Churcher who holds his medals. Photograph from TPC.

Gnr Arthur Race: BR, 1901 and 1911 census, SBR, MR and PR.

Pte George Thornton: SWB with additional information provided by Vince McGarry.

Gnr Sydney Philip Wenmoth: BR, 18911, 1901 and 1911 census, SBR, MR and PR. Additional information provided by Geoff Martin.

Pte Frederick Burrows: MIC, TCBH.

D19 (No 753 male)

Capt Stephen Scott Sellick: BC, 1881 census, MR, WO 339/56595, LT (various), MIC, passenger lists (various), London telephone directory 1934-5 and 1940-47 and PR.

Cpl Charles Walter Luck: BR, CR, 1891 and 1901 census, MR, WO 339/45073, LG (various), MIC, wife's PR, DR and PR.

Gnr James Anthony "Jim" Blackmore: BR, 1891, 1901 and 1911 census, MC, SBR, *The Book of Porlock* – Denis Corner pp 29, 38, 60, 69 and 130. Further information provided by Dr Lita Strapp and Derek Purvis.

Gnr Henry Chapman. BR, SBR, MIC.

Gnr John Cameron Tolson. BR, 1901 and 1911 census, MR, TCBH, LG dated 13 March 1918, *Wiltshire and Gloucestershire Standard* dated 4 May 1918, son's CWGC records, 50th anniversary dinner night at Caxton hall on 15 Sep 1966, letter to Victor Huffam dated 23 October 1956 (L-H Archives) .

Pte Thomas Hinds ASC: CR, 1911 census, SBR, ICRC POW card, SWB and MR.

NO 4 SECTION

D20 "Daphne" (No 744 male)

2Lt Harry Cecil Frank Drader: BR, 1901 and 1911 census, WO374/20651, LG (various), *Bedford Times and Independent* dated 1 December 1916, US naturalization certificate dated 14 January 1938, 1940 US census, Los Angeles telephone directory (various). Family information and photographs provided by David Earl Drader.

Cpl Owen Frank Rowe: BR, 1901 and 1911 census, SWB and DR,

Gunner Walter William Atkins: BR, 1911 census, obituary *The Motor Cycle* dated 22 February. Letters held by the Herbert Museum and Art Gallery in Coventry, courtesy of the Keeper of Collections Huw Jones who also provided the photograph.

Gnr Joseph William Clark: BR, 1891, 1901 and 1911 census, SBR and DR.

Gnr Roland George Elliott: BR, CR, 1901 and 1911 census, *Coventry Evening Telegraph* dated 20 August 1915, WS Atkins' letters and Harry Drader's letter dated 16 November 1916 courtesy of the Herbert Art Gallery and Museum in Coventry, MR, Coventry telephone directory (1938 to 1962), PR. Further information provided by Ian Sutherland and contributors to the *Coventry Local History Forum.*

Gnr Ernest Herbert Statham: BR, CR, 1891, 1901 and 1911 census. MR, MIC, Kelly's directory to Coventry 1928, *Edinburgh Gazette* dated 22 Aug 1950, LG dated 17 Mar 53 and DR.

Pte Frank Rusby Styring: BR, CR, 1901 and 1911 census, SDGW, CWGC, ARSE 522575, LT dated 1 May 17 and PR.

Pte Alfred John Bowerman: BR, 1901 census, MR, MIC and DR.

D21 "Delphine"

Lt Alexander Easson Sharp: BC, 1901 census, WO339/56086, LG (various), *Dundee Courier* dated 16 April 1917, Institution of Civil Engineers application 1919, *Civil Engineer Lists, 1868–1930.* London, UK: Institution of Civil Engineers. Engineers India Office list (various).

Gnr Harold Bertram Wigley: BR, 1901 and 1911 census, *Birmingham Daily Mail* dated 26 September 1916, ICRC POW cards, MC, Bromsgrove telephone directories1940 – 1963, PR.

Gnr George Charles Foote: BC, 1901 and 1911 census, LG dated 14 November 1916, SDGW, CWGC and http://www.tank-cambrai.com/english/personnages/foot.php,

Gnr George Moscrop: BR, 1901 census, SBR, Additional family information provided by Alison Waddell (see D23) and DR.

Gnr Ernest John Shepherd; BR, SDGW, CWGC with additional information from Trevor Harkin.

Pte Herbert Ernest Wilson: MIC.

D22 (No 756 male)

Lt Frederick Andrew "Eric" Robinson: BC, 1901 and 1911 census, RNAS records, WO 339 / 33315, LG (various), MC, *The Motor Cycle* dated 18 January 1917, Ilford War Memorial Gazette published 1930.

Cpl Dudley Nevill White: BR, CR, 1901 and 1911 census, SDGW, CWGC and ARSE 593244. Further information provided by Susan Tall.

Gnr James Anderson: SBR, TCBH, and LG dated 9 July 1917. Additional information provided by David Tattersfield.

Gnr John William Applegate: BR, CR, 1901 and 1911 census, SBR and 4th Battalion crew list dated 30 July 1918.

Gnr Jack Choules: BR, 1901 census, SBR, MR, Slough telephone directory and PR.

Gnr Percy Raworth. BR, *Harrogate Herald* (various 1916-17), LG dated 16 December 1916, *Rushden Echo* dated 5 October 1917, SDGW, CWGC, ARSE 574874 and PR. http://www.harrogatepeopleandplaces.info/ww1/soldiers/r/raworth-percy.htm

Pte Ernest Cecil Howes ASC: BR, 1901 and 1911 census, MIC, sister's PR and DR.

D23 (No 528 female)

Capt George William Mann: BR, WO339 / 45093, MR, LG (Various) SDGW, CWGC, ARSE 54548 and PR. Further information provided in the *War History of the Sixth Tank Battalion*.

John Barnes Starkey: BR, CR, 1901 and 1911 census, MIC, SDGQ, CWGC and ARSE 772848.

Gnr Henry Clifford Tillotson: DR, school records, SBR, 4th Battalion Tank Corps crew list 30 July 1918, MIC, MC, London electoral rolls (various) and DR.

Gnr Douglas Benson Tweddle: BR, SBR, MR, DR, and PR. Additional information provided by his grand-daughter Alison Waddell.

Pte Osmond Woodford "Jack" Rossiter: BR, CR, 1901 and 1911 census, MIC, Marnhull Absent Voters List 1918, MC, DR and PR. Family information provided by his grand-daughter Ann Peters.

D24 (751 male)

Lt Walter Stones: BR, CR, 1891 and 1901 census, WO 339/60444, LG (various), MR and wife's PR, *Doncaster Chronicle* dated 28 August 1947 and DR. Additional family information provided by John Bucklow.

Pte Robert Steele Coffey: DR, 1901 and 1911 census, MR, MIC, ICRC POW record and DR.

Gnr William Ernest (Billy) Foster: BR, 1911 census, Army pension record, MC and DC, Additional information provided by Ralph Lloyd-Jones and http://www.oucs.ox.ac.uk/ww1lit/gwa © Helen Callister

Gnr Leslie Richard Reeve: BR, 1911 census, CWGC, SDGW and ARSE 473794. Additional information provided by Lynette Duggan.

Gnr Frederick Joseph Rule: BR, 1911 census, MR, SBR and PR, additional family information and photograph provided by great-granddaughter Clare Rule.

Pte John Thomas Wells; BR, CR, SDGW, CWGC and ARSE 752594. Additional family information provided by Anne Geary (great niece), Cathryn Ball (great niece) and Geoffrey Churcher holds his medals.

Pte Frederick George Wood ASC: MIC.

D25 (No 511 female)

2Lt Edward Carl Kestell Colle: BR, 1901 and 1911 census, LG (various), service file, MR, passenger list SS Ranpura dated 14 February 1930, LBEC/994/28A (28 Group Officer's History Form (undated) for period August 1914 to August 1941. Application for transfer to the Corps of Military Police dated 22 August 1945. London telephone directory 1952 and 1956, DR.

Cpl Henry Thomas Frederick Reynolds: BR, 1891 and 1901 census, SBR, Exeter telephone directory (various), DR.

Gnr James Brunton Petrie: BR, SBR and DR.

Gnr Herbert Routledge: BR, 1901 and 1911 census and SBR.

Pte John Maude ASC: MIC

REFERENCES AND BACKGROUND READING

Anon., *Denny and Dunipace Roll of Honour* (Uckfield: Naval & Military Press 2006)

Victor Archard, "Diary and Letters" (TMA, unpublished).

Arthur Arnold, "Report to Major F Summers dated September 19, 1916", *The Tank* Volume 45 Edition 529 (May 1963), pp.183-84.

—— "The First Tank Engagement", *The Tank,* Volume 45 Edition 529 (May 1963), pp.200-01.

John Blacker (ed), *Have you forgotten yet – the First World War memories of CP Blacker MC GM* (Barnsley: Pen & Sword, 2000).

Malcom Brown, *The Imperial War Museum Book of the Somme* (London: Pan Books, 2002).

Nigel Cave, *Delville Wood* (Barnsley: Pen & Sword, 1999).

—— *Thiepval* (Barnsley: Pen & Sword, 1995).

Brian Cooper, *The Ironclads of Cambrai* (London: Cassell, 2002).

Dennis Corner, *The Book of Porlock* (Wellington: Halsgrove, 2010).

William Taylor Dawson, "Reminiscences of my experiences in the first tanks" (TMA, unpublished).

John Farquharson Ltd, *The Bell House Book* (London: Hodder and Stoughton, 1979).

David Fletcher (ed), *Tanks* and Trenches, (Stroud: Sutton, 1996).

John Foley, *The Boilerplate War* (London: George Muller, 1963).

Michael Foley, *Rise of the Tank* (Barnsley: Pen & Sword, 2014).

J F G Fuller, *Tanks in the Great War 1914-1918* (London: John Murray, 1920).

Jean-Luc Gibot and Philippe Gorzczynski, *Following the Tanks: Cambrai, 20 November – 7 December 1917* (Privately published, 1998).

John Glanfield, *The Devil's Chariots* (Stroud: Sutton, 2001).

Bryn Hammond, *Cambrai 1917* (London: Weidenfeld & Nicolson, 2008)

Colin Hardy, "Rewriting history – An Alternative account of the death of Lieutenant George Macpherson of the Heavy Section Machine Gun Corps", *Stand To: The Journal of the Western Front Association* No. 89 (August / September 2010), pp. 30 – 32.

B L Q Henriques, *Indiscretions of a Warden* (London: Methuen & Co Limited, 1937).

A Holford Walker letter to Editor of Military Operations: France and Belgium, 1916 Volume 2 dated 22 April 1935 (NAM).

V Huffam, "Flers September 15th and 16th, 1916", *The Tank* Volume 41 No. 476 (December 1958), pp. 89-90.

A M Inglis, "Report of operations of the Tanks of No 1 Section C Company HS MGC dated 16 September 1916" (TMA).

B H Liddell-Hart, *The Tanks Volume 1 1914-1919* (London: Cassell, 1959).

—— "Papers relating to the First Tank Action, Battle of the Somme 15 September 1916", 9/28/63 (LHCMA)

L L Loewe, *Basil Henriques – A Portrait Based on his Diaries, Letters and Speeches as collated by his widow, Rose Henriques* (London: Routledge & Kegan Paul, 1976).

R F G Maurice, *Tank Corps Book of Honour* (reprint Uckfield: Naval & Military Press, 2009).

Frank Mitchell, *Tank Warfare* (Stevenage: Spa Books, 1987).

Jonathan Nicholls, *Cheerful Sacrifice: The Battle of Arras 1917* (Barnsley: Pen & Sword, 2005).

Terry Norman, *The Hell They Called High Wood* (Wellingborough: Patrick Stephens, 1989).

Trevor Pidgeon, *The Tanks at Flers* (Cobham: Fairmile Books, 1995).

Trevor Pidgeon, *Flers and Gueudecourt* (Barnsley: Pen & Sword, 2002).

—— *Tanks on the Somme* (Barnsley: Pen & Sword, 2010).

Douglas Plowman, *The Royston War Memorial* (Royston: Royston and District Local History Society, 2006).

Paul Reed, *Combles* (Barnsley: Pen & Sword, 2002).

Paul Reed, *Courcelette* (Barnsley: Pen & Sword, 1998).

Reginald H. Roy (ed), *The Journal of Private Fraser, 1914-1918* (Victoria, BC: Sono Nis Press, 1985).

Gary Sheffield, *The Chief: Douglas Haig and the British Army* (London, Aurum Press, 2011).

Jack Sheldon, *The German Army on the Somme 1914-1916* (Barnsley: Pen & Sword, 2006).

Andrew R B Simpson, *Another Life: Lawrence after Arabia* (Stroud: Spellmount, 2008).

Sir Albert G Stern, *Tanks 1914-1918: The Log Book of a Pioneer* (Uckfield, Naval & Military Press reprint of 1919 edition).

Richard Van Emden & Steve Humphries, *Veterans: The Last survivors of the Great War* (Barnsley: Pen & Sword, 2005).

Various, *The War History of the Sixth Tank Battalion* (Privately published, 1919).

Ian Verrinder, *Tank Action in the Great War, B Battalion's Experiences.* (Barnsley: Pen & Sword, 2009).

W H Watson, *A Company of Tanks* (London: William Blackwood & Sons, 1920).

Clough Williams-Ellis & Amabel William-Ellis, *The Tank Corps* (London: Country Life, 1919).

ELECTRONIC SOURCES

Ancestry @ http://home.ancestry.co.uk/

British Newspaper Archive @ http://www.britishnewspaperarchive.co.uk/

The Commonwealth War Graves Commission @ http://www.cwgc.org/find-war-dead.aspx

Find My Past @ http://www.findmypast.co.uk/

Google Landships @ https://sites.google.com/site/landships/

Great War Forum @ 1914-1918.invisionzone.com/

London Gazette @ https://www.thegazette.co.uk/

Motor Cycle @ https://archive.org/details/motorcycle05lond and https://archive.org/details/motorcycle16lond

National Archives @ http://www.nationalarchives.gov.uk/

Scotland's People @ http://www.scotlandspeople.gov.uk

Index

INDEX OF PEOPLE

INDEX OF BATTLES

INDEX OF GENERAL & MISCELLANEOUS TERMS

INDEX OF PLACES

INDEX OF MILITARY FORMATIONS & UNITS